MACM

Phrasal
Verbs
plus

Macmillan Education
Between Towns Road, Oxford OX4 3PP
A division of Macmillan Publishers Limited
Companies and representatives throughout the world

ISBN: 978-1-4050-6390-6

First published 2005

The *Macmillan Phrasal Verbs Plus* dictionary was conceived, compiled and
edited by the Reference and Electronic Media Division of Bloomsbury
Publishing Plc.

This Dictionary includes words on the basis of their use in the English
language today. Some words are identified as being trademarks or service
marks. Neither the presence nor absence of such identification in this
Dictionary is to be regarded as affecting in any way, or expressing a
judgement on, the validity or legal status of any trademark, service mark,
or other proprietary rights anywhere in the world.

World English Corpus
The definitions in the *Macmillan Phrasal Verbs Plus* dictionary have been
based on information derived from 200 million words of English which make
up the World English Corpus. This consists of the Bloomsbury Corpus of
World English® and the Macmillan ELT Corpus, as well as a corpus of
common errors made by learners of English.

Cover design by Liz Faulkner
Illustrated by Martin Shovel
Cover illustration by Martin Shovel
Typeset by Butler and Tanner, Frome, United Kingdom

Printed and bound in China

2009   2008
10 9   8   7   6

CONTENTS

Editor-in-Chief
Michael Rundell

Associate Editor
Gwyneth Fox

EDITORIAL TEAM

Editors
Howard Sargeant
Stella O'Shea
Donald Watt
Laura Wedgeworth

Common Particles
Stephen Handorf

Phonetician
Dinah Jackson

Proofreaders
Sandra Anderson
Ruth Hillmore

PROJECT TEAM

Project Manager
Katy McAdam

Database Consultant
Edmund Wright

Project Coordinator
Katalin Süle

Production Editor
Nicky Thompson

Design Manager
Liz Faulkner

Production Director
Penny Edwards

Production Manager
Rowena Drewett

Dictionaries' Publisher
Faye Carney

Publishing Directors
Kathy Rooney
Sue Bale

OTHER CONTRIBUTORS

Illustrations
Martin Shovel

**Editorial, Keyboarding, and
Administrative Assistance**
Heather Bateman
Ian M Spackman

**Common Particles
Design**
Nigel Partridge

ADVISORY PANEL

Chief Adviser
Professor Michael Hoey
Baines Professor of English Language and Director of the Applied
English Language Studies Unit, University of Liverpool, UK

Professor Chen Lin
Professor of English,
Foreign Languages
University, Beijing, China

Simon Greenall
ELT author and trainer

Vaughan Jones
ELT author and trainer

Sue Kay
ELT author and teacher

Cindy Leaney
ELT author and trainer

Jane Magee
Course Director, English
Language Teaching,
University of St Andrews,
UK

Amy Chi Man-lai
Instructor, Language
Centre, Hong Kong
University of Science and
Technology, Hong Kong

Professor Kevin Mark
Professor, School of
Politics and Economics,
Meiji University, Japan

Dr Don R. McCreary
Associate Professor,
Department of English,
University of Georgia,
Athens, Georgia, USA

Professor Rukmini Nair
Professor of Linguistics
and English,
Department of Humanities
and Social Sciences,
Indian Institute of
Technology, Delhi, India

Dr Hilary Nesi
Senior Lecturer, Centre for
English Language Teacher
Education, University of
Warwick, UK

Philip Prowse
ELT author and trainer

Pete Sharma
Lecturer and ELT author

Susan Stempleski
Coordinator of Faculty
Development, Hunter
College International
English Language
Institute, City University of
New York, USA

Adrian Underhill
ELT consultant, trainer,
author

Sara Walker
Coordinator of the English
Programme,
Brazilian Diplomatic
Academy, Ministry of
Foreign Relations,
Brasilia DF, Brazil

Consultant
Jonathan Marks
ELT trainer and author

Introduction

MICHAEL RUNDELL, Editor-in-Chief

The *Macmillan Phrasal Verbs Plus* dictionary has been specially designed to help learners of English deal confidently with phrasal verbs. The dictionary provides all the information that is needed to *understand* phrasal verbs and to *use* them well.

Learners often think that phrasal verbs are difficult, and – as Dr Sylvie De Cock shows in her article – some students try to avoid using them altogether. But phrasal verbs are not only a central feature of the English language, they are also extremely useful. Expert speakers use phrasal verbs in *all* kinds of contexts – not just in informal situations such as conversations or emails, but quite often in formal and technical writing too. There are many contexts where a phrasal verb is simply the best, most natural-sounding way of expressing an idea, and so students should be encouraged to use them. To make this easy, the dictionary deals with all the factors that make phrasal verbs seem difficult:

- it explains their *meanings* using uncomplicated language
- it gives an easy-to-use description of their *syntactic behaviour* – how they combine with other words, where the object of the verb can be placed, where pronouns go, and so on
- it provides guidance on *register* – the types of context in which it is natural and appropriate to use a phrasal verb

We chose the name *Phrasal Verbs Plus* because – as well as explaining the meaning and use of phrasal verbs in English – this dictionary has a wealth of additional features, including:

- 'red words': using data from our large language corpora, we have identified just over 1,000 of the most frequently used English phrasal verbs. These words are shown in red and divided into three bands, each of about 350 verbs (the words with three stars are the most frequent). The same approach is used in the other Macmillan dictionaries, and students and teachers have told us how useful this information is.
- 'menus' for words with five or more meanings, making it easy to find the meaning that you are looking for
- 'collocation boxes', providing invaluable information about the most frequent and natural-sounding combinations
- special entries on the 12 most common particles (such as **back**, **down**, **in**, and **up**), showing how their meanings develop from the literal to the figurative
- an index of single-word verbs that have phrasal verb synonyms: using the index, you can look up a word like **inherit** and find a phrasal verb – **come into** – with the same meaning.
- a collection of articles, in the centre pages, on topics such as syntax, register, and pronunciation, to help students to develop a better awareness of how phrasal verbs work and why they are so useful

Like all Macmillan dictionaries, *Phrasal Verbs Plus* has benefited at every stage in its development from the advice of teachers, students, teacher-trainers, academics, and ELT materials writers. We are convinced that the dictionary will help its users to lose their fear of phrasal verbs and to start using them with confidence.

USING YOUR DICTIONARY

This dictionary includes phrasal verbs and words that are derived from them. A phrasal verb consists of a 'root verb' such as *go, put,* or *set* and a 'particle' (an adverb or preposition, such as *away, on,* or *out*).

Finding a phrasal verb

You will find phrasal verbs listed under their root verb, in alphabetical order.

BOOT /buːt, *American* but/
boots, booting, booted

➤**boot 'out** [often passive] *informal*
to make someone leave a place, their job, their school etc = DISMISS, KICK OUT
be booted out *Anyone caught taking drugs was booted out.* ♦ **+of** *They were booted out of the club for fighting.*
boot sb out *also* **boot out sb** *His girlfriend has booted him out.*

➤**boot 'up**
if a computer boots up, or if you boot it up, it starts working and is ready to use
boot up *Your computer may take a little time to boot up.*
boot sth up *also* **boot up sth** *Try booting your machine up again.*

Phrasal verbs with more than one entry

Sometimes the same phrasal verb is pronounced with a different stress when it has different meanings. In this case each phrasal verb is shown as a separate entry.

LINGER /ˈlɪŋgə, *American* ˈlɪŋgər/
lingers, lingering, lingered

➤**linger 'on**
1 to last or continue for longer than people expected
linger on *Ten years later, the memory still lingers on.* ♦ *Some childish ideas linger on in all of us.*
2 to be alive, although very ill, for a long time after you seemed likely to die
linger on *He did not want to linger on in pain and without dignity.*

➤**'linger on**
to continue looking at someone or something, especially because they are very attractive
linger on sb/sth *His eyes lingered on her face.*

Phrasal verbs that are always used in the passive are shown in the passive form.

➤**be ˌcast a'way**
to be left on an island surrounded by sea without any way of leaving
be cast away (on sth) *He was cast away on a desert island for over 20 years.*

■ **castaway** /ˈkɑːstəˌweɪ/ **noun** [C]
someone who has been left on an island surrounded by sea and cannot get away, especially after their ship has sunk: *The play tells the story of six castaways.*

Phrasal verbs that have the same meaning but a different particle are shown together.

'cushion against (*also* **'cushion from**)
to protect a person or thing from the harmful effects of something
cushion sb/sth against sth *Their savings partly cushioned them against the worst effects of the legal costs.*
♦ *Government subsidies have cushioned farmers from the worst effects of the drought.*

Derived words
Some phrasal verbs have nouns, adjectives, and verbs that are derived from them. These words are shown at the end of the entry for the phrasal verb that they are derived from.

,sleep 'over
to sleep at someone else's house for one night
sleep over *Mum, can Billy sleep over on Saturday?*
■ **sleepover** /'sliːpəʊvə/ [C] **noun** a children's party at which the guests stay the night at one person's house

Word classes
There is a list of word classes on the inside front cover.

Idioms and other fixed expressions
Some phrasal verbs are used in idioms or other fixed expressions. These are shown at the end of the entry for the phrasal verb, following the small box that says **PHRASE** or **PHRASES** .

'end in ★★★
to have something as a final result = *formal* CULMINATE IN
end in sth *The game ended in a draw.*
♦ *His attempt to persuade the boy ended in failure.*
PHRASE **end in tears** if a situation ends in tears, people involved in it become disappointed or angry

Finding the meaning of a phrasal verb
Many phrasal verbs have more than one meaning, and each different meaning is shown by a number.

BOLT /bəʊlt, *American* boʊlt/
bolts, bolting, bolted

,bolt 'down
1 to eat food very quickly
bolt down sth *also* **bolt sth down** *She bolted down her lunch and rushed back to work.*
2 [usually passive] to fix something firmly to the floor
be bolted down *The people here would even steal the chairs if they weren't bolted down.*

Some phrasal verbs have many different meanings. Entries with five or more meanings have a 'menu' at the top to make it easier to find the particular meaning you are looking for.

Definitions

All the definitions are written using a carefully selected 'defining vocabulary' of 2,300 words so that it is easy to understand the definitions.

Finding out more about a phrasal verb

Red phrasal verbs

Some phrasal verbs are printed in red with a 'star rating' to show their frequency. This helps you to identify the ones that you are most likely to need to know. For more information about red phrasal verbs, see the inside back cover.

Pronunciation

The International Phonetic Alphabet shows you how a word is pronounced. A list of the symbols used is given at the end of the dictionary. When British and American pronunciations are different, both are given.

Stress marks tell you which part of a phrasal verb or a compound to stress when you are saying it.

Alternative spellings

Alternative spellings of root verbs are shown separately and cross-referred to the main entry.

Inflections

Inflections of root verbs are shown.

,blow 'up ★★★

1	explode
2	make sth explode
3	fill sth with air/gas
4	when a storm starts
5	when an argument/problem begins
6	become angry
7	make a photograph bigger
+	PHRASE
+	**blow-up** noun

1 if something blows up, it explodes and is destroyed
    blow up *The boiler blew up, wrecking the entire building.*

→ al'low for ★★★
→ ,add 'up ★★
→ ,answer 'back ★

BUOY /bɔɪ, *American* 'buːi/
buoys, buoying, buoyed

,buoy 'up [usually passive]
    1 to encourage someone and make them feel more confident ≠ DEPRESS
    be buoyed up *He has been buoyed up by the news.*
    2 to help a company, market, or economy to be more successful = BOOST
    be buoyed up *The stock market was buoyed up by comments from the Bank of England chairman.*

CENTER the American spelling of **centre**

ADMIT /əd'mɪt/
admits, admitting, admitted

ad'mit of *very formal*
to make it possible for something to happen or be allowed = ALLOW OF
    admit of sth *The incident may admit of another explanation.*

Grammar patterns

Every meaning of a phrasal verb has grammar patterns that show whether the verb takes an object, whether the object is a person (**sb**) or thing (**sth**), and where that object can go.

,charge 'up
to put electricity into a piece of electrical equipment such as a battery
→ **charge up sth** *also* **charge sth up** *I need to charge up my mobile phone.*

Intransitive phrasal verbs that never take an object are shown like this.

,band to'gether ★
to come together as a group in order to achieve something = JOIN TOGETHER
→ **band together** *The various opposition groups have banded together to form a single party.*

Transitive phrasal verbs where the object or pronoun always follow the particle are shown like this.

'act for ★★
if you act for someone, you do something as their representative = REPRESENT
→ **act for sb** *Lawyers acting for the family will issue a statement this morning.*

Transitive phrasal verbs where the object or pronoun can go between the verb and particle, or after the particle, are shown like this.

,hash 'out *informal*
to discuss a plan or agreement in order to agree about the details = THRASH OUT
→ **hash out sth** *also* **hash sth out** *We hashed out some of the details of the plan.*

Transitive phrasal verbs where an object can follow both the verb and the particle are shown like this.

,drag 'out of
to force or persuade someone to tell you something when they do not want to
→ **drag sth out of sb** *He only told me her name, and I had to drag that out of him.*

At red phrasal verbs, all grammar patterns are shown on separate lines.

,cross 'off ★
to draw a line through something on a list to show that you have dealt with it
→ **cross sth off** *The children tell their names to the teacher, who crosses each one off.*
→ **cross off sth** *Cross off the hotels after you've phoned them.*
→ **cross sth off sth** *I'd already crossed several items off the list.*

Other grammar patterns show whether a phrasal verb is often or usually used in the passive, and whether it is followed by a gerund.

,curtain 'off [usually passive]
to separate an area from the rest of a room or area by a curtain
be curtained off *The clean area is curtained off from the rest.*

con'ceive of [usually in negatives or questions]
to imagine something or think of doing something
→ **conceive of (doing) sth** *How can they even conceive of doing such an appalling thing?*

Labels
Labels in *italic* tell you whether
a word is used only in American
or British English, or in formal
or informal contexts. Lists of
these labels are given on the
inside front cover.

Examples
Example sentences in *italic* show
you how a word is used in
context.

Information about collocation
and syntax – how words combine
and which structures they can be
used with – is shown in **bold
type**.

When a phrasal verb has many
collocations, these are shown in
a box at the end of the meaning
or entry.

,ace 'out *American informal*
  to be much better than someone else, or
  to defeat someone in a competition
  ace out sb *also* **ace sb out** *Odelay aced
  out Clapton for the best performance.*

'check on ★★
  to look at someone or something so that
  you are certain they are safe, satisfactory
  etc
  check on sb/sth *I sent Michael to check
  on the kids.* ♦ *The boss arrived to check
  on our progress.*

,bone 'up *informal*
  to learn as much as possible about
  something in order to prepare for a test,
  meeting etc
  bone up *He's boning up for his final
  exams.* ♦ **+on** *She boned up on the
  company before the interview.*

,cast 'off ★★
  1 to get rid of someone or something that
  you do not want or need = DISCARD
  cast off sth *It took many years for
  Chicago to **cast off its reputation** as the
  home of violent gangsters.*
  cast sth off *The company has worked
  hard to cast that image off.*

,die 'down ★★
  if something dies down, it becomes much
  less noisy, powerful, or active = SUBSIDE
  die down *I waited for the noise to die
  down before I spoke.* ♦ *The wind died
  down during the night.*

  Nouns often used as subjects with **die down**
  ■ applause, commotion, excitement,
  fighting, fuss, laughter, noise, protest

Expanding your vocabulary

There are many ways that you can use this dictionary to expand your vocabulary.

Some definitions give you synonyms. _____

Sometimes the opposite of a word is shown. _____

Sometimes you are told to look at another word or page in the dictionary where you will find a related entry or a picture. _____

,**count 'in** [often in imperative]
to include someone in your plans
= INCLUDE ≠ COUNT OUT, EXCLUDE
count sb in *'There's a party on Saturday.' – 'Count me in!'* ♦ *If you need help, you can count me in.*

,**crowd 'round** *same as* **count on**

,**come 'round** *British*
to become conscious again after being unconscious = COME TO ≠ BLACK OUT
—*picture* → PASS OUT
come round *When I came round, I was lying on the back seat of a car.*

If a synonym or opposite is more formal than the phrasal verb it is shown at, it has a *formal* label. _____

,**bottle 'up**
if you bottle up a negative feeling such as anger or disappointment, you stop yourself from showing it over a period of time, so that it often develops in a harmful way = *formal* CONTAIN
bottle up sth *also* **bottle sth up** *She had bottled up her resentment for years.*
♦ *Talking about how you feel can be better than bottling it all up.*

If a synonym or opposite is more informal than the phrasal verb it is shown at, it has an *informal* label. _____

,**hold 'on to** (*also* ,**hold 'onto**)
1 to hold something tightly or carefully so that you do not drop it or lose it
hold on to sth *Hold onto your purse, won't you?*
2 to not lose something or not let someone else have it = *informal* HANG ON TO
hold on to sth *Hold on to the instructions in case you have any problems.*

For more information on synonyms of phrasal verbs, see the **Index of Single-Word Equivalents** at the back of the book, on page 515.

ABANDON /ə'bændən/
abandons, abandoning, abandoned

a'bandon to *literary*
to feel an emotion so strongly that you do not think about anything else = GIVE UP TO
abandon yourself to sth *She hid her face and abandoned herself to grief.*

ABIDE /ə'baɪd/
abides, abiding, abode /ə'bəʊd/ or abided

a'bide by ★ *formal*
to accept a rule, decision, or instruction and obey it = OBEY; *informal* STICK TO
abide by sth *They promised to abide by the rules of the contest.*

ABOUND /ə'baʊnd/
abounds, abounding, abounded

a'bound in (*also* **a'bound with**) *formal*
to be filled with or contain a lot of something
abound in sth *The markets abound with imported goods.*

ABSOLVE /əb'zɒlv, American əb'zɑlv/
absolves, absolving, absolved

ab'solve from (*also* **ab'solve of**) *formal*
to state officially that someone should not be blamed for something or is not responsible for something
absolve sb from sth *also* **absolve sb of sth** *The report absolves the pilot from any blame for the crash.* ◆ *She absolved herself of all responsibility for the failure.*

ABSORB /əb'zɔːb, American əb'sɔrb, əb'zɔrb/
absorbs, absorbing, absorbed

be ab'sorbed in
to be so interested or involved in something that you do not notice anything else = BE WRAPPED UP IN
be absorbed in sth *Phil has been absorbed in his work all morning.*

ABSTAIN /əb'steɪn/
abstains, abstaining, abstained

ab'stain from
1 to deliberately avoid doing something that is enjoyable but may not be healthy, safe, or morally right
abstain from (doing) sth *A high percentage of women said they had abstained from alcohol during pregnancy.* ◆ *We were asked to abstain from eating meat.*
2 *formal* to not do something that is likely to cause serious problems = REFRAIN FROM
abstain from (doing) sth *They agreed to abstain from any actions that might endanger the peace process.* ◆ *Countries agreed to abstain from deploying these weapons.*

ACCEDE /ək'siːd, American ək'sid/
accedes, acceding, acceded

ac'cede to *formal*
1 to do what someone wants, or to agree with what they say = BOW TO
accede to sth *They were forced to accede to all of the hijackers' demands.*
2 to formally take a position of authority, especially as a king, queen, or president
accede to sth *1952 was the year in which Queen Elizabeth acceded to the throne.*

ACCOMMODATE /ə'kɒmədeɪt, American ə'kɑmədeɪt/
accommodates, accommodating, accommodated

ac'commodate to *formal*
to change your attitudes and behaviour in order to deal with a new situation
accommodate to sth *Some colleagues were reluctant to accommodate to new ways of working.*
accommodate yourself to sth *The Masai people hadn't accommodated themselves to the modern world.*

ACCORD /ə'kɔːd, American ə'kɔrd/
accords, according, accorded

ac'cord with *formal*
to be very similar to something, or to be suitable in relation to something = MATCH, MATCH UP WITH
accord with sth *Hemming's account does not accord with the police evidence.*
◆ *The design didn't accord with my idea of how the house should look.*

ACCOUNT /əˈkaʊnt/
accounts, accounting, accounted

acˈcount for ★★★

1 be the reason for sth
2 be an amount or part of sth
3 explain sth bad that you have done
4 say how you will spend money
5 know where sb/sth is
+ PHRASE

1 to be the reason why something exists or happens = EXPLAIN
account for sth *A number of factors account for the differences between the two scores.*

2 to form, use, or produce a particular amount or part of something = MAKE UP
account for sth *Repeat purchases account for 73% of our sales.*

3 to give an explanation for something bad that has happened, especially something you are responsible for = EXPLAIN
account for sth *You will be brought before the head teacher to account for your behaviour.*

4 [often passive] to say how you have used, or how you will use, an amount of money that you are responsible for spending, especially in your job
be accounted for *Investors were told that over half their savings had vanished and could not be accounted for.*
account for sth *She had to account for every cent that she spent.*

5 [always passive] if someone or something is accounted for, you know where they are and so you do not worry about them
be accounted for *One small child from the group was still not accounted for.*
PHRASE **there's no accounting for taste** used for saying that you think what someone likes is strange: *She seems to like him, but I suppose there's no accounting for taste.*

ACCRUE /əˈkruː, American əˈkru/
accrues, accruing, accrued

acˈcrue to *formal*
if things such as benefits and advantages accrue to you, you receive them
accrue to sb *The same pension benefits would accrue to people who retire early.*

ACCUSTOM /əˈkʌstəm/
accustoms, accustoming, accustomed

acˈcustom to [often passive]
to gradually start to feel that something is normal or natural
be accustomed to sth *He was accustomed to living without electricity.*
accustom sb/yourself to sth *The manager is taking his team to train in South Africa in order to accustom them to the heat.* ♦ *It took her a moment to accustom herself to the dim light inside.*

ACE /eɪs/
aces, acing, aced

ˌace ˈout *American informal*
to be much better than someone else, or to defeat someone in a competition
ace out sb *also* **ace sb out** *Odelay aced out Clapton for the best performance.*

ACHE /eɪk/
aches, aching, ached

ˈache for *literary*
to want very much to do or have something
ache for sth *I was aching for the sound of her voice.*

ACKNOWLEDGE /əkˈnɒlɪdʒ, American əkˈnɑlɪdʒ/
acknowledges, acknowledging, acknowledged

acˈknowledge as [usually passive]
to recognize the true character or importance of someone or something
= RECOGNIZE AS
be acknowledged as sth *Wimbledon is widely acknowledged as being the premier tennis tournament.*

ACQUAINT /əˈkweɪnt/
acquaints, acquainting, acquainted

aˈcquaint with *formal*
1 [often passive] to know or learn about something = FAMILIARIZE WITH
be acquainted with sth *Are we all acquainted with the details of the case?*
acquaint yourself with sth *She had failed to acquaint herself with the facts.*

2 to give someone information about something
acquaint sb with sth *We aim to acquaint policy makers with some of these issues.*

ACT /ækt/
acts, acting, acted

'act as ★★★
to do the job of a particular type of person or thing = SERVE AS
act as sth *You speak Greek – will you act as interpreter?* ♦ *Body fat acts as an insulator.*

'act for ★★
if you act for someone, you do something as their representative = REPRESENT
act for sb *Lawyers acting for the family will issue a statement this morning.*

'act on ★★★
1 to do something because you have been given information, advice, or orders
act on sth *I'm acting on the advice of my lawyers.* ♦ *They were acting on the instructions of senior managers.*

Nouns often used as objects with **act on 1**
■ **advice, information, instructions, orders, recommendation, tip-off**

2 to have an effect on something or someone
act on sb/sth *The experiment should show us how sugars act on the enamel of the teeth.*

,act 'out ★
1 to show the events that happened in a situation by doing them again or doing the same things as the people involved = ENACT
act out sth *The girls were asked to act out the events of that night.*
act sth out *Studying history became more important than acting it out.*

2 to express your thoughts or feelings through your words or behaviour = VENT
act out sth *He was acting out his feelings of inferiority by being overly aggressive.*
act sth out *You control this emotion. You do not act it out.*

3 to do something that you have planned or had previously only thought of
act sth out *Just imagining these things is fine, as long as you don't try to act them out.*

,act 'up *informal*
1 if children act up, they behave badly = MISBEHAVE, PLAY UP
act up *The kids have been acting up again.*

2 if a part of your body or a piece of equipment acts up, it starts to become painful or to develop problems = PLAY UP ≠ BEHAVE

act up *I hope my back doesn't start acting up again.*

ADD /æd/
adds, adding, added

,add 'in ★
to add something, or to add more of something
add in sth *We need to add in some information about his family.*
add sth in *Once you add travel costs in the whole scheme begins to look expensive.*

,add 'on ★
1 to include an extra thing or amount in something
add on sth *The referee added on eight minutes of injury time.*
add sth on *Hidden charges could add 25% on the cost of travel.*

2 *American* to build an extra part on to a building = *British* EXTEND
add on *They refurbished the whole place and even added on.*

■ **'add-on** noun [C] something that is added to something else: *I just want the basic blender, with no add-ons.*

,add 'on to
to build an extra part on to a building = EXTEND
add on to sth *You might want to add on to the kitchen at a later date.*

'add to ★★★
1 to make something such as a feeling or quality greater or more extreme
add to sth *The arrival of five more guests only added to the confusion.*

2 [often passive] to make an amount or number greater by adding another amount or number
be added to sth *All her many expenses were added to my bill.*
add sth to sth *Add the amount of tax you paid to the total.*

,add 'up ★★
1 to calculate the total of several numbers or amounts = ADD ≠ SUBTRACT
add up *I'm not very good at adding up in my head.*
add up sth *Now add up the number of calories you have eaten.*
add sth up *I've added it up three times and the answer is different each time.*

2 if small amounts add up, they gradually produce a large total = ACCUMULATE
add up *All these little expenses soon add up.*

PHRASE **not add up** if the different parts of a situation or what someone has told you do not add up, it does not seem reasonable or correct when everything is considered together: *There's something about this case that just doesn't add up.*

,add 'up to

1 if separate amounts add up to a total amount, together they form that total = COME TO, TOTAL
add up to sth *His business expenses add up to around £4,000 a year.*

2 to combine to produce a particular result or effect = AMOUNT TO
add up to sth *These new measures do not add up to genuine reform.* ♦ *We offer a range of attractions that all add up to a great day out for the family.*

ADDRESS /ə'dres/
addresses, addressing, addressed

ad'dress as [often passive]
to call someone by a particular name or title when you speak to them
be addressed as sth *She prefers to be addressed as Lady Black.*
address sb as sth *His stepchildren address him as 'Mr. H'.*

ad'dress by [often passive]
to use a particular name when you speak to someone
be addressed by sth *We were all addressed by our last names.*
address sb by sth *Some callers address you by your full name.*

ad'dress to

1 [often passive] to officially direct your complaints, questions, or comments to a particular person or organization
be addressed to sb *All further inquiries should be addressed to your course professor.*
address sth to sb *You should address your remarks to the chairman.*

2 *formal* to give all your attention to something
address yourself to sth *It's time to address ourselves to the matter of finance.*

ADHERE /əd'hɪə, American əd'hɪr/
adheres, adhering, adhered

ad'here to ★★ *formal*

1 to obey a rule, law, agreement etc = ABIDE BY
adhere to sth *We must strictly adhere to the terms of the contract.*

2 to support or believe in an idea, plan, opinion etc = SUBSCRIBE TO

adhere to sth *His followers adhere to a blend of Buddhist, Hindu, and Christian teachings.*

ADJOURN /ə'dʒɜːn, American ə'dʒɜrn/
adjourns, adjourning, adjourned

ad'journ to ★ *formal*
to leave one place and move to another
adjourn to sth *Let's adjourn to the bar.*

ADMIT /əd'mɪt/
admits, admitting, admitted

ad'mit of *very formal*
to make it possible for something to happen or be allowed = ALLOW OF
admit of sth *The incident may admit of another explanation.*

ADVISE /əd'vaɪz/
advises, advising, advised

ad'vise against
to tell someone that you think they should not do something = WARN AGAINST
advise against (doing) sth *The police are advising against travelling in this weather.*
advise sb against (doing) sth *She advised me against accepting the invitation.*

ad'vise of ★ *formal*
to tell someone about something
advise sb of sth *They advised me of the best route to take home.* ♦ *Please advise us of any changes to these details.*

AFFILIATE /ə'fɪlieɪt/
affiliates, affiliating, affiliated

be af'filiated to (*also* be af'filiated with)
to be officially connected with a larger organization or group
be affiliated to sth *The local youth group was affiliated to the national party.*

AGONIZE /'ægənaɪz/
agonizes, agonizing, agonized

'agonize over (*also* 'agonize about)
to spend a long time making a decision because you are worried that you might not make the right one
agonize over sth *For years I agonized over whether I should have told her.*

AGREE /əˈgriː, American əˈgri/
agrees, agreeing, agreed

aˈgree with ★★★

1 *linguistics* if a word such as a verb or adjective agrees with a noun or pronoun, it has the correct form for the noun or pronoun, according to whether it is singular or plural, masculine or feminine
agree with sth *The verb in the sentence has to agree with the subject.*
2 if a situation or way of living agrees with you, you enjoy it and you feel happy and relaxed
agree with sb *I find that country life really agrees with me.*
PHRASES **not agree with sth** to think that something is the wrong thing to do: *I don't agree with corporal punishment in schools.* ♦ *He doesn't agree with giving money to beggars.*
not agree with sb if something such as food or drink does not agree with you, it makes you feel ill: *Stop taking the medicine if it doesn't agree with you.*

AIM /eɪm/
aims, aiming, aimed

ˈaim at ★★★

1 [often passive] if you aim something you say, write, or create at a particular group, you want that group to listen to or use what you have said or created
be aimed at sb *The book is aimed at people with no specialized knowledge.*
♦ *The remark seemed to be aimed at parents who allow their children to stay off school.*
aim sth at sb *We should be aiming our message at a younger audience.*
2 [always passive] if a plan or idea is aimed at a particular thing, it is intended to achieve that thing
be aimed at sth *The regulations are aimed at the prevention of accidents at work.*
be aimed at doing sth *This country needs an energy programme aimed at reducing our dependence on fossil fuels.*

ALERT /əˈlɜːt, American əˈlɜrt/
alerts, alerting, alerted

aˈlert to *formal*

to tell someone about something that might affect them = WARN OF
alert sb to sth *Something in his voice alerted Paige to the real danger.*

ALIGHT /əˈlaɪt/
alights, alighting, alighted

aˈlight on *literary*

to suddenly notice or think of something
alight on sth *Her eyes alighted on an extraordinary sight.*

ALIGN /əˈlaɪn/
aligns, aligning, aligned

aˈlign with

1 [often passive] to give your support publicly to a group, political party, or country
be aligned with sb/sth *The union's leaders are aligned with the ruling party and the military.*
align yourself with sb/sth *Many women do not want to align themselves with the movement.*
2 to organize activities or systems so that they match or fit well together
align sth with sth *We have closely aligned our research and development work with our business needs.*

ALLOW /əˈlaʊ/
allows, allowing, allowed

alˈlow for ★★★

to consider something when making a plan or calculation = TAKE INTO ACCOUNT
allow for sth *The cost of the new road, allowing for inflation, is around £17 million.* ♦ *The survey does not allow for the fact that some students are attending part-time.*

alˈlow of *formal*

to show that something is possible = ADMIT OF
allow of sth *The evidence allows of no other interpretation.*

ALLUDE /əˈluːd, American əˈlud/
alludes, alluding, alluded

alˈlude to ★★ *formal*

to mention someone or something in an indirect way = REFER TO
allude to sth/sb *She made no mention of the problem she alluded to earlier.*

ALLY /əˈlaɪ, ˈælaɪ/
allies, allying, allied

alˈly with

1 if you ally yourself with someone, you work together to help each other

ally yourself with sb *Bruce had allied himself with the English.*

2 to show your close support for something, for example a belief or an organization

ally yourself with sth *The group allies itself with no political party.* ♦ *He refused to ally himself with Marxist philosophy.*

ALTERNATE /ˈɔːltəneɪt, *American* ˈɔltərˌneɪt/
alternates, alternating, alternated

'alternate between
if someone or something alternates between two things, they keep changing between them

alternate between sth and sth *His mood alternates between joy and despair.*

'alternate with
if one thing alternates with another, it happens after it and keeps being repeated

alternate with sth *Wet days alternated with dry ones.*

AMALGAMATE /əˈmælgəmeɪt/
amalgamates, amalgamating, amalgamated

a'malgamate with [often passive]
to join two or more organizations, businesses etc and make a single large one

be amalgamated with sth *They were amalgamated with the Miners' Union.*
amalgamate sth with sth *There are plans to amalgamate the village school with a larger one nearby.*

AMOUNT /əˈmaʊnt/
amounts, amounting, amounted

a'mount to ★★★
1 to be the same as something else, or to have a very similar effect to something else **=** *formal* CONSTITUTE

amount to sth *They're not calling the operation an attack, but it amounts to the same thing.* ♦ *Two dates in nine years hardly amounts to an active social life.*

2 to add up to a particular total **=** COME TO, TOTAL

amount to sth *His monthly earnings amount to about £2,000.*

> **PHRASE not amount to much/a great deal** to not be very impressive, important etc: *The results of the research don't really amount to much.*

ANCHOR /ˈæŋkə, *American* ˈæŋkər/
anchors, anchoring, anchored

be 'anchored in
if something is anchored in a particular set of ideas or beliefs, it is firmly based on it

be anchored in sth *Their approach is firmly anchored in a Christian world view.*

ANGLE /ˈæŋg(ə)l/
angles, angling, angled

'angle for *informal*
to try to make someone give you something without asking for it directly **=** FISH FOR

angle for sth *She didn't want Ron thinking she was angling for sympathy.*

ANSWER /ˈɑːnsə, *American* ˈænsər/
answers, answering, answered

,answer 'back ★
to reply rudely to someone who has more authority than you

answer sb back *Don't you dare answer me back!*
answer back *I don't like children who answer back.*

answer someone back

'answer for ★★
to agree to be responsible for something
answer for sth *If we allow you to have a party at home you'll have to answer for any damage that happens!*

> **PHRASES can't answer for sb** used for emphasizing that you cannot say what someone else will do or think about something: *I can't answer for my colleagues, but as far as I'm concerned this is a great proposal.*
> **have a lot to answer for** to be responsible for a lot of bad things that

have happened: *I think the parents of these kids have a lot to answer for.*

'answer to ★

to have to explain to someone why you did something = BE ACCOUNTABLE TO
answer to sb *I answer to no one except myself.*

PHRASE **answer to the name of sth** if an animal answers to the name of something, it comes to you when you call it this name: *They have a cat that answers to the name of Harry.*

ANTE /'ænti/
antes, anteing, anted

,ante 'up *American informal*

to pay an amount of money, usually an amount that you owe, or your share of an amount that other people are also paying = PAY UP; *British* COUGH UP
ante up *Tell the other boys to ante up.*
ante up sth *He wants the company to ante up 5 million dollars in compensation.*

APPEAL /ə'piːl, *American* ə'pil/
appeals, appealing, appealed

ap'peal for ★★★

1 to make an urgent request for people to give you something that you need such as help, money, or information
appeal for sth *Once again, the country was appealing for emergency aid.* ♦ *The police have appealed for witnesses.*
appeal to sb for sth *They're appealing to local businesses for sponsorship money.*

Nouns often used as objects with **appeal for 1**

■ aid, assistance, donations, help, information, support, volunteers, witnesses

2 to ask people to behave in a particular way, especially in a difficult situation
appeal for sth *As the crisis grew worse, local community leaders appealed for calm.*

ap'peal to ★★★

1 if something appeals to you, you like it or want it
appeal to sb *The show's direct approach will appeal to children.*

2 to try to get someone to do or accept something by making them think it is a sensible or fair thing to do
appeal to sth *Max tried appealing to her good sense.*

APPERTAIN /ˌæpə'teɪn, *American* ˌæpər'teɪn/
appertains, appertaining, appertained

apper'tain to *very formal*

to affect or be relevant to a particular person or thing = APPLY TO, RELATE TO
appertain to sb/sth *We would especially remind you of the particular regulations appertaining to the army.*

APPLY /ə'plaɪ/
applies, applying, applied

ap'ply to ★★★

to affect or be relevant to a particular person or thing = RELATE TO; *formal* APPERTAIN TO
apply to sb *The discount no longer applies to him because he's over eighteen.* ♦ *She seems to think that the law doesn't apply to her.*
apply to sth *The rule applies to all schools in the area.*

APPRISE /ə'praɪz/
apprises, apprising, apprised

ap'prise of *formal*

to tell someone about something = INFORM
apprise sb of sth *It was my role to apprise them of the current situation.*

ARGUE /'ɑːgjuː, *American* 'ɑrˌgju/
argues, arguing, argued

'argue into

to persuade someone to do something
argue sb into sth *They might be able to argue him into accepting.* ♦ *The judges had argued us into submission.*

'argue out of

to persuade someone not to do something
argue sb out of sth *I argued the bank out of making a decision immediately.* ♦ *We were hoping to argue them out of such a drastic change.*

ARRAY /ə'reɪ/
arrays, arraying, arrayed

be ar'rayed against *literary*

if people are arrayed against you, they are ready to fight or oppose you
be arrayed against sb *Considering the forces arrayed against him, the prime minister put up a pretty good fight.*

be ar'rayed in *literary*

to be dressed in clothes of a particular type

Around and **round** are used with the same meaning, but around is far more common in American English, and **round** is far more common in British English. **About** can also be used with the first two literal meanings listed below.

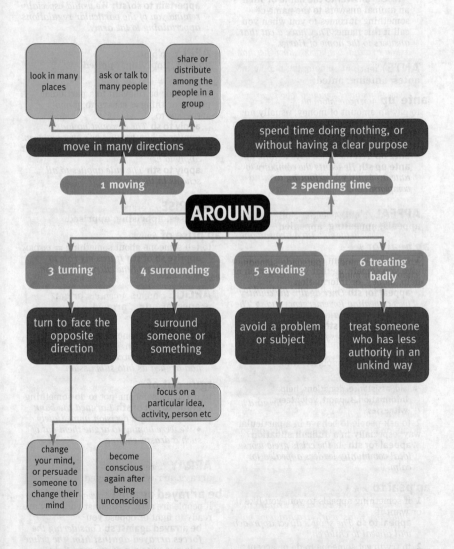

Main meanings	Example verbs		
1 moving			
move in many directions	bustle around	move around	rush around
*The kids were screaming and **running around** the playground.*	go around	run around	show around
look in many places	look around	scout around	snoop around
*We've started **looking around** for a new house.*	nose around	shop around	
ask or talk to many people	ask around	call around	phone around
*I **asked around**, but nobody knew her name.*			
share or distribute among the people in a group	hand around	pass around	spread around
*Do you think there's enough food to **go around**?*			
2 spending time			
spend time doing nothing, or without having a clear purpose	fiddle around	loaf around	play around
	fool around	loll around	sit around
*He just **sits around** the house all weekend and watches TV.* ♦ *Stop **fooling around** and get to work!*	hang around	lounge around	stand around
	kick around	mess around	stick around
	lie around	mope around	wait around
3 turning			
turn to face the opposite direction	spin around	swivel around	wheel around
*When you get to the end, **turn around** and come back.*	swing around	turn around	
change your mind, or persuade someone to change their mind	bring around	talk around	win around
*I knew they'd eventually **come around** to my point of view.*	come around		
become conscious again after being unconscious	bring around	come around	
*The cool night air quickly **brought** her **around**.*			
4 surrounding			
surround someone or something	cluster around	gather around	throw around
*I just wanted to **throw** my arms **around** him and give him a big kiss.*	crowd around		
focus on a particular idea, activity, person etc	centre around	revolve around	
*Village life **revolves around** the harvest.*			
5 avoiding			
avoid a problem or subject	go around	skate around	talk around
*There must be some way to **get around** these regulations.* ♦ *Just **work around** it for now – we'll find a solution later.*	get around	skirt around	work around
6 treating badly			
treat someone who has less authority in an unkind way	boss around	order around	shove around
*My older sister always **bossed** us **around**.*	kick around	push around	

be arrayed in sth *The soldiers were arrayed in Hungarian national dress.*

ARRIVE /əˈraɪv/
arrives, arriving, arrived

arˈrive at ★
to reach a result, decision, or solution to a problem = REACH
arrive at sth *How did they arrive at that figure?* ♦ *The two studies arrive at very different conclusions.*

ARSE /ɑːs/
arses, arsing, arsed

ˌarse aˈround (*also* ˌarse aˈbout) *British impolite*
to behave in a way that is not sensible

ASCRIBE /əˈskraɪb/
ascribes, ascribing, ascribed

aˈscribe to *formal*
1 [usually passive] to believe that something is the cause of something else = ATTRIBUTE TO
be ascribed to sth *Their defeat was ascribed to a poor defence.*
2 to believe that something is a typical quality of someone or something
ascribe sth to sb/sth *We wrongly ascribe human feelings to animals.*
3 [usually passive] to believe that a particular person wrote a book or a piece of music, painted a picture etc so that people generally accept this to be true = ATTRIBUTE TO
be ascribed to sb *The poem is ascribed to Homer.*

ASK /ɑːsk, *American* æsk/
asks, asking, asked

ˈask after
to ask for news about someone = INQUIRE AFTER
ask after sb *I met Bob and he asked after you.*

ˌask aˈlong
to invite someone to go somewhere with you or do something with you = INVITE ALONG
ask sb along *It was generous of them to ask her along.*

ˌask aˈround (*also* ˌask ˈround *British*)
to ask several people for information or advice
ask around *I asked around, but nobody had seen him for days.*

ˌask ˈback ★
to ask someone to come to your home, especially after you have both been somewhere together = INVITE BACK
ask sb back *I'd like to ask you back but my parents are at home.* ♦ **+to** *Did she ask you back to her place?* ♦ **+for** *They asked me back for lunch after the service.*

ˈask for ★★★
1 to speak or write to someone because you want them to give you something = *formal* REQUEST
ask for sth *He's always reluctant to ask for anyone's help.* ♦ *Why don't you ask for a rise?*
ask sb for sth *He asked me for a ride back to the apartment.*
2 to say that you want someone to come and speak to you
ask for sb *There's someone in the shop asking for the manager.*
PHRASES **be asking for sth** to behave in a way that makes it likely that a particular unpleasant thing will happen to you: *She's asking for trouble speaking to people like that.*
be asking for it *Anyone who drives while they're drunk is just asking for it.*
sb couldn't ask for sth *informal* used for emphasizing that something is so good that nothing could be better: *I couldn't ask for a more caring bunch of people to work with.* ♦ *We couldn't have asked for better weather.*

ˌask ˈin
to invite someone who has called to see you to come into your house, your room etc = INVITE IN
ask sb in *She decided not to ask him in.* ♦ **+for** *I'd ask you in for a coffee but I'm just going out.*

ˌask ˈout ★
to invite someone to go with you to a cinema, restaurant etc because you want to start a romantic or sexual relationship with them = INVITE OUT
ask sb out *Finally he asked her out.* ♦ **+for** *He's asked me out for dinner.*

ˌask ˈover (*also* ˌask ˈround)
to invite someone to come to your house, for example to have a meal = INVITE OVER
ask sb over *None of the neighbours has ever asked us over.* ♦ **+for** *They've asked us over for a drink later.*

ˌask ˈround
1 *same as* **ask over**
2 *British same as* **ask around**

ask out

move in

run off with

Goodbye
for ever!
from
your wife

break up/split up

verbs to do with relationships

'ask to

to invite someone to do something or go somewhere with you
ask sb to sth *How many people have you asked to the party?*

ASPIRE /ə'spaɪə, *American* ə'spaɪr/
aspires, aspiring, aspired

a'spire to

to want to achieve something, or want to be successful, especially in your career
aspire to sth *She aspires to nothing less than the chairmanship of the company.*
PHRASE **sth that sb can only aspire to**
used for saying that someone will never achieve something: *She achieved the kind of success that the others could only aspire to.*

ASSIGN /ə'saɪn/
assigns, assigning, assigned

as'sign to [usually passive]

to send someone to a particular place, especially in order for them to work there
be assigned to sth *He was assigned to the company's branch in Cairo.*

ASSOCIATE /ə'səʊsieɪt, *American* ə'soʊʃiˌeɪt/
associates, associating, associated

as'sociate with

1 to spend time with someone = MIX WITH
associate with sb *While she was in Paris, she associated with many well-known artists.*

2 to form a connection in your mind between different people or things
associate sth with sth *We associate babies with crying.* ♦ *The study found that many people associate science with masculinity.*
PHRASE **associate yourself with sb/sth**
to say publicly that you support a person or group or that you agree with something: *It would be bad for us to associate ourselves with the movement.*

ATONE /ə'təʊn, *American* ə'toʊn/
atones, atoning, atoned

a'tone for *formal*

to show that you are sorry for doing something bad or wrong
atone for sth *Gifts are an excellent way of atoning for sins.*

Away has several different meanings when it is used as part of a phrasal verb. Some of these meanings are literal, but many are figurative. This diagram shows how all these meanings are connected, and how the figurative meanings develop from the literal ones.

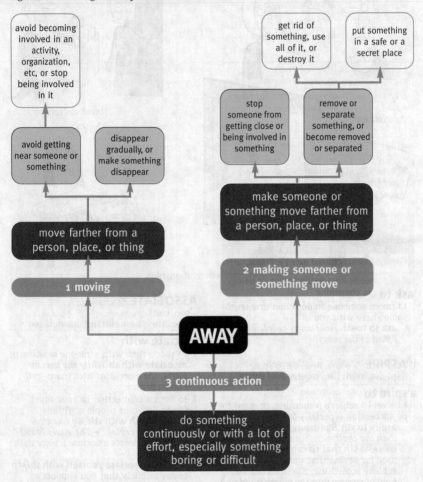

Main meanings	Example verbs		
1 moving			
move farther from a person, place, or thing *The Harrises **moved away** in April.* ♦ *I managed to **slip away** from the meeting without anyone noticing.*	back away break away come away	get away go away move away	run away slip away walk away
avoid getting near someone or something *Police warned us to **stay away** from the area.*	keep away	stay away	
avoid becoming involved in an activity, organization etc, or stop being involved in it *Nick isn't one to **shy away** from hard work.* ♦ *I'd love to just **get away from** it all for a week or two.*	back away break away fall away get away from	grow away from keep away move away from pull away	shy away stay away turn away from walk away from
disappear gradually, or make something disappear *Thomson's critics have continued to **chip away** at his credibility.* ♦ *Many of the old traditions are **dying away**.*	chip away crumble away die away drop away eat away fade away	melt away pass away rot away rust away seep away slip away	trail away waste away wear away whittle away wither away
2 making someone or something move			
make someone or something move farther from a person, place, or thing *The dog quickly **chased away** all the squirrels.*	call away chase away	send away spirit away	tow away wave away
stop someone from getting close or being involved in something *The birds have special markings to **warn away** predators.*	drive away frighten away push away	scare away steer away	warn away wave away
remove or separate something, or become removed or separated *He just can't **tear** himself **away** from the TV.* ♦ *The old paint had begun to **peel away**.*	break away burn away come away	fall away peel away pull away	strip away take away tear away
get rid of something, use all of it, or destroy it *You can't **do away with** racism simply by passing new laws.* ♦ *Over the years, the couple have **given away** millions of dollars.*	blow away brush away chuck away cut away do away with fritter away	gamble away give away kiss away magic away sign away sweep away	throw away toss away wash away while away wipe away wish away
put something in a safe or a secret place ***Put** your toys **away** and go to bed.* ♦ *I'm sure he has the letter **filed away** somewhere.*	clear away file away hide away hoard away lock away	pack away put away salt away shut away squirrel away	stash away store away stow away tidy away tuck away
3 continuous action			
do something continuously or with a lot of effort, especially something boring or difficult *They were still **talking away** when I went to bed.* ♦ *You expect me to **slave away** in the kitchen while you read a book.*	bang away beaver away blaze away chat away hammer away	jabber away peg away plod away plug away slave away	slog away talk away toil away work away

ATTACH /əˈtætʃ/
attaches, attaching, attached

atˈtach to ★★★
1 to believe that something has a certain meaning or importance
attach sth to sth *I don't think you should attach too much importance to their comments.*

Nouns often used as objects with **attach to 1**

■ importance, meaning, significance, value, weight

2 [usually passive] if a quality is attached to someone or something, they have that quality
be attached to sth *There's inevitably an element of risk attached to sports such as skiing.* ♦ *There will be considerable prestige attached to his new position.*
3 [usually passive] to be sent to work with a different group of people or in a different place, especially temporarily
be attached to sth *She is now attached to the American Embassy in Beijing.*
4 to join a particular person or group
attach yourself to sb *They soon attached themselves to a group of women discussing the next day's activities.*

ATTEND /əˈtend/
attends, attending, attended

atˈtend to ★★★
1 to deal with something = SEE TO ≠ IGNORE
attend to sth *We still have a number of other matters to attend to.*
2 [often passive] to deal with someone, for example a customer in a shop or a patient waiting to see a doctor = SEE TO ≠ IGNORE
be attended to *Are you being attended to?*
attend to sb *If you wait here, I'll find someone to attend to you.*
3 *very formal* to pay attention to something
attend to sth *We were required to attend to the tiniest details.*

ATTEST /əˈtest/
attests, attesting, attested

atˈtest to *formal*
to show or prove that something is true
attest to sth *These results attest to the efficiency of the system.*

ATTRIBUTE /əˈtrɪbjuːt, *American* əˈtrɪˌbjut/
attributes, attributing, attributed

atˈtribute to ★★★
1 [often passive] to believe that something is the result of a particular situation, event, or fact
be attributed to sth *His election defeat was attributed by many people to his policy on tax cuts.*
attribute sth to sth *Her teachers attributed her learning difficulties to emotional problems.*
2 [often passive] to believe or say that something was written, said, painted etc by a particular person
be attributed to sb *The remarks attributed to him have been taken out of context.*
attribute sth to sb *Experts originally attributed Marcello's work to his brother Benedetto.*
3 to think of someone or something as having a particular quality or feature
attribute sth to sb/sth *People are attributing qualities to me that I just don't have.*

ATTUNE /əˈtjuːn, *American* əˈtjun/
attunes, attuning, attuned

be atˈtuned to
to be familiar with something and able to deal with it in a sensitive way
be attuned to sth *The company needs people who are attuned to today's youth culture.*

AUCTION /ˈɔːkʃ(ə)n, *American* ˈɔkʃ(ə)n/
auctions, auctioning, auctioned

ˈauction off [often passive]
to sell something at an auction
be auctioned off *Watching my family's possessions being auctioned off was more painful than I'd expected.*
auction off sth *also* **auction sth off** *When I'm dead, they'll auction off the farm.*

AVAIL /əˈveɪl/
avails, availing, availed

aˈvail of *formal*
if you avail yourself of something, you use it = USE
avail yourself of sth *Companies have availed themselves of the free training programme.*

AVENGE /əˈvendʒ/
avenges, avenging, avenged

aˈvenge on
to react to something wrong that has been done to you, your family, or your friends by punishing the person who did it
avenge yourself on sb *They began to avenge themselves on their neighbours.*

AVERAGE /ˈæv(ə)rɪdʒ/
averages, averaging, averaged

ˌaverage ˈout [often passive]
to calculate the average of a set of numbers or amounts
be averaged out *The total amount is averaged out on a daily basis.*
average out sth *also* **average sth out** *We average out the incomes of everyone living in the house.*

ˌaverage ˈout at
to have a particular number or amount as an average
average out at sth *Total contributions average out at over £1,000 a week.*

AWAKE /əˈweɪk/
awakes, awaking, awoke /əˈwəʊk, American əˈwoʊk/, awoken /əˈwəʊkən, American əˈwoʊkən/

aˈwake to *same as* awaken to

AWAKEN /əˈweɪkən/
awakens, awakening, awakened

aˈwaken to (*also* aˈwake to)
to begin to notice something
awaken to sth *It took them many years to awaken to the dangers they were facing.*

B b

BACK /bæk/
backs, backing, backed

ˌback aˈway ★★

1 to move backwards and away from someone, for example because you are afraid = RETREAT
back away *She moved towards me and I began backing away.* ♦ **+from** *The photo showed a woman backing away from a man with a gun.*

2 to gradually become less involved in something
back away *If they sense failure, most companies will back away.* ♦ **+from** *The World Bank is backing away from big infrastructure projects.*

ˌback ˈdown ★
to stop asking for something, or to stop saying that you will do something, because a lot of people oppose you = *formal* YIELD
back down *Neither side will back down because both believe they are right.* ♦ **+on** *We will not back down on the decision to strike.*

ˌback ˈoff ★★
to move backwards in order to get further away from something
back off *Everyone back off and let the doctor through.*
PHRASE **back off!** *informal* used to tell someone to stop criticizing you or stop telling you what to do: *Back off, will you? I'll tell you when I'm ready!*

ˌback ˈonto
if a building, garden etc backs onto a place, that place is directly behind it
back onto sth *The field backs onto a railway line.*

ˌback ˈout ★
to decide not to do something that you agreed to do = PULL OUT
back out *I promised to help and I'm not backing out now.* ♦ **+of** *We're hoping that no one will back out of the deal.*

ˌback ˈup ★★★

1	say sb is right and support them
2	prove sth is right
3	copy computer information
4	traffic: stop moving
5	person: move backwards
6	drive car backwards
7	toilets/pipes etc: become blocked
8	become less efficient
+	PHRASE

1 to give support to someone by saying or showing that you agree with them
back sb up *If I ask for more money will you back me up?*

2 to show that an explanation or belief is probably true = SUPPORT; *formal* CORROBORATE
back up sth *All the evidence backs up her story.*
back sth up *It's an interesting theory, but do you have evidence to back it up?*

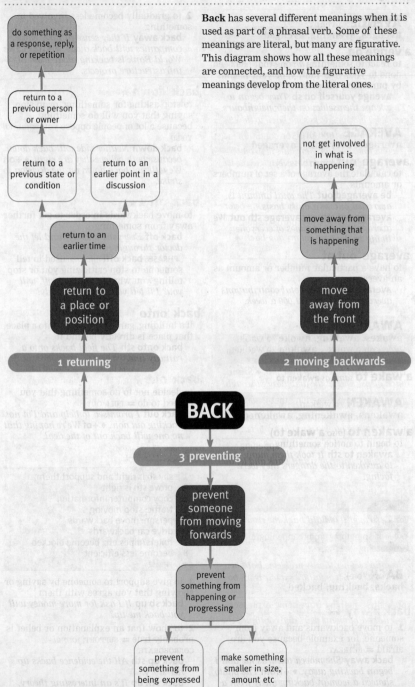

Back has several different meanings when it is used as part of a phrasal verb. Some of these meanings are literal, but many are figurative. This diagram shows how all these meanings are connected, and how the figurative meanings develop from the literal ones.

do something as a response, reply, or repetition

return to a previous person or owner

return to a previous state or condition

return to an earlier point in a discussion

return to an earlier time

return to a place or position

1 returning

not get involved in what is happening

move away from something that is happening

move away from the front

2 moving backwards

BACK

3 preventing

prevent someone from moving forwards

prevent something from happening or progressing

prevent something from being expressed

make something smaller in size, amount etc

Main meanings	Example verbs		
1 returning			
return to a place or position	come back	go back	put back
Come back and visit us again soon ♦ Put that book back where you found it!	double back	head back	start back
	get back	move back	turn back
return to an earlier time	date back	hark back to	take back
Think back to the time when you were a child. ♦ That song takes me back to the 1980s.	flash back to	look back	think back
return to a previous state or condition	bounce back	get back	snap back
It won't take long for your hair to grow back. ♦ We'll soon get things back to the way they were.	bring back	grow back	spring back
return to an earlier point in a discussion	bring back	go back	refer back
Let's go back to what you were saying before.	come back	look back	think back
return to a previous person or owner	buy back	give back	send back
I didn't think I'd ever get my dog back. ♦ Give me back my pen.	claw back	hand back	take back
	get back	pay back	win back
do something as a response, reply, or repetition	answer back	get back at	read back
	bite back	get back to	report back
Write back soon. ♦ Yes, I hit him, but I didn't expect him to hit me back.	call back	hit back	ring back
	come back	pay back	strike back
	fight back	phone back	talk back
	fire back	play back	write back
2 moving backwards			
move away from the front	draw back	settle back	sit back
Louise settled back into the chair. ♦ Stand back please and let the ambulance through!	lie back	sink back	stand back
	pull back		
move away from something that is happening	drop back	get back	pull back
Army command has decided to pull back the troops. ♦ Stay back – it might explode.	fall back	keep back	stay back
not get involved in what is happening	hang back	pull back	stand back
Are you just going to stand back and let this happen?	hold back	sit back	step back
3 preventing			
prevent someone from moving forwards	hold back	keep back	push back
Police struggled to hold back the crowd.			
prevent something from happening or progressing	hold back	put back	set back
	keep back	rein back	
She didn't let her family problems hold her back. ♦ The system failure set our work back a few months.			
prevent something from being expressed	bite back	fight back	gulp back
He choked back his tears and continued the story. ♦ I had the feeling she was holding something back.	choke back	force back	hold back
make something smaller in size, amount etc	cut back	roll back	scale back
We really need to cut back on our use of oil. ♦ Plans for new stores have been scaled back.			

cut in/carve up

back up/snarl up

break down

verbs to do with driving

3 to make a copy of information on your computer = COPY
back up *How often do you back up?*
back up sth *Back up your work regularly.*
back sth up *I forgot to back it up and now it's lost forever!*

4 [often passive] if traffic backs up, or if it is backed up, the vehicles are in a long line and are waiting to continue moving
be backed up *Cars were backed up for miles.*
back up *Traffic is backing up on all out-of-town routes.*

5 *informal* to move backwards a short distance = BACK
back up *I need everyone to back up about ten paces.*

6 to make a car go backwards = REVERSE, BACK
back sth up *Could you back your car up a bit?*
back up *Back up just a few more yards.*
♦ *The driver in front started backing up.*

7 [often passive] if a toilet, sink, or drain backs up, or if it is backed up, water cannot flow through it because something is blocking it
be backed up *All the drains were backed up.*

back up *We had to call in a plumber because the sink was backing up.*

8 [often passive] if a system backs up, or if it is backed up, it has slowed down or stopped working because there is too much of something for it to deal with
be backed up *Orders are really backed up this month.*
back up *If you overload the system, it'll back up.*
PHRASE **back up** *American informal* used for telling someone to return to something that was said earlier: *Back up: didn't you say they already met?*

BAG /bæg/
bags, bagging, bagged

bag 'up [often passive] *British*
to put things into bags
be bagged up *They'll only accept coins that have been bagged up.*
bag up sth *also* **bag sth up** *We spent a few hours bagging up clothes.*

BAIL /beɪl/
bails, bailing, bailed

,bail 'out ★★ (also ,bale 'out British)

1	help sb with problems
2	pay money to a court
3	escape from a situation/project etc
4	jump out of a plane
5	empty water from a boat

1 to help a person or organization that is having problems, especially financial problems
bail out sb/sth *It's wrong to expect businesses to bail out schools.*
bail sth/sb out *The government has already bailed the project out once before.*

2 to give money to a court so that someone is allowed to stay out of prison while they wait for their trial
bail sb out *My father got a lawyer and bailed me out.*

3 to leave a project, situation, or relationship, especially when it becomes difficult
bail out *Investors bailed out as prices plunged.* ♦ **+of** *She's the one who bails out of family responsibilities.* ♦ **+on** *You can't bail out on us now.*

4 to escape from a plane by using a parachute
bail out *He controlled the plane long enough for the crew to bail out.*

5 to empty water from a boat using a small container
bail out *She continued to steer the boat while I bailed out.*
bail sth out *I tried bailing the water out with my hands.*

BALANCE /'bæləns/
balances, balancing, balanced

'balance against ★ (also 'balance with) [often passive]
to create or keep a good or correct balance between the different parts or features of something
be balanced against sth *Economic development has to be balanced against environmental concerns.*
balance sth against sth *There is a need to balance the demands of the workplace against those of family life.*

,balance 'out ★
1 to change, increase, or reduce one of the parts of something with the result that another part is not too strong, noticeable etc = OFFSET, EVEN OUT
balance out sth *The tangy fruit balances*

bail out (sense 4)

out the creaminess of the sauce.
balance sth out *Taller plants are planted behind these to **balance things out**.*

2 if things balance out, the different effects of each thing make the total effect good or acceptable
balance out *Over time, things will balance out.*

'balance up
to make two different things equal in amount or value = EVEN OUT
balance up sth also **balance sth up** *We need to balance up inequality of treatment between men and women.*

'balance with same as balance against

BALE /beɪl/
bales, baling, baled

,bale 'out British same as bail out

BALK another spelling of baulk

BALLS /bɔːlz, American bɔlz/
ballses, ballsing, ballsed

,balls 'up British impolite
to do something very badly and make a lot of mistakes

■ **'balls-up** noun [C] *British impolite* a mistake or difficult situation caused by someone doing something badly

BAND /bænd/
bands, banding, banded

,band to'gether ★
to come together as a group in order to achieve something = JOIN TOGETHER
band together *The various opposition*

groups have banded together to form a single party.

BANDAGE /'bændɪdʒ/
bandages, bandaging, bandaged

,bandage 'up [often passive]
to wrap a bandage around an injured part of your body
be bandaged up *My fingers were all bandaged up.*
bandage up sth *Doctors bandaged up his wounds.*

BANDY /'bændi/
bandies, bandying, bandied

,bandy a'round (*also* ,bandy a'bout
British) *showing disapproval*
to mention something a lot, usually without thinking much about what you are saying
bandy sth around *also* **bandy around sth**
I don't want people bandying my name around in public. ♦ *The press have been bandying around a figure of £5 million.*

BANG /bæŋ/
bangs, banging, banged

,bang a'round (*also* ,bang a'bout)
informal
1 to make a lot of noise as you move around in a place
bang around *I could hear them banging around in the kitchen.*
2 to make a lot of noise as you use something or move something
bang sth around *He banged his tools around angrily.*

,bang a'way *informal*
to make a lot of noise as you do something, especially as you play music
bang away *I could hear him banging away upstairs.* ♦ **+on** *Carl was banging away on the drums.* ♦ **+at** *An entertainer was banging away at the piano.*

,bang 'down
to put something on a surface with a lot of force, making a loud noise
bang down sth *also* **bang sth down**
Kathy yelled and then banged the phone down. ♦ **+on** *He drained the glass and banged it down on the table.*

,bang 'on ★★ *British informal*
to talk about something for a long time in a boring and annoying way = GO ON
bang on *She banged on a bit longer.*
♦ **+about** *Is she still banging on about the neighbours?*

,bang 'out *informal*
1 to play a tune on the piano very loudly and not very well
bang out sth *also* **bang sth out** *He banged out loud blues songs all night.*
2 to write something quickly on a keyboard or typewriter
bang out sth *also* **bang sth out** *Just bang out a few letters saying we're busy.*

,bang 'up [usually passive] *informal*
1 *British* to put someone in prison
be banged up *He spent seven years banged up in a prison cell.*
2 *American* to damage something such as a vehicle
be/get banged up *How did your truck get all banged up?*

BANISH /'bænɪʃ/
banishes, banishing, banished

'banish from
1 [often passive] to make someone stop thinking about something or having particular feelings
be banished from sth *The fear was banished from his heart.*
banish sth from sth *The news of her pregnancy had banished all other thoughts from her mind.*
2 [often passive] to get rid of something
be banished from sth *These shows have been banished from our TV screens.*
banish sth from sth *The aim is to banish litter from our streets.*
3 [usually passive] *often humorous* to make someone leave a place
be banished from sth *After dinner, children were banished from the dining room.*

'banish to [usually passive] *often humorous*
to make someone go somewhere else
be banished to sth *We were banished to our rooms.*

BANK /bæŋk/
banks, banking, banked

'bank at *same as* **bank with**

'bank on ★
to depend on something happening or on someone doing something = COUNT ON
bank on sb/sth *We're banking on good weather for tomorrow.* ♦ **+to do sth** *They're banking on him to find a solution to the problem.*
bank on doing sth *I was banking on being able to get a meal at the hotel.*
bank on sb doing sth *We were banking on him coming up with an idea.*

PHRASE don't bank on it or **I wouldn't bank on it** *informal* used for telling someone that you think something will probably not happen: *'He said he'd come.' 'Don't bank on it – he's still in bed.'*

,bank 'up

1 [usually passive] to make something into a pile
be banked up *Soil was banked up against the wall.*

2 to put a lot of coal onto a fire so that it will burn slowly and for a long time
bank up sth *also* **bank sth up** *Before going to bed, she banked up the fire.*

'bank with (*also* 'bank at)

to have a bank account with a particular bank
bank with sth *Who do you bank with?*
♦ *We bank at Barclays in the high street.*

BARGAIN /'bɑːgɪn, *American* 'bɑːgən/
bargains, bargaining, bargained

'bargain for

PHRASE more than you bargained for or **not what you bargained for** different from what you expected, especially different in a worse way: *It took a lot more time than we bargained for.*

'bargain on

to expect something to happen, often when something else depends on it
bargain on doing sth *We'd bargained on finding them quickly.*
bargain on sb doing sth *She's bargaining on me changing my mind.*
PHRASE not bargain on sth used for saying that something bad happens that you do not expect to happen: *We hadn't bargained on being stuck in traffic for hours.* ♦ *What she didn't bargain on was being ordered to leave.*

BARGE /bɑːdʒ, *American* bɑːrdʒ/
barges, barging, barged

,barge 'in

1 barge in or **barge into** to enter a room suddenly and noisily, usually interrupting someone in a rude way
barge in *The kids just barge in without knocking.* ♦ *+on He just barged in on us in the middle of a meeting.*
barge into sth *She barged into my bedroom in the middle of the night.*

2 to interrupt what someone is doing or saying, or start to get involved with something that does not concern you
= BUTT IN

barge in *She never misses an opportunity to barge in.* ♦ *+on Sorry to barge in on you like this, but have you got a moment?*

barge in

BARK /bɑːk, *American* bɑːrk/
barks, barking, barked

,bark 'out

to say or shout something in a loud angry voice
bark out sth *also* **bark sth out** *A man was barking out instructions.*

BASE /beɪs/
bases, basing, based

'base in [often passive]

to have somewhere as your main office or place of work, or the place where you live
be based in sth *Many well-known research companies are based in London.*
base sth in sth *We decided to base our training operations in the New York office.*

'base on ★★★ [often passive]

1 to use particular ideas or facts to make a decision, do a calculation, or develop a theory
be based on sth *Prices are based on two people sharing a room.* ♦ *Her lectures are based mainly on the teachings of Marx.*
base sth on sth *I based this theory on the fact that he was never there when I was around.*

Nouns often used as objects with
base on 1

■ assumption, concept, criterion, fact, idea, information, notion, premise, principle

2 to use something as a model for a film, piece of writing, or work of art
be based on sth *The film is based on a true story.*

base sth on sth *He bases his designs on Roman mosaics.*

BASH /bæʃ/
bashes, bashing, bashed

ˌbash aˈbout *informal*
to treat someone or something roughly or violently
bash sb/sth about *You can bash the toy about and it still won't break.* ♦ *Her ex-boyfriend had bashed her about.*

ˌbash aˈway at *British informal*
to continue to work hard on something
bash away at sth *She's still bashing away at her last chapter.*

ˌbash ˈdown *informal*
if someone bashes down a door, they get into a place by destroying the door
bash down sth *also* **bash sth down** *She complained that the police had bashed down her door.*

ˌbash ˈin [often passive] *informal*
to damage something or injure someone by hitting them hard and violently
be bashed in *One side of his head had been bashed in.*
bash sth in *Someone had bashed the door in.*

ˌbash ˈon *British informal*
to continue to do something when you would prefer to stop = CRACK ON
bash on *I'll bash on for another hour or so.* ♦ **+with** *I'd better bash on with this – I'll see you later.*

ˌbash ˈout *informal*
to produce something very quickly and without working very hard = CHURN OUT, PRODUCE
bash out sth *also* **bash sth out** *She bashes out two or three songs a week.* ♦ *I'm bashing the new chapter out now.*

ˌbash ˈup *informal*
to hit someone hard and violently several times
bash sb up *He's always trying to bash his little brother up.*

BASK /bɑːsk, *American* bæsk/
basks, basking, basked

ˈbask in
1 to enjoy people's attention and approval, especially when you have achieved a great success
bask in sth *For now, she is content to bask in her new-found fame.*

2 to relax and enjoy yourself by lying in the sun
bask in sth *We'll soon be basking in the sun on a tropical beach.*

BAT /bæt/
bats, batting, batted

ˌbat aˈround
to discuss ideas or plans in an informal way = TOSS AROUND
bat around sth *also* **bat sth around** *Let's try batting around some thoughts on the project.* ♦ *Economists are always batting new theories around.*

BATHE /beɪð/
bathes, bathing, bathed

be ˈbathed in
1 *mainly literary* if a place is bathed in light, it is filled with light
be bathed in sth *The valley was bathed in moonlight.*

2 if you are bathed in sweat, you are covered in sweat
be bathed in sth *Her face was bathed in perspiration.*

BATTEN /ˈbæt(ə)n/
battens, battening, battened

ˌbatten ˈdown
1 to make something such as a door or window safe by closing it tightly or fastening it with a piece of wood
batten down *The ship had battened down, ready for the storm.*
batten down sth *The plastic sheeting can be used to cover a roof but it has to be securely battened down.*

2 to prepare for a difficult or dangerous situation
batten down *Residents on the east coast have been warned to batten down for Hurricane Freddie.*
batten down sth *Here are some useful precautions you can take to batten down your home for winter.* ♦ *With interest rates set to rise, it's time to batten down our budgets.*
PHRASE **batten down the hatches** to prepare for a difficult or dangerous situation by taking action to protect yourself: *When the stock market is looking frail, the investor's instinct is to batten down the hatches and sit tight.*

ˈbatten on *mainly literary*
to use someone or something for your own purposes, in an unfair or unkind way
batten on sb/sth *He struggled to support*

*his large family of aunts and uncles,
who battened on him relentlessly.*
♦ *Opponents criticized a bureaucratic
state that was out of control, battening
on taxpayers' money.*

BATTER /'bætə, *American* 'bætər/
batters, battering, battered

'batter down

to hit something such as a door or gate
several times until it is broken, in order
to get through it = BREAK DOWN
 batter sth down *also* **batter down sth**
*Firefighters had to batter the door down
to reach the family.* ♦ *Rioters battered
down the gates and streamed into the
compound.*

BATTLE /'bæt(ə)l/
battles, battling, battled

,battle 'out

PHRASE **battle it out** if two people or groups
battle it out, they compete with each
other until there is a definite winner:
*Twelve teams will battle it out to see who
is the new European champion.*

BAULK /bɔːk, *American* bɔk/
baulks, baulking, baulked

'baulk at

1 to be unwilling to do or accept
something because you think it will cause
problems
 baulk at sth *They wanted the house, but
they baulked at the price.*
2 if a horse baulks at something, it stops
suddenly and refuses to go forwards
 baulk at sth *The horse baulked at the
fence and I was thrown off over its head.*

BAWL /bɔːl, *American* bɔl/
bawls, bawling, bawled

,bawl 'out *informal*

to speak angrily to someone because of
something wrong that they have done
= TELL OFF
 bawl out sb *also* **bawl sb out** *He got mad
and started bawling out the waiter.*
♦ *Don't bawl me out just because you
messed up!*

BEAM /biːm, *American* bim/
beams, beaming, beamed

,beam 'down

in science-fiction stories, to send someone
down onto a planet from a space vehicle
using special electronic equipment that

makes them appear there suddenly
 beam sb down *also* **beam down sb** *Beam
us down, Mr Scott.* ♦ *We beamed down
reinforcements.*

,beam 'up

in science-fiction stories, to bring someone
back to their space vehicle using special
electronic equipment that makes them
appear there suddenly
 beam sb up *also* **beam up sb** *She gave
the order to beam them up.* ♦ *It was time
to beam up the landing party.*

BEAR /beə, *American* ber/
bears, bearing, bore /bɔː, *American*
bɔr/, **borne** /bɔːn, *American* bɔrn/

,bear 'down

1 to push or press downwards = PUSH
DOWN
 bear down *It's a natural instinct for a
woman giving birth to bear down.*
2 *American* to try very hard
 bear down *We need to bear down if we
want to make this work.*

,bear 'down on

to move towards someone in a determined
and threatening way = ADVANCE ON
 bear down on sb *I could see a police car
bearing down on us.* ♦ *The black line of
a storm bore down on them from the
west.*

'bear on (*also* 'bear upon)

to be relevant to something, or to influence
something
 bear on sth *Do you have any information
bearing on his disappearance?* ♦ *We
discussed matters bearing upon
relationships and self-esteem.*

,bear 'out ★★

to show that something is true or that
someone is telling the truth = SUPPORT
 bear out sb/sth *Scientific evidence bears
out the claim that stress and disease are
linked.*
 bear sb/sth out *I always said – and Rick
will bear me out – that this wouldn't
work.* ♦ *The results seem to bear this
theory out.*

,bear 'up

to behave bravely in a sad or difficult
situation = HOLD UP ≠ GIVE IN
 bear up *'How is she?' 'She's bearing up
remarkably well.'* ♦ *'Bear up!' he said
cheerfully. 'It'll soon be over.'* ♦ **+under**
*Let's see how he bears up under the
pressure.*

'bear upon *same as* **bear on**

,bear 'with ★

PHRASE **bear with me** used to ask someone to be patient with you while you do or finish something = BE PATIENT WITH: *Just bear with me – I'll explain everything shortly.*

BEAT /biːt, *American* bit/
beats, beating, beat, beaten

'beat against (*also* **'beat on**)
to hit something continuously or over a long period of time
beat against sth *The rain was beating against the window.*

,beat 'down
1 if the sun beats down, it shines very brightly making the weather very hot
beat down *The sun beat down mercilessly.* ♦ **+on** *I could feel the sun beating down on my head.*
2 if the rain beats down, it rains very hard
beat down *Outside, the rain was beating down.* ♦ **+on** *The rain beat down on the sodden fields.*
3 to persuade someone to sell you something at a lower price than their first offer = KNOCK DOWN
beat sb down *We'll have to beat them down or there's no way the deal can proceed.* ♦ **+to** *The original price was £50, but we beat them down to £40.*

beat down

'beat off ★
1 to succeed in winning or gaining something from an opponent
beat off sth *Virgin Airlines must beat off stiff competition to win the contract.*
beat sb/sth off *Having beaten their*

closest rivals off, they were ready to start developing the area.
2 to prevent someone from physically attacking you by hitting them with your hands or with an object
beat off sb/sth *She nearly died in an attempt to beat off her attacker.*
beat sb/sth off *He had to beat the dogs off with a stick.*
3 *American very informal* if a man beats off, he strokes his sexual organ in order to get sexual pleasure = *formal* MASTURBATE

'beat on
1 *American informal* to hurt someone by hitting them a lot of times
beat on sb *According to the witness, the police ran up and started beating on him.*
2 *same as* **beat against**

'beat out
1 to stop a fire from burning by hitting it with something
beat out sth *also* **beat sth out** *She beat out the flames with a branch.*
2 to make a pattern of sounds by hitting an instrument or other object
beat out a rhythm *The audience were beating out the rhythm with their feet.*
3 *American informal* to succeed in winning or gaining something that someone else wants
beat out sb *also* **beat sb out** *Atlanta beat out Athens for the privilege of hosting the 1996 Olympics.*

,beat 'out of [usually passive]
to force someone to tell you something by using physical violence against them
be beaten out of sb *He claims the confession was beaten out of him.*

,beat 'up ★★ [often passive]
to hurt someone by hitting or kicking them a lot of times = ATTACK
be beaten up *Prisoners claim that they were regularly beaten up by guards.*
beat sb up *They threatened to beat me up if I didn't give them my wallet.*
beat up sb *There was little sympathy for a man who allegedly beat up his wife.*
PHRASE **beat yourself up** to blame or criticize yourself for something wrong that you have done: *It's time you stopped beating yourself up over this.*

■ **'beat-up** adj *informal* old and in bad condition: *She used to drive round in a beat-up old van.*

,beat 'up on *American informal*
1 to hurt someone by hitting or kicking them a lot of times

beat up on sb *He and his brother are always beating up on each other.*
2 to blame or criticize yourself or someone else
beat up on sb *I'm not here to beat up on single parents.*
beat up on yourself *She can't stop beating up on herself about it.*

BEAVER /ˈbiːvə, *American* ˈbivər/
beavers, beavering, beavered

ˌbeaver aˈway *informal*
if you beaver away at something, you work very hard at it
beaver away *Meanwhile the talented young director has been beavering away on his latest film.* ♦ **+at** *He was beavering away at his homework until after midnight.*

BECOME /bɪˈkʌm/
becomes, becoming, became /bɪˈkeɪm/, **become**

beˈcome of ★★
PHRASE **what has/will become of sb/sth?**
used for asking what has happened to someone or something, because you have not seen them for a long time, or for asking what will happen to them, because you are worried about them
= HAPPEN TO: *If she is sent to prison, what will become of her children?* ♦ *What became of the painting that used to be in your grandfather's library?*

BED /bed/
beds, bedding, bedded

1	lie down to sleep
2	arrange for sb to sleep
3	begin to work well
4	start to do well
5	have sex

ˌbed ˈdown
1 to lie down somewhere to sleep, especially in a place that is not your usual bed = *informal* DOSS DOWN
bed down *We ate our meal round the campfire then bedded down for the night.*
2 to arrange for a person or animal to sleep in a bed or some other place
bed sb/sth down *After we'd bedded the kids down we went downstairs to eat.*
3 if a new system beds down, it begins to work well after a period of time when there are problems
bed down *It will probably take a little time for the new Assembly to bed down.*
4 if someone beds down in a new job or

organization, they start to do well in it because they have been there for some time
bed down *After a shaky start, the new midfielder has bedded down well.*
5 *American informal* to have sex with someone
bed sb down *also* **bed down sb** *I think he bedded her down once.*

ˌbed ˈout [usually passive]
to plant young plants outdoors = PLANT OUT
be bedded out *Bean plants can be bedded out in late April.*

BEEF /biːf, *American* bif/
beefs, beefing, beefed

ˌbeef ˈup [often passive] *informal*
to increase or improve something, or to make something better or more interesting = STRENGTHEN ≠ WEAKEN
be beefed up *Security has been considerably beefed up in advance of the President's visit on Thursday.*
beef up sth *also* **beef sth up** *They used slides to beef up their presentation.*

■ **ˈbeefed-up adj** [only before noun]
made bigger or stronger than before: *A new beefed-up police force has done little to reduce crime in the area.*

BEETLE /ˈbiːt(ə)l, *American* ˈbit(ə)l/
beetles, beetling, beetled

ˌbeetle ˈoff (*also* ˌbeetle aˈway) *British informal*
to go somewhere quickly = DASH OFF
beetle off *He beetled off to find some extra chairs.*

BEG /beg/
begs, begging, begged

ˌbeg ˈoff *informal*
to say that you are not going to do something that you had previously agreed to do = CRY OFF
beg off *I'm afraid I'm going to have to beg off this time.* ♦ **+from** *Two of our usual players have already begged off from tomorrow's game.*

BEGIN /bɪˈgɪn/
begins, beginning, began /bɪˈgæn/, **begun** /bɪˈgʌn/

beˈgin with ★★★
1 if an activity or process begins with something, that is the first thing that happens in it

begin with sth *All their meals begin with a short prayer.*

2 to do something as the first part of an event, process etc

begin with sth *She began with a short introduction to the topic.*

begin sth with sth *We began our tour with a visit to the Royal Palace.*

PHRASE **to begin with** *informal* **1** used for introducing the first thing in a list of things you are going to say = FIRSTLY: *'Why were you annoyed?' 'Well, to begin with, she arrived late.'* **2** during the first part of an activity or process = AT FIRST: *She didn't seem very enthusiastic to begin with, but she gradually came round to the idea.*

BELCH /beltʃ/
belches, belching, belched

,belch 'out *showing disapproval*

if smoke or steam belches out of something, or if something belches it out, it comes out in large amounts

belch sth out *also* **belch out sth** *It's a bleak landscape, with factory chimneys belching thick smoke out into the air.*
belch out *Fumes were belching out towards them.*

BELIEVE /bɪˈliːv, *American* bɪˈliv/
believes, believing, believed

be'lieve in ★★★

1 to think that something exists
believe in sth *I don't believe in miracles.* ♦ *I'm beginning to think you actually believe in ghosts!*

2 to think that an idea or a way of doing something is good or right
believe in sth *She used to say she didn't believe in marriage.*

3 to feel confident that a person or an organization is good or reliable
believe in sb/sth *Some of his previous supporters have stopped believing in him.*
believe in yourself *You need to believe in yourself a bit more.*

BELLY /ˈbeli/
bellies, bellying, bellied

,belly 'out

if sails belly out, they fill with air and become large and round
belly out *The sails of the yacht bellied out as the breeze quickened.*

BELONG /bɪˈlɒŋ, *American* bɪˈlɔːŋ/
belongs, belonging, belonged

be'long to ★★★

1	be owned by sb
2	be a member of sth
3	benefit particular people
4	come from a time/place
5	come from a group/set
6	when sb deserves sth

1 to be owned by someone
belong to sb *The sports car belongs to the woman next door.* ♦ *Who does this coat belong to?* ♦ *A purse belonging to the missing girl was found near the scene.*

2 to be a member of an organization or club
belong to sth *She belongs to the school computer club.*

3 if something such as a period of time belongs to someone, they get the most benefit from it, they control it, or they have the most success in it
belong to sb *The future belongs to people with good computing skills.*

4 to come from or be related to a particular time or place
belong to sth *This painting clearly belongs to a later period.*

5 to come from or be part of a particular group
belong to sth *This belongs to the same family of drugs as Prozac.* ♦ *They belong to a different generation.*

6 to be the thing that someone deserves or has a right to
belong to sb *Of course all the credit really belongs to my partner, Sam.*

BELT /belt/
belts, belting, belted

,belt 'down *American informal*

to drink alcoholic drinks quickly, one after another
belt down sth *also* **belt sth down** *She was belting down shots of whiskey.*

,belt 'out

to shout or sing something loudly, or to play something loudly on a musical instrument
belt out sth *also* **belt sth out** *The band were belting out some old rock'n'roll songs.*

,belt 'up *informal*

1 to fasten the belt that keeps you safe in your seat in a car, on a plane etc = BUCKLE UP belt up *Make sure the kids belt up.*

2 *British impolite* used for telling someone to be quiet = SHUT UP

belt up *I wish you'd just belt up and get on with your work.*

BEND /bend/
bends, bending, bent /bent/

,bend 'down ★★
to lean forwards and downwards, or to move the top part of your body forwards and downwards

bend down *Helen bent down to pick up her pen.*

,bend 'over ★★
to lean forwards and downwards, or lean over something

bend over *She bent over to look more closely at my face.* ♦ *Bend over and touch your toes.*

bend over sth *He bent over the table and picked up the dirty plates.*

BESTOW /bɪ'stəʊ, *American* bɪ'stoʊ/
bestows, bestowing, bestowed

be'stow on (*also* be'stow upon) *formal*
to give someone something valuable such as property or a prize

bestow sth on sb *He bestowed all his land upon his daughter and her husband.* ♦ *The general bestowed the highest honour at his disposal on his captain.*

BET /bet/
bets, betting, bet

'bet on ★★
1 to risk an amount of money by saying what you think will happen, especially in a race or game = GAMBLE ON

bet sth on sth *I bet £25 on the Czech Republic to win the tournament.*

bet on sth *He regularly bets on the horses* (=*on the results of horse races*).

2 to feel sure that something will happen = GAMBLE ON

bet on sth *Many homeowners are betting on further price rises.* ♦ *She might turn up later but I **wouldn't bet on it**.*

BEWARE /bɪ'weə, *American* bɪ'wer/

be'ware of ★★ [usually in imperative]
used, especially on signs and notices, for warning people that there might be danger or problems

beware of sth *There was a sign on the door saying 'Beware of the Dog'.*

beware of doing sth *You should beware of giving your credit-card details out over the Internet.*

BIG /bɪg/

,big 'up *informal*
to praise or support someone or something in an enthusiastic way, and attract attention to them by doing this

big up sth *also* big sth up *It was an article bigging up some new dj.*

PHRASE big it up *informal* to enjoy yourself in a social situation, often by spending a lot of money: *This time next week we'll be bigging it up in Ibiza.*

BILL /bɪl/
bills, billing, billed

'bill as [often passive]
to advertise or describe someone or something in a particular way, especially in order to make them sound interesting or important

be billed as sth *Electric cars are being billed as the automobiles of the future.*

bill sb/sth as sth *The press billed Sharapova as the next world champion.*

BIND /baɪnd/
binds, binding, bound /baʊnd/

,bind 'over [usually passive]
if a court of law binds someone over, it orders them to do something and usually makes them pay money if they do not obey

be bound over *The three youths were bound over for a year.* ♦ *They were **bound over to keep the peace**.*

,bind to'gether [often passive]
to make two people or groups feel that they have a very strong connection or relationship with each other

be bound together *There is a feeling that European nations are inevitably bound together in some way.*

bind sb together *The troubles they had shared bound them much closer together.*

be ,bound 'up with
to be connected very closely

be bound up with sth *His political philosophy was closely bound up with his religious beliefs.*

BITCH /bɪtʃ/
bitches, bitching, bitched

,bitch 'out [often passive] *American very informal*
to criticize or shout at someone angrily

because they have done something wrong
be/get bitched out *I had to stand there and get bitched out by my sergeant.*
bitch sb out *also* **bitch out sb** *I could hear him bitching them out.*

BITE /baɪt/
bites, biting, bit /bɪt/, bitten /'bɪt(ə)n/

'bite at
to try to bite something without in fact managing to bite it
bite at sth *The animals might bite at your fingers if you put them through the fence.*

,bite 'back
1 to stop yourself from saying what you really think, or showing what you really feel
bite back sth *also* **bite sth back** *Paul bit back an angry reply.* ♦ *She wanted to tell him he was a fool, but bit the words back.*
2 to react angrily to someone who has done or said something unpleasant to you
bite back *It was his instinct to bite back if anyone criticized him.*

,bite 'into
to press hard into a surface
bite into sth *The metal collar bit into his neck.*

,bite 'off ★ [often passive]
to separate something from the main part by biting
be bitten off *His right leg had been bitten off by a shark.*
bite off sth *I bit off a chunk of chocolate.*
bite sth off *The fingernail was broken so I bit it off.*
  PHRASE **bite off more than you can chew** to try to do too much, or try to do something that is too hard for you: *I'm afraid he might have bitten off more than he can chew with this new job.*

BLACK /blæk/
blacks, blacking, blacked

,black 'out ★
1 to suddenly become unconscious
= FAINT, PASS OUT ≠ COME TO —*picture* → PASS OUT
black out *He had blacked out as his car hit the tree.*
2 [often passive] to prevent someone from reading or seeing something by covering it with something dark
be blacked out *Half the pages in the report had been blacked out for security reasons.*

black out sth *We blacked out all the sensitive information first.*
black sth out *I blacked everyone's name out before releasing the report.*
3 [usually passive] to make a place dark by turning off all the lights, for example so that the enemy cannot see a place at night
be blacked out *The whole city had been blacked out.*

■ **blackout** /'blækaʊt/ noun [C] **1** a short period when the electricity supply to a building or district is stopped, especially at night: *We had a supply of candles for the blackout.* **2** a period during a war when the lights are turned off so that an enemy cannot see them at night: *She arrived home shortly before the blackout.* **3** a period when you suddenly become unconscious, usually for a few minutes: *What would happen if you had a blackout in the street?* **4** a situation in which journalists are officially prevented from reporting news about something: *a news blackout*

,black 'up
if a white person blacks up, they put a dark colour on their face in order to look like a black person for a performance, dance, song etc. This practice is now considered to be offensive to black people.
black up *Some of the performers refused to black up.*

BLANK /blæŋk/
blanks, blanking, blanked

,blank 'out
1 if you blank out a feeling, memory, warning etc, you deliberately try not to think about it or try to forget it = BLOCK OUT ≠ ACKNOWLEDGE
blank out sth *also* **blank sth out** *He had blanked out everything that happened at that time.*
2 [usually passive] to hide or cover something so that you cannot see it
= BLOCK OUT
be blanked out *The headline had been blanked out.*
3 to suddenly be unable to remember something
blank out *I just blanked out when they asked me what I'd read on the subject.*

BLANKET /'blæŋkɪt/
blankets, blanketing, blanketed

'blanket in (*also* 'blanket with) [often passive]

to cover something with a layer of something such as snow
be blanketed in sth *When I woke, the valley was blanketed with snow.*
blanket sth in sth *Forest fires had blanketed most of the capital in a haze of smoke.*

BLARE /bleə, *American* bler/
blares, blaring, blared

ˌblare ˈout
to make a loud and unpleasant noise
blare out *The radio has been blaring out that dreadful music all day.*

BLAST /blɑːst, *American* blæst/
blasts, blasting, blasted

ˌblast aˈway
1 if a gun blasts away, or if a person blasts away, they shoot at someone or something several times
blast away *Machine guns were blasting away in the distance.* ♦ **+at** *The rebels were blasting away at everything in sight.*
2 if music is blasting away, it is playing very loudly
blast away *The radio was blasting away downstairs.*

ˌblast ˈoff
if a space vehicle blasts off, it leaves the ground at the beginning of its journey to space ≠ TOUCH DOWN
blast off *Apollo 13 blasted off the following afternoon.*

blast off

■ **ˈblast-off** noun [C] *informal* the moment when a space vehicle leaves the ground at the beginning of its journey to space = LIFT-OFF: *The rocket crashed into the ocean 20 minutes after blast-off.*

BLAZE /bleɪz/
blazes, blazing, blazed

ˌblaze aˈway
1 if a fire blazes away, it burns very brightly and strongly
blaze away *A fire was blazing away in the grate.*
2 if guns blaze away, they continue firing for a long time
blaze away *Artillery blazed away throughout the night.*

BLEEP /bliːp, *American* blip/
bleeps, bleeping, bleeped

ˌbleep ˈout [often passive]
to replace a swearword in a television or radio broadcast with a short high sound, so that people are not offended
be bleeped out *About half the performance had to be bleeped out.*
bleep out sth *also* **bleep sth out** *The producers wanted to bleep out the last word.*

BLEND /blend/
blends, blending, blended

ˌblend ˈin ★
1 if someone or something blends in, they are similar to the other people, objects, buildings etc around them, so that they seem to suit their environment, or you do not notice them in particular
blend in *She seemed to blend in easily wherever she went.* ♦ **+with** *The new library blends in perfectly with the surrounding buildings.* ♦ *Security men were trying to blend in with the crowd.*
2 to mix one food or substance with another
blend in sth *Blend in the flour and water mixture.*
blend sth in *Add the beaten egg white and blend it in carefully.*

ˈblend ˌinto
1 to seem to gradually change into something else
blend into sth *Her dreams had a way of blending into her waking thoughts.*
2 if someone or something blends into a place, you do not notice them because they are similar in colour, shape etc to the things that are around them
blend into sth *She had the ability to blend into any crowd.* ♦ *Wild cats can **blend into the background** quite easily.*
3 to mix one food or substance with another

blend sth into sth *Blend some crushed rosemary into the oil.*

BLISS /blɪs/
blisses, blissing, blissed

bliss 'out *informal*
to go into a happy relaxed state, or to make someone feel relaxed and happy

bliss out *Just curl, up, relax, and bliss out to the sound of your favourite love songs.*

bliss sb out *The oil has a beautiful scent that will bliss you out.*

BLOCK /blɒk, *American* blɑk/
blocks, blocking, blocked

block 'in
1 [often passive] to leave your car or some other object so close to someone else's car that they do not have enough room to move = BOX IN

be blocked in *When I came back to the car park my car was blocked in.*

block sb/sth in *Rubbish was dumped across the driveway, blocking us in.*

2 to completely cover a large area of something such as a painting with one colour

block in sth *also* block sth in *Broad flat brushes are useful for blocking in colour.*

3 to plan a time for doing or dealing with something

block in sth *also* block sth in *Try to block in half an hour every day for regular exercise.*

block 'off
to completely cover or close an entrance, gate, road etc so that nothing can move through it = CLOSE OFF

block off sth *also* block sth off *Snow had blocked off several streets.* ♦ *Troops blocked the whole area off.*

block 'out ★
1 to stop light or sound from reaching a place = SHUT OUT

block out sth *That tree in the neighbour's garden blocks out a lot of the light.*

block sth out *The netting is thick enough to block sunlight out.*

2 to stop yourself from thinking about or remembering something = BLANK OUT, BLOT OUT ≢ ACKNOWLEDGE

block out sth *He had always managed to block out the incident.*

block sth out *When I'm working, I try to block everything else out of my mind.* ♦ *If something is bothering you, it's hard to block it out.*

block 'up ★
to stop something moving through or along something else, for example a pipe = BLOCK, OBSTRUCT ≢ FREE

block up sth *We had continual problems with leaves blocking up the gutters.*

block sth up *Paper towels were blocking the toilet up.* ♦ *More sand in the tubes would block them up completely.*

■ '**blocked-up** adj [only before noun] a blocked-up pipe, tube etc has something blocking it so that water, oil, or gas cannot flow through it: *Would you know how to deal with a blocked-up drain?*

BLOT /blɒt, *American* blɑt/
blots, blotting, blotted

blot 'out ★★
1 to cover something so that you can no longer see it = CONCEAL

blot out sth *Dark clouds overhead had blotted out the sun.*

blot sth out *The trees were blotting sunlight out.*

2 to stop yourself from remembering something unpleasant = BLANK OUT, BLOCK OUT ≢ RECALL

blot out sth *She tried hard to blot out the bitter memories of the divorce.*

blot sth out *She was unable to blot these images out.* ♦ *The memory is a painful one, and I've been unable to blot it out.*

blot 'up
to remove liquid from the surface of something by using a piece of paper or cloth

blot up sth *also* blot sth up *Blot up any excess ink.* ♦ *With paper towels you can blot any spills up easily.*

BLOW /bləʊ, *American* bloʊ/
blows, blowing, blew /bluː/ **blu/, blown** /bləʊn, *American* bloʊn/

blow a'part
1 [often passive] to destroy something with an explosion

be blown apart *Several vehicles were blown apart in the high winds.*

blow sth apart *also* blow apart sth *The blast blew the whole administration block apart.*

2 to show that an idea is completely false or wrong

blow apart sth *also* blow sth apart *The book blew apart the myth of their perfect marriage.*

ˌblow aˈway ★★

1 if something blows away, or if the wind blows it away, the wind moves it away from you through the air

blow away *His hat blew away on the roller coaster.*

blow away sth *She switched on the fan to blow away the smoke.*

blow sth away *The wind was blowing any fallen leaves away.* ♦ *A jet of air directed onto the fumes blows them away.*

2 *informal* to kill someone by shooting them = SHOOT

blow sb away *'So what happened?' asked Jimmy. Al shrugged. 'The cops blew him away.'*

blow away sb *They blew away the first guy and wounded the second.*

3 [often passive] *informal* to impress someone very much, or to make them very excited

be blown away *I saw her in the dress and was blown away.* ♦ *We were blown away by their skill and confidence.*

blow sb away *When I heard that song for the first time it just blew me away.*

4 *American informal* to defeat someone completely and easily

blow sb away *In the second game we completely blew them away.*

blow away sb *She continued to blow away any player she came up against.*

ˌblow ˈdown [often passive]

if something blows down or if the wind blows it down, it falls

be blown down *Several trees were blown down.*

blow down *The old ash tree had blown down in the storm.*

blow down sth *also* **blow sth down** *A sudden gust of wind could blow down that fence.*

ˌblow ˈin ★

1 to come towards you in the air

blow in *A cool breeze blew in from the coast.*

2 if a window blows in, or if something blows it in, it breaks into pieces that fall inside the building

blow in *The window at the front of the building had blown in.*

blow in sth *The gale blew in every window in the house.*

blow sth in *The force of the blast had blown the windows in at the front of the building.*

3 *informal* to arrive unexpectedly

blow in *Charlie and May just blew in for a visit.*

ˌblow ˈoff ★★

1 [often passive] if the wind blows something off, or if it blows off, the wind makes it come off

be blown off *Part of the chimney had been blown off.*

blow off *The roof blew off in the storm.*

blow sth off *A gust of wind blew her hat off.* ♦ *If the wind catches the aerial, it could blow it off.*

blow off sth *The wind had once blown off his glasses.*

blow sth off sth *The force of the wind had blown some tiles off the roof.*

2 [often passive] if a bomb or an explosion blows off part of something, or part of someone's body, it removes it and destroys it

be blown off *Both of his legs had been blown off by a land mine.*

blow sth off *An explosion blew one of the wings off.*

blow off sth *The explosion would be strong enough to blow off a man's arm.*

blow sth off sb/sth *The blast had blown one of the arms off a man standing next to me.*

3 *American informal* to not do something that you had agreed or arranged to do

blow off sth *I can't believe you blew off the exam.*

blow sth off *We were expecting her to make a speech, but she blew it off.*

4 *American informal* to behave as if you think that someone or something is unimportant

blow sb off *I invited her to join us but she just blew me off.*

blow off sb *He had already blown off several girls in my class.*

ˌblow ˈout ★★

1	stop burning
2	window: break into pieces
3	tyre: burst
4	fail to meet
5	defeat in sport
6	storm: end
+	**blowout** noun

1 if you blow out a flame, or if it blows out, it stops burning because you blow on it or because of the wind ≠ IGNITE

blow out sth *He blew out all 60 candles on his birthday cake.*

blow sth out *A sudden gust of wind blew the flame out.*

blow out *What do we do if the lamp blows out?*

2 if a window blows out, or if something blows it out, it breaks into pieces that fall outside the building

blow out sth *The bomb blew out all the windows on the bus.*
blow sth out *Even a small explosion would blow the glass out. ♦ There were no windows left at all. The blast had blown them all out.*
blow out *There was a bang and the windscreen blew out.*

3 if a tyre blows out, or if something blows it out, it bursts
blow out *Our front tyre blew out when we were halfway here.*
blow sth out *Those rocks will blow your tyres out in two minutes if you try to go that way.*
blow sth out *I hit something that blew out my front tyre.*

4 *British informal* to not meet someone that you have arranged to meet, and so make them feel annoyed or disappointed
blow sb out *Frances was supposed to be here, but she's blown us out.*

5 *mainly American informal* to defeat someone easily in sport
blow out sb *They've blown out every team they've played this season.*
blow sb out *We didn't imagine they could blow our team out like this. ♦ It feels great to blow them out for once.*

6 if a storm blows itself out, it ends
blow itself out *By morning the storm had blown itself out.*

■ **blowout** /ˈbləʊaʊt/ noun [C] **1** an occasion when a tyre on a moving vehicle suddenly bursts: *We had a blowout on the motorway.* **2** [usually singular] a celebration during which people eat and drink a lot: *Jim's having a birthday blowout at the Hacienda.* **3** an occasion when oil or gas suddenly escapes from a well (=a deep hole in the ground): *The team is trained to deal with blowouts.* **4** an easy victory in a game or competition: *When the Yankees scored ten runs in the first inning, we knew the game would be a blowout.*

,blow 'over ★★

1 [often passive] if something blows over or is blown over, the wind makes it fall
be blown over *Several trees had been blown over in the gale.*
blow over *The dustbins have blown over and there's rubbish everywhere.*
blow sth over *The storm had blown the huts right over.*
blow over sth *The wind blew over my neighbour's fence.*

2 if a storm blows over, it gradually becomes less strong and ends
blow over *We can't go now – we'll have to wait till the storm blows over.*

3 if a dangerous or embarrassing situation blows over, people stop worrying about it and forget about it
blow over *It was a major scandal, and we all hoped it would soon blow over. ♦ I decided to lie low for a while and wait for it all to blow over.*

,blow 'up ★★★

1	explode
2	make sth explode
3	fill sth with air/gas
4	when a storm starts
5	when an argument/problem begins
6	become angry
7	make a photograph bigger
+	PHRASE
+	**blow-up** noun

1 if something blows up, it explodes and is destroyed
blow up *The boiler blew up, wrecking the entire building.*

2 to make something explode, especially with a bomb
blow up sth *Separatist forces had blown up the only surviving bridge.*
blow sth up *Bomb disposal experts blew the van up in a controlled explosion.* ♦ *Terrorists had taken control of the building and were threatening to blow it up.*

3 to fill something with air or gas = INFLATE
blow up sth *We blew up lots of balloons and hung them around the room.*
blow sth up *Check your tyres for wear and blow them up before you go.*

4 if a storm or strong wind blows up, it suddenly starts
blow up *The race had to be cancelled when a sudden storm blew up.*

5 if a serious argument or problem blows up, it begins suddenly
blow up *A political row has blown up over the minister's remarks.*

6 to suddenly become angry and shout at someone = LOSE YOUR TEMPER
blow up *He seems to blow up whenever I mention the subject.* ♦ **+at** *She just blew up at me.*

7 to make a photograph bigger = ENLARGE ≠ REDUCE
blow sth up *Why not take the first photo and blow it up?*
blow up sth *They had blown up the picture to make a huge poster of his face.*
PHRASE **blow up in sb's face** *informal* if your plans blow up in your face, they do not happen as you expected and cause a lot of problems: *I wondered*

what stupid idea had blown up in his face.

blow up

■ **'blow-up** noun [C] **1** a photograph or part of a photograph that has been made bigger: *On the wall is a huge blow-up of a family portrait.* **2** *informal* a sudden angry argument: *The star player had a much-publicized blow-up with his manager last season.*

BLUDGEON /'blʌdʒ(ə)n/
bludgeons, bludgeoning, bludgeoned

'bludgeon into [usually passive]
to force someone into doing something by using repeated arguments or threats
  be bludgeoned into (doing) sth *We were bludgeoned into accepting their offer.*

BLUNDER /'blʌndə, American 'blʌndər/
blunders, blundering, blundered

,blunder a'round (*also* **,blunder a'bout** *British*)
to move or progress in a clumsy or accidental way, making mistakes or creating problems as you go
  blunder around *Someone was blundering around in the darkness.*

,blunder 'into
to become involved in something by accident
  blunder into sth *The book tells the story of how Europe blundered into World War I.*

BLURT /blɜːt, American blɜrt/
blurts, blurting, blurted

,blurt 'out ★
to say something suddenly and without thinking about the effect it will have, usually because you are nervous or excited

blurt out sth *She blurted out his name, then gasped as she realized what she'd done.*
blurt sth out *I'd blurted a reply out before I could stop myself.*

BOARD /bɔːd, American bɔrd/
boards, boarding, boarded

,board 'off [usually passive]
to hide or protect something by putting wooden boards over or around it
  be boarded off *Part of the garage had been boarded off during building works.*

,board 'out [often passive] *British*
to arrange for a person or animal to stay with someone who is paid to look after them for a period of time
  be boarded out with sb *The children were boarded out with foster parents.*
  board out sb *also* **board sb out** *Many pet owners dislike the thought of boarding out their dog or cat while they are away.*

,board 'over
to cover something with wooden boards
  board over sth *also* **board sth over** *They boarded over all the old fireplaces.*

,board 'up [often passive]
to cover a window or door with wooden boards, especially to stop people getting in when a building is empty
  be boarded up *All the windows were either broken or boarded up.*
  board up sth *also* **board sth up** *Those people who stayed boarded up their windows.*

■ **'boarded-up** adj [only before noun] a boarded-up window, door, or building has wooden boards fixed over it, for example to stop people getting in when a building is empty: *Across the road was a disused laundry with boarded-up windows.*

BOB /bɒb, American bɑb/
bobs, bobbing, bobbed

,bob 'up
to move up and come into view with a short quick movement = POP UP
  bob up *A head bobbed up from behind the fence.*

BODGE /bɒdʒ, American bɑdʒ/
bodges, bodging, bodged

,bodge 'up *British informal*
to do something badly, especially to make or repair something badly because you do not have enough time or the right

materials to do it properly = BOTCH UP

bodge up sth *also* **bodge sth up** *The builders completely bodged up the plastering.* ♦ *If I do the decorating myself I'll only bodge it up.*

BOG /bɒg, *American* bɑg/
bogs, bogging, bogged

get ,bogged 'down ★ (*also* be ,bogged 'down)

1 to become so involved with one particular part of a process that you cannot make any progress

get bogged down with sth *The meeting got bogged down with disputes about who was going to do what.*

get bogged down in sth *It's difficult to make any real changes without getting bogged down in bureaucracy.*

2 to be or become stuck in soft wet ground

get bogged down *The wheels were getting bogged down in the mud.*

,bog 'off [always in imperative] *British impolite*
used for telling someone rudely to go away = BUG OFF

BOGGLE /'bɒg(ə)l, *American* 'bɑg(ə)l/
boggles, boggling, boggled

'boggle at
to be so surprised or shocked at something that you are almost unable to believe it

boggle at sth *I just boggle at how much these lawyers earn.*

BOIL /bɔɪl/
boils, boiling, boiled

,boil a'way
if a liquid boils away, or if you boil it away, it disappears and turns to gas after reaching a very high temperature

boil away *Check every 20 minutes to make sure the water has not boiled away.*

boil away sth *also* **boil sth away** *Boil away about a third of the sauce.*

,boil 'down
1 to become smaller in quantity after cooking because some of the liquid has turned to gas, or to make something do this = REDUCE

boil down *When the sauce has boiled down, add the chopped herbs.*

boil sth down *also* **boil down sth** *Boil the meat juices down to make a thick sauce.*

2 to make something such as a piece of writing shorter until only the basic, most important facts remain

boil sth down to sth *You need to boil*

whole pages of information down to just one paragraph.

,boil 'down to ★
to be the main reason for something or the most basic part of something
= AMOUNT TO

boil down to sth *It's difficult to choose which appliance to buy, but in the end it usually boils down to cost.* ♦ *What it really boils down to is the fact that they don't like each other.*

,boil 'over ★
1 if a situation or feeling boils over, people cannot control their anger and they start to fight or argue

boil over *Racial tensions in the area were boiling over.* ♦ **+into** *The dispute finally boiled over into a series of violent protests.*

2 if a liquid boils over, it rises so much when it boils that it flows over the top of the container that it is in = OVERFLOW

boil over *There was a hissing sound as the soup boiled over.*

,boil 'up
1 if a situation or feeling boils up, people start to feel angry

boil up *The dispute boiled up when three people were fired for lateness.* ♦ *Anger was boiling up inside me.*

2 to heat liquid, or to heat something in a liquid, until it boils

boil up sth *also* **boil sth up** *Will you boil up some water?* ♦ *Keep the chicken bones and boil them up to make stock.*

BOLSTER /'bəʊlstə, *American* 'boʊlstər/
bolsters, bolstering, bolstered

,bolster 'up
to make something stronger or more effective = REINFORCE

bolster up sth *also* **bolster sth up** *The campaign is designed to bolster up the government's image as being tough on crime.*

BOLT /bəʊlt, *American* boʊlt/
bolts, bolting, bolted

,bolt 'down
1 to eat food very quickly = WOLF DOWN

bolt down sth *also* **bolt sth down** *She bolted down her lunch and rushed back to work.*

2 [usually passive] to fix something firmly to the floor

be bolted down *The people here would even steal the chairs if they weren't bolted down.*

BOMB /bɒm, _American_ bɑm/
bombs, bombing, bombed

,bomb 'out

1 _mainly American informal_ to be very unsuccessful
>**bomb out** _The play bombed out – it only ran for two nights._

2 [usually passive] to force someone to leave a place by attacking them with bombs
>**be bombed out** _After we were bombed out, my family moved to the country._
>♦ _Hundreds of people were bombed out of their homes in the raid._

■ **'bombed-out** adj [only before noun] a bombed-out building, vehicle, or place has been destroyed or very badly damaged by bombs: _The bombed-out presidential palace was rebuilt after the war._ ♦ _Families huddled in the ruins of their bombed-out homes._

,bomb 'out of _informal_

to have to leave something such as an industry or a competition because you have failed badly or you have been easily defeated
>**bomb out of sth** _After only six months, the company bombed out of the computer software business._

BOMBARD /bɒm'bɑːd, _American_ bɑm'bɑrd/
bombards, bombarding, bombarded

bom'bard with ★

1 to ask someone so many questions, or give them so much information, that it is difficult for them to deal with it all
>**bombard sb/sth with sth** _She bombarded him with faxes and called his office repeatedly._

2 to attack someone or something by hitting them with a lot of objects or by hitting them many times
>**bombard sb/sth with sth** _Protesters bombarded the building with ink, paint, and bottles._

BONE /bəʊn, _American_ boʊn/
bones, boning, boned

,bone 'up _informal_

to learn as much as possible about something in order to prepare for a test, meeting etc
>**bone up** _He's boning up for his final exams._ ♦ **+on** _She boned up on the company before the interview._

BOOK /bʊk/
books, booking, booked

,book 'in ★ _British_

1 book in or **book into** to say that you have arrived when you get to a hotel, clinic etc, so that your name can be put on an official record or list = CHECK IN ≠ LEAVE
>**book in** _I'd just arrived at the conference and hadn't had time to book in._

2 [often passive] to arrange for yourself or someone else to stay at a hotel, hospital etc
>**be booked in** _He's been booked in at the Royal Palace Hotel._
>**book sb in** _I'll book you in right away._
>♦ **+at** _He's booked himself in at a health spa._
>**book sb into sth** _Officials booked the family into a guesthouse for the night._

'book on (_also_ 'book onto)

to buy tickets for someone for a specific journey on a plane, train, or bus
>**book sb on sth** _Could you book me on the 8.30 flight?_

be ,booked 'up

if a restaurant, tour, concert etc is booked up, all the places or seats have already been taken
>**be booked up** _I'm sorry, sir, but the restaurant is booked up until the middle of next week._

BOOM /buːm, _American_ bum/
booms, booming, boomed

,boom 'out

to make a deep loud sound that continues for some time
>**boom out** _A voice boomed out from the loudspeakers._

BOOT /buːt, _American_ but/
boots, booting, booted

,boot 'out [often passive] _informal_

to make someone leave a place, their job, their school etc = DISMISS, KICK OUT
>**be booted out** _Anyone caught taking drugs was booted out._ ♦ **+of** _They were booted out of the club for fighting._
>**boot sb out** _also_ **boot out sb** _His girlfriend has booted him out._

,boot 'up

if a computer boots up, or if you boot it up, it starts working and is ready to use
>**boot up** _Your computer may take a little time to boot up._
>**boot sth up** _also_ **boot up sth** _Try booting your machine up again._

BORDER /ˈbɔːdə, American ˈbɔrdər/
borders, bordering, bordered

ˈborder on ★★

1 to be very close to a particular unpleasant quality, feeling, state etc, especially an extreme one = APPROACH, VERGE ON

border on sth *She had a feeling of dislike for him that bordered on hatred.* ♦ *There was an atmosphere of excitement bordering on hysteria.*

2 to be next to another country or region
border on sth *Jordan borders on both Israel and Iraq.*

BORE /bɔː, American bɔr/
bores, boring, bored

ˈbore into
if someone's eyes bore into you, they look at you very hard and this makes you feel nervous
bore into sb *She felt Alan's eyes boring into her.*

BORROW /ˈbɒrəʊ, American ˈbɔroʊ/
borrows, borrowing, borrowed

ˈborrow from ★ [often passive]
to use an idea, method, phrase etc that was first used by another person or in another place or situation
be borrowed from sb/sth *English is full of words that have been borrowed from other languages.*
borrow sth from sb/sth *His speech was, to borrow a phrase from Shakespeare, 'full of sound and fury'.*

BOSS /bɒs, American bɔs, bɑs/
bosses, bossing, bossed

ˌboss aˈround (also ˌboss aˈbout)
informal
to keep telling other people what to do in a way that is annoying
boss sb around *He's used to bossing his little brother around.* ♦ *Stop bossing me around!*

BOTCH /bɒtʃ, American bɑtʃ/
botches, botching, botched

ˌbotch ˈup *informal*
to do something very badly or carelessly
botch up sth *also* **botch sth up** *Police officers had botched up the entire investigation.*

BOTTLE /ˈbɒt(ə)l, American ˈbɑt(ə)l/
bottles, bottling, bottled

ˌbottle ˈout *British informal*
to not do something because you do not feel brave enough = CHICKEN OUT
bottle out *He was supposed to come with us but he bottled out at the last minute.*

ˌbottle ˈup
if you bottle up a negative feeling such as anger or disappointment, you stop yourself from showing it over a period of time, so that it often develops in a harmful way = *formal* CONTAIN
bottle up sth *also* **bottle sth up** *She had bottled up her resentment for years.*
♦ *Talking about how you feel can be better than bottling it all up.*

BOTTOM /ˈbɒtəm, American ˈbɑtəm/
bottoms, bottoming, bottomed

ˌbottom ˈout
if something such as the economy or a price bottoms out, it reaches its lowest and worst level before starting to improve or rise again
bottom out *Property prices are still falling, and show no signs of bottoming out.*

BOUNCE /baʊns/
bounces, bouncing, bounced

ˌbounce aˈround
to discuss something in an informal way
bounce sth around *The festival was a chance for groups of musicians to bounce their ideas around.* ♦ *There are a few points I'd like to bounce around.*

ˌbounce ˈback ★★

1 to become healthy, happy, or successful again after something bad has happened to you = *formal* RECOVER
bounce back *He's sad about Sally leaving him, but he'll bounce back.*
♦ *After an early defeat, she bounced back to win the championship.*

2 *business* if the economy or a price bounces back, it improves or rises again after being at a low level = *formal* RECOVER
bounce back *BT's shares fell dramatically, but bounced back before the end of the day.*

ˌbounce ˈinto [often passive]
to make someone do something that they do not really want to do by not giving them enough time to think about it
be bounced into (doing) sth *They complained that they were being*

*bounced into accepting last-minute
decisions.*
bounce sb into (doing) sth *The
opposition is trying to bounce them into
an election while interest rates are still
high.*

,bounce 'off

1 if light, sound etc bounces off a surface,
it hits it and then moves away from it
again = GLANCE OFF
bounce off sth *Radar waves bounce off
objects in their path.*

2 to discuss an idea with someone else in
order to get their opinion and make a
decision
bounce sth off sb *OK, I'd now like to
bounce another idea off you.*

BOW /baʊ/
bows, bowing, bowed

,bow 'down

to show a lot of respect to someone or
something that is more powerful than you
bow down *His captors forced him to bow
down before their leader.*

,bow 'down to *same as* bow to

,bow 'out ★

to give up a job or position, especially one
that you have had for a long time
bow out *I've had a great decade with
this company, but now it's time to bow
out.* ♦ **+of** *She has no plans to bow out
of politics just yet.*

'bow to *(also ,bow 'down to)*

to agree to do what someone wants you to
do, although you do not want to = ACCEPT
bow to sth/sb *The government has
repeated its message that it will not bow
to the terrorists' demands.* ♦ *Laura did
not usually bow down to her husband's
wishes.*

BOWL /bəʊl, *American* boʊl/
bowls, bowling, bowled

,bowl a'long

to move along quickly and smoothly,
especially in a vehicle
bowl along *We were bowling along
beside the edge of the cliffs.*

,bowl 'out *[often passive]*

in the sport of cricket, to get all of one
team's players out and so end their turn
at hitting the ball
be bowled out *England were bowled out
and lost by 66 runs.*
bowl sb out *They bowled the West Indies
out for 247 runs.*

,bowl 'over ★

1 [usually passive] to impress someone very
much by being extremely beautiful,
exciting, attractive etc = IMPRESS
be bowled over *We were bowled over by
the sheer beauty of the landscape.*

2 to knock someone over, because you are
hurrying somewhere
bowl sb over *Another boy ran into him
and bowled him over.*

BOX /bɒks, *American* bɑːks/
boxes, boxing, boxed

,box 'in *[usually passive]*

1 to surround a person or vehicle so that
they cannot move or leave a place
be boxed in *I was completely boxed in
until the other driver came back.*

2 to limit someone's freedom to choose
what to do = CONSTRAIN
be boxed in *Reformers are boxed in by
all sorts of out-dated laws.*

■ **'in box** noun [C] **1** the file in an email
program where new email messages
arrive: *I switched the machine on but
there was nothing in my in box.*
2 *American* a flat open container on your
desk where you put documents that you
have not dealt with yet: *My office is a
mess and my in box is bursting at the
seams.*

,box 'off

to separate an area from the rest of a
place, especially by building a wall
around it
box off sth *also* **box sth off** *They've boxed
off the bathroom.*

,box 'up

to put something in a box, or to put things
in boxes
box sth up *also* **box up sth** *I'll ask my
colleague to box the computer up for you.*
♦ *I've boxed up all my stuff.*

BRANCH /brɑːntʃ, *American* bræntʃ/
branches, branching, branched

,branch 'off

1 if a road or path branches off, part of it
becomes a separate road or path that goes
in a different direction ≠ MERGE
branch off *Several tracks branch off in
different directions.* ♦ *A tunnel branched
off to the left.*
branch off sth *Lanes branch off the main
road, leading to the coast.*

2 if you branch off, you leave one road or
path and go onto another road or path
that is joined to it = TURN OFF

branch off *A small group of soldiers branched off into the jungle.*

branch 'out ★

to start doing something new or different, especially a new activity = DIVERSIFY

branch out *The company grew and began branching out.* ♦ *Quinn wanted to leave the company and branch out on his own.* ♦ **+into** *In the longer term, the company wants to branch out into providing investment advice.* ♦ *Several singers have successfully branched out into the movie business.* ♦ **+from sth into/to sth** *Designers have branched out from clothes to cosmetics and toiletries.*

BRAVE /breɪv/
braves, braving, braved

brave 'out

PHRASE **brave it out** to deal with an unpleasant situation in a confident, patient, and determined way: *Grim though our situation was, we had no choice but to brave it out.*

BRAZEN /ˈbreɪz(ə)n/
brazens, brazening, brazened

brazen 'out

PHRASE **brazen it out** if someone brazens it out, they deal with a difficult or embarrassing situation by pretending that they do not care if people are shocked or offended by their behaviour, especially when they are in fact embarrassed: *He knew the decision would upset a lot of people but he was confident he could brazen it out.*

BREAK /breɪk/
breaks, breaking, broke /brəʊk, *American* broʊk/, **broken** /ˈbrəʊkən, *American* ˈbroʊkən/

Break is often used with adverbs and prepositions when it means 'to separate, or make something separate, into two or more pieces, for example by hitting or dropping it': *She **broke** the stick **over** her knee.* ♦ *The glass slipped from her hand and **broke into** a dozen pieces.* ♦ *Heat makes the two surfaces **break apart**.* These uses are not included here.

break a'way ★★

1 to leave a political party or other group, especially in order to start another one = SPLIT OFF ≠ JOIN

break away *More than 30 Labour MPs broke away to form the SDP.* ♦ **+from**

Several members decided to break away from the church and start their own group.

2 to move away from someone, often someone who is trying to prevent you from leaving = PULL AWAY

break away *Anna tried to break away but he held her tight.* ♦ **+from** *He tried to break away from the man's grasp.*

3 if a part of something breaks away from the rest, it becomes separated from it = BREAK OFF

break away *Part of the wood had broken away.* ♦ **+from** *Two carriages broke away from the train when it crashed.*

■ **breakaway** /ˈbreɪkəˌweɪ/ adj [only before noun] consisting of people who have decided to separate from a larger group: *They formed their own breakaway theatre company.*

■ **breakaway** /ˈbreɪkəˌweɪ/ noun [C] an occasion when some people in a large group leave the group to form a smaller, separate group, usually because of a disagreement: *The rebels were considering a breakaway.*

break a'way from

to stop doing something and start doing something different

break away from sth *The younger generation is eager to break away from tradition.*

break 'down ★★★

1	about machines/vehicles
2	when a relationship/discussion ends
3	divide a total
4	start to cry
5	make a door/wall fall down
6	make progress by removing difficulty
7	separate sth into parts
8	become mentally ill
+	**breakdown** noun; **broken-down** adj

1 if a machine or vehicle breaks down, it stops working = *informal* CONK OUT —*picture* → BACK UP

break down *The car broke down just outside London.* ♦ *I didn't make a copy of the letter because the photocopier had broken down.*

2 if something such as a relationship or discussion breaks down, it stops being successful = COLLAPSE

break down *At one point, the talks seemed close to breaking down.*

3 to divide something such as a total amount into separate parts = DIVIDE UP

break sth down *The amount doesn't seem quite so bad when you break it down.* ♦ **+into** *It's best to break the* *information down into manageable chunks.*

4 to start crying, especially in public
break down *Many people broke down and wept.*

5 to hit something such as a door or wall very hard so that it falls down
break down sth *Firefighters had to break down the door to get into the house.*
break sth down *They got into the compound by breaking the gates down.*
♦ *If a door is locked, our officers break it down.*

6 to remove a difficulty that prevents something from happening = OVERCOME
break down sth *The aim of the agreement is to break down barriers to trade.*
break sth down *When we meet with resistance, we break it down.*

7 [often passive] if a substance breaks down or is broken down into parts, it separates into the parts that it is made up of
be broken down *Like all natural substances, it is easily broken down by bacteria.*
break sth down *The body has the task of breaking food down and digesting it.*
break down sth *Enzymes in the liver break down caffeine.*

8 if someone breaks down, they become mentally ill, especially as a result of difficult events in their life = *informal* CRACK UP
break down *Most people would break down under that kind of pressure.*

■ **breakdown** /ˈbreɪkdaʊn/ **noun**
1 [C/U] a situation in which something has failed or is beginning to fail: *The breakdown of his marriage soon followed.* **2** [C] a situation in which a machine or vehicle stops working: *We had a breakdown on the motorway.* **3** [C] *health* a mental condition in which you are so upset or unhappy that you cannot look after yourself: *Then the mother had a breakdown.* **4** [C] information that has been separated into different groups: *This section gives a detailed breakdown of how the money is spent.*

■ **,broken-'down** **adj** no longer working or in good condition: *The floor is littered with broken-down machinery.*

'break for
to go somewhere quickly, especially in order to escape
break for sth *We're assuming they'll break for the border.*

,break 'in ★★★

1	enter a place in order to steal things
2	interrupt
3	about new shoes/clothes
4	help sb do sth new
5	train a horse
+	**break-in** noun

1 to enter a building by force, especially in order to steal things = FORCE ENTRY
break in *Someone had broken in through the bedroom window.*

2 to interrupt when someone is talking
break in *'Hilary,' he broke in gently, 'I'm just trying to help.'*

3 to make new shoes comfortable by wearing them, especially by making the leather less stiff
break in sth *Make sure you break in new boots a few weeks before you go hiking.*
break sth in *My shoes were rubbing my heels. I was still breaking them in.*

4 to help someone get used to something new, for example a new job
break sb in *To break me in, they gave me little jobs to do.*
break in sb *They break in newcomers by making them answer the phones.*

5 to train a horse that is young or wild
break in sth *One of his jobs was breaking in young horses.*
break sth in *It took us all day to break him in.*

■ **'break-in** noun [C] an act of entering a building illegally using force, especially in order to steal things: *There's been an increase in the number of break-ins in the area.*

,break 'into ★★★

1	enter a place in order to steal things
2	start laughing/singing
3	interrupt sb
4	become involved in sth
5	use money
6	open a container

1 [often passive] to enter a building by force, especially in order to steal things = BURGLE
be broken into *A house in our street was broken into last night.*
break into sth *Some kids had broken into the school at night.*

2 to start doing something such as running, laughing, or singing = BEGIN
break into sth *The kids saw the beach and broke into a run.* ♦ *We watched her puzzled face break into a wide grin.* ♦ *I almost expected him to break into song.* ♦ *My legs were shaking with*

*exhaustion, but Phil hadn't even **broken into a sweat**.*

3 to interrupt someone when they are talking or thinking = DISTURB, INTERRUPT
break into sth *Christopher's voice broke into her thoughts.*

4 to start to become involved in an activity or business, especially successfully
break into sth *We see the deal with China as a way of breaking into markets in the Far East.* ♦ *It's always been his ambition to break into broadcasting.*

5 to start to use an amount of money
break into sth *We had to break into our savings to pay the fine.* ♦ *I didn't want to break into a twenty-pound note.*

6 to open a container in order to use some of the substance contained in it
break into sth *I didn't want to break into another packet.*

ˌbreak 'off ★★★

1	stop speaking
2	end a relationship
3	end sth because of a disagreement
4	become separated from sth
5	remove sth from sth

1 to stop speaking, especially suddenly
break off *Linda broke off, realizing that she was wrong.*
break off sth *People would break off their conversations when she came into the room.*

2 to end a romantic or sexual relationship
break off sth *Did you know they've broken off their engagement?*
break sth off *I've decided to break it off with her.*

3 to end something such as a discussion that you are involved in with other people, because of a disagreement
break off sth *The two countries have broken off diplomatic relations.* ♦ *The unions have broken off all negotiations.*

Nouns often used as objects with
break off 3

■ **conversation, discussion, negotiations, talks**

4 if a part of something breaks off, it becomes separated from the main part = BREAK AWAY, DETACH
break off *Part of the chimney broke off and fell to the ground.* ♦ **+from** *Chunks of ice breaking off from the glacier create icebergs.*

5 if you break a piece off something, you remove it from the main part = DETACH
break off sth *Each child broke off a slice of pizza.*

break sth off *He took the bread and broke a large piece off.* ♦ *When new shoots appeared on the plant, I broke them off.*
break sth off sth *Someone had broken the rotten pieces off the top of the fence.*

ˌbreak 'out ★★★

1	start
2	skin: get spots
3	spots: appear
4	end a situation
5	leave prison
+	**breakout** noun, adj; **outbreak** noun

1 if something bad such as a war or a disease breaks out, it starts = START ≠ END
break out *We got married a month before the war broke out.* ♦ *The fire must have broken out during the night.*

Nouns often used as subjects with
break out 1

■ **fighting, fire, hostilities, rioting, row, scuffles, trouble, violence, war**

2 if your skin breaks out in something such as spots or a rash, they start to appear on your skin
break out *If I drink wine, my skin starts to break out.* ♦ **+in** *The skin on my arms was breaking out in a rash.*

3 if something such as spots or a rash break out on your skin, they start to appear on your skin = APPEAR
break out *Spots started to break out all over his face.* ♦ **+on** *Sweat was beginning to break out on his forehead.*

4 to escape from something such as a situation or way of life
break out of sth *He felt the desire to break out of the boring routine of normal daily living.*

5 to escape from a prison
break out *Some of the guys were planning to break out.*
break out of sth *Six prisoners have broken out of a top-security jail.*

■ **breakout** /ˈbreɪkaʊt/ noun [C] **1** an occasion when prisoners escape from a prison: *Myers and two other guys were planning a breakout.* **2** *business* one of several groups that a larger group of people has divided into to discuss something, especially at a conference: *We've organized a number of breakout sessions.* **3** a sudden appearance of a disease = OUTBREAK: *the 2004 breakout of bird flu* **4** *American* an appearance of spots on your skin: *Consuming any of these substances might trigger a breakout.*

■ **breakout** /ˈbreɪkaʊt/ adj [only before noun] *American* involving great success that makes someone or something very popular: *We haven't seen a real breakout series from NBC since 'Friends'.*

■ **outbreak** /'aʊtbreɪk/ noun [C] the sudden start of war, disease, violence etc: *an outbreak of food poisoning* ♦ *the outbreak of war*

,break 'through ★★

1	push yourself through sth
2	make progress despite difficulties
3	about sunlight
4	become seen
5	become noticed
+	**breakthrough** noun

1 to force your way through something that is stopping you from moving forward
break through sth *A group of young demonstrators attempted to break through police lines.*
break through *The rock was several feet thick and we had difficulty breaking through.*

2 to successfully deal with something that is stopping you from making progress = OVERCOME
break through sth *There were attempts to break through prejudice in the workplace.*

3 if sunlight breaks through, or if it breaks through cloud, you can see the sunlight because the cloud has disappeared
break through sth *Sunshine was breaking through the clouds.*
break through *The sun had finally broken through.*

4 if something breaks through something, you can see it after it has been hidden by something
break through sth *Maggie's head broke through the surface of the pool.*

5 if a quality breaks through, it starts to be noticed when it could not be noticed before
break through *Her sense of humour kept breaking through.*

■ **breakthrough** /'breɪkθruː/ noun [C] **1** a discovery or achievement that comes after a lot of hard work: *Scientists predict a major breakthrough within six months.* **2** a time when you begin to be successful at something: *The breakthrough came in the 20th minute with a header from John Barnes.*

,break 'up ★★★

1	when a relationship ends
2	end a relationship
3	when an event ends
4	make a fight end
5	about radios/phones
6	about schools/students
7	divide an area/period
8	break sth into pieces
9	become broken into pieces
10	make sb laugh
+	**breakup** noun

1 if a relationship breaks up, or if something breaks it up, it ends = END
break up *The marriage broke up just a few years later.*
break up sth *There were suggestions that her involvement had broken up the partnership.*
break sth up *He blamed my mother for breaking our marriage up.* ♦ *Things can happen to damage the relationship or break it up.*

2 if two people break up, they end their relationship = SEPARATE, SPLIT UP —*picture* → ASK OUT
break up *He hasn't seen her since they broke up.*
break up with sb *He's just broken up with his girlfriend.*

3 if a meeting or other event breaks up, or if you break it up, it ends and people leave
break up *The talks didn't break up until after midnight.*
break up sth *Sorry to break up the party, but I have to go.*
break sth up *The police made no attempt to break the demonstration up.* ♦ *The session was going so well I didn't want to break it up.*

4 to stop a fight
break up sth *She was injured when she tried to break up a fight between two boys.*
break sth up *Okay, you two. Break it up.* ♦ *Several people tried to break the fight up, but still the punches flew.*

5 if a person talking on a radio or a mobile phone breaks up, the sound keeps disappearing so it is difficult to hear or understand them
break up *I can't hear you, you're breaking up.*

6 *British* if schools break up, or if students or teachers break up, the students and teachers stop working at the end of term
break up *That's the week that the schools break up.* ♦ *+for Have the kids broken up for the summer yet?*

break up (sense 4)

7 to divide a large area or a period of time into smaller parts so that it does not seem so big or long

break up sth *I usually go for a walk around three o'clock to break up the afternoon.*
break sth up *Hang pictures on a long wall to break it up.* ♦ *I look forward to my husband coming home at lunchtime. It breaks the day up.*

8 to break something to make smaller pieces = DIVIDE ≠ JOIN

break sth up *Break the chocolate up into squares.* ♦ *She stabbed at the clumps of earth with a spade to break them up.*
break up sth *The thieves had broken up most of my furniture.*

9 if something breaks up, it breaks into smaller pieces = DISINTEGRATE

break up *The plane broke up in mid-air.*

10 *American informal* to make someone laugh a lot = *British* CRACK UP

break sb up *The way he talks just breaks us up.*

■ **breakup** /ˈbreɪkʌp/ **noun** [C] **1** the end of a serious relationship or marriage: *I haven't spoken to her since the breakup.* **2** the division of something such as an organization or country into smaller parts: *This happened before the breakup of the Soviet Union.*

'break with

1 to leave a group of people, or end a friendship or relationship, usually because of a disagreement ≠ JOIN

break with sb/sth *Soon afterwards, he broke with the Labour Party.* ♦ *That was the year she broke with her songwriting partner.*

2 if you break with a tradition or the way things have always been done, you disagree with it and start doing things in a completely new way

break with tradition/the past etc *Some women broke with tradition by going to study abroad.*

BREATHE /briːð, *American* brið/
breathes, breathing, breathed

breathe 'in ★★

1 to take air into your lungs through your nose or mouth = INHALE

breathe in *It hurts when I breathe in.*

2 to take something such as smoke or a particular smell into your lungs through your nose or mouth = INHALE

breathe in sth *They needed medical treatment after breathing in toxic fumes.*
breathe sth in *There was the scent of rosemary in the air and she breathed it in.* ♦ *It was impossible not to breathe the smoke in.*

breathe 'out ★★

1 to send air out of your lungs through your nose or mouth = EXHALE

breathe out *Now breathe out slowly.*

2 to send something such as smoke or a particular gas out of your lungs through your nose or mouth = EXHALE

breathe out sth *We breathe in air and breathe out carbon dioxide.*
breathe sth out *She breathes the smoke out quickly.* ♦ *The smoke filled my lungs, and I breathed it out with a sense of relief.*

BREEZE /briːz, *American* briz/
breezes, breezing, breezed

breeze 'in (*also* **breeze 'into**) *showing disapproval*

to enter a place in a confident way, especially when you do not seem to care what other people think = ROLL IN

breeze in *He breezes in and starts giving people orders.*
breeze into sth *He breezed into the meeting and took charge.*

ˈbreeze through

to do something very easily or confidently
= SAIL THROUGH
breeze through sth *We're expecting the champion to breeze through the first few rounds.*

BREW /bruː, *American* bru/
brews, brewing, brewed

ˌbrew ˈup

1 *informal* to develop as a situation that will cause difficulty
brew up *I sense a scandal brewing up.*
2 *informal* to create a situation that causes difficulty
brew up sth *He's brewing up a nasty shock for his old friend.*
3 *informal* to make a drink of tea
brew up *Haven't you brewed up yet?*
brew up sth *I was just about to brew up some tea.*

BRICK /brɪk/
bricks, bricking, bricked

ˌbrick ˈin *same as* brick up

ˌbrick ˈup [often passive]

to fill a space in a wall with bricks
be bricked up *The windows were all bricked up.*
brick up sth *also* **brick sth up** *Someone had bricked up the old entrance.* ♦ *We would have to brick the hole up afterwards.*

BRIEF /briːf, *American* brif/
briefs, briefing, briefed

ˌbrief aˈgainst

to say things that are intended to give people a bad opinion of someone, especially a politician
brief against sb *She accused him of briefing against Gordon Brown.*

BRIGHTEN /ˈbraɪt(ə)n/
brightens, brightening, brightened

ˌbrighten ˈup ★

1 to make something more interesting or attractive by adding things = LIVEN UP
brighten up sth *You could brighten up that skirt with a red blouse.*
brighten sth up *Try brightening your marriage up by giving each other treats.*

2 to become happier or more hopeful
= CHEER UP, PERK UP
brighten up *Sarah brightened up considerably when she saw him.*

3 if the weather brightens up, it becomes sunnier ≠ CLOUD OVER
brighten up *I think it's beginning to brighten up.* ♦ *Let's hope the weather brightens up a bit.*

brighten up

BRIM /brɪm/
brims, brimming, brimmed

ˌbrim ˈover

1 [usually progressive] if a container is brimming over, it is so full of liquid that some is falling out = OVERFLOW
brim over *The cup was nearly brimming over.* ♦ **+with sth** *The bowls were brimming over with soup.*
2 to be full of something such as a strong emotion = OVERFLOW
brim over *Their eyes met, and his heart brimmed over.* ♦ **+with** *I was brimming over with excitement.*

ˈbrim with ★ [usually progressive]

to be full of something
brim with sth *I handed him a cup brimming with tea.* ♦ *The greenhouse was brimming with plants.* ♦ *Her eyes were brimming with tears.*

BRING /brɪŋ/
brings, bringing, brought /brɔːt, *American* brɔt/

Bring is often used with adverbs and prepositions when it means 'to take someone or something from one place and have them with you when you arrive somewhere else': *Can I bring the children to work?* ♦ *I'll bring another plate from the kitchen.* ♦ *When I come downstairs, I'll bring the photos down.* These uses are not included here.

bring a'bout ★★★ [often passive]

to make something happen, especially to cause changes in a situation = CAUSE, MAKE HAPPEN

be brought about *These social changes have been brought about by new technology.*

bring about sth *We will have to work harder to bring about changes in the system.*

bring sth about *We wanted change but were doing nothing to bring it about.*
♦ *How do you plan to bring these improvements about?*

Nouns often used as objects with **bring about**

■ (changes) change, developments, improvements, revolution, transformation
(bad events) collapse, decline, demise, destruction, downfall, end, fall

bring a'long ★★

to take someone or something with you when you go somewhere = BRING

bring sb/sth along *Bring some friends along if you like.* ♦ *My mother is staying with me at the moment. Is it OK if I bring her along too?*

bring along sb/sth *They are expected to bring along enough school work to keep themselves busy.*

bring a'round ★

1 to take someone or something somewhere, especially to someone's house

bring sb/sth around *He promised to bring the letter around in the morning.*

2 *American* to persuade someone to agree with you

bring sb around *Sam was sure he could bring them around to the deal.*

3 *American* to make someone who is unconscious become conscious

bring sb around *We threw water in his face to try to bring him around.*

bring a'round to

to gradually change the subject of a conversation or discussion to one that you want to talk about

bring sth around to sth *Eventually I brought the conversation around to the subject of money.*

bring 'back ★★★

1	make sb remember sth
2	start doing sth again
3	give sb a job they had before
4	bring sth when you return
5	discuss sth mentioned before
6	make a dead person live
7	save sb from dying

1 to cause ideas, feelings, or memories to be in your mind again = *formal* EVOKE

bring back sth *Do these stories bring back any memories?*

bring sth back *Seeing him again brought it all back.* ♦ *Just talking about what happened brings the fear back.*

2 to start using or doing things that were used or done in the past = RESTORE, REINSTATE

bring back sth *They'll never bring back the death penalty.*

bring sth back *We want to bring some of that old glamour back to the place.* ♦ *The club used to have a male-only rule, and they're talking about bringing it back.*

3 [often passive] to give someone a job or position that they had in the past = *formal* REINSTATE

be brought back *I know I can help them win if I am brought back into the team.*

bring back sb *I didn't agree with the decision to bring back Smith.*

bring sb back *The rebels are attempting to bring the exiled president back.* ♦ *Now she has resigned and nothing we say can bring her back.*

4 to bring something with you when you come back from a place

bring back sth *Travellers brought back news of the outside world.*

bring sth back *We didn't bring any presents back this year.* ♦ *Would you like a burger? I could go around the corner and bring some back.*

bring sb back sth *He always brings me back something nice when he goes abroad.*

5 used for saying that you are going to talk about a subject that you have already talked about = TAKE BACK

bring sb back to sth *This brings us back to the obvious question: why do we bother to watch the programme at all?*

6 to make a dead person live again

bring sb back *'Anger won't bring Jim back,' she said.*

7 to save someone's life when they have almost died = REVIVE, RESUSCITATE

bring sb back *Her heart stopped three times, but they brought her back.*

‚bring be'fore

1 [often passive] to make someone go to court because they have been accused of doing something wrong

  be brought before sb/sth *He had never been charged or brought before a judge.*

  bring sb before sth/sb *We proposed bringing him before a tribunal of officers.*

2 to arrange for a case to be discussed in a court, committee, or parliament

  bring sth before sth *They plan to bring the issue before the UN Security Council.*

‚bring 'down ★★★

1	about governments/politicians
2	reduce a rate/level
3	push sb to the ground
4	make sth fall
5	shoot a person/animal
6	shoot a bird/plane
7	make a plane land safely
8	make sb sad

1 to cause a government or politician to lose power = TOPPLE, OVERTHROW

  bring down sb/sth *Opposition parties are threatening to bring down the government.*

  bring sb/sth down *The plan was to bring the whole regime down.* ♦ *The Prime Minister criticized the rebels who were trying to bring him down.*

2 to reduce the rate, level, or amount of something = REDUCE, LOWER ≠ RAISE

  bring down sth *Our principal responsibility is to bring down the level of unemployment.*

  bring sth down *All the major shops were bringing their prices down.* ♦ *If your child has a fever, try to bring it down by giving him a cool bath.*

3 [often passive] to make someone fall to the ground, for example by attacking them

  be brought down *Johnson was brought down by an aggressive tackle just a few feet from the goal.*

  bring sb down *Your aim is to bring him down before he reaches the line.* ♦ *He made two attempts to bring his man down, but failed.*

  bring down sb *She can bring down a man twice her size.*

4 to make something fall to the ground = TOPPLE

  bring down sth *Strong winds brought down power lines across the region.*

  bring sth down *A powerful gust could bring the whole fence down.* ♦ *The gales were striking the wall straight on and eventually brought it down.*

5 to shoot a person or animal and make

them fall to the ground = SHOOT DOWN

  bring down sb/sth *Could this small dart bring down such a huge creature?*

  bring sb/sth down *These weapons can bring a man down from over 500 yards.*

6 to make a bird or plane fall out of the sky, for example by shooting at it = SHOOT DOWN

  bring down sth *We brought down twenty enemy aircraft in a couple of hours.*

  bring sth down *We didn't bring a single plane down.* ♦ *The bird avoided all attempts to bring it down.*

7 when someone flying a plane brings it down, they make it come down from the sky onto the ground safely = LAND

  bring sth down *He managed to bring the plane down safely with only one engine.* ♦ *Only a skilled pilot could bring her down in weather like that.*

8 to make someone feel sad, or to make someone have no hope = DEPRESS

  bring sb down *She's always trying to bring me down.*

‚bring 'forth *formal*

to produce something, or to cause a particular reaction = PRODUCE, ELICIT

  bring forth sth *Her letter to the paper brought forth a flood of supportive comments.* ♦ *America brings forth new technology on a daily basis.*

‚bring 'forward ★★

1 [often passive] to change the date or time of an event so that it happens earlier ≠ PUT BACK

  be brought forward *The match has been brought forward to 1.00 pm.*

  bring sth forward *They brought the date of the wedding forward so her cousins could attend.* ♦ *We planned the meeting for the 28th May but had to bring it forward.*

2 to announce plans or ideas officially so that people can discuss them = PUT FORWARD, PUT ON THE TABLE

  bring forward sth *The various departments have not yet brought forward their spending plans.*

  bring sth forward *Thank you for bringing that forward.* ♦ *We will bring the matter forward at the next meeting.*

3 [often passive] to take the total of a column of numbers from the bottom of one page to the top of the next page

  be brought forward *I wasn't sure which number should be brought forward.*

  bring sth forward *Then you bring that figure forward.*

,bring 'in ★★★

1 [often passive] to use the skills of a particular group or person = CALL IN

be brought in *An independent investigator will be brought in to look at the allegations.*

bring in sb *They're bringing in experts from all over the world.*

bring sb in *The hostage negotiators did a good job, but the authorities were criticized for bringing them in too late.* ♦ *The company has brought a new management team in.*

2 to be the reason that someone or something receives a particular amount of money = ATTRACT

bring in sth *Overseas students bring in more than £30 million a year in tuition fees.*

bring sth in *He had all sorts of ideas for bringing extra money in.* ♦ *We didn't think the scheme would bring that much in.*

3 [often passive] to introduce a new law or system = INTRODUCE

be brought in *New measures will be brought in to ensure that this never happens again.*

bring in sth *She said the government would bring in the necessary legislation to deal with the problem.*

> Nouns often used as objects with **bring in 3**
>
> ■ bill, law, legislation, measures, regulations

4 to involve someone in a radio or TV discussion

bring in sb *And here I'd like to bring in James Walker to hear his comments.*

bring sb in *Let's bring your mother in and see what she has to say.*

PHRASE **bring in a verdict** to say officially whether someone is guilty or not: *There were gasps when the jury brought in a verdict of not guilty.*

'bring into ★★★

1 to cause someone or something to be involved in something

bring sb/sth into sth *Why are you bringing money into the conversation?* ♦ *We risk bringing politics into sport.* ♦ *I don't want them bringing me into their arguments.*

2 to be the reason that someone or something receives money = ATTRACT

bring sth into sth *Tourists bring millions of pounds into the domestic economy.*

,bring 'off ★

to succeed in doing something difficult = PULL OFF

bring off sth *If they can bring off the deal, they'll be able to retire.*

bring sth off *The concerto is a huge challenge but she brought it off magnificently.*

,bring 'on ★★★

1 [often passive] to be the cause of something bad, especially an illness = CAUSE

be brought on *She nearly died of a heart attack brought on by fear.*

bring sth on *I don't know what's brought this on – he's usually so friendly.* ♦ *What do you think brought your depression on this time?*

bring on sth *The slightest thing can bring on the pain.*

2 to make something bad happen to someone

bring sth on sb *He accused her of bringing shame and disgrace on the family.* ♦ *I don't feel sorry for her – she brought it all on herself.*

3 to help someone to improve their talents or skills = DEVELOP

bring sb on *We need a scheme for bringing our youngsters on.* ♦ *He's a very good teacher. He's bringing her on very well.*

bring on sb *The company has set up a centre for film production to bring on new talent.*

PHRASE **bring it on** *very informal* you say this to show that you feel brave and confident enough to deal with any situation or face any opponent: *If he thinks he can beat me, tell him to bring it on!*

,bring 'out ★★★

1 to produce a new product and start to sell it = PUBLISH, RELEASE

bring out sth *The next year they brought out a low-priced car to compete with Ford.*

bring sth out *She is bringing a new album out next month.* ♦ *With her second book, the publishers decided to bring it out as a mass-market paperback.*

2 to make someone or something show a quality that they have = HIGHLIGHT ≠ SUPPRESS

bring out sth *The wine really brings out the spicy flavour of the meat.*

bring sth out *A small amount of makeup can bring that natural beauty out.*

bring out the sth in sb *Fear brings out the child in us.* ♦ *There's something about her that brings out the worst in me* (=makes me show my worst personal qualities).

3 to make someone feel less shy and start to behave more confidently

> **bring sb out** *Take him to your party. That might bring him out.*
> **bring sb out of himself/herself** *She needs friends who can bring her out of herself.*

‚bring 'out in

to make particular marks appear on someone's skin

> **bring sb out in spots/a rash/ goosepimples etc** *The medicine brought her out in a rash.*

‚bring 'over ★★

to take someone or something from one place to the place where someone else is, especially their home

> **bring sb/sth over** *I'll bring my holiday photos over when I come.* ♦ **+to** *He's bringing his new girlfriend over to our house tonight.*

‚bring 'round ★ British

1 to take someone or something somewhere, especially to someone's house = BRING

> **bring sb/sth round** *He promised to bring the letter round in the morning.* ♦ *I've got loads of spare paper. I'll bring some round when I come.*
> **bring round sb/sth** *I'll bring round more chairs later.*

2 to persuade someone to agree with you = WIN OVER, TALK ROUND

> **bring sb round** *Do you think you can bring them all round?* ♦ *She's adamant she's not going to be brought round.*
> ♦ **+to** *Sam was sure he could bring them round to the deal.*

3 to make someone who is unconscious become conscious again = BRING TO, REVIVE ≠ KNOCK OUT

> **bring sb round** *We threw water in his face to try and bring him round.*

‚bring 'round to *same as British* **bring around to**

‚bring 'through

to take someone or something from one place and have them with you when you arrive somewhere else

> **bring sb/sth through** *also* **bring through sb/sth** *I'm bringing a form through for you to sign.* ♦ *When the letter arrives, can you ask Pam to bring it through?*
> ♦ *Please bring through the next candidate.*

‚bring 'to

to make someone who is unconscious

become conscious again = BRING ROUND, REVIVE ≠ KNOCK OUT

> **bring sb to** *He fainted but we managed to bring him to.*

‚bring to'gether ★★★

1 to create a situation in which people meet and do something together, especially when they would not usually do so

> **bring together sb and sb** *The event was unique in bringing together politicians, business leaders, and academics.*
> **bring sb together** *The group aims to bring residents together to solve local problems.*
> **bring together sb** *The organization brings together a number of teaching unions.*

2 to put a number of different things into one place so that people can see or experience them all = ASSEMBLE, GATHER TOGETHER ≠ SEPARATE

> **bring together sth** *The exhibition brings together a stunning collection of maps and charts.*
> **bring sth together** *The program then brings the images together to make one colour image.*

‚bring 'up ★★★

1	look after a child
2	teach a child how to behave
3	where sb lived as a child
4	mention/discuss sth
5	when sb is ill
6	about information on a computer screen
+	PHRASE
+	**upbringing** noun

1 [often passive] to take care of a child until he or she becomes an adult = RAISE

> **be brought up** *He was brought up by his grandmother.*
> **bring up sb** *She brought up three sons on her own.*
> **bring sb up** *It was our grandparents who really brought us up.* ♦ *It's not easy bringing four children up on £50 a week.*

2 to teach a child to behave in a particular way or to have particular beliefs = RAISE

> **bring sb up** *That's not how we brought you up!* ♦ **+to do sth** *Our parents brought us up to believe in our own abilities.*

3 [always passive] used for saying where or how someone lived when they were a child = BE RAISED

> **be brought up** *I was brought up on a farm.* ♦ *He was born and brought up in India.* ♦ *These kids have been brought up on a diet of junk food and endless television.*

4 [often passive] to start discussing a subject that was not being discussed before = MENTION, RAISE

be brought up *Brown said the issue would be brought up again at the next climate convention.*

bring sth up *I hate to bring this up, but you still owe me £50.* ♦ *I don't want you to bring this subject up again.*

bring up sth *You brought up an excellent point and we need to clarify it right here.*

5 to make food or drink come back up from your stomach through your mouth = *formal* VOMIT; *informal* HEAVE UP

bring sth up *The dog has brought his food up.*

bring up sth *It looks like he's brought up his whole breakfast.*

6 to make something appear on a computer screen

bring up sth *I'll bring up the prices for you now.*

bring sth up *It'll take a while to bring that information up.* ♦ *I've got her details here. Let me just bring them up on the screen.*

PHRASE **bring sb up short** to make someone stop what they are doing or saying because they are very surprised: *He started walking across to the door, only to be brought up short by the sound of Tamara's voice.*

■ **upbringing** /ˈʌpˌbrɪŋɪŋ/ **noun** [singular] the way that parents look after their children and teach them to behave: *She had a strict Protestant upbringing.*

ˌbring ˈup against
to make someone have to deal with something

bring sb up against sth *His work constantly brought him up against this problem.*

ˌbring uˈpon (*also* ˌbring ˈon) *formal*
to make something bad happen to someone

bring sth upon sb *They had brought discredit upon Congress.*

ˌbring ˈup to
to make someone or something reach a particular standard

bring sb/sth up to sth *We need to bring all our employees up to the required standard.*

BRISTLE /ˈbrɪs(ə)l/
bristles, bristling, bristled

ˈbristle with

1 if something bristles with long, thin things, it has a lot of them on its surface

bristle with sth *The rooftops bristled with aerials.*

2 to be full of things or people

bristle with sth/sb *The town is bristling with tourists.*

3 to be full of a particular emotion

bristle with sth *The new bands bristle with confidence.* ♦ *Andy was bristling with rage.*

BROADEN /ˈbrɔːd(ə)n, *American* ˈbrɔd(ə)n/
broadens, broadening, broadened

ˌbroaden ˈout

1 to become wider = BROADEN, WIDEN ≠ NARROW

broaden out *The stream broadens out into a pool.*

2 to make something include more things or people = EXPAND, WIDEN

broaden out sth *also* **broaden sth out** *We decided to broaden out the debate slightly.* ♦ *The students wanted to broaden their discussions out to include moral issues.*

3 to change and start to include more things or people = EXPAND

broaden out *Her life was broadening out.*

BROOD /bruːd, *American* brud/
broods, brooding, brooded

ˈbrood over (*also* **ˈbrood on**)
to keep thinking about something that makes you worried or unhappy

brood over sth *Look, I know she's being unfair, but there's no point in brooding over it.*

BROWN /braʊn/
browns, browning, browned

be browned ˈoff *old-fashioned*
to be bored or discouraged

be browned off *It's a good thing to do if you're feeling a bit browned off.*

BROWSE /braʊz/
browses, browsing, browsed

ˌbrowse ˈthrough
to look at information or pictures in a book or magazine, without looking for anything in particular = FLICK THROUGH

browse through sth *I browse through the jobs pages from time to time.*

BRUSH /brʌʃ/
brushes, brushing, brushed

ˌbrush aˈgainst ★
to touch someone or something lightly while passing them
brush against sb/sth *I felt something soft brush against my knee.*

ˌbrush aˈside [often passive] *showing disapproval*
to refuse to accept that something is important or true = DISMISS
be brushed aside *These longstanding traditions, values, and attitudes cannot be brushed aside quickly.*
brush aside sth *also* **brush sth aside** *The minister brushed aside accusations that he had lied.*

> Nouns often used as objects with
> **brush aside**
>
> ■ accusations, complaints, criticism, doubts, protests, questions, suggestions

ˌbrush aˈway
1 to remove something from somewhere with a movement of your hand
brush sth away *also* **brush away sth** *Jean brushed her tears away as she listened.* ♦ *He brushed away a strand of hair that had fallen across my face.*
2 to refuse to accept or listen to something that someone says = DISMISS
brush sth away *also* **brush away sth** *She brushes this criticism away.* ♦ *The minister has brushed away all allegations of corruption.*

ˌbrush ˈdown
to clean someone or something using your hands or a brush
brush down sth *also* **brush sth down** *Brush down the paintwork before applying a fresh coat.* ♦ *She feeds the horse and brushes him down.*
brush yourself down *He stood in the doorway brushing himself down.*

ˌbrush ˈoff *showing disapproval*
to refuse to listen to someone, or refuse to accept that something is true = DISMISS
brush off sth *The Foreign Secretary brushed off suggestions that he had considered resigning.*
brush sb off *I tried to tell him, but he just brushed me off.*

■ **ˈbrush-off** noun [singular] *informal* a clear sign to someone that you are not interested in them or in their ideas: *I try to start a conversation but she gives me the brush-off.*

ˌbrush ˈout
to use a brush to remove something from a person's or animal's hair
brush sth out *also* **brush out sth** *If you get paint in your hair, you won't be able to brush it out.* ♦ *The hairdresser gently brushed out her curls so her hair fell in long waves.*

ˌbrush ˈpast
to pass someone and rub against them gently as you do so
brush past sb/sth *I felt an electric shock as she brushed past me.*

ˌbrush ˈup
to practise and improve your skills or knowledge of something = FRESHEN UP
brush up sth *I took a class to brush up my German before the trip.*
brush up on sth *The course offers students the opportunity to brush up on various techniques.*

BUBBLE /ˈbʌb(ə)l/
bubbles, bubbling, bubbled

ˌbubble ˈover
1 if a happy or excited feeling bubbles over, you feel it very strongly and usually show that you are feeling it
bubble over *His optimism bubbled over.*
2 [usually progressive] if you are bubbling over with a feeling or a thought, you feel it very strongly and usually show that you are feeling it
be bubbling over with sth *His voice was bubbling over with delight.* ♦ *She was petite, vivacious and bubbling over with ideas.*

ˌbubble ˈunder [usually progressive]
to have some success but not yet be extremely successful and famous
be bubbling under *Their albums have been bubbling under for a couple of years now.*

ˌbubble ˈup
to increase and become more obvious
bubble up *Tension could bubble up again at any time.* ♦ *These hidden feelings bubble up occasionally.*

ˈbubble with
1 to be full of a strong feeling
bubble with sth *Everybody's bubbling with enthusiasm.*
2 used for saying that a lot of something is happening, or that there are many things in a place
bubble with sth *Science rooms bubble with ongoing experiments.* ♦ *The*

neighbourhood bubbles with political activity.

BUCK /bʌk/
bucks, bucking, bucked

'buck for *American*
to try hard to get something, especially in your job
buck for sth *I think she's bucking for a raise.*

,buck 'up
1 *informal* to try to make someone happier, or to become happier = CHEER UP
buck sb up *I took him out to lunch to try to buck him up a bit.*
buck up *She seems to have bucked up a lot.*
2 *British old-fashioned* used for telling someone to hurry = HURRY UP
buck up *Come on, you two. Buck up!*
PHRASE **buck your ideas up** *British informal* to try harder or do something better = IMPROVE: *I told him to buck his ideas up, or he'd be out of a job.*

BUCKET /'bʌkɪt, American 'bʌkət/
buckets, bucketing, bucketed

'bucket down *British informal*
to rain very hard = POUR DOWN
bucket down *It had been bucketing down all morning.*

BUCKLE /'bʌk(ə)l/
buckles, buckling, buckled

,buckle 'down *informal*
to start working hard and seriously
= KNUCKLE DOWN
buckle down *If you don't buckle down, you're not going to graduate.* ♦ **+to** *Everyone should buckle down to work.*

,buckle 'under
to stop trying to do something, or to stop opposing someone, because you have no energy or determination left = GIVE IN
buckle under *Threats might have caused him to buckle under.*

,buckle 'up
to fasten your seat belt in a car, plane etc
= *British* BELT UP
buckle up *Has everyone buckled up?*

BUDDY /'bʌdi/
buddies, buddying, buddied

,buddy 'up
1 if two or more people buddy up, they form a group in order to do something together
buddy up *Dan and I buddied up for the next game.*
buddy up with sb *She'd decided to buddy up with an older girl.*
2 *American* to make friends with someone
buddy up to sb *They knew who I was and buddied up to me.*
buddy up with sb *Who are the kids he's buddied up with?*

BUDGE /bʌdʒ/
budges, budging, budged

,budge 'up *British informal*
to move so that there is space for someone else = MOVE UP
budge up *Ask the people on the end to budge up.*

BUDGET /'bʌdʒɪt, American 'bʌdʒət/
budgets, budgeting, budgeted

'budget for
to decide or expect to spend a particular amount of money
budget for sth *We'd budgeted for about two thousand pounds' worth of household repairs.* ♦ *It wasn't an expense that I'd budgeted for.*

BUFF /bʌf/
buffs, buffing, buffed

,buff 'up
to make something shine by rubbing it with something such as a soft cloth
buff up sth *also* **buff sth up** *Buff up paintwork with silicone polish.* ♦ *Let the polish soak into the leather before you buff it up.*

BUG /bʌg/
bugs, bugging, bugged

,bug 'off [usually in imperative] *American impolite*
if someone tells you to bug off, they want you to go away = *British* BOG OFF

,bug 'out *American*
1 if someone's eyes bug out, they open very wide, for example because the person is shocked by something
bug out *Her eyes will bug out when she sees that pile of work.*

2 *informal* if someone bugs out, they leave quickly
bug out *If you're finished, let's bug out.*

3 *informal* if someone bugs out, they become too scared to do something
bug out *If things get tough, don't bug out.*

■ **bugout** /'bʌgaʊt/ **noun** [C] *American informal* an occasion when someone leaves a place quickly, often because they are scared: *All these resignations suggest a mass bugout.*

BUGGER /'bʌgə, *American* 'bʌgər/
buggers, buggering, buggered

,bugger a'bout (*also* ,bugger a'round)
British impolite
1 to waste time behaving in a silly way
= MESS ABOUT
2 to cause problems for someone = MESS ABOUT

,bugger 'off *British impolite*
1 [usually in imperative] used for telling someone rudely to go away
2 to leave, or to go away

,bugger 'up *British impolite*
to spoil something or do something badly
= COCK UP, MESS UP

BUILD /bɪld/
builds, building, built /bɪlt/

,build a'round [often passive]
to make a particular aim or idea the main part of something
be built around sth *Her whole campaign was built around economic recovery.*
build sth around sth *They build a whole show around that one song.*

,build 'in ★★★ (*also* ,build 'into) [often passive]
1 to build something such as a piece of furniture so that it becomes part of a wall or room = *formal* INCORPORATE
be built in *If you want bookcases, they could be built in.*
be built into sth *The baths were built directly into the walls of the house.*
build in sth *They built in a beautiful stainless steel sink.*
2 to make something part of a plan, system, calculation etc = INCLUDE; *formal* INCORPORATE ≠ EXCLUDE
be built in *The cost of hiring equipment should be built in.*
build sth in *We build these costs in wherever possible.*

build in sth *Remember to build in travelling time.*
build sth into sth *We build that figure into the total cost.*

■ **,built-'in** **adj** forming part of something, and not separate from it: *The walls have built-in bookcases.*

■ **inbuilt** /'ɪnbɪlt, *American* 'ɪn,bɪlt/ **adj** existing as a natural or basic part of something: *The body has an inbuilt ability to heal itself.*

'build on ★★★
to do something in addition to what you have already achieved
build on sth *We need to build on the ideas we have had so far.*

,build 'on
to build a new room or part on the outside of a building
build on sth *They're building on an extension at the side of the house.*
build on *If you ever needed an extra room you could always build on.*

,build 'up ★★★

1	gradually increase
2	make sth improve/increase
3	make sth successful
4	make sb/sth seem impressive
5	make sb healthy and strong
6	collect things
7	gradually understand sth
+	PHRASE
+	**build-up** noun; **built-up** adj

1 if something bad or unwanted builds up, it gradually increases in size or amount
build up *Don't allow resentment to build up between you and your partner.*
♦ *Traffic was building up on all the roads out of town.*

Nouns often used as subjects with
build up 1
■ frustration, pressure, resentment, tension

2 to gradually improve or increase something = BOOST
build up sth *These exercises are good for building up leg strength.* ♦ *They soon built up a reputation for reliability and good value.*
build sth up *More experience would help you build your confidence up.* ♦ *Your former strength will return, but you have to build it up gradually.*

Nouns often used as objects with **build up 2**
■ confidence, expertise, immunity, profile, reputation, resistance, stamina, strength

3 to make something such as a business bigger and more successful = DEVELOP
build up sth *Stevens played a key role in building up the company.*
build sth up *We've built the organization up into a major political force.* ♦ *I started a furniture business, building it up gradually.*

4 to talk about someone or something in a very positive way so that people are impressed with them = TALK UP
build sb up *They've built him up to be something that he isn't.*

5 to make someone bigger, healthier, and stronger, especially by making them eat more
build sb up *You need lots of fresh fruit to help build you up.*

6 to form a collection by gathering things together, usually gradually
build up sth *We've built up a portfolio of techniques for dealing with these tasks.*
build sth up *It's taken him years to build this collection up.* ♦ *It's a wonderful assembly of South American artefacts and she sacrificed a lot to build it up.*

7 to gradually gather information that allows you to know what something or someone is like
build up sth *Witnesses help us build up a picture of who the attacker is.* ♦ *The results allow us to build up a profile of the system's strengths and weaknesses.*
PHRASE **build up sb's hopes** or **build sb's hopes up** to make someone think that something good is going to happen when in fact it is very unlikely: *I don't want to build up her hopes if he's not coming back.* ♦ *Try not to build your hopes up too much.*

■ **'build-up** noun [C usually singular] **1** a gradual increase in the amount or level of something: *A build-up of gas in the system could be dangerous.* **2** the time before an event when people are talking about it and preparing for it: *There were a few problems in the build-up to the Games.* **3** a description of someone or something in which you make people think they are very good: *If you give the audience this great build-up, you have to produce a spectacular show.*

■ **,built-'up** adj a built-up area has a lot of buildings in it

'build upon
to do something in addition to what you have already achieved
build upon sth *The project will build upon existing knowledge.*

build 'up to
to gradually prepare yourself or someone else for something that you are going to say or do = WORK UP TO
build up to (doing) sth *He seemed to be building up to a confession.* ♦ *She'd been building up all week to telling them she was leaving.*

BULK /bʌlk/
bulks, bulking, bulked

,bulk 'out
to add something to something else to make it bigger or more satisfactory
bulk out sth *also* **bulk sth out** *You can always bulk out a meal with bread or rice.* ♦ *Sausages are often filled with horrible things to bulk them out.*

,bulk 'up
if someone bulks up, they become bigger and heavier
bulk up *After bulking up for his last film role, he's now down to a slim 11 stone.*

BULLY /'bʊli/
bullies, bullying, bullied

,bully 'off British old-fashioned
to start a game of hockey by hitting another player's stick and then the ground before trying to hit the ball
bully off *The girls bully off at two o'clock this afternoon.*

BUM /bʌm/
bums, bumming, bummed

,bum a'round (also ,bum 'round British) informal
1 to spend time relaxing and doing nothing
bum around *It's nice to have a day off to just bum around.*

2 to spend time travelling around a place without having any particular plans about where you will go next
bum around sth *She's bumming around Europe for a couple of months.*

,bum 'off
to ask someone to give you something such as a cigarette, drink, or money without giving them anything in return
= PONCE OFF, CADGE
bum sth off sb *He bummed another cigarette off a passer-by.*

,bum 'out American informal
to annoy someone, or to make them disappointed

bum sb out *All this rain is really bumming me out.*

BUMBLE /ˈbʌmb(ə)l/
bumbles, bumbling, bumbled

ˌbumble aˈround (*also* ˌbumble aˈbout British)
to move somewhere without a clear purpose, often in a way that is not organized, effective, or graceful

bumble around *He was bumbling around in the lobby.* ♦ *Some of the passengers were still bumbling about in the car park.*

BUMP /bʌmp/
bumps, bumping, bumped

ˌbump aˈlong
to continue at around the same level, rising and falling only slightly

bump along *Their standard of living bumped along without any significant increase.*

PHRASE bump along the bottom to continue at around the same low level, rising and falling only slightly: *Their economy was still bumping along the bottom.*

ˌbump ˈinto ★★
1 to meet someone unexpectedly = RUN INTO

bump into sb *I bumped into your mother at the supermarket.*

2 to accidentally hit against something = COLLIDE WITH

bump into sth *As I turned round, I bumped into a filing cabinet.*

bump into

ˌbump ˈoff *informal*
1 [often passive] to murder someone = DO IN, KILL

be bumped off *He was scared of being bumped off.*

bump off sb *also* **bump sb off** *He's the guy who bumped off the professor.* ♦ *She paid someone to bump him off.*

2 [usually passive] if you are bumped off a computer system, you can no longer use the Internet because the connection with your computer is suddenly broken

be/get bumped off *If you don't have the right software installed, you may be bumped off the system.* ♦ *I got bumped off my connection while I was trying to reserve a flight.*

ˌbump ˈup *informal*
1 to increase something = INCREASE, RAISE ≠ DECREASE

bump up sth *also* **bump sth up** *She's doing some teaching in the evenings to bump up her income.* ♦ *If they see you're a tourist, they bump the price up.*

2 [usually passive] to give someone or something a better position

be bumped up *We were bumped up to first class when two seats became available.* ♦ *The system has been bumped up from experimental status to an actual product.*

ˌbump ˈup against
to experience a problem that slows down your progress = COME UP AGAINST, RUN INTO

bump up against sth *We're now bumping up against the limits of our expansion in the present manufacturing facility.*

BUNCH /bʌntʃ/
bunches, bunching, bunched

ˌbunch ˈup (*also* ˌbunch toˈgether)
[usually passive]
if people or things are bunched up or are bunched together, they are very close to each other, in a group

be bunched up *The girls were bunched up on one side of the room.* ♦ *The guests were all bunched together near the buffet table.*

BUNDLE /ˈbʌnd(ə)l/
bundles, bundling, bundled

ˌbundle ˈinto [often passive]
to make someone go into a place or vehicle by pushing them in a rough way

be bundled into sth *He was bundled into the back of a police car.*

bundle sb into sth *They bundled her into the nearest office.*

,bundle 'off [often passive]

to make someone go somewhere, especially in order to get rid of them

> **be bundled off** *He was bundled off to boarding school when he was ten years old.*
> **bundle sb off** *We bundled her off on the next train.*

,bundle 'out of [often passive]

to make someone leave a place or get out of a vehicle by pushing them in a rough way

> **be bundled out of sth** *People were bundled out of their homes and workplaces.*
> **bundle sb out of sth** *The larger man bundled me out of the car.*

,bundle 'up

1 to put warm clothes on yourself or someone else, or to wrap someone in something warm = WRAP UP

> **bundle sb up** *I bundled him up in a thick sweater and fur hat.*
> **bundle up** *You'll have to bundle up, it's cold outside.*

2 to gather things together and wrap them up or tie them up = GATHER UP

> **bundle up sth** *also* **bundle sth up** *She bundled up her belongings and put them in a bag.* ♦ *We cut the straw and bundled it up.*

BUNG /bʌŋ/
bungs, bunging, bunged

,bung 'up [usually passive]

1 if something such as a pipe or a drain is bunged up, liquid does not flow through it normally because it is blocked = BLOCK, STOP UP

> **be bunged up** *The toilet is bunged up again.*

2 *British informal* to have a blocked nose because you have a cold

> **be bunged up** *Her voice sounded different because she was so bunged up.*

BUNK /bʌŋk/
bunks, bunking, bunked

,bunk 'off *British informal*

to not go to school or work when you do not have a good reason for staying away

> **bunk off sth** *Lee's been suspended for bunking off school.*
> **bunk off** *Her parents don't know that she bunks off.*

BUOY /bɔɪ, *American* ˈbuɪ/
buoys, buoying, buoyed

,buoy 'up [usually passive]

1 to encourage someone and make them feel more confident ≠ DEPRESS

> **be buoyed up** *He has been buoyed up by the news.*

2 to help a company, market, or economy to be more successful = BOOST

> **be buoyed up** *The stock market was buoyed up by comments from the Bank of England chairman.*

BURN /bɜːn, *American* bɜrn/
burns, burning, burned or **burnt** /bɜːnt/

,burn a'way

1 to remove something by burning it

> **burn away sth** *also* **burn sth away** *They use lasers to burn away the cancerous cells.* ♦ *When the acid touches skin, it burns it away.*

2 to disappear or be removed by burning

> **burn away** *The paraffin finally burned away.*

,burn 'down ★★

1 to destroy a building or something large with fire, or to be destroyed in this way

> **burn down** *The entire house burnt down in 20 minutes.*
> **burn down sth** *There are laws against burning down forests.*
> **burn sth down** *The soldiers had burned her house down.* ♦ *They had lit a fire in the school, but never intended to burn it down.*

2 if a fire or flame burns down, it becomes smaller and less hot

> **burn down** *The fire in the grate gradually burnt down.*

,burn 'off

1 to remove something by burning it

> **burn off sth** *also* **burn sth off** *They managed to burn off the excess wax.* ♦ *The treatment burns part of your skin off.*

2 to use up energy or get rid of fat from your body by doing physical activity

> **burn off sth** *also* **burn sth off** *Swimming can help you burn off those unwanted calories.*

,burn 'out ★★

1	when a fire stops burning
2	destroy inside of sth with fire
3	about electrical equipment
4	when a strong feeling stops
5	become ill after working hard
+	**burned-out** adj; **burnout** noun; **burnt-out** adj

1 if a fire burns out, or if it burns itself out, it stops burning
　　burn out *All the candles had burnt out.*
　　burn itself out *Leave the fire to burn itself out.*

2 [usually passive] to completely destroy with fire the inside of something such as a vehicle or building = GUT
　　be burnt out *The house had been burnt out by kids.*

3 if a piece of electrical equipment burns out, it gets too hot and stops working
　　burn out *Be careful that the motor doesn't burn out.*

4 if a strong feeling burns out, or if it burns itself out, you stop feeling it
　　burn itself out *His rage had been intense, but it had burnt itself out.*
　　burn out *What love he had burnt out years ago.*

5 if you burn out, or if you burn yourself out, you make yourself ill or unable to continue working because you have worked too hard
　　burn yourself out *If he carries on like this, he'll burn himself out.*
　　burn out *Some young players burn out at 25.*

■ **,burned-'out** adj　*same as* **burnt-out**

■ **burnout** /'bɜːnaʊt/ **noun** [singular/U]
1 *informal* the mental and physical condition of having no energy left or becoming ill after a period of very hard work: *Any extra responsibilities might lead to burnout.* **2** a situation in which a plane or spacecraft has used all of its fuel and has no more power: *A number of safeguards were introduced to prevent burnout during a mission.* **3** damage caused to a piece of electrical equipment when it gets too hot: *Only good insulation can prevent burnout.*

■ **,burnt-'out** adj **1** a burnt-out building or vehicle has had everything inside it destroyed by fire: *We found her burnt-out car at the side of the road.* **2** someone who is burnt-out is very tired and has no energy, usually because of too much work or worry: *You wind up burnt-out by the time you're forty.*

,burn 'up ★

1	be destroyed by fire
2	use your body's fat/energy
3	use fuel
4	be hot with a fever
5	make sb angry

1 if something burns up, or if it is burned up, fire completely destroys it
　　burn up *The spacecraft has a heat shield to prevent it burning up when it re-enters the Earth's atmosphere.*
　　burn up sth *The explosion burns up everything around it.*
　　burn sth up *We threw the papers on the fire and the fire burned them up.*

2 to use fat or energy in your body
　　burn up sth *Dancers burn up a lot of calories.*
　　burn sth up *Breathing alone burns some of that unwanted fat up.* ♦ *You feel there's extra fuel there in your body and you look for ways to burn it up.*

3 if a machine or vehicle burns up fuel, it uses the fuel to work
　　burn up sth *My van seems to be burning up too much fuel.*
　　burn sth up *I kept putting in more and more petrol but the car just seemed to burn it up.*

4 [usually progressive] if someone is burning up, they are very hot, especially because they have a fever
　　be burning up *Poor child! She's burning up.*

5 *American informal* to make someone very angry
　　burn sb up *That guy burns me up.*

'burn with

if you burn with a strong feeling such as anger, you feel it very strongly
　　burn with sth *I was burning with curiosity.* ♦ *She's someone who burns with enthusiasm.*

BURST /bɜːst, *American* bɜrst/
bursts, bursting, burst

,burst 'in ★

to go into a place quickly and suddenly
　　burst in *I heard a noise in the hallway, then a man burst in.*

,burst 'in on

to suddenly enter a room where someone is doing something and interrupt them
= WALK IN ON
　　burst in on sb/sth *The headmaster could have burst in on them at any moment.*
　　♦ *She burst in on the meeting to protest.*

ˈburst into ★★★

1 to go into a place quickly and suddenly
burst into sth *She has this habit of bursting into my office.*

2 to suddenly start doing something such as crying, singing, laughing etc
burst into tears/song/laughter etc *Terri keeps* ***bursting into tears*** *for no reason.* ♦ *The audience* ***burst into*** *wild* ***applause****.*

PHRASES **burst into flames** to suddenly start burning with large flames: *Their helicopter burst into flames after hitting a power line.*
burst into life to suddenly start working or becoming active: *Banks of electronic equipment burst into life.*

ˈburst onto

to become noticeable or successful quickly and suddenly
burst onto sth *She burst onto the racing scene in 1998.*

ˌburst ˈout ★★

1 to suddenly start laughing or crying
burst out doing sth *I almost burst out laughing when I saw what she was wearing.*

2 to suddenly say or shout something = EXCLAIM
burst out sth *'I hate you!' Julia suddenly burst out.*

■ **outburst** /ˈaʊtbɜːst/ noun [C] **1** a sudden spoken expression of a strong feeling, especially anger: *emotional outbursts* ♦ *his outbursts of temper* **2** the sudden start of an activity or emotional reaction among a lot of people: *an outburst of patriotic fervour*

ˈburst upon

to become noticeable or successful quickly and suddenly
burst upon sth *All at once gene therapy has burst upon the scene as a potential new treatment for genetic disorders.*

ˈburst with [usually progressive]

to have a lot of a particular quality
be bursting with sth *The dancers are bursting with energy and joy.* ♦ *You can see that the parents are bursting with pride.*

BURY /ˈberi/
buries, burying, buried

ˌbury aˈway [usually passive]

if something is buried away somewhere, it is in a place where you cannot easily notice or find it
be buried away *She had the photograph buried away at the bottom of her bag.*

ˈbury in

1 to push one thing into another very hard = SINK
bury sth in sth *Diane screamed as the dog buried its teeth in her arm.* ♦ *The bullet had buried itself in the floorboards.*

2 to spend all your time doing and thinking about a particular activity
bury yourself in sth *Some people bury themselves in their work when their relationships end.*

BUST /bʌst/
busts, busting, busted or **bust**

ˌbust ˈout *informal*

1 to escape from prison = BREAK OUT
bust out *They're thinking of busting out.* ♦ **+of** *You couldn't bust out of a place like that.*

2 *American* to escape from the boring situation you are in and make your life more exciting
bust out *He was the typical teenager who couldn't wait to bust out.*

ˌbust ˈup *informal*

1 *British* to have an argument and end a relationship = SPLIT UP ≠ MAKE UP
bust up *We bust up six months ago.*

2 to stop an activity from continuing to happen, or stop an organization from continuing to exist = BREAK UP
bust up sth *also* **bust sth up** *Customs officers have bust up a major gun smuggling operation.* ♦ *Word comes through of a demonstration and armed troops are sent in to bust it up.*

■ **ˈbust-up** noun [C] *British informal* **1** a serious argument or fight: *She had a big bust-up with her boss over pay.* **2** the end of a relationship: *He started drinking after the bust-up of his marriage.*

BUSTLE /ˈbʌs(ə)l/
bustles, bustling, bustled

ˌbustle aˈround (*also* **ˌbustle aˈbout**)

to do something or go somewhere quickly, usually because you are very busy
bustle around *Maggie was bustling around doing the housework.*

BUTT /bʌt/
butts, butting, butted

,butt 'in
to interrupt a conversation or activity,
especially rudely = INTERRUPT
butt in *How can I tell you what happened
if you keep butting in? ♦ Sorry, I didn't
mean to butt in.*

,butt 'out *mainly American informal*
used for telling someone rudely to go away
or not get involved in something
butt out *It's my problem, so butt out!*

,butt 'up
to have one side or edge touching
something, or to put something in this
position
butt up against sth *The shop butted up
against the end of a row of houses.*
butt up sth *Butt up the edges of
adjoining floorboards so they fit together
tightly. ♦ +to Butt up one tile to the next.*

BUTTER /'bʌtə, American 'bʌtər/
butters, buttering, buttered

,butter 'up
to be especially nice to someone so that
they will help or support you = FLATTER
≠ INSULT
butter up sb *also* **butter sb up** *He was
trying to butter up the electorate with
promises of tax cuts. ♦ I'm sure we can
get the principal on our side – just butter
her up a bit.*

BUTTON /'bʌt(ə)n/
buttons, buttoning, buttoned

,button 'up
to fasten something with buttons, or to be
fastened with buttons = FASTEN
button sth up *also* **button up sth** *He had
buttoned his jacket up all the way to his
neck. ♦ Button up your shirt!*
button up *Women's jackets button up on
the left side, men's on the right.*

- **,buttoned-'up** adj *British informal*
unwilling to talk about or show your
feelings: *He would be too buttoned-up to
discuss it.*

BUY /baɪ/
buys, buying, bought /bɔːt, American
bɒt/

,buy 'in *British*
to buy a large quantity of something
buy in sth *also* **buy sth in** *Supermarkets
have been buying in champagne for*

*Christmas. ♦ We've had to buy extra
supplies in.*

- **'buy-in** noun [C] a situation in which
a group of managers get some control
over a company that they do not work
for by investing a lot of money in the
company: *We couldn't raise the cash for
a buy-in.*

'buy into
1 to start to believe something that a lot
of other people believe
buy into sth *You don't buy into all this
nonsense, do you? ♦ It seems a lot of
people have bought into the idea that
working longer hours makes you more
productive.*
2 to buy part of a business, especially in
order to get control of it
buy into sth *Moves to buy into other
companies have failed.*

,buy 'off ★★
1 [often passive] to pay money to someone
or to give them something so that they
will do something dishonest or something
that is against their principles = BRIBE
be bought off *It seemed the whole of the
management team had been bought off.*
buy off sb *He knew he'd be able to buy
off a few local politicians.*
buy sb off *They tried unsuccessfully to
buy him off. ♦ +with There had been
attempts to buy her off with a major
promotion.*
2 to pay someone money so that they will
stop threatening you or causing trouble
for you
buy sb off *Is there any way you can buy
them off?*
buy off sb *It was no use trying to buy off
a bully like Jenkins.*

,buy 'out ★★
1 to pay money to someone so that you
can control all of something that you
previously owned together
buy sb out *The other directors have
offered to buy me out.*
buy out sb *Could he afford to buy out
his partner?*
2 *British* to pay money so that someone can
leave an organization, especially the
armed forces, before the time that they
had originally agreed
buy sb out *He was desperate to leave the
army, so we raised the cash to buy him
out.*
buy yourself out *Her only choice was to
buy herself out. ♦ +of People who buy
themselves out of the services at an early
stage often regret it later.*

■ **buyout** /ˈbaɪaʊt/ noun [C] a situation in which the managers or people employed in a company take control of it by buying all of its shares: *a management buyout*

buy 'up ★★

to buy large amounts of something or all of something that is available

buy up sth *Developers have been buying up vast areas of land just outside the town.*

buy sth up *Someone is going to buy all this furniture up before long.*

BUZZ /bʌz/
buzzes, buzzing, buzzed

buzz a'round (also buzz a'bout British)

1 if an insect buzzes around, it flies around making its usual continuous noise

buzz around *I could hear a mosquito buzzing around somewhere.*

2 to move quickly around a place in a busy way

buzz around *The director buzzed around checking camera angles.*

buzz around sth *I watched the children buzzing around the room, getting things ready.*

3 if thoughts buzz around in your head, you are thinking about a lot of things at the same time

buzz around *With all these **questions buzzing around** in my head, I couldn't sleep.*

buzz 'in

to allow someone to enter your building by operating the electric lock on the door

buzz in sb *also* **buzz sb in** *Don't buzz in any visitors until you're sure you know who they are.* ♦ *I arrived at her apartment and she buzzed me in.*

buzz 'off [usually in imperative] informal

used for telling someone rudely to go away

buzz off *Buzz off, will you – I'm trying to work!*

Cc

CALCULATE /ˈkælkjʊleɪt, American ˈkælkjə,leɪt/
calculates, calculating, calculated

'calculate on [often with a negative or in questions]

to expect something to happen

calculate on sth *We had not calculated on having any problems with our application.*

CALL /kɔːl, American kɔl/
calls, calling, called

'call after [often passive]

to give a baby the same name as someone else, especially a member of your family

= NAME AFTER; *American* NAME FOR

be called after sb *She was called after her grandmother.*

call sb after sb *I wanted to call him after the Greek emperor, Alexander.*

call a'way [usually passive]

to ask someone to leave a place, usually by telephoning them or sending them a message

be called away *He was called away unexpectedly today, which is why I came to meet you instead.* ♦ **+to do sth** *The doctor has been called away to deal with an emergency.*

call 'back ★★

1 to telephone someone again, or telephone someone who telephoned you earlier = RING BACK

call sb back *I'll call you back when I've heard something.*

call back *He wasn't in. I'll call back later.*

2 [often passive] to ask someone who is trying to get something such as a job or a part in a play, to return for another interview

be called back *I feel lucky just to be called back.*

call sb back *I was sure they'd call me back.*

call back sb *From an initial field of 30 candidates, we called back just 6.*

3 to go and see someone again, usually for a short time

call back *I'll call back later and see how you are.*

be 'called before

to be ordered to go to a place so that people can officially ask you questions

be called before sb/sth *Only two of the men had been called before the judge.* ♦ *She will be called before the parliamentary committee.*

,call 'by *British*

to visit someone, usually for a short time = DROP BY, VISIT

call by *Do you want me to call by tomorrow?*

,call 'down on *literary*

to pray for something bad to happen to someone = INVOKE

call down sth on sb *He called down vengeance on those who had wronged him.*

'call for ★★★

1 to say publicly that something must happen = DEMAND

call for sth *Several of his colleagues were calling for his resignation.* ♦ *Protesters were calling for a ban on the production of GM foods.*

Nouns often used as objects with **call for 1**

■ ban, boycott, change, end, halt, reform, removal, resignation, review, shake-up

2 if a situation calls for a particular quality, that quality is needed in order to deal with it successfully = REQUIRE

call for sth *The present crisis calls for mature judgement on the part of our leaders.*
be called for *Extreme caution is called for when dealing with unsolicited callers.* ♦ *Remarks like that are just **not called for** (=they are unnecessary and unpleasant)!*

Nouns often used as objects with **call for 2**

■ ability, imagination, ingenuity, initiative, judgement, knowledge, skill

3 to go somewhere and get someone or something in order to take them to another place

call for sb/sth *I'll call for you at eight.* ♦ *Has he called for his parcel yet?*

4 *American* to say that something, especially a particular kind of weather, will probably happen

call for sth *For this afternoon the forecast calls for partly cloudy skies with only widely scattered showers.*

,call 'forth *formal*

to produce a particular reaction = ELICIT

call forth sth *Their latest move called forth nothing but contempt from their opponents.*

,call 'in ★★★

1	visit a place/person
2	about a radio/television programme
3	ask sb to come and help
4	ask sb to come and discuss sth
5	phone to say where you are
+	PHRASES
+	call-in noun

1 to visit someone or visit a place, usually for a short time = *formal* VISIT; *informal* DROP IN

call in *I'll try to call in this afternoon if I have time.* ♦ **+on** *She wondered whether to call in on Mark on the way home.* ♦ **+at** *She usually calls in at her grandmother's on Friday evenings.* ♦ **+ to do sth** *I called in to see Jeff yesterday.*

2 to telephone a radio or television programme with a comment or question = PHONE IN

call in *It's a hot topic, and people have been calling in all morning.*

3 to ask a person or organization that provides a service to come and deal with something = *formal* SUMMON

call in sb *The company have called in the police to investigate.*
call sb in *We'd better call a plumber in before it gets worse.*

4 to ask or tell someone to come to a place, usually so that you can talk to them = SEND FOR; *formal* SUMMON

call sb in *The manager called me in and demanded an explanation.*
call in sb *It was time to call in the next candidate.*

5 to phone the place where you work and say where you are or what you are doing

call in *Over five people **called in sick** this morning (=phoned to say they would not be at work because they are ill).*

PHRASES **call in a favour** to ask someone to help you because you helped them in the past: *There are a few favours I can call in.*

call in a loan to ask someone to pay you the money that you lent them: *We were worried the bank would call in the loan.*

■ **'call-in** noun [C] *American* a radio or television programme that people phone with their questions or complaints = *British* PHONE-IN: *He hosts a weekly call-in radio show in San Francisco.*

,call 'off ★★

1 to decide that something that has been arranged will not now happen = CANCEL

call off sth *She's called off the wedding.*

♦ *The mayor is urging rail workers to call off their strike.*
call sth off *We might have to call the game off if there's any more rain.*

> **Nouns often used as objects with call off 1**
>
> ■ **campaign, deal, game, match, search, strike, talks, wedding**

2 to order an animal or a person to stop attacking or chasing someone
call off sb/sth *I yelled to the man to call off his dog.*
call sb/sth off *Call your men off and we'll try to deal with this in a civilized manner.*

3 to decide to stop something that is already happening = ABANDON
call off sth *With the weather worsening, they've called off the search for survivors.*
call sth off *Unless people calm down, we'll have to call the meeting off.*

'call on ★★★ (*also* 'call upon *formal*)

1 to visit someone in order to spend a short time with them = VISIT
call on sb *Edward called on them last night.*

2 [often passive] to make a formal or official request for someone to do something = ASK
be called on *British troops were being called on to act as peacekeepers in the region.*
call on sb *The petition calls on the council to reverse its decision.*

3 to decide to use something that someone can offer you
call on sth *We may need to call on professional help.*

4 to produce a particular quality in yourself, especially by making a great effort
call on sth *She called on all her reserves of courage to face the ordeal ahead of her.*

,call 'out ★★★

1 to shout or say something in a loud voice, especially when you are trying to get someone's attention = SHOUT OUT
call out *If you need help, put up your hand. Don't call out.* ♦ **+to** *I tried to call out to him through the window.*
call out sth *She called out the names of the winners.*
call sth out *We don't want people calling the answers out.*

2 [often passive] to ask a person or organization that provides a service to come and deal with something for you = *formal* SUMMON
be called out *The lifeboat was called out yesterday.*

call out sb *If you call out the engineer, they charge you £55.* ♦ **+to do sth** *Governor Ross called out the militia to deal with the riot.*
call sb out *Why don't they call an electrician out?*

call out (sense 2)

■ **'call-out** noun [C] a visit to your home or office by someone who provides a service: *How much do you charge for a call-out?*

,call 'over

to call someone and ask them to come across to where you are, so that you can speak to them, ask them for something etc
call sb over *She called Robert over so that he could meet her new boyfriend.*

,call 'round *British informal*

to visit someone in their home, usually for a short time = CALL BY, DROP BY, VISIT
call round *I called round yesterday, but you weren't in.* ♦ **+at** *Could you call round at her flat on your way?*

'call to

to speak loudly to someone or to shout something to them
call to sb *He called to the man standing at the door.* ♦ **+to do sth** *I called to the driver to stop.*

,call 'up ★★★

> **1** phone sb
> **2** make sb join the army etc
> **3** invite sb to play in a team
> **4** about computer information
> **5** make sb remember sth
> **6** about a dead person's spirit
> **+** **call-up** noun

1 *mainly American* to phone someone = CALL, PHONE, RING
call sb up *I called him up and told him.*
♦ **+to do sth** *I called her up to tell her as soon as I heard the news.*

call up sb *She immediately called up all her friends.*

2 [usually passive] to officially tell someone that they must join an army, navy etc, especially in a war = CONSCRIPT, DRAFT

be/get called up *Two of her brothers had already been called up.* ♦ *If I get called up, I'll try to escape across the border.*

3 [usually passive] to ask someone to play in a sports team, especially in an international match

be/get called up *He was called up for England last season.*

4 to make information in a computer appear on the screen

call up sth *Call up the menu and click on 'Documents'.*

call sth up *She called the map up onto the screen.*

5 to make you remember something = EVOKE

call up sth *Seeing Paula in that white dress called up memories of his wife.*

call sth up *The idea is buried at the back of her mind but an experience like this could call it up again.*

6 to use magic to try to make the spirit of a dead person appear = CONJURE UP

call up sth *The spell is supposed to be a way of calling up demons.*

call sth up *They claim they can call the spirits up.*

■ **'call-up** noun **1** [singular] a situation in which people are officially ordered to join the armed forces, or an order for an individual person to do this: *He was only 17 when he received his call-up.* = DRAFT **2** [C] an invitation to someone to play in a sports team, especially in an international game: *His performance earned him a call-up for Saturday's match against Italy.*

CALM /kɑːm, *American* kɑm/
calms, calming, calmed

ˌcalm ˈdown ★★★

1 to begin to feel more relaxed and less anxious or emotional = QUIETEN DOWN, SETTLE DOWN

calm down *Just calm down and tell us what the problem is.*

2 to make someone feel more relaxed and less anxious or emotional = SETTLE DOWN, QUIETEN DOWN ≠ AGITATE

calm sb down *He was shaking with anger, but we managed to calm him down.*

calm yourself down *She tried to calm herself down, but her heart was racing.*

3 if a situation calms down, there is less activity and people are not so busy = SETTLE DOWN, STABILIZE

calm down *In general the stock market has calmed down after a busy few weeks.* ♦ *We'll wait for things to calm down a bit before we make an announcement.*

CAMP /kæmp/
camps, camping, camped

ˌcamp ˈout

1 to sleep outside, usually in a tent

camp out *The children love camping out in the garden.*

2 to stay somewhere temporarily, without the furniture and equipment that you normally have

camp out *We're camping out at my parents' place until our new apartment is ready.*

3 to stay outside a place until you get what you want

camp out *Journalists had camped out on the lawn in front of his office.*

SALE BEGINS TOMORROW

camp out

ˌcamp ˈup

PHRASE **camp it up** *informal* to behave in a way that is deliberately artificial in order to make people laugh: used especially about a man who behaves in a way that is thought to be typical of the way that gay men behave

CANCEL /ˈkæns(ə)l/
cancels, cancelling, cancelled

ˌcancel ˈout ★★

to have an equal and opposite value to something else and therefore prevent it from having any effect = OFFSET

cancel sth out *Our votes will cancel each other out.*

cancel out sth *For most households the*

fall in interest rates will cancel out the effects of the new tax.

CANNON /'kænən/
cannons, cannoning, cannoned

,cannon 'into
to knock into something or someone with a lot of force
cannon into sb/sth *Turning the corner, he cannoned straight into Mr Wilson.*

CAPITALIZE /'kæpɪtəlaɪz, *American* 'kæpɪt(ə)l,aɪz/
capitalizes, capitalizing, capitalized

'capitalize on ★
to use an opportunity or situation to help you achieve something or get an advantage = EXPLOIT, TAKE ADVANTAGE OF; *informal* MAKE THE MOST OF, CASH IN ON
capitalize on sth *Looking to capitalize on his military gains, Napoleon launched an attack on Russia.*

CARE /keə, *American* ker/
cares, caring, cared

'care for ★★★
1 to love someone, especially in a way that is based on friendship rather than sex = LIKE ≠ DISLIKE
care for sb *He really cared for her.* ♦ *She made him feel special and cared for.*
2 to do the necessary things for someone who needs help or protection = LOOK AFTER ≠ NEGLECT
care for sb *The inspectors make sure that the elderly residents are well cared for.* ♦ *Teach your children how to care for their pets.*
3 to treat something carefully so that it stays in good condition = LOOK AFTER
care for sth *Your clothes won't last if you don't care for them properly.* ♦ *Her teeth looked healthy and well cared for.*
PHRASES **not care for sb/sth** to dislike someone or something: *I knew she didn't much care for my brother.* ♦ *Marianne didn't really care for big crowds.*
would you care for sth *formal* used for asking politely if someone would like something: *Would you care for a coffee?*

CARRY /'kæri, *American* 'keri/
carries, carrying, carried

Carry is often used with adverbs and prepositions when it means 'to hold something and take it somewhere': *She carried the bucket on her head.* ♦ *The waiter carried away our empty plates.* ♦ *I carried my bags out to the taxi.* These uses are not included here.

get ,carried a'way ★★ (*also* be ,carried a'way)
to become so excited and involved in something that you lose control of your feelings or behaviour
be/get carried away *Let's not get carried away – they haven't signed the contract yet.* ♦ *I found myself being carried away in the general mood of excitement.*

,carry 'forward
1 *business* to take something such as money or holidays that are available for you to use in one period of time into the next period of time
carry sth forward *also* **carry forward sth** *Your tax allowance for capital equipment can be carried forward into the next financial year.* ♦ *Good sales enabled us to carry forward substantial cash reserves to the following year.*
2 to help something to continue and develop
carry sth forward *also* **carry forward sth** *His successors carried forward his programme of reforms.*

,carry 'off
1 to deal successfully with something difficult ≠ FAIL IN
carry off sth *also* **carry sth off** *Both actors have the stylish self-confidence needed to carry off these roles.*
2 to win a prize = WIN
carry off sth *also* **carry sth off** *They remain on course to carry off the league championship.*

,carry 'on ★★★

1	continue doing sth
2	continue going somewhere
3	continue sth started by sb else
4	behave in an emotional way
5	have a sexual relationship
+	**carry-on noun, adj**

1 to continue doing something = GO ON ≠ STOP
carry on *Carry on. You're doing fine.* ♦ *For the moment we've been told to carry on as usual.*

carry on sth *He moved to London to carry on his work.*
carry on with sth *Just carry on with what you were doing.*
carry on doing sth *If you carry on spending money like that, you'll end up in debt.*

2 to continue going in the same direction = GO ON
carry on *Turn left at the traffic lights and carry on up the high street.*

3 to continue something that someone else started
carry on sth *Her daughter intends to carry on her mother's research.*
carry sth on *Younger members are needed to carry the reforms on.* ♦ *We develop and implement the programme and other agencies carry it on.*

4 *informal* to behave in an angry, excited, or emotional way = GO ON, MAKE A FUSS
carry on *'It's no good you carrying on, Mother,' said Sally. 'I'm not going to marry him.'*

5 [usually progressive] *old-fashioned showing disapproval* if two people are carrying on, they are having a sexual relationship but they are not married to each other = HAVE AN AFFAIR
carry on *She'd told him his wife had been carrying on with other men.*

■ **'carry-on** noun [singular] *British informal* an annoying, silly, or unreasonable situation that wastes your time: *I always hate making reservations on the Internet – it's always such a carry-on.*

■ **'carry-on** adj [only before noun] carry-on bags or cases are ones that you can keep with you on a plane: *Passengers' carry-on baggage is always X-rayed.*

ˌcarry 'out ★★★ [often passive]

1 to do a particular piece of work, research etc = DO
be carried out *The building work was carried out by a local contractor.* ♦ *An investigation is being carried out by the prison governor.*
carry out sth *We are planning to carry out a survey of our customers' needs.*

Nouns often used as objects with
carry out 1

■ **assessment, check, experiment, inquiry, inspection, investigation, research, review, search, study, survey, test**

2 to do something that you have said you will do or that you have been told to do = DO; *formal* DISCHARGE, FULFIL
be carried out *I expect my instructions to be carried out promptly.*

carry out sth *Too much paperwork is preventing police officers from carrying out their duties.*
carry sth out *They carried his instructions out speedily and efficiently.*

Nouns often used as objects with
carry out 2

■ **duties, instructions, order, promise, threat**

■ **carryout** /ˈkæriaʊt/ noun [C] a takeaway meal or restaurant

ˌcarry 'over

1 [often passive] if something carries over or is carried over from one situation into another, it has a similar effect in the new situation as it had in the old one
be carried over into sth *Stresses at work can often be carried over into your home life.*
carry over into sth *This same enthusiasm for life carried over into her charitable work.*

2 to take something that you earn or are given in one period of time into the next period of time
carry sth over *also* **carry over sth** *You are not allowed to carry over holiday entitlement from one year into the next.*

■ **'carry-ˌover** noun [singular]
1 something that happens now that is the result of a situation that existed in the past: *This attitude is a carry-over from the Korean War days.* **2** an amount of money that has not been used within a period of time and that can be kept and used later: *This carry-over allowed them to continue offering loans.*

ˌcarry 'through

1 to complete something that was planned, often despite difficulties or opposition
carry sth through *also* **carry through sth** *It's a tough job, and we're relying on you to carry it through.* ♦ *Attlee carried through these reforms in the face of considerable opposition.*

2 to make it possible for someone to deal successfully with a difficult or unpleasant situation
carry sb through *In the end, her passionate belief in justice carried her through.*
carry sb through sth *It was my parents' support that carried me through this crisis.*

CART /kɑːt, American kɑrt/
carts, carting, carted

,cart a'round (also ,cart a'bout British)
to carry or take something with you wherever you go, especially something that is heavy or difficult to hold
  cart sth around *I've been carting this rucksack around all day.*

,cart 'off *informal*
to take someone somewhere, especially to a prison or hospital = HAUL OFF
  cart sb off *also* **cart off sb** *I was carted off in an ambulance with the sirens blaring.*

CARVE /kɑːv, American kɑrv/
carves, carving, carved

,carve 'out ★
to develop a career or position for yourself by working hard = ESTABLISH, FORGE
  carve out sth *After leaving college she carved out a successful career for herself as a freelance fashion journalist.*
  carve sth out *If you want to carve a living out for yourself in this industry you have to work hard.*

Nouns often used as objects with **carve out**
  ■ **career, living, niche, position**

,carve 'up ★
1 to divide something valuable and share it between different people, organizations, or countries, especially in a way that seems unfair = DIVIDE UP
  carve sth up *The two most profitable routes were carved up by the two major bus companies.*
  carve up sth *In a treaty of 1916, France and Britain had carved up Turkey's Arab provinces.*
2 *British informal* to drive past another car that is travelling in the same direction as you and then move in front of it too quickly = CUT UP —*picture* → BACK UP
  carve sb up *His defence was that the other driver had carved him up.*
  ■ **'carve-up** noun [singular] *informal* a situation in which something is divided into several parts, often in a way that seems unfair: *The collapse of the old regime led to the carve-up of the former Yugoslavia.*

CASH /kæʃ/
cashes, cashing, cashed

,cash 'in ★★
1 *showing disapproval* to use an opportunity

to make a profit or gain an advantage
= PROFIT, BENEFIT
  cash in *Copying programs is a simple operation and the software pirates are cashing in.*
  cash in on sth *They accused him of trying to cash in on his daughter's fame.*
2 to exchange something such as an insurance policy or a voucher for its value in money = REDEEM
  cash sth in *You can cash your vouchers in at any petrol station.*
  cash in sth *You can cash in your investment after three years.*

,cash 'out *American*
to exchange something for money, especially at the end of a game
  cash out *Having won a thousand dollars in chips at the casino, Bob cashed out and went home.*

,cash 'up *British*
to count and check all the money that a shop has received in a day
  cash up *Your responsibilities will include cashing up at the end of each day.*

CAST /kɑːst, American kæst/
casts, casting, cast

,cast a'round for (also ,cast a'bout for British or ,cast 'round for British)
to look for or try to think of something, especially when you feel pressure to do something quickly
  cast around for sth *Casting around for a safe topic, she made a comment about the weather.* ♦ *He was clearly casting around for an excuse in his mind.*

'cast as
1 [often passive] to choose someone as a performer for a particular part or type of part in a play, film etc
  be cast as sth *Ben admits he gets fed up with being cast as the comic gay character.*
  cast sb as sb *He cast Nicole Kidman as Virginia Woolf.*
2 [usually passive] to describe someone or something as a particular type of person, thing etc
  be cast as sth *From his earliest days on the team he was cast as a troublemaker.*

,cast a'side [often passive]
to get rid of someone or something because it is no longer useful or interesting to you
= GET RID OF ≠ KEEP
  be cast aside *Many of the unique*

qualities of these cultures are being cast aside.
cast aside sth *Cast aside all fears of failure and you can only succeed.*

be ˌcast aˈway

to be left on an island surrounded by sea without any way of leaving
be cast away (on sth) *He was cast away on a desert island for over 20 years.*

■ **castaway** /ˈkɑːstəˌweɪ/ **noun** [C] someone who has been left on an island surrounded by sea and cannot get away, especially after their ship has sunk: *The play tells the story of six castaways.*

ˌcast ˈback

if you cast your mind back to something, or if your mind casts back to something, you think about something that happened in the past
cast your mind back *Try to cast your mind back to the last conversation you had with her.*
cast back *My mind cast back to the winter of last year.*

ˌcast ˈdown

1 [always passive] *mainly literary* if you are cast down, you are very unhappy about something
be cast down *He was a little cast down by the rejection of his painting.*
2 *mainly literary* to look down
cast your eyes down *She cast her eyes down and started blushing.*

■ **downcast** /ˈdaʊnkɑːst, *American* ˈdaʊnˌkæst/ **adj** **1** sad or upset: *Anna went off looking very downcast.*
2 downcast eyes are looking downwards, especially because you are sad, embarrassed, or shy

ˌcast ˈoff ★★

1 to get rid of someone or something that you do not want or need = DISCARD, SHED
cast off sth *It took many years for Chicago to cast off its reputation as the home of violent gangsters.*
cast sth off *The company has worked hard to cast that image off.*
2 to untie the rope fastening your boat to the land so that you can sail away
cast off *Roger was given the job of casting off.*
3 if a boat casts off, it is untied and moves away from the land
cast off *The oil tanker cast off and backed away from the wharf.*
4 to finish a piece of knitting by removing the wool from the needle and making a tidy edge = CAST ON
cast off *Now you need to cast off.*

cast off sth *Cast off the stitches at the start of the next four rows.*

■ ˈcast-off **noun** [C] *British* a piece of clothing that you no longer want and give to someone else: *You wore your big sister's cast-offs.*

ˌcast ˈon

to start a piece of knitting by putting wool onto the needles to make the first row of stitches = CAST OFF
cast on *I'll show you how to cast on.*
cast on sth *Cast on 75 stitches and knit 3 rows.*

ˌcast ˈout [often passive] *literary*

to force someone or something to leave a place or organization = THROW OUT
be cast out of sth *Those considered to be 'revisionists' were cast out of the Party.*
cast sb out *also* **cast out sb** *They cast her out into the street with all of her belongings.*

■ **outcast** /ˈaʊtkɑːst, *American* ˈaʊtˌkæst/ **noun** [C] someone that other people will not accept as a member of society or a member of a particular group or community: *Parents of child criminals are often treated as social outcasts.*

ˌcast ˈround for *British same as* **cast around for**

ˌcast ˈup [usually passive] *literary*

if something is cast up by the sea, the sea carries it somewhere and leaves it there
be cast up *He was searching for objects that had been cast up by the tides.*

CATAPULT /ˈkætəpʌlt/
catapults, catapulting, catapulted

ˈcatapult to (*also* ˈcatapult into)

to suddenly make someone very successful or famous
catapult sb to sth *Her role in the film 'Bend it like Beckham' catapulted her to international stardom.*

CATCH /kætʃ/
catches, catching, caught /kɔːt, *American* kɔt/

ˈcatch at *British*

to reach out and try to get hold of something
catch at sth *He caught at her arm as she tried to move away.*

be ˈcaught in *same as* **be caught up in**

ˌcatch ˈon ★★

1 to become popular or fashionable ≠ FLOP
catch on *Sports drinks have caught on*

as consumers have become more health-conscious. ♦ **+with** *Long-haul vacations quickly caught on with the public.*

2 to begin to understand something
= COTTON ON, UNDERSTAND
catch on *He didn't catch on at first.*
♦ **+to** *Then I caught on to what the guy was actually saying.*

catch on

,catch 'out ★★ *British*

1 [often passive] to show that someone has made a mistake or is not telling the truth, especially by asking them questions
= EXPOSE
be caught out *She had been **caught out** in a lie more than once* (=proved to have been lying).
catch sb out *He asked her some seemingly casual questions, to see if he could catch her out.*

2 [usually passive] to put someone in an unpleasant or difficult situation that they are not prepared for
be caught out *They came close to being caught out by a storm during another climb on Mont Blanc.*

3 [usually passive] to cause someone to be out in a game such as cricket by catching the ball after it has been hit and before it touches the ground
be caught out *He was caught out after only one ball.*

,catch 'up ★★★

1 to go faster so that you reach the person or vehicle in front of you ≠ FALL BEHIND
catch sb/sth up *We left before them, but they soon caught us up again.* ♦ **+with sb/sth** *We need to catch up with that van before it reaches the bridge.* ♦ *We left first, but they caught up with us.*
catch up *Kelly went into the lead but the US runner soon caught up.*

2 to improve in order to reach the same

standard or rate as someone or something
≠ FALL BEHIND
catch up *He's missed so much school that he's going to find it hard to catch up.*
♦ **+with** *I did have a bit of a battle to catch up with the rest of the team in terms of fitness.*
catch sb/sth up *I was determined to catch my brother up however much it took.*

3 to do something that should have been done before
catch up *The deadline's tomorrow. How are we ever going to catch up in time?*
♦ **+on** *I just want to go home and catch up on some sleep.* ♦ **+with** *Staff are struggling to catch up with the backlog.*

4 to talk to someone you have not seen for some time and find out what they have been doing
catch up *Come over tomorrow and we can catch up.* ♦ *You two must have a lot of **catching up to do**.* ♦ **+with** *I'll catch up with you another time, Kevin.* ♦ *It'll give them a chance to talk and catch up with all their news.*

■ **'catch-up** noun PHRASE **play catch-up** *American* to try to make as much progress as someone or something that you are competing with: *Europe has been playing catch-up for decades.*

be ,caught 'up in ★★ (*also* **be 'caught in**)

to be unexpectedly involved in an unpleasant or annoying situation
be/get caught up in sth *My brother seems to be caught up in something pretty sinister.* ♦ *She got caught up in a clash between protesters and the police.*
♦ *My parents are always arguing, and it's me who gets **caught up in the middle** (=involved in an argument between other people).*

,catch 'up with ★★★

1 to find and arrest someone who has committed a crime after searching for them or chasing them
catch up with sb *The police will catch up with you sooner or later.*

2 to begin to have an effect on someone
catch up with sb *The lack of sleep caught up with her, and she began to doze off.*

CATER /ˈkeɪtə, *American* ˈkeɪtər/
caters, catering, catered

'cater for ★★★ *British*
to provide people with everything that they want or need
cater for sb/sth *The school caters for the*

needs of children with learning
difficulties.
be catered for *Visiting fans are
generally **well catered for**.*

Nouns often used as objects with **cater for**

- **demands, interests, needs, requirements,
tastes**

'cater to
to provide people with something that
they want or need, especially something
that is particularly suitable for them
cater to sb/ sth *There are plenty of TV
shows catering to young male audiences.*
♦ *We try to cater to every taste.*

CAVE /keɪv/
caves, caving, caved

,cave 'in ★
1 if a roof or wall caves in, it falls down
or inwards **=** COLLAPSE
cave in *The tunnel caved in and over 20
miners were trapped.*
2 *showing disapproval* to finally agree to do
what someone is asking you to do, after
they have spent a long time trying to
persuade you **=** GIVE IN; *formal* YIELD
cave in *My parents eventually caved in
and let me go to the festival.* ♦ **+to** *The
prime minister seems to have caved in to
US pressure on this issue.*

Nouns often used as objects with **cave in 2**

- **demands, intimidation, pressure, threats**

cave in

- **'cave-in** noun [C] **1** *showing disapproval*
an occasion when someone suddenly
stops opposing something, usually
because people have persuaded them:
A humiliating cave-in would be avoided.
2 an occasion when the roof of a mine
or cave suddenly falls down: *Not many
men survived the cave-in.*

CENTER the American spelling of
centre

CENTRE /'sentə, *American* 'sentər/
centres, centring, centred

'centre around (*also* 'centre round
British) [often passive]
1 to have something as the main subject
of attention, interest, or activity **=** CENTRE
ON
be centred around sth *Too many of our
social activities are centred around
drinking.*
centre around sth *The debate centred
around the issue of finance.*
2 if something centres around a place,
that is where it usually happens
be centred around sth *Most new
development is centred around existing
towns.*
centre around sth *Recreation is centred
around the local bars.*

'centre on ★★★ (*also* 'centre upon)
1 [often passive] to have something as the
basis or most important aspect of
something
be centred on sth *The college's
curriculum was centred mainly on
music, art, and drama.* ♦ *A baby's world
is entirely centred on itself.*
centre sth on sth *We centre most of our
research on environmental issues.*
2 if something centres on a place, that is
where it mainly happens
centre on sth *Village life often used to
centre on the local pub.*

'centre round *British same as* **centre around**

'centre upon *same as* **centre on**

CHAIN /tʃeɪn/
chains, chaining, chained

'chain to
to use a chain to tie someone or something
to something
chain sb/sth to sth *You can chain your
bike to the railings outside.*

,chain 'up
to use a chain to fasten someone or
something to something so that they
cannot escape
chain sb/sth up *also* **chain up sb/sth** *At
night we chain the dogs up in the yard.*

CHALK /tʃɔːk, American tʃɔk/
chalks, chalking, chalked

,chalk 'up

1 to score points or achieve success in a game = SCORE
chalk up sth also **chalk sth up** In 1989, she chalked up the first of her five successive championships.
2 [usually passive] American to consider something as having a particular cause = ATTRIBUTE TO, PUT DOWN TO
be chalked up to sth Low voter turnout was chalked up to a dull campaign.
3 to achieve a particular level or number
chalk up sth also **chalk sth up** He has already chalked up over 100 hours of solo flying time. ♦ The stock market fell back after chalking up record gains.
PHRASE **chalk sth up to experience** to consider something bad that happens to you as an experience that will help you to deal better with similar situations in the future: Accept that you've lost the money and chalk it up to experience.

CHALLENGE /'tʃælɪndʒ, American 'tʃæləndʒ/
challenges, challenging, challenged

'challenge to
to invite someone to compete or fight with you, or to show that they can do something difficult
challenge sb to sth I challenged him to a contest there and then.
challenge sb to do sth I challenge you to prove that any of this is true.

CHANCE /tʃɑːns, American tʃæns/
chances, chancing, chanced

'chance on (also 'chance upon) mainly literary
to find something or see someone when you did not expect or plan to find or see them = STUMBLE ON
chance on sb/sth I was browsing in a bookshop when I chanced upon an old friend.

CHANGE /tʃeɪndʒ/
changes, changing, changed

,change a'round ★ (also ,change 'round British) [often passive]
to move things so that they are in different places or positions
be changed around The desks have been changed around since I was here last.

change sth around She's always changing the furniture around.

,change 'back ★
1 if something changes then changes back, it returns to how it was originally
change back to sth Do you think things will ever change back to the way they were?
2 to put on the clothes you were wearing originally, before you took them off
change back into sth She changed back into her painting clothes.

,change 'down British
to change the gear in a vehicle to a lower gear, for example when you reduce your speed
change down You should change down when going round corners.

'change for
to take something you have bought back to a shop and get something different instead
change sth for sth Can I change this shirt for one in a different colour?

,change 'into ★★
1 to stop being in one state or form and start being in another, or to put something into another state or form
change into sth At what point does boiling water change into water vapour?
change sth into sth Tourism has changed the quiet town into a bustling resort.
2 in stories, if a person or thing changes into something, or is changed into something, they become that thing by magic
change into sb/sth The frog changed into a handsome prince.
change sb/sth into sth The witch threatened to change her into a tree.
3 to put on different clothes after taking off the ones you are wearing
change into sth If you're going to paint the door, you ought to change into some old jeans.

,change 'out of
to take off your clothes and put different clothes on
change out of sth I change out of my school uniform as soon as I get home.

,change 'over
1 to stop doing or using one thing and start doing or using something else = SWITCH
change over to sth When did the UK change over to the metric system?

2 to start doing something that another person was doing before

change over *The drivers changed over at the halfway point.*

,change 'round *British same as* **change around**

,change 'to ★

to stop doing or using one thing and start doing something different

change to sth *Shoppers are increasingly changing to organic produce.*

change sth to sth *I changed the payments to once a month instead of weekly.*

,change 'up *British*

to change the gear in a vehicle to a higher gear, for example when you increase your speed

change up *Once you're on a straight road, you change up immediately.*

CHANNEL /'tʃæn(ə)l/
channels, channelling, channelled

,channel 'into

1 to use your energy, abilities, ideas etc for a particular purpose

channel sth into sth *She channelled all her energies into her career.*

2 to use money or supplies for a particular purpose

channel sth into sth *The company has channelled over $2m into developing new projects.*

,channel 'through [usually passive]

to use a particular system for doing or dealing with something

be channelled through sth *All information about courses is channelled through our admissions office.*

CHARACTERIZE /'kærɪktəraɪz, American 'kerəktə,raɪz/
characterizes, characterizing, characterized

'characterize as ★ [often passive]

to describe someone or something as being a particular type of person or thing

be characterized as sth *The military is often characterized as being very conservative.*

characterize sb/sth as sth *The media characterize him as talented but stupid.*

CHARGE /tʃɑːdʒ, American tʃɑrdʒ/
charges, charging, charged

be 'charged at

if something is charged at a particular amount of money, that is how much you must pay for it

be charged at sth *All calls will be charged at £1 a minute.*

'charge to [often passive]

to arrange for a payment to be made by a particular person or from a particular account

be charged to sth/sb *The bill was charged to my father's hotel room.*

charge sth to sth/sb *Could you charge it to my current account please?*

,charge 'up

to put electricity into a piece of electrical equipment such as a battery

charge up sth *also* **charge sth up** *I need to charge up my mobile phone.*

'charge with ★★★

1 [often passive] to officially accuse someone of committing a particular crime

be charged with sth *The man was arrested and charged with assault.*

charge sb with sth *The police charged her with dangerous driving.*

2 [usually passive] *formal* if someone is charged with doing something, they are responsible for doing it

be charged with sth *As senior officer he was charged with overall responsibility for the discipline of his troops.*

be charged with doing sth *The estate staff were charged with organizing the event.*

CHARM /tʃɑːm, American tʃɑrm/
charms, charming, charmed

,charm 'into

to deliberately make someone like you so that they do what you want them to do

charm sb into (doing) sth *He was able to charm my mother into helping him financially.*

CHASE /tʃeɪs/
chases, chasing, chased

,chase 'after

1 to try hard to get something you want

chase after sth *I drove from coast to coast, chasing after non-existent contracts.*

2 to try hard to make someone interested in having a romantic or sexual relationship with you

chase after sb *All they seem interested in is chasing after boys.*

,chase a'way (*also* ,chase 'off)

to move towards someone quickly so that they run away

chase away sb/sth *also* **chase sb/sth away** *His job seemed to consist of chasing away kids that trespassed on the premises.* ♦ *The male fish will chase other males away if they approach.*

,chase 'down *mainly American*

to try hard to catch someone or to get something you need

chase down sb/sth *also* **chase sb/sth down** *Police chased down two suspects seen fleeing the scene of the crime.* ♦ *See if you can chase the data down.*

,chase 'off *same as* chase away

,chase 'up

1 to find out what is being done about something

chase up sth *also* **chase sth up** *My department is responsible for chasing up deliveries.*

2 to ask someone who should have done something why they have not done it

chase up sb *also* **chase sb up** *Why don't you chase up those software people today?*

CHAT /tʃæt/
chats, chatting, chatted

,chat a'way

to talk to someone for a long time in a relaxed way

chat away *Within minutes she was chatting away cheerfully to the nurses.*

,chat 'up ★ *British informal*

to start a conversation with someone because you want to start a sexual or romantic relationship with them = HIT ON

chat up sb *She was trying to chat up a couple of guys standing at the bar.*

chat sb up *For some men, chatting women up is just a game.* ♦ *He spent the whole evening chatting us up.*

CHEAT /tʃiːt, *American* tʃit/
cheats, cheating, cheated

'cheat on ★

1 to secretly have sex with someone other than your husband, wife, or partner

cheat on sb *He discovered she'd been cheating on him.*

2 *mainly American* to behave dishonestly by not obeying the rules on something

cheat on sth *It's generally richer people who cheat on their taxes.*

,cheat 'out of

to get something for yourself from someone else by doing something dishonest

cheat sb out of sth *He was accused of cheating investors out of their life savings.*

CHECK /tʃek/
checks, checking, checked

'check against

to find out whether information is accurate or useful by comparing it with other information

check sth against sth *The police are checking his fingerprints against their database.*

,check 'in ★★

1 to arrive at a hotel or a private hospital where you have arranged to stay and give your personal details to the person working at the reception desk = REGISTER

check in *Have you checked in yet?*

2 to arrive at an airport and show your ticket to an official

check in *You must check in at least one hour before your flight.*

3 to give your bags and cases to an official at an airport so that they can be put on the plane

check in sth *Roger checked in his suitcase.*

check sth in *We'll have to check our bags in first.*

4 to deal with someone when they arrive at a hotel or a private hospital where they have arranged to stay, or at an airport from which they have arranged to fly = REGISTER

check sb in *The receptionist checked us in.*

■ **'check-in** noun **1** [singular] the place you go to when you arrive at an airport or hotel: *We were still standing at check-in.* **2** [U] the process you go through when you arrive at an airport: *Then you have to go through check-in.*

,check 'into

1 to try to find out more information about something

check into sth *I'll check into the tours and see how much they cost.*

2 to arrive at a hotel or a private hospital where you have arranged to stay and give your personal details to the person working at the reception desk

check into sth *Greg checked into a top*

London clinic for his operation.

‚check 'off *American*

to mark things on a list to show that you have dealt with them or that they are correct = *British* TICK OFF

check sth off *also* **check off sth** *Check their names off as they come in.*

'check on ★★

to look at someone or something so that you are certain they are safe, satisfactory etc

check on sb/sth *I sent Michael to check on the kids.* ♦ *The boss arrived to check on our progress.*

‚check 'out ★★★

1	leave a hotel
2	examine sth
3	look at sb/sth and judge them
4	seem to be true
5	borrow a book
6	pay for things in a shop/supermarket
+	**checkout** noun

1 to leave a hotel or a private hospital after paying the bill = LEAVE

check out *What time did they check out?* ♦ **+of** *Joan had already checked out of the hotel.*

2 [often passive] to examine someone or something in order to be certain that everything is correct, true, or satisfactory = INSPECT

be/get checked out *Go to the doctor and get yourself checked out.*
check sb/sth out *The police are checking the woman out.*
check out sb/sth *I've been taking loads of photographs, just to check out the camera.*

3 *informal* to look at someone or something to see whether you like them

check out sth/sb *Have you checked out the local sports centre yet?*
check sth/sb out *The man at the bar is checking us out.*

4 *mainly American* if information checks out, it seems to be true after you examine it

check out *Their story just didn't check out.*

5 *American* to borrow a book from a library = BORROW

check sth out *I'll check those out for you.*
check out sth *You can't check out any book if you don't have your card.*

6 *American* to pay for your goods before leaving a supermarket or other large shop

check out *Customers generally leave the store once they've checked out.*

■ **checkout** /'tʃekaʊt/ noun [C] the

place where you pay in a supermarket or other large shop: *The woman at the checkout said she didn't know.*

‚check 'over

1 to look at something again to make sure that everything is correct and that there are no mistakes = LOOK OVER

check sth over *also* **check over sth** *Check your work over for spelling mistakes.*

2 to examine someone to find out whether there is anything wrong with them = LOOK OVER

check sb over *The nurse began checking him over.*

‚check 'through

to examine the whole of something, or a set of things, in order to find out whether it is how it should be

check through sth *We've been checking through our files and can find no record of your payment.* ♦ *When you've written your essay, check through it for spelling mistakes.*

‚check 'up *British*

to make certain about something by checking it

check up *I'm not sure what time it leaves – we'd better check up.*

■ **'check-up** noun [C] an examination by a doctor to make sure that you are healthy, or by a dentist to make sure that your teeth are healthy: *Come for another check-up in six months' time.*

‚check 'up on ★

to find out information about someone, especially secretly

check up on sb *We checked up on him and it seems he was nowhere near the house that night.* ♦ *Have you been checking up on me?*

CHEER /tʃɪə, *American* tʃɪr/
cheers, cheering, cheered

‚cheer 'on

to shout loudly in order to encourage someone, especially someone taking part in a race or competition = ENCOURAGE ≠ HECKLE

cheer sb on *also* **cheer on sb** *I'll be there to cheer you on when the race starts.*

‚cheer 'up ★★

1 to become less sad, or to make someone feel less sad = PERK UP

cheer up *Tommy seems to have cheered up a lot recently.*
cheer sb up *I tried to cheer him up, but he just kept staring out of the window.*

2 if you cheer a place up, you make it

look brighter by adding colourful things
= BRIGHTEN UP
>**cheer up sth** *Cheer up a dull room with fresh flowers.*
>**cheer sth up** *We thought a few posters would cheer the place up a bit.*

3 [always in imperative] *informal* used for telling someone to try to be happier
>**cheer up** *'Cheer up,' he said. 'It can't be that bad.'*

CHEESE /tʃiːz/
cheeses, cheesing, cheesed

‚cheese 'off [usually passive] *informal*
to feel annoyed, bored, or frustrated
>**be cheesed off** *Customers are cheesed off with the poor service.*

CHEW /tʃuː, American tʃu/
chews, chewing, chewed

'chew on *informal*
to think about something carefully for a long time, before making a decision about it = MULL OVER
>**chew on sth** *After chewing on the idea for a while, he agreed to meet her.* ♦ *The investors have several economic reports to chew on.*

‚chew 'out *American informal*
to speak angrily to someone because they have done something wrong = LAY INTO
>**chew sb out** *Mom really chewed me out the time I got in a fight.*

'chew over *informal*
to think about something carefully or discuss it carefully with other people before making a decision about it
= PONDER, CONSIDER
>**chew over sth** *also* **chew sth over** *Officials meet regularly to chew over the future of the company.* ♦ *I'll need some time to chew this over.*

‚chew 'up
1 to use your teeth in order to bite food in your mouth for a long time, until it is very soft or in very small pieces and easy to swallow = CHEW
>**chew sth up** *also* **chew up sth** *Make sure you chew your food up well.*

2 [usually passive] *informal* to crush something or tear something apart so that it is damaged or destroyed
>**be/get chewed up** *My new top got chewed up by the washing machine.*

CHICKEN /'tʃɪkɪn, American 'tʃɪkən/
chickens, chickening, chickened

‚chicken 'out *showing disapproval*
to not do something that you were going to do because you are too frightened
= WIMP OUT
>**chicken out** *I was going to tell him what I thought of him, but I chickened out.*
>♦ **+of (doing) sth** *She chickened out of going to the party at the last minute.*

CHILL /tʃɪl/
chills, chilling, chilled

‚chill 'out
1 [usually in imperative] *informal* to relax and stop being angry or nervous = CALM DOWN
>**chill out** *Chill out, Karen. There's nothing to worry about.*

2 *informal* to spend time relaxing = LAZE AROUND, RELAX
>**chill out** *We spent most of the holiday chilling out on the beach.*

■ **chillout** /'tʃɪlaʊt/ **adj** chillout time, space etc is time or space when you can relax and be calm: *A long working week and two young daughters leave me very little chillout time.*

■ **chillout** /'tʃɪlaʊt/ **noun** [U] a type of music that uses relaxing electronic sounds: *We don't buy chillout albums.*

CHIME /tʃaɪm/
chimes, chiming, chimed

‚chime 'in
to join a conversation by saying something = CHIP IN
>**chime in** *Feel free to chime in if you've got something to add.* ♦ **+with** *George couldn't resist chiming in with his 'helpful hints' about investments.*

'chime with *formal*
to be similar to someone else's ideas, plans, or feelings etc, or to be correct, suitable, or sensible in relation to them
= BE IN TUNE WITH, FIT IN WITH
>**chime with sth** *His idea of a happy life did not exactly chime with mine.*

CHIP /tʃɪp/
chips, chipping, chipped

‚chip a'way
1 [often progressive] to gradually make something weaker, smaller, or less effective
>**chip away** *I kept chipping away, hoping to persuade them eventually.* ♦ **+at** *Her comments were beginning to chip away*

at his self-confidence. ♦ *They chipped away at the problem in the hope of finding a solution.*

chip away sth *also* **chip sth away**
Informative TV shows can help to chip away prejudice. ♦ *The company's dominance of the market is gradually being chipped away.*

2 to remove small pieces from something hard by hitting it with a tool = CHIP OFF

chip away sth *also* **chip sth away** *Use a hammer to chip away the edge.* ♦ *First, he chipped the rotten wood away.*

chip away *Picking up the chisel, he began chipping away again.* ♦ **+at** *She was chipping away at the ground with a trowel.*

ˌchip 'in ★

1 *informal* to add something to someone else's conversation

chip in *I'd just like to chip in, Bill, if I might.* ♦ **+with** *We all chipped in with suggestions.*

chip in sth *'Give her a kiss, Robbie!'* one of the photographers chipped in.

2 *informal* if people chip in, or if they chip something in, they each give some money to help to pay for something = CONTRIBUTE

chip in *The three of us chipped in and bought the boat between us.*

chip in sth *Both companies chipped in sizeable sums of money to finance the project.*

ˌchip 'off

to remove small pieces from something hard by hitting it with a tool = CHIP AWAY

chip off sth *also* **chip sth off** *Chip off any loose paint.* ♦ *We started chipping the rust off.*

chip sth off sth *The weather was so bad that we had to chip ice off the windscreen.*

CHIVVY /ˈtʃɪvi/
chivvies, chivvying, chivvied

ˌchivvy aˈlong *British*

to try to persuade someone to do something more quickly, especially when they do not really feel like it or are being too slow

chivvy sb along *I have to chivvy the kids along so they're ready for school in time.*

CHOKE /tʃəʊk, *American* tʃoʊk/
chokes, choking, choked

ˌchoke 'back (*also* ˌchoke 'down)

to stop yourself from showing a strong feeling or emotion such as anger or disappointment = SUPPRESS ≠ LET OUT

choke back sth *also* **choke sth back** *Ms*

Ross **choked back tears** as she described what had happened. ♦ *He was finding it hard to choke back his emotion.* ♦ *A protest rose to her lips but she choked it back.*

ˌchoke 'down

1 to eat or drink something with difficulty because you do not like it or because you are ill or upset

choke down sth *also* **choke sth down** *Emma managed to choke down half of her meal.*

2 *same as* **choke back**

ˌchoke 'off

to stop someone or something from developing or from being successful

choke off sth *also* **choke sth off** *The government's policy is to choke off all dissent.* ♦ *If prices are too high, demand is choked off.*

ˌchoke 'up

1 if someone chokes up, or if something chokes them up, they cannot speak because they are starting to cry

choke up *When we met again after five years, I just choked up.*

choke sb up *It choked me up to see him so upset.*

2 to fill a place so that it is difficult for people or traffic to move = CHOKE

choke up sth *also* **choke sth up** *Cars and trucks are choking up our streets.*

CHOP /tʃɒp, *American* tʃɑp/
chops, chopping, chopped

ˌchop 'down ★

to make a tree or tall plant fall to the ground by cutting through it at the bottom = CUT DOWN

chop down sth *He used an axe to chop down the tree.* ♦ *The rainforests are being chopped down at a very fast rate.*

chop sth down *It seems a shame to chop such a beautiful tree down.*

ˌchop 'off

to remove something by cutting, especially a part of someone's body = CUT OFF

chop sth off *also* **chop off sth** *He threatened to chop her hands off.* ♦ *He accidentally chopped off the top of his finger with a knife.*

chop sth off sth *She kept chopping bits off my hair.*

ˌchop 'up ★

to cut something such as food or wood into pieces = CUT UP

chop up sth *Sarah was busy chopping up onions.*
chop sth up *They chopped the chairs up for firewood.*

CHOW /tʃaʊ/
chows, chowing, chowed

,chow 'down *American informal*
to eat food, especially a lot of food, quickly or in an enthusiastic way
chow down *Many office workers chow down at their desks.* ♦ **+on** *They chowed down on pizza after the game.*

CHUCK /tʃʌk/
chucks, chucking, chucked

,chuck a'way *informal*
1 to get rid of something that you do not want = BIN, CHUCK OUT, THROW AWAY ≠ KEEP
chuck sth away *also* **chuck away sth** *Go and chuck all that rubbish away.* ♦ *Why are you chucking away all this good stuff!*
2 to waste an advantage or an opportunity that you have = THROW AWAY
chuck sth away *We've given you the best education money can buy – don't **chuck** it all away.*

,chuck 'down
PHRASE **be chucking it down** *British informal*
to be raining very hard: *It's been chucking it down all day.*

,chuck 'in *British informal*
to give up something such as your job or course of study and go somewhere else = PACK IN, GIVE UP
chuck in sth *also* **chuck sth in** *She decided to chuck in her job.* ♦ *He dreamt of chucking it all in (=leaving his job, possessions etc) to sail around the world.*

,chuck 'out ★ *informal*
1 to force someone to leave a place or a job, usually because they have done something wrong = THROW OUT, KICK OUT
chuck sb out *My dad said if I ever got pregnant he'd chuck me out.* ♦ **+of** *Do you think they'll chuck her out of school?* ♦ *He was chucked out of office for taking bribes.*
2 to get rid of something that you do not want = BIN, CHUCK AWAY, THROW AWAY ≠ KEEP
chuck out sth *I chucked out all the newspapers yesterday.*
chuck sth out *Those old shoes are disgusting. It's time you chucked them out.*

,chuck 'up *informal*
if you chuck up, or if you chuck up something, food comes up from your stomach and out of your mouth because you are ill = THROW UP; *formal* VOMIT
chuck up *I felt as though I was going to chuck up.*
chuck up sth *also* **chuck sth up** *She chucked up all her dinner.*

CHUG /tʃʌg/
chugs, chugging, chugged

,chug a'long
to make progress in a slow but steady way
chug along *The project had been chugging along nicely until she took over.*

CHUM /tʃʌm/
chums, chumming, chummed

,chum 'up with *British old-fashioned*
to become friends with someone
chum up with sb *She's chummed up with a girl her parents don't approve of.*

CHURN /tʃɜːn, *American* tʃɜrn/
churns, churning, churned

,churn 'out ★
to quickly produce large quantities of things, often things of poor quality = KNOCK OUT
churn out sth *The director has been churning out action movies for years.*
churn sth out *You'd think people would be tired of his books, but he keeps churning them out.*

,churn 'up
1 [often passive] to damage the surface of the ground by walking or driving over it and making it rough
be/get churned up *The muddy field had been churned up by farm vehicles.*
churn up sth *also* **churn sth up** *Motorbikes churned up the sand as they rode along the beach.*
2 to move something such as dust or water around violently = STIR UP
churn up sth *also* **churn sth up** *The rainstorm churned up the rivers.*
3 to produce strong emotions in someone, for example anger or sadness = PRODUCE, STIR UP
churn up sth *also* **churn sth up** *Going back to his home town churned up a lot of emotions in him.*

CLAIM /kleɪm/
claims, claiming, claimed

,claim 'back

to say that you want someone to give something, often money you have paid, back to you

claim sth back also **claim back sth** *You can claim back the tax on these items.*

CLAM /klæm/
clams, clamming, clammed

,clam 'up *informal*

to suddenly stop talking or explaining something, because you are embarrassed, unhappy, or want to keep a secret = DRY UP, CLOSE UP

clam up *He clammed up when I asked him who else was involved.* ♦ *Don't put any pressure on her, or she might clam up.*

CLAMP /klæmp/
clamps, clamping, clamped

,clamp 'down ★

to make a determined attempt to stop people doing something bad or illegal = CRACK DOWN

clamp down *If there are any further protests, the authorities are expected to clamp down even harder.*
clamp down on sth *The government plans to clamp down on illegal militant groups.*

■ **clampdown** /'klæmpdaʊn/ **noun** [C usually singular] a determined attempt by someone in authority to stop people doing something bad or illegal = CRACKDOWN: *It's all part of the government's clampdown on smoking.*

,clamp 'on (also ,clamp 'onto or ,clamp 'to)

1 [often passive] if you clamp something on something, you put it there firmly so that it cannot move easily

be clamped on sth *A pair of headphones were clamped on his head.* ♦ *She always has her mobile phone clamped to her ear.*
clamp sth on sth *He clamped his hand on her arm.*

2 if something clamps on another thing, it attaches itself there very firmly

clamp on sth *The animal's jaws clamped on the stick as I tried to beat it off.*

CLAP /klæp/
claps, clapping, clapped

,clap 'in

to suddenly put someone somewhere that they cannot escape from

clap sb in sth *The regime's response was to clap him in jail.*

,clap 'to

to put something somewhere with a sudden quick movement

clap sth to sth *She clapped her hand to her mouth in mock surprise.*

,clap 'out

to hit your hands together at the same speed and beat as a piece of music or poetry

clap out sth also **clap sth out** *Ask your students to clap out the rhythm of the song.*

CLASS /klɑːs, American klæs/
classes, classing, classed

'class among (also **'class with**) [usually passive]

to include someone or something in a particular group because they have similar features or qualities

be classed among sb/sth *Wilfred Owen is classed among the truly great First World War poets.* ♦ *This could be classed with the worst experiences of his life.*

'class as ★★ [usually passive]

if someone or something is classed as a particular kind of person or thing, people think they have the same features or qualities as that person or thing

be classed as sb/sth *She is now classed as a professional athlete.* ♦ *Razor blades are not classed as a medical necessity.*

CLAW /klɔː, American klɔ/
claws, clawing, clawed

'claw at

to try to attack someone or tear something using your fingernails

claw at sth *He clawed at the muddy soil, desperately trying to uncover the buried gun.*

,claw 'back *British*

1 to get something again that you had lost, for example power, especially gradually and with difficulty = RECOVER

claw back sth also **claw sth back** *The company has managed to claw back its share of the market.* ♦ *The team needed to claw a goal back.*

2 if a government or company claws back money after losing it or spending it, it gets it again, for example by making people pay higher taxes or by charging higher prices = RECOVER
claw back sth also **claw sth back** *The government clawed back £10 million in taxes.* ♦ *You might be able to claw some of the money back.*

■ **clawback** /ˈklɔːbæk/ noun [C] an act of getting money back after losing it or spending it, for example by making people pay higher taxes or by charging shoppers higher prices for goods: *The scheme provided a clawback for investors.*

CLEAN /kliːn, *American* klin/
cleans, cleaning, cleaned

,clean 'down
to remove the dirt from something, especially from an upright surface
clean down sth also **clean sth down** *Clean down all the timbers before you spray them.* ♦ *They clean the machines down at the end of every shift.*

,clean 'off
to remove the dirt from something
clean off sth also **clean sth off** *He was told to clean off the graffiti.* ♦ *There was mud all over his boots and he was cleaning it off.*
clean sth off sth *How do you clean red wine off carpets?*

,clean 'out ★★
1 to make a place or container clean or tidy by removing objects that are not wanted and getting rid of any dirt or dust in it = CLEAR OUT
clean out sth *They spent the day cleaning out the garage.* ♦ *The animals' cages have to be cleaned out every week.*
clean sth out *We need to clean these cupboards out.*
2 to remove objects from a place or container in order to make it tidy = CLEAR OUT
clean out sth *I had to clean out all the rubbish before I could fit my bike in the shed.*
clean sth out *Clean the old bedding out before putting the hamsters back in their cage.*
3 *informal* to empty a place of objects or goods, especially by stealing or buying them in large quantities
clean sth out *Government soldiers moved in and cleaned the village out.*
♦ *The supermarkets were cleaned out by panicking shoppers.*

4 *informal* to use all of someone's money = BANKRUPT
clean sb out *The divorce will clean me out. I'll have to sell the house.*

■ **cleanout** /ˈkliːnaʊt/ noun [C] *British* an act of emptying and cleaning a place to make it clean and tidy and get rid of things you do not need: *We needed to give the spare room a thorough cleanout.*

,clean 'up ★★★

1	make a place tidy
2	remove a mess
3	wash sb
4	remove pollution
5	get rid of crime
6	earn a lot of money
+	PHRASE
+	**clean-up** noun

1 to make a place completely clean and tidy = TIDY UP, CLEAR UP
clean up sth *Go and clean up your room.* ♦ *We really ought to make a start on getting this place cleaned up.*
clean sth up *He helped me clean the house up after the party.*
clean up *I'm going to clean up in here this afternoon.*
2 to remove objects or dirt from a place in order to make it completely clean and tidy = TIDY UP, CLEAR UP
clean up sth *Joe can clean up the mess.*
clean sth up *There was oil all over the floor and I had to clean it up.* ♦ *Clean any spills up immediately to stop them staining the carpet.*
3 to wash someone who is dirty = WASH
clean sb up *Once the nurses had cleaned him up he looked a little better.* ♦ *Come into the bathroom and I'll get you cleaned up.*
clean yourself up *I cleaned myself up and got ready for dinner.*
4 to remove pollution from a place or from an industrial process
clean up sth *We need a systematic plan for identifying and cleaning up waste sites.*
clean sth up *They have been successful in cleaning their beaches up.*
5 to stop bad, unfair, or criminal behaviour in a place or activity
clean up sth *He led a popular campaign to clean up the voting system and prevent electoral fraud.*
clean sth up *They were elected on a promise to clean the city up.* ♦ *The system operates along corrupt lines and it's our intention to clean it up.*
6 *informal* to make a lot of money = MAKE A FORTUNE, PROFIT

clean up *He really cleaned up on the stock market.*

PHRASE **clean up your act** *informal* to start behaving in a more suitable and sensible way and stop doing things that are dishonest or harmful: *She has cleaned up her act since her drug-taking days.*

■ **'clean-up** noun **1** [C] the process of removing pollution or waste from a place or an industrial process: *clean-up costs* **2** [singular] an occasion when you make a person or place clean and tidy: *We gave the place a bit of a clean-up.* **3** [C] an attempt to stop bad, unfair, or criminal behaviour in a place or activity: *This latest drugs clean-up doesn't go far enough.*

,clean 'up after

to clean a place after someone has made it dirty or untidy = TIDY UP AFTER, CLEAR UP AFTER

    clean up after sb *I'm always having to clean up after the kids.*

clean up after

CLEANSE /klenz/
cleanses, cleansing, cleansed

'cleanse of [often passive] *literary*
to get rid of something bad or unpleasant from someone or something
    be cleansed of sth *Anyone who touched the sacred stone would be cleansed of sin.*
    cleanse sb/sth of sth *The mayor has promised to cleanse the city streets of crime.*

CLEAR /klɪə, American klɪr/
clears, clearing, cleared

,clear a'way

to remove something that you have finished using or no longer want in order to make a place tidy = TIDY AWAY

clear away sth *also* **clear sth away** *A young woman cleared away their empty cups.* ♦ *I cleared all my books away and put them in my bag.*
    clear away *You sit down – I'll clear away.*

'clear for [usually passive]
to give a plane, ship, or person permission to enter or leave a place
    be cleared for sth *The aircraft had not been cleared for take-off.*

'clear of [usually passive]
to prove officially that someone did not do something wrong
    be cleared of (doing) sth *He was cleared of killing his ex-wife.* ♦ *Even though he was cleared of the charges, the allegations ruined his career.*

,clear 'off ★ British informal

1 to leave a place quickly = GO OFF, GO AWAY ≠ STAY
    clear off *They've all cleared off and left me to clean this mess up.*

2 [usually in imperative] used for telling someone rudely to go away = GO AWAY
    clear off *Clear off, both of you!*

,clear 'out ★★

1 to make a place or container clean or tidy by removing objects that are not wanted and getting rid of any dirt or dust in it = CLEAN OUT
    clear out sth *I'm going to clear out the cupboards tomorrow.*
    clear sth out *Will you help me clear her wardrobe out?*

2 to remove things that are not wanted from a place or a container in order to make it tidy = CLEAN OUT
    clear out sth *It's time you cleared out some of your junk.*
    clear sth out *When are you going to clear your things out?*

3 *informal* to leave a place quickly and often permanently
    clear out *Would it be better for you if I just cleared out?* ♦ **+of** *I sometimes feel like clearing out of here altogether.*

4 [usually in imperative] *informal* used for telling someone rudely to leave a room or building = GET OUT
    clear out *Just clear out!*

■ **'clear-out** noun [C] *British* an occasion when you get rid of all the things that you have kept but do not need: *She generally has a good clear-out before Christmas.*

,clear 'up ★★★

1 if the weather clears up, the clouds or rain go away = BRIGHTEN UP
clear up *It's supposed to clear up this afternoon.*

2 to make a place tidy by removing things that you have finished using or no longer want = CLEAN UP, TIDY UP
clear up *I'll clear up if you want to go to bed.*
clear up sth *They started clearing up the mess.*
clear sth up *Have you cleared the broken glass up yet?*

3 to find an explanation for a mystery or misunderstanding, or a solution to a problem = SORT OUT
clear sth up *I hope we can clear the matter up once and for all.*
clear up sth *He contacted Mr Jones the following day and cleared up the misunderstanding.*

> Nouns often used as objects with **clear up 3**
> ■ confusion, matter, misunderstanding, mystery, problem, uncertainty

4 if an illness or condition clears up, or if something clears it up, you stop being affected by it
clear up *Most colds clear up after a few days.*
clear up sth *a lotion to clear up spots*
clear sth up *I've had dandruff for some time and nothing seems to clear it up.*

■ **'clear-up** noun [C] *British* an occasion when you make a place tidy by removing things that you have finished using or no longer want: *It's time we had a clear-up in here.*

,clear 'up after

to make a place tidy after someone else has made it untidy = CLEAN UP AFTER, PICK UP AFTER
clear up after sb *I'm sick to death of clearing up after you.*

CLEAVE /kliːv, *American* kliv/
cleaves, cleaving, cleaved

'cleave to *literary*

1 to stay very close to someone
cleave to sb *They cleaved to each other, lips against lips.*

2 to keep believing an idea or following a tradition even when other people disagree with you = CLING TO
cleave to sth *Like many children, she cleaved to the conviction that her divorced parents would get back together again.*

3 to become fixed to something
cleave to sth *Her mouth was dry and*

her tongue cleaved to the roof of her mouth.

CLIMB /klaɪm/
climbs, climbing, climbed

,climb 'down *British*

to admit that you were wrong, especially after expressing an opinion or argument very firmly = BACK DOWN
climb down *In the end Western Bank plc had to climb down and admit its computer systems were faulty.*

■ **'climb-down** noun [C] *British* a change of attitude in which someone admits that they were wrong: *The company has already been forced to make a humiliating climb-down and apologize to customers.*

CLING /klɪŋ/
clings, clinging, clung /klʌŋ/

,cling 'on *same as* cling to 1

'cling to ★★★ (*also* ,cling 'onto)

1 to hold onto someone or something tightly with your hands or arms, for example because you are afraid or about to fall
cling to sth/sb *Crossing the bridge, she felt dizzy and clung to the rails.* ♦ *Some children were sobbing and clinging to their mothers.*

2 to stick to something or fit very tightly on something
cling to sth *Gareth's dripping clothes clung to his body.* ♦ *The smooth surface prevents dirt from clinging to it.*

3 to try very hard to stay in a position of power or authority
cling to sth *The Prime Minister is still clinging to power.*

4 to keep believing that something is right or real, even though other people do not = CLEAVE TO
cling to sth *He still clings to his old beliefs.* ♦ *They still cling to the hope that all this will end happily.* ♦ *Fifteen years after independence, private businesses are still clinging to colonial attitudes.*

> Nouns often used as objects with **cling to 4**
> ■ attitude, belief, hope, idea, notion, the past, tradition

CLOCK /klɒk, *American* klɑk/
clocks, clocking, clocked

,clock 'in (*also* ,clock 'on)

in a factory, to pass a special card through a piece of equipment to record that you

have arrived at work = PUNCH IN ≠ CLOCK
OFF, CLOCK OUT
> **clock in** *We have to clock in by 9 in the
> morning.*

ˌclock 'in at
to take a particular amount of time or to
last for a particular amount of time
> **clock in at sth** *The CD clocks in at 45
> minutes.*

ˌclock 'off (*also* ˌclock 'out)
in a factory, to pass a special card through
a piece of equipment to record that you
are leaving work = PUNCH OUT ≠ CLOCK IN,
CLOCK ON
> **clock off** *The day shift was clocking off.*

ˌclock 'up
to reach a particular number or amount
= NOTCH UP
> **clock up sth** *Dawson has clocked up 34
> years as a police officer.*

CLOG /klɒg, *American* klɑg/
clogs, clogging, clogged

ˌclog 'up
1 to block something such as a pipe, tube,
or passage, or to become blocked, so that
nothing can get through = CLOG, BLOCK UP
> **clog up** *Too much fatty food makes your
> arteries more likely to clog up.*
> **clog up sth** *also* **clog sth up** *The mud and
> slime that were deposited after the flood
> had clogged up the drains.* ♦ *All this
> extra traffic is clogging local roads up.*
> **be/get clogged up** *In a hard-water area
> your pipes get clogged up more quickly.*

2 to slow down a process or an activity
= CLOG
> **clog up the system** *If all minor traffic
> offences were prosecuted it would clog up
> the system.*

CLOSE /kləʊz, *American* kloʊz/
closes, closing, closed

ˌclose a'round
to put your fingers, hands, or arms around
someone or something
> **close sth around sb/sth** *She reached for
> the keys and closed her hand around
> them.*
> **close around sb/sth** *His arms closed
> around her.*

'close at
to close at a particular value at the end of a
day in which shares have been bought
and sold
> **close at sth** *The company's shares closed
> at 517p yesterday.*

ˌclose 'down ★★★
1 if a factory, shop, company etc closes
down, or if someone closes it down, it
stops doing business permanently = SHUT
DOWN ≠ OPEN
> **close down** *Hotels are closing down all
> over the country.*
> **close down sth** *Their intention is to close
> down the factory.*
> **close sth down** *They closed a lot of coal
> mines down in the 1980s.* ♦ *It's a good
> hospital. I really hope they don't close it
> down.*

2 if a computer program closes down, or
if you close it down, it stops operating
and disappears from your computer
screen
> **close down** *The computer makes a noise
> when a program closes down.*
> **close down sth** *Close down all programs
> that are running before you install the
> software.*
> **close sth down** *How do I close this
> program down?*

close down

■ **close-down** /'kləʊz daʊn/ **noun** [C] a
situation in which a factory, shop,
company etc permanently stops doing
business: *The policy will lead to the
close-down of small local businesses.*

ˌclose 'in ★
1 if people close in on someone, they move
nearer to them, especially in order to
surround them and stop them from
escaping = MOVE IN
> **close in** *Enemy troops began closing in
> at dawn.* ♦ **+on** *The police finally closed
> in on Connors and captured him.*

2 if cloud or fog closes in, it gets closer or
thicker as the weather gets worse
> **close in** *Black clouds began closing in.*

3 *literary* if night or darkness closes in, it
gets darker
> **close in** *It was only six o'clock, but*

already the darkness was closing in.

4 if the days are closing in, there are fewer hours of light each day because autumn is starting = DRAW IN

close in *It was now late September and the days were already starting to close in.*

,close 'off

to prevent people from entering a place, using a road etc = BLOCK OFF, CORDON OFF, SEAL OFF

close off sth *Police used barriers to close off certain streets.* ♦ *Some parts of the palace are closed off, and visitors may not go there.* ♦ **+ to** *The police have closed off the high street to traffic.*

,close 'out

1 *American informal* to finish, or to make something finish

close out sth *also* **close sth out** *The Rangers' four-game series against the Mariners closes out the season's first half.* **close out** *The marathon race closed out in record time.*

2 *American* to sell a product at a low price in order to get rid of it = SELL OFF

close out sth *also* **close sth out** *The manufacturers decided to close out last year's model.* ♦ *The product was still selling well so we were reluctant to close it out.*

,close 'up ★

1 to lock the doors of a building or business for a period of time = SHUT UP

close up sth *As the storm approached, everyone began closing up their businesses.*

close up *All the shops had closed up for the night.*

2 if a group of people or things close up, they move closer together ≠ OPEN UP, SPREAD OUT

close up *The runners had closed up and were moving in a tight little pack.*

3 if an injury or cut in your skin closes up, or if someone closes it up, the edges join so that the skin can become healthy again = HEAL ≠ OPEN

close up *The cut has closed up without a scar.*

close up sth *The doctor used a special kind of glue to close up the cut.*

4 to refuse to talk about your true feelings or thoughts = CLAM UP

close up *Why do you close up every time I mention your father?*

PHRASE **close up shop** *American* to stop an activity or close a business, either for a short time or permanently: *At one*

stage, we considered closing up shop for good.

CLOUD /klaʊd/
clouds, clouding, clouded

,cloud 'over

1 to become darker because grey clouds are forming in the sky ≠ BRIGHTEN UP

cloud over *It's beginning to cloud over – we should go back now.* ♦ *A breeze started up and the sky clouded over.*

2 if your face or eyes cloud over, you start to look sad, worried, or angry

cloud over *Her face clouded over with the pain of the memories.*

CLOWN /klaʊn/
clowns, clowning, clowned

,clown a'round (*also* ,clown a'bout British*)

to do silly things in order to make people laugh

clown around *Harvey was clowning around pretending to be a singer.*

CLUB /klʌb/
clubs, clubbing, clubbed

,club to'gether

if people club together, each of them gives some money so that all the money collected can be used to buy something

club together *We could all club together and buy her something really special.* ♦ **+to do sth** *Friends clubbed together to buy him an electric wheelchair.*

CLUE /kluː, American klu/
clues, cluing or clueing, clued

,clue 'in *informal*

to provide someone with information about someone or something

clue sb in *I've no idea what to do. I'm waiting for someone to clue me in.* ♦ **+on/about** *Someone must have clued him in on the correct answer.* ♦ *Philip had clued her in a bit about how to behave.*

■ **,clued-'in** **adj** informed about something: *We're now more clued-in to the risks of this approach.*

CLUMP /klʌmp/
clumps, clumping, clumped

,clump to'gether

to form a solid mass

clump together *The loose dirt had clumped together and blocked the pipe.*

CLUSTER /'klʌstə, *American* 'klʌstər/
clusters, clustering, clustered

cluster 'round (*also* ,cluster a'round)
to form a close group around someone or something = GATHER ROUND
  cluster round sb/sth *She spotted Luke standing in the crowd who had clustered round the entrance.*

CLUTCH /klʌtʃ/
clutches, clutching, clutched

'clutch at
to try to take hold of someone or something because you are afraid or in pain, or in order to stop yourself from falling = GRAB AT
  clutch at sb/sth *She clutched at him to stop herself from falling.* ♦ *He fell to the ground, clutching at his throat.*
  PHRASE **clutch at straws** to try to find anything at all that will help you or give you hope in a difficult situation, even though it is likely that you will find nothing: *What we have is a government clutching at straws.*

CLUTTER /'klʌtə, *American* 'klʌtər/
clutters, cluttering, cluttered

clutter 'up [often passive]
to put too many things in a place so that it looks untidy
  be cluttered up *Her desk was cluttered up with empty coffee cups.*
  clutter up sth *also* **clutter sth up** *I try not to clutter up the room with too many books.*

COAST /kəʊst/
coasts, coasting, coasted

coast a'long
to achieve success very easily or with very little effort
  coast along *In the 1980s Britain was coasting along as the fourth-largest West European spender on space.*

COAX /kəʊks, *American* koʊks/
coaxes, coaxing, coaxed

coax 'into
to gently persuade someone to do something
  coax sb into (doing) sth *After dinner Lynne was coaxed into singing several songs.*

coax 'out of
to gently persuade someone not to do something
  coax sb out of (doing) sth *Rescuers told how they had coaxed a man out of a suicide attempt.*

COBBLE /'kɒb(ə)l, *American* 'kɑb(ə)l/
cobbles, cobbling, cobbled

cobble to'gether ★ *informal*
to make something quickly and without a lot of care, using whatever is available
= THROW TOGETHER; *formal* IMPROVISE
  cobble together sth *I cobbled together a meal from leftovers in the fridge.*
  cobble sth together *He pretended to have spent a long time on the report, when in fact he had cobbled it together in a couple of days.*

COCK /kɒk, *American* kɑk/
cocks, cocking, cocked

cock 'up
1 *British impolite* to spoil something by doing it wrongly = BUGGER UP
  cock sth up *also* **cock up sth** *Try not to cock things up this time.* ♦ *One small mistake can cock up the whole system.*
2 *British impolite* to make a bad mistake
= MESS UP
  cock up *Every time you cock up, I have to take the blame.*
■ **'cock-up** noun [C] *British impolite* a bad mistake, or something that has been done wrongly

COIL /kɔɪl/
coils, coiling, coiled

coil 'up
1 to wind something into a shape like a series of rings
  coil up sth *also* **coil sth up** *McCabe taught me how to coil up a rope.* ♦ *She took lengths of wool and coiled them up.*
2 to move in a curve
  coil up *A column of smoke was coiling slowly up into the air.*

COLLECT /kə'lekt/
collects, collecting, collected

col,lect 'up
to get things from different places or people, after people have finished using them
  collect up sth *also* **collect sth up** *Can someone collect up the dirty cups?* ♦ *Pass*

your exam papers to the end of the line then we'll collect them all up.

COLOR the American spelling of colour

COLOUR /'kʌlə, *American* 'kʌlər/
colours, colouring, coloured

,colour 'in
to use pens, pencils etc in order to add colour to a picture
colour in sth *also* **colour sth in** *She was colouring in the letters on a big poster.* ♦ *I'll draw a picture and you can colour it in.*

,colour 'up
if you colour up, your face becomes pink or red because you are embarrassed
colour up *He kissed Mary on the cheek, and she coloured up instantly.*

COMB /kəʊm, *American* koʊm/
combs, combing, combed

,comb 'out
to pull a comb through your hair in order to make it smooth or straight
comb out sth *also* **comb sth out** *She was combing out her hair in front of the mirror.* ♦ *Set the hair in rollers, then comb it out after 30 minutes.*

,comb 'through
to search carefully among things
comb through sth *Accident investigators are continuing to comb through the wreckage.* ♦ *Researchers have been combing through data files trying to detect problems.*

COMBINE /kəm'baɪn/
combines, combining, combined

com'bine with ★★★
1 to use, do, or put two or more things together
combine sth with sth *It can be hard to combine motherhood with a career.* ♦ *Combine the excitement of a week in Athens with a week on the unspoilt beaches of Crete.* ♦ *Napoleon's superior speed, combined with his tactical brilliance, made the French forces irresistible.*
2 when one chemical element combines with another, they form a new substance
combine with sth *When hydrogen burns, it combines with the oxygen in the air.*

COME /kʌm/
comes, coming, came /keɪm/, **come**

Come is often used with adverbs and prepositions when it means 'to move or travel to the place where you are': *Come here, children.* ♦ *A tall woman was coming across the lawn towards me.* ♦ *Why don't you come into the garden with me?* These uses are not included here.

,come a'bout ★★★
1 to happen, especially by chance
come about *We don't understand how that situation came about.* ♦ *The increase in production has come about through the use of technology.* ♦ **+that** *I don't know how it came about that we stopped loving each other.*
2 *technical* if a ship comes about, it changes direction
come about *She gave the order to come about.*

,come a'cross ★★★
1 to meet someone or find something by chance = COME ON, STUMBLE ACROSS; *formal* ENCOUNTER
come across sb/sth *Have you ever come across such a horrible person in all your life?* ♦ *I came across a word I'd never seen before.*
2 if someone or something comes across in a particular way, you have a particular opinion of them when you meet them or see them = APPEAR, COME OVER
come across *A lot depends on how well you come across in the interview.* ♦ **+as** *She comes across as very self-confident.* ♦ *He didn't want to come across as being impatient.*
3 if something such as a feeling or idea comes across when you speak, you make it very clear to people = COME OVER
come across *His sense of enthusiasm comes across very clearly.*

,come a'cross with *British informal*
to provide something that is needed or wanted = COME UP WITH, PRODUCE
come across with sth *There was one person I thought might come across with a few facts.*

,come 'after
to try to find or catch someone, usually in order to punish or harm them = PURSUE
come after sb *Even if she left the country, she knew the police would come after her.*

,come a'long ★★★

1	appear or become available
2	go with sb
3	go to be with sb
4	make progress or improve
5	used for telling sb to hurry
6	I do not believe you
+	PHRASE

1 to arrive, or to become available **=** TURN UP, APPEAR

come along *He decided to give the money to the first stranger who came along.*
♦ *He told me to work hard and take every opportunity that comes along.*

2 to go somewhere with someone **=** TAG ALONG

come along *I've never seen a baseball game – do you mind if I come along?*

3 to go somewhere so that you can be with someone who went there earlier

come along *Ray had some work to finish and decided to come along later.*

4 [usually progressive] to make progress or get better in quality, skill, or health
= COME ON, PROGRESS

be coming along *The building work was coming along nicely.* ♦ **+with** *How's Kathleen coming along with her swimming?*

5 [always in imperative] *old-fashioned* used for telling someone to hurry **=** COME ON, HURRY UP

come along *Come along! The train leaves in ten minutes.*

6 [always in imperative] *old-fashioned* used for telling someone that you do not believe or accept what they are saying **=** COME ON

come along *Come along, now! It can't have been as bad as that!*

PHRASE **come along for the ride** to take part in an activity that other people are doing although you are not really interested in it: *He's not really interested in going to the exhibition but he just wants to come along for the ride.*

,come a'part ★

1 if an object comes apart, it separates into pieces, either because it has been made that way or because it is very old or in very bad condition **=** FALL APART

come apart *I picked up the book and it just came apart in my hands.* ♦ *It's designed to come apart for easy repair and cleaning.*

2 to fail completely, or to come to an end

come apart *At this point, the policy began to come apart.* ♦ *It was clear that the relationship was coming apart at the seams (=no longer being successful).*

,come a'round ★★★ *(also* ,come 'round *British)*

1	happen regularly
2	go to visit sb
3	talk to each person
4	be sent to several people
5	change your opinion/decision

1 if a regular event comes around, it happens again **=** RECUR

come around *Before we knew it, Christmas had come around again.*

2 to go to a place where someone is, especially their house, in order to visit them **=** VISIT

come around *Why don't you come around after work?* ♦ **+to** *You could come around to our house for drinks.*

3 to go to several people in a room, one after another, for example in order to talk to them

come around *The manager came around and congratulated everyone.* ♦ *A waiter came around with a tray of drinks.*

4 if something such as a letter or a message comes around, it is sent to several people in a place

come around *A note came around asking for new ideas.*

5 to change your opinion or decision because someone has persuaded you to agree with them **=** AGREE

come around *We were sure she'd come around in the end.* ♦ **+to** *I knew she would come around to our way of thinking.*

'come at

1 to move towards someone in order to threaten them or attack them physically **=** COME FOR

come at sb *A stranger came at him with a knife.*

2 if things such as questions or pieces of information come at you, they are directed at you in order to influence or affect you

come at sb *Disturbing images come at you from the television set.*

3 to examine or deal with something such as a problem in a particular way **=** APPROACH

come at sth *Try coming at it from a different angle.*

,come a'way ★★

1 if one thing comes away from another that it was fixed to, it becomes separated from it by accident **=** COME OFF

come away *The doorknob just came away in my hand.* ♦ **+from** *Another block of stone came away from the wall.*

2 to leave a place, often in a particular state or condition

come away *It was a great party. We didn't come away until after midnight.* ♦ **+with** *We came away with the feeling that they didn't really approve of us.*

3 [often in imperative] to move away from someone or something

come away *The man looked drunk, so we came away.* ♦ **+from** *Come away from that dog.*

,come a'way with

1 **come away with** or **come out with** British informal to say something

come away with sth *You should hear some of the things she comes away with!*

2 to succeed in achieving something or winning something

come away with sth *She'll be pleased if she can come away with a medal.* ♦ *You want to be sure you come away from college with a decent qualification.*

,come 'back ★★★

1	return
2	happen/exist again
3	be remembered again
4	be fashionable again
5	be successful/effective again
6	reply
+	**comeback** noun

1 to return to a place ≠ GO AWAY

come back *We'll definitely come back next year.* ♦ **+to** *We decided to come back to Scotland for another holiday.*

2 to start to happen or exist again = RECUR ≠ GO AWAY

come back *The pain has never come back since.* ♦ *The good weather seemed to be coming back at last.*

3 to start to be remembered again

come back *Details of his ordeal slowly began to come back.* ♦ **+to** *I can't think of her name right now, but I'm sure it'll come back to me.*

4 to become fashionable again

come back *You can't say that short hair is coming back, because it never really went away.*

5 to become successful or effective after being in a bad situation, especially in a sports event

come back *They came back from behind to win 3–2.*

6 to reply or react to what someone has said = RESPOND

come back *I asked them for a price, but they haven't come back yet.* ♦ **+with** *Jane came back with a strong response.*

■ **comeback** /'kʌmbæk/ noun [C] **1** a

period when someone or something becomes successful or popular again: *The film sparked something of a comeback for Astaire.* ♦ *Seventies styles are making a comeback.* **2** British a way of making someone accept responsibility for something bad that they have done to you: *You signed away your rights, so you have no comeback.* **3** a quick clever reply to a comment or criticism: *This time she has no snappy comeback.*

,come 'back to ★★★

to deal again with something that you were dealing with earlier = RETURN TO

come back to sth *Can we come back to my original question?*

,come be'fore

1 to be more important than someone or something else

come before sb/sth *In these situations, your family comes before everything else.*

2 to be considered, discussed, or judged by someone in authority

come before sb/sth *The case comes before the magistrates again in June.*

,come be'tween ★

1 to cause a disagreement or argument between people ≠ UNITE

come between sb (and sb) *He didn't want this to come between them.* ♦ *Never come between a husband and wife.*

2 to prevent you from doing or getting something = STAND BETWEEN

come between sb and sth *She was determined that nothing would come between her and the manager's job.*

,come 'by ★★

1 to get something, especially something that is hard to get = GET, OBTAIN

come by sth *How did you come by such a beautiful house?* ♦ *At that time, teaching jobs abroad were **hard to come by**.*

2 to make an informal visit to someone for a short time = DROP BY, VISIT

come by *I'll come by later on my way home.*

,come 'down ★★★

1	move downwards
2	about levels/prices etc
3	about buildings
4	about rain/snow
5	about aircraft
6	travel further south
7	decide to support/oppose sth
8	reach a lower point/level
9	agree about a lower price
10	feel normal again after excitement
11	leave a university
+	PHRASES
+	**comedown** noun

1 to move down to the ground or to a lower level
come down *He was sitting in a tree and refused to come down.*

2 to become less in amount, level, price etc = DECREASE, FALL ≠ GO UP
come down *Interest rates have come down significantly in the last three years.*

3 if a building or part of it comes down, it is destroyed and falls to the ground = FALL DOWN ≠ GO UP
come down *The ceiling looked ready to come down any minute.*

4 if rain, snow etc comes down, it falls to the ground, especially in large amounts = FALL
come down *The heavens opened and the rain came down.* ♦ *It's **coming down in torrents** (=a lot of rain is falling) outside.*

5 if an aircraft comes down, it lands, or it crashes
come down *The plane came down in a nearby field.*

6 to travel to a place that is further south or that is smaller or less important than the place you are leaving ≠ COME UP
come down *My parents are coming down for the weekend.*

7 to make a decision that supports or opposes someone or something
come down *It's difficult to predict which way the board will come down.* ♦ **+in favour of** *The council came down in favour of closing the road.* ♦ **+against** *The Commission is likely to come down against the takeover.* ♦ **+on** *Everything depends on which side the judge comes down on.*

8 to be long enough or deep enough to reach a particular lower point or level ≠ COME UP
come down *How far does the skirt come down?* ♦ **+to** *The jacket came down almost to his knees.*

9 to agree to ask for or pay a lower price
come down *If you're interested, I think they'll come down a bit.*

10 *informal* to start to feel normal again after feeling very excited, for example after an exciting experience or after taking an illegal drug
come down *It'll take the kids a few hours to come down.*

11 *British old-fashioned* to leave a university, especially Oxford or Cambridge, at the end of a period or course of study = GO DOWN ≠ COME UP, GO UP
come down *That was the year I came down.*

PHRASES **come (back) down to earth** to start normal life again after a time of great excitement or happiness: *Sooner or later, you come back down to earth.*
come down in sb's estimation/opinion to become less respected by someone than you were before, because of something that you have done: *I knew I had come down a lot in their estimation.*
come down in the world to become less rich, powerful, successful etc than you were previously: *We didn't want others to think we'd come down in the world.*

■ **comedown** /ˈkʌmdaʊn/ **noun**
[C usually singular] **1** a situation in which you suddenly have less status or fewer advantages than you had previously: *The place was a comedown after the comfort of a luxury hotel.* **2** an unpleasant physical and mental feeling someone gets when an illegal drug stops affecting them: *It's not so great when the comedown kicks in.*

,come 'down on

to criticize or punish someone severely = TAKE TO TASK
come down on sb *She came down pretty hard on the kids for making a mess.*

,come 'down to ★★

1 to be the most important aspect of a situation or problem = BOIL DOWN TO
come down to sth *In the end, it all comes down to money.*

2 to become someone's property because the previous owner has died = COME TO
come down to sb *The necklace had come down to her from her grandfather.*

3 if something such as knowledge or a tradition comes down to you, you learn about it from people who lived a long time before you
come down to sb *This is the version of the story that has come down to us.*

ˌcome ˈdown with

to become ill with a particular disease, usually one that is not serious = GO DOWN WITH; *formal* CONTRACT ≠ FIGHT OFF

come down with sth *You look terrible. Are you coming down with the flu?*

ˈcome for

1 to come to a place so that you can take someone or something away with you

come for sb/sth *The taxi will come for us at around 8 o'clock.* ♦ *I've just come for the book your brother borrowed from me.*

2 to move towards someone in order to threaten them or attack them physically = COME AT

come for sb *The dog was coming for me.*

3 to come to a place in order to arrest someone

come for sb *The police came for him in the middle of the night.*

ˌcome ˈforward ★★★

to offer help or information = VOLUNTEER

come forward *The National Blood Service is anxious for more donors to come forward.* ♦ **+with** *Police said that several people had come forward with information about the attack.*

ˈcome from ★★★

1	be produced by sth
2	about an origin
3	where sb was born
4	where sb's home is
5	about a family/social group
6	be the result of sth
+	PHRASES

1 to be obtained from, produced by, or found in a particular place or thing

come from sb/sth *Opposition may also come from people within his own party.* ♦ *I can't tell where the noise is coming from, can you?* ♦ *The serum comes from a tropical plant.*

2 to have something as an origin = STEM FROM, DERIVE FROM

come from sth *The word comes from an African language.*

3 to have been born in a particular place = BE FROM

come from sth *My parents came from Italy.*

4 to have your home in a particular place = BE FROM

come from sth *We come from London.*

5 to belong to a particular type of family or social group = BE FROM

come from sth *His wife comes from a pretty rich family.* ♦ *They all come from similar backgrounds.*

6 to be the result of something

come from sth *His air of confidence came from his firm belief that he was the best candidate for the job.*

come from doing sth *It's the kind of accident that comes from being careless.*

PHRASES **coming from sb** used for emphasizing that what someone is saying is surprising, annoying, or funny: *Coming from him, that's praise indeed!*

where sb is coming from *informal* the ideas, intentions, or feelings that make someone say a particular thing or behave in a particular way: *I understand where you're coming from, but I think you're mistaken.*

ˌcome ˈin ★★★

1	enter
2	arrive
3	when a message is received
4	when money is earned/received
5	go to work
6	come to your house to work
7	start to be used/done
8	when the sea gets higher
9	join a conversation/discussion
10	become involved too
11	become fashionable
12	finish a race
+	PHRASES
+	**income** noun; **incoming** adj

1 to enter a room, building, or other place = ENTER ≠ GO OUT

come in *Come in and sit down.*

2 to arrive somewhere = ARRIVE, GET IN

come in *What time does his train come in?* ♦ *Phone the shop and ask if our order has come in yet.*

3 if something such as a message comes in, it is received by someone

come in *Reports are coming in of a major air accident.* ♦ *Have any messages come in for me?*

4 if money comes in, it is earned or received by someone

come in *We've got absolutely no money coming in at the moment.*

5 to go to work

come in *He's too ill to come in today.*

6 if someone comes in, they come to your house in order to do work

come in *I've got the plumber coming in tomorrow.* ♦ *She's the woman who comes in to clean.*

7 if something such as a law or practice comes in, it starts to be used or done = BE INTRODUCED

come in *When the new legislation comes*

in, the police will have even greater powers.

8 when the tide comes in, the sea moves higher up the beach ≠ GO OUT
come in *The tide was coming in fast.*

9 to join a conversation or discussion by saying something
come in *I'd like to come in here and make a suggestion.* ♦ **+on** *Let's get some of the others to come in on the discussion.*

10 to join other people who are involved in something such as a business project
come in *Are you ready to come in now or do you need more time to think about it?* ♦ **+on** *If your friend wants to come in on the deal, he'll need to put a lot of money on the table.* ♦ **+with** *I'm looking for people to come in with me on a new restaurant venture.*

11 to become fashionable at a particular time ≠ GO OUT
come in *When did the miniskirt first come in?*

12 to finish a race in a particular position = FINISH
come in *The British runner came in a long way behind the rest.* ♦ *My horse came in third.*

PHRASES **come in useful/handy** to be useful for a particular situation: *A big sheet of plastic always comes in handy when you're camping.*
where sb/sth comes in what someone or something is needed for: *We'll need new information systems, and that's where Steve comes in.*

■ **income** /ˈɪnkʌm/ noun [C/U] money that someone gets from working or from investing money: *Most of the villagers rely on farming for income.*

■ **incoming** /ˈɪnkʌmɪŋ/ adj **1** coming in or arriving: *Incoming calls can be forwarded to another phone extension.*
2 recently elected or chosen for a job or position: *the incoming president*

‚come ˈin at
to cost a particular amount
come in at sth *That particular carpet comes in at around £40 a square yard.*

‚come ˈin for ★
to receive criticism, blame, or unpleasant comments
come in for sth *You may come in for some negative comments from your competitors for the job.*

‚come ˈinto ★★★

1 to be an aspect of a situation
come into sth *The argument was over artistic freedom – money never came into*

it. ♦ *The question of cost inevitably comes into the equation.*

2 if you come into something, it becomes yours when someone dies = INHERIT
come into sth *She came into a lot of money after her father died.*

PHRASES **come into being/existence** to start to exist: *The organization came into being in 1926.*
come into force/effect/play/operation to start to have an effect or influence on something: *When does the new legislation come into force?* ♦ *That's where his greater experience came into play.*
come into your own to show how effective or useful you can be: *In the wintry conditions the Norwegian team really came into their own.*
come into use to start being used by people: *Computers first came into use in the early 1950s.*
come into view/sight if something comes into view or into sight, you can see it now, although you could not see it before: *As we turned the corner, the house came into view.*

‚come ˈof ★
to be the result of something
come of sth *I wrote to over twenty companies asking for work, but nothing came of my efforts.*
come of doing sth *Don't complain about being tired – that's what comes of watching TV until three in the morning.*

‚come ˈoff ★★★

1	fall off a horse/bicycle etc
2	about dirt/paint etc
3	stop being fixed
4	stop taking medicine/drugs
5	succeed
6	happen
7	win or lose
8	be replaced by another player
+	PHRASE

1 to fall off something that you are riding = FALL OFF
come off sth *She'd come off her new bike and hurt her knee.*
come off *The second horse hit the fence, and the rider came off.*

2 if something such as dirt or paint comes off something, it is removed by washing or rubbing
come off sth *The chewing gum wouldn't come off my shirt.*
come off *It's the kind of grease that won't come off with ordinary soap.*

3 to stop being fixed to something = COME AWAY

come off *I pulled at the drawer, and the handle came off.*
come off sth *One of the legs has come off the table.*

4 to stop taking something such as a medicine or drug

come off sth *She'd been advised to come off the medication immediately.*

5 to succeed ≠ FAIL

come off *What if their plan doesn't come off?* ♦ *The party didn't quite come off as we had hoped.*

6 to happen = TAKE PLACE

come off *Another competition is coming off in the summer.*

7 to achieve a particular result in an activity, especially a competition or fight

come off *He* **came off** *quite* **badly** *in the exchange of insults.* ♦ *I wouldn't take him on if I were you. You're bound to* **come off worst.** ♦ *Surprisingly, the champion* **came off second-best.**

8 to leave a sports field and be replaced by another member of your team = BE TAKEN OFF

come off *Beckham had to come off after five minutes of the second half.*

<u>PHRASE</u> **come off it!** *informal* used for telling someone that you do not believe them or that what they are saying is stupid: *Oh, come off it, Tom – that's just ridiculous!*

ˌcome ˈoff as *American*

used for talking about your opinion of someone or something when you see them or meet them = APPEAR, COME ACROSS AS, COME OVER AS

come off as sth *Luckily, the speech comes off as professional.* ♦ *I don't want to come off as desperate.*

ˌcome ˈon ★★★

1	develop or progress
2	when equipment starts to work
3	about rain/snow
4	be broadcast
5	appear in a programme
6	be affected by illness
7	improve
8	when you tell sb to hurry
9	when you encourage sb
10	I do not believe you
11	arrive on stage
12	arrive on a sports field
13	meet sb or find sth by chance
14	when you want to fight sb
+	PHRASE
+	**come-on** noun; **oncoming** adj

1 to develop or make progress = COME ALONG, PROGRESS

come on *How's your essay coming on?* ♦ **+with** *She's coming on fine with her music.*

2 to start working by being switched on = GO ON ≠ GO OFF

come on *I saw a light come on in an upstairs window.*

3 if something such as rain or snow comes on, it starts to fall ≠ STOP

come on *The snow came on pretty heavily, so we decided to go home.* ♦ **+to do sth** *It came on to rain.*

4 to start to be broadcast

come on *We all had to be quiet when the news came on.*

5 to start to appear in a television or radio programme

come on *Then the president comes on and tells everyone to spend more money.*

6 if an illness comes on, it starts to affect you

come on *I can feel another headache coming on.*

7 to improve

come on *His French has really come on since last year.*

8 [always in imperative] *informal* used for telling someone to hurry = HURRY UP

come on *Come on! We're going to be late.*

9 [always in imperative] *informal* used for encouraging someone to do something such as make a greater effort or stop being sad = COME ALONG

come on *Come on! It's not the end of the world.*

10 [always in imperative] *informal* used for telling someone that you do not believe what they are saying = COME ALONG

come on *Oh, come on! Only a fool would believe a story like that!*

11 to arrive on a stage = ENTER ≠ GO OFF

come on *When he came on, the audience finally began to show some interest.*

12 to arrive on a sports field in order to replace another member of your team ≠ GO OFF

come on *She came on at the beginning of the second half.* ♦ **+as** *He came on as a substitute.* ♦ **+for** *Miller came on for his injured team-mate with only two minutes of the game left.*

13 *literary* to meet someone, or to find something by chance = COME ACROSS, COME UPON, HAPPEN ON; *formal* ENCOUNTER

come on sb/sth *We came on an injured deer lying at the side of the road.*

14 [always in imperative] *informal* used for trying to make someone fight you

come on *Come on, then! Or are you too scared?*

PHRASE **come on strong** *informal* to start to show that you are determined to do something, especially to defeat an opponent or to start a sexual relationship with someone: *He came on strong towards the end of the round.* ♦ *I think I came on a bit too strong.*

■ **'come-on** **noun** [C] *informal*
1 something you say or do to let someone know that you are interested in them sexually: *She seemed to be giving me the come-on.* **2** something that a business offers at a low price to encourage you to buy more: *CDs are the supermarkets' biggest come-ons.*

■ **oncoming** /ˈɒnˌkʌmɪŋ/ **adj** [only before noun] **1** moving towards you: *oncoming traffic* **2** going to happen very soon: *our hopes for success in the oncoming season*

ˌcome 'on to

1 to start to deal with a new subject in a discussion
come on to sth *We'll come on to the politics of the situation in a moment.*

2 *informal* to behave towards someone in a way that shows you would like to have a sexual relationship with them
come on to sb *I couldn't believe it when he started coming on to me.*

ˌcome 'out ★★★

1	become known
2	stop being fixed
3	when dirt is removed
4	how sth is heard/understood
5	book/film: become available
6	about the sun/moon/stars
7	about a photograph
8	about how sb/sth appears in a photograph
9	have a particular result
10	be noticed
11	state sth officially
12	arrive from somewhere far away
13	about flowers
14	stop work to protest
15	about being gay
16	about an upper-class young woman
+	PHRASES
+	**outcome** noun

1 if something comes out, it becomes known = EMERGE
come out *He said it'll all come out in court.* ♦ **+that** *It eventually came out that he was married.*

2 to stop being fixed somewhere = FALL OUT

come out *Another of her baby teeth came out yesterday.*

3 to be removed from something such as clothing or cloth by washing or rubbing
come out *We scrubbed the carpet with soap but the stains still wouldn't come out.*

4 to be spoken, heard, or understood in a particular way
come out *It was meant as a compliment, but that wasn't how it came out.* ♦ *She had only meant to defend herself, but it had come out all wrong.* ♦ **+as** *I didn't mean it to come out as a criticism.*

5 if something such as a book or a film comes out, it becomes available to buy or see = BE RELEASED, BE PUBLISHED
come out *We've recorded a new album, and it's coming out in the spring.*

6 if the sun, moon, or stars come out, they start to appear in the sky = COME UP, APPEAR ≠ GO IN
come out *The sun came out and bathed the whole garden in its summer light.*

7 if a photograph comes out, the chemical process that produces it is successful
come out *None of my holiday photos came out.*

8 to have a particular appearance in a photograph
come out *The colour of her eyes hasn't really come out.*

9 to have a particular result, or to end in a particular way
come out *It's impossible at this stage to judge how the vote will come out.* ♦ *I'm sure it will all come out all right in the end.*

10 to become easy to notice
come out *These differences don't come out until you put the two groups in a room together.*

11 to state a decision or opinion officially or publicly
come out *We still have no idea which way the committee will come out.* ♦ **+in favour of** *The commission has come out in favour of the takeover.* ♦ **+against** *The government has come out against privatizing the industry.*

12 if someone comes out, they travel to the country that you are in, for example to visit you
come out *My parents are coming out for Christmas.* ♦ *We first came out here in 1978.*

13 if a flower comes out, it opens = OPEN
come out *The first of the spring flowers had already come out.*

14 *British* to stop working as a protest = STRIKE

come out *We decided to come out in support of the miners.* ♦ *It seemed clear that the workers would come out on strike.*

15 to tell people that you are gay
come out *She'd decided she was brave enough to come out.* ♦ **+to** *Coming out to her parents was the hardest part.*

16 *old-fashioned* if a young upper-class woman comes out, she formally becomes part of upper-class society by going to a special party or other social event for the first time
come out *Their youngest girl comes out next month.*

PHRASES **come out on top/come out tops** to be the best or the winner: *Phil always comes out on top.*

come (right) out and say sth to say something in an open, honest, or public way that often makes someone feel surprised, embarrassed, or offended: *We were all thinking he'd made a mistake, but nobody would come out and say it.*

■ **outcome** /'aʊtkʌm/ noun [C usually singular] the final result of a process, meeting, event etc: *A second game will be played to determine the outcome.* ♦ *He refused to comment on the outcome of the election.*

,come 'out at

to be a particular number or amount that is the result of a calculation or measurement
come out at sth *The total comes out at well over £10,000.*

,come 'out in British

to become covered in spots because you are ill or because your body reacts to a food or medicine
come out in sth *She can't eat shellfish without coming out in a rash.*

,come 'out of

to be the result of something = EMERGE FROM
come out of sth *I hope some good will come out of all this.*

PHRASE **come out of yourself** to stop being shy and become more confident and relaxed with other people: *He soon came out of himself when the music started.*

,come 'out with

to say something suddenly, usually something that surprises or shocks people
= COME AWAY WITH
come out with sth *You never know what the children are going to come out with.*

,come 'over ★★★

1	be affected by a strong feeling
2	react
3	visit sb's house
4	travel to a place far away
5	have a particular opinion of sb/sth
+	PHRASE

1 if a feeling comes over you, it suddenly affects you in a strong way
come over sb *A wave of anger came over him.*

2 *British informal* to react in a particular way
come over *I came over all emotional when I saw him.*

3 to visit someone in the place where they are, especially their house = VISIT
come over *Why don't you come over one evening?* ♦ **+to** *Come over to my place and we'll discuss it.*

4 to travel to a place, especially a long way across water in order to live in a new country
come over *He came over when he was just eighteen.* ♦ **+from** *Her great-grandparents came over from Ireland in the nineteenth century.*

5 if someone or something comes over in a particular way, you have a particular opinion of them when you meet them or see them = COME ACROSS, APPEAR
come over *Everything depends on how you come over at the meeting.* ♦ **+as** *He tends to come over as rather shy.*

PHRASE **not know what has come over sb** to be unable to explain why someone is behaving in such a strange way: *He's not normally so rude – I don't know what's come over him.*

,come 'over to

1 to change your position or opinion and start supporting someone you were arguing or fighting with
come over to sb *The president announced that there would be an amnesty for all who now came over to him.*

2 to change your opinion and accept someone else's opinion instead
come over to sth *We were sure they would come over to our way of thinking.*

,come 'round British

to become conscious again after being unconscious = COME TO ≠ BLACK OUT
—*picture* → PASS OUT
come round *When I came round, I was lying on the back seat of a car.*

,come 'through ★★★

1	not be killed/defeated
2	about a signal/message
3	receive sth that sb sends
4	about a feeling/quality
5	do what you agreed/promised

1 to be still alive, working, or making progress after a difficult or dangerous experience = SURVIVE
come through sth *It's been a very upsetting time but we've come through it together.*

2 if something such as a signal or a message comes through, you receive it
come through *The call to the police came through at 5.40 pm.*

3 if a document that you are expecting comes through, you receive it after it has been sent to you
come through *The job offer still hasn't come through.*

4 if a feeling or quality that someone or something has comes through, it can be clearly understood or seen
come through *Her disbelief comes through in the questions she asks.*

5 *informal* to do something that you have agreed or promised to do
come through *The team came through when it mattered.* ♦ **+with** *She came through with the script ahead of schedule.*

'come to ★★★

1	remember sth
2	reach a total
3	start dealing with sth
4	reach a bad point/state
5	when you are shocked/upset by sth
6	become owned by sb
+	PHRASES

1 if something comes to you, you think of it or remember it = OCCUR TO
come to sb *The idea came to me when we were on holiday.* ♦ *Her name will come to me in a minute.* ♦ **+that** *It came to her that it was foolish to expect him to help.*

2 to reach a particular total when everything is added together = ADD UP TO, AMOUNT TO, TOTAL
come to sth *With salaries and overtime the bill came to £752,000.*

3 to start to talk about something or start to deal with something
come to sth *We'll come to the legal argument in a minute.* ♦ *'What about an explanation?' 'I'm just coming to that.'*

4 to reach a particular state or point, especially one that is bad or unpleasant
come to sth *If it comes to war, NATO*

forces will be stronger in the air.

5 used for emphasizing how bad a situation is and how shocked or upset you are about it
come to sth *It comes to something when you don't even remember your own mother's birthday.* ♦ *So, has our relationship come to this?* ♦ *When you see children starving, you wonder what the world is coming to.*

6 to become someone's property, especially because the previous owner has died = COME DOWN TO
come to sb *The farm will come to you when I die.*

PHRASES **come to nothing** or **not come to anything/much** to fail to be successful or useful: *In the end, all our plans came to nothing.* ♦ *His teachers all agreed that he wouldn't come to anything.*
when it comes to (doing) sth when the subject being discussed is a particular thing: *When it comes to holidays, I prefer something lazy.* ♦ *When it comes to writing letters, she's hopeless.*

,come 'to

to become conscious again after being unconscious = COME ROUND ≠ BLACK OUT
—*picture* → PASS OUT
come to *She would sometimes wander off in her sleep, and when she came to she had no recollection of doing it.*

,come to'gether ★★

1 to start to be good or effective because different parts are combining well
come together *After several weeks of rehearsals, the play finally started to come together.*

2 if several people or groups come together, they meet or join in order to do something = MEET
come together *The convention gives us a chance to come together.* ♦ **+to do sth** *We come together to share our thoughts and experiences.*

'come under ★★★

1 to be forced to experience something unpleasant
come under sth *The department had come under criticism for poor performance.* ♦ *Airport security will now come under increased scrutiny.* ♦ *The president is coming under pressure to take action.*

Nouns often used as objects with **come under 1**

■ attack, criticism, fire, pressure, scrutiny, strain, threat

2 to be the responsibility of a particular person or institution

come under sb/sth *Issues relating to pay come under the personnel department.*

3 to belong to a particular group or class

come under sth *Libraries and swimming pools come under Leisure Services.*

,come 'up ★★★

1	go to speak to sb
2	become available
3	problem: need to be dealt with
4	be mentioned
5	be happening soon
6	travel further north
7	about computer information
8	when sb is sick
9	reach a higher point/level
10	about the sun/moon/stars
11	win money with a ticket
12	plant: start to grow
13	be judged in court
14	go to university
+	PHRASES
+	**upcoming** adj

1 to move towards someone, usually because you want to talk to them = APPROACH

come up *A woman came up and started complaining about the noise.* ♦ **+to** *Strangers come up to him in the street and say how much they enjoy his books.*

2 if something such as a job comes up, it becomes available = ARISE

come up *She's hoping a vacancy will come up at the local college.*

3 if a problem comes up, it happens and needs to be dealt with immediately = ARISE

come up *I'm going to have to cancel our lunch – something's come up.*

4 to be mentioned and to need to be considered = ARISE

come up *A number of interesting points came up at today's meeting.*

5 [always progressive] to be about to happen soon

be coming up *We've got a busy period coming up in a couple of weeks.*

6 to travel to a place that is further north or that is larger or more important than the place you are leaving ≠ COME DOWN

come up *Why don't you come up for the weekend?* ♦ **+from** *My mother's coming up from England for the weekend.*

7 if information about something comes up on something such as a computer screen, it appears there

come up *Our flight hasn't come up yet.*

8 if food that you have eaten comes up, your stomach forces it out through your mouth

come up *He could feel his breakfast coming up.*

9 to be tall, deep, or long enough to reach a particular higher point or level

come up *The water came up about this high.* ♦ **+to** *The grass in the garden came up to her knees.*

10 if the sun, moon, or stars come up, they start to appear in the sky = COME OUT ≠ GO DOWN

come up *We sat on the beach and watched the sun come up.*

11 if your ticket or name comes up in a game such as a lottery, it is chosen as a winner

come up *None of my numbers ever comes up.*

12 if a plant comes up, it starts to appear above the ground

come up *The first of the spring bulbs were coming up.*

13 to be judged in a court of law

come up *His case comes up next week.*

14 *British old-fashioned* to go to a university, especially Oxford or Cambridge, at the beginning of a period or course of study = GO UP ≠ COME DOWN, GO DOWN

come up *My younger brother is coming up next year.*

PHRASES **come up in sb's estimation/opinion** to become more respected by someone than you were before, because of something you have done: *He's really come up in my estimation since I heard what he did for you.*

come up in the world to become richer, more powerful, or more successful than before: *Judging by that car, he's come up in the world.*

coming (right) up used for saying that you will bring what someone has asked for very soon: *'Two burgers, please.' 'Coming right up!'*

■ **upcoming** /ˈʌpˌkʌmɪŋ/ adj **1** an upcoming event will happen soon: *the upcoming elections* **2** an upcoming book, record, or film will soon be available to buy or see: *She is starring in an upcoming TV serial.*

,come 'up against

to have to deal with something difficult or unpleasant = EXPERIENCE

come up against sth *In the first week, we came up against a pretty tricky problem.*

PHRASE **come up against a brick wall** to reach a point in a process where there are problems that seem impossible to solve: *In a lot of cases, you come up against a brick wall.*

,come 'up for ★

to reach the time when something should happen

come up for sth *The contract comes up for review next month.* ♦ *The matter failed to come up for discussion.* ♦ *The issue will come up for debate in parliament shortly.* ♦ *The house comes up for sale next month.* ♦ *The painting is coming up for auction at Sotheby's.*

'come upon ★★ *mainly literary*

1 to meet someone or find something by chance = COME ACROSS, COME ON, STUMBLE ACROSS; *formal* ENCOUNTER

come upon sb/sth *We turned a corner and came upon an old church.*

2 if a thought or feeling comes upon you, you have it

come upon sb *A feeling of great excitement had suddenly come upon me.*

,come 'up to

1 to get nearer to a particular time or stage in a process = APPROACH

come up to sth *As we come up to the end of the first half, the score remains France 3, Italy 3.*

2 to be as good as you want, need, or expect something to be = MATCH

come up to sth *It's hard for others to come up to the very high standards she sets for herself.* ♦ *Did the holiday come up to your expectations?* ♦ *The hotel didn't really come up to scratch* (=it was not as good as it should have been).

,come 'up with ★★★

1 to think of something such as an idea or a plan = THINK OF

come up with sth *Is that the best you can come up with?*

Nouns often used as objects with **come up with 1**

■ compromise, idea, plan, proposal, solution, suggestion

2 to produce or provide something that people want = PRODUCE; *British informal* COME ACROSS WITH

come up with sth *We're in big trouble if we don't come up with the money by 6 o'clock.*

'come with ★★★

1 to exist or develop as a result of something

come with sth *It's the kind of skill that comes with years of practice.*

2 to be included with something

come with sth *In those days, the house came with the job.* ♦ *All these computers come with a 3-year guarantee.*

COMMIT /kəˈmɪt/
commits, committing, committed

comˈmit to ★★

1 to make someone agree or promise to do something

commit sb to sth *The treaty commits member states to a 20% reduction in pollution.*

commit sb to doing sth *The agreement commits them to giving a minimum number of performances per year.*

commit yourself to sth *I do not want to commit myself to any particular date.*

commit yourself to doing sth *Both sides have committed themselves to finding a peaceful solution to the conflict.*

2 to promise to do something

commit to doing sth *He would have to commit to spending several thousand pounds.*

commit to sth *We were prepared to commit to a second meeting.*

COMMUNE /kəˈmjuːn, American kəˈmjun/
communes, communing, communed

comˈmune with *literary*

to communicate with someone or something without using words because you feel especially close to them

commune with sb/sth *Peter felt he could commune with the trees.* ♦ *She had wandered out into the countryside to commune with nature.*

COMPARE /kəmˈpeə, American kəmˈper/
compares, comparing, compared

comˈpare to ★★★ [often passive]

to say that one person or thing is similar to another

be compared to sb/sth *His poems have been compared to those of the English Romantics.*

compare sb/sth to sb/sth *The minister compared the economic crisis to the dropping of a bomb.*

comˈpare with ★★★

used for saying how good or bad one thing is in relation to another

compare with sth *How does the UK's*

record compare with that of other European countries? ♦ *Our performance* **compares** *very* **favourably with** *the national average.*

PHRASE **sth doesn't compare with sth** used for saying that one thing is not as good as another thing: *The architecture of these buildings doesn't compare with that of older institutions.*

COMPLAIN /kəm'pleɪn/
complains, complaining, complained

com'plain of ★★
1 *formal* to say that something bad has happened
complain of sth *Foreign tourists complain of bureaucratic delays when trying to enter the country.*
complain of doing sth *Refugees had complained of being robbed and beaten by officials.*
2 to say that you have a pain or are ill
complain of sth *She'd been complaining of headaches.*

COMPOSE /kəm'pəʊz, American kəm'poʊz/
composes, composing, composed

be com'posed of ★★★
to be made of particular parts or things
be composed of sth *Muscle is composed of two different types of protein.* ♦ *The organization is composed almost entirely of women.*

CONCEIVE /kən'siːv, American kən'siv/
conceives, conceiving, conceived

con'ceive of [usually in negatives or questions]
to imagine something, or to think of doing something
conceive of (doing) sth *How can they even conceive of doing such an appalling thing?*

CONCENTRATE /'kɒns(ə)ntreɪt, American 'kɑns(ə)ntreɪt/
concentrates, concentrating, concentrated

'concentrate on ★★★
to give most of your attention to one aim or activity
concentrate on sth *Luke wants to concentrate on his film career.*
concentrate on doing sth *The government is concentrating on controlling interest rates.* ♦ *You should*

concentrate your efforts on *passing these exams.*

CONDEMN /kən'dem/
condemns, condemning, condemned

con'demn to ★
1 [usually passive] to give a punishment to someone who has committed a crime
be condemned to sth *Both men have been condemned to life imprisonment.* ♦ *Fifty rebels were* **condemned to death**.
2 [often passive] if something condemns you to an unpleasant situation, it forces you to experience it
be condemned to sth *These youngsters will be condemned to a life of boredom.*
condemn sb to sth *A late goal condemned them to their first defeat since March.*

CONE /kəʊn, American koʊn/
cones, coning, coned

,cone 'off [often passive] British
to put cones (=plastic objects with a circular base that rise to a point) across a road to prevent traffic from going along the road
be coned off *One side of the road had been completely coned off.*
cone off sth *Police coned off the accident site.*

CONFER /kən'fɜː, American kən'fɜr/
confers, conferring, conferred

con'fer on (also con'fer upon) formal
to give something such as authority, a legal right, or an honour to someone
confer sth on sb *The university conferred an honorary doctorate on her.*

CONFIDE /kən'faɪd/
confides, confiding, confided

con'fide in ★★
to tell someone a secret or discuss your private feelings with them
confide in sb *I hope you know that you can always confide in me.*

CONFINE /kənˈfaɪn/
confines, confining, confined

conˈfine to ★★★

1 affect only one person/place
2 make sb stay somewhere
3 stay somewhere because ill/disabled
4 limit sth dangerous
5 limit an activity

1 [always passive] if something is confined to one place, person, or group of people, it happens only in that place or affects only that person or group of people
be confined to sb/sth *Before 1914 divorce was largely confined to the upper classes.* ♦ *The risk of infection is confined to relatively small groups.*

2 [usually passive] to force someone to stay in a place and prevent them from leaving
be confined to sth *Many prisoners are confined to their cells for long periods of time.* ♦ *All the soldiers were confined to barracks for twenty-four hours.*

3 [usually passive] to make someone stay in a place because they are too ill, weak, or disabled to leave
be confined to sth *Ill health meant he was confined to his room.*

4 to prevent something dangerous from spreading
confine sth to sth *They managed to confine the fire to the engine room.*

5 *formal* to keep an activity within particular limits
confine sth to sth *I shall attempt to confine the discussion to broad principles.*

CONFORM /kənˈfɔːm, American kənˈfɔrm/
conforms, conforming, conformed

conˈform to ★★★ (also conˈform with)

1 to obey something such as a rule or law
conform to sth *All fireworks must conform to British safety standards.*

2 to be similar to an idea of what is usual or normal
conform to sth *He doesn't conform to the stereotype of a military man.*

CONFRONT /kənˈfrʌnt/
confronts, confronting, confronted

conˈfront with ★★ [often passive]
if you confront someone with information, you give it to them and they must say whether it is true
be confronted with sth *Confronted with the evidence, I had to admit it was true.*

confront sb with sth *I confronted her with the letters I had found.*

CONFUSE /kənˈfjuːz, American kənˈfjuz/
confuses, confusing, confused

conˈfuse with ★★ [often passive]
to think wrongly that a person or thing is someone or something else
be confused with sb/sth *Robert should not be confused with his father, who has the same name.*
confuse sb/sth with sb/sth *It's easy to confuse success with happiness.*

CONJURE /ˈkʌndʒə, American ˈkʌndʒər/
conjures, conjuring, conjured

ˌconjure ˈup ★★

1 to create or achieve something difficult or unexpected
conjure up sth *They managed to conjure up a goal and won the match.*
conjure sth up *You hope that Brando will conjure some magic up to save the movie.* ♦ *They need a miracle but there are no signs of them conjuring one up.*

2 to bring something such as a feeling or memory to your mind = *formal* EVOKE
conjure up sth *The company's name conjures up the romance of the 1920s.*
conjure sth up *Hearing the song conjured those feelings up again.*

3 to make something or somebody appear using magic powers = CALL UP
conjure up sth/sb *They found her at the bottom of her garden, conjuring up the spirits of her ancestors.*
conjure sth/sb up *By saying his name over and over to herself, had she magically conjured him up?*

CONK /kɒŋk, American kɑŋk/
conks, conking, conked

ˌconk ˈout *informal*

1 to suddenly stop working = FAIL ≠ START UP
conk out *Suddenly the copier just conked out.*

2 to go to sleep, especially suddenly = FLAKE OUT, CRASH OUT ≠ WAKE UP
conk out *He conked out on the couch.*

CONNECT /kəˈnekt/
connects, connecting, connected

conˈnect to ★★★ (also conˈnect with)

1 to join two things together
connect sth to sth *It has speakers inside,*

which you can connect to your sound card.

2 [usually passive] to join two places, making it possible for people and things to move between them
  be connected to sth *The upper town is connected to the lower town by cable car.*

3 to show a relationship between one person or thing and another
  connect sb/sth to sb/sth *There is no evidence to connect him to the murder.*
  ♦ *The public connects him with sport not politics.*

con,nect 'up

1 to join several things or places together
  connect up sth *also* **connect sth up** *A network of canals connects up all the major ports.*

2 to join something to a supply of electricity, water, or gas
  connect up sth *also* **connect sth up** *The plumber came and connected up the dishwasher.* ♦ **+to** *We need to connect the cable up to the mains.*

3 to make it possible for someone to communicate using a set of computers that are all joined to one another
  connect up to sth *I'm just trying to connect up to the email server.*
  connect sth up to sth *The aim is to connect all these machines up to the Internet.*

CONNIVE /kəˈnaɪv/
connives, conniving, connived

con'nive at (*also* con'nive in)
to ignore behaviour or an activity that is wrong, or do nothing to stop it, so that you seem to approve of it
  connive at sth *It seems that the legal system connives at such crimes.*

CONSIGN /kənˈsaɪn/
consigns, consigning, consigned

con'sign to ★★ *formal*

1 to put someone in an unpleasant situation that usually lasts a long time
  consign sb/sth to sth *His policies consigned the people to starvation.*
  ♦ *Enemies of the king were consigned to the dungeons.*

2 to give someone or something to someone else to look after
  consign sb/sth to sb *We consign our children to the care of the teacher for the day.*

3 to put someone or something somewhere, especially because you do not want to deal with them

  consign sb/sth to sth *He consigned his work suits to the back of the wardrobe.*

CONSIST /kənˈsɪst/
consists, consisting, consisted

con'sist in *formal*
to have something as the most important aspect or the only aspect
  consist in (doing) sth *True strength does not consist in mere muscle.* ♦ *Plato believed that progress consisted in trying to achieve pre-existing ideals.*

con'sist of ★★★
to be made of particular parts, things or people
  consist of sth *His breakfast consists of dry bread and a cup of tea.* ♦ *A task force was set up, consisting of several senior economists.*
  consist of doing sth *My role seemed to consist of standing and smiling at people.*

> Adverbs often used with **consist of**
>
> ■ chiefly, essentially, largely, mainly, predominantly, primarily, principally, solely

CONSORT /kənˈsɔːt, *American* kənˈsɔrt/
consorts, consorting, consorted

con'sort with *formal*
to spend time with someone who is considered bad, for example a criminal or an enemy = ASSOCIATE WITH
  consort with sb *Do you deny you were consorting with a known criminal?*

CONSTRUE /kənˈstruː, *American* kənˈstru/
construes, construing, construed

con'strue as [often passive] *formal*
to understand the meaning of something in a particular way = INTERPRET AS
  be construed as sth *Can that be construed as an apology?*
  construe sth as sth *Please do not construe this as any criticism of yourself.*

CONTEND /kənˈtend/
contends, contending, contended

con'tend with
to have to deal with problems or difficulties, especially in order to achieve something
  contend with sth *They had to contend with winds of over 40 miles an hour.*

♦ *With three kids to bring up, I've got* **enough to contend with**.

CONTENT /kənˈtent/
contents, contenting, contented

conˈtent with
if you content yourself with something, you are willing to accept what you have, although you would prefer to have something else
content yourself with (doing) sth *Initially, she contented herself with simply looking after her family.* ♦ *You'll have to content yourself with the company of older people.*

CONTRACT /kənˈtrækt/
contracts, contracting, contracted

ˌcontract ˈin *British*
to agree by a written legal agreement to be included in something
contract in *Union members were expected to contract in.* ♦ **+to** *Most employees chose to contract in to the savings scheme.*

ˌcontract ˈout ★★
1 *British* to agree by a written legal agreement not to be included in something
contract out *They were trying to persuade employees to contract out.* ♦ **+of** *Some teachers prefer to contract out of the state pension scheme.*
2 to give work to another company by a written legal agreement instead of using your own company to do the work
contract out sth *The firm contracts out most of the basic building work.*
contract sth out *There are plans to contract some of this work out.* ♦ *They get rid of these services altogether or contract them out.*

CONTRAST /kənˈtrɑːst, *American* kənˈtræst/
contrasts, contrasting, contrasted

conˈtrast with ★★★
1 to compare two people or things in order to show how they are different
contrast sb/sth with sb/sth *He contrasted his party's record on unemployment with that of the last government.*
2 if one person or thing contrasts with another, the two are different from each other, often in a noticeable or interesting way
contrast with sb/sth *Her dark hair*

contrasted sharply with her pale silk gown.

CONTRIBUTE /kənˈtrɪbjuːt, *American* kənˈtrɪbjut, ˈkɑntrɪˌbjut/
contributes, contributing, contributed

conˈtribute to ★★★ (*also* conˈtribute towards)
to be one of the things that help to make something happen
contribute to sth *The scandal certainly contributed to their defeat at the last election.*

Nouns often used as objects with **contribute to**

■ (positive) development, formation, improvement, success
(negative) decline, demise, downfall, erosion, failure, fall, loss, reduction

CONVERGE /kənˈvɜːdʒ, *American* kənˈvɜrdʒ/
converges, converging, converged

conˈverge on ★ (*also* conˈverge upon)
if people converge on a place, they come to it from different places
converge on sth *World leaders were converging on Washington.*

CONVERT /kənˈvɜːt, *American* kənˈvɜrt/
converts, converting, converted

conˈvert into ★★★
to change something from one use to another, or to be changed to a different use
convert sth into sth *They're converting the old church into flats.* ♦ *Old ambulances can be converted into motor homes.*
convert into sth *The sofa converts into a bed.*

CONVULSE /kənˈvʌls/
convulses, convulsing, convulsed

be conˈvulsed with
if you are convulsed with something such as laughter, you are laughing in an uncontrolled way
be convulsed with sth *Her audiences are regularly **convulsed with laughter**.*

COOK /kʊk/
cooks, cooking, cooked

,cook 'up

1 *informal* to invent a story, excuse, or plan
= INVENT, MAKE UP
cook up sth *also* **cook sth up** *Between them they cooked up some story to tell their parents.* ♦ *I assumed she and Donald had cooked it up between them.*

2 to prepare and cook food without spending a lot of time and effort on it
= PREPARE; *informal* KNOCK UP
cook up sth *also* **cook sth up** *She quickly cooked up some pasta.* ♦ *I can cook a meal up for us in no time!*

COOL /ku:l, *American* kul/
cools, cooling, cooled

,cool 'down ★★

1 to become cooler, or to make something cooler ≠ WARM UP
cool down *We had to wait until the engine had cooled down before restarting the car.*
cool sth down *The rain had cooled everything down.*

2 *informal* to become, or cause someone to become, less angry or excited = CALM DOWN
cool down *Just try to cool down and think rationally.*
cool sb down *Nothing I say will cool her down.*

,cool 'off

1 to become cooler after being very hot
≠ WARM UP
cool off *We went for a swim to cool off.*

2 to become calm again after being angry
= CALM DOWN
cool off *Let him cool off. You can talk about it later.*

3 to become less busy or active after being very busy or active = CALM DOWN
cool off *I'm really busy, but when things cool off, I'll come and see you.*

4 to fall in amount or value
cool off *Most experts expect interest rates to cool off soon.*

■ **,cooling-'off** adj PHRASE **cooling-off period 1** a pause in an argument, especially one between a company's management and employees, that gives people time to think calmly about how to reach an agreement: *Talks between staff and management will resume after a two-week cooling-off period.* **2** a period of time in which you are allowed to change your mind about a contract or agreement that you have signed: *a ten-day cooling-off period*

COOP /ku:p, *American* kup/
coops, cooping, cooped

be ,cooped 'up

if a person or an animal is cooped up in a place, they have to stay there without being able to move around much = BE CAGED UP
be cooped up *I've been cooped up in this office all day.*

COP /kɒp, *American* kɑp/
cops, copping, copped

,cop 'off with British *very informal*

to meet someone and start a sexual relationship with them = GET OFF WITH
cop off with sb *So, did you cop off with anyone?*

,cop 'out *informal*

to avoid doing something that you should do because it is difficult = DUCK OUT, BACK OUT
cop out *They accused him of trying to cop out.*

■ **'cop-out** noun [C] something you say or do to avoid doing what you should do: *Telling him you're ill sounds like a cop-out to me.*

'cop to *mainly American informal*

to admit to something embarrassing or something you have done wrong
cop to sth *We didn't expect him to cop to it straightaway.*

COPY /'kɒpi, *American* 'kɑpi/
copies, copying, copied

,copy 'down

to write exactly what someone has written or said
copy down sth *also* **copy sth down** *We carefully copied down the chemical formula.* ♦ *Let me copy that address down.*

,copy 'in

to send someone a copy of an email or letter that you are sending to another person
copy sb in *I'll email her about it, and copy you in.*

,copy 'out

to write something again exactly as it has been written
copy out sth *also* **copy sth out** *We had to copy out sentences from a book.* ♦ *I was forced to copy the whole page out again.*

'copy to

1 to send a copy of an email or letter to someone

copy sth to sb *I accidentally copied the email to everyone in the company.*

2 to put a copy of a piece of computer information in another place on the computer

copy sth to sth *Have you copied it to the hard drive?*

CORDON /'kɔːd(ə)n, *American* 'kɔrd(ə)n/
cordons, cordoning, cordoned

,cordon 'off [often passive]

1 if the police or soldiers cordon off an area, they guard it to stop people from entering = CLOSE OFF

be cordoned off *The embassy had been cordoned off.*
cordon off sth *Police had cordoned off the area.*

2 to stop people from entering an area by putting something such as a rope around it

be cordoned off *A corner of the restaurant had been cordoned off.*
cordon off sth *They cordon off their private living quarters.*

CORK /kɔːk, *American* kɔrk/
corks, corking, corked

,cork 'up [usually passive]

to close something, especially a bottle, with a cork

be corked up *Make sure the bottles are properly corked up.*

CORRELATE /'kɒrəleɪt, *American* 'kɔrə,leɪt/
correlates, correlating, correlated

'correlate with *formal*

1 [often passive] if one thing correlates with, or is correlated with, another thing, they are connected in a way that is not caused by chance

be correlated with sth *Quick reactions are correlated with high intelligence.*
correlate with sth *This response to the question did not correlate significantly with age or gender.*

2 to examine two things and find out whether they are connected

correlate sth with sth *Attempts will be made to correlate our findings with various environmental factors.*

CORRESPOND /ˌkɒrɪ'spɒnd, *American* ˌkɔrə'spɑnd/
corresponds, corresponding, corresponded

corre'spond to ★★★

1 correspond to or **correspond with** to be the same as something else, or very much like it

correspond to sth *In 60% of the patients, all symptoms corresponded to what we expected.* ♦ *What is printed out corresponds exactly with what is seen on the screen.*

2 used about something in a different country or system that is very much like something in yours

correspond to sth *His first post was as an Associate Professor, which roughly corresponds to Lecturer here.*

3 correspond to or **correspond with** to be connected or related to something

correspond to sth *In machine code, one instruction corresponds directly to one operation of the computer.* ♦ *The timing of the gift closely corresponded with Robert's return from Italy.*

COST /kɒst, *American* kɔst/
costs, costing, costed

,cost 'out (*also* ,cost 'up)

to calculate exactly how much something will cost

cost out sth *also* **cost sth out** *Have you costed out the job?* ♦ *We'll have to cost these proposals up.*

COSY /'kəʊzi, *American* 'koʊzi/
cosies, cosying, cosied

,cosy 'up

to move close to someone for warmth or love

cosy up *It was a cold night outside, so we cosied up under the blankets.* ♦ *In the morning we found all the children cosied up in the same bed.*

,cosy 'up to *showing disapproval*

to try to become friendly with someone in order to get some benefit for yourself
= SUCK UP TO

cosy up to sb *He has been accused of cosying up to the new US president.*

COTTON /'kɒt(ə)n, *American* 'kɑt(ə)n/
cottons, cottoning, cottoned

,cotton 'on *informal*

to begin to realize or understand something = CATCH ON, UNDERSTAND

cotton on *Suddenly I cottoned on – she'd been lying from the start.* ♦ **+to** *It took him a while to cotton on to what I was saying.*

'cotton to *American informal*
to begin to like someone or something
cotton to sb/sth *I didn't cotton to him at first.*

COUCH /kaʊtʃ/
couches, couching, couched

'couch in [often passive] *formal*
to express something in a particular way
be couched in sth *Couched in generalities, the report named no one responsible for the incident.*
couch sth in sth *He would have to couch the thing in the right words.*

COUGH /kɒf, *American* kɑf/
coughs, coughing, coughed

ˌcough 'up ★
1 to force something such as blood out of your lungs by coughing
cough up sth *You might cough up a little blood.*
cough sth up *The medicine will help you to cough the mucus up.*
2 *informal* to give money to pay for something, especially when you would prefer not to = PAY UP
cough up *Come on, cough up: it's your turn to pay.* ♦ **+for** *I had to cough up for the medical bills.*
3 *British informal* to admit something or give information about something that you would prefer other people not to know = CONFESS
cough up sth *He was eventually forced to cough up details of the crime.*
cough sth up *She had important information but refused to cough any of it up.*

COUNT /kaʊnt/
counts, counting, counted

ˌcount a'gainst
to be a disadvantage in a particular situation = WEIGH AGAINST ≠ HELP
count against sb *I'm worried that my age might count against me.*

ˌcount a'mong
to think of someone or something as belonging to a group of people or things that you have a particular opinion about
count sb/sth among sb/sth *He counts John Lennon among his musical*

influences. ♦ *I don't really count her among my friends.*

'count as [often passive]
to think of someone or something as a particular type of person or thing, or to be thought of as a particular type of person or thing
be counted as sb/sth *Is geography counted as a science subject?*
count as sb/sth *That counts as a lie as far as I'm concerned.*
count sb/sth as sb/sth *Beth is a good player, but you would never count her as a real musician.*

ˌcount 'down
to say numbers one after the other from a bigger number to a smaller number, especially zero
count down *Try counting down from a hundred.*
PHRASE be counting down the days/minutes etc to be very impatient for something good that is about to happen: *We're counting down the days until the end of the exams.*
■ **countdown** /'kaʊntdaʊn/ **noun** [C]
1 the counting of numbers backwards, for example from ten to zero, before something important happens: *The countdown for the shuttle launch has already begun.* **2** the period of time just before an important event: *This was a countdown to civil war.*

'count for ★★
PHRASE count for nothing or **not count for much** to not be any advantage to you in a particular situation: *Expertise and experience count for nothing if a fighter isn't mentally prepared when he enters the ring.* ♦ *Qualifications don't count for much in the music industry.*

ˌcount 'in [often in imperative]
to include someone in your plans
= INCLUDE ≠ COUNT OUT, EXCLUDE
count sb in *'There's a party on Saturday.' – 'Count me in!'* ♦ *If you need help, you can count me in.*

ˌcount 'off
to count things as you deal with them or as they pass
count off sth *also* **count sth off** *'There's lots we could do,' she said, counting off the points on her fingers.* ♦ *He counted the seconds off by the hands of his watch.*

'count on ★★ (*also* **'count upon**)
1 to depend on someone to do what you want or expect them to do for you = BANK ON

count on sb *The whole team was counting on me, and I let them down.* ◆ **+for** *You can always count on him for good advice.* ◆ **+to do sth** *I knew I could count on you to be on time.* ◆ **+doing sth** *I was counting on Jane driving me home.*

2 to plan or expect that someone will do something or that something will happen = BANK ON

count on sb/sth *Tournament directors are counting on good weather.*

count on sb/sth doing sth *We're counting on about 20 people coming to the meal.* ◆ *She hadn't counted on it raining.*

3 used in a humorous way for saying that you know someone will behave in a particular way

count on sb *If there's a wrong way to do something, you can always count on her.* ◆ **+to do sth** *You can always count on Ted to make a mess of the cooking.*

ˌcount ˈout ★

1 to count things one by one
count out sth *She counted out £100 in £5 notes.*
count sth out *Jackson counts the money out slowly and deliberately.* ◆ *He took a handful of sweets and counted them out.*

2 [often in imperative] to not include someone in a plan or activity = EXCLUDE ≠ INCLUDE, COUNT IN
count sb out *If you're going to watch the football, count me out.*

3 [usually passive] in sports such as boxing, to say that someone has lost a fight because they are not ready to fight again after remaining hurt for ten seconds
be counted out *He was counted out in his last three fights.*

ˌcount ˈtowards

to be included in a calculation
count towards sth *Marks for project work count towards your final grade.*

ˌcount ˈup ★

to count all the things or people in a group = TOTAL, ADD UP
count up sth *Have you counted up how many times the team has lost?*
count sth up *When you count all their achievements up, it's a pretty impressive record.* ◆ *There are six empty bottles here. Count them up.*

ˈcount upon *same as* count on

ˈcouple to [usually passive]

if one vehicle or part of a machine is coupled to another, they are joined so that they work together
be coupled to sth *A trailer was coupled to the tractor.*

be ˈcoupled with ★★★

if one thing is coupled with another, they are combined and produce a particular effect
be coupled with sth *Her intelligence, coupled with her experience, makes her a perfect candidate for the job.* ◆ *The weather, **coupled with the fact that** the trains were on strike, meant that few reporters turned up.*

ˈcover for

1 to do someone's work while they are away or ill
cover for sb *I'm just covering for Mrs Tyler, so please bear with me.*

2 to protect someone from punishment, for example by telling a lie for them
cover for sb *If Pauline asks where I am, will you cover for me?*

be ˈcovered in ★★★ (*also* be ˈcovered with)

if a surface or object is covered in a substance, the substance is all over the surface or object
be covered in sth *His clothes were covered in mud.* ◆ *All the furniture was covered with dust.*

ˌcover ˈover

to cover something, especially in order to protect it or hide it
cover over sth *also* **cover sth over** *She put a cloth on the table to cover over the marks.* ◆ *We cover over the swimming pool in the winter.* ◆ **+with** *Cover the food over with cloths until it is time to eat.*

ˌcover ˈup ★★

1 to put one thing over another thing in order to protect or hide it ≠ EXPOSE
cover sth up *Use dust sheets to cover the furniture up if you are away for long periods.* ◆ **+with** *Cover the food up with a cloth.*
cover up sth *She wears powder to cover up the scar.*

2 to put more clothes or covers on your

body, to hide it or keep it warm

cover up *It's freezing outside, so cover up.*

cover yourself up *You wish these young girls would cover themselves up more.*

3 to hide the truth about something by not telling what you know or by preventing other people from telling what they know = SUPPRESS ≠ EXPOSE

cover sth up *It was a real scandal, but the school tried to cover the whole thing up.*

cover up sth *She had tried to cover up her shameful past.*

cover up *Alice, as usual covering up, said that Jasper had gone to visit his brother.* ♦ **+for** *He got his powerful friends to cover up for him.*

■ **'cover-up** noun [C] an attempt to stop people from discovering the truth about something, especially a crime or a serious mistake: *People suspected another government cover-up.*

COZY the American spelling of **cosy**

CRACK /kræk/
cracks, cracking, cracked

,crack 'down ★

to start dealing with someone or something much more strictly = CLAMP DOWN

crack down *Crime is rising. Isn't it time the government cracked down hard?* ♦ **+on** *The school is cracking down on smoking.*

■ **crackdown** /'krækdaʊn/ noun [C usually singular] strong action that someone in authority takes to stop a particular activity: *Police are launching a crackdown on gun crime in the capital.*

,crack 'on British informal

to continue doing something as quickly as possible = GET ON

crack on *There's only two hours left. We'd better crack on.* ♦ **+with** *We really need to crack on with this painting.*

,crack 'up ★ informal

1 to become mentally ill = BREAK DOWN

crack up *He just cracked up from the stress.*

2 to suddenly laugh a lot at something = CREASE UP

crack up *The girls all cracked up when they saw him.*

3 to make someone laugh a lot = CREASE UP

crack sb up *Little kids just crack me up with the things they say.*

PHRASE **sth is not all/what it's cracked up to be** informal used for saying that something is not as good as people say that it is: *Italian football isn't all it's cracked up to be.*

CRAM /kræm/
crams, cramming, crammed

,cram 'in (also ,cram 'into)

1 to put people or things into a space that is too small = SQUEEZE IN

cram in sb/sth also **cram sb/sth in** *The case was full, but she tried cramming in another few files.* ♦ *The room was tiny, but we crammed everyone in.*

cram sb/sth into sth *Guards cram 40 prisoners into cells designed for 12.*

2 to do a lot of activities in a short time

cram in sth also **cram sth in** *I wanted to cram in visits to a few more places before we left.* ♦ *We only have two days. How are you going to cram all that in?*

cram sth into sth *How much surfing can you cram into an afternoon?*

CRANK /kræŋk/
cranks, cranking, cranked

,crank 'out informal

to produce things in large numbers, often without caring much about their quality = CHURN OUT, TURN OUT

crank out sth also **crank sth out** *He cranked out hit song after hit song.* ♦ *You don't normally expect great performances every time, but he keeps cranking them out.*

,crank 'up informal

1 to increase the level or degree of something = INCREASE

crank up sth also **crank sth up** *We are determined to crank up the pressure on the government.* ♦ *We'll have to crank the air conditioning up tonight.*

2 to make a machine or a piece of equipment start to work = START, START UP ≠ TURN OFF

crank up sth also **crank sth up** *It was time to crank up the boiler.* ♦ *I heard him crank the engine up.*

CRAP /kræp/
craps, crapping, crapped

,crap 'on impolite

to talk continuously in an annoying or boring way = DRIVEL ON, DRONE ON

crap on *They just crap on for hours.*

♦ **+about** *The newspapers are all crapping on about how wonderful he is.*

CRASH /kræʃ/
crashes, crashing, crashed

,crash a'round (also ,crash a'bout British)
to make a lot of noise as you move around in a place = BANG AROUND
crash around *I hear him crashing about in the bathroom.*

,crash 'down
to stop existing or stop being successful, or to make someone or something stop existing or stop being successful
come crashing down *Their rivals hoped and expected them to come crashing down.*
bring sb/sth crashing down *We imagined we could bring capitalism crashing down.*

,crash 'out *informal*
1 to suddenly start sleeping, usually when you are very tired = FLAKE OUT
crash out *I crashed out around ten in front of the TV.*
2 *mainly journalism* to be badly defeated so that you have to leave a competition
crash out *The world No. 1 also crashed out, comprehensively beaten by No. 6 Chang.* ♦ **+of** *England crashed out of the European Cup again today.*

CRATE /kreɪt/
crates, crating, crated

,crate 'up
to put something into a large wooden box in order to move or store it
crate up sth also **crate sth up** *He paid 65 labourers for nine months to dismantle the monastery, crate it up, and move it.*
♦ *The paintings were crated up and shipped to the US.*

CRAWL /krɔːl, American krɔl/
crawls, crawling, crawled

'crawl with [usually progressive]
1 to be full of people in a way that is unpleasant
be crawling with sb *The town was crawling with police.*
2 to be covered in insects in a way that is unpleasant
be crawling with sth *The food was crawling with flies.*

CREAM /kriːm, American krim/
creams, creaming, creamed

,cream 'off
1 to take the best people or things from a larger group in order to form a smaller special group
cream off sb/sth also **cream sb/sth off** *They always cream off all the best students.*
2 to take a lot of money or profit, especially an unfair amount, in a business deal
cream off sth also **cream sth off** *He wondered how much Lawton had creamed off while he was running the business.*

CREASE /kriːs, American kris/
creases, creasing, creased

,crease 'up British informal
1 to laugh a lot = CRACK UP
crease up *It's an old joke, but I crease up every time I hear it.*
2 to make someone laugh a lot = AMUSE
crease sb up *You really crease me up!*

CREDIT /'kredɪt/
credits, crediting, credited

'credit to
1 [usually passive] to add an amount of money to a bank account
be credited to sth *The money will be credited to your account in about three days.*
2 to say that someone has achieved something because of a particular thing
credit sth to sth *The team credited their victory to sheer hard work.*

'credit with ★★ [often passive]
1 to say or believe that someone is responsible for something that has happened, especially something important or successful
be credited with sth *She's rarely credited with the enormous amount she actually achieved.*
be credited with doing sth *As finance minister he is **widely credited with** restoring economic stability to the country.*
credit sb with doing sth *The police chief credited his regional commander with bringing peace to the area.*
credit sb with sth *I'd be reluctant to credit her with all the hard work.*
2 to say or believe that someone has a particular quality

be credited with sth *It'd be nice to be credited with some sense of humour!*
credit sb with sth *Surely you credit me with more intelligence than that!*

CREEP /kriːp, *American* krip/
creeps, creeping, crept /krept/

,creep 'by
if time creeps by, it passes very slowly
creep by *The minutes seemed to be creeping by.*

,creep 'in (*also* ,creep 'into)
1 to appear gradually and begin to affect something or someone, especially in a negative way
creep in *Politicians have warned of voter cynicism creeping in unless there's an immediate inquiry.*
creep into sth *A few errors had crept into the text.*
2 if an emotion or feeling creeps in somewhere, someone gradually starts to experience it
creep in *She smiled, but a sense of uneasiness seemed to have crept in.*
creep into sth *Suspicion began to creep into her mind.*
3 if a word or meaning creeps in, it gradually becomes used
creep in *French worries about the number of English words continuing to creep in*
creep into sth *A new meaning of 'sexy' crept into the language a few years ago.*

,creep 'over
to gradually affect someone or something
creep over sb/sth *Tiredness crept over her, making her eyelids droop.* ♦ *When she saw Paul a slight flush crept over her face.*

,creep 'up
to gradually become larger in number or amount = SNEAK UP
creep up *The sales figures keep creeping up.* ♦ *+to The number of missing people has crept up to 40.*

,creep 'up on
1 to move towards someone quietly and slowly, especially because you want to surprise them = SNEAK UP ON
creep up on sb *I didn't notice him creeping up on me.*
2 if something creeps up on you, it happens slowly or gradually, or without you noticing that it is happening = SNEAK UP ON
creep up on sb *It's funny how old age suddenly creeps up on you.* ♦ *The final*

deadline seemed to have crept up on all of us.

CROP /krɒp, *American* krɑp/
crops, cropping, cropped

,crop 'up ★★ informal
1 if a problem crops up, it appears or happens, especially suddenly or unexpectedly = COME UP
crop up *Take your phone with you in case anything crops up.*
2 if a subject, word, or name crops up, someone mentions it, for example in a conversation or a discussion = COME UP
crop up *I've noticed Alice's name keeps cropping up in our conversations.*

CROSS /krɒs, *American* krɔs/
crosses, crossing, crossed

,cross 'off ★
to draw a line through something on a list to show that you have dealt with it
cross sth off *The children tell their names to the teacher, who crosses each one off.*
cross off sth *Cross off the hotels after you've phoned them.*
cross sth off sth *I'd already crossed several items off the list.*

,cross 'out ★★
to draw an X or a line through writing because it is wrong or because you have decided to write something else = DELETE, SCORE OUT
cross out sth *Just cross out the old address.*
cross sth out *Someone had crossed my name out.*

■ **crossings-out** /ˌkrɒsɪŋz ˈaʊt/ noun [plural] where one or more words have been crossed out in a piece of writing: *There were only three crossings-out in the whole essay.*

,cross 'over
1 to walk from one side of a room, road etc to the other
cross over *Coming to the bridge, we crossed over and followed the path along the river.* ♦ *+to I crossed over to her and took her arm gently.*
2 to stop supporting one group and start supporting another = *formal* DEFECT
cross over *Sheila Jones may well be the next senior cabinet member to cross over.* ♦ *+to Another member of the government has crossed over to the opposition.*
3 to start to belong to a different group or type from before

cross over *He is a thriller writer trying to cross over and reach a more intellectual readership.* ♦ **+into** *Several Latino singers have crossed over into mainstream rock.*

■ **crossover** /ˈkrɒsəʊvə/ **noun** a change from one situation or style to another: *He never quite made the crossover from classical to pop.*

CROWD /kraʊd/
crowds, crowding, crowded

,crowd a'round ★ (also ,crowd 'round)
if people crowd around, they surround someone or something, especially because they want to see what is happening
crowd around *Everyone crowded around to see what was going on.*
crowd around sb/sth *The children were crowding around the dead dog.*
♦ *Everyone in the restaurant crowded around them and started singing.*

,crowd 'in ★
1 crowd in or **crowd into** to move into a particular place at the same time as a lot of other people
crowd in *They opened the doors and we all crowded in.*
crowd into sth *Thousands of demonstrators had crowded into a few square miles.*
2 if unpleasant thoughts or worries crowd in, they seem to threaten you and make you feel upset
crowd in *She tried to shut her mind to the fears that kept crowding in.* ♦ **+on** *Everything was crowding in on me and I felt that I couldn't cope.*

,crowd 'in on (also ,crowd 'in upon formal)
if people crowd in on someone, they move close to them and then surround them
crowd in on sb *Some youths he did not know began crowding in on him.*

,crowd 'out [often passive]
to become bigger, stronger, or more successful than another group so that they can no longer successfully compete with you
be crowded out *The old inhabitants are being crowded out by rich young professionals.*
crowd out sb/sth *The idea is that the harmless bacteria crowd out the harmful ones.*

,crowd 'round same as crowd around

CRUISE /kruːz, American kruz/
cruises, cruising, cruised

'cruise through
to succeed easily in a competition, test, game etc = BREEZE THROUGH
cruise through sth *She cruised through her midterm exams.*

'cruise to
to achieve success easily in a game, race, or competition
cruise to victory/a win/the finals etc *They cruised to an effortless 5–0 win over AC Milan.*

CRUMBLE /ˈkrʌmb(ə)l/
crumbles, crumbling, crumbled

,crumble a'way
to break into very small pieces
crumble away *The bricks were soft and crumbled away when he lifted them.*

CRUMPLE /ˈkrʌmp(ə)l/
crumples, crumpling, crumpled

,crumple 'up
1 to crush something such as paper or cloth so that it forms untidy folds, or to be crushed in this way
crumple sth up *also* **crumple up sth** *I quickly crumpled up the letter and shoved it in my pocket.*
crumple up *The car crumpled up with the force of the impact.*
2 [often passive] to fall to the ground suddenly, with your body, legs, and arms bent, because you are injured, ill, or upset
be crumpled up *He lay on the bed, crumpled up in pain.*
crumple up *He swayed, then crumpled up in a heap at our feet.*

CRY /kraɪ/
cries, crying, cried /kraɪd/

'cry for
to cry because you want someone or miss them
cry for sb *Children often cry for their mothers on their first day of school.* ♦ *She cried for her dead husband every night.*

,cry 'off informal
to decide not to do something that you had promised or agreed to do = CANCEL
cry off *Their guest speaker cried off at the last minute.*
cry off (doing) sth *In the end he cried off taking the kids swimming.*

,cry 'out ★★

1 to make a loud noise because you are in pain, frightened, or shocked = YELL
cry out *I tried not to cry out when a guard suddenly appeared in the doorway.*
♦+in/with *One of the women cried out in fear.* **♦** *He cried out in pain when she tried to move him.*

2 to shout something, especially when you are surprised or worried = SHOUT
≠ WHISPER
cry out sth *'Be careful!' Miss Honey cried out.* **♦** *He seemed to be crying out someone's name.*
cry out *I thought I heard a woman's voice crying out in the distance.* **♦ +for** *Someone was crying out for help.* **♦ +to** *She cried out to the man standing on the beach.*

■ **outcry** /ˈaʊtkraɪ/ **noun** [usually singular] an angry expression of protest or shock by a lot of people, as a reaction to something someone has done or to something that has happened: *A massive public outcry followed the revelation.*

,cry 'out against
to feel or show very strongly that you do not want to do something or that you think something is wrong
cry out against (doing) sth *My instincts cried out against leaving him there all alone.* **♦** *Part of me cried out against the idea of being someone's wife.*

,cry 'out for [usually progressive]
to clearly need something a lot
cry out for sth *This room is crying out for some new furniture.* **♦** *Local schools are crying out for more investment.*

CUDDLE /ˈkʌd(ə)l/
cuddles, cuddling, cuddled

,cuddle 'up [often passive]
to sit or lie with your body resting against someone else's and with your arms around them because you want to feel warm, protected, or loved = SNUGGLE UP
be cuddled up *The two children were cuddled up on the sofa.*
cuddle up *They cuddled up and went to sleep.* **♦ +to** *She came over and sleepily cuddled up to him.* **♦ +together** *In the evenings, they would cuddle up together and watch TV.*

CUE /kjuː, *American* kju/
cues, cueing, cued

,cue 'in
to give news or information to someone
cue sb in *What's going on? Can someone cue me in?* **♦ +on** *I'll cue you in on the morning's events before the meeting.*

CULL /kʌl/
culls, culling, culled

'cull from
to collect something such as information from different places
cull sth from sth *We used recipes culled from magazines.*

CULMINATE /ˈkʌlmɪneɪt/
culminates, culminating, culminated

'culminate in ★★
to happen or exist as the final result of a process or series of actions = END IN
culminate in sth *The scandal eventually culminated in the collapse of the government.* **♦** *The raids continued all night, culminating in the arrest of over 40 suspected terrorists.*

CURE /kjʊə, *American* kjʊr/
cures, curing, cured

'cure of [often passive]
if an event, situation, feeling etc cures someone of something such as a bad habit, feeling, or attitude, it gets rid of it
be cured of sth *She hasn't been cured of her infatuation for him yet, unfortunately.*
cure sb of sth *A month working with local street kids should cure him of any sense of self-pity.*

CURL /kɜːl, *American* kɜrl/
curls, curling, curled

,curl 'up ★★

1 [often passive] to sit in a comfortable position, with your legs bent and your feet up off the floor
be curled up *We sat curled up on the sofa, watching the late film.*
curl up *I curled up in an old armchair in front of the fire.*

2 to form a curved or round shape, or to give something this shape
curl up *Smoke curled up from their cooking fire.*
curl sth up *He curled his hands up into fists.*

3 [often passive] to lie, usually on your side,

with your back curved and your legs and arms close to your chest

be curled up *Anna lay curled up in bed, thinking about what happened.*

curl (yourself) up *The dog curled himself up in the grass and closed his eyes.* ♦ *She wanted to curl herself up into a ball, to make herself invisible.*

curl up (sense 3)

PHRASE **want to curl up and die** *informal* used to tell someone about how you felt when something very embarrassing happened: *When they all started laughing I just wanted to curl up and die!*

■ **,curled-'up** **adj** forming a curved shape, or curved at the edges, because of being dried-up or old: *There were a few curled-up sandwiches left on the plate.*

CURSE /kɜːs, *American* kɜrs/
curses, cursing, cursed

,curse 'out *American informal*
to use impolite or offensive language to someone, especially because they have made you angry = CUSS OUT
curse sb out *Neighbours had heard him cursing her out before she was found dead.*

be 'cursed with
to have a serious problem, disadvantage, or condition that is often permanent
be cursed with sth *The area is cursed with the lowest wages in the whole country.* ♦ *Since childhood, he had been cursed with acute shyness.*

CURTAIN /'kɜːt(ə)n, *American* /'kɜrt(ə)n/
curtains, curtaining, curtained

,curtain 'off [usually passive]
to separate an area from the rest of a room or area by a curtain
be curtained off *The clean area is curtained off from the rest.*

CUSHION /'kʊʃ(ə)n/
cushions, cushioning, cushioned

'cushion against (*also* **'cushion from**)
to protect a person or thing from the harmful effects of something
cushion sb/sth against sth *Their savings partly cushioned them against the worst effects of the legal costs.* ♦ *Government subsidies have cushioned farmers from the worst effects of the drought.*

CUSS /kʌs/
cusses, cussing, cussed

,cuss 'out *American informal*
to use impolite or offensive language to someone, especially because they have made you angry = CURSE OUT
cuss sb out *Dad cussed me out good for taking the car without asking.*

CUT /kʌt/
cuts, cutting, cut

,cut a'cross
1 to go across an area of land, instead of going around the edge of it, in order to save time
cut across sth *We cut across the field because we were late.*
2 to pass through or across something
cut across sth *A river cut across the track about a hundred metres further on.*
3 to affect two or more different groups in the same way
cut across sth *These problems cut across class boundaries.*

,cut a'way
to remove the parts of something that you do not want by cutting them
cut away sth *also* **cut sth away** *Cut away any dead growth on your roses.*

■ **cutaway** /'kʌtə,weɪ/ **noun** [C] a short shot in a film that shows something that is not happening in the main scene: *There's a brief but hilarious cutaway to the glazed faces of the audience.*

,cut 'back ★★★

1 to reduce the amount of money that you spend or the amount of something that you use = REDUCE ≠ INCREASE

> **cut back** *We'll have to cut back a little.*
> ♦ **+on** *We're trying to cut back on the amount we spend on food.*
> **cut back sth** *They strongly oppose any plans to cut back investment in education.*

2 to start doing or using less of something, especially because it is bad for your health = REDUCE —*picture* → CUT DOWN

> **cut back** *Pete smokes but he's trying to cut back.* ♦ **+on** *If you cut back on fat and sugar, you'll definitely lose weight.*

3 to remove parts of a plant or tree in order to reduce its size = PRUNE

> **cut back sth** *I had to cut back several branches that were blocking the path.*
> **cut sth back** *It'll soon be time to cut the roses back.*

■ **cutback** /ˈkʌtbæk/ **noun** [C] a reduction in something such as the amount of money available to spend: *Many hospitals face cutbacks in services.*

,cut 'down ★★★

1	reduce an amount
2	do less of sth bad
3	make speech/writing shorter
4	make a tree fall down
5	kill or injure sb

1 to reduce an amount of something, or the number or size of something = REDUCE ≠ INCREASE

> **cut down sth** *How can you cut down the risk of cancer?* ♦ *Accidents were cut down by about 25%.* ♦ **+on** *These improvements should help cut down on traffic noise.*

2 to start eating, drinking, or smoking less of something because it is bad for your health = REDUCE ≠ INCREASE

> **cut down sth** *Cut down your alcohol intake and take more exercise.* ♦ **+on** *I'm trying to cut down on salt.*
> **cut down** *If you really can't give up smoking, at least try to cut down.*

3 to make something such as a speech or piece of writing shorter = SHORTEN

> **cut down sth** *Can you cut down the article by about 100 words?*
> **cut sth down** *You need to cut your essay down a little – it's still too long.*

4 [often passive] to cut through the main part of a tree in order to make it fall to the ground = FELL

> **be cut down** *Huge areas of the rainforest are being cut down.*
> **cut down sth** *Protesters tried to stop them cutting down the trees.*

cut sth down *They plan to cut the big old oak in the park down.*

5 [often passive] *literary* if a weapon, bullet, or illness cuts someone down, or if they are cut down by it, it kills or injures them = KILL

> **be cut down** *Hundreds of men were cut down in battle.*
> **cut sb down** *Cancer cut him down while he was still in his prime.*

cut down/cut back (sense 2)

,cut 'in

1 to interrupt someone who is speaking by saying something = INTERRUPT

> **cut in** *'That's rubbish,' Sue cut in.*
> ♦ **+on** *Alex cut in quickly on Sandra's response.* ♦ **+with** *Ann cut in with the occasional sarcastic comment.*

2 to drive past a vehicle and move quickly in front of it in a dangerous way —*picture* → BACK UP

> **cut in** *An old white van cut in in front of us.*

3 if a piece of equipment cuts in, it starts operating automatically when it is needed = START ≠ CUT OUT

> **cut in** *The cooling system cuts in when the temperature gets too high.*

4 *informal* to allow someone to get part of the profits of something

> **cut sb in** *They refused to cut her in.*
> ♦ **+on** *They wouldn't cut me in on the deal.*

,cut 'into

1 to reduce an amount of something that is available, especially time or money = REDUCE ≠ INCREASE

> **cut into sth** *The teaching days I do really cut into my time at home.* ♦ *The recession has cut into company budgets.*

2 to interrupt an activity or process = INTERRUPT

> **cut into sth** *A loud rap on his office door cut into his thoughts.*

cut 'off ★★★

1	remove sth by cutting
2	stop a supply
3	block sb's way
4	make place difficult to communicate with
5	make sb difficult to communicate with
6	make sb stop talking
7	prevent sb from getting your money
8	stop being friends with sb
9	make a phone conversation stop
10	refuse to serve alcohol to sb
+	PHRASE
+	cutoff noun; offcut noun

1 to remove something by cutting it
cut sth off *The kidnappers cut his ear off and sent it to his family with a ransom note.*
cut off sth *Why did you cut off all your hair?* ♦ *All the cat's fur had been cut off.*
cut sth off sth *Cut the tops off the carrots.*

2 [often passive] to stop providing a supply of something, especially gas, water, or electricity ≠ CONNECT, RECONNECT
be cut off *Their phone must have been cut off.*
cut off sth *The government has threatened to cut off our funding.*
cut sth off *They cut the electricity off last week.*

3 to stop someone from going somewhere, especially by blocking their way = BLOCK
cut off sb/sth *A second policeman cut off his escape.*
cut sb/sth off *They advanced rapidly to try to cut the enemy forces off before they could reach the river.*

4 [often passive] to make a place difficult or impossible to enter, leave, or communicate with = ISOLATE
be cut off *The town was completely cut off for over three days.* ♦ *The area was cut off by heavy flooding.*
cut off sth *The floods completely cut off the town.*
cut sth off *Heavy snowfalls would cut the community off for weeks in the winter.*
cut sth off from sth *Our house was cut off from the rest of the village.*

5 to prevent someone from leaving a place, or from communicating with people in another place = ISOLATE
cut sb off *He needed the company of other children, but his parents' wealth cut him off.*
♦ **+from** *Having a new baby can cut a young mother off from the adult world.*

6 to prevent someone from continuing what they are saying = INTERRUPT

cut sb off *Don't cut me off when I'm talking.*
cut off sb *It's rude to cut off the poor boy in mid sentence like that.*

7 to refuse to allow someone to get your money or property = *formal* DISINHERIT
cut sb off *Her father cut her off without a penny.*

8 to stop having a close or friendly relationship with someone
cut sb off *Why did all his friends suddenly cut him off?*
cut off sb *Everyone in the village cut off the couple completely when the news got out.*

9 [often passive] if someone or something cuts you off when you are talking on the telephone, you suddenly can no longer talk to the other person because of a problem with the telephone line ≠ CONNECT, RECONNECT
be/get cut off *We got cut off in the middle of the call.*
cut sb off *Someone must have cut her off.*
cut off sb *Cut off another caller and you're fired!*

10 *American informal* to not allow someone to buy any more alcoholic drinks in a bar because they have already drunk too many
cut sb off *I'm sorry, but I'm going to have to cut you off.*

PHRASE **cut off your nose to spite your face** *informal* to do something that is intended to harm someone even though you know that it will harm you too: *Changing your mind now would be cutting off your nose to spite your face.*

cut off (sense 2)

■ **cutoff** /ˈkʌtɒf/ **noun** **1** [C] a level or limit at which something stops: *the cutoff date by which all applications must be received* **2** [C] a part of a pipe that can be closed to stop a gas or liquid flowing: *Fuel can be re-routed by means* *of this cutoff.* **3 cutoffs** [plural] short trousers that you make by cutting part of the legs off old trousers: *She's wearing a T-shirt and denim cutoffs.*

■ **offcut** /ˈɒfkʌt/ **noun** [C] a piece of something such as paper or wood that is left after the main part has been cut off: *A neighbour makes children's toys from workshop offcuts.*

,cut 'out ★★★

1	remove a piece by cutting
2	make sth by cutting
3	remove parts of sth
4	stop eating/doing sth
5	stop annoying sb
6	stop noise/light etc from entering
7	not include sb
8	engine/machine: stop working
9	join a new line of traffic
+	PHRASES
+	**cutout** noun

1 to remove something from a larger piece by cutting
  cut sth out of sth *I cut this article out of a magazine for you.*
  cut out sth *She carefully cut out the picture.*
  cut sth out *Why don't you cut the photo out and paste it in your scrapbook?*

2 to make something by cutting it from a larger piece
  cut out sth *He cut out several star shapes.*
  ♦ **+from** *Cut out six circles from a large sheet of paper.*
  cut sth out *She cut a large rectangle out in the middle of the lawn to form a flowerbed.*

3 to remove parts from something such as a piece of writing, a speech, a film etc = REMOVE ≠ PUT IN
  cut out sth *They've cut out several scenes in which I appeared.*
  cut sth out *The piece will read better if you cut that paragraph out.*

4 to stop eating something or doing something, especially because it is bad for your health
  cut out sth *I've cut out chocolate completely.*
  cut sth out *If you'd any sense, you'd cut cigarettes out.*

5 [usually in imperative] *informal* to stop doing something that someone considers is annoying
  cut sth out *That's enough fighting – cut it out!*
  cut out sth *Cut out the dramatics! You're not fooling anyone.*

6 to stop something such as noise or light from reaching a place = BLOCK OUT

cut out sth *The thick curtains cut out most of the light.*
cut sth out *Fitted carpets should cut the noise from downstairs out.*

7 to not allow someone to do something or get something = EXCLUDE
  cut sb out *We're not trying to cut you out: you'll get your share.* ♦ **+of** *I don't want to cut the children out of our plans.* ♦ *Frank's mother threatened to **cut him out of her will**.*

8 if an engine or machine cuts out, it suddenly stops working = STOP ≠ CUT IN
  cut out *He heard the plane's engine cut out seconds before the crash.*

9 *mainly American* to suddenly leave a line of traffic and join another one
  cut out *The car in front cut out suddenly without signalling.*
  PHRASES   not be cut out for sth/to do sth to not have the right qualities or character for doing something: *Bill was never cut out to be a parent.*
  cut out the middleman to deal directly with someone instead of talking to their representatives, in order to avoid unnecessary stages in a process: *Ordering over the Internet is one way of cutting out the middleman.*

■ **cutout** /ˈkʌtaʊt/ **noun** [C] **1** a shape cut out of a piece of card or wood, usually with a picture stuck on it: *a cardboard cutout* **2** a piece of equipment that automatically switches off a machine when something goes wrong: *Unbelievably, they built the system without a cutout.*

,cut 'through ★★

1 to go through an area instead of going around the edge of it
  cut through sth *He decided to cut through the forest.*

2 to make a path through something by cutting
  cut through sth *She tried to cut through the undergrowth.*
  cut a way/path/route through sth *He cut his way through the jungle with a machete.*

3 to deal quickly and effectively with something that causes problems or is confusing
  cut through sth *We need to cut through the political rhetoric and see what really lies behind the policy.*

4 to move quickly and smoothly through something
  cut through sth *England cut through the French defence and scored a try.*

,**cut 'up** ★★

1 to cut something into several pieces
= CHOP UP

cut sth up *At this stage, your child will need someone to cut up her food for her.*
cut up sth *You may need a power saw to cut up the wood.*

2 *British* to drive past a vehicle and move quickly in front of it in a dangerous way
= CARVE UP

cut sb/sth up *Did you see the way he cut me up there?*
cut up sb/sth *He cut up a BMW whose driver sounded his horn angrily.*

3 *American informal* to behave in a noisy silly way

cut up *They were in the habit of cutting up whenever the teacher left the room.*

> PHRASE **cut up nasty/rough** *British old-fashioned* to become angry, threatening, or violent: *When Steve cut up rough, she realized she'd gone too far.*

■ ,**cut 'up** adj *informal* **1** upset or offended: *It's clear from his face that he's still cut up about it.* **2** injured by being cut many times: *He staggers into casualty battered and cut up.*

Dd

DAB /dæb/
dabs, dabbing, dabbed

'**dab at**

to touch a surface gently several times with something such as a piece of cloth, in order to make it clean or dry

dab at sth *Marge dabbed at her eyes with a handkerchief.*

,**dab 'off**

to remove something from a surface by gently touching it several times with something such as a piece of cloth

dab off sth *also* **dab sth off** *He put his hand to his face and dabbed off a tear.*
♦ +**with** *If you spill coffee on your clothes, dab it off immediately with a cloth.*
dab sth off sth *'This won't take long', said the nurse, dabbing the blood off his arm.*

,**dab 'on** (*also* ,**dab 'onto**)

to quickly put small amounts of a substance on a surface

dab sth on *also* **dab on sth** *She dabbed some cream on gently.* ♦ *I dabbed on a little more paint.*

dab sth on sth *If it hurts, dab some cream on it.* ♦ *Dab some lotion onto the affected area.*

DABBLE /'dæb(ə)l/
dabbles, dabbling, dabbled

'**dabble in**

1 dabble in or **dabble with** to be involved in an activity for a short time in a way that is not very serious

dabble in sth *When he was younger he dabbled in astrology.*

2 to put your hands or feet in water and make small quick movements with them

dabble sth in sth *The children were dabbling their feet in the warm water.*

DALLY /'dæli/
dallies, dallying, dallied

'**dally with**

1 to consider an idea or course of action but not in a serious way = TOY WITH

dally with sth *She had often dallied with the thought of leaving him.*

2 *old-fashioned* to have a sexual relationship with someone that lasts only a short time and is not serious

dally with sb *She's the girl that he dallied with and then cast aside.*

DAM /dæm/
dams, damming, dammed

,**dam 'up** *literary*

to control your feelings so that you do not show them

dam up sth *also* **dam sth up** *I tried to dam up my tears.*

DAMP /dæmp/
damps, damping, damped

,**damp 'down**

1 to use water to put out a fire or to stop it spreading = DAMPEN

damp down sth *also* **damp sth down** *The firemen had planned to use water from beneath the bridge to damp down a blaze in the copse.*

2 *same as* **dampen down**

DAMPEN /'dæmpən/
dampens, dampening, dampened

,**dampen 'down** (*also* ,**damp 'down**)

1 to make something such as a feeling or hope less strong

dampen down sth *also* **dampen sth down** *They tried to dampen down our* enthusiasm. ♦ *She works hard to dampen that anger down.*

2 to control a situation in order to reduce something or make something weaker
dampen down sth *also* **dampen sth down** *The government has attempted to dampen down this controversy.*
♦ *Military action hasn't dampened the crisis down at all.*

DANGLE /ˈdæŋg(ə)l/
dangles, dangling, dangled

'dangle be,fore (*also* 'dangle in ,front of)
to offer someone something attractive as a way of persuading them to do something
dangle sth before sb *Other teams were dangling huge pay offers before him.*
♦ *The possibility of real democracy was dangled in front of them.*

DASH /dæʃ/
dashes, dashing, dashed

'dash a,gainst
1 if water dashes against something, it hits it violently
dash against sth *Huge waves dashed against the side of the boat.*
2 to throw or hit something very violently onto a surface, usually so that it breaks
dash sth against sth *Picking up the glass, he dashed it against the wall.*

,dash a'round (*also* ,dash a'bout)
to go from place to place very quickly because you are in a hurry = RUSH AROUND
dash around *She was dashing around, trying to get things ready for the party.*

,dash 'off ★
1 to leave quickly or suddenly because you are in a hurry = RUSH OFF, SHOOT OFF
dash off *I've got to dash off after lunch to meet a client.*
2 to write or draw something quickly because you are in a hurry
dash off sth *I sat down and dashed off a letter to the paper.*
dash sth off *If Mozart really did compose these pieces, he must have dashed them off as fast as he could.*

DATE /deɪt/
dates, dating, dated

,date 'back ★★
to be made or begun at a particular time in the past = GO BACK
date back *a tradition dating back five centuries* ♦ *Some of the roads are Roman,*

dash off

and some date back even earlier. ♦ **+to**
The building probably dates back to the 15th century.

'date from ★★★
to be made at a particular time in the past
date from sth *These sculptures must date from the middle of the 7th century.*

DAUB /dɔːb, *American* dɔb/
daubs, daubing, daubed

,daub 'on [often passive]
to spread a wet substance such as paint on a surface in a careless way = SMEAR ON
be daubed on *The words were daubed on every wall.*
daub sth on sth *Like a soldier, she'd daubed dirt on his face.*

'daub with [usually passive]
if you daub a surface with a wet substance such as paint, you spread the substance on the surface in a careless way
be daubed with sth *The windows are smashed and the walls daubed with graffiti.*

DAWN /dɔːn, *American* dɔn/
dawns, dawning, dawned

'dawn on ★★
if something dawns on you, you realize it for the first time
dawn on sb *It was several months before the truth finally dawned on me.* ♦ **+that**
Little by little it dawned on Archie that his wife was not coming back.

DEAL /diːl, *American* dil/
deals, dealing, dealt /delt/

'deal in

1 to buy and sell something
deal in sth *a small company that deals in rare books* ♦ *The police said she was dealing in stolen goods.*

2 *informal* to behave in a particular way, or to be involved in a particular activity
deal in sth *Lawrence was not a man who dealt in rumours.* ♦ *Our schools have been dealing in failure for too long.*

,**deal 'in** ★★★ *mainly American informal*
to allow someone to take part in something with you = COUNT IN
deal sb in *If you're going hiking this weekend, deal me in.*

,deal 'out

1 *informal* to give a punishment or bad treatment to someone = ADMINISTER
deal out sth *also* **deal sth out** *It is up to the courts to deal out the right punishments.* ♦ *The treatment is the same no matter who's dealing it out.*

2 to give cards to the people playing a game of cards = DEAL ≠ COLLECT
deal out sth *also* **deal sth out** *He dealt out all the cards.* ♦ *Just deal the cards out quickly.*

'deal with ★★★

1	do sth
2	control an emotional situation
3	buy and sell things
4	take necessary action
5	be about sth
6	talk about sth
7	punish sb

1 [often passive] to take action to do something, for example to solve a problem = HANDLE, TACKLE
be dealt with *This is a matter that should be dealt with by the police.* ♦ *The subject is probably best dealt with by simply ignoring it.*
deal with sth *The government must now deal with the problem of high unemployment.* ♦ *I spent the morning dealing with my emails.*

Nouns often used as objects with
deal with 1

▪ **complaint, crisis, emergency, enquiry, issue, matter, problem, question, situation**

2 to accept and control a difficult emotional situation so that you can start to live a normal life again despite it = COPE WITH, HANDLE

deal with sth *She's dealing with her father's death very well.*

Nouns often used as objects with
deal with 2

▪ **anxiety, emotion, feeling, grief, pain, pressure, stress**

3 to buy goods or services from someone, or to sell them to someone = DO BUSINESS WITH, TRADE WITH
deal with sb *We have dealt with the company for years.* ♦ *Most small shops deal directly with their suppliers.*

4 to take the action that is necessary when you are involved with a particular person or type of person = HANDLE
deal with sb *Nurses find it difficult to deal with violent patients.*

5 to be about a subject = BE ABOUT, COVER, GO INTO
deal with sth *Chapter 5 deals only briefly with this issue.*

6 to talk about something = DISCUSS; *formal* ADDRESS ≠ AVOID
deal with sth *We'll deal with the question of poverty in a moment.*

7 [often passive] to punish someone or speak to someone angrily because they have done something wrong = PUNISH
be dealt with *He believes young offenders should be dealt with quickly and harshly.*
deal with sb *Wait in your room – I'll deal with you in a minute.*

DEBAR /dɪˈbɑː, *American* dɪˈbɑr/
debars, debarring, debarred

de'bar from [often passive]

1 to officially prevent someone from doing something or having something
be debarred from (doing) sth *Some students have been debarred from taking the examination.* ♦ *Why should I be debarred from a military career?*
debar sb from (doing) sth *The decision debars him from the European Cup final.* ♦ *The rule debars the President from holding any such position.*

2 to refuse to allow someone to enter a place
be debarred from (doing) sth *The five men were debarred from entering France for five years.*
debar sb from (doing) sth *They did away with the old practice of debarring women from golf clubs.*

DECIDE /dɪˈsaɪd/
decides, deciding, decided

deˌcide aˈgainst ★★

1 to decide not to do something or not to choose someone or something
decide against sb/sth *In the end we decided against the house because it was too small.* ♦ *The police have decided against further action.*
decide against doing sth *We decided against making a public statement immediately.*

2 to state officially that someone is wrong or that someone will not be allowed to do something, after considering their case carefully in a court of law, committee etc
decide against sb *The court decided against Mrs McLoughlin.*

deˈcide on ★★★

to choose someone or something from a number of possible choices = SETTLE ON
decide on sb/sth *We decided on Spain for our holiday this year.* ♦ *The party has already decided on his successor as leader.*

DECK /dek/
decks, decking, decked

ˌdeck ˈout [usually passive]

1 to decorate something, usually a room or building, for a special occasion
be decked out *The office was already decked out for Christmas.* ♦ **+with** *The streets are decked out with flags and streamers.* ♦ **+in** *The dining table is decked out in fine linen and porcelain.*

2 if someone is decked out in particular clothes, they are wearing those clothes
be decked out *I look ridiculous decked out like this.* ♦ **+in** *The children were all decked out in national costume.*

DECLARE /dɪˈkleə, American dɪˈkler/
declares, declaring, declared

deˈclare against

to say publicly that you oppose someone or something
declare against sb/sth *Others followed him and declared against the monarchy.*

deˈclare for

to say publicly that you support someone or something
declare for sb/sth *Senator Hopkins has now declared for the tax cuts.*

DEDICATE /ˈdedɪkeɪt/
dedicates, dedicating, dedicated

ˈdedicate to ★★★

1 to spend your time and effort doing something = DEVOTE
dedicate sth to doing sth *This woman has dedicated her whole life to helping others.*
dedicate sth to sth *Andy wants to dedicate more time to his hobbies.*
dedicate yourself to doing sth *They dedicated themselves to restoring the family home.*
dedicate yourself to sth *He dedicated himself to academic work.*

2 [often passive] to say at the beginning of something such as a book or song that it has been written for someone you love or admire
be dedicated to sb *This song is dedicated to Ginny, my wife and my inspiration.*
dedicate sth to sb *Lynne has dedicated the novel to her friend Norma.*

3 to use space, time, or money for a particular thing
dedicate sth to sth *The newspaper dedicated three whole pages to pictures of the princess.*

4 [usually passive] to say at an official ceremony that a new building will have a special connection with a particular person as a sign of admiration or respect for them
be dedicated to sb *The church was dedicated to Saint Francis.*

DEFER /dɪˈfɜː, American dɪˈfɜr/
defers, deferring, deferred

deˈfer to ★ *formal*

to accept someone's opinion or decision, especially because you respect them
defer to sb/sth *I will defer to Mr Walters on this point.*

DEGENERATE /dɪˈdʒenəreɪt/
degenerates, degenerating, degenerated

deˈgenerate into

if a situation or an event degenerates into something bad, bad things start to happen that make it unpleasant
degenerate into sth *These demonstrations usually degenerated into violence.* ♦ *The show soon degenerated into farce.*

DELIGHT /dɪˈlaɪt/
delights, delighting, delighted

deˈlight in
to get a lot of pleasure or enjoyment from something
delight in (doing) sth *He delights in corresponding with his old students.*
♦ *She delighted in his company.*

DELIVER /dɪˈlɪvə, American dɪˈlɪvər/
delivers, delivering, delivered

deˌliver ˈup *formal*
to give something to someone officially and formally = HAND OVER
deliver up sth to sb *All the firm's accounting records have now been delivered up to the court.*

DELUGE /ˈdeljuːdʒ, American ˈdeljudʒ/
deluges, deluging, deluged

ˈdeluge with [usually passive]
to give someone a lot of things to deal with = FLOOD WITH
be deluged with sth *The Commission has been deluged with complaints.*

DELVE /delv/
delves, delving, delved

ˌdelve ˈinto
1 to look for information by searching through something thoroughly
delve into sth *This biography delves deep into the artist's private life.*
2 to search for something in a bag, pocket etc = DIG INTO
delve into sth *Frank delved into his pocket and brought out a few coins.*

DEPART /dɪˈpaːt, American dɪˈpart/
departs, departing, departed

deˈpart from
to not use the usual way of doing something or thinking about something
depart from sth *He did not depart from his usual morning routine.* ♦ *Some schools are now departing from the traditional idea of homework.*

DEPEND /dɪˈpend/
depends, depending, depended

deˈpend on ★★★ (*also* deˈpend upon *formal*)
1 [never progressive] if one thing depends on another, it is changed or affected by the other thing

depend on sth *Their future depends on how well they do in these exams.*
♦ *Cooking time depends on the size of the joint of meat.* ♦ *How much money you get* **depends entirely on** *your circumstances.*
♦ *The method of advertising used* **depends largely on** *the budget.*
2 to need someone or something in order to continue to exist or in order to be successful = NEED
depend on sb/sth *We realized how much we depended on each other.* ♦ *The project's success depends on the support of everyone concerned.* ♦ **+for** *The young birds depend on their parents for food.*
♦ *Some countries depend on tourism for their economic survival.* ♦ **+to do sth** *The animals all depend on Mr Jackson to feed them.* ♦ *She depended on luck to get her through her exams.*
3 if you can depend on someone, you are sure that they will help you or do what you expect them to do = RELY ON
≠ MISTRUST
depend on sb *I wasn't worried: I knew I could depend on you.* ♦ **+to do sth** *You can always depend on Kim to be calm in a crisis.*
4 if you can depend on something, you are sure that you will get it or that it will happen = RELY ON
depend on sth *Can I depend on your vote?* ♦ *I won't let you down. You can depend on that.*
PHRASES **as if/as though your life depends on it** with as much effort as possible: *He pedalled furiously, as if his life depended on it.*
depending on according to: *House prices vary greatly depending on area.*

DEPRIVE /dɪˈpraɪv/
deprives, depriving, deprived

deˈprive of ★★★ [often passive]
if you deprive someone of something they want or need, you take it away from them or prevent them from having it
be deprived of sth *He had been deprived of love and attention.*
deprive sb of sth *You cannot deprive me of the right to see my child.*
deprive yourself of sth *Why are you depriving yourself of so much pleasure?*

DERIVE /dɪˈraɪv/
derives, deriving, derived

deˈrive from ★★★ [often passive]
1 to obtain something from something else = COME FROM
be derived from sth *A number of*

products also contained ingredients that were derived from animals, for example gelatine.
derive sth from sth *Parasitic fungi derive food from living plants and animals.* ♦ *She seems to derive pleasure from hurting others.*

2 to have something as an origin
be derived from sth *The symbol for sodium, Na, is derived from its Latin name natrium.*
derive from sth *The title of the film derives from the name of its hero.*

DESCEND /dɪ'send/
descends, descending, descended

des'cend from ★★

1 [often passive] to be related to a person or animal that lived long ago
be descended from sb *She claims to be descended from royalty.*
descend from sb *the idea that modern creatures descended from earlier, very different ones*

2 *formal* to develop from something that happened or existed earlier
descend from sth *the cultural traditions that descend from the Bible*

des'cend into

if an activity, place, or organization descends into a bad state, the situation becomes very bad
descend into sth *Filming descended into chaos after further arguments.* ♦ *There are fears that the country is descending into civil war.*

des'cend on

1 if people descend on a person or a place, a lot of them arrive, often unexpectedly
descend on sb/sth *Crowds of tourists descended on the tiny church.* ♦ *The whole family descended on me for lunch.*

2 to suddenly arrive, happen, or be felt
descend on sb/sth *Waves of sadness descended on him.* ♦ *Silence descended on the room.*

des'cend to

if someone descends to behaving in a bad way, they start behaving in that way
descend to (doing) sth *She won't descend to using that kind of language.* ♦ *I would never descend to physical violence.*

DESCRIBE /dɪ'skraɪb/
describes, describing, described

de'scribe as ★★★

to say that someone or something is a particular type of person or thing
describe sb/sth as sth *Would you describe him as a reasonable man?*
describe yourself as sth *She describes herself as an old-fashioned teacher.*
be described as sth *The meeting was described as constructive.*

DESPAIR /dɪ'speə, *American* dɪ'sper/
despairs, despairing, despaired

de'spair of

to feel that a bad situation will never change or get better, or that something you want badly will ever happen = GIVE UP ON
despair of sb/sth *I despair of the state of the health service in this country!*
despair of doing sth *Mike had begun to despair of ever seeing her again.*

DETER /dɪ'tɜː, *American* dɪ'tɜr/
deters, deterring, deterred

de'ter from ★★

to make someone decide not to do something by showing them that it would be difficult, dangerous, or unpleasant
deter sb from doing sth *The rain didn't deter people from coming to the game.*
♦ *People are being deterred from making complaints because of fear of discovery.*

DETRACT /dɪ'trækt/
detracts, detracting, detracted

de'tract from ★★

to make something seem less good, attractive, or important
detract from sth *We should not allow her personal difficulties to detract from her public achievements.*

DEVIATE /'diːvieɪt, *American* 'diviˌeɪt/
deviates, deviating, deviated

'deviate from

to start doing something different from what is expected or has been agreed
deviate from sth *Try not to deviate too much from the script.*

DEVOLVE /dɪ'vɒlv, *American* dɪ'vɑlv/
devolves, devolving, devolved

de'volve on (*also* de'volve upon *or* de'volve onto) *formal*

if work or responsibility devolves on someone, it is transferred to that person
devolve on sb *As he grew older, more of Father Jack's duties devolved on a curate.*

de'volve to

1 [often passive] to give power or responsibility to someone else, especially a smaller organization or one that is at a lower level
be devolved to sb/sth *Responsibility for minor cases was devolved to the local courts.*
devolve sth to sb/sth *A decision was taken to devolve more power to the regions.*
2 to become someone's property when someone else dies
devolve to sb *Rights to the land devolve to his heirs upon his death.*

DEVOTE /dɪ'vəʊt, *American* dɪ'voʊt/
devotes, devoting, devoted

de'vote to ★★★

1 to spend a lot of your time or effort doing something = DEDICATE
devote sth to sth *He's devoted most of his time to his painting.*
devote yourself to sth *Few people are able to devote themselves fully to their career.*
2 to use something such as money for a particular purpose
devote sth to sth *We have devoted over £50m to healthcare in the past year.*
3 to use a particular amount of time or space for dealing with something
devote sth to sth *The newspaper has begun devoting more review space to children's books.*
4 [always passive] if you are devoted to someone or something, you love them very much
be devoted to sb/sth *She's completely devoted to her pets.* ♦ *He was clearly devoted to his beautiful young wife.*

DIAL /'daɪəl/
dials, dialling, dialled

dial 'up (*also* dial 'in)

to get connected to the Internet on your computer by using a modem and telephone line
dial up *The service allows customers of*
the bank to dial up from their home computer.

■ **'dial-up** (*also* **'dial-in**) adj a dial-up service needs a computer modem and telephone line in order to communicate with the Internet or another computer: *dial-up Internet access*

DICTATE /dɪk'teɪt, *American* 'dɪk,teɪt/
dictates, dictating, dictated

dic'tate to

to tell someone exactly what to do and how to behave
dictate sth to sb *Washington is in no position to dictate terms to Moscow.*
dictate to sb *I won't be dictated to by some spotty-faced boy!*

DIE /daɪ/
dies, dying, died

die a'way ★

if something such as a sound dies away, it becomes quieter or weaker and finally stops = FADE AWAY
die away *The echoes gradually died away.* ♦ *The laughter died away, and there was silence.*

die 'back

if a plant dies back, the part above the ground dies but the roots stay alive
die back *The weeds had turned brown and almost died back.*

die 'down ★★

if something dies down, it becomes much less noisy, powerful, or active = SUBSIDE
die down *I waited for the noise to die down before I spoke.* ♦ *The wind died down during the night.*

Nouns often used as subjects with **die down**

■ applause, commotion, excitement, fighting, fuss, laughter, noise, protest

be 'dying for ★ [always progressive]
informal

to want to have something or to do something very much
be dying for sth *I'm dying for a drink.* ♦ *Can we stop soon? I'm dying for the toilet.*

die 'off

if a group dies off, its members die one by one until none are left
die off *The generation that fought in the war are all dying off.*

,die 'out ★★

1 to become weaker or less common and then disappear completely = BECOME EXTINCT
> **die out** *The tribe's traditional way of life is dying out.* ♦ *The species has died out.*

2 *same as* **die away**

DIFFER /ˈdɪfə, *American* ˈdɪfər/
differs, differing, differed

'differ from ★★★

to be different from someone or something else
> **differ from sb/sth** *English differs from Spanish in that it is not pronounced as it is written.* ♦ *How does the latest version differ from the last one?*

DIFFERENTIATE /ˌdɪfəˈrenʃiˌeɪt/
differentiates, differentiating, differentiated

diffe'rentiate from

to be the quality or fact that makes one person or thing different from another
> **differentiate sb/sth from sb/sth** *The ability to use speech differentiates humans from other animals.*

DIG /dɪg/
digs, digging, dug /dʌg/

,dig a'round (*also* **,dig a'bout** *British*)

1 to try to find something inside a place or container by searching in every part of it = RUMMAGE AROUND
> **dig around** *She dug around in her handbag for a pen.*

2 to try very hard to find information about someone, usually when they do not want you to
> **dig around** *Several journalists started digging around in his past.*

,dig 'in ★★

1	press hard into sth
2	mix sth with soil
3	prepare for difficulties
4	soldiers: make a place by digging
5	start eating
+	PHRASE

1 if something digs in, it presses hard into something else
> **dig in** *There was a red mark on his shoulder where the buckle had dug in.*

2 to mix something into the soil by digging
> **dig sth in** *I need to dig the compost in.*
> **dig in sth** *He started to dig in the cow*

dung which was kindly supplied by a neighbouring farmer.

3 to prepare yourself for a difficult situation, especially one that will last for a long time
> **dig in** *We just have to dig in and hope we can turn things around.* ♦ **+for** *Both sides are digging in for a long and bitter dispute.*

4 if soldiers dig in, or if they dig themselves in, they dig long narrow open holes in the ground where they can wait for an attack
> **dig in** *British troops dug in and organized their defences rapidly.*
> **dig yourself in** *They dug themselves in and prepared for battle.*

5 *informal* to start eating food with a lot of enthusiasm = TUCK IN
> **dig in** *Come on, everybody – dig in!*
> **PHRASE** **dig your heels in** or **dig in your heels** to refuse to do something even though other people are trying to persuade you to do it: *We had hoped she'd come round, but she's really digging her heels in.*

,dig 'into ★★

1	search in pocket/bag
2	use money
3	try to find sth out
4	press hard into sth
5	make sth press hard into sth else
6	mix sth with soil

1 to put your hand in your pocket or bag in order to find something = DELVE INTO
> **dig into sth** *She dug into her bag and took out a pen.*
> **dig sth into sth** *He dug his hands deeper into the pockets of his coat.*

2 *informal* to start using money that you had been saving = DIP INTO
> **dig into sth** *I've had to dig into my savings this month to pay for my car insurance.*

3 *informal* to try to find information about something = INVESTIGATE
> **dig into sth** *Someone was digging into his past and he was determined to find out who it was.*

4 to press hard into something
> **dig into sth** *The seat belt was digging into my shoulder.*

5 to make something press hard into another thing
> **dig sth into sth** *Jenny dug her nails into the palms of her hand.*

6 to mix something into the soil by digging
> **dig sth into sth** *He was digging manure into the soil.*

ˌdig 'out ★★

1 to get someone or something out of a place or out of the ground by digging
= UNCOVER, UNEARTH ≠ BURY

dig out sb/sth *Firefighters dug out a terrier which got stuck underground.*
dig sb/sth out *It snowed so much that I spent two hours digging my car out.*
♦ **+of** *Rescuers are still digging people out of the rubble.*

2 to find something that you have not used or seen for a long time = RETRIEVE
dig out sth *I'll dig out my old college notes later.*
dig sth out *You'll need to dig your old walking boots out for next weekend.*

■ **dugout** /ˈdʌɡaʊt/ **noun** [C] **1** a small shelter by the side of a sports field where team members sit during a game when they are not playing: *He shouts instructions from the dugout.* **2** a hole or tunnel in the ground used as a shelter by soldiers during a battle: *We stayed in the dugout until the firing stopped.* **3** a boat made by cutting out the inside of a log (=long piece of wood from a tree): *We made fishing expeditions in our dugout.*

ˌdig 'over

to dig ground in order to prepare it for new plants

dig over sth *also* **dig sth over** *The first job was to dig over the flowerbeds.* ♦ *Dig the area over well and incorporate plenty of organic matter.*

ˌdig 'up ★★

1 to remove something from under the ground by digging = UNEARTH ≠ BURY
dig sth up *We will have to dig that tree up.*
dig up sth *They dug up a body in his garden.*

2 to dig holes in the ground
dig up sth *They've been digging up the road outside our house.*
dig sth up *He's planning to dig the lawn up and put a garage there.*

3 to find information by searching carefully = DREDGE UP, UNEARTH
dig up sth *When we investigated his background, we dug up some interesting facts.*
dig sth up *The media are still trying to dig everything they can up on her.*

DIGNIFY /ˈdɪɡnɪfaɪ/
dignifies, dignifying, dignified

ˈdignify with *formal*

to make someone or something seem better or more important than they really are, especially by describing them or reacting to them in a particular way
dignify sb/sth with sth *I then embarked on my acting career – if I could dignify it with such a name.*

DIN /dɪn/
dins, dinning, dinned

ˌdin 'into

to teach something to someone by repeating it a lot of times in a very determined way = DRUM INTO
din sth into sb/sth *She was tired of trying to din Physics into the heads of bored teenagers.*

DINE /daɪn/
dines, dining, dined

ˌdine 'in

to eat your evening meal at home, or at a hotel when you are staying there, instead of at a restaurant = EAT IN ≠ EAT OUT
dine in *Will you be dining in tonight, sir?*

ˈdine on (*also* ˈdine off) *formal*

to eat a particular type of food, especially an expensive one
dine on sth *They dined on caviar and strawberries.*

ˌdine 'out *formal*

to eat your evening meal in a restaurant instead of at home = EAT OUT ≠ EAT IN
dine out *We can't dine out every night.*

ˌdine 'out on *humorous*

if you dine out on an experience you have had, people invite you to meals so that you can entertain them by telling them about it
dine out on sth *I dined out on that story for quite a while.*

DIP /dɪp/
dips, dipping, dipped

ˌdip 'into ★

1 to read parts of something such as a book or magazine, without reading the whole thing from start to finish = SKIM
dip into sth *I haven't read the book all the way through, but I dipped into it occasionally.*

2 to take some money from an amount you have saved

dip into sth *I want to avoid **dipping into** my **savings** again.*

3 to put your hand into a bag or a container in order to get something

dip sth into sth *Dipping his hand into his pocket, he produced the letter I'd sent him.*

dip into sth *She just can't stop dipping into the cookie jar!*

PHRASES **dip into your (own) pocket** to use your own money to pay for something, especially when it is not your responsibility to pay for it: *Leeds signed the Barnsley defender yesterday after the directors dipped into their pockets to meet a £30,000 fee.*

dip a/your toe into sth to try something new in a very careful way because you are not confident about it: *The company has recently dipped a toe into the computer games market.*

DISABUSE /ˌdɪsəˈbjuːz, *American* ˌdɪsəˈbjuz/
disabuses, disabusing, disabused

ˌdisabˈuse of *formal*
to make someone realize that they were wrong to believe something

disabuse sb of sth *He seeks to disabuse people of the notion that they live in a real democracy.*

DISAGREE /ˌdɪsəˈɡriː, *American* ˌdɪsəˈɡri/
disagrees, disagreeing, disagreed

ˌdisaˈgree with ★★★
1 to not approve of something because you think that it is dishonest or immoral ≠ AGREE WITH

disagree with sth *Most people strongly disagree with any cruelty to animals.*

2 if something that you have eaten or drunk disagrees with you, it makes you feel ill ≠ AGREE WITH

disagree with sb *Spicy food always disagrees with me.*

DISAPPROVE /ˌdɪsəˈpruːv, *American* ˌdɪsəˈpruv/
disapproves, disapproving, disapproved

ˌdisapˈprove of ★★
to not approve of someone or something = FROWN ON ≠ APPROVE OF

disapprove of sth *Why do you always have to disapprove of everything I do?*
♦ *She was going out with a boy that her parents disapproved of.*

disapprove of doing sth *The school*

strongly disapproves of students taking part-time jobs.

DISCOURAGE /dɪsˈkʌrɪdʒ/
discourages, discouraging, discouraged

disˈcourage from ★★
to try to prevent someone from doing something, or to make it less likely that they will want to do it

discourage sb from doing sth *How can we discourage people from using their cars?* ♦ *Higher tuition fees will discourage less wealthy students from going to university.*

DISCOURSE /dɪsˈkɔːs, *American* dɪsˈkɔrs/
discourses, discoursing, discoursed

disˈcourse on (*also* **disˈcourse upon**)
formal
to talk for a long time about a particular subject that you know a lot about

discourse on sth *She spent over an hour discoursing on the merits of the new technology.*

DISGUISE /dɪsˈɡaɪz/
disguises, disguising, disguised

disˈguise as
1 [often passive] to change your appearance in order to look like someone or something else

be disguised as sb/sth *She would arrive at his home disguised as a man.*

disguise yourself as sb/sth *Soldiers disguised themselves as ordinary civilians.*

2 to change the appearance of something so that it looks like something else

disguise sth as sth *They disguised their look-out posts as town rubbish dumps.*

DISH /dɪʃ/
dishes, dishing, dished

ˌdish ˈout ★
1 *informal* to give things to a number of people = DISTRIBUTE, GIVE OUT, DOLE OUT

dish out sth *Some doctors are dishing out drugs their patients do not need.*

dish sth out *A woman stood by the door dishing brochures out as the audience left.*

2 *informal* same as **dish up**

3 *informal* if someone dishes out something such as criticism or advice, they often criticize people or give them advice = HAND OUT

dish out sth *He's always ready to dish out criticism.*

dish sth out *She dishes advice out as if she were an expert on relationships.*

PHRASE **sb can dish it out but they can't take it** *informal* used for saying that someone often criticizes other people but does not like being criticized: *There's the feeling that politicians can dish it out but they can't take it.*

,dish 'up

1 to put food into dishes or onto plates so that it is ready to be eaten = SERVE UP

dish up sth *also* **dish sth up** *She dished up the meal and they ate in silence.*

2 *British informal* to produce something for a lot of people to see, read, listen to etc

dish up sth *also* **dish sth up** *They're dishing up the usual diet of propaganda and patriotic movies.* ♦ *If you want a controversial speech, you can always rely on Jim to dish one up.*

DISPENSE /dɪ'spens/
dispenses, dispensing, dispensed

di'spense with ★★ *formal*

to not use or do something because it is not necessary or is no longer useful

dispense with sth *I think we can dispense with the introduction and get straight to the main points.* ♦ *We all know each other, so we can dispense with the formalities* (=not make formal introductions etc). ♦ *We have reluctantly decided to dispense with Porter's services* (=no longer employ him).

DISPOSE /dɪ'spəʊz, American dɪ'spoʊz/
disposes, disposing, disposed

dis'pose of ★★★

1 to get rid of something that you no longer need or want = THROW AWAY

dispose of sth *Please dispose of all litter in the containers provided.*

2 to remove something such as a problem by dealing with it successfully

dispose of sth *Most complaints can be disposed of pretty quickly.*

3 *formal* to kill someone = KILL

dispose of sb *The regime had many ingenious ways of disposing of its opponents.*

4 to defeat someone easily in a game, competition etc = DEFEAT

dispose of sb *Federer disposed of Henman in straight sets.*

DISSOCIATE /dɪ'səʊsɪeɪt, American dɪ'soʊʃi,eɪt/
dissociates, dissociating, dissociated

di'ssociate from

to say that someone is not connected with or not responsible for something and so is not to blame for it

dissociate sb/yourself from sth *The royal spokesperson was anxious to dissociate the monarchy from any involvement in the incident.* ♦ *The prime minister tried to dissociate himself from the foreign secretary's comments.*

DISSOLVE /dɪ'zɒlv, American dɪ'zɑlv/
dissolves, dissolving, dissolved

di'ssolve in

to mix a solid substance with a liquid so that it becomes mixed with the liquid and it seems to disappear into it

dissolve sth in sth *Dissolve the sugar in one tablespoon of water.*

dis'solve into

if you dissolve into something such as tears or laughter, you begin to cry or laugh in an uncontrolled way

dissolve into sth *She dissolved into helpless giggles when she saw his haircut.*

DISTANCE /'dɪstəns/
distances, distancing, distanced

'distance from

to act in a way that shows you are not connected with someone or something, usually because you do not approve of them

distance yourself from sb/sth *The company is trying to distance itself from remarks made by its former director.*

DISTINGUISH /dɪ'stɪŋgwɪʃ/
distinguishes, distinguishing, distinguished

di'stinguish from ★★★

1 to recognize the difference between two or more similar things = TELL FROM

distinguish sth from sth *It's quite difficult to distinguish her voice from her sister's.*

2 to be a feature that makes someone or something clearly different from someone or something else

distinguish sb/sth from sb/sth *There's very little to distinguish it from hundreds of other websites devoted to the subject.*

DIVE /daɪv/
dives, diving, dived *or American* **dove**
/dəʊv, *American* doʊv/, **dived**

,dive 'in *informal*

1 to start doing something in a very
enthusiastic way, especially without
thinking much about it first
   dive in *Sometimes you've just got to take
   a chance and dive in.*
2 to start eating in a very enthusiastic
way = TUCK IN, DIG IN
   dive in *Food's on the table, just dive in!*

DIVERT /daɪˈvɜːt, *American* dɪˈvɜrt,
daɪˈvɜrt/
diverts, diverting, diverted

div'ert from (*also* div,ert a'way from)
to do something to take people's attention
away from something that you do not
want them to concentrate on or notice
   divert sth from sth *The government is
   using the war to divert attention from
   their appalling economic performance.*

DIVEST /daɪˈvest, *American* dɪˈvest,
daɪˈvest/
divests, divesting, divested

div'est of

1 [often passive] *formal* to officially take
away someone's power, position, or
authority = STRIP OF
   be divested of sth *He had been divested
   of all his previous power.*
   divest sb of sth *On 1 March 1198 the
   assembly divested Philip of his title.*
2 *very formal* to take off clothes
   divest yourself of sth *The guests divested
   themselves of their overcoats.*
3 *very formal* to get rid of something, for
example by selling it
   divest yourself of sth *The court ruled
   that she had voluntarily divested herself
   of the property.*

DIVIDE /dɪˈvaɪd/
divides, dividing, divided

di'vide by ★★
if you divide a larger number by a smaller
number, you do a calculation using
mathematics in order to find out how
many times the larger number contains
the smaller one
   divide sth by sth *Divide 24 by 4.* ♦ *I'm
   trying to work out 282 divided by 2.5.*

di'vide into
if you divide a smaller number into a
larger number, you do a calculation using

mathematics in order to find out how
many times the smaller number can be
contained in the larger one
   divide sth into sth *Divide 3 into 9.*
   ♦ *What's 9 divided into 27?*

di,vide 'off
to keep one area separate from another
   divide off sth *also* **divide sth off** *A fence
   divided off the women's section.*

di,vide 'up ★★

1 to separate people or things into smaller
parts or groups = BREAK DOWN
   divide sb/sth up *Even in quite small
   gardens you can divide the available
   space up with walls and hedges.* ♦ **+into**
   *Divide the children up into groups of
   four.*
   divide sb/sth *Different languages
   divide up the colour spectrum differently.*
2 to separate something into smaller
parts and share the parts between people
= SHARE OUT
   divide sth up *His heirs would divide the
   land up after his death.*
   ♦ **+among/between** *Divide the money
   up between the four of you.*
   divide up sth *There was a secret pact for
   dividing up Europe in 1940.*

DIVORCE /dɪˈvɔːs, *American* dɪˈvɔrs/
divorces, divorcing, divorced

be di'vorced from
to be completely separated from
something else and have no connection
with it at all
   be divorced from sth *Politics should not
   be divorced from ordinary people's lives.*
   ♦ *I'm afraid his thinking is completely
   divorced from reality.*

DIVVY /ˈdɪvi/
divvies, divvying, divvied

,divvy 'up *informal*
to divide or share something such as
money or profits between people
   divvy up sth *also* **divvy sth up** *He says
   he'll divvy up the winnings.*
   divvy up *It's time to divvy up – let's see
   how much money we've made.*

DO /duː, *American* du/
does /dəz, dʌz/, **doing, did** /dɪd/, **done**
/dʌn/

,do a'bout ★★★
to do something to help deal with a
situation or solve a problem
   do sth about sth *My son started taking
   drugs and I couldn't do anything*

about it. ♦ *We should recognize the problem and then try to* **do something about it.** ♦ *The doctor said he* **couldn't do much about** *the swelling.*

'do as

PHRASE **do as sb asks/says/suggests** to do what someone asks you to do or what they say or suggest you should do: *Do as I say or there'll be trouble.* ♦ *I'll do as you suggest and see if it works.*

,do a'way with ★★

1 to get rid of something = ABOLISH, ELIMINATE ≠ KEEP, RETAIN
do away with sth *If we do away with the monarchy, what will we have in its place?* ♦ *I think we should do away with private education once and for all.* ♦ *A lot of the restrictions on imports have already been done away with.*

2 do away with or **do in** *informal* to murder someone = BUMP OFF, MURDER
do away with sb *There were rumours that Doug had done away with his wife.*

,do 'down *British*

informal to criticize someone in a way that makes them seem stupid or unsuccessful = *formal* DISPARAGE
do sb down *also* **do down sb** *Why are you always doing your kids down?*
do yourself down *You mustn't do yourself down – you have a lot of ability.*

'do for

1 [usually with a negative] *informal* to make someone feel interested or excited
do sth for sb *Ken wants to buy a new Porsche, but sports cars* **don't do anything for** *me.*

2 *British old-fashioned* to regularly clean someone else's house and cook for them
do for sb *Mrs Bradley used to come in twice a week to do for us.*

,be 'done for ★ *informal*

1 to be likely to be punished, hurt, or killed
be done for *If the guards see us, we're done for.*

2 if something is done for, it is in such bad condition or so badly damaged that it cannot be used
be done for *We're going to have to buy a new photocopier – that one's done for.*

3 *old-fashioned* to be so tired that you cannot continue
be done for *I'm afraid Oates is pretty well done for – he can't walk any farther.*

,do 'in *informal*

1 *same as* **do away with 2**

2 [usually passive] to feel very tired
be done in *I'm completely done in after all that running around.*
do sb in *It was climbing that last hill that really did them in.*

,do 'out *British*

1 *informal* to make a room, cupboard, or drawer thoroughly tidy and clean = CLEAR OUT
do out sth *also* **do sth out** *While I'm down here, I'll do out these cupboards.* ♦ *The cleaner's coming to do the big room out.*

2 to decorate a room in a particular way = DECORATE
do sth out in sth *They've had their kitchen done out in light wood and blue tiles.*

,do 'out of *informal*

to stop someone from getting or having something that they should have, especially in a way that is unfair or dishonest
do sb out of sth *That guy at the garage did me out of £50 last night.* ♦ *We've got a letter from a widow who claims she's been done out of her pension.*

,do 'over *informal*

1 [often passive] *British* to illegally enter someone's house, steal things from it, and cause a lot of damage
be done over *As soon as I opened the door, I could see the place had been done over.*
do sth over *also* **do over sth** *Someone did their house over last night.*

2 *British* to attack someone and hit and kick them = BEAT UP
do sb over *also* **do over sb** *A gang of kids did him over on the way back from school.*

3 *mainly American* to decorate a building or room again in a completely different way
do sth over *also* **do over sth** *Can we afford to have the house done over?*

'do to ★★★

to affect someone in a way that makes them happy, sad, or excited
do sth to sb *When I hear that song, it always does something to me.*

,do 'up ★★

1	improve sth old
2	tie/arrange hair
3	be dressed
4	fasten sth
5	how sth fastens

1 *British* to repair, paint, and improve an old building, car, boat etc
do sth up *It's a lovely cottage, but we need to do it up a bit.*
do up sth *We spent our weekends doing up a 1934 Rolls Royce.*

2 [usually passive] to tie or arrange your hair in a particular way
be done up *Her shiny dark hair was done up in a ponytail.*

3 [often passive] to dress yourself in very nice clothes or put make-up on your face in order to look attractive
be done up *Angie was done up in a silky black dress and fishnet stockings.*
do yourself up *She had spent hours doing herself up for the party.*

4 to fasten something = FASTEN ≠ UNDO —*picture* → PUT ON
do sth up *Do up your shoelaces.*
do sth up *You don't need to do the top button up.*

5 if clothes do up in a particular way, they fasten in that way
do up *The dress does up at the back.*

'do with ★★★

1 used for asking what arrangements someone makes for something
do with sth *What do you usually do with the cat when you're away?*

2 used for asking where someone puts something
do with sth *'What have you done with my calculator?' 'I put it on your desk.'*

3 used for asking how someone uses something
do with sth *What am I going to do with all this food if no one turns up?*
PHRASES **could do with sth** *informal* used for saying that you want or need something: *I could do with a drink.* ♦ *I'm sure James could do with some help.*
have/be nothing to do with sb/sth
1 to not be connected with or caused by someone or something: *I'm sure Nancy's resignation has nothing to do with her health.* **2** used for saying that something is personal and private and there is no reason for someone to know about it or be involved in it: *What I do in my own time has nothing to do with you!*
have/be (sth) to do with sb/sth to be connected with someone or something: *Most of the articles have to do with America's role in the world since the end of the Cold War.* ♦ *Was the dispute anything to do with safety regulations?*
what sb does with themselves used for asking how someone spends their time:

What are you going to do with yourself during the school holidays? ♦ *He won't know what to do with himself while Julie is gone.*
what has sth (got) to do with...? used for asking, often in an angry way, how two people or things are connected or why someone is interested in something: *What have her personal problems got to do with my holiday plans?* ♦ *As a matter of fact I do have a boyfriend, but what's that got to do with you?*
what is sb doing with sth? *informal* used for asking why someone has something: *What are you doing with my trainers? I never said you could borrow them.*
what sb is going to do with sb *informal* used for asking how you are going to make someone behave better: *I don't know what we're going to do with you, Tony. You're always in trouble.*

'do with'out ★★

to succeed in living or working without someone or something = GO WITHOUT
do without *There's no more milk, so I guess we'll just have to do without.*
do without sth *Now that they have a regular income, they should be able to do without any help from us.*
do without sb *You'll be gone for six days? I think we can do without you for that long.*
PHRASE **can/could do without sth** *informal* used for saying that something is annoying you and causing problems for you: *I could do without all these interruptions.*

DOB /dɒb, *American* dɑb/
dobs, dobbing, dobbed

dob 'in *informal old-fashioned*
to tell someone such as a parent or teacher about something bad that someone else has done = TELL ON, GRASS ON
dob sb in *We knew the others would dob us in.*

DOLE /dəʊl, *American* doʊl/
doles, doling, doled

dole 'out *informal*
to give something such as food or money to a particular group of people or to every person in a group
dole out sth *also* **dole sth out** *The government has agreed to dole out an additional £5 million to schools.*

DOLL /dɒl, *American* dɑl/
dolls, dolling, dolled

ˌdoll ˈup *informal*
to make yourself look attractive for a
special occasion = DRESS UP, DO UP
doll yourself up *We used to doll ourselves
up and go into town.*
be/get dolled up *She's all dolled up for
the office Christmas party.*

DOOM /duːm, *American* dum/
dooms, dooming, doomed

be ˈdoomed to
to be certain to experience something such
as failure or unhappiness
be doomed to sth *The project was
doomed to failure from the start.*
♦ *With the loss of so many habitats,
hundreds of species were doomed to
extinction.*

DOPE /dəʊp, *American* doʊp/
dopes, doping, doped

ˌdope ˈup *informal*
to give someone a drug in order to take
away their pain or make them sleep
dope sb up *They've doped her up quite
heavily because she was in such pain.*

DOSE /dəʊs, *American* doʊs/
doses, dosing, dosed

ˌdose ˈup with [often passive]
to give an amount of a legal drug to
someone in order to make them sleep or
feel better
be dosed up with sth *Most of the patients
here are dosed up with sedatives.* ♦ *I had
flu and was dosed up to the eyeballs
with paracetamol.*
dose yourself up with sth *I used to dose
myself up with Valium every day.*

DOSS /dɒs, *American* dɑs/
dosses, dossing, dossed

ˌdoss aˈround (*also* ˌ**doss aˈbout**) *British
informal*
to spend time in a place in a lazy way,
doing very little
doss around sth *We spent the weekend
dossing around the house.*
doss around *He's just been dossing
around for the last year.*

ˌdoss ˈdown *British informal*
to sleep somewhere = BED DOWN, KIP DOWN
doss down *Is it ok if I doss down here
tonight?*

DOT /dɒt, *American* dɑt/
dots, dotting, dotted

be ˌdotted aˈround (*also* **be ˌdotted
aˈbout** *British*)
to exist or be present in several places
around an area, especially with a fairly
large amount of space in between
be dotted around sth *The company has
more than thirty branches dotted around
Spain.*
be dotted around *There may be one or
two farmhouses dotted around, but there
are no villages.*

ˈdot with
to cover a surface with small amounts of
something in different places
dot sth with sth *Dot the top of the pie
with butter then put it in the oven.*

be ˈdotted with
if an area is dotted with something, it
exists in several parts of the area
be dotted with sth *There was a large
lawn that was dotted with fruit trees.*

DOTE /dəʊt, *American* doʊt/
dotes, doting, doted

ˈdote on
to love someone very much, often so much
that you do not notice their faults
dote on sb *She absolutely dotes on the
grandchildren.*

DOUBLE /ˈdʌb(ə)l/
doubles, doubling, doubled

ˈdouble as (*also* ˌ**double ˈup as**)
to have a second use or purpose
double as sth *In the corner was an old
sofa that doubled as Simon's bed.*

ˌdouble ˈback
to turn and go back in the direction that
you have just come from
double back *We doubled back through
the fields to the village.*
double back on yourself *When you get
to the roundabout, you need to double
back on yourself.*

ˈdouble for
to take the place of an actor by pretending
to be them in difficult or dangerous parts
of a film
double for sb *He doubled for Roger
Moore in the film Octopussy.*

ˌdouble ˈover
1 [usually passive] to fold something so that
one surface lies flat against the other
be doubled over *The map on his desk*

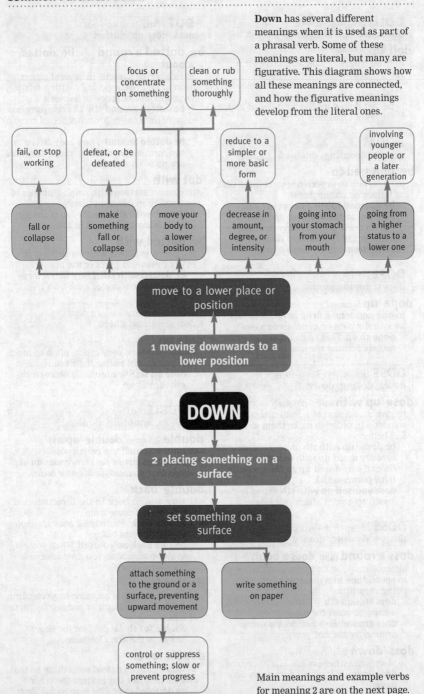

Down has several different meanings when it is used as part of a phrasal verb. Some of these meanings are literal, but many are figurative. This diagram shows how all these meanings are connected, and how the figurative meanings develop from the literal ones.

focus or concentrate on something

clean or rub something thoroughly

fail, or stop working

defeat, or be defeated

reduce to a simpler or more basic form

involving younger people or a later generation

fall or collapse

make something fall or collapse

move your body to a lower position

decrease in amount, degree, or intensity

going into your stomach from your mouth

going from a higher status to a lower one

move to a lower place or position

1 moving downwards to a lower position

DOWN

2 placing something on a surface

set something on a surface

attach something to the ground or a surface, preventing upward movement

write something on paper

control or suppress something; slow or prevent progress

Main meanings and example verbs for meaning 2 are on the next page.

Main meanings	Example verbs		
1 moving downwards to a lower position			
move to a lower place or position *The rain's really **coming down** out there.* ♦ *You'd better **get down** before Mum sees you.*	bucket down climb down come down	fall down get down go down	pelt down pour down touch down
fall or collapse *The old house just **fell down**.*	blow down break down	burn down come down	fall down tumble down
make something fall or collapse *A black sports car nearly **ran** her **down**.* ♦ *Giant bulldozers were **tearing down** the old apartment block.*	batter down beat down blow down break down bring down	burn down chop down cut down knock down mow down	pull down run down shoot down take down tear down
fail, or stop working *Many businesses have had to **shut down**.* ♦ *The car just **broke down** on the motorway.*	break down close down	fall down go down	run down shut down
defeat, or be defeated *The committee quickly **voted down** the proposal.* ♦ *Ed **backed down** when we confronted him.*	back down bow down break down bring down	do down drag down howl down shoot down	shout down stand down vote down wear down
move your body to a lower position *Please **sit down** – I want to talk to you.* ♦ *I'm just going to **lie down** for a few minutes.*	bed down bend down bow down flop down	hunker down kneel down lie down plop down	plump down put down sink down sit down
focus or concentrate on something *It's about time we **got down** to work.*	buckle down get down to	knuckle down	settle down
clean or rub something thoroughly ***Wipe down** the cooker when you've finished.*	brush down clean down	hose down rub down	wash down wipe down
decrease in amount, degree, or intensity *You should really **cut down** on the amount of fat you eat.* ♦ *Could you **turn** the volume **down**?*	boil down calm down cool down cut down dampen down die down drive down mark down	melt down narrow down play down quieten down round down run down scale down simmer down	slim down slow down thin down tone down turn down water down wear down whittle down
reduce to a simpler or more basic form *Critics complain that reporters are **dumbing down** the news.* ♦ *What it **boils down to** is that we need more money.*	boil down boil down to	break down dumb down	pare down strip down
going into your stomach from your mouth *He quickly **wolfed down** the sandwich.* ♦ *She can't **keep down** anything she eats.*	bolt down drink down gobble down	go down gulp down keep down	stay down wash down wolf down
going from a higher status to a lower one *The court **handed down** a four-year sentence.* ♦ *I wish you wouldn't **talk down to** me.*	hand down look down on	put down step down	talk down to trickle down
involving younger people or a later generation *The traditions **are handed down** from father to son.*	come down	hand down	pass down

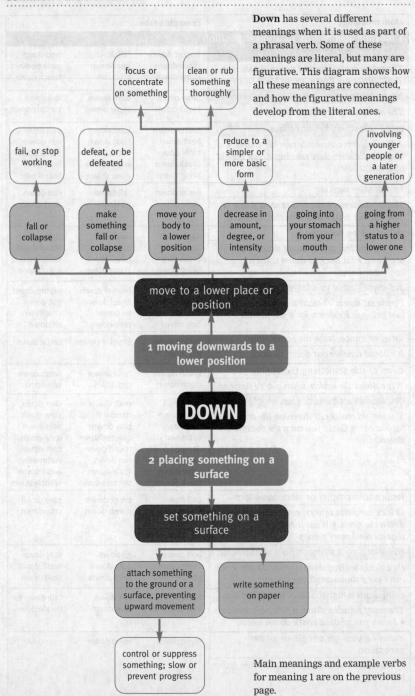

Down has several different meanings when it is used as part of a phrasal verb. Some of these meanings are literal, but many are figurative. This diagram shows how all these meanings are connected, and how the figurative meanings develop from the literal ones.

focus or concentrate on something

clean or rub something thoroughly

fail, or stop working

defeat, or be defeated

reduce to a simpler or more basic form

involving younger people or a later generation

fall or collapse

make something fall or collapse

move your body to a lower position

decrease in amount, degree, or intensity

going into your stomach from your mouth

going from a higher status to a lower one

move to a lower place or position

1 moving downwards to a lower position

DOWN

2 placing something on a surface

set something on a surface

attach something to the ground or a surface, preventing upward movement

write something on paper

control or suppress something; slow or prevent progress

Main meanings and example verbs for meaning 1 are on the previous page.

Main meanings	Example verbs		
2 placing something on a surface			
set something on a surface *Put your pencils **down**. ♦ You can set that tray **down** over there.*	bang down lay down	plunk down put down	set down throw down
attach something to the ground or a surface, preventing upward movement *Why did they **nail down** the furniture? ♦ You'd better **tie** that stuff **down** or it will fall off.*	nail down pin down	tamp down tie down	weigh down weight down
control or suppress something; slow or prevent progress *Authorities **are cracking down** on drug dealers. ♦ I'm not going to let a bad loss **keep** me **down**.*	bog down clamp down come down on	crack down hold down keep down	pin down slap down tie down
write something on paper *Can you **write down** your name for me? ♦ These are just a few notes I **jotted down**.*	copy down get down jot down mark down	note down put down scribble down set down	stick down take down write down

was doubled over so I couldn't see it.

2 double over or **double up** [often passive]
to suddenly bend forwards, because you
are in pain or because you are laughing a
lot = BEND OVER
> **be doubled over** *Steve was doubled over
> holding his knee.* ♦ *She was **doubled
> over with pain**.*
> **double over** *Frank **doubled over** with
> laughter, wiping tears from his eyes.*

,double 'up ★

1 *same as* **double over 2**

2 if two people double up, they share
something, especially a bedroom
> **double up** *The children won't mind
> doubling up.*

,double 'up as *same as* **double as**

DOZE /dəʊz, *American* doʊz/
dozes, dozing, dozed

,doze 'off ★

to go to sleep for a short time, especially
when you are not in bed and without
intending to = FALL ASLEEP ≠ WAKE UP
> **doze off** *I dozed off in front of the
> television.*

DRAFT /drɑːft, *American* dræft/
drafts, drafting, drafted

,draft 'in (*also* **,draft 'into**) [usually passive]
to bring someone into a team or group of
people in order to help them do something
> **be drafted in** *Extra police officers have
> been drafted in.* ♦ **+to do sth** *Various
> sports personalities have been drafted in
> to boost their bid to host the Olympics.*
> **be drafted into sth** *Tsai was drafted into
> the Taiwan team after the regular player
> was omitted.*

DRAG /dræg/
drags, dragging, dragged

Drag is often used with adverbs and
prepositions when it means 'to pull
someone or something along with
difficulty', for example because they are
heavy': *Police **dragged away** a handful
of protesters.* ♦ *Three men attacked him
and tried to **drag** him **into** an alley.*
♦ *The prisoners were **dragged through**
the streets in front of jeering crowds.*
These uses are not included here.

,drag a'way

to make someone leave a place when they
would prefer to stay, or stop doing
something when they would prefer to
continue to do it = TEAR AWAY, DRAG OFF

> **drag sb away from sth** *If you could drag
> yourself away from that computer for a
> second, I could do with some help here!*

,drag 'by

if time drags by, it seems to pass very
slowly
> **drag by** *The minutes seemed to drag by.*

,drag 'down ★

1 to make someone have a lower social
position or worse standards of behaviour,
so that other people lose respect for them
> **drag sb down** *If you're not careful he'll
> end up dragging you down with him.*
> ♦ *Don't let yourself be **dragged down to
> her level**.*

2 to make someone feel unhappy or less
hopeful
> **drag sb/sth down** *I don't mean to drag
> you down with all my problems.*
> **drag down sb/sth** *The conversation was
> dragging down her spirits.*

,drag 'in (*also* **,drag 'into**)

1 to start talking about someone or
something that is not connected with
what you are discussing and that other
people do not want to talk about
> **drag in sth** *also* **drag sth in** *He seemed
> determined to drag in irrelevant details
> about my personal life.*
> **drag sb/sth into sth** *Don't start
> dragging my mother into this!*

2 to make someone become involved in a
situation when they do not want to be
involved = SUCK IN ≠ EXCLUDE
> **drag sb in** *also* **drag in sb** *I don't know
> anything about the project, so don't try
> and drag me in.*
> **drag sb into sth** *We don't want them
> dragging us into another war.* ♦ *Don't
> try and drag me into this!*

,drag 'off

to make someone leave a place, especially
when they do not want to = DRAG AWAY
> **drag sb off** *His girlfriend turned up and
> dragged him off somewhere.*

,drag 'on

to continue for longer than you want or
think is necessary
> **drag on** *This affair does seem to have
> dragged on, doesn't it?* ♦ **+for** *Some trials
> drag on for years.*

,drag 'out

to make something continue for longer
than necessary = EXTEND ≠ CUT SHORT
> **drag out sth** *also* **drag sth out** *They
> dragged out the meeting endlessly.*

ˌdrag ˈout of

to force or persuade someone to tell you
something when they do not want to
> **drag sth out of sb** *He only told me her
> name, and I had to drag that out of him.*

ˌdrag ˈup

to start talking about something when it
is not necessary, usually something
unpleasant that happened in the past and
that other people want to forget
> **drag up sth** *also* **drag sth up** *Must you
> drag up that old argument?*

DRAGOON /drəˈguːn, *American*
drəˈgun/
dragoons, dragooning, dragooned

draˈgoon into

to make someone do something that they
do not want to, often in a way that
seems unfair to them
> **dragoon sb into (doing) sth** *She spent
> most of her time trying to dragoon the
> village women into attending
> philosophical lectures.* ♦ *I was dragooned
> into helping at the school fundraising
> day.*

DRAIN /dreɪn/
drains, draining, drained

ˌdrain ˈoff (*also* ˌdrain aˈway)

to flow away from something, or let liquid
flow away
> **drain off** *Allow the liquid from the can
> to drain off before cooking the beans.*
> **drain off sth** *also* **drain sth off** *Drain off
> any excess oil.*

DRAW /drɔː, *American* drɔ/
draws, drawing, drew /druː, *American*
druː/, **drawn** /drɔːn, *American* drɔn/

ˌdraw aˈway

to move away from a person or place
= PULL AWAY ≠ APPROACH
> **draw away** *People started waving as the
> train drew away.* ♦ **+from** *Ann suddenly
> drew away from me.*

ˌdraw ˈback ★

1 to move backwards and away from
someone or something ≠ APPROACH
> **draw back** *She drew back in horror.*

2 to pull something such as a curtain into
an open position
> **draw sth back** *Draw the curtains back
> and let some light in.*
> **draw back sth** *They heard the sound of
> a bolt being drawn back.*

draw back

ˌdraw ˈdown *business*

to reduce an amount of money by using it
> **draw down sth** *Some firms have dealt
> with the problem by drawing down their
> cash reserves.*

ˈdraw from

to get ideas, information, or knowledge
from something
> **draw sth from sth** *She drew inspiration
> for her stories from her childhood.* ♦ *I
> drew little encouragement from his
> remarks.*

ˌdraw ˈin

1 when the nights or days draw in, it gets
dark earlier in the evening because
autumn is starting = CLOSE IN ≠ DRAW OUT
> **draw in** *It was that time of year when the
> nights seemed to draw in quickly.*

2 **draw in** or **draw into** if a vehicle draws
in or draws into a place, it arrives in that
place = ARRIVE, PULL IN ≠ DRAW OUT, PULL
OUT
> **draw in** *Someone was waving as the car
> drew in.*
> **draw into sth** *The train drew into the
> station.*

3 **draw in** or **draw into** [often passive] to
involve someone in a conversation or
situation, often when they do not want to
be involved = INVOLVE
> **be/get drawn in** *The remark was
> directed at me, but I refused to be drawn
> in.* ♦ *We do not want to get drawn into a
> long and expensive conflict.*
> **draw sb in** *also* **draw in sb** *Her low,
> musical voice soon drew in her listeners.*

4 **draw in** or **draw into** to take something
such as air into your body
> **draw in sth** *also* **draw sth in** *He drew in
> a deep breath.*
> **draw sth into sth** *She drew the smoke
> deep into her lungs.*
> **PHRASE draw in your horns** to start

spending less money than you usually do: *We're going to have to draw in our horns a bit now that you're unemployed again.*

,draw 'off

to take some of the liquid out of something = SIPHON OFF

draw off sth *also* **draw sth off** *Doctors drew off over a litre of fluid from his lungs.*

'draw on ★★★

1 draw on or **draw upon** to use part of something that you have gradually gained or saved

draw on sth *As an actor, you often draw on your own life experiences.* ♦ *Your body draws on its reserves of fat during the times when you are fasting.*

2 to put a cigarette between your lips and suck smoke from it

draw on sth *She drew heavily on her cigarette, searching for the words.*

3 [often passive] to take money from a bank account by writing a cheque

be drawn on sth *He paid with a cheque drawn on his company's account.*

draw sth on sth *As soon as the payment reaches your account you will be able to draw cheques on it.*

,draw 'out ★★

1 to make something continue longer than usual = PROLONG ≠ CUT SHORT

draw out sth *This action could draw the dispute out for another six months.*

draw sth out *People with southern accents tend to draw their vowels out.*

2 if a vehicle draws out or draws out of a place, it moves out of that place = LEAVE, PULL OUT ≠ DRAW IN, PULL IN

draw out *The 9.30 to Oxford was just drawing out as we got to the platform.* ♦ *+of Slowly the train drew out of the station.*

3 to encourage someone to talk more by making them feel more relaxed and confident

draw sb out *I tried to put him at his ease, but it still wasn't easy to draw him out.*

4 when the nights or days draw out, it becomes light earlier because spring is starting ≠ CLOSE IN, DRAW IN

draw out *The worst of the weather is behind us and the days are drawing out.*

,draw 'up ★★★

1 to prepare and write something such as a document or plan = DRAFT

draw sth up *Can you draw the contract up by tomorrow?*

draw up sth *Guidelines have been drawn up for dealing with emergencies.*

> Nouns often used as objects with **draw up 1**
>
> ■ budget, constitution, contract, guidelines, list, plan, proposal, schedule, shortlist, timetable

2 if a vehicle draws up, it arrives at a place and stops = PULL UP

draw up *A taxi drew up outside the hotel.*

PHRASES draw up a chair to move your chair so that you are sitting closer to someone or something: *She came in and drew up a chair beside us.*

draw yourself up to stand up very straight so that you look as tall as possible, because you want to impress or frighten someone: *He drew himself up to his full height and glared at me.*

'draw upon *same as* **draw on**

DREAM /driːm, *American* drim/ **dreams, dreaming, dreamed** or **dreamt** /dremt/

,dream a'way

to spend your time thinking pleasant thoughts but not really achieving anything

dream away sth *also* **dream sth away** *I don't concentrate properly in class. I just dream away the time.* ♦ *She just dreams her life away at home.*

'dream of ★★★

to think about something that you would very much like to do, have, or achieve

dream of sth *They have wealth that ordinary people could only dream of.*

dream of doing sth *I used to dream of being a movie star.*

PHRASE wouldn't dream of doing sth used for emphasizing that you definitely would not do something: *I wouldn't dream of telling you how to do your job!*

,dream 'on [always in imperative] *impolite* used for telling someone that you think there is no chance that something that they have just mentioned will happen

dream on *If you think she's going to agree to that, dream on!*

,dream 'up ★★

to think of a new idea or plan, especially one that is silly or unusual = COME UP WITH

dream up sth *Whoever dreamt up that idea?* ♦ *It was stranger than anything I could have dreamed up.*

dream sth up *The theory must have*

sounded wonderful to the people who dreamed it up.

DREDGE /dredʒ/
dredges, dredging, dredged

ˌdredge ˈup
1 to tell people about something that someone did in the past that they would prefer to keep secret = DIG UP ≠ BURY
dredge sth up *also* **dredge up sth** *Details of his previous affairs were dredged up by the media.*
2 to remember with difficulty something that you learned or knew long ago = RECALL
dredge up sth *also* **dredge sth up** *He dredged up an old song from somewhere deep in his memory.*

DRESS /dres/
dresses, dressing, dressed

ˌdress ˈdown
to wear clothes that are less formal than the clothes that you usually wear ≠ DRESS UP
dress down *It's not the kind of place where you can dress down for work.*
■ ˌdressing-ˈdown **noun** **PHRASE** **give sb a dressing-down** to speak angrily to someone because they have done something wrong = SCOLD: *He's upstairs being given a dressing-down.*

ˈdress for
to put on clothes that are suitable for a particular occasion or situation
dress for sth *We hadn't thought to dress for such cold weather.* ♦ *I see you've all dressed for the occasion.*

ˌdress ˈup ★★★
1 to put on special clothes that make you look like someone else, especially for fun—*picture* → PUT ON
dress up *All children love dressing up.*
♦ **+as** *They had dressed up as princes and princesses.*
dress sb up *She dresses that child up like a little doll.*
2 to put on clothes that are more formal than the clothes that you usually wear
dress up *Jonah had obviously made an effort to dress up for the occasion.*
3 to make something seem more impressive than it really is
dress sth up *He tries to dress it up, but he's basically a waiter.*
dress up sth *The actual events were so dramatic in themselves that it seems a little unnecessary to dress up the facts in this way.*

■ ˌdressed ˈup **adj** **1** wearing formal clothes: *Why are you dressed up? Are you going somewhere special?* **2** something that is dressed up is made to look better than it really is: *This is an average performance dressed up as some fantastic achievement.*

■ ˌdressing-ˈup **noun** [U] *British* the children's game of putting on different clothes and pretending to be someone else: *She pulled another shirt out of the dressing-up box.*

DRIFT /drɪft/
drifts, drifting, drifted

ˌdrift aˈpart
if two or more people drift apart, their relationship gradually ends = GROW APART
drift apart *We used to share a room at college, but we drifted apart over the years.*

ˌdrift ˈoff
to gradually go to sleep
drift off *I was just drifting off when the door slammed.*

DRILL /drɪl/
drills, drilling, drilled

ˈdrill in
to teach someone something by making them repeat it a lot of times until they know it thoroughly
drill sb in sth *She spent the rest of the afternoon drilling us in the new safety procedures.* ♦ *They had all been thoroughly drilled in the correct thing to say.*

ˌdrill ˈinto [often passive]
to make someone learn or understand something by telling them about it many times = DRUM INTO, DIN INTO
be drilled into sb *Not to talk to strangers is something that is drilled into children from an early age.*
drill sth into sb *If you do something you should never do it half-heartedly. My parents drilled that into us when we were young.*

DRINK /drɪŋk/
drinks, drinking, drank /dræŋk/, drunk /drʌŋk/

ˌdrink ˈdown
to drink all of something, especially quickly = DOWN
drink sth down *also* **drink down sth** *She made a face but drank the medicine down.* ♦ *He silently drank down his beer.*

,drink 'in

to experience something with great
enjoyment
drink in sth *also* **drink sth in** *Sit out on
the terrace and drink in the stunning
view.*

'drink to

to wish for health, happiness, or success
for someone or something, and then lift
your glass and drink from it
drink to sb/sth *Then we all drank to
John and wished him luck on his
expedition.*
drink sth to sb/sth *Let's all drink a
toast to the bride and groom.*
PHRASE **I'll drink to that** *informal* used
for saying that you strongly agree with
what someone has said: *'I don't think I
want to die yet'. 'I'll drink to that', I
laughed.*

,drink 'up ★

to drink all of your drink
drink up *Drink up, everyone: it's time to
go.*
drink up sth *She quickly drank up her
milk.*
drink sth up *We drank the last of the
wine up and left the restaurant.*

DRIP /drɪp/
drip, dripping, dripped

'drip with [always progressive]

1 if you are dripping with a liquid, it is
running off you in small drops
be dripping with sth *The temperature
rose and I was **dripping with sweat**.*

2 *showing disapproval* to have a lot of a
particular quality or thing
be dripping with sth *She was dripping
with expensive jewellery.* ♦ *He wrote a
review of the book that was dripping
with sarcasm.*

DRIVE /draɪv/
drives, driving, drove /drəʊv, *American*
droʊv/, **driven** /'drɪv(ə)n/

Drive is often used with adverbs and
prepositions when it means 'to control a
vehicle so that it moves somewhere': *We
decided to **drive to** the airport.* ♦ *The
truck reversed and **drove back down** the
road.* ♦ *He **drove** his car **into** a tree.* These
uses are not included here.

'drive at
PHRASE **what sb is driving at** what someone
is really trying to say: *I can see now
what you're driving at.* ♦ *I've read his
book, but I'm still not sure what he's
driving at.*

,drive a'way ★

to make someone stop wanting something
or stop wanting to be with someone
drive sb away *Peter's behaviour was
driving his wife away.* ♦ *I don't want to
drive you away with impossible
demands.*
drive away sb *Increasing prices will only
drive away customers.*

,drive 'back [usually passive]

if something drives you back, it forces you
to stop trying to reach a person or place
and move back
be driven back *They were driven back
by police gunfire.*

,drive 'down ★

to make a price or amount fall to a lower
level = BRING DOWN ≠ DRIVE UP
drive down sth *Fierce competition
among restaurants has driven down
prices.*
drive sth down *The aim is to drive
unemployment down.* ♦ *If your blood
pressure is high, special drugs can drive
it down.*

,drive 'off ★

1 if a vehicle or driver drives off, the
vehicle starts moving and leaves = MOVE
OFF
drive off *They stood and waved as we
drove off.*

2 [often passive] to force people or animals
to go away, especially when they are
attacking or threatening you
be driven off *Invaders were driven off or
captured.*
drive sb off *The burglars had tried to
enter by a side gate, but the dogs had
driven them off.*
drive off sb *A herd of cattle can drive off
wolves.*

,drive 'on

to continue driving
drive on *When I give you the instruction,
I want you to drive on.* ♦ *Let's drive on a
bit further.*

,drive 'out ★★ [often passive]

to force someone or something to leave a
place = *formal* EXPEL
be driven out of sth *They were driven
out of their homes.*
drive sb out *Government forces have
driven the rebels out.* ♦ *Demonstrators
broke into the embassy compound but
troops later drove them out.*
drive out sb *A priest was invited to the
house to drive out evil spirits.*

'drive to [often passive]

to force someone into a bad state, or into behaviour that is dangerous or harmful

be driven to sth *People are being driven to violence by police action.*

drive sb to sth *His behaviour eventually drove her to drink.*

PHRASE **drive sb to distraction** *informal* to annoy someone by doing something repeatedly over a period of time: *The way the kids behave drives me to distraction.*

drive 'up ★

1 if a vehicle or driver drives up, the vehicle moves near to a person or place and stops

drive up *A huge Rolls Royce drove up.* ♦ **+to** *Drive up to the gates, and they will open automatically.*

2 to make a price or amount rise to a higher level = PUSH UP ≠ DRIVE DOWN

drive up sth *The government's policies are driving up interest rates.*

drive sth up *The crisis in policing is driving crime up.* ♦ *We need to maintain current standards or even drive them up.*

DRIVEL /'drɪv(ə)l/
drivels, drivelling, drivelled

drivel 'on *informal*

to talk for a long time about stupid or unimportant things = BANG ON, DRONE ON

drivel on *I knew he would drivel on for another twenty minutes.* ♦ **+about** *She started drivelling on about happiness.*

DRONE /drəʊn, *American* droʊn/
drones, droning, droned

drone 'on

to talk about something for a long time in a very boring way and in a very boring voice = BANG ON, DRIVEL ON

drone on *I wish he'd stop droning on.* ♦ **+about** *He droned on about America's importance in the world.*

DROOL /druːl, *American* drul/
drools, drooling, drooled

'drool over *informal*

to look at someone or something in a foolish way that shows you desire them very much or find them very attractive

drool over sth/sb *The boys were all drooling over her.*

DROP /drɒp, *American* drɑp/
drops, dropping, dropped

drop a'way

1 to become smaller in amount or number

drop away *Support for him has begun to drop away.* ♦ *As time went on customers began to drop away.*

2 if the ground drops away, it slopes downwards = FALL AWAY

drop away *The land drops steeply away into a small valley.*

drop 'back ★

1 to fall to a lower amount or value

drop back *Inflation dropped back a little last year.* ♦ *The temperature had dropped back a few degrees.* ♦ **+to** *Economic growth will drop back to 3% this year.*

2 drop back or **drop behind** to move into a lower position in a race or competition = FALL BEHIND

drop back *He dropped back towards the end of the race and finished in sixth place.*

3 drop back or **drop behind** to move more slowly than other people so that you are behind them = FALL BEHIND

drop back *Alex dropped back to let me pass.*

drop be'hind same as **drop back 2, 3**

drop 'by *informal*

to make a short visit somewhere = DROP ROUND, POP IN

drop by *I'll drop by and see you on my way home.* ♦ **+for** *Why don't you drop by for coffee some time?*

drop 'in ★

1 to make a short visit somewhere, usually without making a formal arrangement in advance = POP IN, VISIT, CALL IN

drop in *I dropped in to see how he was.* ♦ **+on** *She often drops in on me for a chat.* ♦ **+at** *I dropped in at the newspaper office to speak to him.*

2 to take something to a place and not stay there very long = DROP OFF

drop sth in *I'll drop those photos in later.* ♦ **+to** *I'll drop the book in to you later.*

■ **drop-in centre** /'drɒp ɪn ˌsentə/ noun [C] a place where people can go to get information or help without having to make an arrangement first: *The town has just opened a new drop-in centre for young people.*

,drop 'off ★★

1	take sb in car
2	take sth somewhere
3	became weaker/smaller
4	sleep
5	stop being attached

1 to take someone to a place in a car, usually without getting out of the car yourself
drop sb off *Can you drop the kids off at school this morning?* ♦ *Gary dropped me off outside her house.*
drop off sb *I'm going to Gill's house to drop off my mother.*

2 to take something to a place and not stay there very long = DELIVER, DROP IN
drop sth off *Can I drop the documents off later?* ♦ *Your sweater's here. Jon dropped it off when you were out.*
drop off sth *She'll drop off the posters for you to have a look at.*

3 to become weaker or smaller in amount = FALL OFF
drop off *Her popularity has dropped off recently.* ♦ *Your energy levels tend to drop off in the middle of the afternoon.*

4 *informal* to start to sleep = DOZE OFF, NOD OFF, FALL ASLEEP ≠ WAKE UP
drop off *He usually drops off in front of the telly.*

5 to stop being fixed to something and fall to the ground
drop off *The exhaust on my car dropped off when I was driving home.*

drop off

■ **'drop-off** adj used about the time or place that you deliver something somewhere: *We agreed on a drop-off point.*

■ **'drop-off** noun [singular] a reduction in the amount or level of something: *We often see a drop-off in business during the winter season.*

,drop 'out ★★

1 to leave college or university before you have finished your course
drop out *She dropped out after the first term.* ♦ **+of** *Too many students drop out of college after only one year.*

2 to stop taking part in an activity or a competition before it has finished ≠ CARRY ON
drop out *She was injured in the first round and had to drop out.*

3 to decide not to have an ordinary job or life because you do not want to be part of society
drop out *He decided to drop out and spend his life travelling.*

■ **dropout** /'drɒpaʊt, *American* 'drɑpˌaʊt/ noun [C] **1** someone who leaves school or college without finishing their course of study: *He was determined not to become just another dropout.* **2** someone who does not live like most people because they do not agree with society's values: *Long hair was the trademark of the hippy and the dropout.*

,drop 'round British informal

to make a short visit to someone who lives near you, often without arranging it formally in advance
drop round *The children drop round to see her occasionally.*

DROWN /draʊn/
drowns, drowning, drowned

'drown in

to cover something completely in a liquid, especially in a way that spoils it
drown sth in sth *If you cook potatoes properly you don't have to drown them in butter.*

,drown 'out ★

to prevent a sound from being heard by making a louder noise = HOWL DOWN
drown out sth/sb *The music almost drowned out the sound of his voice.*
drown sb/sth out *The guitars were drowning him out.* ♦ *I turned up the radio to drown the kids out.*

DRUG /drʌg/
drugs, drugging, drugged

,drug 'up [often passive]

to give someone a lot of drugs or medicine with the result that they cannot behave normally
be drugged up *Everyone in the hospital seemed to have been drugged up.*

drop out (sense 2)

drug sb up *Doctors can't just drug people up for their own convenience.*

■ **,drugged 'up** **adj** if someone is drugged up, they cannot behave normally because they have been given a lot of drugs: *He was still drugged up after the operation.* ♦ *The painting looked as though it was the work of a drugged up madman.*

DRUM /drʌm/
drums, drumming, drummed

,drum 'into
to make someone learn or understand something by repeating it many times
= DIN INTO, DRILL INTO
drum sth into sb *Latin isn't an easy language to learn. You have to drum it into students.*

,drum 'out [usually passive]
to force someone to leave an organization because they have done something bad
= THROW OUT
be drummed out of sth *She risks being drummed out of the army.*

,drum 'up ★
to try to make people support you or buy something from you
drum up sth *Advertisements should help to drum up some business.* ♦ *He's trying to drum up more support for his proposals.*

DRY /draɪ/
dries, drying, dried

,dry 'off
if something dries off, or if you dry it off, all the water dries or is wiped from its surface = DRY
dry off *Wash the salad and leave it to dry off.*
dry sth off *also* **dry off sth** *She washed*

her hair and dried it off quickly.
dry yourself off *He got out of the shower and dried himself off.*

,dry 'out ★★
1 if something dries out, some or all the water comes out of it and it becomes too dry or too hard = DRY UP
dry out *Water the ground regularly to stop it from drying out.*

2 *informal* to stop drinking alcohol, especially by getting medical treatment
dry out *She went into a clinic to dry out.*

,dry 'up ★★

1	become too dry
2	when a supply ends
3	make dishes dry
4	stop talking
5	telling sb to stop talking

1 if something dries up, all the water comes out of it and it becomes too dry or too hard = DRY OUT
dry up *The land had dried up and no crops would grow.* ♦ *She rubs cream into her face every day to prevent her skin from drying up.*
dry up sth *The drought had dried up the rivers.*
dry sth up *The harsh sun had dried her complexion up.*

2 if a supply of something dries up, it stops being available = STOP
dry up *What will happen to the project when the money dries up?* ♦ *Complaints virtually dried up when he took over.*

Nouns often used as subjects with **dry up 2**

■ **cash, demand, funding, investment, money, orders, supply**

3 to wipe the water off dishes after they have been washed
dry up *Whose turn is it to dry up?*
dry up sth *I left John drying up the pots and pans.*

dry sth up *Don't worry, I'll dry the breakfast dishes up for you.*

4 *informal* to stop talking because you do not know what to say

dry up *She is terrified that when she gets on stage she'll just dry up.*

5 [usually in imperative] *informal* used for rudely telling someone to stop talking

dry up *Why don't you dry up!*

DUB /dʌb/
dubs, dubbing, dubbed

ˌdub ˈin [usually passive]
to change an existing recording by adding new sound to it

be dubbed in *The sound of the train was dubbed in afterwards.*

ˌdub ˈinto [usually passive]
to replace the speech in a film with a different language, so that the actors seem to be speaking the other language

be dubbed into sth *It was an English film dubbed into German.*

ˌdub ˈout
to remove the original sound from a recording, especially a film

dub sth out *also* dub out sth *They dubbed the background noise out.*

ˌdub ˈover
to replace the original sound from a recording with new sound

dub over sth *They dubbed over the American dialogue and replaced it with Russian.*

DUCK /dʌk/
ducks, ducking, ducked

ˌduck ˈout
1 to leave a place, especially in a way that is not noticed by other people = NIP OUT

duck out *She ducked out for a smoke.*

2 to avoid doing something that you were intending to do or had promised to do = BACK OUT

duck out *We're not going to allow him to duck out now.* ♦ **+of** *He said he would come, but now he's trying to duck out of it.*

DUFF /dʌf/
duffs, duffing, duffed

ˌduff ˈup *British informal old-fashioned*
to hit someone repeatedly and injure them = BEAT UP

duff sb up *They duffed him up because he's smaller than them.*

DUKE /djuːk, *American* duk/
dukes, duking, duked

ˌduke ˈout
PHRASE duke it out *American informal* to fight: *We watched as the two men duked it out.*

DUMB /dʌm/
dumbs, dumbing, dumbed

ˌdumb ˈdown *showing disapproval*
to make something simpler and easier to understand in a way that reduces its quality

dumb down sth *also* dumb sth down *The pass rate was so high that the school was accused of dumbing down the exam.*

■ ˌdumbing-ˈdown **noun** [U] *showing disapproval* changes that are intended to make something easier to understand but that also reduce its quality: *Alterations to the degree programme brought accusations of dumbing-down.*

DUMP /dʌmp/
dumps, dumping, dumped

ˈdump on *informal*
1 to treat someone in an unfair way, especially by criticizing or blaming them for something

dump on sb *Why do you let him dump on you like that?*

2 to give someone an unpleasant or difficult job to do instead of doing it yourself or helping them with it

dump sth on sb *You can't dump all that responsibility on a teenager.*

DUST /dʌst/
dusts, dusting, dusted

ˌdust ˈdown *British*
to wipe dust or dirt off the surface of something

dust down sth *also* dust sth down *She came in from the snow, dusting down her jacket.* ♦ *She took the tools out of the bag and dusted them down.*

dust yourself down *He fell awkwardly, but got up and dusted himself down.*

PHRASE dust yourself down to quickly try something again or continue to do what you were doing after a problem or failure, without getting upset: *You have to learn to just dust yourself down and try again.*

ˌdust ˈoff ★
to get something ready to use that you have not used for a long time

dust off sth *I'm dusting off my old typing skills and returning to work.*
dust sth **off** *We're dusting our old songsheets off for the occasion.* ♦ *Most retired people have talents they can draw on, if they're prepared to dust them off.*

DWELL /dwel/
dwells, dwelling, dwelled or dwelt /dwelt/

'dwell on ★★ (*also* 'dwell upon)
to spend a lot of time thinking or talking about something unpleasant
dwell on sth *He tends to dwell on the negative aspects of his performance.*
♦ *Don't allow your mind to dwell upon the past.*

Nouns often used as objects with **dwell on**

■ matter, the past, problem, subject

DWINDLE /'dwɪnd(ə)l/
dwindles, dwindling, dwindled

,dwindle a'way
to become gradually less or smaller over a period of time until there is very little left
dwindle away *Her hopes for success dwindled away to nothing.*

E e

EARTH /ɜːθ/
earths, earthing, earthed

,earth 'up
to put soil around a plant in order to protect it or help it to grow
earth up sth *also* **earth** sth **up** *In cold areas, earth up the stems.*

EASE /iːz, *American* iz/
eases, easing, eased

,ease 'off ★
1 ease off or **ease up** if something unpleasant or annoying eases off, it becomes less unpleasant or annoying
= LET UP ≠ INTENSIFY
ease off *If the rain eases off overnight, we'll leave in the morning.* ♦ *The pain should ease off after a couple of hours.*
2 to go more slowly, especially when you are driving or running fast = SLOW DOWN
ease off *Ease off a bit as you go around the bend.* ♦ *He was so far in front of the*

other runners that he was able to ease off on the home straight.
3 to give something less effort or energy, especially when you have been working very hard = SLOW DOWN
ease off *If she doesn't ease off at work, she'll make herself ill.*

,ease 'out [often passive]
to make someone leave a job or position in such a way that they seem to have left it by choice = ELBOW OUT
be eased out *Senior party sources say Liddell will be eased out during the next few weeks.*
ease sb **out** *They were looking for a chance to ease him out.*

,ease 'up
1 *same as* ease off 1
2 to become less angry, serious, or severe towards someone = LET UP
ease up *He needs to relax – ease up a little.* ♦ **+on** *Government forces appear to be easing up on the rebels.*

EAT /iːt, *American* it/
eats, eating, ate /et, eɪt/, eaten /'iːt(ə)n, *American* 'it(ə)n/

,eat a'way
to gradually destroy something = ERODE
eat away sth *also* **eat** sth **away** *Within a few years inflation had eaten away all the economic gains.*

,eat a'way at
to make someone feel more and more unhappy or worried
eat away at sb *You could see that jealousy was eating away at her.*

,eat 'in
to have a meal at home instead of in a restaurant ≠ EAT OUT, DINE OUT
eat in *We only ate in twice a week.*

,eat 'into
1 if an activity or cost eats into your time or money, it uses more of it than you intended = USE UP
eat into sth *The cost of new computer systems is eating into the bank's profits.*
2 to gradually destroy something = ERODE
eat into sth *The river had eaten into the bank, and part of it had collapsed.*

,eat 'out ★
to have a meal in a restaurant instead of at home = DINE OUT ≠ EAT IN
eat out *People are eating out more than ever before.*

‚eat 'up ★★

1	eat everything
2	use a lot of time/money
3	be affected by a bad feeling
4	travel quickly
5	want to hear/see more

1 to eat all of something = EAT; *formal* CONSUME

eat up sth *Come on, eat up your broccoli.*
eat sth up *If you ask for more, I want you to eat it all up.* ♦ *He ate his dinner up nicely today.*
eat up *Eat up, and we'll go for a walk.*

2 to use large amounts of your available time or money = *formal* CONSUME

eat up sth *Having children eats up a lot of a family's income.*
eat sth up *You'll find that studying eats all that spare time up.* ♦ *We'd all have more energy if modern life didn't eat it all up.*

Nouns often used as objects with **eat up 2**

■ capital, funds, income, money, profits, time

3 [often passive] to feel a negative emotion such as anger or hate so strongly that it is difficult to think about anything else = *formal* CONSUME

be eaten up *Paula was eaten up by guilt for days.*
eat sb up *You could see the embarrassment was eating her up.*

4 *informal* to travel a particular distance easily and steadily

eat up sth *They drove on, eating up the distance between themselves and home.*

5 *informal* to like something so much that you want to hear or see more = LAP UP ≠ HATE

eat sth up *The press ridiculed the book while the public was eating it up.*
eat up sth *Most celebrities eat up the attention they get from the media.*

EBB /eb/
ebbs, ebbing, ebbed

‚ebb a'way *mainly literary*
if a feeling or your energy or strength ebbs away, it gradually becomes weaker until it disappears

ebb away *Her happiness had begun to ebb away.*

PHRASE **sb's life is ebbing away** if someone's life is ebbing away, they are slowly dying

EDGE /edʒ/
edges, edging, edged

‚edge 'out [often passive]
to beat someone in a competition by a small amount

be edged out *The Welsh star was edged out by two seconds.*
edge out sb *also* **edge sb out** *Eileen Petersen edged out Victor Frazer by 27 votes.* ♦ *She managed to edge her rival out.*

‚edge 'up
to gradually increase

edge up *Inflation has been edging up recently.* ♦ *The newspaper has seen profits edge up from £25.3 million to £26.6 million.*

EDIT /'edɪt/
edits, editing, edited

‚edit 'out [often passive]
to remove parts of a film or of a television or radio show that are not wanted before it is shown or broadcast = CUT, DELETE

be edited out *Much of the violence has been edited out.*
edit out sth *also* **edit sth out** *The show is taped, so we can edit out the mishaps later.* ♦ *We can always edit that bit out.*

EFF /ef/

‚eff 'off *British impolite*
used as a less offensive way of saying 'fuck off', which is a very offensive way of telling someone to go away, or saying that you do not agree with them

EGG /eg/
eggs, egging, egged

‚egg 'on [often passive]
to encourage someone to do something that they should not do = ENCOURAGE ≠ DISSUADE

be egged on *He'd been egged on by the other boys.*
egg sb on *He'd never have stolen it if she hadn't egged him on.*

EKE /iːk, *American* ik/
ekes, eking, eked

‚eke 'out ★
to make something such as money or food last as long as possible

eke out sth *They have to eke out their fuel supplies throughout the winter.*
eke sth out *My mother used to eke the*

food out by making soup from the leftovers. ♦ *Water is added to the juice to eke it out.*

PHRASE **eke out a living/existence** to get just enough money or food to be able to continue to exist: *The family barely manages to eke out a living from their small farm.*

ELABORATE /ɪˈlæbəreɪt/
elaborates, elaborating, elaborated

eˈlaborate on
to give more details or information about something
  elaborate on sth *He would not elaborate on the reasons for his decision.*

ELBOW /ˈelbəʊ, American ˈelboʊ/
elbows, elbowing, elbowed

ˌelbow ˈout (also ˌelbow aˈside) [often passive]
to make someone leave a job or position so that someone else can take their place = EASE OUT
  be elbowed out *She found herself elbowed out by her colleagues.*
  elbow sb out *Younger men would come and elbow him out.*

ELEVATE /ˈeləveɪt/
elevates, elevating, elevated

ˈelevate to [often passive] formal
to give someone a more important job or position = PROMOTE TO
  be elevated to sth *In 1922, he was elevated to the House of Lords.*
  elevate sb to sth *The President elevated him to the chairmanship of the council.*

EMANATE /ˈeməneɪt/
emanates, emanating, emanated

ˈemanate from
1 *formal* to come from a particular place = COME FROM
  emanate from sth *She could hear raised voices emanating from her parents' room.* ♦ *Wonderful smells emanated from the kitchen.*
2 *formal* if a quality or feeling emanates from you, you show it without expressing it in words
  emanate from sb *A sense of joy emanated from him.*

EMBARK /ɪmˈbɑːk, American ɪmˈbɑrk/
embarks, embarking, embarked

emˈbark on ★★★ (also emˈbark upon)
1 to start a new project or activity, usually one that will be difficult and will take time = ENTER ON
  embark on sth *After leaving college, Lucy embarked on an acting career.* ♦ *The new government embarked upon an energetic legislative programme.*

Nouns often used as objects with **embark on 1**

■ campaign, career, course, policy, programme, project, process, series, venture

2 to start a journey by ship
  embark on sth *We embarked on a voyage to the Caribbean.*

EMBED /ɪmˈbed/
embeds, embedding, embedded

emˈbed in
1 [often passive] to fix something firmly in a surface or object
  be embedded in sth *We discovered the cause of the puncture – a two-inch nail that was embedded in the tyre.*
  embed itself in sth *The bullet had embedded itself in the skull.*
2 [usually passive] to make something a fixed and important part of something else
  be embedded in sth *Traces of earlier ways of life are embedded in modern society.*
3 [usually passive] if a journalist is embedded with part of an army, they are allowed to travel with it and report on what is happening to it
  be embedded in sth *Lawrence was embedded in a US military unit during the fighting in southern Iraq.*

EMBROIDER /ɪmˈbrɔɪdə, American ɪmˈbrɔɪdər/
embroiders, embroidering, embroidered

emˈbroider on
to make a story or an account more interesting or impressive by adding details that you have invented = EMBELLISH
  embroider on sth *She gave a clear account of the events to the police, resisting the temptation to embroider on the details.* ♦ *It was a melodramatic story, the kind that had no doubt been embroidered on over the years.*

EMBROIL /ɪmˈbrɔɪl/
embroils, embroiling, embroiled

be/become em'broiled in

to be involved in, or become involved in,
a difficult situation
> **be/become embroiled in sth** *They were
> anxious to avoid becoming embroiled in
> another scandal.* ♦ *At that time both
> governments were embroiled in foreign
> wars.*

EMPTY /ˈempti/
empties, emptying, emptied

ˌempty 'out ★

1 to make something empty by taking
everything out of it ≠ FILL UP
> **empty out sth** *He was told to empty out
> his desk and leave.*
> **empty sth out** *She ordered me to empty
> my bags out.* ♦ *When the bucket was full,
> he'd empty it out and put it back.*

2 to remove the substance or the objects
inside a container
> **empty sth out** *She lifted the bag and
> emptied the money out onto the bed.*
> ♦ **+of** *You have to empty the water out of
> the tank first.*

3 if a place empties out, all the people
who are in it leave
> **empty out** *All the pubs empty out at the
> same time.*

ENAMOR the American spelling of
enamour

ENAMOUR /ɪˈnæmə, American
ɪˈnæmɔr/
enamours, enamouring, enamoured

be e'namoured of (*also* be
e'namoured with)

1 *formal* if you are enamoured of
something, you like it very much = LIKE
> **be/become enamoured of sth** *I've
> become very enamoured of free software.*
> ♦ *Farmers were not so enamoured with
> the idea.*

2 *old-fashioned* if you are enamoured of
someone, you love them = LOVE
> **be/become enamoured of sb** *She
> became enamoured of a young dancer.*

ENCASE /ɪnˈkeɪs/
encases, encasing, encased

en'case in [often passive]

to completely cover or enclose an object
in something
> **be encased in sth** *The pipe is encased in
> a plastic tube.*
> **encase sth in sth** *It's difficult to encase
> the upper arm in plaster.*

ENCROACH /ɪnˈkrəʊtʃ, American
ɪnˈkroʊtʃ/
encroaches, encroaching, encroached

en'croach on (*also* en'croach upon)

1 *showing disapproval* to gradually take
something such as power or authority
from someone else
> **encroach on sth** *The federal government
> is encroaching on a state issue.*

2 *showing disapproval* to gradually cover
more and more land
> **encroach on sth** *Housing developments
> continue to encroach on wildlife
> habitats.*

3 *showing disapproval* to gradually reduce
the amount of time that someone has
available to do what they want to do
> **encroach on sth** *I didn't want work to
> encroach any more on my spare time.*

END /end/
ends, ending, ended

'end in ★★★

to have something as a final result = FINISH
IN; *formal* CULMINATE IN
> **end in sth** *The game ended in a draw.*
> ♦ *His attempt to persuade the boy **ended
> in failure**.*
> **PHRASE** **end in tears** if a situation ends
> in tears, people involved in it become
> disappointed or angry

ˌend 'up ★★★

to be in a particular place or state after
doing something or because of doing it
= FINISH UP, WIND UP ≠ START OUT
> **end up** *Somehow they all ended up at my
> house.* ♦ *Keep on doing that and you'll
> end up in serious trouble.*
> **end up doing sth** *I ended up spending
> the night in the airport.*

'end with ★★★

to have or add something as the final part
> **end with sth** *The festival ended with
> fireworks.*
> **end sth with sth** *Why did you end your
> essay with a quotation from Shakespeare?*

ENDEAR /ɪnˈdɪə, American ɪnˈdɪr/
endears, endearing, endeared

en'dear to ★

if someone's behaviour or personality
endears them to you, it makes you like
them

endear sb to sb *His warm personality endeared him to everyone he met.* ♦ *Her brusque manner did not exactly endear her to colleagues.*
endear yourself to sb *He had endeared himself to French society.*

ENDOW /ɪnˈdaʊ/
endows, endowing, endowed

enˈdow with
1 *formal* to give a particular quality to something, or to say that something has a particular quality = GIVE
endow sth/sb with sth *The General's supporters endow him with an almost godlike status.*
2 [always passive] if you are endowed with a good ability or quality, you have it = HAVE
be endowed with sth *She was endowed with both brains and beauty.*

ENGAGE /ɪnˈɡeɪdʒ/
engages, engaging, engaged

enˈgage in ★★★ *formal*
1 to take part in a particular activity, especially one that involves competing with or talking to other people
engage in sth *These men are used to engaging in urban warfare.* ♦ *We actively encourage the students to engage in debate with us.*
2 [always passive] if you are engaged in something, you are involved in it
be engaged in sth *He is currently engaged in a dispute with his former business partner.*
PHRASE **engage sb in conversation** to start having a conversation with someone: *I felt sorry for her and attempted to engage her in conversation.*

be enˈgaged on (*also* be enˈgaged upon)
if you are engaged on something, you are doing it
be engaged on sth *Her team knew they were engaged on work of great importance.*

enˈgage with *formal*
1 to make an effort to understand and deal with someone or something
engage with sb/sth *They accused the company of failing to engage with the local community.*
2 to start to fight an enemy in battle
engage with sb *The first army to engage with the Christians was Motamid's.*

be enˈgaged upon *literary same as* be engaged on

ENGROSS /ɪnˈɡrəʊs, *American* ɪnˈɡroʊs/
engrosses, engrossing, engrossed

be enˈgrossed in
to be doing something with all your attention and energy because you are very interested in it
be engrossed in (doing) sth *She pretended to be engrossed in reading the newspaper.*

ENLARGE /ɪnˈlɑːdʒ, *American* ɪnˈlɑrdʒ/
enlarges, enlarging, enlarged

enˈlarge on (*also* enˈlarge upon)
to give more information about something that you have already mentioned = EXPAND ON
enlarge on sth *Would you like to enlarge on that remark?* ♦ *He refused to enlarge upon his reasons for leaving his job.*

ENQUIRE another spelling of inquire

ENSHRINE /ɪnˈʃraɪn/
enshrines, enshrining, enshrined

be enˈshrined in *formal*
if something such as an idea or principle is enshrined in a document, it is recorded there so that it cannot be ignored
be enshrined in sth *These fundamental freedoms are enshrined in the Universal Declaration of Human Rights.*

ENTER /ˈentə, *American* ˈentər/
enters, entering, entered

ˌenter ˈinto ★★★
1 to start to take part in a discussion or activity with someone = BECOME INVOLVED IN
enter into sth *The government had entered into a genuine dialogue with the terrorists.* ♦ *It was not the time to enter into a debate about sports policy.*

Nouns often used as objects with
enter into 1

■ correspondence, debate, dialogue, discussions, negotiations, talks

2 to be an important aspect of a situation = COME INTO
enter into sth *When companies are trying to save money, loyalty to workers doesn't enter into it.*

3 to agree to be part of an official agreement or contract

> **enter into sth** *In 1986, the organization entered into an agreement with a private firm to operate the security system.*

> Nouns often used as objects with **enter into 3**
>
> ■ agreement, alliance, arrangement, contract, partnership, relationship, transaction, treaty

> PHRASE **enter into the spirit (of sth)** to behave in the enthusiastic way that people expect in a particular situation, for example in a game or at a party: *Guests entered into the spirit of the occasion by dressing in period costumes and learning to dance in eighteenth century style.*

'enter on (*also* **'enter upon**) *formal*
to begin something, or to begin to take part in something = EMBARK ON

> **enter on sth** *He realized he had entered on a futile course of action.* ♦ *Montgomery entered upon a brilliant political career.*

ENTITLE /ɪnˈtaɪt(ə)l/
entitles, entitling, entitled

en'title to ★★★ [often passive]
to give someone the right to do something

> **be entitled to sth** *You're entitled to free use of the pool at a neighbouring hotel.*
> **entitle sb to sth** *Membership entitles you to reduced season tickets.*

ENTRUST /ɪnˈtrʌst/
entrusts, entrusting, entrusted

en'trust to ★★ [often passive]
to give the responsibility for something important to a particular person

> **be entrusted to sb** *He gambled away the money that had been entrusted to him.*
> **entrust sth to sb** *We cannot entrust the country's telecommunications to unqualified people.*

en'trust with ★ [often passive]
to make someone responsible for something important

> **be entrusted with sth** *I've been entrusted with the task of getting him home safely.*
> **entrust sb with sth** *He had entrusted her with his secret.*

EQUATE /ɪˈkweɪt/
equates, equating, equated

e'quate with (*also* **e'quate to**)
1 to consider something to be the same as something else

> **equate sth with sth** *These people seem to equate honesty with weakness.* ♦ *Don't make the mistake of equating high test scores to intelligence.*

2 to be the same as something

> **equate with sth** *Market rates don't always equate with reasonable prices.*
> ♦ *20% of the population equates to around 6 million people.*

ERODE /ɪˈrəʊd, *American* ɪˈroʊd/
erodes, eroding, eroded

e,rode a'way [often passive]
1 if something such as soil or rock erodes away or is eroded away, it is gradually damaged by water or wind so that it begins to disappear

> **be eroded away** *We aim to plant more trees to prevent the beach from being eroded away.*
> **erode away** *The coastline is eroding away.*

2 if something erodes away or is eroded away, its strength, value, or importance is gradually reduced until it disappears completely

> **be eroded away** *She fears his confidence is being eroded away.*
> **erode away** *Western support for Yeltsin was slowly eroding away.*

ETCH /etʃ/
etches, etching, etched

be 'etched on *mainly literary*
PHRASES **be etched on sb's memory/mind** if something is etched on your memory, mind or brain, you can still remember it very clearly, sometimes when you would prefer to forget it: *It was a scene that will be etched on my memory for ever.*

> **be etched on/into sb's face** used for saying that someone's face shows clearly what they are feeling or what experiences they have had, usually when the feelings or experiences are bad: *Weariness was etched into his face.* ♦ *Mockery was etched on every line of her face.*

EVEN /ˈiːv(ə)n, *American* ˈiv(ə)n/
evens, evening, evened

,even 'out
1 if things even out, or if you even them out, the differences between them change so that they become fewer or smaller
= BALANCE UP, BALANCE OUT

> **even out sth** *also* **even sth out** *The company saw overseas growth as a way*

to even out swings in the UK market.
♦ **+between** *We're trying to even things out between London and the regions.*

2 to share or divide something equally, or to be shared or divided equally
even out sth *also* **even sth out** *We would like to be able to even out the workload more fairly.*

,even 'up
to make something fairer or more equal
= EQUALIZE
even sth up *also* **even up sth** *A second player was sent off, from the other team this time, which did even things up a bit.*
♦ *Another goal would even up the score.*

EXPAND /ɪk'spænd/
expands, expanding, expanded

ex'pand on (*also* **ex'pand upon**)
to talk or write more about something, adding more details or information
= ENLARGE ON
expand on sth *I do not care to expand any further on my earlier statement.*

EXPATIATE /ek'speɪʃieɪt/
expatiates, expatiating, expatiated

ex'patiate on (*also* **ex'patiate upon**)
literary
to talk or write a lot or in great detail about something
expatiate on sth *The issue is whether the nonspecialist has any right to expatiate on scientific matters.*

EXPLAIN /ɪk'spleɪn/
explains, explaining, explained

ex,plain a'way ★
to give someone reasons for something unusual that has happened in order to make them think it is less serious or important than it really is or to stop them asking questions about it
explain away sth *She made up stories to explain away the missing money.*
explain sth away *How are they going to explain that away?* ♦ *Some people try to explain miracles away and say that they do not happen.*

EXPOSE /ɪk'spəʊz, *American* ɪk'spoʊz/
exposes, exposing, exposed

ex'pose to ★★★ [often passive]
1 to fail to protect someone or something from something harmful or dangerous
be exposed to sth *Many of the soldiers had been exposed to radiation.*

expose sth/sb to sth *The sale exposed the company to widespread criticism.*
♦ *Take care when you expose your skin to the sun.*

2 to introduce new ideas, activities etc to someone so that they can learn about them
be exposed to sth *Some of these kids have never been exposed to art.*
expose sb to sth *Schools are again exposing children to the classics.*

EXTRICATE /'ekstrɪkeɪt/
extricates, extricating, extricated

'extricate from ★ *formal*
1 to get someone out of a difficult or unpleasant situation
extricate yourself from sth *Pete had managed to extricate himself from a very embarrassing situation.*
extricate sb from sth *China's role in extricating Asia from economic crisis could be vital.*

2 to get someone or something out of a place, when this is difficult or dangerous
extricate sb/sth from sth *It took two hours to extricate him from the rubble.*
♦ *We have to extricate the bigger fish from the nets.*

EYE /aɪ/
eyes, eyeing *or* eying, eyed

,eye 'up *British informal*
1 to look at someone in a way that shows that you are sexually attracted to them
eye sb *also* **eye sb up** *As usual, there were men standing at the bar eyeing up women.* ♦ *I think she's eyeing you up.*

2 to look at something in a way that shows that you want it or that you are very interested in it
eye up sth *also* **eye sth up** *They were eyeing up new business opportunities in the area.* ♦ *He was eyeing my beer up, so I offered him one.*

Ff

FACE /feɪs/
faces, facing, faced

,face a'bout
to turn and face in the opposite direction
= TURN AROUND
face about *The soldiers faced about and starting marching south.*

,face 'down

to appear strong and confident when someone is threatening or criticizing you
face down sb/sth *also* **face sb/sth down** *They showed they could face down the opposition.* ♦ *You have to face your opponent down.*

,face 'off

1 *mainly American informal* if people or groups face off, they compete or fight with each other
face off *Soldiers and protesters faced off during riots.* ♦ **+against** *It was Clinton's turn to face off against Castro.*
2 to begin a game of ice hockey
face off *The teams face off at 3 o'clock.*
■ **'face-off** noun [C] **1** *informal* a disagreement or fight between two people or groups: *The Cold War was a face-off between two military superpowers.* = CONFRONTATION **2** the method used for starting a game of ice hockey: *It's only a few minutes until the face-off.*

,face 'onto

if something faces onto a place, the front of it is in the direction of that place
face onto sth *The hotel faces onto the park.* ♦ *All the houses face onto inner courtyards.*

,face 'up to

to accept that a bad situation exists and try to deal with it = FACE
face up to sth *He was the only one who faced up to the problem.*

be 'faced with ★★

to have a particular problem or situation to deal with
be faced with sth *Now he was faced with the problem of how to break the news to his wife.* ♦ *They are faced with some very tough decisions.*

FACTOR /'fæktə, *American* 'fæktər/
factors, factoring, factored

,factor 'in (*also* ,factor 'into)

to include a particular amount or fact when you calculate the total amount of something or when you consider something = INCLUDE
factor in sth *also* **factor sth in** *Total spending was virtually the same in real terms after factoring in inflation.*
factor sth into sth *You have to factor his age into it.*

,factor 'out

to not include a particular amount or fact when you calculate the total amount of

something or when you consider something = EXCLUDE, DISCOUNT
factor out sth *also* **factor sth out** *This would allow investors to factor out inflation.* ♦ *The situation looks different once you factor these elements out.*

FADE /feɪd/
fades, fading, faded

,fade a'way ★★

1 if something that you can see or hear fades away, it gradually becomes less loud, bright etc until it disappears = DISAPPEAR
fade away *Her footsteps faded away down the staircase.* ♦ *She thought she saw his face, then the vision faded away.*
2 if someone or something well-known fades away, they gradually become less famous or less important until they are forgotten about
fade away *Most of these fashions just fade away and are forgotten.*
3 if a person fades away, they gradually lose their strength, lose weight, and become ill or die = WASTE AWAY
fade away *If you don't start eating properly you're going to fade away.*

,fade 'in (*also* ,fade 'up)

if a sound or picture fades in, or if you fade it in, it gradually becomes louder or clearer
fade in sth *also* **fade sth in** *The DJ faded in another record.*
fade in *Her voice begins to fade in at the beginning of the record.*

,fade 'out

if a sound or picture fades out, or if you fade it out, it gradually disappears
fade out *The voice on the radio faded out.*
fade sth out *also* **fade out sth** *I'll fade the music out at that point.* ♦ *You fade out one image and replace it with another.*

,fade 'up *same as* fade in

FAFF /fæf/
faffs, faffing, faffed

,faff a'bout (*also* ,faff a'round) *British informal*

to waste time doing things that are not important or necessary, or to waste time by doing things in a way that is not organized = MESS ABOUT, MESS AROUND
faff about *Let's stop faffing about and make a decision.*

FAG /fæg/
fags, fagging, fagged

be ˌfagged 'out *British informal*
to be very tired
  be fagged out *It was late and we were
  all fagged out.*

FAKE /feɪk/
fakes, faking, faked

ˌfake 'out *American*
to trick someone by pretending something
or by behaving dishonestly
  fake sb out *also* **fake out sb** *The animal
  fakes out its prey by pretending to be
  hurt.* ♦ *The company has faked investors
  out.*

FALL /fɔːl, *American* fɔl/
falls, falling, fell /fel/, fallen /ˈfɔːlən,
American ˈfɔlən/

Fall is often used with adverbs and
prepositions when it means 'to move
quickly downwards from a higher
position': *I keep **falling off** my bike.*
♦ *Stay away from the pond – I don't want
you **falling in**.* ♦ *Bombs continued
falling on the city.* These uses are not
included here.

ˌfall a'bout *British informal*
if you fall about or fall about laughing,
you laugh a lot at something = CRACK UP
  fall about *His behaviour made us all fall
  about.* ♦ *He forgot his lines and we all
  fell about laughing.*

ˌfall a'part ★★
1 if something falls apart, it breaks
because it is old or badly made = *formal*
DISINTEGRATE
  fall apart *I've read this book so often it's
  falling apart.* ♦ *Those shoes are falling
  apart. Why don't you buy some new ones?*
2 if something such as a system or
relationship falls apart, it stops existing
or working normally = COLLAPSE
  fall apart *The entire system of
  government was falling apart.* ♦ *Our
  marriage was rapidly **falling apart at
  the seams**.*
3 if someone falls apart, they lose control
of their emotions and become unable to
deal with a difficult situation = CRACK UP
  fall apart *A lot of things happened and
  I just fell apart.*

ˌfall a'way ★
1 if something falls away, it breaks off
from the thing it was part of
  fall away *The wood was falling away in
  chunks.* ♦ **+from** *Plaster was falling
  away from the walls.*
2 if the amount, level, value etc of
something falls away, it becomes smaller
or lower = DECREASE, FALL OFF
  fall away *Sales have fallen away
  sharply.*
3 if land falls away, it slopes down
suddenly from a particular point = DROP
AWAY
  fall away *The ground fell away below us
  to the sea.*
4 *British literary* if something such as a
sound or feeling falls away, it becomes
weaker and disappears
  fall away *The noise of gunfire was
  beginning to fall away.*

ˌfall 'back
1 to move more slowly than the group of
people you are with so that you are behind
them = DROP BACK
  fall back *Oliver and Sara fell back and
  started talking.*
2 if an amount, level, value etc falls back,
it becomes smaller or lower = DROP
  fall back *Profits fell back slightly this
  month.* ♦ **+to** *The value of the company
  fell back to £200 million.*

ˌfall 'back on ★★
to use or do something else after other
things have failed
  fall back on sth *They always fall back
  on their old slogans.* ♦ *She always has
  her teaching experience to fall back on.*

■ **fallback** /ˈfɔːlbæk/ **adj** a fallback
position, plan, option etc is one that
you can use when your first plan or idea
fails: *If they refuse our offer, what's our
fallback position?*

■ **fallback** /ˈfɔːlbæk/ **noun** [C usually
singular] something that you can use if
your first plan or idea fails: *It's a risky
plan, so we need a fallback of some kind.*

ˌfall be'hind ★★
1 to move more slowly than other people
in the group you are with so that you get
further and further behind them ≠ KEEP UP
  fall behind *After five miles Tara was
  tired and started to fall behind.*
  fall behind sb *On the bend he fell behind
  the other runners.*
2 to make less progress or be less
successful than other people who are
doing a similar job or activity = GET BEHIND
≠ KEEP UP
  fall behind *If you miss classes, you soon
  start to fall behind.* ♦ **+with** *My daughter
  is falling behind with her school work.*

fall behind sb/sth *Britain has fallen behind the rest of Europe in this area.*

3 to fail to do something or pay something at the time that you should
fall behind *I'd lost my commitment to my work and things started to fall behind.* ♦ **+with** *We started to fall behind with the rent.*

,fall 'down ★★★

1 if something such as an argument or system falls down, it fails because a particular part of it is weak or not correct
= FAIL
fall down *This is where your theory falls down.* ♦ **+on** *Their argument falls down on several important points.*

2 [always progressive] if a building is falling down, it is in very bad condition
= COLLAPSE
be falling down *The truth was that the school was falling down.*

3 if something that you are wearing falls down, it slips down your legs
fall down *The boy came into the room with his trousers falling down.*
PHRASE **fall down on the job** to do a particular job or activity in a careless way so that you are not successful
≠ SUCCEED: *The figures suggest schools are falling down on the job.*

'fall for ★★

1 to fall in love with someone
fall for sb *He fell for Rosie when he was in hospital and she was his nurse.*

2 to believe that a trick or a joke is true
= BE DUPED BY ≠ SEE THROUGH
fall for sth *How could you fall for such an obvious trick?*

3 to like something immediately and decide that you want to have it
fall for sth *I fell for this car as soon as I saw it.*

,fall 'in

1 if a roof or wall falls in, it falls to the ground = CAVE IN
fall in *The ceiling fell in.*

2 if soldiers fall in, they form a line by standing next to each other or behind each other ≠ FALL OUT
fall in *He gave the order for the men to fall in.*

,fall 'in behind

to start walking behind someone or something
fall in behind sb/sth *He fell in behind the procession.*

,fall 'in beside

to start walking next to someone or something
fall in beside sb/sth *He fell in beside her and they started chatting.*

'fall into

1 to start doing something by chance
fall into sth *She fell into modelling quite by accident.*

2 to belong to a particular group or class
fall into sth *The students fall into three distinct groups.*
PHRASES **fall into conversation** to start having a conversation with someone, especially someone you have just met: *The two men just fell into conversation.*
fall into disuse/disrepair to get into a bad condition: *A large number of churches have fallen into disuse.* ♦ *The station gradually fell into disrepair.*
fall into sb's hands if something falls into someone's hands, they start to own or control it when you did not want them to: *All the western provinces had fallen into enemy hands.* ♦ *We don't want this information to fall into the wrong hands.*
fall into sb's lap to suddenly happen or be given to someone without them having to make any effort: *The reporter couldn't believe it when the story fell into his lap.*
fall into step if you fall into step beside someone, you start walking beside them: *The old man fell into step beside the boy.*

,fall 'in with

1 to accept or agree with someone else's ideas, way of behaving etc = GO ALONG WITH
fall in with sth *I tried to fall in with the general mood of celebration.*

2 to begin to be involved with a person or group of people after meeting them by chance = JOIN
fall in with sb *At university she fell in with a group of student radicals.*

,fall 'off

1 if the amount, level, or value of something falls off, it gets smaller = DROP OFF, DECLINE, DECREASE ≠ INCREASE
fall off *Sales always fall off in the winter months.*

2 if part of something falls off, or if it falls off something, it separates from the thing that it was attached to
fall off sth *One of the buttons has fallen off my jacket.*
fall off *The handle of the knife fell off.*

■ '**fall-off** **noun** [singular] a reduction

in the amount or level of something: *There has been a noticeable fall-off in sales.*

ˈfall ˈon ★★

1	happen on particular day
2	be sb's responsibility
3	get hold of
4	happen to sb
5	start eating, drinking etc

1 if a date or an event falls on a particular day, it happens on that day
fall on sth *Christmas Day falls on a Thursday this year.*

2 fall on or **fall upon** *formal* if a job or duty falls on someone, it is their responsibility to do it
fall on sb *The burden of caring for elderly parents often falls on women.*
♦ **+to do sth** *It fell on me to give them the bad news.*

3 fall on or **fall upon** *formal* to take hold of someone suddenly, either to attack them or as a sign of affection
fall on sb *She fell on him and kissed him.*

4 if something unpleasant falls on someone, it happens to them
fall on sb *Unfortunately the consequences of these new regulations fell on the people they were originally meant to protect.*

5 fall on or **fall upon** *literary* to start eating, drinking, or using something as soon as it arrives, in a way that shows that you want it very much
fall on sth *Food was produced, and the hungry men immediately fell on it.*
   PHRASE **fall on deaf ears** if something such as a warning or request falls on deaf ears, it is completely ignored by the person who hears it: *All their appeals for help fell on deaf ears.*

ˌfall ˈout ★★

1 *informal* to stop being friendly with someone because you have had an argument or a disagreement with them
≠ MAKE UP —*picture →* TAKE AFTER
fall out *Have you two fallen out?* ♦ **+with** *I'd fallen out with my parents.* ♦ **+over** *The two friends had fallen out over a girl they both liked.*

2 if something such as your hair or a tooth falls out, it stops being attached to your body = COME OUT
fall out *I'd noticed my hair was falling out.*

3 if soldiers fall out, they stop standing in a formal line ≠ FALL IN
fall out *Tell the men to fall out.*

fall out

■ ˌfalling-ˈout **noun** [C] an occasion when you have a disagreement with someone: *Tom's had a falling-out with his brother.*

■ **fallout** /ˈfɔːlaʊt/ **noun** **1** [singular/U] the unpleasant effects of something that has happened: *The fallout from the Asian financial crisis has continued to affect businesses.* **2** [U] the dangerous dust that falls to the ground after a nuclear explosion: *fallout from the Chernobyl nuclear disaster*

ˌfall ˈover ★★★

1 if something falls over, it falls so that its front is on the ground
fall over *My foot hit the chair and it fell over.* ♦ *The bookshelf looked as though it was going to fall over on top of him.*

2 if you fall over, or if you fall over something, you fall or almost fall to the ground = TRIP
fall over *She fell over and grazed her knee.*
fall over sth *The room is full of boxes and people keep falling over them.*

3 *British informal* if a computer program falls over, it stops working = CRASH
fall over *The system keeps falling over.*
   PHRASE **be falling over themselves to do sth** to be very keen to do something: *The neighbours were falling over themselves to help us.*

ˌfall ˈthrough ★★

if something such as a deal, plan, or arrangement falls through, it fails to happen = FAIL
fall through *If the house purchase falls through, you still have to pay the lawyer.*

ˈfall ˈto *formal*

1 if a particular job or duty falls to someone, it is their responsibility
fall to sb *The politicians had drawn up*

a peace plan, but it fell to the military commander in the area to make it work.

♦ **+to do sth** *It fell to me to explain to him what happened.*

2 *literary* if you fall to doing something, you start to do it with energy and enthusiasm

fall to doing sth *The dogs fell to fighting with each other.*

ˌfall 'under

1 to belong to a particular group or class

fall under sth *This work fell under a different branch of science.*

2 to be controlled or influenced by someone or something

fall under sth *The policy falls under direct control from Whitehall.* ♦ *This project falls under my authority.*

PHRASE **fall under sb's spell** or **fall under the spell of sth** to start to like someone or something very much, often so much that you are unable to control your feelings or behaviour: *The boys all fell under her spell.* ♦ *We visited the island and I immediately fell under its spell.*

'fall upon *formal same as* **fall on** 2, 3, 5

FAMILIARIZE /fəˈmɪliəraɪz, *American* fəˈmɪljəˌraɪz/
familiarizes, familiarizing, familiarized

faˈmiliarize with
to make someone learn or experience something so that they know about it

familiarize sb with sth *It's my job to familiarize new employees with office procedures.*

familiarize yourself with sth *I need to familiarize myself with the subject first.*

FAN /fæn/
fans, fanning, fanned

ˌfan 'out ★

1 if a group of people fan out, they move forwards and apart in a straight line = SPREAD OUT

fan out *Officers fanned out across the field to look for clues.*

2 to spread objects or parts out, often in the shape of half a circle = SPREAD OUT

fan out *Her long dark hair fanned out across the pillow.*

fan sth out *Take your cards and fan them out.*

fan out sth *The bird fans out her feathers to attract the males.*

FARM /fɑːm, *American* fɑrm/
farms, farming, farmed

ˌfarm 'out

1 to arrange for part of your work to be done by people outside your company

farm out sth *also* **farm sth out** *We could always farm out some of the typing.*

♦ *They farm the research out.* ♦ **+to** *Why don't we farm these jobs out to an agency?*

2 [usually passive] *showing disapproval* to arrange for someone to be looked after by someone else because you are too busy to do it yourself

be farmed out to sb *The children are farmed out to a childminder.*

FART /fɑːt, *American* fɑrt/
farts, farting, farted

ˌfart a'round (*also* ˌfart a'bout *British*)
impolite

to waste time when you should be doing something more important or more serious = MESS AROUND

fart around *She's been farting around all day instead of getting on with her homework.*

FASTEN /ˈfɑːs(ə)n, *American* ˈfæs(ə)n/
fastens, fastening, fastened

'fasten on

1 if your eyes fasten on someone or something, you start to look at them very carefully or for a long time

fasten on sb/sth *Seven pairs of eyes fastened on him at this news.*

2 fasten on or **fasten onto** if your attention fastens on someone or something, you start to pay close attention to them

fasten on sth *My mind fastened on this new and terrible thing that was happening.*

3 fasten on or **fasten onto** to accept and start to use an idea or suggestion very quickly and with enthusiasm

fasten on sth *It was a brilliant idea, and I fastened on it immediately.*

4 to keep following or talking to someone and not let them go

fasten on sb *He fastened on her, following her and whispering continuously in her ear.*

'fasten to
to fix one thing to another using something such as string or nails

fasten sth to sth *We fastened a rope to the door handle and pulled.* ♦ *There was a hand-written notice fastened to the door.*

ˌfasten 'up

to close something such as a piece of clothing or a bag using the buttons etc on it

fasten up sth *also* **fasten sth up** *It's getting cold out, so fasten up your coat.*
♦ *Can you help me fasten my dress up please?*

'fasten upon

1 if your attention fastens upon someone or something, you start to pay close attention to them = FASTEN ON

fasten upon sb/sth *At that moment, my thoughts fastened upon Peter.*

2 if your eyes fasten upon someone or something, you start to look at them very carefully or for a long time = FASTEN ON

fasten upon sb/sth *He could not describe the horror of what his eyes had fastened upon.*

FATHOM /ˈfæðəm/
fathoms, fathoming, fathomed

ˌfathom 'out *British*

to understand something complicated or mysterious after thinking about it carefully for some time = WORK OUT

fathom out sth *also* **fathom sth out** *It's impossible to fathom out how such a small amount of money can save the situation.* ♦ *Why had she left? I couldn't fathom it out.*

FATTEN /ˈfæt(ə)n/
fattens, fattening, fattened

ˌfatten 'up

1 to make an animal fatter so that it will be nicer to eat = FEED UP

fatten up sth *also* **fatten sth up** *We're fattening up the turkey for slaughter.*
♦ *The feed is designed to fatten the birds up.*

2 *humorous* to make someone fatter, often deliberately because you think they look too thin

fatten sb up *also* **fatten up sb** *Mother's always trying to fatten us up.* ♦ *Her recipes are fattening up the nation.*

FAVOR the American spelling of **favour**

FAVOUR /ˈfeɪvə, *American* ˈfeɪvər/
favours, favouring, favoured

'favour with *mainly literary*

to give someone something such as a look, smile, or answer to a question

favour sb with sth *They have not favoured us with a reply.*

FAWN /fɔːn, *American* fɔn/
fawns, fawning, fawned

'fawn over (*also* 'fawn on) *showing disapproval*

to praise someone and do things for them because you want them to like you or give you something

fawn over sb *Politicians fawn over him when he comes to town.*

FAX /fæks/
faxes, faxing, faxed

ˌfax 'through

to send a message to someone using a fax machine

fax sth through *also* **fax through sth** *I can fax the figures through later.* ♦ *The shop faxed through a copy of the original estimate.*

FEAR /fɪə, *American* fɪr/
fears, fearing, feared

'fear for

to feel worried about someone or something because you think that something bad may happen to them or has happened to them

fear for sb/sth *Police now fear for the children, who have not yet been found.*
♦ *He fears for the future of the restaurant if customer numbers continue to fall.*
♦ *Hundreds of innocent civilians fear for their lives.*

FEAST /fiːst, *American* fist/
feasts, feasting, feasted

'feast on (*also* 'feast upon)

to eat a lot of a particular food with great enjoyment

feast on sth *We feasted on strawberries and cream.*

FEED /fiːd, *American* fid/
feeds, feeding, fed /fed/

ˌfeed 'in

to push something into a machine, especially slowly and gently

feed sth in *Feed the paper in slowly.*

ˌfeed 'into ★★

1 to push something into a machine, especially slowly and gently

feed sth into sth *She kept feeding coins into the machine.*

2 [often passive] to provide a supply of something for a machine
be fed into sth *Information is fed into the computer and stored in a database.*
feed sth into sth *A modified carburettor feeds air and gas into the engine.*

'feed off (*also* 'feed on)

1 if animals feed off something, they eat it as their usual food = EAT, LIVE ON
feed off sth *The ducklings feed off small water plants.*

2 to use something in order to continue to exist or become stronger, especially something that is bad for another person
feed off sth *Both sides in the conflict feed off old suspicions.* ♦ *She seemed to feed on his despair.*

,feed 'up British informal

to give someone more food than usual in order to make them stronger or less thin
feed sb up *My mother always tries to feed me up when I come home from college.*

FEEL /fiːl, *American* fil/
feels, feeling, felt /felt/

,feel a'round

to feel somewhere with your hands, especially because you cannot see clearly and you are looking for something
feel around *Why didn't you put the light on instead of feeling around in the dark?*
♦ **+for** *He felt around for the bedside table.*

'feel for ★

1 to feel sympathy for someone
= SYMPATHIZE WITH
feel for sb *Poor Jane, I really feel for her.* ♦ *As a man who would like to marry and have a family, I feel for women who also long to have children.*

2 to try to find something with your hands, especially because you cannot see clearly
feel for sth *He felt for the light switch.*

,feel 'out informal

to try to discover in a careful or indirect way what a situation is like or what someone's attitude is
feel out sth *Try to feel out the vendor's position, collecting as much information as you can.*

,feel 'up informal

to touch someone sexually when they do not want you to touch them = TOUCH UP
feel sb up *He tried to feel me up on the back of the bus.*

FENCE /fens/
fences, fencing, fenced

,fence 'in

1 [often passive] to put some kind of fence around something
be fenced in *The school grounds were fenced in with barbed wire.*
fence sth in *also* **fence in sth** *They fenced the animals in.* ♦ *Villages are being urged to fence in their rubbish dumps.*

2 to limit someone's freedom = HEM IN
fence sb in *We would no longer be bound by the rules that had fenced us in for so long.*

,fence 'off ★ [often passive]

to separate an area by surrounding it with some kind of fence
be fenced off *Part of the grounds are fenced off so the public cannot go there.*
fence off sth *Farmers are fencing off the fields used for animal feeding.*
fence sth off *Why don't they fence the whole area off?* ♦ *Someone fell in the pond and drowned so they fenced it off.*

FEND /fend/
fends, fending, fended

'fend for ★

PHRASE **fend for yourself** to look after yourself without help from anyone else: *She had always had to fend for herself, even as a child.*

,fend 'off ★★

1 to defend yourself against an attack, especially by pushing someone away
= WARD OFF
fend off sb/sth *She used a chair to fend off her attacker.* ♦ *His opponent jumped back and tried to fend off the blows.*
fend sb/sth off *He wasn't strong enough to fend his attackers off.*

2 to protect yourself from criticism or a difficulty, especially by ignoring it or not dealing directly with it = DEFLECT
fend off sth *So far, he has managed to fend off criticism of his policies.*
fend sth off *She was besieged by media inquiries, but managed to fend them off.*

FERRET /'ferɪt, *American* 'ferət/
ferrets, ferreting, ferreted

,ferret 'out

to discover a person or a piece of information by searching for it in a determined way
ferret out sb/sth *also* **ferret sb/sth out** *Journalists have to be good at ferreting*

out information. ♦ *They hired spies to ferret out union sympathizers.* ♦ *If they returned to London, the police would soon ferret them out.*

FESS /fes/
fesses, fessing, fessed

,**fess 'up** *informal*
to admit that something is true or that you have done something wrong
= CONFESS, OWN UP
fess up *How was the money spent? It's time for the government to fess up.*

FETCH /fetʃ/
fetches, fetching, fetched

,**fetch 'up** *British informal old-fashioned*
to arrive at a place by accident or without intending to go there = LAND UP
fetch up *The men had somehow fetched up on a remote Pacific island.* ♦ *It was unlikely that he was killed at the spot where his body fetched up.*

FIDDLE /ˈfɪd(ə)l/
fiddles, fiddling, fiddled

,**fiddle a'round** (*also* ,**fiddle a'bout**
British)
1 to touch, move, or change something many times in order to improve it or make it work better = MESS AROUND
fiddle around with sth *He's been fiddling around with the video player again.*
♦ *Children are the losers when they keep fiddling around with education.*
2 to touch or move something with many small quick movements of your fingers because you are bored, nervous or concentrating on something else
fiddle around *She was constantly fiddling around in her bag.* ♦ **+with** *She took a tin of beans out of the cupboard and fiddled around with it.*
3 to waste time doing things that are not important or useful
fiddle around *For three years he fiddled around, doing part-time jobs.*

FIGHT /faɪt/
fights, fighting, fought /fɔːt, *American* fɔt/

,**fight 'back** ★★
1 to hit or kick someone who is attacking you = RETALIATE
fight back *He was wounded several times, but continued to fight back.*
2 to try to stop someone from criticizing

you or doing something harmful to you
= HIT BACK
fight back *Small firms hit by crime are fighting back.* ♦ **+against** *The concert organizers have fought back against their critics.* ♦ *It's time to fight back against firms that are trying to take over the market.*

3 if you fight back an emotion, you try very hard not to show it = FORCE BACK, REPRESS
fight back sth *He fought back the urge to look over his shoulder.*
fight sth back *Tears came to her eyes, but she bit her lip and fought them back.*

■ **fightback** /ˈfaɪtbæk/ **noun** [C] *British*
a situation in which you end by defeating an opponent who was winning before: *Schmidt looked set for an easy win but Taylor staged a dramatic fightback in the second half.*

,**fight 'down**
to try hard not to feel or express an emotion that you are starting to feel
fight down sth *also* **fight sth down** *She stood still, fighting down a feeling of panic.* ♦ *He could feel anger rising inside him but he fought it down.*

,**fight 'off** ★★
1 to defend yourself against someone who is trying to attack you = FEND OFF
fight off sb *The woman managed to fight off her attackers.*
fight sb off *With a massive effort she tried to fight him off.*
2 to try to prevent a competitor from defeating you, especially in sport or business
fight off sb/sth *They had successfully fought off a takeover bid from one of the major airlines.*
fight sb/sth off *The reigning champion successfully fought her challenger off.*

Nouns often used as objects with
fight off 2

■ **attempt, bid, challenge, competition, competitor, rival**

3 if your body fights off an illness, it prevents the illness from making you ill
fight off sth *Regular exercise helps the body to fight off illnesses.*
fight sth off *She got an infection and her immune system wasn't strong enough to fight it off.*

,**fight 'out** ★ [often passive]
if people fight something out, they fight, argue, or compete until one of them wins
be fought out *In Pakistan, family feuds are fought out between men.*

figure 154 **fill**

fight out sth *England and Germany fought out a thrilling 4–4 draw.*
fight sth out *This is nonsense. I'm going to leave them to **fight it out**.*

FIGURE /'fɪgə, *American* 'fɪgjər/
figures, figuring, figured

'figure on
to think that something will happen in a particular way
figure on (doing) sth *She hadn't figured on him reacting this way.* ♦ *This was something he hadn't figured on.*

,figure 'out ★★
1 to be able to understand something or solve a problem = WORK OUT
figure out sth *We had to figure out the connection between the two events.*
figure out how/what/who etc *I couldn't figure out what the teacher was talking about.* ♦ *She couldn't figure out why she was making no progress.*
figure sth out *You can figure the rest out for yourself.* ♦ *Why would anyone want to kill him? He just couldn't figure it out.*
2 to understand what someone is like and why they behave in the way they do = WORK OUT, MAKE OUT
figure sb out *I find Steve very strange – I can't figure him out at all!* ♦ *He sat quietly, saying nothing, trying to figure Kay out.*

FILE /faɪl/
files, filing, filed

,file a'way [often passive]
to put a document away in a file
be filed away *All the relevant documents are filed away with the property deeds.*
file sth away *also* **file away sth** *Can you file this lot away for me please?* ♦ *File away your lecture notes carefully.*

,file 'down [often passive]
to rub something with a metal tool in order to make it smooth or to cut it
be filed down *The horse had to have its teeth filed down.*
file sth down *File the edges down in order to give a smooth finish.*

'file for
PHRASES **file for bankruptcy** to officially ask a court to state that you are unable to pay the money that you owe people: *The company was forced to file for bankruptcy.*
file for divorce to officially ask a court to legally end your marriage: *She made a tearful phone call to her parents,* *saying she was going to file for divorce.*

FILL /fɪl/
fills, filling, filled

,fill 'in ★★★
1 to add information such as your name or address in the empty spaces on an official document = FILL OUT; *formal* COMPLETE
fill in sth *Fill in the missing words.*
♦ *Please fill in your name and address in the space provided.* ♦ *There were loads of forms to fill in.*
fill sth in *You might need some help filling the application form in.*
2 [usually passive] to put something into a hole or space so that the hole or space no longer exists = BLOCK, PLUG
be filled in *The canal is now disused and partly filled in.*
3 *informal* to give someone details about something
fill sb in *I don't know what's happened. I'm waiting for someone to fill me in.*
♦ *I'll tell you the situation, then maybe you can fill the others in.* ♦ **+on** *My secretary will fill you in on the details.*
♦ *Who's going to fill me in on the gossip?*
4 to do someone's job for them while they are away = STAND IN
fill in *I'm not the usual secretary. I'm just filling in.* ♦ **+for** *I'm filling in for the receptionist at the moment.*
PHRASE **fill in the blanks** to give or learn information that is needed in order to understand something properly: *We know roughly how the system works, but Brian is here to fill in the blanks.*

■ **'fill-in** **noun** [C] **1** someone who does another person's work while they are away: *I was just a fill-in when she wasn't available.* **2** a job that you do temporarily, while you look for another job: *This might suit me for a while, as a fill-in.*

,fill 'out ★★
1 to add information such as your name or address in the empty spaces on an official document = FILL IN; *formal* COMPLETE
fill out sth *It took me several hours to fill out the application form.* ♦ *Not everyone enjoys filling out questionnaires.*
fill sth out *I've just got to fill this order form out.*
2 *informal* if someone fills out, their body becomes less thin = PUT ON WEIGHT ≠ SLIM DOWN
fill out *He looked different. He had filled out and he had less hair.*

,fill 'up ★★★

1	make sth full
2	become full
3	food: make you no longer hungry
4	give sb a lot of food
5	eat a lot of food
+	fill-up noun

1 to make something full ≠ EMPTY
fill up sth *He turned on the tap and filled up the kettle.* ♦ **+with** *They go over the border to fill up their cars with cheap petrol.*
fill sth up *When the machine runs out of cans, a man comes round and fills it up.* ♦ *I can't eat any more. You've already filled my plate up.* ♦ **+with** *She kept filling my glass up with champagne.* ♦ *Put a layer of pebbles in the bottom of a plant pot and fill it up with damp soil.*
2 to become full of something ≠ EMPTY
fill up *By eight o'clock the restaurant was beginning to fill up.* ♦ **+with** *Waves were crashing over the sides of the boat, and it was filling up with water.*
3 if a particular food fills you up, it makes you feel full and no longer hungry
= SATISFY
fill sb up *It doesn't taste very nice but it fills you up.*
4 to give someone enough food so that they feel full and no longer feel hungry
fill sb up *I try and fill the kids up at lunchtime so that they don't need any more food until the evening.* ♦ **+with** *They filled me up with cakes and sandwiches.*
5 to eat enough of a particular kind of food so that you feel full and no longer hungry
fill up on sth *If you're very hungry, fill up on rice, pasta and potatoes.*
■ **'fill-up** noun [C] an act of filling something until it is completely full, especially the act of filling a car's petrol tank with petrol: *With this network of service stations, drivers are never very far from a fill-up.*

FILM /fɪlm/
films, filming, filmed

,film 'over
to become covered in a thin layer of something = MIST OVER ≠ CLEAR
film over *Her eyes filmed over and she began to cry.*

FILTER /'fɪltə, *American* 'fɪltər/
filters, filtering, filtered

,filter 'out
1 if an object or substance filters out something that is not wanted, it removes it as it passes through it
filter out sth *also* **filter sth out** *Reed beds filter out much of the pollution.* ♦ *His mask filtered the horrible smell out.*
2 to remove things from a group
filter out sb/sth *also* **filter sb/sth out** *At the first meeting we filter out all unsuitable candidates.* ♦ *Use what methods you need to filter non-essential material out.*

FIND /faɪnd/
finds, finding, found /faʊnd/

,find a'gainst
to formally decide that someone is wrong after listening to all the facts
find against sb *The court found against the plaintiff.*

,find 'for
to formally decide that someone is right after listening to all the facts
find for sb *In the end, the jury found for the defendant.*

,find 'out ★★★
1 to discover a fact or piece of information
= DISCOVER
find out sth *We may never find out the truth about what happened.*
find out who/what/why etc *The police are determined to find out who killed Louise.* ♦ *I don't know where she lives but I'll try and find out.*
find out (that) *Her parents found out that she had a boyfriend.*
find out about sth *I don't want anyone else to find out about this.*
find sth out *It's only by asking questions that you find things out.*
2 [often passive] to discover that someone has been dishonest or has tricked you
= CATCH OUT
be found out *He knew he would be found out sooner or later.*
find sb out *It was only a matter of time before someone found him out.*

FINISH /'fɪnɪʃ/
finishes, finishing, finished

,finish 'off ★★★
1 to do the last part of something so that it is complete = COMPLETE
finish off *We're just finishing off now.*

finish off sth *They hired a smaller company to finish off the job.* ♦ *I just need to finish off a few things first.*

finish sth off *The children will enjoy finishing this cake off.* ♦ *I've done most of my essay. I just need to finish it off.*

finish off doing sth *Do you mind if I finish off eating my lunch while we talk?*

finish off by doing sth *He finished off by lightly blow-drying her hair.*

2 to eat, drink, or use all of something so that there is none left = FINISH UP

finish off sth *Do you want to finish off these sandwiches?* ♦ *They finished off their meal and left the restaurant.*

finish sth off *He finished the bottle of wine off and slammed it down on the table.* ♦ *There's only a little brandy left. We might as well finish it off.*

3 *informal* to kill someone, especially someone who is already injured = KILL

finish sb off *It was the drink that really finished him off.*

4 *informal* to make someone feel extremely tired = TIRE OUT; *formal* EXHAUST

finish sb off *That walk round the lake just about finished me off!*

ˌfinish ˈup ★★

1 to be in a particular place or situation at the end of a long series of events = END UP ≠ START OFF

finish up in/at/under etc *She eventually finished up in London.* ♦ *We spent the day shopping and finished up at an expensive restaurant.*

finish up doing sth *Lisa always finishes up doing most of the work.*

finish up with sth *I never thought I'd finish up with a famous husband.*

finish up dead/broke etc *He finished up dead after a street fight.*

2 to eat, drink, or use all of something so that there is none left = FINISH OFF

finish up sth *Finish up your drinks, please.*

finish sth up *Did you finish that cement up?* ♦ *If there's any chicken left, I finish it up for lunch the day after.*

ˈfinish with ★★

1 if you have finished with something, you have stopped using it and no longer need it

finish with sth *Have you finished with the red pen?* ♦ *When you've finished with the sponge, simply rinse it in cold water.*

2 *informal* to end a relationship with someone so that they are no longer your boyfriend or girlfriend = BREAK UP WITH

finish with sb *She's terrified he'll finish with her.*

3 to punish someone, or to tell someone that you are very angry with them

finish with sb *I'll talk to you when I've finished with Tom.* ♦ *He won't be laughing when I've finished with him.*

FIRE /faɪə, *American* faɪr/
fires, firing, fired

ˌfire aˈway [always in imperative]

used for telling someone that they can ask a question or begin asking questions

fire away *'Can I ask you a question?'* – *'Fire away'.*

ˌfire ˈback at

to answer a question or remark quickly and in an angry way

fire back at sb *The government has fired back at those who oppose their action.*

ˌfire ˈoff

1 [often passive] to quickly send a message or give instructions

be fired off to sth *The commands are fired off to the database.*

fire off sth *also* **fire sth off** *First thing the next morning I was going to fire off a letter.* ♦ *I usually fire a few emails off before I settle down to work.* ♦ **+to** *I sat down and fired off a letter to my MP.*

2 to shoot with a gun or other weapon = FIRE

fire off sth *also* **fire sth off** *The British ship fired off a few warning shots.*

ˌfire ˈup ★ [usually passive]

to make someone feel very enthusiastic or angry

be/get fired up *She's all fired up about this new course she's taking.* ♦ *He was getting fired up because no one was agreeing with him.*

■ ˌfired-ˈup **adj** *informal* feeling very excited about something or eager to do something: *The new scheme was the product of fired-up managers.*

FIRM /fɜːm, *American* fɜrm/
firms, firming, firmed

ˌfirm ˈup

1 [often passive] to make something more definite, or to become more definite

be firmed up *The agreement has still to be firmed up.*

firm up sth *also* **firm sth up** *Negotiators will meet later this week to firm up the deal.* ♦ *Can we firm that up as a date for the meeting?*

firm up *Voting preferences have firmed up over the past few months.*

2 to make the muscles in a part of your

body stronger = TONE UP, STRENGTHEN

firm up sth *also* **firm sth up** *This exercise is good for firming up your abdominal muscles.*

3 to give someone or something what they need in order to be stronger

firm up sth *also* **firm sth up** *They've agreed to firm up their peacekeeping force.*

FISH /fɪʃ/
fishes, fishing, fished

ˈfish for
to try to make someone tell you something or say something to you, for example by asking them questions = ANGLE FOR

fish for sth *He's always fishing for information about my sister.* ♦ *Are you fishing for compliments?*

ˌfish ˈout ★
1 to pull someone or something out of the water

fish sb/sth out *A tourist jumped into the canal to fish the boy out.* ♦ **+with** *I dropped my keys in the pond and had to fish them out with a fishing net.*

fish out sth *He took a spoon and fished out the teabag.*

2 to pull something out of a bag or other container = PULL OUT ≠ PUT IN

fish sth out *She reached into her bag and fished a pen out.* ♦ **+from** *He fished out a bottle of whisky from his bag.*

FIT /fɪt/
fits, fitting, fitted *or American* **fit**

ˈfit for
1 [usually passive] to measure a person and then provide the correct size of clothing or piece of equipment

be fitted for sth *The soldiers were being fitted for their uniforms.*

2 to provide the necessary skills or experience for a particular job, situation, or way of life

fit sb for sth *His background seemed to fit him for government.* ♦ *The object of parenthood is to fit your children for an independent existence.*

ˌfit ˈin ★★

1	belong to a group etc
2	be accepted by a group etc
3	have enough time for sb/sth
4	have enough space for sth
5	be correct/suitable/sensible

1 to belong to a group, plan, or situation

fit in *He explained the project to me and how my job fits in.* ♦ **+with** *He didn't fit in with her plans, so she left him.*

2 to be accepted by a group of people because you are similar to them = *formal* CONFORM

fit in *I tried to fit in but they were all much younger than I was.* ♦ **+with** *She fitted in with her new colleagues straight away.*

3 to have enough time to deal with someone or something = SLOT IN

fit sb/sth in *Dr Halden can fit you in this morning at 10.* ♦ *There's so much going on in her life, I don't know how she fits it all in.* ♦ **+around** *He fits his work in around his family commitments.*

fit in sth *Some days I simply can't fit in my daily walk.*

4 fit in or **fit into** to have space for someone or something

fit sb/sth in *I'll come in your car, if you can fit me in.* ♦ *My suitcase is full – I can't fit anything else in.*

fit in sth *I can only fit in one more person.*

fit sb/sth into sth *Could you fit a double bed into the small bedroom?*

5 to be correct, suitable, or sensible in relation to something else

fit in *Her account of things didn't quite fit in.* ♦ **+with** *Western ideas were modified to fit in with Japanese reality.*

ˌfit ˈout
1 [usually passive] to put equipment into a room or building so that it can be used for a particular purpose = EQUIP

be fitted out *The office had been fitted out in style.* ♦ **+with** *The kitchen has been fitted out with pine cupboards.*

2 [often passive] to give someone clothes or equipment for a particular purpose

be/get fitted out *This is where they bring new members to get fitted out.*

fit sb out *also* **fit out sb** *It costs a lot of money to fit both children out.* ♦ *Can we afford to fit out the whole team?* ♦ **+ with** *We fitted them out with wet suits and surf boards.*

■ **outfit** /ˈaʊtfɪt/ **noun** [C] **1** a set of clothes that are worn together: *I need a new outfit for the wedding.* **2** an organization, especially a small firm: *Is this a nationwide company, or a local outfit?*

■ **outfit** /ˈaʊtfɪt/ verb [T] to provide someone or something with the clothes or equipment that they need for a particular purpose: *a van that is outfitted with modems and laptop computers*

,fit to'gether ★★

1 if things fit together, you can join them together because they are the right size or shape

fit together *The ends of the tube fit together.* ♦ *He had a technical mind and loved to see how all the working parts fit together.* ♦ *All the pieces had to fit together without any gaps.*

2 if ideas or facts fit together, they can be joined to make a sensible story or explanation

fit together *The facts were beginning to fit together.* ♦ *We have all the evidence but we don't know yet how it fits together.*

3 if you fit things together, you join them in the right way to make something

fit sth together *I've got all the pieces; now I just have to fit them together.* ♦ *The instructions told you how to fit the bed together.*

,fit 'up [often passive] British

1 to provide the equipment that is needed for a particular purpose or activity
= EQUIP

be fitted up *The boat was fitted up in an elegant style.* ♦ **+with** *The den was fitted up with electric light.*

fit up sb/sth *He fitted up a laboratory in his house.*

fit sb/sth up with sth *He asked the coach to fit him up with a pair of boxing gloves.*

2 *informal* to make it seem that someone is guilty of a crime when they are not
= FRAME

be fitted up *I'm innocent. I've been fitted up.*

fit sb up *The police were trying to fit me up.*

'fit with ★★ [often passive]

to put a particular kind of equipment into something such as a vehicle, room, or building

be fitted with sth *The new trains are fitted with air conditioning.*

fit sth with sth *They fitted the engine with a new piston.*

FIX /fɪks/
fixes, fixing, fixed

'fix on

1 to choose someone or something after considering the situation = DECIDE ON

fix on sth *We've finally fixed on the Lake District for our summer holiday.*

2 [often passive] if you fix your eyes or your attention on someone or something, you look straight at them and at nothing else

be fixed on sth/sb *I kept my eyes fixed on the horizon.*

fix sth on sth *She fixed her gaze on Jeff.*

3 [always passive] *informal* if you are fixed on something, you think about it so much, or you are so determined to do it, that you do not think about anything else

be fixed on (doing) sth *He was fixed on a career in the army.* ♦ *Why are you so fixed on causing trouble for me?*

,fix 'up ★★

1	make sth happen
2	arrange sth for sb
3	repair, clean etc
4	find romantic partner for sb
5	get dressed up, made up etc

1 to arrange for something to happen
= SORT OUT, ARRANGE

fix up sth *Perhaps we can fix up a meeting for next week.* ♦ *I went to the bank to fix up a loan.*

fix sth up *We should be able to fix the interview up for some other time.* ♦ *If you want to go on a date with my brother, I'll fix it up.*

2 *informal* to arrange for someone to have something that they need = SORT OUT

fix sb up *If you need more equipment, Mark will fix you up.* ♦ **+with** *I can fix you up with a place to live.* ♦ *His father fixed him up with a job in the family business.*

3 to clean, repair, or decorate something
= DO UP

fix sth up *We know someone who fixes old cookers up.* ♦ *They take old furniture and fix it up.*

fix up sth *I'm going to fix up the house before my mother-in-law arrives.*

4 *informal* to arrange for two people to meet so that they might begin a romantic relationship

fix sb up *Teresa's always trying to fix me up.* ♦ **+with** *Jimmy wants to fix Joe up with his sister.*

5 [often passive] *mainly American* to make yourself look nice, for example by putting on nice clothes

be fixed up *I got all fixed up for the party.*

fix yourself up *Go and fix yourself up – the Clarks are coming over.*

'fix with

if you fix someone with your eyes, you look directly in their eyes so that they feel they cannot turn away

fix sb with sth *Mary fixed him with a cool gaze.*

FIZZLE /ˈfɪz(ə)l/
fizzles, fizzling, fizzled

,fizzle 'out
to gradually fail, become less enthusiastic, or disappear, especially after starting successfully = PETER OUT
fizzle out *The group's efforts at reform fizzled out after their leader left.*

FLAG /flæg/
flags, flagging, flagged

,flag 'down
to wave at the driver of a car so that they stop = WAVE DOWN
flag down sb/sth *also* **flag sb/sth down**
A couple of tourists were trying to flag down a cab. ♦ *The police finally managed to flag him down.*

,flag 'up
to mention something so that people know about it
flag up sth *also* **flag sth up** *They've already flagged up several problems.*
♦ *They were one of the first public bodies to flag this issue up.*

FLAIL /fleɪl/
flails, flailing, flailed

,flail a'round (*also* ,flail a'bout *British*)
to move your arms and legs about in an uncontrolled way = THRASH AROUND
flail around *Bob was still flailing around on the ice.*

FLAKE /fleɪk/
flakes, flaking, flaked

,flake 'off
to come off a surface in small flat pieces
flake off *After a while, cheap nail polish starts to flake off.*
flake off sth *The skin was beginning to flake off her face.*

,flake 'out *informal*
to go to sleep very quickly because you are very tired = COLLAPSE
flake out *He had flaked out on the bed.*

FLARE /fleə, American fler/
flares, flaring, flared

,flare 'off [usually passive]
to burn gas and let it go into the atmosphere
be flared off *Some natural gas is flared off as a by-product of oil production.*

,flare 'out
to spread out or become wider at one end
flare out *The trousers flare out below the knee.*

,flare 'up ★
1 if fighting, trouble, or a disagreement flares up, it begins or becomes worse
= ERUPT ≠ DIE DOWN
flare up *It looked as if long-feared violence might flare up.* ♦ *He is worried that the row might flare up again.*
2 if an illness or medical condition flares up, it becomes worse
flare up *In moments of stress, his asthma always flares up.*
3 to suddenly burn or shine brightly
flare up *The fire could flare up again at any time.* ♦ *Novae are stars which flare up suddenly and shine brightly for a few days.*

■ **'flare-up** noun [C] **1** an occasion when people suddenly start behaving in an angry or violent way: *There was a flare-up involving three of the players.* **2** an occasion when a disease suddenly returns after you have not had it for some time: *The symptoms are largely under control, but there's still the occasional flare-up.*

FLASH /flæʃ/
flashes, flashing, flashed

,flash a'round
to show something to a lot of people because you want to impress them
flash sth around *If you're carrying a lot of cash, don't flash it around.* ♦ *She enjoyed flashing her bandaged arm around to gain sympathy.*

,flash 'back to
to suddenly remember something that happened in the past
flash back to sth *His memory flashed back to the last time he was in a prison cell.*

■ **flashback** /ˈflæʃbæk/ noun **1** [C] a very clear memory of something unpleasant or painful that happened in the past: *I kept getting flashbacks of her lying there on the ground.* **2** [C/U] a part of a book, film, or play that tells you what happened during an earlier time: *The story is told in flashbacks as the brothers learn of their parents' first meeting.*

,flash 'by (*also* ,flash 'past)
to go past very quickly
flash by *A car flashed by on the other side of the road.*

flash by sth *His first shot flashed by the post.*

'flash on *American informal*
to realize or remember something
flash on sth *He suddenly flashed on the girl's name.* ♦ *It was then that I flashed on the fact that the two were related.*

,flash 'past *same as* flash by

FLATTEN /'flæt(ə)n/
flattens, flattening, flattened

'flatten against
to press your body, or part of your body, against a surface so that the part that is touching the surface becomes flat
flatten sth against sth *She flattened her breasts against his chest.*
flatten yourself against sth *He jumped round the corner and flattened himself against the wall.*

,flatten 'out
1 if something flattens out, or if you flatten it out, it becomes flat or flatter
flatten out *After the town of Kendal, the countryside starts to flatten out.*
flatten out sth *also* **flatten sth out** *Her long fingers began to flatten out the creased piece of paper.* ♦ *I flattened the magazine out in front of me.*
2 if the price or amount of something flattens out, or if something flattens it out, it becomes lower or less likely to change
= LEVEL OFF
flatten out *Over the last few years the sales increase has flattened out.*
flatten out sth *This agreement is expected to flatten out the price of crude oil.*

FLESH /fleʃ/
fleshes, fleshing, fleshed

,flesh 'out [often passive]
to add more details about something in order to make it easier to understand or imagine = AMPLIFY ≠ CONDENSE
be fleshed out *The story needs to be fleshed out a bit.*
flesh out sth *also* **flesh sth out** *He tried to flesh out his party's economic philosophy.* ♦ *It is time to flesh these remarks out a little more.*

FLICK /flɪk/
flicks, flicking, flicked

,flick 'off
to move a switch in order to turn

something such as a light or machine off
= FLIP OFF
flick sth off *also* **flick off sth** *Just flick the bathroom light off, will you?* ♦ *She flicked off the TV set and went to bed.*

,flick 'on
to move a switch in order to turn something such as a light or machine on
= FLIP ON
flick sth on *also* **flick on sth** *There's a fan heater over there. Just flick it on for a few minutes.* ♦ *He flicked on the bedroom light.*

,flick 'through ★
1 to turn the pages of a book, magazine, newspaper etc and look at some of the pages for a very short time only = LOOK THROUGH
flick through sth *She flicked through a hairstyle magazine.* ♦ *He was curled up in an armchair, flicking through a book.*
2 to quickly change from one television channel to another, having a very quick look at each to see what programme is on
flick through sth *He flicked through the channels but there was nothing interesting on.*

FLING /flɪŋ/
flings, flinging, flung /flʌŋ/

'fling at *showing disapproval*
to show that you are interested in someone sexually, in a way that shows a lack of control = THROW AT
fling yourself at sb *You can't fling yourself at every man you meet.*

'fling into
to start doing something with a lot of energy or enthusiasm
fling yourself into sth *He flung himself into his work.*

'fling off
if you fling off your clothes, you take them off quickly = THROW OFF
fling off sth *also* **fling sth off** *She flung off her clothes and left them in a pile on the floor.* ♦ *He hurried inside, flinging his coat off.*

'fling on
if you fling on your clothes, you put them on quickly = THROW ON
fling on sth *also* **fling sth on** *Going into the hall she flung on a coat.* ♦ *I just flung yesterday's clothes on.*

FLIP /flɪp/
flips, flipping, flipped

'flip for *American informal*
to immediately like someone or something very much
flip for sb/sth *Fashionable clients have flipped for her designs.*

,flip 'off
1 *mainly American* to move a switch in order to turn something such as a light or machine off = FLICK OFF
flip off sth *also* **flip sth off** *He flipped off the kitchen light.* ♦ *Flip the light off before you go down to sleep.*
2 *American informal* to make a very rude and offensive sign that you are angry by showing someone your raised middle finger
flip sb off *That guy just flipped me off.*

,flip 'on *mainly American*
to move a switch in order to turn something such as a light or machine on = FLICK ON
flip on sth *also* **flip sth on** *He went into the room and flipped on the TV set.*
♦ *She sits down and flips the radio on.*

,flip 'out *informal*
to become very angry
flip out *He's going to flip out when he finds out what they're saying about him.*

,flip 'over
to turn over quickly, or to make something turn over quickly
flip over *I saw the little boat flip over.*
flip sth over *also* **flip over sth** *He took the tape and flipped it over in his hand.*
♦ *She's flipping over the pages of a magazine.*

'flip through
1 to turn the pages of a book, magazine, newspaper etc very quickly, looking at some of the pages for a very short time
= FLICK THROUGH, LOOK THROUGH, LEAF THROUGH
flip through sth *He flipped through his address book looking for someone to take to the dance.*
2 to quickly change from one television channel to another, having a quick look at each to see which programme is on
= FLICK THROUGH
flip through sth *When the adverts come on, he starts flipping through the channels.*

FLIRT /flɜːt, *American* flɜrt/
flirts, flirting, flirted

'flirt with ★★
to consider an idea or plan, but not very seriously = TOY WITH
flirt with sth *They've been flirting with the idea of selling up.* ♦ *She seems to be flirting with the possibility of changing careers.*
PHRASE **flirt with danger/disaster** to do something that you know you should not do and that may cause you serious trouble: *John, a keen rock climber, has always enjoyed flirting with danger.*

FLOAT /fləʊt, *American* floʊt/
floats, floating, floated

,float a'round (*also* ,float a'bout *British*) *informal*
1 [always progressive] if something is floating around, you have seen it somewhere near but you are not certain where it is
be floating around *There's a pen floating around here somewhere.* ♦ *Don't buy any more plant pots. There are loads of them floating around in the garden.*
2 [usually progressive] if an idea is floating around, it has been suggested but not yet considered
float around *We have various issues floating around that we need to discuss.*

FLOOD /flʌd/
floods, flooding, flooded

,flood 'back
if memories or feelings flood back, you suddenly remember them very clearly
flood back *The memory of the previous evening flooded back.* ♦ *When he told me his name, it all **came flooding back**.*
♦ *The smell of a certain perfume can bring memories flooding back.*

,flood 'in ★★
to arrive somewhere quickly in very large numbers = POUR IN
flood in *Applications have been flooding in since we advertised the jobs last week.*
♦ *Aid workers tried to cope with the thousands of refugees flooding in across the border.*

Nouns often used as subjects with **flood in**

■ applications, calls, complaints, entries, letters, messages, suggestions, tributes

,flood 'out [usually passive]

if a place is flooded out, it becomes filled with water and the people who live there are forced to leave

be flooded out *The ground floor was flooded out.*

FLOP /flɒp, *American* flɑp/
flops, flopping, flopped

,flop 'down

1 to sit or lie down in a heavy way by relaxing your muscles and letting your body fall = PLOP DOWN

flop down *Jamie flopped down beside me.*

2 to move or hang in a loose, heavy, and uncontrolled way

flop down *Her long hair flopped down over her eyes.*

FLOUNDER /'flaʊndə, *American* 'flaʊndər/
flounders, floundering, floundered

,flounder a'round (*also* **,flounder a'bout** *British*)

to move with great difficulty and in an uncontrolled way

flounder around *We floundered around in the dark for a few minutes.*

FLOW /fləʊ, *American* floʊ/
flows, flowing, flowed

'flow from *formal*

to be a natural result of something

flow from sth *Important consequences flow from this decision.* ♦ *There are many benefits flowing from such research.*

FLUFF /flʌf/
fluffs, fluffing, fluffed

,fluff 'out (*also* **,fluff 'up**)

to shake something so that more air goes into it and it becomes larger and softer

fluff sth out *also* **fluff out sth** *Fluff out the pillows after you use them.*

fluff out *When the cat's annoyed his tail fluffs out!*

FLUNK /flʌŋk/
flunks, flunking, flunked

,flunk 'out *mainly American informal*

to have to leave a school because your work is not satisfactory

flunk out *Not many of the kids who enrol flunk out.* ♦ **+of** *Marie has flunked out of college.*

FLUSH /flʌʃ/
flushes, flushing, flushed

,flush a'way

to get rid of an object or a substance by directing a current of water onto it

flush away sth *also* **flush sth away** *You can flush away the debris later.* ♦ *Empty the contents into the sink and flush it away.*

,flush 'out ★

1 to clean something using a lot of water

flush sth out *You need to remove the radiator so that you can flush it out.* ♦ **+with** *Flush the pipes out with cold water.*

flush out sth *Drink at least eight glasses of water a day to flush out your system.*

2 to remove something by pouring a lot of water through the place where it is

flush out sth *Use plain water to flush out the debris.*

flush sth out *The best way of removing embryos is using a fine needle and a syringe to flush them out.* ♦ **+of** *Drinking plenty of water helps to flush harmful substances out of your body.*

3 to force a person or animal to leave the place where they have been hiding = HUNT OUT

flush out sb/sth *The hounds are sent in to flush out the fox.*

flush sb/sth out *They now had an even greater chance of flushing the killer out.*

FLY /flaɪ/
flies, flying, flew /fluː, *American* flu/, **flown** /fləʊn, *American* floʊn/

,fly a'round (*also* **,fly a'bout** *British*)

[usually progressive]

if things such as rumours or stories are flying around, a lot of people are telling each other about something, often something that is not true

fly around *There was a rumour flying around that the factory was closing.*

'fly at

to rush towards someone and attack them violently

fly at sb *She suddenly flew at me, kicking and scratching.*

,fly 'by

if time flies by, it seems to pass very quickly

fly by *The weeks flew by.*

,fly 'in (*also* **,fly 'into**)

1 to arrive in a place by plane

fly in *The President is flying in later*

today to attend the meeting. ♦ *They flew into London late last night.*

2 [often passive] to send something or someone to a place by plane
be flown in *More troops will be flown in next month.*
fly in sth/sb *also* **fly sth/sb in** *We're flying in the tools and equipment needed.* ♦ *The British flew more troops into the southern region.*

,fly 'off

if something flies off, a sudden strong force pushes it away from the thing that it was resting on or was attached to
fly off *She shook her foot and her sandal flew off.*
fly off sth *I saw the watch fly off his wrist.*
PHRASE **fly off the handle** *informal* to suddenly become very angry: *He won't fly off the handle if you're there.*

,fly 'out

1 to go somewhere by plane
fly out *We're flying out to join them next week.* ♦ **+to** *I flew out to California, where the company was based.*
2 to send something or someone to a place by plane
fly out sth/sb *also* **fly sth/sb out** *The company is flying out its own team of experts.* ♦ *They've arranged to fly a replacement out as soon as possible.*

FOB /fɒb, *American* fɑb/
fobs, fobbing, fobbed

,fob 'off

1 [often passive] to give someone an answer or explanation that is not true or complete, in order to make them stop asking questions or complaining
= MISLEAD
be fobbed off *I'm tired of being fobbed off.*
fob sb off *I'm not going to let him fob me off.* ♦ **+with** *It was impossible to fob her off with vague statements.*
2 [usually passive] to give someone something that is not what they want or need
be fobbed off with sth *Customers complain they're being fobbed off with an inferior model.*

FOCUS /'fəʊkəs, *American* 'foʊkəs/
focuses or **focusses, focusing** or **focussing, focused** or **focussed**

'focus on ★★★ (*also* 'focus upon *formal*)

[often passive]
to concentrate on something and pay particular attention to it

be focused on sth *Efforts are now focused on cleaning up the beaches.*
focus on sth *We will focus on three main topics.* ♦ *It's time to focus upon important issues.* ♦ *When I play sports I focus solely on doing my best.* ♦ *Inevitably, much* **attention has focused on** *the wording of the agreement.*
focus sth on sth *The report has focused attention on the dangers of passive smoking.*

FOG /fɒg, *American* fɔg/
fogs, fogging, fogged

,fog 'up

if something such as a window or mirror fogs up, it becomes covered with steam so that you cannot see through it or in it
= STEAM UP
fog up *My glasses had fogged up.*

FOIST /fɔɪst/
foists, foisting, foisted

'foist on (*also* 'foist upon *formal*)

to force someone to accept or deal with something that they do not want
foist sth on sb *The company attempted to foist a defective brake system on a customer.* ♦ *We are not trying to foist our conclusions on you.*

FOLD /fəʊld, *American* foʊld/
folds, folding, folded

,fold a'way

1 if something large such as a piece of furniture folds away, you can fold some of its parts to make it easier to store when you are not using it
fold away *Ideally, we need a bed that folds away.*
2 if you fold something away, you make it flat by folding it and then you store it somewhere
fold sth away *also* **fold away sth** *Jack folded the letter away in his pocket.* ♦ *He folded away the blankets and the sheets.*

,fold 'in

to use a spoon or knife to add something slowly and gently to a mixture
fold sth in *also* **fold in sth** *Slowly fold the flour in.* ♦ *Fold in the egg whites.*

,fold 'into

1 to combine something with something else so that the two things can be dealt with together
fold sth into sth *The bill would fold three agencies into the State Department in a cost-saving plan.*

2 to use a spoon or knife to add something slowly and gently to a mixture
fold sth into sth *Fold the cocoa into the cake mixture.*

,**fold 'over**
to bend a piece of paper or cloth and press one part of it over another part
fold sth over *also* **fold over sth** *Fold the left flap over and hold it down.* ♦ *He took the scrap of paper and folded it over.* ♦ *Make sure you fold over the top of the bag.*

,**fold 'up** ★
1 [often passive] to make something smaller by bending it over on itself more than once ≠ UNFOLD
be folded up *His clothes were neatly folded up on a chair.*
fold sth up *He folded the newspaper up and put it on the table.*
fold up sth *Let me show you how to fold up a map properly.*
2 if a business folds up, it closes because it is not able to make enough money
= CLOSE DOWN, FOLD
fold up *Two months later the company folded up.*

FOLLOW /ˈfɒləʊ, *American* ˈfɑloʊ/
follows, following, followed

,**follow a'round** ★ (*also* ,**follow a'bout** *British*)
to follow someone wherever they go, especially in a way that annoys them
follow sb around *Henry's been following me around like a puppy!* ♦ *Stop following me about!*

,**follow 'on from**
to happen after something, and often as the next part or stage of it
follow on from sth *Following on from last year's success, we'll be offering other similar courses.* ♦ *What I'm going to say follows on from what Elizabeth was saying.*

,**follow 'out**
to take action according to things such as orders or suggestions from other people, or according to your own feelings or plans
follow out sth *We followed out a tip we had from a witness.* ♦ *They had followed out all my instructions.*

,**follow 'through** ★★
1 to continue doing something until it has been completed
follow through *Jack is always starting projects, but he rarely follows through.* ♦ **+with** *The government needs to follow*

through with some very necessary reforms.
2 to continue the movement of your arm or leg after you have hit, kicked, or thrown a ball in a sport
follow through *He put the full force of his boot on the ball, following through flawlessly.*
■ ˈ**follow-through** noun **1** [C/U] the final part of the movement you make when you hit, kick, or throw the ball in a sport: *He has a good swing with a full follow-through.* **2** [U] action that is taken in order to finish something: *Although many claims are lodged with the organization, evidence suggests that follow-through is patchy.*

,**follow 'through on** *mainly American*
1 to do something that you have promised or threatened to do
follow through on sth *Voters will expect Washington to follow through on its promises.*
2 to do something that a situation suggests you should do
follow through on sth *There isn't a system for following through on these reports.* ♦ *People don't follow through on what they see.*

,**follow 'up** ★★★
1 to try to find out more about something or do something more to deal with it
follow sth up *They never followed my complaint up.* ♦ *She started the investigation but never followed it up.*
follow up sth *The police are now following up some new leads.* ♦ **+on** *You'll want to follow up on this report.*
2 to do something in addition to what you have already done, in order to be certain of achieving your aim
follow up sth *The project follows up a previous research programme.* ♦ **+with** *Follow up the phone call with a written confirmation.* ♦ *How many people did not follow up their enquiry with an application?*
follow sth up *It was a brilliant victory, but he was unable to follow it up.* ♦ **+with** *Always follow your question up with a more specific one.*
3 to check the health of someone who has received medical treatment, in order to be certain that it has been effective
follow up sb *The study followed up over 200 heart patients.*
follow sb up *Recurrence of the symptoms is higher among young children, and we recommend following these up.*
■ ˈ**follow-up** noun **1** [C/U] something

that is done in order to complete something: *Everyone liked my proposal, but there hasn't been any follow-up.* ♦ *Researchers conducted a follow-up study two years later.* **2** a check carried out after medical treatment to make sure that the treatment was effective: *These patients did not require a proper medical follow-up.* ♦ *Patients were given a questionnaire about their diet at every follow-up visit to the hospital.* **3** [C] a book, film, or article that is based on or develops an earlier one = SEQUEL: *The author refused to write a follow-up.* **4** [C] *mainly journalism* a question that you ask immediately after another question, in order to get more information: *You are trained always to ask a follow-up.* ♦ *He then asked a follow-up question, which the spokeswoman refused to answer.*

FOOL /fuːl, *American* ful/
fools, fooling, fooled

,fool a'round (*also* ,fool a'bout *British*)
1 to behave in a silly way for fun = MESS AROUND, CLOWN
fool around *Mark admits he used to fool around in class.*
2 to have a sexual relationship with someone who is not your usual partner = HAVE AN AFFAIR
fool around *He had been fooling around behind her back.* ♦ **+with** *I think he's fooling around with someone from the office.*

,fool a'round with (*also* ,fool a'bout with)
to handle or use something in a stupid or careless way = MESS AROUND WITH
fool around with sth *Someone had been fooling about with the controls.*

'fool with *mainly American*
1 to touch or use something in a stupid or careless way that could cause accidents or trouble = MESS WITH
fool with sth *The first thing you learn is not to fool with acid.*
2 to become involved with something or someone that is dangerous
fool with sth/sb *It's time you stopped fooling with these kids.*

FOOTLE /'fuːt(ə)l, *American* 'fut(ə)l/
footles, footling, footled

,footle a'round (*also* ,footle a'bout *British*) *informal*
to waste time doing things that are not important or necessary

footle around *Dad spent the afternoon footling around with an old typewriter I was planning to throw away.*

FORCE /fɔːs, *American* fɔrs/
forces, forcing, forced

,force 'back
to try very hard not to show your emotion = FIGHT BACK
force back sth *also* **force sth back** *'Why are you leaving me?' she said, forcing back the tears.* ♦ *A wave of nausea came over her, but she forced it back.*

,force 'down
1 to make something become lower
force down sth *also* **force sth down** *Staffing cuts are forcing down standards.* ♦ *More competition will force prices down.*
2 to eat or drink something even though you do not want to
force down sth *also* **force sth down** *I managed to force down a sandwich.* ♦ *Don't force the food down if you are satisfied with less.*
3 [usually passive] to force a plane to land
be forced down *His plane was forced down in enemy territory.*

,force 'into ★★ [often passive]
to make someone do something that they do not want to do, for example by using threats
be forced into sth *I only went to church because I was forced into it.*
be forced into doing sth *He had been forced into making a quick decision.*
force sb into sth *Her father had forced her into an arranged marriage.*
force sb into doing sth *You can't force him into going out with you.*

'force on
1 to make someone accept something that they do not want = PRESS
force sth on sb *You took over the meeting and forced your views on everyone.* ♦ *He thinks states should not force their will on other nations.*
2 to try and kiss someone or have sex with them when they do not want you to
force yourself on sb *He said he had never forced himself on a woman.*

,force 'out of
to force someone to tell you something
force sth out of sb *He eventually forced the names out of her.*

,force 'through
to do something so that a proposal is accepted or an issue is dealt with quickly

force through sth also **force sth through**
*The Senate hopes to force through
legislation before its summer vacation.*
♦ *The government has a majority and
can usually force its measures through.*
force sth through sth *The company is
determined to force the case through the
courts.*

force 'up
to make something increase
force up sth also **force sth up** *The latest
interest rate rise could force up inflation.*
♦ *Increased demand has forced prices up.*

FORGE /fɔːdʒ, *American* fɔrdʒ/
forges, forging, forged

forge a'head
1 to make strong steady progress = STEAM
AHEAD ≠ LAG BEHIND
forge ahead *Export sales continue to
forge ahead.* ♦ **+with** *He forged ahead
with his plans.*
2 forge ahead or **forge on** to move
forwards in a strong steady way = PRESS
ON ≠ LAG BEHIND
forge ahead *Panting and breathless, she
forged ahead.* ♦ *Napoleon's soldiers
forged on through the snow.*

FORK /fɔːk, *American* fɔrk/
forks, forking, forked

fork 'out *informal*
to spend money on something, especially
when you do not want to
fork out sth *I discovered my car had
been towed away and I'd have to fork
out £70 if I wanted it back.* ♦ **+on/for** *I'm
not forking out 400 quid on ski clothes!*

fork 'over *American informal same as* **fork
out**

FORM /fɔːm, *American* fɔrm/
forms, forming, formed

'form into
to make something into a particular shape
form sth into sth *She formed the clay
into the shape of a head.*

form 'up [often military]
if a military formation forms up, it moves
together in order to create a group that is
correctly or tidily arranged
form up *The procession formed up and
began to march towards the town hall.*

FOUL /faʊl/
fouls, fouling, fouled

foul 'out *American*
in basketball, to be forced to leave a game
after failing to obey the rules more often
than is allowed
foul out *Both players fouled out in the
last five minutes of the game.*

foul 'up [informal]
1 to do something wrong or spoil
something, especially by making
mistakes
foul up *We can't afford to foul up this
time.*
foul sth up also **foul up sth** *Our leaders
should be humble enough to admit when
they completely foul things up.*
2 to become twisted around part of an
engine, machine etc, so that it cannot
move or work properly
foul up sth also **foul sth up** *Watch out for
driftwood which may foul up the boat's
engine.*
■ **'foul-up** noun [C] *informal* a mistake
in a process or system that means it
cannot work effectively: *We don't want
any more foul-ups.*

FOUND /faʊnd/
founds, founding, founded

be 'founded on ★★ (also **be 'founded
upon**)
to be based on a particular idea, principle,
quality etc
be founded on sth *A good relationship
has to be founded on trust.* ♦ *Our political
system is founded upon the idea that all
people are equal.*

FRATERNISE another spelling of
fraternize

FRATERNIZE /'frætənaɪz, *American*
'frætər,naɪz/
fraternizes, fraternizing, fraternized

'fraternize with *showing disapproval*
to spend time with someone and talk to
them in a friendly way, especially
someone you should not be talking to
fraternize with sb *They were told not to
fraternize with journalists.* ♦ *Masters
was accused of fraternizing with the
enemy.*

FREAK /friːk, *American* frik/
freaks, freaking, freaked

,**freak 'out** *informal*

if you freak out, or if someone freaks you out, you become so angry, surprised, excited, or frightened that you cannot control yourself = TRIP OUT
> **freak out** *She just freaked out when she saw the police.*
> **freak sb out** *Meeting my dad again after all these years really freaked me out.*

FREE /friː, *American* fri/
frees, freeing, freed

'**free from** (*also* '**free of**)

to remove controls or obligations from someone, so that they are more able to do what they want to do
> **free sb from sth** *Steps will be taken to free the media from government control.*
> ♦ *He is to be freed of direct responsibility for his staff.*

,**free 'up**

to make someone or something such as time or money available to be used for another purpose
> **free up sb/sth** *also* **free sb/sth up** *We can probably free up £20,000 to buy new computer equipment.* ♦ *We need to free more police officers up for street duties.*

FREEZE /friːz, *American* friz/
freezes, freezing, froze /frəʊz, *American* froʊz/, **frozen** /'frəʊz(ə)n, *American* 'froʊz(ə)n/

,**freeze 'out** *informal*

to stop someone joining a group of people, or taking part in an event or activity, by being deliberately unfriendly to them = EXCLUDE ≠ WELCOME
> **freeze out sb** *also* **freeze sb out** *The rest of the team were starting to freeze me out.* ♦ **+of** *He complained he was being frozen out of family gatherings.*

,**freeze 'over**

to become covered with a layer of ice = ICE OVER
> **freeze over** *It was so cold that the rivers froze over.*
> **PHRASE** **till hell freezes over** *humorous* used for saying that something is very unlikely to happen: *He can wait till hell freezes over, but I'm not going out on a date with him!*

,**freeze 'up** *informal*

1 if something freezes up, it gets so cold that it does not work or cannot move = ICE UP
> **freeze up** *All the locks had frozen up.*

2 to be unable to think of anything to say, especially because you are nervous
> **freeze up** *I can't speak in public – I just freeze up.*

FRESHEN /'freʃ(ə)n/
freshens, freshening, freshened

,**freshen 'up** ★

1 to make something fresher, cleaner, or more attractive
> **freshen up sth** *Freshen up your room with a new coat of paint.*
> **freshen sth up** *Have one of these mints. It will freshen your mouth up.*

2 to wash your hands and face and make yourself cleaner and tidier = WASH
> **freshen yourself up** *Would you like to freshen yourself up before dinner?*
> **freshen up** *I went to the washroom to freshen up.*

3 *American* to improve your skill or knowledge of something = BRUSH UP
> **freshen up sth** *You could freshen up your Spanish with some conversation classes.*
> **freshen sth up** *I need to freshen my French up before we go on vacation.*

FRIG /frɪg/
frigs, frigging, frigged

,**frig a'round** (*also* ,**frig a'bout**) *British offensive*

1 to spend time doing things that are not important

2 to treat someone with no respect

FRIGHTEN /'fraɪt(ə)n/
frightens, frightening, frightened

,**frighten a'way** ★ (*also* ,**frighten 'off**)

1 to make a person or animal so afraid that they run away
> **frighten sb/sth away** *He fired his gun in the air to frighten the dogs away.*
> **frighten away sb/sth** *We leave that there to frighten away the crows.*

2 to make someone so worried or nervous that they decide not to become involved with something
> **frighten away sb** *The fall in share prices frightened off possible investors.*
> **frighten sb away** *These policies are frightening voters away.*

FRITTER /ˈfrɪtə, *American* ˈfrɪtər/
fritters, frittering, frittered

ˌfritter aˈway
to waste time or money on things that are not necessary or important, especially until there is none left = SQUANDER, WASTE
fritter away sth *also* **fritter sth away**
Over the next year he frittered away all his winnings.

FRONT /frʌnt/
fronts, fronting, fronted

ˈfront for
to be a person or company that hides an illegal or secret activity for another person or organization
front for sb/sth *He fronted for banned scriptwriters during the McCarthy era.*

ˌfront ˈonto (*also* ˈfront on) *British*
if a building fronts onto something, it faces it = FACE
front onto sth *The house fronted on to a main road.* ♦ *The building fronts on Bristol Street.*

FROST /frɒst, *American* frɔst/
frosts, frosting, frosted

ˌfrost ˈover (*also* ˌfrost ˈup)
to become completely covered with a thin white layer of ice = ICE OVER, ICE UP
frost over *The windscreen was already starting to frost over.*
be frosted over *The windows were all frosted over.*

FROWN /fraʊn/
frowns, frowning, frowned

ˈfrown on ★ (*also* ˈfrown upon) [often passive]
to not approve of something = DISAPPROVE OF ≠ FAVOUR
be frowned on *Personal phone calls are frowned on at work.*
frown on sth *Her parents frowned on the idea of her becoming an actress.*

FRY /fraɪ/
fries, frying, fried

ˌfry ˈup
to cook food in hot oil or fat
fry up sth *also* **fry sth up** *Heat the oil in a large pan and fry up the onion and garlic for 5 minutes.*

■ ˈfry-up noun [C] *British informal* a meal of fried food, especially consisting of eggs, bacon, and sausages: *You can't beat a fry-up for breakfast.*

FUCK /fʌk/
fucks, fucking, fucked

ˌfuck aˈround (*also* ˌfuck aˈbout *British*)
very offensive
1 to waste time, especially by doing things that are silly or unnecessary
2 to waste someone else's time, or to treat them in a very annoying way

ˌfuck ˈoff *very offensive*
1 [always in imperative] an expression used for telling someone to go away when you are angry with them
2 *British* to make someone very angry

ˌfuck ˈover *very offensive*
to treat someone in a bad or unfair way

ˌfuck ˈup *very offensive*
1 to spoil or damage something completely
2 to make a serious mistake, or to fail completely
3 to make someone very confused, unhappy, or mentally ill

■ ˌfucked ˈup adj *very offensive* **1** so confused, unhappy, or mentally ill that it is hard to live a normal life **2** completely broken, or in a very bad state

■ ˈfuck-up noun [C] *very offensive* **1** a serious mistake, or a complete failure **2** someone who often makes serious mistakes or fails completely

ˈfuck with *very offensive*
to treat someone in an unfair way, or to trick them

FUEL /ˈfjuːəl, *American* ˈfjuəl/
fuels, fuelling, fuelled

ˌfuel ˈup
to put petrol into your vehicle
fuel up *I always make sure I fuel up before starting a long journey.*

FUMBLE /ˈfʌmb(ə)l/
fumbles, fumbling, fumbled

ˌfumble aˈround (*also* ˌfumble aˈbout *British*)
to try to find something using your hands in a way that is not skilful or graceful
fumble around *I fumbled around on the floor and eventually found one of the coins.*

'fumble for

1 to try to hold, move, or find something using your hands in a way that is not skilful or graceful

fumble for sth *She fumbled for her keys in her bag.*

2 to try to find the right words to express something, especially because you are nervous, upset, or embarrassed

fumble for sth *He just stood there, fumbling for the words to tell her it was all over.*

FUNCTION /ˈfʌŋkʃ(ə)n/
functions, functioning, functioned

'function as ★★

to operate as a particular thing or in a particular way

function as sth *A little room over a shop functioned as party headquarters.* ♦ *I felt I could no longer function as their leader.*

FUR /fɜː, American fɜr/
furs, furring, furred

,fur 'up British

1 if one of the tubes in your body that carries blood from the heart furs up, or if it is furred up, it becomes covered inside with a thick substance that stops it working normally

fur up *Smoking causes your arteries to fur up.*

be furred up *The arterial walls are furred up and narrow.*

2 if a pipe or container for water furs up, or if it is furred up, it becomes covered inside with a hard white substance that stops it working normally

fur up *Hard water makes your kettle fur up faster.*

be furred up *The washing machine is furred up again.*

FURNISH /ˈfɜːnɪʃ, American ˈfɜrnɪʃ/
furnishes, furnishing, furnished

'furnish with

to provide someone with something that they need, especially information
= PROVIDE

furnish sb with sth *His evidence may have furnished police with a vital lead.*

FUSS /fʌs/
fusses, fussing, fussed

'fuss at American

to annoy someone by frequently complaining to them about something that they do

fuss at sb *I'm sorry I fussed at her that way.*

'fuss over

to give a person or animal a lot of attention and make sure that they have everything they need

fuss over sb/sth *Everyone was fussing over the new baby.*

'fuss with

to touch or handle something continuously, especially in a nervous way
= FIDGET WITH

fuss with sth *He kept fussing with his tie.*

FUTZ /fʌts/
futzes, futzing, futzed

,futz 'around American informal

to spend time doing silly or unimportant things

futz around *She futzed around in Paris for two years.*

G g

GAD /gæd/
gads, gadding, gadded

,gad a'round (also ,gad a'bout British) old-fashioned showing disapproval

to go from place to place enjoying yourself, especially when you should be doing something else

GAG /gæg/
gags, gagging, gagged

be 'gagging for [always progressive] very informal

to want something very much, especially sex

be gagging for sth *It's obvious he's absolutely **gagging for it**.*

GAIN /geɪn/
gains, gaining, gained

'gain from

to get a benefit or advantage for yourself from something

gain sth from (doing) sth *What do you hope to gain from your stay here?*
♦ *There's a lot to be gained from schools working together.*

'gain in ★

to get more of a particular quality

gain in sth *These new programmes are gaining in popularity.* ♦ *It's good to see her gaining in confidence.*

'gain on

to gradually get closer to someone or something that you are following or trying to catch = CATCH UP WITH

gain on sb/sth *After a slow start, my horse started to gain on the leader.* ♦ *She's beginning to gain on the other children in her group.*

GALLIVANT /'gælɪvænt/
gallivants, gallivanting, gallivanted

ˌgallivant aˈround (also ˌgallivant aˈbout) *informal old-fashioned*

to go from place to place looking for enjoyment

GALLOP /'gæləp/
gallops, galloping, galloped

ˌgallop ˈthrough

to do something very quickly

gallop through sth *I galloped through the last few chapters of the book.*

GALVANIZE /'gælvənaɪz/
galvanizes, galvanizing, galvanized

'galvanize into

to shock or affect someone so strongly that they react by doing something about a situation

galvanize sb into (doing) sth *The shocking pictures of starving children finally galvanized the government into action.*

GAMBLE /'gæmb(ə)l/
gambles, gambling, gambled

ˌgamble aˈway

to lose all of an amount of money by risking it in the hope of winning more = SQUANDER

gamble away sth *also* **gamble sth away** *Before the night was over he'd gambled away all his wife's savings.*

'gamble on

to do something that involves risks and hope, or to expect that things will happen in the way you want = BET ON

gamble on sth *Simone had gambled on the fact that Lucy would come as well.* ♦ *I hadn't gambled on quite so many people coming to the party.*

GANG /gæŋ/
gangs, ganging, ganged

ˌgang ˈup on

to join together in a group in order to hurt, frighten, or fight someone = UNITE AGAINST

gang up on sb *They feel that the international community is ganging up on them.*

GAS /gæs/
gases *or* gasses, gassing, gassed

ˌgas ˈup *American informal*

to put petrol in a car or other vehicle

gas up *Let's gas up before we get on the highway.*

gas up sth *also* **gas sth up** *They'll gas up your car and check your oil.* ♦ *I gassed the Chevy up for a long drive.*

GASP /gɑːsp, American gæsp/
gasps, gasping, gasped

ˌgasp ˈout *mainly literary*

to say something while you are breathing with difficulty, for example because you need more air, or are in pain

gasp out sth *also* **gasp sth out** *He managed to gasp out the enemy's location before collapsing to the ground.*

GATHER /'gæðə, American 'gæðər/
gathers, gathering, gathered

ˌgather aˈround ★ (also ˌgather ˈround *British*)

if people gather around, they come together to form a group or crowd around someone or something

gather around *She started talking so we all gathered around.*

gather around sb/sth *The men had gathered around the fire.* ♦ *Worshippers gathered around the holy man.*

ˌgather ˈin *literary*

to collect crops from the fields when they are ready = HARVEST

gather in sth *also* **gather sth in** *We didn't stop until all the wheat was safely gathered in.*

ˌgather ˈround *British same as* **gather around**

ˌgather ˈup ★★ (also ˌgather toˈgether)

to pick up things from several different places and put them together = PICK UP ≠ PUT DOWN

gather up sth *Janet quickly gathered up her books and left the classroom.*

gather sth up *Gather your things up and bring them with you.*

GEAR /gɪə, *American* gɪr/
gears, gearing, geared

'gear to ★★ (*also* **'gear towards**) [usually passive]
to make something suitable for a particular situation, purpose, or group
be geared to sb/sth *As it stands, the system isn't geared to the needs of children.*

'gear 'up
to prepare yourself for an activity or event
= GET READY
gear up *Now the Foundation, which sponsored the campaign, is gearing up again.* ♦ **+to do sth** *The tobacco companies are gearing up to fight the new tax.*
gear yourself up *Japan and South Korea have already been gearing themselves up, fully aware of the importance of this tournament.* ♦ **+for** *Most banks were gearing themselves up for the electronic age back in the 1970s.*

GEE /dʒiː/
gees, geeing, geed

gee 'up [usually in imperative] *old-fashioned*
used for urging a horse, cow, or similar animal to move, or move faster

GEN /dʒen/
gens, genning, genned

gen 'up on *British informal old-fashioned*
to learn all you can about a particular subject

GET /get/
gets, getting, got /gɒt, *American* gɑt/

Get is often used with adverbs and prepositions when it means 'to move to or from a position or place': *She forgot her keys and got into the house through the kitchen window.* ♦ *They helped him upstairs and managed to get him on the bed.* ♦ *I don't know how we'll get this box up the steps.* These uses are not included here.

get a'bout *British*
1 to go or travel to different places = GET AROUND
get about *You really need a car to get about here.*
get about sth *The scheme is designed to*

help people with disabilities get about the town centre.
2 if news gets about, a lot of people hear it = GET AROUND, GET ROUND
get about *Rumours get about so quickly in this office.* ♦ **+that** *Somehow it got about that Jenny was having a baby.*

get a'bove
PHRASE get above yourself *showing disapproval* to start to think that you are better or more important than other people: *There were signs that she was getting above herself.*

get a'cross ★ (*also* **get 'over**)
to make people understand something
= PUT ACROSS, CONVEY, PUT OVER
get sth across *He sometimes has trouble getting his meaning across in English.* ♦ **+to** *What message are you trying to get across to the consumer?*
get across how/what etc *I was trying to get across how much I admired them.*

get 'after
1 to chase someone or something
get after sb/sth *Don't stand here talking. Get after them!*
2 *American* to keep complaining to someone because they have not done something
get after sb *She's always getting after me about the dirty toilet.*

get a'head
to be more successful or progress more quickly than other people = ADVANCE
≠ FAIL
get ahead *The best way to get ahead is through hard work.* ♦ *Sometimes you have to be ruthless to get ahead in business.*

get a'long ★★
1 if people get along, they like each other and are friendly to each other
get along *Richard and his sister don't really get along.* ♦ **+with** *I get along well with most of my colleagues.*
2 to manage to continue doing something or make progress in a situation = COPE
get along *I got along much better in my new job.* ♦ **+with** *How are you getting along with your schoolwork?* ♦ **+without** *I couldn't get along without you.*
3 *informal* to leave a place
get along *You'd better be getting along now.*

get a'round ★★

1	travel to many places
2	be able to move
3	news: be told to many people
4	avoid or deal with problem
5	persuade sb
6	have many sexual relationships

1 to go or travel to different places
get around *She was in Japan last week – she certainly gets around, doesn't she?*
get around sth *Cycling is often the best way of getting around a big city.*

2 to be able to move around and do things without much difficulty, despite being old or ill
get around *At the age of 85 Milly still gets around quite well.*

3 get around or **get about** *British* or **get round** *British* if news gets around, a lot of people hear it
get around *It didn't take long for news of his resignation to get around.* ♦ **+that** *Very quickly, word got around that she was leaving the band.*

4 get around or **get round** *British* to find a way of dealing with a problem or avoiding it
get around sth *There are ways of getting around the tax rules.* ♦ *You can't get around the fact that smoking kills.*

5 get around or **get round** *British* to persuade someone to do something, especially by being nice to them
get around sb *She really knows how to get around her dad.*

6 *informal* to have sexual relationships with a lot of different people
get around *She really gets around, doesn't she?*

get a'round to (also get 'round to *British*)

to finally do something that you have intended to do for some time = WORK AROUND TO
get around to (doing) sth *I meant to call you, but somehow I never got around to it.* ♦ *We must get around to cleaning those windows.*

'get at ★★★

1 to manage to reach or touch something = REACH
get at sth *I keep the sweets up here where the kids can't get at them.*

2 [usually progressive] to try to suggest something without saying it directly
get at sth *What are you getting at?* ♦ *I wasn't quite sure what he was getting at.*

3 to discover the true facts about something = UNCOVER

get at sth *This was an attempt to stop journalists getting at the truth.*

4 *British informal* to criticize someone again and again in a way that is unfair
get at sb *Why are you always getting at me?*

get a'way ★★★

1 to escape from a person or place = ESCAPE
get away *A police officer grabbed him, but he got away.* ♦ **+from** *The dog got away from me in the park.*

2 to manage to leave a place, especially your work = LEAVE
get away *He said he'd meet me for lunch if he could get away.*

3 to go somewhere different from where you live in order to have a rest or holiday
get away *We usually manage to get away for a few weeks in the summer.* ♦ *On days like today, I just want to get away from it all.*
PHRASE get away! *British old-fashioned* used for saying that you are very surprised by what someone has told you

get away

■ **getaway** /ˈɡetəˌweɪ/ **noun** **1** a place away from home where you can relax: *They bought a little getaway in the country.* **2** a short holiday: *a weekend getaway*
PHRASES getaway car/van/vehicle the vehicle that criminals use when they are driving away, for example from a bank where they have stolen money: *Police found the getaway car abandoned.*
make a getaway 1 to escape after committing a crime **2** to get away from a boring social situation

get a'way from ★

1 to stop believing something that is not true or is no longer useful or relevant
get away from sth *We want to get away*

from this idea that in a divorce one partner has to be blamed.

2 to talk about something that is different from what you should be talking about
get away from sth *I think we're getting away from the point.*

3 [always in imperative] *informal* used for telling someone to move away from a person or place
get away from sb/sth *Get away from there! It's hot!*
PHRASE **you can't get away from sth/there's no getting away from sth** used for saying that a fact or situation must be accepted and cannot be avoided: *There's no getting away from the fact that we're all getting older.*

ˌget aˈway with ★★★

1 to manage to do something bad without being punished or criticized for it
get away with sth *They have repeatedly broken the law and got away with it.*
get away with doing sth *How can he get away with speaking to her like that?*

2 *informal* to manage to do something that is not the best you can do but is just acceptable
get away with sth *You ought to allow three sandwiches per person, although you could get away with two.*
PHRASE **get away with murder** *informal* to do something extremely bad without being punished or criticized for it: *She lets those kids get away with murder.*

ˌget ˈback ★★★

1	return
2	have sth again
3	hurt sb who has hurt you
4	move away because of danger
5	put sth in its old condition/state
6	receive money paid before

1 to return to a place, often to your home
get back *It's late, I ought to get back.*
♦ *Dad always got back home in time for tea.* ♦ **+from/to** *What time does Sara get back from work?*

2 to receive or have something again after it was taken or lost = RETRIEVE ≠ LOSE
get sth back *She left her briefcase on the train and she doesn't know how to get it back.*

3 to do something in order to hurt or upset someone because they have done something to hurt or upset you = GET EVEN WITH
get sb back *I swore I'd get him back.*
♦ *I'll get you back for this! You just wait!*

4 [always in imperative] *informal* used for

telling someone to move away because they are in danger
get back *Get back! He's got a knife.*

5 to make something return to the state or condition it was in before
get sth back *It won't take long for us to get things back the way they were.*

6 if you get your money back, the money that you paid for something is given back to you ≠ LOSE
get sth back *I went back to the shop to try to get my money back.*
get back sth *You'll get back every penny if you're not completely satisfied.*

ˌget ˈback at

to do something in order to hurt or upset someone after they have hurt or upset you = GET EVEN WITH
get back at sb *She was trying to get back at him for humiliating her.*

ˌget ˈback ˈinto

to start being involved in something again after not doing it for a while
get back into sth *A year after his band broke up, he wants to get back into music again.*

ˌget ˈback to

1 *informal* to phone, write, or speak to someone at a later time because you were busy or could not answer their question earlier
get back to sb *Tell her I'm busy and I'll get back to her.* ♦ **+on** *Can you get back to me on those figures by the end of the day?*

2 to begin doing something again after not doing it for some time
get back to sth *She was eager to get back to work after she had her baby.* ♦ *I woke early and couldn't get back to sleep.*

ˌget ˈback toˈgether

if two people who ended their sexual or romantic relationship get back together, they start having a relationship with each other again
get back together *I kept hoping they would get back together.*

ˌget ˈback with

to start to have a sexual or romantic relationship with someone that you had a relationship with before
get back with sb *He's getting back with his ex-wife.*

ˌget beˈhind ★

1 if you get behind with work or payments, you have not done as much work or made as many payments as you should have = FALL BEHIND

get behind *Once you get behind it's quite hard to catch up again.* ♦ **+with** *The family got behind with the rent and were evicted.*

2 to support someone or something, either in practical ways or with a lot of enthusiasm = SUPPORT ≠ OPPOSE
get behind sb/sth *The crowd are really getting behind their team now.*

get 'by ★★

to have just enough of something such as money or knowledge to be able to do what you need to do = SURVIVE, MANAGE
get by *My arithmetic isn't very good, but I get by.* ♦ **+on** *I couldn't possibly get by on £500 a month.* ♦ **+with** *You could probably get by with that computer, but a more powerful one would be better.*

get 'down ★★

1 to make someone feel sad or lose hope = DEPRESS
get sb down *Doing the same thing day after day can sometimes get you down.* ♦ *I know she's a difficult person, but try not to let her get you down.*

2 to write something quickly, so that you will not forget it
get down sth *Someone managed to get down the registration number of the car.* **get sth down** *Try to get your thoughts down on paper.*

3 to manage to swallow food or drink
get down sth *You should try to get down a little food even if you don't feel like it.* **get sth down** *I tried to get the tablet down, but it stuck in my throat.*

4 to lower your head and body quickly in order to avoid being hit by something
get down *Incoming fire! Get down!*

get 'down on *American informal*

to keep criticizing someone or something
get down on sb/sth *She's always getting down on the kids.*
get down on yourself *He gets down on himself a lot.*

get 'down to

to start doing something seriously or with a lot of effort ≠ PUT OFF
get down to (doing) sth *It was hard to get down to work again after all the excitement.* ♦ *After lunch we got down to discussing the issue of job cuts.*

PHRASES get down to brass tacks *informal* to start discussing the most important issue: *It took the better part of an hour to get down to brass tacks.*
get down to business to start doing something that you need to do without wasting any more time: *If you don't*

mind, I'd like to get down to business straight away.

get 'in ★★★

1	arrive at home/work
2	go/come into place
3	be accepted/chosen
4	be elected
5	deliver/send sth
6	ask sb to come
7	have enough time for sth
8	buy/collect things
9	train/plane: arrive
10	buy things for people
11	start being angry

1 to arrive at home or at work = ARRIVE
get in *You got in very late last night!*

2 to go or come into a place
get in *The door was locked and I had to get in through the bathroom window.*
get in sth *Hurry up and get in the car!*

3 to be accepted to study at a school, chosen to play for a team etc
get in *It's a very exclusive school and you have to pass an exam to get in.*

4 to be elected to a political position
get in *The Labour Party got in again in 2001.*

5 to deliver or send something to a person or place, especially by a particular time
get sth in *I have to get this homework in by the end of the week.*

6 *British* to ask someone to come to your house, office etc in order to do something for you
get sb in *We're getting a plumber in to fix the leak.*
get in sb *They got in an expert to give them advice.*

7 to manage to fit something such as an activity or comment into a small amount of time = FIT IN
get in sth *I try to get in an hour or so playing with the kids every day after work.*
get sth in *She just talked and talked and I couldn't get a word in.*

8 *British* to buy or collect things that you need
get sth in *Kara's friends are coming at the weekend, so get lots of chocolate in.*
get in sth *I got in extra food just in case they came over.*

9 if a train, plane etc gets in, it arrives somewhere = ARRIVE ≠ DEPART
get in *Our flight got in on time.* ♦ *What time does your train get in?*

10 *British* to buy and bring something for a group of people, usually drinks in a bar
get sth in *You paid last time – I'll get the drinks in this time.*

get in sth *You can get in the next round.*

11 if you get in something such as a bad mood, you start being in a bad mood
get in sth *Alan always gets in a filthy mood when his father comes to stay.*

get 'in on

to become involved in something that other people are doing that is fun or interesting, or that makes money
get in on sth *The venture looked as if it would succeed, and rival companies wanted to get in on it.* ♦ *I think she's quite desperate to get in on the act (=get involved with something that someone else is doing).*

get 'into ★★★

1	start enjoying sth
2	start discussing sth
3	train, plane: arrive
4	arrive at work/school
5	be accepted/chosen
6	be elected
7	become involved in sth bad
8	be in bad mood
9	start doing sth
10	wear sth
+	PHRASE

1 to start enjoying something, or to become enthusiastic about it
get into sth *You feel nervous when you start your speech, but you soon get into it.* ♦ *He's really getting into baseball at the moment.*

2 *informal* to begin to discuss something
get into sth *I don't think we have time to get into that now.*

3 if a train, plane etc gets into a place, it arrives there
get into sth *We should get into JFK in a couple of hours.*

4 to arrive at work or school
get into sth *Mark never gets into work before 9.30.*

5 to be accepted to study at a school, chosen to play for a team etc
get into sth *I never managed to get into university.*

6 to be elected to a political position
get into sth *She got into parliament at the last election.*

7 to become involved in a bad situation
get into sth *I don't want to get into an argument with him.* ♦ *Those kids are always getting into trouble.* ♦ *She got into a fight on her way home from school.*
get sb **into** sth *Oh dear, now I've got him into trouble with the boss.* ♦ *Nina's got herself into a bit of a mess.*

8 if you get into something such as a bad mood etc, you start being in a bad mood
get into sth *He always gets into a temper if he's kept waiting.*

9 to start doing something regularly in a particular way
get into sth *We soon got into the routine of the camp.* ♦ *Try to get into the habit of drinking a glass of water every hour.*

10 to put on a piece of clothing = PUT ON
get into sth *I'll just get into some more suitable shoes for walking.* ♦ *After I had the baby I couldn't get into my old jeans for months.*

> **PHRASE** **what's got into sb?** *informal* used for asking why someone is behaving in an unusual or annoying way: *I don't know what's got into her – she never used to be so argumentative!*

get 'in with

1 *showing disapproval* to begin to be involved with a particular person or group
get in with sb *Sue seems to have got in with a very strange bunch of people.*

2 to persuade someone who can help you to be your friend or to like you
= INGRATIATE WITH
get in with sb *If you want to be elected to the club, she's the person you need to get in with.*

get 'off ★★★

1	have a holiday
2	leave work
3	send sth
4	avoid being punished
5	help sb avoid being punished
6	borrow/take sth
7	stop touching sb/sth
8	prevent sb from touching sb/sth
9	make sb sleep
10	help sb leave on time
11	talk about a different subject
12	about sex
13	leave a bus, train etc
+	PHRASES

1 to have a particular period of time as a holiday = TAKE OFF
get sth **off** *I'll try to come, but I'm not sure I'll be able to get that week off.* ♦ *Do you get much time off at Christmas?*

2 to leave the place where you work at the end of the day = LEAVE
get off *We get off early on Fridays.*
get off sth *What time do you get off work?*

3 to send something, for example in the post = SEND OFF
get sth **off** *Have you got your application form off yet?* ♦ *+to I'll get the documents off to you this afternoon.*

4 to not be punished severely or at all for something that you have been accused of in court

get off *He was charged with manslaughter, but got off.* ♦ **+with** *At best you can hope to get off with a £100 fine.*

5 to help someone to avoid being punished by a court, or to help them to get a punishment that is not too severe

get sb off *Do you think his lawyer will be able to get him off?* ♦ **+with** *She got him off with a suspended sentence.*

6 *informal* to borrow or take something from someone

get sth off sb *She got that old bike off her brother.*

7 [usually in imperative] used for telling someone to stop touching someone or something

get off *Get off – you're hurting my back.*
get off sb/sth *Get off the grass right now!*

8 [usually in imperative] used for telling someone to stop another person or thing touching someone or something

get sb/sth off sb/sth *Get your dog off me!* ♦ *Would you please get your feet off the table?*

9 *British* to help someone to go to sleep, especially when they find it difficult

get sb off *I was upstairs trying to get the baby off.*

10 to help someone to be ready to leave a place at the right time

get sb off *I try to get the kids off in the mornings by 8.30.*

11 to stop talking about something because you have become interested in talking about something else

get off sth *She's not a good public speaker – she keeps getting off the subject and rambling.*

12 *mainly American informal* to have an orgasm, or to make someone have an orgasm

13 to leave a bus, plane, or train = *formal* ALIGHT

get off *I asked the bus driver where to get off.*
get off sth *We were told to get off the plane by the exit at the back.*

PHRASES **get off my back** *informal* used for telling someone you want them to stop annoying or criticizing you: *For heaven's sake get off my back! I'm tired of your always nagging me.*

get off on the right/wrong foot to immediately establish a good/bad relationship with someone when you first meet them or first start working with them: *We appear to have got off on the wrong foot.*

get off scot-free to avoid punishment for doing something that deserves punishment: *The bigger companies are getting off scot-free.*

get off to sleep *British* to go to sleep, especially when you find it difficult: *She finally got off to sleep around midnight.*

tell sb where they can get off/where to get off *informal* to tell someone rudely that you are angry or annoyed at them: *If anyone questions her, she tells them where to get off.*

get 'off on *informal*
to enjoy and become very excited about something, especially in a sexual way

get off on sth *You never know what some people will get off on.*

get 'off with *British informal*
to start a new sexual relationship with someone = COP OFF WITH

get off with sb *That's the girl he got off with at your party.*

get 'on ★★★

1	enter a bus, train etc
2	continue doing sth
3	be friends with sb
4	be chosen for a group/team
5	choose sb for a group/team
6	make progress
7	be successful
8	appear on a programme
9	put sb on a programme
10	be old
11	be late
12	finally do sth
13	remind sb
+	PHRASES

1 to get into a bus, plane, or train = BOARD

get on *The bus driver waited until we got on.*
get on sth *I'm hoping to get on the 9 o'clock flight to Glasgow.*

2 *British* to continue doing something, especially with more effort or more quickly than before

get on *Can we please get on, because there are a lot of things still to discuss.* ♦ *I need to get on and cook this chicken before everyone gets here.*

3 to have a friendly relationship with someone = GET ALONG

get on *Pat and Heather don't really get on.* ♦ **+with** *How do you get on with your boss?*

4 to be chosen to be part of a group or team

get on sth *How on earth did she get on the local council?*

5 to persuade or choose someone to be part of a group or team

get sb on sth *They want to get more women on the editorial team.*

6 *British* to manage to continue doing something or make progress in a situation
= GET ALONG

get on *I forgot she had her driving test yesterday – how did she get on?* ♦ **+in** *How did you get on in your exams?* ♦ **+with** *Jim seems to be getting on very well with the cleaning.*

7 *British* to be successful in life or at work
= SUCCEED

get on *He is prepared to do anything in order to get on.*

8 to appear on a television or radio programme

get on sth *She'd do anything to get on TV.*

9 to put someone on a television or radio programme

get sb on sth *A famous TV interviewer wanted to get her on his show.*

10 [always progressive] *informal* to be fairly old

be getting on *My dad is getting on a bit now.*

11 [always progressive] *British* to be fairly late

be getting on *It's getting on: we'd better go.*

12 *mainly American* to finally do something you have been intending to do for a while

get on sth *I'll get on it as soon as I can.*

13 *American* to remind someone to do something, especially when you have to do it more than once

get on sb *Get on Bill to see if he can come up with those numbers for you.*

> PHRASES **get it on** *American impolite* to have sex

get on like a house on fire to become good friends very quickly and have a lot to talk to each other about: *Alice and my mother were getting on like a house on fire.*

get 'on at *British informal*
to ask or tell someone a lot of times about something in a way that they do not like

get on at sb *Don't keep getting on at me like that.*

get 'on for [always progressive]
to be almost a particular time, number, age etc

be getting on for sth *It was getting on for ten o'clock when she got home from work.*

get 'onto (*also* **get 'on to**)

1	write/speak to sb
2	start talking about sth
3	start dealing with sth
4	be chosen for a group/team
5	choose sb for a group/team
6	appear on a programme
7	put sb on a programme

1 *British* to write or speak to someone in order to ask them to do something for you

get onto sb *I'll get onto head office immediately.* ♦ **+about** *You need to get onto your landlord about that leaky roof.*

2 to start talking about a subject

get onto sth *Let's get onto the next item on the agenda.* ♦ *How did we get onto this subject?*

3 to start dealing with a problem

get onto sth *Have you got onto that problem with the supplier yet?*

4 to be chosen to be part of a group or team

get onto sth *Things changed when he got onto the selection committee.*

5 to persuade or choose someone to be part of a group or team

get sb onto sth *She's trying to get more of her supporters onto the board.*

6 to appear on a television or radio programme

get onto sth *He managed to get onto a local radio show.*

7 to put someone on a television or radio programme

get sb onto sth *They're hoping to get her onto the show next week.*

get 'on with ★★★
to give your time to something and make progress with it

get on with sth *The sooner we finish the speeches, the sooner we can get on with the celebration.* ♦ *Our priority now is to get on with the job of developing a comprehensive test ban treaty.*

get on with doing sth *The government must get on with addressing these long-standing issues.*

> PHRASES **get on with it!** used for telling someone to hurry up: *Get on with it, then. We're waiting.*

get on with your life to stop thinking or worrying about something bad that happened in the past and start living a normal life again: *This process gives victims a chance to get on with their lives.*

get 'out ★★★

1	leave
2	make sb leave
3	have an enjoyable time
4	remove sth from inside
5	become known
6	remove sb from their job/position
7	say sth
8	make sth available
+	PHRASES
+	get-out adj

1 to leave a place, building, car etc
= LEAVE
get out *The teacher screamed at him to get out.* ♦ *The place was on fire – we got out just in time.* ♦ **+of** *Get out of my house!*

2 to make someone leave a place
get sb out *They got the injured people out as quickly as they could.* ♦ **+of** *Get that man out of here!*

3 to go to different places and spend time enjoying yourself
get out *We don't get out much these days.*

4 to remove something that is inside or is mixed with something else
get sth out *I washed the shirt twice, but I couldn't get the stain out.* ♦ **+of** *Mike got a splinter of glass out of Jenny's foot.*

5 if something secret gets out, a lot of people find out about it
get out *There was a huge public outcry when the news got out.* ♦ **+that** *It quickly got out that Mariel was leaving Danny.*

6 to remove someone from their job, especially from a position of political power
get sb out *They were confident they could get the Conservatives out.*

7 to manage to say something
get sth out *He tried to protest, but couldn't get the words out.*

8 to make something such as a new book or newspaper available for people to buy
= PUBLISH
get sth out *If you can get your book out in reasonable time, I can see it being a real winner.*
get out sth *They got out a special edition to cover the bombings.*
PHRASES get out! *American informal* used for saying you are surprised by something or do not believe it: *Get out! He looks old enough to be her father!*
you should get out more used for saying in a humorous way that you think that someone is boring and should spend more time doing things and enjoying themselves: *If they think this is exciting, they should get out more.*

■ **'get-out** adj *informal* allowing you to avoid an obligation or a difficult situation: *a get-out clause*

get 'out of ★★

1	get pleasure/benefit
2	avoid doing what you promised
3	help sb avoid sth
4	take clothes off
5	make sb give you sth
+	PHRASE

1 to get pleasure or a benefit from something
get sth out of sth *He gets a lot of satisfaction out of being a teacher.* ♦ *I don't understand what she gets out of that relationship.*

2 to avoid doing something that you should do or that you said you would do
get out of sth *I said I'd meet him, but now I wish I could get out of it.*
get out of doing sth *Ruth always tries to get out of doing the washing up.*

3 to help someone avoid doing something that they do not want to do
get sb out of sth *I'll try to get you out of lunch with my parents if you really are too busy.*
get sb out of doing sth *Can you get me out of going to this meeting?*

4 to take off clothes, especially because they are uncomfortable
get out of sth *I'll just go upstairs and get out of these wet things.*

5 to persuade someone to give you something such as information or money
get sth out of sb *Take him for a drink or something and see whether you can get anything out of him.* ♦ *We managed to get a firm commitment out of them.*
PHRASE get out of here! *mainly American* used for saying you do not believe what someone is telling you: *Get out of here! She can't be 54!*

get 'over ★★

1	feel happy or well again
2	forget problems with your relationship
3	solve a problem
4	do sth that you want to finish
+	PHRASES

1 to start to feel happy or well again after something bad has happened to you
= RECOVER FROM
get over sth *It can take weeks to get over an illness like that.* ♦ *Don's pretty upset, but he'll get over it.*

2 to start to forget someone and feel happy again after a relationship has ended

get over sb *It took her a long time to get over Rob.*

3 to find a way to solve or deal with a difficult problem = OVERCOME

get over sth *There are many hurdles still to get over before the new restaurant can open.*

4 to do something or allow something to happen, because you want it to be finished or you want to start something else

get sth over *We decided to get the holidays over before we started decorating the house.*

5 *same as* **get across**

PHRASES **can't get over sth** used for saying that you are very surprised by something: *I just can't get over how well we played!*

get over here/there *informal* used for telling someone to come or go somewhere: *Hey, Peter! Get over here!*

get over it *informal* used for telling someone to stop worrying, complaining, or being upset about something, in a way that is not sympathetic to them: *You lost. Get over it!*

get 'over with

to do something difficult or unpleasant or allow it to happen, because you want it to be finished or you want to start something else

get sth over with *I wanted to get the interview over with as quickly as possible.* ♦ *Once I've got my assignment over with, I'll have a bit more time.*

get 'past

to manage to get something such as a proposal accepted by people who have the power to stop it happening

get past sb *The plan for the new library first has to get past the local authority.*

get sth past sb *This will be the most sweeping package of changes yet, if Mr MacSharry can get it past his colleagues on the board.*

get 'round *British same as* get around

get 'round to *British same as* get around to

get through ★★★

1	deal with a difficult situation
2	help sb deal with a difficult situation
3	talk by phone
4	finish doing sth
5	pass a test etc
6	use/finish sth
7	become law

1 to manage to deal with a difficult

situation or stay alive until it is over = SURVIVE

get through sth *The refugees will need help to get through the winter.* ♦ *I just have to get through the first five minutes of my speech, and then I'll be fine.*

2 to help someone to deal with a difficult situation or to stay alive until it is over

get sb through *She was relying on luck to get her through.*

get sb through sth *He needs a lot of coffee to get him through the day.*

3 to be connected to a place by telephone so that you can talk to someone

get through *I couldn't get through – the line was engaged.* ♦ +to *I finally got through to Warren on his mobile.*

4 to finish dealing with something = FINISH

get through sth *There was a lot to get through in the meeting.*

5 to pass a test or stage of something

get through sth *How did he ever get through his driving test?*

6 *British* to use or finish something faster than you expected

get through sth *How do we get through so much milk?*

7 if a law gets through, or someone gets it through something, it is accepted by a parliament

get through *The proposals got through after a second vote.*

get sth through sth *Getting a bill though Congress is a long process.*

get 'through to ★★

1 to finally succeed in making someone understand what you are trying to say

get through to sb *The teacher feels he is not getting through to some of the kids in his class.*

2 to go forward to the next stage of a process, for example a competition, because you have succeeded in the previous stage

get through to sth *She got through to the final round of interviews.*

'get to *informal*

1 if something gets to you, it annoys you or upsets you, although you try not to let that happen = ANNOY

get to sb *After a while his teasing started to get to me.*

2 to start doing something

get to doing sth *He got to thinking that it was all his fault.*

PHRASE **where has sth/sb got to?** *informal* used for asking where something or someone is: *Where's my laptop got to?*

get to'gether ★★★

1	spend time together
2	ask people to come
3	organize sth with many parts
4	collect things you need
5	start a romantic/sexual relationship
6	get money
7	control your life
+	PHRASES
+	**get-together** noun

1 if people get together, they meet in order to do something or to spend time together = MEET UP

get together *The whole family usually gets together at Christmas.* ♦ **+with** *He got together with some friends to plan a party for her.*

2 to arrange for people to meet in order to do something with them or to tell them something

get sb together *Lou got the girls together and told them about Anna's accident.*

3 to organize or produce something that has a lot of separate parts

get sth together *We've got to get this report together by tomorrow.*

4 to find or collect things that you need, so that they are in one place and ready to use = COLLECT

get together sth *I got together a list of all their names and phone numbers.*
get sth together *Can you get all the information together by this afternoon?*

5 *informal* if two people get together, they start a romantic or sexual relationship = HOOK UP

get together *I can't believe they're getting married – they only got together 2 months ago!*

6 to obtain an amount of money that you need

get sth together *He promised me he'd get the money together by Friday.*

7 to start to be in control of your life, so that you are successful and are doing what you want to do

get sth together *I realized it was time to get my life together.*
PHRASES **get it together** *British informal* if two people get it together, they start a romantic or sexual relationship: *So when did you two get it together?*
get yourself together to become calm and in control of your emotions: *I hope she can get it together in time for the performance.*

■ **'get-to₁gether** noun [C] an informal social occasion: *We should organize a get-together.*

get 'up ★★★

1	get out of bed
2	make sb get out of bed
3	ask many people to take part
4	dress sb
5	wind: start blowing strongly
+	PHRASES
+	**get-up** noun; **get-up-and-go** noun

1 to get out of bed after sleeping = RISE
—*picture* → STAY UP

get up *He never gets up before nine.*
♦ *What time did you get up this morning?*

2 to wake someone up and make them get out of bed

get sb up *Will you get me up at six tomorrow?*

3 *British* to organize something by asking different people to take part in it or support it

get up sth *Local people got up a petition against the factory closure.*
get sth up *We managed to get a team up to play them at football.*

4 [often passive] *British* to dress someone in a particular way

be got up *The children were got up in fairy costumes.*
get yourself up *She got herself up as Queen Victoria.*

5 if the wind gets up, it starts blowing strongly
PHRASES **get it up** *very informal* if a man gets it up, his penis becomes stiff because he is sexually excited
get it up for sth *American informal* to become enthusiastic about doing something that you expect to be an effort: *I'm not sure I can get it up for this party tonight.*

■ **'get-up** noun [C] *informal* the clothes that someone is wearing, used especially when you think they look silly: *Where did you buy that get-up?*

■ **'get-up-and-'go** noun [U] *informal* energy and enthusiasm: *She certainly has plenty of get-up-and-go.*

₁get 'up to *showing disapproval*

informal to do something, especially something that you should not do
get up to sth *The children get up to all sorts of mischief when I'm not here.*

'get with

PHRASES **get with it** *mainly American* to know about what is happening or what things that are fashionable at the present time: *If you've never used the Internet then you need to get with it.*

get with the program *mainly American* to pay attention to what is happening and start doing what you should be doing: *He's not doing very well in school – it'll be too late if he doesn't get with the program soon.*

GINGER /ˈdʒɪndʒə, *American* ˈdʒɪndʒər/
gingers, gingering, gingered

ˌginger 'up *British*
to make something more interesting and exciting

ginger sth up *also* **ginger up sth** *Unfortunately the director of the new production has tried to ginger things up with a number of inappropriate touches.*

GIVE /gɪv/
gives, giving, gave /geɪv/, **given** /ˈgɪv(ə)n/

ˌgive a'way ★★★

1	give sth without getting money
2	give secret information
3	show your feelings/intentions
4	allow opponents to win
5	walk with a woman at her wedding
6	tell sb in authority sth

1 to give someone something without asking for any payment
give away sth *We're giving away 10,000 copies of the software absolutely free.* ♦ **+to** *Any plants that were left I gave away to neighbours.*
give sth away *He gave all his old records away years ago.*

2 to tell someone information or facts that you should keep secret, often by mistake = REVEAL ≠ KEEP SECRET
give away sth *If captured, they might give away vital military secrets.*
give sth away *Careful, Mike – you don't want to **give the game away** (=give away a secret).*

3 to show a feeling or intention that you are trying to hide = BETRAY ≠ KEEP SECRET
give sth away *Her face gave nothing away.*
give away sth *Only Edward's eyes gave away the measure of his dismay.*

4 in sport, to allow an opponent to gain an advantage because you make a silly mistake
give sth away *He gave a penalty away as a result of a violent tackle.*
give away sth *They gave away two goals in the first half.*

5 if a man gives a woman away on her wedding day, he leads her towards the man she is going to marry
give sb away *She still wanted her father to give her away.*

6 to tell someone in authority about someone who is trying to hide from them or hide something from them = BETRAY
give sb away *She promised not to give me away whatever happened.*

ˌgive 'back ★★★
to give something to the person who already owns it, or who gave it to you before = RETURN
give back sth *The company had to give back all the money customers had paid.*
give sb back sth *We just want them to give us back our home.* ♦ *I felt I had been given my life back.*
give sth back *I'll give your books back tomorrow.* ♦ **+to** *Did I give your keys back to you?*
PHRASE **give something back** to do something to help a person, group, or organization that has done something for you: *Some tourists contribute funds for the local school as a way of giving something back.*

ˌgive 'in ★★★
1 to stop competing or arguing and accept that you cannot win = YIELD; *formal* CAPITULATE
give in *The champion refused to give in and went on to win the set.* ♦ *My parents eventually gave in and let us go to the festival.* ♦ **+to** *The government has said all along that it will never give in to terrorist threats.*

2 *British* to give something, especially a piece of work, to someone in authority who is expecting it = HAND IN
give in sth *She gave in her homework a week late.*
give sth in *I have to give two assignments in before the end of term.*
PHRASE **give in your notice** to tell your employer that you are leaving your job, especially in a letter: *He's waiting until the end of the week to give in his notice.*

ˌgive 'in to
to finally allow yourself to do something that you want to do
give in to sth *She had to struggle not to give in to her desire to laugh.*

ˈgive of *formal*
if you give of yourself or your time, you do helpful things for people
give of yourself *We gave of ourselves in what way we could to help those who needed our support.*
give of sth *Thanks were also extended to all the club members who gave of their time to ensure that fun was had by all.*

give 'off ★★

to produce something such as heat or a
smell = EMIT

give off sth *When they die, plants give
off gases such as carbon dioxide and
methane.*

> Nouns often used as objects with **give off**
>
> ■ aroma, fumes, gas, odour, scent, smell

'give onto *formal*

if something such as a door or window
gives onto a place, it leads to that place
or you can see through it to that place

give onto sth *The soldier bolted the door
which gave onto the platform and sat
down opposite me.*

give 'out ★★★

> 1 give sth to many people
> 2 machine etc: stop working
> 3 no longer be available
> 4 produce sound/light etc
> 5 give many people information

1 to give something to several people
= HAND OUT

give out sth *She earned a little money
giving out leaflets in front of the train
station.* ♦ **+to** *The office gives out
financial advice to students who ask for
it.*

give sth out *The teacher gave out the test
papers in total silence.* ♦ **+to** *Now give
the cards out to the players.*

2 if something such as a machine or a
part of your body gives out, it stops
working = FAIL ≠ HOLD OUT

give out *His heart finally gave out under
the strain.*

3 if a supply of something gives out, all
of it has been used = RUN OUT

give out *Their water gave out two days
ago.*

4 to produce something such as a sound,
light, or a signal = EMIT

give out sth *The quietest devices give out
only a low, almost inaudible hum.*
♦ *Somewhere a transmitter was giving
out a weak signal.*

5 *British* to give a lot of people information
about something, for example in a
television broadcast

give out sth *Details of the accident were
given out on the nine o'clock news.*

give sth out *The government will give
the unemployment figures out tomorrow.*

give 'over *British informal*

used to tell someone to stop doing
something that is annoying you = STOP

give over *'You know how fond I am of
you.' 'Oh, give over, will you?'*

give over doing sth *Give over making
that noise!*

give 'over to

1 [usually passive] *formal* to use something
for a particular purpose = BE DEVOTED TO

be given over to (doing) sth *The major
part of the garden was given over to
growing vegetables.*

2 to give something to someone so that
they become responsible for it

give sth over to sb *All weapons should
be given over to the police.*

give 'up ★★★

> 1 stop doing sth
> 2 stop trying
> 3 stop thinking/believing sth
> 4 allow sb to have sth
> 5 allow yourself to be caught
> 6 stop looking for sb
> 7 use your time for sth

1 to stop doing something that you do
regularly = QUIT

give up sth *Giving up his job was the
last thing we expected him to do.*

give sth up *Have you ever tried to give
alcohol up?*

give up *I used to go to the gym, but I
gave up years ago.*

give up doing sth *His wife finally
persuaded him to give up working late.*

2 to stop doing something that you are
trying hard to do

give up sth *I gave up the fight and let
him have his way.*

give up doing sth *We've given up trying
to persuade them to change.*

give up *Decide what you want and then
don't give up until you've achieved it.*

3 to stop thinking or believing something
= *formal* ABANDON

give up sth *He had given up the idea of
marriage altogether.* ♦ *It was a difficult
time, but we never **gave up hope**.*

4 to allow someone to have something
that was yours = SURRENDER

give up sth *The new arrangement would
mean giving up some of their political
independence.*

give sth up *The land is ours and we
don't intend to give it up without a fight.*
♦ **+to** *They agreed to give half their office
up to the temporary staff.*

5 if you give yourself up, you allow
yourself to be arrested by the police, or
caught by someone who is chasing you
= SURRENDER, TURN IN

give yourself up *Police are urging the
man to give himself up before any
further damage is caused.* ♦ **+to** *She*

eventually gave herself up to a US commander.

6 to accept that you will not find someone or something and stop looking for them

give sb up *The men who were still in the boat had given him up for dead.*

7 to use your time for one activity instead of another = SACRIFICE

give up sth *Doing this course will mean giving up a lot of my spare time.*

give sth up *Mum wants me to look after my little brother, which means giving my weekend up.*

give up

,give 'up on

1 to stop hoping that someone will improve and stop trying to help or change them = DESPAIR OF

give up on sb *Most of the teachers gave up on her years ago.*

2 to stop believing that an idea or activity is good, right, or useful

give up on sth *I gave up on exercise a long time ago.* ♦ *Never give up on your ideals.*

,give 'up to *literary*

to let yourself feel or experience something completely

give yourself up to sth *She gave herself up to the excitement of the moment.*

GLAM /glæm/
glams, glamming, glammed

,glam 'up *informal*

to make someone or something glamorous

glam sb/sth up *It won't cost much to glam the place up a bit.*

GLANCE /glɑːns, *American* glæns/
glances, glancing, glanced

,glance 'off

to hit something quickly and without much force and then move away in a different direction = BOUNCE OFF, RICOCHET OFF

glance off sth *The bullet glanced off the tree and went through the window.*

GLAZE /gleɪz/
glazes, glazing, glazed

,glaze 'over

if your eyes glaze over, they show that you are not at all interested in something that is being discussed

glaze over *His eyes always glaze over at the mention of technology.*

GLEAN /gliːn, *American* glin/
gleans, gleaning, gleaned

'glean from

to learn small pieces of information from someone or something by asking questions or listening or watching carefully

glean sth from sb/sth *The report is based on what I could glean from the Internet.*

GLOM /glɒm, *American* glɑm/
gloms, glomming, glommed

,glom 'onto *American informal*

to immediately become very interested in something that you have just discovered

glom onto sth *The media glommed onto the story and seemed to revel in the couple's breakup.*

GLORY /'glɔːri, *American* 'glɔri/
glories, glorying, gloried

'glory in

to get a lot of pleasure or satisfaction from something = REVEL IN ≠ DESPISE

glory in sth *He writes about physical violence well, without glorying in it.*

GLOSS /glɒs, *American* glɔs/
glosses, glossing, glossed

,gloss 'over

to deliberately avoid unpleasant facts and say as little about them as possible = SKIM OVER ≠ DWELL ON

gloss over sth *He could no longer gloss over his failures.* ♦ *I tried to **gloss over the fact** that I knew all about the affair from the beginning.*

GLUE /gluː, American gluː/
glues, gluing, glued

be 'glued to
to be looking at something, especially a television or computer screen, continuously and with all your attention
be glued to sth *The kids have been glued to the TV all night.*

GNAW /nɔː, American nɔː/
gnaws, gnawing, gnawed

'gnaw at (*also* ,gnaw a'way at)
if something gnaws at you, you keep worrying about it or feeling upset about it
gnaw at sb *Doubts continued to gnaw at me for several more days.*

GO /gəʊ, American goʊ/
goes, going, went /went/, gone /gɒn, American gɔn/

Go is often used with adverbs and prepositions when it means 'to move or travel to a place': *She **went into** the bathroom. ♦ We're planning to **go to** Spain this winter. ♦ I'm **going out** into the garden for some fresh air.* These uses are not included here.

,go a'bout ★★★
1 to do something that you normally do in your usual way
go about sth *Most people went about their daily life as usual.*
2 to start dealing with a problem, situation, or job in a particular way = TACKLE
go about sth *I think I'd go about it quite differently.*
go about doing sth *How did you go about finding a job?*
3 *same as* go around 2
4 *same as* go around 3
PHRASE **go about your business** to do the things that you normally do: *I respected the quiet way they went about their business.*

,go 'after ★★
1 to try to get something that other people are also competing for
go after sth *Our company is going after the software market in western Europe.*
2 to try to catch someone in order to talk to them
go after sb *You'd better go after her and tell her you're sorry.*

3 to try to catch someone in order to arrest or attack them = PURSUE
go after sb *It would be dangerous to go after the killer on your own.*

,go a'gainst ★★
1 to oppose someone or something
go against sb/sth *You can't go against your family.* ♦ *Building it here would go against the wishes of the local community.*
2 if something such as a decision or judgment goes against you, you do not get the decision or judgment you wanted
go against sb/sth *It appears likely the judge's ruling will go against them.*
3 if someone's behaviour or action goes against something such as a principle or a rule, it is opposed to the principle or rule = *formal* VIOLATE
go against sth *This goes against everything I've been brought up to believe in.*
PHRASE **go against the grain** to be completely different from what you feel is right, natural, or normal for you: *Admitting you're wrong really goes against the grain, doesn't it?*

,go a'head ★★★
1 to start or continue to do something, especially after waiting for permission
go ahead *If you want another beer, just go ahead.* ♦ *Go ahead and eat before everything gets cold.* ♦ **+with** *The club will be going ahead with its plans for a new stadium in the summer.*
2 to go to a place before someone else you are with = GO ON
go ahead *You go ahead and we'll wait here for Sally.* ♦ **+of** *Don went ahead of the others to try to find help.*
3 to happen in the way that people expect, even though there are difficulties
go ahead *The party went ahead as planned.*
■ **'go-a,head** adj with a lot of energy and new modern ideas: *an exciting, go-ahead company*
■ **'go-a,head** noun **PHRASE** **give/get the go-ahead** to give/get permission to do something: *Rosenthal had been given the go-ahead by his doctor to resume training.*

,go a'long ★★★
1 to travel somewhere with someone else
go along *He's going to York tomorrow and I think I might just go along too.*
2 [usually progressive] to continue to happen or develop

be going along *Everything was going along just fine until she turned up!*

3 if you do something as you go along, you do it without planning it first

go along *The teacher seemed to be making up the lesson as he went along.*

> PHRASE **go along for the ride** to take part in an activity that other people are doing although you are not really interested in it: *I went along for the ride, since I'd nothing better to do.*

¡go a'long with

1 to agree with someone or something

go along with sb/sth *I would tend to go along with what Tim was saying.*

2 to agree to do something together with other people = *formal* ACQUIESCE IN

go along with sth *They describe him as a weak man who went along with the scheme out of fear.*

¡go a'round ★★ (*also* ¡go 'round *British*)

1	visit a person/place
2	how sb behaves
3	how sb dresses
4	be given/told to many people
5	spend time with sb
6	be enough for everyone
7	move in a circle
+	PHRASE

1 to visit a person or a place

go around *I went around last night, but no one was in.* ♦ **+to** *Are you going around to Tom's after work?*

2 to behave in a particular way

go around *You've been going around in a dream all morning.* ♦ **+doing sth** *You can't go around saying things like that!*

3 to be dressed in a particular way

go around *He's been going around like that all day.* ♦ *Why does he go around with no shoes on?*

4 [usually progressive] if something such as an illness or a piece of news is going around, people are giving or telling it to each other

go around *He caught the bug that's been going around.*

go around sth *There's a story going around the office that you're thinking of leaving.*

5 to spend a lot of time with someone, going to different places and doing things together

go around with *She used to go around with Susannah all the time.* ♦ **+together** *We went around together, the three of us.*

6 to be enough so that everyone can have one or some

go around *In some classes, there aren't*

even *enough books to go around.*

7 to move in a circle = REVOLVE

go around *The hands of the clock seemed to go around so slowly.*

> PHRASE **what goes around comes around** used for saying that the way you behave towards other people will influence the way that other people behave towards you in the future: *Those people had been killed because of what they had done, he said. What goes around comes around.*

'go at

1 to attack someone violently

go at sb *The two boys were going at each other like mad dogs.*

2 to do something with a lot of enthusiasm or energy

go at sth *Harbury was young and ambitious and went at things with a daunting eagerness.*

> PHRASE **go at it hammer and tongs** *British* to fight or argue with a lot of energy: *They obviously didn't resolve their differences because an hour later they were still going at it hammer and tongs.*

¡go a'way ★★★

1 to stop existing or being noticeable = DISAPPEAR

go away *The pain should go away in a couple of hours.*

2 to move or travel away from a person or place

go away *If he's bothering you, tell him to go away.*

3 to leave your home for a period of time, especially for a holiday ≠ STAY

go away *We've decided to go away for a long weekend.*

¡go 'back ★★★

1	return
2	have existed for a long time
3	have known each other for a long time
4	when classes begin again in school
5	when clocks show an earlier time
+	PHRASE

1 to return to a person, place, subject, or activity = RETURN

go back *It started to rain, so we decided to go back.* ♦ **+for** *I'd left my keys in the office and had to go back for them.* ♦ **+to** *We didn't think he'd go back to his wife after everything that's happened.* ♦ *I'd like to **go back to what** Abby was saying just a minute ago.* ♦ *She should be well enough to **go back to work** on Wednesday.* ♦ **+to doing sth** *The computer breaks down and you go back* *to writing things down on pieces of paper.*

2 to have existed since or for a particular time = DATE BACK

go back *My interest in the subject goes back many years.* ♦ **+to** *Some of these houses go back to the early 19th century.*

3 *informal* if two people go back a particular period of time, they have known each other for that period of time

go back *We go back a long time, don't we?*

4 *British* when the schools or students go back, classes begin again after a long holiday

go back *Our schools don't go back until September.*

5 *British* when the clocks go back in the autumn in some countries, everyone changes the time on their clocks so that it shows a time that is one hour earlier than before

go back *Don't forget the clocks go back this weekend.*

PHRASE **go back to the drawing board** to try to think of a completely new idea because the one you tried before was not successful: *The trials of the new product had mixed success, so there was nothing for it but to go back to the drawing board.*

ˌgo ˈback on

to fail to do something that you have promised or agreed to do = CHANGE YOUR MIND ≠ KEEP YOUR WORD

go back on sth *Both leaders feared that the other would go back on his word.*

ˈgo beˌfore

1 to be considered by a judge, committee, or other authority as part of an official process

go before sb/sth *The case is scheduled to go before the Appeal Court next week.* ♦ *Changes will be made before the bill goes before Parliament.*

2 to happen before something else

go before *This is a brief summary of what has gone before.*

ˌgo beˈyond ★★★

1 to be more than something = *formal* EXCEED

go beyond sth *The cost of a project often goes beyond the original estimate.*

2 to refer to, deal with, or include more things than something

go beyond sth *The British representative argued against any major changes that would go beyond the 1992 Treaty.*

ˌgo ˈby ★★★

1	time: pass
2	go past sb/sth
3	stop during a journey
4	base an opinion on sth
5	use sb's opinion in your judgment
6	use a false name
+	**bygone** adj

1 if time goes by, it passes = PASS BY

go by *Last month went by so fast.*

2 to go past a place or person = PASS BY

go by *Another bus just went by.*
go by sb/sth *I went by his house on my way home.*

3 to stop at a place for a short time during a journey

go by sth *I went by the post office on the way home.*

4 to base an opinion or decision on something = JUDGE BY, GO ON

go by sth *It's never very wise to go by appearances.*

5 to accept what someone or something says when you are deciding what to do or think

go by sth *Going by what Tim said, we should be there by mid-afternoon.*
♦ *Police officers protect themselves from criticism by going by the book* (=obeying official rules carefully).

6 to use a particular name for yourself that is not your real name

go by sth *In the 1970s she went by the name of Ricki.*

■ **bygone** /ˈbaɪɡɒn/ **adj** [only before noun] happening or existing during a period of time in the past: *These photos belong to a bygone age.*

ˌgo ˈdown ★★★

1	become less
2	be remembered/recorded
3	make people react
4	become worse
5	sun/moon: stop being seen
6	computer etc: stop working
7	lights: become less bright
8	be long
9	go under water
10	fall
11	travel south
12	swallow food
13	stop being swollen
14	be defeated
15	be moved to a lower group in sport
16	go to prison
17	happen
18	travel to a smaller place
19	leave university
+	PHRASES

1 to become less = DECREASE ≠ GO UP
go down *No one expects house prices to go down in the near future.* ♦ *The crime rate shows no signs of going down.*

2 to be remembered or recorded in a particular place or way
go down as *Hansen will go down as one of the best teachers this school has ever had.* ♦ **+in** *Both their names went down in the referee's notebook.*

3 to produce a particular reaction
go down well/badly (with sb) *The plan to increase charges has not gone down well with tenants.*

4 if something such as a standard goes down, it becomes worse = DETERIORATE
go down *The quality of their products has really gone down in the past few years.*

5 when the sun or moon goes down, it moves below the horizon so you cannot see it any longer = SET ≠ RISE
go down *The sun was just starting to go down as we reached the farm.*

6 if something such as a computer or an electrical system goes down, it stops working for a period of time = CRASH
go down *The airline's entire booking system had gone down.*

7 if lights go down, especially in a theatre or cinema, they gradually become less bright and are switched off = DIM ≠ COME UP, GO UP
go down *Finally the lights went down and the performance started.*

8 to be long enough to reach a particular lower point or level ≠ GO UP
go down *The path didn't go down as far as the water.* ♦ **+to** *There were steps going down to what had once been a lawn.*

9 if a ship goes down, it sinks below the surface of the water = SINK
go down *The ship went down off the coast of Africa.*

10 to fall to the ground
go down *We watched as the plane went down in a fiery blaze.*

11 to travel towards the south ≠ GO UP
go down *We're going down for her birthday.* ♦ **+to** *The family is going down to Brighton for a few days.*

12 if food or drink goes down, you swallow it
go down *You need smaller pills that go down more easily.*

13 if an area of your body that has increased in size as a result of an injury or illness goes down, it becomes its normal size again

go down *How long will it take for the swelling to go down?*

14 to be defeated in a competition, especially in sport = LOSE ≠ WIN
go down *United went down 2–1 last night.* ♦ **+to/against** *Canada went down 3–1 to the Russian team.*

15 *British* to move to a lower group in a series of groups of sports teams = BE RELEGATED ≠ GO UP
go down *They'll be very sad if they go down at the end of the season.*

16 *British informal* to go to prison
go down *How long did he go down for?*

17 *mainly American informal* to happen
go down *I was nowhere near here when the robbery went down.*

18 *British old-fashioned* to travel to a place that is smaller or less important than the place you are leaving ≠ GO UP
go down to *We're going down to the country next weekend.*

19 *British old-fashioned* to leave a university, especially Oxford or Cambridge, at the end of a period or course of study ≠ GO UP
go down *By the time he went down from Cambridge, he was already a published novelist.*

PHRASES **go down a bomb/storm (with sb)** *informal* to be very successful or popular: *The T-shirts go down a bomb with tourists.*

go down in history to be remembered by many people in a country for having done something unusual or impressive: *The efforts they made will go down in history.*

go down in sb's opinion to become less respected by someone than you were before, because of something you have done: *By taking part in such a show, he'd gone down in people's opinion.*

go down like a lead balloon if something such as a joke or suggestion goes down like a lead balloon, people do not like it at all: *I imagine that comment went down like a lead balloon.*

,go 'down on *impolite*
to use your mouth on someone else's sexual organs in order to give them pleasure

,go 'down with *British*
to become ill with a particular illness = CATCH, COME DOWN WITH
go down with sth *Three people in my office have gone down with the flu.*

'go for ★★★

1	walk/drive somewhere
2	compete for sth
3	like sb/sth
4	choose sth
5	be sold
6	go somewhere to get sth
7	be true/relevant
8	attack sb
9	speak to sb angrily
+	PHRASES

1 to go on a short journey on foot, in a car, on a horse, etc, usually for enjoyment
go for sth *Would you like to go for a drive in my new car?* ♦ *First we went for a tour of the college.*

2 *informal* to try to get something that you have to compete for
go for sth *There were 200 people going for just three jobs.* ♦ *She's trying to go for the world record.*

3 *informal* to like a particular type of person or thing **=** LIKE **≠** DISLIKE
go for sb/sth *I don't really go for horror stories.* ♦ *So what type of men do you go for?*

4 *informal* to choose a particular thing **=** CHOOSE
go for sth *I think I'll go for the steak. What are you having?*

5 to be sold for a particular amount of money **=** FETCH
go for sth *We expect the house to go for more than the asking price.*

6 to go somewhere in order to get someone or something
go for sb/sth *She's just gone for the kids – she'll be back any minute.* ♦ *I'm going to go for a newspaper.*

7 to be true or relevant for someone or something **=** APPLY TO
go for sb/sth *We expect you boys to behave yourselves, and the same goes for the girls.*

8 to attack someone physically **=** ATTACK
go for sb *Apparently, she went for her husband with a knife.*

9 to speak to someone very angrily, for example in order to criticize or blame them
go for sb *As soon as he walked in, she went for him.*

PHRASES **go for broke** to try as hard as you can to get or achieve something, even if this involves taking risks or doing dangerous things: *Jacob decided to go for broke and gave up his job to become a writer.*

go for it *informal* used for encouraging someone to do something or to try very hard: *It sounds a fantastic offer to me – go for it!*

go for the jugular to attack an opponent, especially in an argument, in the way that will immediately do the most damage: *A harsher critic would have gone for the jugular.*

go for nothing to achieve nothing or be completely wasted: *I'd hate all that work to go for nothing.*

have sth going for you if a person or thing has something going for them, they have an advantage, skill, or other positive quality: *With its wide variety of hotels and restaurants, the town has a lot going for it.*

go for (sense 8)

go 'in ★★★

1 when the sun or moon goes in, clouds move in front of it **≠** COME OUT

2 if information goes in, you understand it completely
go in *She'd heard what I said, but I could tell it hadn't really gone in.*

3 if people such as police officers or soldiers go in, they enter an area in order to take action of some kind **=** ENTER
go in *Our unit will be going in first.*

go 'in for

1 to enjoy a particular thing or activity **=** LIKE **≠** DISLIKE
go in for sth *I don't go in for golf much.*

2 *British* to take part in a competition, or to take an examination **=** ENTER
go in for sth *His school had suggested he go in for the Young Musician of the Year competition.*

3 *British* to choose something as a subject of study or as your career
go in for sth *I think he's planning to go in for politics.*

go 'into ★★★

1	start a job/activity
2	change to a different state
3	talk about in detail
4	be used/spent
5	begin a long explanation
6	be divided by a smaller number
7	crash

1 to start working in a particular type of job or business = ENTER
go into sth *Alex has decided to go into nursing.* ♦ *Eric went into the army right after school.*

2 to change to a different movement, state, or condition, usually a worse one
go into sth *Her car went into a dangerous spin.* ♦ *Fur sales went into a steep decline last month.*

3 to talk about something in a lot of detail = DISCUSS
go into sth *That's a good question, but I don't want to go into it now.* ♦ *The company is refusing to go into detail about its offer.*

4 to be used or spent in order to do something
go into sth *Over 50% of the budget went into the design of the equipment.*
go into doing sth *Months of hard work have gone into making tonight's ceremony a success.*

5 to start an explanation or statement, especially a long and boring one
go into sth *He went into a long rant about the price of food.*

6 if a smaller number goes into a larger number, the larger number can be divided by the smaller one a particular number of times
go into sth *5 goes into 25 5 times.* ♦ *9 into 23 won't go.*

7 to crash into something
go into sth *The truck swerved violently and went into a wall.*

go 'in with

to join together with someone else in order to do something such as start a business
go in with sb *She's gone in with a friend on a new restaurant idea.*

go 'off ★★★

1	explode
2	electricity etc: stop working
3	stop liking sb/sth
4	leave
5	start making a noise
6	food/drink: be no longer fresh
7	become worse
8	happen
9	begin sleeping
+	PHRASES

1 to explode, or to be fired = EXPLODE
go off *The gun went off while he was cleaning it.*

2 if something such as a light or an electricity supply goes off, it stops working or being available
go off *All the lights in the building suddenly went off.*

3 *British* to stop liking someone or something
go off sb/sth *I went off the idea of buying a sports car after I found out how much it would cost.*

4 to leave a place, especially for a particular purpose = LEAVE ≠ STAY
go off *He went off without saying a word.*
♦ **+to** *Dave's gone off to the south of France for the summer.* ♦ **+to do sth** *He went off to have lunch in the canteen at one o'clock.*

5 to start making a noise as a signal or warning = SOUND
go off *I was just going to sleep when the alarm clock went off.*

6 *British* if food or drink goes off, it stops being fresh = GO BAD
go off *We'd better cook the fish today, it will have gone off by tomorrow.*

7 *British informal* to become worse in quality = DETERIORATE
go off *His work has really gone off recently.*

8 to happen in the way that had been planned
go off *The whole conference went off just as we had planned.*

9 *British informal* to go to sleep ≠ WAKE UP
go off *He sits in the chair and goes off within seconds.* ♦ **+to** *The baby's just gone off to sleep.*
　PHRASES **go off at half-cock** to start doing something without being properly prepared, so that the results are not successful: *The French army's attack went off at half-cock.*
go off the deep end to unexpectedly become very angry, especially without a good reason: *He accused Saunders, who went off the deep end.*

go off (sense 5)

go 'off on *American informal*
to become very angry and start shouting at someone
>**go off on sb** *He just went off on her for no reason.*

go 'off with

1 *showing disapproval* to start a new relationship with someone after leaving the person you were previously having a relationship with
>**go off with sb** *Apparently he's gone off with someone he met at a conference last year.*

2 to leave with something that belongs to someone else
>**go off with sth** *Someone's gone off with my coffee cup.*

go 'on ★★★

1	continue happening
2	happen
3	begin an activity/state
4	start taking a drug
5	used for encouraging sb
6	electricity etc: start working
7	do sth after
8	time: pass
9	base an opinion on sth
10	go to a place before sb
11	continue travelling
12	begin talking again
13	talk a lot
14	go to another place
15	receive a payment from the government
16	be spent on sth
17	begin performing
18	replace another player in sport
+	PHRASES
+	**goings-on** noun; **ongoing** adj

1 to continue happening as before, or to continue doing something as before
= CONTINUE ≠ STOP

go on *The meeting went on a lot longer than I expected.* ♦ *We **can't go on like this** any more. Things have got to change.* ♦ **+with** *Burton smiled and went on with his work.*
>**go on doing sth** *She can't go on pretending that everything is okay when it clearly isn't.*

2 to happen = OCCUR
>**go on** *I wonder what's going on next door – they're making a lot of noise.* ♦ *There's a lot going on at the festival this week.*

3 to start doing a particular activity, or to start being in a particular state
>**go on sth** *We're **going on holiday** next week.* ♦ *Workers voted by a large majority to **go on strike**.* ♦ *It will **go on sale** this summer.* ♦ *I really must go on a diet!*

4 to start taking a particular medicine or drug
>**go on sth** *He needs to go on stronger medication.*

5 [always in imperative] used for encouraging someone to do something
>**go on** *Go on, try it – it's really good.*

6 if something such as a light or an electricity supply goes on, it starts working or becomes available ≠ GO OFF
>**go on** *I heard the TV go on in the next room.*

7 to do something after you have finished doing something else
>**go on** *If Mary wishes to, she can go on and train to be an accountant.* ♦ **+to** *When you finish the first section of the test, go on to the next.* ♦ **+to do sth** *They eventually went on to win the championship.*

8 if time goes on, it passes
>**go on** *As the day went on, they got more and more exhausted.*

9 to base an opinion or decision on something = JUDGE BY
>**go on sth** *Since there were no witnesses, the police **had little to go on**.*

10 to go to a place before someone else that you are with
>**go on** *Why don't you go on without me?*

11 to continue travelling and not stop = CONTINUE
>**go on** *We went on for another two or three miles before resting.*

12 to start talking again after a pause or interruption = CONTINUE
>**go on** *Please go on – I didn't mean to interrupt you.* ♦ **+with** *He encouraged her to go on with her story.*

13 to talk so much that people become bored or annoyed = PRATTLE ON

go on *You do go on, don't you?* ♦ **+about** *She tends to go on about how clever her children are.*

14 to go to another place after being somewhere else
go on *We stopped for a drink before going on again.* ♦ **+to** *After Moscow, we went on to St Petersburg for a couple of days.*

15 to stop working and start to receive a particular type of payment, for example because you are ill or unemployed
go on sth *You go on sick pay after the first week.*

16 *British* if money goes on something, it is spent on it
go on sth *Most of my earnings go on childcare.*

17 to walk onto a stage in order to begin your part in a performance
go on *I don't go on until the final act.*

18 to walk onto a sports field in order to replace a member of your team
go on *Owen went on in the 75th minute.*
PHRASES **go on!** *British informal* used for saying that you do not believe what someone is telling you: *Go on! She didn't really say that.* ♦ **go on with you!** *old-fashioned 'Don't you look nice!' 'Oh, go on with you!'*
going on (for) sth almost a particular age, time, or amount: *Tina is six, going on seven.* ♦ *We waited for going on an hour.*
go on the offensive to begin to take action against someone that you think is attacking you: *Opposition parties were going on the offensive.*
go on (the) TV/radio to decide to appear on television or radio in order to say something: *The President went on television to appeal for calm.*

■ **goings-'on** **noun** [plural] *informal* events or activities that are strange, dishonest, or illegal: *She often told stories of weird goings-on in the house, which she claimed was haunted.*

■ **ongoing** /ˈɒnˌɡəʊɪŋ/ **adj** still happening or being done: *an ongoing discussion*

ˌgo 'on at *informal*
to criticize someone regularly or for a long time
go on at sb *He was always going on at the kids.* ♦ **+about** *My mum keeps going on at me about my friends and the way I dress.* ♦ **+to do sth** *Everyone's been going on at me to get a haircut.*

ˌgo 'out ★★★

1	have a romantic/sexual relationship
2	stop burning/shining
3	leave a competition after a defeat
4	stop being fashionable
5	go somewhere for enjoyment
6	travel far away
7	about the level of the sea
8	be broadcast
9	be told to people
10	be sent
+	PHRASES
+	**outgoing** adj; **outgoings** noun

1 [usually progressive] to have a romantic or sexual relationship with someone and spend a lot of time with them
go out *How long have Rob and Sue been going out?* ♦ **+with** *Greg used to go out with Katy.* ♦ **+together** *We've been going out together for three months now.*

2 to stop burning or shining
go out *The fire must have gone out during the night.* ♦ *Suddenly, all the lights went out.*

3 to not be allowed to take part in the next stage of a competition because you have been defeated
go out *Last year's champion went out in the second round.* ♦ **+of** *England went out of the World Cup amid great controversy.*

4 to stop being fashionable at a particular time
go out *That hairstyle went out about ten years ago.* ♦ **+of** *Classic styles like this will never go out of fashion.*

5 to leave your house and go somewhere, especially in order to do something enjoyable = SOCIALIZE
go out *I never seem to go out at night any more.* ♦ *She wasn't allowed go out and play with the other kids.* ♦ **+to do sth** *Let's go out to eat tonight.*
go out doing sth *We haven't gone out dancing for a long time.*

6 to travel to a place that is far away
go out *My partner's been in Australia since June and I'm going out next year.* ♦ **+to** *She wished she had been able to go out to South Africa with Nicola.*

7 when the tide goes out, the water in the sea flows away from the land = EBB
≠ COME IN

8 to be broadcast on the radio or television
go out *The show doesn't go out until after most children have gone to bed.*

9 to be told to people
go out *The order went out an hour ago.*

♦ +**that** *Word went out that the factory was in danger of closing.*

10 to be sent by post

go out *The invitations haven't gone out yet.*

PHRASES **go out like a light** *informal* to go to sleep very quickly: *A minute later he went out like a light.*

go out on strike to stop working as a protest: *If the postal workers go out on strike, other unions may well join them.*

■ **outgoing** /aʊt'gəʊɪŋ/ **adj** **1** [only before noun] soon to leave a position of authority or power ≠ INCOMING: *the outgoing prime minister* **2** someone who is outgoing is friendly and enjoys meeting and talking to people = SOCIABLE: *Norm is very shy, but his wife's outgoing.* **3** [only before noun] going out of or away from a place ≠ INCOMING: *outgoing mail* ♦ *outgoing flights*

■ **outgoings** /'aʊtgəʊɪŋz/ **noun** [plural] amounts of money that you have to spend regularly, for example on your rent or fuel bills: *Her outgoings include $60 per month on gas and electricity.*

go 'out of

if a feeling or quality goes out of someone or something, they do not have it any longer

go out of sb/sth *All the excitement had gone out of living in the city.* ♦ *When I saw him years later, all the life had gone out of him.*

PHRASES **go out of business** if a company goes out of business, it stops doing business permanently, especially because it has failed

go out of use to stop being used: *This practice went out of use in the 1950s.*

go 'out to *British*

to be defeated by someone in a competition

go out to sb *Sampras went out to young Swiss star Roger Federer.*

PHRASE **sb's heart/sympathy/ thoughts go out to sb** used for saying that someone is sympathetic to someone else who is in a difficult situation: *Our thoughts go out to the victims of yesterday's earthquake.*

go 'over ★★★

1	check sth
2	practise sth
3	move towards sb/sth
4	search a place
5	repeat things
6	clean sth
7	how people react
+	PHRASE

1 to check something carefully

go over sth *Could you go over this report and correct any mistakes?*

2 to practise and repeat something in order to learn it

go over sth *Sue's going to help me go over my lines for the play.*

3 to move or travel towards someone or something

go over *Why don't you go over and say hello?* ♦ +**to** *He went over to the window and closed the curtains.* ♦ +**to do sth** *We had met a year ago, when I went over to Paris to see an exhibition.*

4 to search a place thoroughly

go over sth *We went over this whole area with the greatest of care.*

5 to repeat a series of things or think about them again in order to understand them completely

go over sth *My mind was going over the curious events at Ingard House.*

6 to clean something, especially quickly = CLEAN

go over sth *Using a damp sponge, she'd gone over all the surfaces in the kitchen in a matter of seconds.* ♦ +**with** *He'd gone over the car with a cloth, wiping fingerprints from the steering wheel and the door handles.*

7 *mainly American* to produce a particular reaction

go over *Last night's performance went over very well.* ♦ +**with** *How did the news go over with your parents?*

PHRASE **go over sb's head** if something goes over someone's head, they cannot understand it: *I tried to explain it to him but I could see it went straight over his head.*

go 'over to

1 to change to a new system or way of behaving

go over to sth *The school went over to mixed-ability teaching three years ago.*

2 to change to a report or broadcast from a different place

go over to sb/sth *We'll be going over to Sydney for live coverage in just a couple of minutes.* ♦ *Let's go over to John for a look at the weather.*

3 to join a different group, organization, or political party

go over to sb/sth *What makes them go over to a party they once fought against?*

go 'round British *same as* **go around**

go 'through ★★★

1	examine/search sth
2	experience sth bad
3	be dealt with in a system
4	follow official system
5	use/spend/eat sth
6	practise sth
7	perform regular actions
8	be officially accepted
9	become law
+	PHRASES

1 to examine or search something very carefully = SEARCH THROUGH

go through sth *Someone had broken into the office and gone through all the drawers.* ♦ *Collins went through every legal book she could find.*

2 to experience something difficult or unpleasant = EXPERIENCE

go through sth *We can't really imagine what they're going through.*

3 to be dealt with by a particular person or department in an organization, according to a system

go through sb/sth *All such requests have to go through my section.* ♦ *Your application must go through the proper channels.*

4 to do all the things that are necessary in order to follow an official system or method

go through sth *Even existing employees had to go through the whole application procedure again.*

Nouns often used as objects with
go through 4

■ **formalities, procedure, process, rigmarole, ritual, routine**

5 to use, spend, or eat all of something, especially quickly = RUN THROUGH ≠ KEEP

go through sth *He'd gone through all his money by the end of the first week.*

6 to practise all of something such as a speech, song, or play = REHEARSE

go through sth *Let's go through your lines one more time.*

7 to perform a set of actions that you regularly perform = PERFORM

go through sth *She went through her daily routine of clearing the breakfast table before settling down to handle the correspondence.*

8 if something such as a request,

proposal, or contract goes through, it is officially accepted or approved

go through *If the proposal goes through, there'll be big changes in all offices.*

9 if a law goes through, or goes through a law-making institution, it is officially approved

go through *The legislation went through without a hitch.*

go through sth *The bill is currently going through Parliament.*

PHRASES **go through the floor** to fall to an extremely low level: *Share prices have gone through the floor.*

go through sb's mind/head if a thought or idea goes through your mind or your head, you consider it for a short time: *I knew what was going through her head at that time.*

go through your paces to show other people how good you are at a particular activity: *The Scottish team went through their paces for the press yesterday.*

go 'through with ★

to do something that you have planned or agreed to do, especially after not being sure that you want to do it

go through with sth *I can't believe he went through with the divorce.*

go to ★★★

1 to start doing a particular activity or being in a particular state

go to sth *I was just going to sleep when the phone rang.* ♦ *He went to work on the car and had it repaired by lunchtime.* ♦ *The two countries have gone to war twice over the disputed territory.*

2 to be given to someone or something

go to sb/sth *Our thanks go to everyone who helped make this celebration a success.* ♦ *The house was supposed to go to her children when she died.*

PHRASES **go to pot** *informal* if something goes to pot, it loses all of its good qualities because no one takes care of it: *The garden has completely gone to pot.*

go to the wall British *informal* to fail, especially when this involves losing all your business and money: *No-one was surprised when the company finally went to the wall.*

go to'gether ★★

1 if two or more things go together, they frequently exist together

go together *Too often greed and politics seem to go together.*

2 if two things go together, they seem good, natural, or attractive in combination with each other

go together *I don't think these colours go together very well.*

3 [usually progressive] *informal* if two people are going together, they have a romantic or sexual relationship with each other
be going together *Matt and Michelle have been going together since April.*

ˌgo toˈwards

to be used to help to pay for something
go towards (doing) sth *The proceeds from the sale of the land will go towards the construction of a new stadium.* ♦ *The money raised will go towards rebuilding the children's hospital.*

ˌgo ˈunder ★

1 to sink below the surface of the water
go under *The crowd watched as the ship went slowly under.*

2 if something such as a business goes under, it fails completely and stops operating = FAIL
go under *It looked as though the company was going under.*

3 to become unconscious when a doctor gives you a drug or gas before an operation in order to stop you feeling pain = LOSE CONSCIOUSNESS —*picture* → PASS OUT
go under *I could feel myself going under.*

ˌgo ˈup ★★★

1	increase
2	be built
3	start burning
4	be tall/high
5	be put somewhere for people to see
6	lights: become brighter
7	curtain in a theatre: be raised
8	travel north
9	travel to an important place
10	be moved to a higher group in sport
11	when people make a noise
12	go to university

1 if something such as a level or a price goes up, it increases = INCREASE ≠ GO DOWN
go up *We'd like to see the baby's weight going steadily up.* ♦ *The price of oil has gone up by over 50 per cent in less than a year.*

2 to be built ≠ COME DOWN
go up *New houses are going up all over town.*

3 to start burning quickly or explode
go up *The whole building went up in just a few minutes.* ♦ *From the air, it looked as if the entire city were going up in flames.*

4 to be long or tall enough to reach a particular higher point or level ≠ GO DOWN
go up *We don't want the tiles to go up*

that far. ♦ **+to** *The fire escape only went up to the second floor.*

5 if something such as a notice or sign goes up somewhere, it is put in a place where people can see it
go up *Posters for the show are going up all over town.*

6 if lights go up, especially in a theatre or cinema, they are switched on and gradually become brighter ≠ GO DOWN

7 if the curtain goes up in a theatre, it is raised or opened at the beginning of a performance = RISE ≠ COME DOWN

8 to travel towards the north ≠ GO DOWN
go up *Are you going up for the wedding?* ♦ **+to** *Max goes up to Scotland to fish every summer.*

9 *British old-fashioned* to travel to a place that is larger or more important than the place you are leaving ≠ GO DOWN
go up *We're going up to London to do some shopping.*

10 *British* to move to a higher group in a series of groups of sports teams = BE PROMOTED ≠ GO DOWN
go up *Another defeat would ruin their dream of going up.*

11 if a noise goes up from a group of people, they all start to make it
go up *At the second announcement, a huge groan went up.* ♦ **+from** *A cheer went up from the crowd.*

12 *British old-fashioned* to go to a university, especially Oxford or Cambridge, at the beginning of a period or course of study ≠ GO DOWN
go up *His eldest boy goes up to Oxford next week.*

ˈgo with ★★★

1	seem good/natural
2	usually exist with sth
3	be offered as well as sth
4	choose/accept sth
5	have a romantic/sexual relationship
6	have sex

1 to seem good, natural, or attractive in combination with something
go with sth *Which of the shoes go best with this dress?*

2 to exist frequently with something
go with sth *A fair amount of stress seems to go with jobs like this.*

3 to be provided or offered together with something
go with sth *Does a car go with the job?*

4 to choose or accept something = GO FOR
go with sth *I think we should go with yellow for the walls.*

5 [usually progressive] *informal* to have a

romantic or sexual relationship with
someone = DATE

go with sb *I heard that Carol is going
with the guy who works downstairs.*

6 *informal* to have sex with someone

ˌgo withˈout ★★

to live without something that you need
or would like to have = DO WITHOUT

go without *When there's not enough food
for everyone, some families inevitably go
without.*

go without sth *Three villages have gone
without water for days.*

PHRASE **it goes without saying (that)**
used when you think that someone will
already know what you are going to tell
them because it is so obvious: *It goes
without saying that consumers would be
happier if prices were lower.*

GOAD /gəʊd, *American* goʊd/
goads, goading, goaded

ˈgoad into [often passive]

to get someone to react in a particular
way by making them feel very angry or
upset

be goaded into (doing) sth *She was
finally goaded into losing her temper.*
goad sb into (doing) sth *He refused to
let her goad him into an argument.*

ˌgoad ˈon [often passive]

to encourage someone to react by making
them feel very angry or upset

be goaded on *Goaded on by the crowd,
he turned and hit the umpire.*
goad sb on *His friends were shouting
and goading him on.*

GOBBLE /ˈgɒb(ə)l, *American* ˈgɑb(ə)l/
gobbles, gobbling, gobbled

ˌgobble ˈdown

to eat something quickly and often noisily
= DEVOUR

gobble down sth *also* **gobble sth down**
He gobbled down his lunch and left. ♦ *I
gobbled a sandwich down as fast as I
could.*

ˌgobble ˈup ★

1 to use a lot of something very quickly
= EAT UP

gobble up sth *The armed forces gobble
up all the money.*
gobble sth up *Its huge engine really
gobbles fuel up.*

2 [usually passive] if a larger company or
organization gobbles up a smaller one,
the larger one takes control of the smaller
one

be gobbled up *Many smaller firms are
now being gobbled up by large
corporations.*

3 to eat something quickly and often
noisily = DEVOUR

gobble sth up *The animal gobbled it up
in one.*
gobble up sth *She gobbled up the cake
with relish.*

GOOF /guːf, *American* guf/
goofs, goofing, goofed

ˌgoof aˈround *American informal*

to spend your time behaving in a silly way
goof around *We were goofing around
and I broke my arm.*

ˌgoof ˈoff *American informal*

to have fun or waste time when you should
be working

goof off *I liked the idea of goofing off for
an afternoon.*

ˌgoof ˈup *American informal*

to make a stupid mistake, or to spoil
something by making a stupid mistake
goof up *They were scared I would goof
up.*
goof sth up *also* **goof up sth** *My parents
know we won't goof it up.* ♦ *I had goofed
up dinner once before.*

■ ˈgoof-up noun [C] *American informal* a
situation in which you make a stupid
mistake: *another embarrassing goof-up*

GORGE /gɔːdʒ, *American* gɔrdʒ/
gorges, gorging, gorged

ˈgorge on

1 to eat or drink so much of something
that you cannot eat or drink any more
gorge (yourself) on sth *We gorged
ourselves on fresh sardines and salads.*

2 to have so much of an enjoyable
experience that you do not want any more
gorge (yourself) on sth *I gorged myself
on memories.*

GOUGE /gaʊdʒ/
gouges, gouging, gouged

ˌgouge ˈout

to remove something from a surface by
cutting or digging with a sharp object
gouge sth out *also* **gouge out sth** *They
threatened to gouge his eyes out.* ♦ *The
insect gouges out a channel in the leaf.*

GRAB /græb/
grabs, grabbing, grabbed

'grab at
1 to try to take hold of someone or something in a rough or rude way
= CLUTCH AT
grab at sth *Suddenly he was on his feet, grabbing at her sleeve.*
2 to try to get possession of something such as an opportunity that you are very keen to own or use
grab at sth *Their leader was quick to grab at the notion.*

GRAFT /grɑːft, *American* græft/
grafts, grafting, grafted

'graft off *American informal*
to use your position in business or politics in a dishonest way in order to obtain money or advantages from someone
graft off sb *We had a list of the people she had grafted off.*

,graft 'onto
1 [usually passive] to take a piece of skin, bone etc from one part of someone's body and use it to replace or repair a damaged part of their body
be grafted onto sth *Skin was grafted onto the wound to help it heal.*
2 to add something and make it become a part of another thing
graft sth onto sth *Many different peoples have settled here and grafted their own cultures onto native Malaysian culture.*
3 to take a piece from a plant and join it to a cut made in another plant so that it can grow there
graft sth onto sth *We graft these samples onto existing trees.*

GRAPPLE /'græp(ə)l/
grapples, grappling, grappled

'grapple with ★★
to try hard to understand a difficult idea or solve a difficult problem = WRESTLE WITH
grapple with sth *The government continued to grapple with the issue of public transport.*

GRASP /grɑːsp, *American* græsp/
grasps, grasping, grasped

'grasp at
1 to try to take hold of someone or something
grasp at sth *Hands were grasping at his coat as he walked past.*
2 to try to take the opportunity to do something
grasp at sth *She was grasping at the chance to escape her problems.*
PHRASE grasp at straws to try to find anything at all that will help you or give you hope in a difficult situation, when it is likely that you will find nothing: *We had the feeling the police were grasping at straws.*

GRASS /grɑːs, *American* græs/
grasses, grassing, grassed

'grass on *British informal*
to tell someone in authority, especially the police, about something bad that someone else has done = BETRAY
grass on sb *He was too loyal to grass on his own brother.*

,grass 'over
to cover an area of ground with grass, or to become covered with grass
be grassed over *Should the area be grassed over or concreted?*
grass over *The water channel had dried out and grassed over.*

,grass 'up *British informal*
to tell someone in authority, especially the police, about something bad that someone else has done = BETRAY
grass up sb *also* **grass sb up** *You wouldn't grass up an old mate, would you?* ♦ +to *Who grassed him up to the police?*

GRAVITATE /'grævɪteɪt/
gravitates, gravitating, gravitated

'gravitate towards (*also* 'gravitate to)
1 to go to be with someone because you like them
gravitate towards sb *He was the sort of politician whom people gravitated towards.*
2 to tend to prefer something, or tend to prefer doing something
gravitate towards (doing) sth *Customers gravitate to the products that best reflect their social status.*

GRAY the American spelling of grey

GREY /greɪ/
greys, greying, greyed

be ,greyed 'out
if a part of a computer screen has been greyed out, the writing in it appears in a dull colour in order to show that you cannot use it

be greyed out *When the box is greyed out, nothing happens when you click on it.*

GRIND /graɪnd/
grinds, grinding, ground /graʊnd/

,grind a'way
to work hard and in a determined way over a long period of time, often on something that is boring or difficult
grind away *Many authors grind away for years and produce nothing.*

,grind a'way at *mainly American*
to gradually reduce the strength, value, or importance of something
grind away at sth *Powerful economic forces have been grinding away at the position of workers.*

,grind 'down
to treat someone in a cruel way over a long period and gradually destroy their confidence or strength = WEAR DOWN
grind sb down *also* **grind down sb** *Don't let his stupid remarks grind you down.* ♦ *The army pounded the city, trying to grind down rebel troops.*

,grind 'on
if something boring, unpleasant, or difficult grinds on, it continues happening slowly for a long period of time
grind on *As the negotiations grind on, the deadline for a settlement gets ever closer.*

,grind 'out
1 to achieve something after a lot of effort or difficulty
grind out sth *also* **grind sth out** *The players did exceptionally well to grind out their fifth win on the trot.*
2 to produce something in large quantities, especially when this is boring, unpleasant, or difficult
grind out sth *also* **grind sth out** *He has to grind out poems for every royal occasion.* ♦ *He grinds these stories out at an alarming rate.*
3 to make a cigarette stop burning by pressing on it with your fingers or foot
grind sth out *also* **grind out sth** *Boyd ground his cigarette out.* ♦ *She ground out the cigarette with her heel.*

,grind 'up [often passive]
to break something into very small pieces or into powder, by using a machine or by crushing it between two hard surfaces
be ground up *The seeds are ground up and later digested.*
grind up sth *also* **grind sth up** *They grind*

up plants with their teeth. ♦ *The factory grinds old carpets up to produce synthetic wood.*

GROAN /grəʊn, *American* groʊn/
groans, groaning, groaned

'groan under
1 if one thing groans under another, it can only just support or bear it
groan under sth *The system was groaning under an avalanche of applications.* ♦ *The curriculum was **groaning under the weight of** other priorities.*
2 groan under or **groan with** *British* if a table or other surface groans under something such as food, there is a lot of food on it
groan under sth *The long tables were **groaning under the weight of** fresh fish.* ♦ *The platforms groaned with passengers.*

GROPE /grəʊp, *American* groʊp/
gropes, groping, groped

'grope for
to search for an idea or a way to say something without being certain of what you are doing
grope for sth *She hesitated, seeming to grope for words.*

'grope towards
to make slow progress in an effort to achieve something
grope towards sth *We're groping towards a solution to the problem.*

GROSS /grəʊs, *American* groʊs/
grosses, grossing, grossed

,gross 'out [often passive] *informal*
if something grosses you out, you think it is so unpleasant that it almost makes you feel sick = DISGUST ≠ DELIGHT
be grossed out *Her language was disgusting – I was grossed out by it.*
gross sb out *Some of the scenes will gross you out.*

■ **'gross-out** noun [C] *mainly American informal* something that you think is very unpleasant, especially so unpleasant that it makes you feel sick. This word is used mainly by young people: *For younger kids, nakedness is still a major gross-out.*

,gross 'up [usually passive]
to increase an amount of money recorded in financial accounts by adding an amount, usually tax, that is normally

taken away when calculations are made
be grossed up *The value will have to be grossed up to include tax.*

GROUND /graʊnd/
grounds, grounding, grounded

be 'grounded in ★★

1 be grounded in or **be grounded on** to be based on something
be grounded in sth *Her theories are grounded on sound research.* ◆ *Any new policies need to be firmly grounded in careful analysis of the issues.*

Nouns often used as objects with **be grounded in 1**

■ concept, doctrine, evidence, experience, principles, research, theory

2 to have the basic knowledge or skills relating to a particular subject
be grounded in sth *Candidates should be well grounded in the history of the period.*

ground 'out *American*

in baseball, to be put out of the game temporarily because you hit the ball along the ground
ground out *Smith grounded out, and that was the end of the St. Louis scoring opportunities for the evening.*

GROUP /gruːp, *American* grup/
groups, grouping, grouped

'group into [usually passive]

to put people or things into groups, especially groups in which the members are similar in some way
be grouped into sth *The topics have been grouped into broad categories.*

group to'gether ★ [usually passive]

to put people or things into a group
be grouped together *All the cleaning services will be grouped together for convenience.*

GROW /grəʊ, *American* groʊ/
grows, growing, grew /gruː, *American* gruː/, **grown** /grəʊn, *American* groʊn/

grow a'part

if people grow apart, their relationship gradually changes and they become less close
grow apart *They had simply grown apart over the years.*

grow a'way from

if you grow away from someone, your relationship gradually changes and you become less close to them

grow away from sb *She gradually grew away from her family.*

'grow in

to begin to have more of a quality
grow in sth *She was growing in confidence every day.* ◆ *In recent years cycling has grown in popularity.*

grow 'into ★★

1 to develop and become a particular thing or person
grow into sb/sth *This seedling should grow into a tall attractive plant.* ◆ *She had grown into a beautiful woman.*

2 if children grow into clothes, they become the right size to wear clothes that were too big
grow into sth *If the shirt's a little big, he'll soon grow into it.*

3 if you grow into a situation or activity, you gradually start knowing what to do because you have more experience
grow into sth *She needs time to grow into her new role.*

'grow on

if someone or something grows on you, you start to like them more
grow on sb *The new house slowly began to grow on her.*

grow 'out

if hair that has been coloured, cut, or treated with chemicals to make it curly grows out, it grows so that it no longer has the colour or style that it had
grow out *I'm going to let the colour grow out.*

grow 'out of ★

1 if children grow out of clothes, they grow bigger and the clothes become too small for them = OUTGROW
grow out of sth *In a few weeks, she will have grown out of the dress.*

2 if someone grows out of a habit, they stop doing it, because they are older or wiser = OUTGROW
grow out of sth *They thought I would grow out of my fear of spiders.*

3 to develop from something, or exist as a result of it
grow out of sth *Other issues grew out of the policy review.* ◆ *The poems grew out of her disturbed imagination.*

grow 'up ★★★

1 to change from being a baby or young child to being an older child or adult
grow up *She's really starting to grow up now.* ◆ *He never saw his father while he was growing up.* ◆ *I grew up in London.*

2 to stop behaving like a child, and become wiser = MATURE

grow up *It wasn't until my marriage ended that I really started to grow up.*

3 to start existing or being seen

grow up *It was one of the many small religious sects that grew up and flourished in the area.*

4 [often in imperative] *informal* to stop being silly and behaving like a child

grow up *I wish you would grow up!*

ˌgrow 'up on

used for talking about things that you did a lot, or things that you had a lot of, when you were a child

grow up on sth *We grew up on these stories.*

GRUB /grʌb/
grubs, grubbing, grubbed

ˌgrub a'round (also ˌgrub a'bout British)

to try to find something by moving things around somewhere, especially somewhere that is dirty or difficult to reach

grub around *He was grubbing around in the earth.* ♦ *Jasper was on the floor grubbing about under the carpet.*

ˌgrub 'up [usually passive]

to dig something out of the ground

be grubbed up *Most of the hedges in the area have been grubbed up.*

GUARD /gɑːd, American gɑrd/
guards, guarding, guarded

'guard against ★★

1 to help to prevent something from happening

guard against sth *Eating plenty of fruit is thought to guard against heart disease.*

2 to try to prevent something from happening

guard against sth *We need to guard against the possibility of people losing interest.*

GUESS /ges/
guesses, guessing, guessed

'guess at ★

to say or decide what you think is true, without being certain about it

guess at sth *It was impossible to guess at the purpose of his inquiry.*

PHRASE sb can only guess at sth used for saying that someone does not know something, often because it is difficult or impossible to know: *Experts admit*

they can only guess at the cause of the problem.

GULP /gʌlp/
gulps, gulping, gulped

ˌgulp 'back

to stop yourself from showing tears or an emotion = STIFLE

gulp back sth *Sonia sat in the corner, gulping back the tears.*

ˌgulp 'down

to swallow food or drink quickly in a way that shows you are very hungry or thirsty

gulp down sth *also* **gulp sth down** *I gulped down some coffee and left.* ♦ *We sat and watched him gulp it down.*

ˌgulp 'in

to quickly take in large breaths of air

gulp in sth *He came up from the water, greedily gulping in air.*

GUM /gʌm/
gums, gumming, gummed

ˌgum 'up *informal*

to cause things to be stuck together or covered in a sticky substance so that they no longer work smoothly

gum up sth *Something's gumming up the filters.*

PHRASE gum up the works *informal* to stop a process from working smoothly: *Getting students involved will only gum up the works.*

GUN /gʌn/
guns, gunning, gunned

ˌgun 'down ★ [usually passive] *mainly journalism*

to shoot someone and kill them or injure them badly, especially someone who is not guilty of anything, or who is not carrying a gun = KILL, SHOOT DOWN

be gunned down *He was gunned down in his own doorway.*

'gun for [usually progressive] *informal*

1 to try to hurt someone or damage their reputation

be gunning for sb *He knew the party leadership was gunning for him.*

2 to try to get something, for example a job or prize

be gunning for sth *Brown was gunning for his fifth title in a row.*

GUNGE /gʌndʒ/
gunges, gunging, gunged

be ˌgunged ˈup
to be blocked or covered with a dirty sticky substance
be gunged up *The mechanism was all gunged up.*

GUSSY /ˈgʌsi/
gussies, gussying, gussied

ˌgussy ˈup [often passive] *American*
1 *informal* to make something very attractive or interesting
be/get gussied up *Look at all the TV shows that are getting gussied up.*
gussy up sth *She plans to gussy up the dining area.*
2 *old-fashioned* to dress in very nice clothes in order to make yourself look attractive
be/get gussied up *She gets the children all gussied up.*
gussy yourself up *Mary was busily gussying herself up for the party.*

GUT /gʌt/
guts, gutting, gutted

ˌgut ˈout *American informal*
PHRASE **gut it out** to be brave enough to continue doing something that is difficult or unpleasant: *Brad spent his whole career winning matches he shouldn't have won, just by gutting it out.*

Hh

HACK /hæk/
hacks, hacking, hacked

ˌhack aˈbout [usually passive] *British showing disapproval*
to make a lot of changes to something in a rough or careless way
be hacked about *The old door had been hacked about over the years.*

ˌhack aˈway *showing disapproval*
to cut something many times in a rough or careless way
hack away *He grabbed a branch and started hacking away.* ♦ **+at** *She hacked away at the bushes with her knife.*

ˌhack ˈdown [usually passive] *showing disapproval*
to cut a tree so that it falls to the ground
be hacked down *Old forests are being hacked down with no thought for the environmental damage.*

ˌhack ˈinto
to use a computer in order to connect to someone else's computer secretly and often illegally, so that you can find or change information on it
hack into sth *They hack into banks and transfer huge amounts of cash.*

ˌhack ˈoff
1 to remove something by cutting it in a rough way
hack off sth *also* **hack sth off** *Holding onto one horn, he hacked off the buffalo's head.*
hack sth off sth *Jo hacked a piece off the block of cheese.*
2 [usually passive] *British informal* to annoy someone
be/get hacked off *She's really hacked off about the changes they've made to her timetable.*

ˌhack ˈup
1 [often passive] to cut something into pieces using a knife or other sharp tool in a rough or violent way
be hacked up *They had been hacked up in their own home.*
hack up sb/sth *also* **hack sb/sth up** *The killer had hacked up the body.* ♦ *He hacked the smaller branches up with his machete.*
2 to remove something from your throat or lungs by coughing in a loud rough way
hack up sth *also* **hack sth up** *The cat was hacking up a hairball.* ♦ *It sounded like he was hacking his lungs up.*

HAIL /heɪl/
hails, hailing, hailed

ˈhail as ★★ [usually passive]
to say publicly how good or important someone or something is
be hailed as sb/sth *She's been hailed as the new Margot Fonteyn.* ♦ *The court's ruling was immediately hailed as a victory for freedom.*

ˈhail from *formal*
to be from a particular place
hail from sth *My father hails from Missouri.*

HAM /hæm/
hams, hamming, hammed

ham 'up
PHRASE **ham it up** *informal* to act or behave in an artificial way with too much expression in your voice and movements, especially in order to make people laugh = OVERACT: *He is guilty of hamming it up terribly in a cheap attempt to get laughs.*

HAMMER /'hæmə, American 'hæmər/
hammers, hammering, hammered

hammer a'way at *informal*
1 to keep attacking someone or something
hammer away at sb/sth *Our lawyers hammered away at their witness's credibility.*
2 to do something with great energy and with all your attention
hammer away at sth *She spent all weekend hammering away at her novel.*
3 hammer away at or **hammer at** to keep talking about something, often in order to show people that you think it is important or to try to make them agree with you
hammer away at sth *I keep hammering away at this point but nobody believes me.* ♦ *His speech hammers at the same old themes.*

hammer 'into [often passive]
to keep telling someone something in order to make them understand or accept it = DRUM INTO
be hammered into sb *These are the values that were hammered into us by or parents.*
hammer sth into sb *A good teacher will hammer these principles into students.*

hammer 'out ★ [often passive]
to reach a decision or agreement after discussing it or arguing about it for a long time = THRASH OUT
be hammered out *A new deal was hammered out between the two banks.*
hammer out sth *We'll have to hammer out a new contract first.*

Nouns often used as objects with **hammer out**

■ **agreement, compromise, deal, plan, policy, strategy, terms**

HAND /hænd/
hands, handing, handed

hand a'round (*also* **hand 'round** *British*)
to give things to different people in a group
= GIVE OUT, HAND OUT ≠ TAKE IN
hand around sth *also* **hand sth around**
Nina handed around mugs of hot coffee.
♦ *Will someone hand these printouts around?*

hand 'back ★★
1 to give something back to someone
hand sth back *Jean handed the letter back to Doug.* ♦ *The officer handed me my passport back.*
hand back sth *Ask him to hand me back my pen.*
2 used by someone making a television or radio report from a place for saying that they have finished their report and that someone in the studio will speak now
hand sb back to sb *Now I'll hand you back to Fiona in the studio.*

hand 'down ★★
1 [usually passive] to give knowledge or skill to someone who is younger than you and will live after you have died = PASS DOWN
be handed down *These skills have been handed down from generation to generation.*
2 [usually passive] to give clothes, toys etc to a younger child when an older child no longer needs them
be handed down *When I was a child, all my clothes were handed down.* ♦ **+to** *The best clothes were always handed down to the younger children in the family.*
3 to say officially that someone will receive a particular punishment
hand down sth *In 1954 the US Supreme Court handed down its decision in the case of Brown v. the Board of Education of Topeka, Kansas.*
hand sth down *A lower court cannot hand that sentence down.* ♦ *They formulate policy in Brussels and hand it down to member states.*

Nouns often used as objects with **hand down 3**

■ **decision, judgment, sentence, verdict**

■ **'hand-me-,downs** noun [plural] clothes that have been worn by someone and then given to someone else in the same family: *The younger children are clothed in hand-me-downs.*

,hand 'in ★ [often passive]

to give something to a person in authority = SURRENDER

  hand in sth *Please hand in your keys when you leave the hotel.*

  hand sth in *He was told to hand his uniform in.*

  be handed in *All essays must be handed in by Tuesday.*

  PHRASE **hand in your notice/ resignation** to say officially that you have decided to leave your job: *He's going on Friday. He's already handed in his notice.*

,hand 'on [often passive] *British*

to give someone something that was given to you so that they have it or have to deal with it = PASS ON

  be handed on *These traditions were handed on by my parents.* ♦ **+to** *The farm will be handed on to his son.*

  hand on sth *also* **hand sth on** *He handed on the correspondence between himself and the bishop as requested.* ♦ **+to** *I decided not to hand this information on to the police.*

,hand 'out ★★

1 to give things to different people in a group = GIVE OUT, HAND AROUND ≠ TAKE IN

  hand out sth *Ralph was handing out drinks.*

  hand sth out *Would you hand these papers out for me?*

2 to give something such as advice or information to people

  hand out sth *They won't hand out your phone number without permission.*

  hand sth out *I don't hand my bank details out to people in the street.* ♦ *The problem with criticism is that the people who hand it out are often not good at taking it.*

3 [often passive] to say officially that someone should receive a particular punishment

  be handed out *Harsher punishments are now being handed out for reckless driving.* ♦ **+to** *A three-month sentence was handed out to the teenage boy for making hoax bomb telephone calls.*

  hand out sth *In Albany, a judge 60 years ago handed out a famous verdict.* ♦ **+to** *The Committee handed out a four-week suspension to the jockey.*

■ **handout** /'hændaʊt/ **noun** [C]

1 money or goods given to people who need them: *He's forty and still living on handouts from his parents.* **2** a piece of paper with information on it that is given to everyone in a group, especially a class of students: *You'll find some of the references on the handout.*

,hand 'over ★★★

1 to give something to someone by holding it in your hand and offering it to them = PASS ≠ WITHHOLD

  hand over sth *Albert bowed and handed over the letter.*

  hand sth over *Seeing that the man was armed, she handed the money over immediately.* ♦ **+to** *They've handed their weapons over to the troops.*

2 to give power or control to someone else = *formal* RELINQUISH ≠ WITHHOLD

  hand over sth *They are against handing over control of the region.*

  hand sth over *Britain formally handed sovereignty over in 1997.* ♦ **+to** *They formally hand power over to the new government next week.*

■ **handover** /'hændəʊvə/ **noun** [singular] the process of giving responsibility for something to someone else: *the British handover of Hong Kong to the Chinese*

,hand 'over to

1 [often passive] to give someone to the police or another authority that will become responsible for them = TURN OVER TO

  be handed over to sb *The suspects have now been handed over to the French authorities.*

  hand sb over to sb *Another member of the same gang handed him over to police.*

2 used for saying that someone else will speak now or will deal with someone or something now

  hand sb over to sb *I'm going to hand you over to John, who will show you round.*

,hand 'round *British same as* **hand around**

HANG /hæŋ/
hangs, hanging, hung /hʌŋ/

Hang is often used with adverbs and prepositions when it means 'to put something in a position, or be in a position, where the top part is held in position but the bottom part can move easily and smoothly without being stopped': *Philip **hung** his hat **on** a hook behind the door.* ♦ *She **hung** her bag **over** a chair.* ♦ *Her dark hair **hung down** over her shoulders.* These uses are not included here.

,hang a'bout

1 *informal same as* **hang around**

2 [always in imperative] *informal same as* **hang on 2**

3 [always in imperative] *British informal same as* **hang on 5**

> **PHRASE** **not hang about** *informal* to move or do something quickly = NOT HANG AROUND: *We'd better not hang about: it's 10 o'clock already.*

,hang a'round ★★ (*also* ,hang a'bout

British or ,**hang 'round** *British*) *informal*
to spend time in a place waiting or doing nothing

> **hang around sth** *I hung around the bar, waiting for the others.*
> **hang around** *She's always hanging around backstage, talking to the actors.*
> **PHRASE** **not hang around** *informal* to move or do something quickly = NOT HANG ABOUT: *Let's not hang around or we'll be late!*

,hang a'round to,gether *informal*

to spend time with each other

> **hang around together** *We used to hang around together when we were students.*

,hang a'round with (*also* ,hang a'bout

with *British*) *informal*
to spend time with someone

> **hang around with sb** *Marie always hung around with boys.*

,hang 'back

1 to not do something immediately because you are not confident or you do not feel certain about it = HESITATE ≠ FORGE AHEAD

> **hang back** *She tends to hang back and let others make the decisions.*

2 to stay in a place after other people have left

> **hang back** *She's the kid who hangs back to speak to the teacher.*

,hang 'in *informal*

to be brave or determined enough to continue doing something, even though there are difficulties

> **hang in** *All you have to do is hang in for a couple of days.* ♦ *It'll soon be over. Just hang in there.*

,hang 'on ★★★

1	hold sth tightly
2	wait
3	continue doing sth
4	depend on sth
5	when you realize sth

1 to hold tightly to something = HOLD ON ≠ LET GO

> **hang on** *I hung on as tightly as I could.*

2 hang on or **hang about** [often in imperative] *British informal* to wait or be patient = WAIT ≠ GIVE UP

> **hang on** *I think we should hang on and see the end of the game.* ♦ *Hang on. I've left my keys in the car.*

3 to continue doing something and achieve success even though there are difficulties

> **hang on** *The visiting team hung on for a narrow victory.*

4 to depend on something

> **hang on sth** *Everything hangs on the result of the blood test.*

5 [always in imperative] *British informal* used for saying that you have just realized something

> **hang on** *Hang on a minute. That isn't the dress she was wearing earlier.*
> **PHRASES** **hang on sb's every word** to listen very carefully to what someone is saying: *The children lean forward and hang on his every word.*
> **hang on by your fingernails** to just manage to avoid failure or danger: *The company was hanging on by its fingernails.*

,hang 'onto *informal*

1 to keep something and not lose it, get rid of it, or sell it

> **hang onto sth** *She still hung onto her wedding ring, even after the divorce.*
> ♦ *These are the books I want to hang onto.* ♦ *It looks like they'll manage to hang onto power.*

2 to hold tightly to someone or something

> **hang onto sb/sth** *He hung onto me with his little hand.*

,hang 'out

1 to hang wet clothes outside to dry ≠ TAKE DOWN

> **hang sth out** *also* **hang out sth** *He even had time to hang the washing out.* ♦ *I need to hang out these wet things.*

2 *informal* to spend time in a particular place or with a particular person

> **hang out** *She knew all the clubs where he usually hung out.* ♦ *+with She doesn't like the people I hang out with.*

■ **hangout** /ˈhæŋaʊt/ **noun** [C] a place where a particular group of people like to spend time: *The bar looked like every student hangout in the country.*

,hang 'out of

to lean out of a window so that the top part of your body is outside

> **hang out of sth** *The window was open*

and two of his friends were hanging out of it.

hang 'over

if something hangs over you, you worry about it or feel upset about it

hang over sb/sth *The threat of homelessness hangs over hundreds of families.* ♦ *A sense of doom hung over the town.*

■ **hangover** /ˈhæŋəʊvə/ **noun** [C] **1** the feeling of being tired and sick because you have drunk too much alcohol or taken too many drugs: *A walk might help to lift my hangover.* **2** something from the past such as an idea or attitude that is no longer suitable today: *The style is a hangover from his classical training.*

■ **hungover** /hʌnˈəʊvə/ **adj** tired and ill in the morning because you drank too much alcohol the night before: *At lunch, I was still feeling hungover.*

■ **overhang** /ˈəʊvəhæŋ/ **noun** [C usually singular] a part that sticks out from the edge above something: *The climbers descended the cliff to an overhang about thirty feet above the water.*

■ **overhang** /ˌəʊvəˈhæŋ/ **verb** to stick out from an edge above something

■ **overhanging** /ˌəʊvəˈhæŋɪŋ/ **adj** sticking out above something: *The road sign was partly covered by an overhanging bush.*

hang 'round *British informal same as* hang around

hang to'gether *informal*

if something hangs together, the different parts of it combine well so that it seems well planned and organized = MAKE SENSE

hang together *The speech doesn't really hang together.*

hang 'up ★★

1 to put the telephone down at the end of a conversation = RING OFF

hang up *Greg hung up and sat back in his chair.* ♦ **+on** *'Get lost!' she shouted, and hung up on me.*

2 to hang a piece of clothing on something

hang up sth *The women hung up their coats and sat down.*

hang sth up *Hang your jackets up by the fire.*

3 *informal* to stop using something because you are no longer doing a particular sport or activity

hang up sth *Nicola has decided it's time to hang up her dancing shoes.*

PHRASES **hang up your hat** *informal* to leave your job, especially when you are old enough to stop working: *I wasn't ready to hang up my hat.*

be/get hung up about/on sth *informal* to be or become very worried about something in a way that seems unreasonable: *Even boys as young as 8 are getting hung up about their hair and their clothes.*

be/get hung up on sb *American informal* to like someone very much and want to start a relationship with them, especially so much that it seems unreasonable: *She was hung up on this guy from her drama class.*

get hung up *American informal* to be delayed: *I'm sorry I'm late – I got hung up at the office.*

hang up

■ **'hang-up** **noun** [C] *informal* **1** something that you are worried or embarrassed about, especially something that is not very important: *She doesn't have any hang-ups about her appearance.* **2** *American* a problem that causes a delay or difficulty: *We worried about last-minute hang-ups.*

'hang with *American informal*

to spend time with someone

hang with sb *I'll swim, go for walks, hang with my friends.*

HANKER /ˈhæŋkə, *American* ˈhæŋkər/
hankers, hankering, hankered

'hanker ,after (*also* 'hanker for)

to have a strong feeling of wanting something

hanker after sth *She had always hankered after thick curly hair.*

HAPPEN /'hæpən/
happens, happening, happened

,happen a'long (also ,happen 'by) old-fashioned
to come to a particular place without planning to = COME ON
happen along *He would start a conversation with anyone who happened along.*

'happen on (also 'happen upon) old-fashioned
to meet someone or find something without planning to
happen on sb/sth *Did the film team just happen on him by chance?* ♦ *An explorer happened upon this city many years ago.*

'happen to ★★★
1 if something happens to you, an event or action takes place which affects you
happen to sb *This is the best thing that's ever happened to me.* ♦ *She's very late. I hope nothing bad's happened to her.*
2 if something happens to something, it changes or develops in a particular way = BECOME OF
happen to sth *We don't understand what is happening to the economy.* ♦ *Your hair's all green. What happened to it?*
PHRASES **if anything happens to sb** used as a way of avoiding talking directly about something bad that might take place: *I'd never forgive myself if anything has happened to her because I didn't go to meet her.* ♦ *If anything happens to me (=if I die), you'll have plenty of money to live on.*
what (has) happened to sth *informal* used for asking where something is = BECOME OF: *What's happened to the newspaper that was on the table?*
what/whatever happened to sb used for asking where someone is now and what they are doing: *Whatever happened to your friend George?*
what/whatever happened to sth *informal* used for asking why something does not happen or exist now: *Whatever happened to the idea of being innocent until proven guilty?*

HARDEN /'hɑːd(ə)n, American 'hɑrd(ə)n/
hardens, hardening, hardened

'harden to [usually passive] mainly literary
to become less affected or upset by unpleasant things and to show less kindness or sympathy to other people
be hardened to sth *Years of reporting on wars hardened them to human suffering.*

HARE /heə, American her/
hares, haring, hared

,hare 'off British informal
to go somewhere very quickly
hare off *The dog hared off across the garden.*

HARK /hɑːk, American hɑrk/
harks, harking, harked

'hark at [usually in imperative] British old-fashioned
used for showing that you are surprised, impressed, or offended by something that someone has just said
hark at sb *Just hark at her, with her big fancy words!*

,hark 'back to
1 to remember or talk about something that happened in the past
hark back to sth *They always hark back to what they call the 'good old days'.*
2 to be similar to something from the past
hark back to sth *The style of dress harks back to the 1950s.*

HARP /hɑːp, American hɑrp/
harps, harping, harped

'harp on American informal
to keep talking or complaining about something in a way that makes people bored or annoyed = KEEP ON
harp on sth *He's always harping on the need to reform the economy.*

,harp 'on about British informal same as harp on

HASH /hæʃ/
hashes, hashing, hashed

,hash 'out informal
to discuss a plan or agreement in order to agree about the details = THRASH OUT
hash out sth *also* **hash sth out** *We hashed out some of the details of the plan.*

,hash 'over American informal
to talk about a subject in great detail
hash over sth *also* **hash sth over** *We all need to sit down and hash over what we're going to do.*

,hash 'up British informal
to do something very badly
hash up sth *also* **hash sth up** *I hashed up*

my first attempt at the letter, so I started again.

HATCH /hætʃ/
hatches, hatching, hatched

,hatch 'out

1 if a baby bird, fish, insect etc hatches out, it comes out of its egg and is born
= HATCH
hatch out *Mosquito larvae are hatching out in the pond.*
2 if an egg hatches out, it breaks open so that the baby bird, fish, or insect can come out = HATCH
hatch out *The fertilized egg floats to the surface where it hatches out.*

HAUL /hɔːl, *American* hɔl/
hauls, hauling, hauled

,haul be'fore *same as* haul up

,haul 'in *informal*

1 to earn a lot of money = BRING IN
haul in sth *Their new business venture managed to haul in over £4 million in its first year.*
2 *British same as* haul up

,haul 'off [usually passive]

to take someone away to a place they do not want to go to, usually using force
= CART OFF
be hauled off to sth *Most of the protesters were hauled off to the police station.*

,haul 'up (*also* ,haul be'fore *or* ,haul 'in

British) [usually passive] *British informal*
to make someone appear before a court or other authority because they are accused of doing something wrong = PROSECUTE
be/get hauled up *If we do get hauled up, we'll plead not guilty.* ♦ *He was* **hauled up before** *the board of directors.* ♦ **+for** *They were continually being hauled in for petty crime and drunkenness.*

HAVE /əv, həv, hæv/
has /əz, həz, hæz/, **having, had** /əd, həd, hæd/

,have a'gainst [never progressive]

1 to dislike someone or not approve of them for a particular reason
have sth against sb *I have nothing against you personally, it's just I don't trust politicians.* ♦ *I don't know what he's got against me, but he's always criticizing my work.*

2 to be opposed to a plan or suggestion for a particular reason
have sth against sth *I have nothing against intelligence tests as long as they're done properly.* ♦ *I think it's a great idea. What do you have against it?*

,have a'way

PHRASE **have it away (with sb)** *British informal*
to have sex with someone

,have 'by

to be holding someone by a particular part of their body so that they cannot get away
have sb by sth *He had me by the throat.*

,have 'in [never progressive]

1 if you have someone in, they have come to your house, office, factory etc to do some work there
have sb in *We've had the health and safety inspectors in this week, asking all sorts of questions.* ♦ *They've got the builders in this week.*
2 *British* to have a supply of something that you regularly use in your house, for example food, drink, or fuel
have sth in *Stay for lunch – we've got plenty of food in.*
3 if a shop has something in, it is available in the shop for you to buy
have sth in *We'll have some more guide books in next week.*

,have 'in for

PHRASE **have (got) it in for sb** *informal* to want to cause trouble for someone because you dislike them: *The police stopped him again last night. He thinks they've got it in for him.*

,have 'off

PHRASE **have it off (with sb)** *British very informal* to have sex with someone

,have 'on ★★ (*also* **have ,got 'on**) [never progressive]

1	be wearing sth
2	radio/television etc: be working
3	prove that sb does dishonest things
4	not be free for sth
5	hold/carry sth
+	PHRASE

1 to be wearing particular clothes, shoes etc
have sth on *I'm not answering the door. I've got nothing on.* ♦ *I couldn't see the sign. I didn't have my glasses on.* ♦ *Melissa had her new dress on.*
2 if you have the radio, television, heating etc on, you have switched it on and it is working
have sth on *I can't talk to him while he's*

got the television on. ♦ *We haven't had the air conditioning on all summer.*

3 to have information about someone that shows they have done something dishonest or illegal

have sth on sb *They haven't got anything on Marlowe, so they can't arrest him.*

4 to have arranged to do something at a particular time, so that you are not available to do anything else = TEASE

have sth on *I have a lot on at the moment.* ♦ *Have you got much on tomorrow?* ♦ **+for** *Do you have anything on for tomorrow afternoon?*

5 to be holding something or carrying something with you

have sth on sb *Do you have a pen on you?* ♦ *I haven't got any money on me.*

PHRASE **be having sb on** *British informal* to be trying to make someone believe something that is not true, as a joke: *He's not really annoyed with you. He's just having you on.*

,have 'out

to have a tooth removed from your mouth or an organ removed from your body

have sth out *I'd been to the dentist to have a tooth out.* ♦ *The poor girl's in hospital – she's having her appendix out.*

PHRASE **have it out (with sb)** to talk to someone honestly and directly about something you do not agree about, or about something they have done that is making you angry: *He decided to have it out with Rose there and then.*

,have 'over (also ,have 'round British)

if you have someone over, they come to your house to visit you, usually for a meal or for drinks

have sb over *We're having the Simpsons over on Tuesday evening.* ♦ **+for** *They're having us over for a meal tomorrow.*

,have 'up for [usually passive] British informal

to send someone to a court of law because they have been accused of a crime = PROSECUTE

be had up for sth *He's been had up for dangerous driving once or twice before.*

HAZE /heɪz/
hazes, hazing, hazed

,haze 'over

if the sky or the air hazes over, a mist forms so that you cannot clearly see what is there

haze over *The sun went in and the sky hazed over.*

HEAD /hed/
heads, heading, headed

,head 'for ★★★

1 to go in a particular direction = MAKE FOR

head for sth *We decided to head for home.* ♦ *We asked them where they were headed for.*

2 if you are heading for or headed for something, it is likely to happen to you

be heading/headed for sth *It appears that the rebels are heading for victory.*

,head 'off ★★

1 to prevent something from taking place = PREVENT

head off sth *The police acted quickly and managed to head off a violent confrontation.*

head sth off *A humanitarian catastrophe is looming, and aid workers are battling to head it off.*

2 *informal* to leave = LEAVE

head off *We should be heading off soon.* ♦ *They headed off straight after lunch.*

3 to prevent someone from going somewhere by getting in front of them

head sb off *Let's try and head them off before they cross the bridge.*

head off sb *Special equipment tells soldiers which way to go to head off the enemy.*

,head 'up ★

to be in control of a group or an organization = LEAD, HEAD

head up sth *Maria DeCruz was chosen to head up the department.*

head sth up *We need some bright young person to head this agency up.* ♦ *They've set up a new regulatory body but they don't have anyone to head it up.*

HEAL /hi:l, American hil/
heals, healing, healed

,heal 'over

if an injury heals over, new skin forms over it and it becomes healthy again

heal over *It shouldn't take long for the cut to heal over.*

,heal 'up

if an injury heals up, the skin or bone grows back together and becomes healthy again

heal up *The cut wasn't healing up the way it should.*

HEAP /hiːp, *American* hip/
heaps, heaping, heaped

'heap on (*also* **'heap upon**)
if you heap something such as praise or blame on someone, you praise or blame them a lot = PILE ON
heap sth on sb *The press heaped enormous praise on the new prime minister at first.*

heap 'up [often passive]
to make a big untidy pile of things = PILE UP
be heaped up *Clothes were heaped up on the floor.*
heap up sth *also* **heap sth up** *They heaped up the wood then set fire to it.*
♦ *Someone had heaped the mats up in the corner.*

HEAR /hɪə, *American* hɪr/
hears, hearing, heard /hɜːd, *American* hɜrd/

'hear a'bout ★★★
to be told about something and therefore to know about it or know that it exists
hear about sth *We've heard about a man who might be able to help us.* ♦ *Have you heard about my brother (=has anyone told you the news about my brother)?*

'hear from ★★★
1 if you hear from someone, they write to you, phone you, email you etc
hear from sb *It's years since I heard from Jill.* ♦ *The police would like to hear from anyone who witnessed the accident.*
2 to listen to someone who is speaking about a particular thing
hear from sb *The Commission heard from over thirty witnesses.* ♦ *Next we'll hear from a listener in Scotland.*
PHRASE she'll/they'll/you'll etc be hearing from me *informal* used for saying that you are angry with someone, and you will tell them this: *He'd better apologize to you or he'll be hearing from me.*

'hear of ★★★
1 to find out that something has happened
hear of sth *I was shocked to hear of his death.*
2 to receive news about someone = LEARN OF
hear sth of sb *Do you ever hear anything of Edward these days?* ♦ *Not much was heard of him until his reappearance last night.*
PHRASES have heard of to know about

the existence of someone or something: *'It was James Bomford.' 'Never heard of him!'* ♦ *Have you heard of these phones that let you take pictures?*
not hear of it to refuse to accept a suggestion or offer: *I said he could stay with us, but he wouldn't hear of it.*
the first sb hears of sth the moment that someone finds out about something new, especially when other people already know about it: *'She's getting married next week'. 'Well that's the first I've heard of it!'*

'hear 'out
to let someone finish what they are saying without interrupting
hear sb out *I'm serious about this, so hear me out, please.*

HEAT /hiːt, *American* hit/
heats, heating, heated

'heat 'through
to heat food that has already been cooked, until every part of it is hot
heat sth through *You can get food poisoning if you don't heat food through properly.*

'heat 'up ★★
1 to make something hot or warm = HEAT
heat up sth *I was just heating up some soup.* ♦ *Pollution may be heating up the Earth's atmosphere.*
heat sth up *A boiler's job is to heat the water up.* ♦ *If you don't want your dinner now you can always heat it up later.*
2 to become hot or warm
heat up *The metal expands as it heats up.* ♦ *I stood in the kitchen waiting for the water to heat up.*
3 if a situation heats up, it becomes more exciting, dangerous, or serious
heat up *The dispute was already heating up.* ♦ *At night, the action really starts to heat up.*

HEAVE /hiːv, *American* hiv/
heaves, heaving, heaved

'heave 'to *literary*
if a ship heaves to, it stops moving
heave to *The order came to heave to.*

'heave 'up *informal*
to send food from your stomach out through your mouth, for example because you are ill = BRING UP; *formal* VOMIT
heave up *I could hear someone heaving up in the bathroom.*

HEDGE /hedʒ/
hedges, hedging, hedged

be ˌhedged aˈbout with
if something is hedged about with something such as rules or conditions, these things apply to it

be hedged about with sth *The offer was hedged about with conditions.*

ˈhedge against
to do something that will prevent you from being affected by any problems that might happen

hedge against sth *The purpose of this is to hedge against financial risk.*

ˌhedge ˈin [usually passive]
1 to surround someone or something

be hedged in *His motorbike was hedged in by other cars.*

2 to limit someone's freedom or ability to do something

be hedged in *We were hedged in by rules and regulations.*

ˈhedge with (also ˌhedge ˈin with)
[usually passive]
to make special conditions for something so that you do not have to follow the usual rules

be hedged with sth *Most insurers' conditions are hedged with all sorts of exclusions.*

HEEL /hiːl, American hil/
heels, heeling, heeled

ˌheel ˈover
if a boat heels over, it leans over to one side = LIST

heel over *The ship heeled over and sank.*

HELP /help/
helps, helping, helped

ˌhelp aˈlong
to make something happen more quickly or easily

help sth along *The use of drugs can sometimes help nature along.* ♦ *To help matters along, she decided to give John a call.*

ˌhelp ˈoff with
to help someone to take off a piece of clothing

help sb off with sth *'Let's have a look at this rash', said the doctor, helping him off with his shirt.*

ˌhelp ˈon with
to help someone to put on a piece of clothing

help sb on with sth *He helped me on with my coat.*

ˌhelp ˈout ★★★
to help someone, especially by doing a particular job or by giving them money

help out *My mother helped out a lot when my kids were small.* ♦ **+with** *He always helped out with the housework.*
help sb out *If you run out of money, don't expect me to help you out.*
help out sb *On Fridays I used to help out my grandmother in the shop.*

ˌhelp ˈthrough
to help someone to deal with a difficult situation by giving them support or information

help sb through sth *My friends helped me through a very difficult time.*

ˈhelp to
to give someone something, especially food or drink

help yourself to sth *Help yourself to more coffee.*
help sb to sth *His mother helped him to potatoes and peas.*

ˌhelp ˈup
to help someone stand up when they are sitting down or have fallen down

help sb up *He extended his hand to help her up.* ♦ *When they helped him up, blood was streaming from his face and hands.*

HEM /hem/
hems, hemming, hemmed

ˌhem ˈin [often passive]
1 to enclose someone or something and prevent them from moving or leaving
= FENCE IN

be hemmed in *When she returned to her car, it was hemmed in by a white van.*
hem sb/sth in *The police moved around the crowd, hemming them in.*

2 to prevent someone from making their own choices or doing what they want
= formal CONSTRAIN

be hemmed in *She felt hemmed in by the demands of her family.*
hem in sb/sth also **hem sb/sth in** *You shouldn't hem in teenagers with endless restrictions.*

HERD /hɜːd, American hɜrd/
herds, herding, herded

ˌherd toˈgether [usually passive]
to make people come together to form a group

be herded together *The rest of us were herded together in the room opposite.*

HEW /hjuː, *American* hju/
hews, hewing, hewed /hjuːn, *American* hjun/ or **hewn**

,hew 'out [usually passive] *mainly literary*
to cut something solid such as rock or wood into a rough shape, using a large heavy blade
be hewn out of *A primitive basin had been hewn out of the rock.*

'hew to *American*
to continue to use or do something, and not change to something new
hew to sth *They hewed to the narrow principles of the old school.*

HIDE /haɪd/
hides, hiding, hid /hɪd/, **hidden** /'hɪd(ə)n/

,hide a'way ★★
1 to go to a place where no one can find you because you want to be alone
hide away *Kate's experiences would have made most people want to hide away.*
hide yourself away *When he gets depressed he hides himself away and we never see him.*
2 [often passive] to put something in a place where no one can find it = HIDE
be hidden away *The letters were hidden away in a drawer.*
hide sth away *She buys Christmas presents early, then hides them away.*
■ **hideaway** /'haɪdə,weɪ/ **noun** [C] a private place where someone goes to relax or to be away from other people: *Miller wrote in a hideaway at the bottom of the garden.*

'hide behind
if you hide behind something, you use it as a way of preventing people from discovering something, usually something bad about you
hide behind sth *People think the company is trying to hide behind this report.*

'hide from ★★
1 to try not to accept something or not to be affected by something
hide from sth *She could no longer hide from the truth.* ♦ *You can't hide from the fact that there's something seriously wrong.*
2 to prevent someone from knowing the truth about something
hide sth from sb *I couldn't hide the facts from her any longer.* ♦ *The secret of his birth had been hidden from him all his life.*

,hide 'out
to go somewhere where no one can find you
hide out *He had been hiding out in the woods for three days.* ♦ **+from** *We used to hide out from our parents here.*
■ **hideout** /'haɪdaʊt/ **noun** [C] a place where someone can hide from other people, especially the police or an enemy: *The gang usually has a hideout in the hills somewhere.*

HIKE /haɪk/
hikes, hiking, hiked

,hike 'up *informal*
1 to pull up a piece of your clothing, usually in order to be more comfortable = HITCH UP
hike up sth *also* **hike sth up** *She hiked up her skirt and waded through the water.*
2 to suddenly increase the amount or level of something = JACK UP
hike up sth *also* **hike sth up** *TV networks are trying to hike up their viewing figures by broadcasting cheap game shows.* ♦ *They're hiking gas prices up again.*

HINGE /hɪndʒ/
hinges, hinging, hinged

'hinge on (*also* 'hinge upon)
to depend on something = DEPEND ON
hinge on sth *A lot hinges on the result of tomorrow's match.* ♦ *The fate of the new Europe hinged upon France.*

HINT /hɪnt/
hints, hinting, hinted

'hint at ★★
to say what you are thinking or feeling in an indirect way
hint at sth *Officials are hinting at the possibility of signing an agreement this week.*

HIRE /'haɪə, *American* 'haɪr/
hires, hiring, hired

,hire 'on *American*
to begin working at a particular job, especially a temporary one
hire on *Thousands of desperate people were waiting in line to hire on.* ♦ **+as** *Justin hired on as a construction worker.*

,hire 'out ★
1 *British* to allow someone to use something that you own in return for payment = RENT OUT

hire out sth *There are several companies in the area that hire out bikes.*
hire sth out *Only myself and my family use the boat. I've no intention of hiring it out.*

2 to send someone to work for other people for short periods of time in return for payment
hire yourself out *You're a great cook. You should hire yourself out!* ♦ **+to** *He hires himself out to companies that are in financial trouble.*
hire sb out *also* **hire out sb** *I contacted the agency that hired him out.* ♦ **+to** *Our business is hiring out IT people to companies.*

HIT /hɪt/
hits, hitting, hit

Hit is often used with adverbs and prepositions when it means 'to move quickly onto someone or something, touching it with force': *He accidentally **hit** me **in** the eye.* ♦ *It's thought he may have fallen and **hit** his head **on** the kerb.* ♦ *James was **hit with** a stick.* These uses are not included.

ˌhit ˈback ★★

1 to criticize someone who has criticized you = RETALIATE
hit back *If you criticize the way someone brings up their kids, they're bound to hit back.* ♦ *The president hit back by accusing his rival of double standards.* ♦ **+at** *He has hit back at claims he did not do enough to help.*

2 to deliberately hit someone because they have hit you = RETALIATE
hit sb back *Dan hit me so I hit him back.*
hit back *Just because someone hits you doesn't mean you have to hit back.*

3 to start to play well against an opponent who was winning = FIGHT BACK
hit back *It wasn't until the second half that England started to hit back.* ♦ **+with** *The Ireland team hit back with two more goals.*

ˈhit for *same as* hit up for

ˈhit on ★

1 hit on or **hit upon** to suddenly have an idea = COME UP WITH
hit on sth *They hit on the idea of celebrating the occasion with a concert.* ♦ *James hit upon a radical solution to the problem.*

2 hit on or **hit upon** to discover something by chance = HAPPEN ON
hit on sth *She was scared he might hit on the truth.* ♦ *Somehow they hit upon*

the number that opened the bank's safe.

3 *informal* to try to start a conversation with someone because you are sexually attracted to them = CHAT UP
hit on sb *Hey, are you trying to hit on my sister?*

ˌhit ˈout ★

1 to say something that criticizes or expresses anger towards someone or something = LASH OUT, ATTACK
hit out *The sneer was obvious, but she didn't hit out.* ♦ **+at** *Ms Wallis hit out at the court's decision.* ♦ **+against** *She eventually hit out against the club's petty rules.*

2 to try to hit someone or something in an uncontrolled way = STRIKE OUT
hit out *She raised her arm, trying to hit out.* ♦ **+at** *He screamed and hit out at her.* ♦ **+with** *The police hit out with their truncheons.*

ˌhit ˈup for (*also* ˈhit for) [often passive]
American informal
to ask someone for something, especially money
be hit up for sth *Some companies would be hit up for millions of dollars in fines.*
hit sb up for sth *You know he'll try to hit us up for cash.*

ˈhit upon

1 *same as* hit on 1
2 *same as* hit on 2

ˈhit with

1 to make someone do something or experience something that is unpleasant
hit sb with sth *They may decide to hit him with a lawsuit.*

2 to tell someone something that is unpleasant or surprising
hit sb with sth *Come on, hit me with it – what happened?*

HITCH /hɪtʃ/
hitches, hitching, hitched

ˌhitch ˈup

1 to pull something that you are wearing to a higher position = HIKE UP
hitch up sth *also* **hitch sth up** *She hitched up her skirt and ran.* ♦ *She hitched her dress up over her long skinny legs.*

2 to move a part of your body or something that you are carrying to a higher position
hitch up sth *also* **hitch sth up** *He hitched up the rucksack he was carrying on his back.* ♦ *Hitching up her long skirt, she climbed out of the train.*

3 to fasten a horse to something such as a post or cart

hitch up sth *also* hitch sth up *They can just hitch up their horses and head off.* ♦ **+to** *He hitched up his horse to the fence.*

4 to fasten something such as a trailer to the back of a car
hitch up sth *also* hitch sth up *They hitched up the caravan and set off to the coast.* ♦ **+to** *They hitched up the trailer to the back of the car.*

HIVE /haɪv/
hives, hiving, hived

,hive 'off *business*
to separate part of an organization or service and sell it
hive off sth *also* hive sth off *The company decided to hive off its less profitable activities.* ♦ **+to** *The plan was to hive off IT work to sub-contractors.*

HOARD /hɔːd, *American* hɔrd/
hoards, hoarding, hoarded

,hoard a'way
to get and keep a large amount of something because it might be valuable or useful later
hoard away sth *also* hoard sth away *People panicked and started hoarding away food.*

HOLD /həʊld, *American* hoʊld/
holds, holding, held /held/

,hold a'gainst [usually with a negative]
to feel angry with someone, because of something that they have done in the past
hold sth against sb *He knows it was an accident – I don't think he'll hold it against her.*

,hold 'back ★★

1	prevent sb/sth moving forwards
2	prevent sb from succeeding
3	not do/say sth
4	make sb not do/say sth
5	keep thoughts/feelings secret
6	not allow sb to have sth
7	stop sth from progressing/developing

1 [often passive] to stop someone or something from moving forwards = KEEP BACK, RESTRAIN
be held back *Her hair was held back with two clips.*
hold sb/sth back *Ollie had to hold Tom back to prevent him retaliating.*
hold back sb/sth *The police desperately tried to hold back the crowd.*

2 to stop someone from being as successful as they should be = KEEP BACK

hold sb back *Her parents worried that her classmates were holding her back.*
hold back sb *The legislation was intended to prevent employees from holding back bright young women.*

3 to decide not to do or say something = KEEP BACK
hold back *He held back, remembering the mistake he had made before.* ♦ **+from** *She held back from questioning him any further.*
hold sth back *I think he's holding something back.*
hold back sth *They had held back one or two vital points.*

4 to make someone decide not to do or say something = KEEP BACK
hold sb back *She wanted to tell him what had happened, but loyalty to her friend held her back.*

5 to not show what you are thinking or feeling = CONTAIN, KEEP BACK
hold back sth *Joe held back his anger.* ♦ *She bit her lip to* **hold back the tears**.
hold sth back *Then the excitement burst inside her – she could not hold it back.*

6 to not allow someone to have something, for example money = WITHHOLD
hold back sth *They held back the final payment because they weren't satisfied with the work.*
hold sth back *My parents held some of the money back until I'd finished my studies.*

7 to stop something from progressing or developing as it should = HINDER
hold back sth *What is holding back investment?*
hold sth back *Long-term water shortages can hold economic development back and cause environmental problems.*

,hold 'down ★★

1	prevent sb from standing
2	prevent sb from rising
3	prevent progress/development
4	keep prices/numbers low
5	remove sb's freedom/rights
+	PHRASE

1 to hold someone who is lying down, so that they cannot move
hold sb down *Four people held him down.*
hold down sb *We managed to hold down the mugger until the police arrived.*

2 to hold something so that it does not move upwards
hold sth down *They put stones on the edge of the rug to hold it down.*
hold down sth *Hold down the ALT key and hit return.*

3 to prevent something from developing, or to prevent someone from doing what they want = KEEP DOWN

hold sb down *She proved that being a woman wouldn't hold her down.*

4 to stop prices or numbers from rising

hold down sth *The measure was intended to hold down wages and prices.*
hold sth down *The airline wants to hold fare increases down.* ◆ *The government failed to hold spending down.*

Nouns often used as objects with **hold down 4**

■ cost, increase, inflation, price, rate, wages

5 to stop someone having their freedom or rights

hold sb down *The regime had been holding its people down for years.*
PHRASE **hold down a job** to succeed in keeping a job: *Half of them have never held down a job.*

ˌhold ˈforth

to talk for a long time about something, often in a way that other people think is boring

hold forth *As usual, my father was holding forth.* ◆ **+on/about** *Dave was holding forth on the subject of politics.*

ˌhold ˈin

1 to not allow your feelings to show = RESTRAIN ≠ LET OUT

hold in sth *also* **hold sth in** *It can be bad for you to hold in anger.* ◆ *I was so excited I could hardly hold it in.*

2 to keep something inside a place so that it is safe

hold sth in *also* **hold in sth** *Close the lid firmly to hold the contents in.*
PHRASE **hold your stomach in** to pull in the muscles in your stomach so that it does not stick out

ˌhold ˈoff ★★

1 to deliberately delay doing something

hold off *He may decide to hold off for a few days.* ◆ **+on** *How much longer can they hold off on political reform?*
hold off doing sth *She held off calling him until the last possible moment.*

2 to keep away someone who is trying to attack you

hold sb off *She could not hold him off.* ◆ **+with** *I held them off with bricks and stones.*
hold off sb *He managed to hold off his attacker and get away.*

3 *mainly journalism* to stop an opponent from starting to win or lead

hold off sb/sth *Will Woods manage to hold off Ernie Else's challenge?*

hold sb/sth off *The young Russian player fought hard, but the champion managed to hold her off.*

4 if rain or snow holds off, it does not fall, although you expected it to = KEEP OFF

hold off *I hope the rain holds off for the barbecue.*

ˌhold ˈon ★★★

1 to hold something tightly or carefully so that you do not fall = HANG ON ≠ LET GO

hold on *Hold on tight everyone, the boat's ready to go.* ◆ *You'll fall if you don't hold on.* ◆ **+to** *She held on to the rail and walked unsteadily down the steps.*

2 to wait = HANG ON

hold on *Hold on! You forgot your card!* ◆ **+(for)** *Can you hold on for a moment?* ◆ *We'll hold on another minute, then we'll have to go.*

3 to manage to stay alive or continue to do or deal with something in a difficult or dangerous situation = HANG ON

hold on *You just have to hold on until the ambulance arrives.*
PHRASE **hold on!** *informal* used for telling someone to listen or think: *Hold on, that won't work.* ◆ *Now **hold on a minute!** I never said that.*

ˌhold ˈon to (*also* ˌhold ˈonto)

1 to hold something tightly or carefully so that you do not drop it or lose it

hold on to sth *Hold onto your purse, won't you?*

2 to not lose something or not let someone else have it = *informal* HANG ON TO

hold on to sth *Hold on to the instructions in case you have any problems.*

3 to continue feeling or believing something

hold on to sth *I always held on to the belief that one day he would succeed.*

4 to stop someone from leaving you or from doing what they want

hold on to sb *A mother can't hold on to her children for ever.*

ˌhold ˈout ★★★

1 to hold something where other people can reach it

hold out sth *'Pull me up will you?' she said, **holding out her hand**.* ◆ *Gail held out her glass to be refilled.* ◆ **+to** *She held out a cup of coffee to me.*
hold sth out *He held the book out and I took it.* ◆ **+to** *'It's for you', she said, holding the phone out to me.*

2 to continue to be enough or continue to exist = LAST

hold out *How long will your money hold*

out? ♦ *I wonder whether her stamina will hold out.*

3 to continue to defend a place that is being attacked

hold out *We can only hold out for a few more hours.*

4 to say or show that something may or will happen

hold out a possibility/prospect/ promise etc *Officials held out the possibility of prisoners being released.*

PHRASE **not hold out much hope** to think that something is not likely to happen or succeed: *I don't hold out much hope that they'll come.*

,hold 'out for

to not accept an offer because you want a better one = STAND OUT FOR, STICK OUT FOR

hold out for sth *They've been holding out for an even higher price.*

,hold 'out on

to refuse to tell someone something

hold out on sb/sth *They've been holding out on the details of the plan.* ♦ *Why have you been holding out on me?*

,hold 'over

1 to make someone do what you want by threatening to tell people about something bad that you know about them

hold sth over sb *If I tell them about my past they might hold it over me.*

2 to do something or deal with something at a later time or date = POSTPONE

hold sth over *Do you think they'll hold the offer over if I ask them?* ♦ **+until/to** *Let's hold the session over until this evening.* ♦ **+for** *They intend to hold the article over for the next edition.*

3 [usually passive] *American* to let a play or film continue for longer than was planned because it is so successful

be held over *The movie was held over for an extra two months.*

'hold to ★

1 to do what you have promised or decided

hold to sth *The western democracies held to their policy of non-intervention.*

2 to refuse to change particular beliefs, opinions, or standards

hold to sth *She still holds to the view that violence is never justified.*

3 to make someone do what they have promised or decided to do

hold sb to sth *They didn't hold me to a month's notice.*

4 [usually passive] to make someone continue to behave according to particular beliefs or standards

be held to sth *Anyone appointed to this position should be held to the highest ethical standards.*

PHRASE **I'll hold you to that** *informal* a friendly way of accepting an invitation or offer for a later date: *'We must have dinner together sometime'. 'I'll hold you to that'.*

,hold to'gether

1 [often passive] to remain in one piece and not break apart, or to make something do this

be held together *The piles of letters were held together by rubber bands.*

hold sth together *She removed the metal clips that held the pages together.*

hold together *I can't see how this sculpture holds together.*

2 to stay together and continue to have a good relationship in a difficult situation

hold together *How can any family hold together under these circumstances?*

hold sth together *I was trying to hold my marriage together.*

,hold 'up ★★★

1	hold sth high
2	prevent sb/sth from falling
3	cause a delay
4	steal things by threatening violence
5	stay in good condition
+	PHRASE
+	**hold-up** noun

1 to hold something in a high position, so that people can see it

hold up sth *She held up her hand for silence.*

hold sth up *Can you all hold your pictures up so I can see them.*

2 to support someone or something so that they do not fall down = SUPPORT

hold sb/sth up *Her legs were almost too shaky to hold her up.*

hold up sb/sth *A series of wooden beams hold up the roof.*

3 [often passive] to cause a delay or make someone late = DELAY

be held up *Sorry I'm late, but my train was held up.* ♦ *She got **held up** at work.*

hold up sb/sth *What's holding up the traffic?*

hold sb/sth up *All these telephone calls are holding me up.*

4 to steal from a business, from a vehicle, or from people by threatening violence, usually having a gun or other weapon = ROB

hold up sb/sth *An armed raider held up the village store last week.*

hold sb/sth up *The hero then plans to hold the bank up.* ♦ *They stopped the train and held the passengers up.*

5 to remain strong or in a fairly good condition

hold up *There were fears that her ankle might not hold up for the competition.* ♦ *Prices had held up well until late 1997.*

PHRASE **hold your head up** to not be ashamed of yourself: *My father was so ashamed he said he would never be able to hold his head up again.*

hold up (sense 4)

■ **'hold-up** noun [C] **1** a short delay: *We had a hold-up at the station.* **2** a situation in which traffic does not move, or moves only very slowly: *There's a hold-up on the Forth Road Bridge.* **3** a situation in which someone threatens people in a bank or shop with a gun in order to get money or goods: *He was shot at during an armed hold-up.*

hold 'up as [usually passive]
to say that someone or something is an example of something, usually something good

be held up as sth *He was held up as a hero.* ♦ *We were held up as the best example of working practice.*

'hold with
PHRASE **not hold with sth** to not approve of an activity or action = APPROVE OF ≠ DISAPPROVE OF: *She doesn't hold with going out with younger men.*

HOLE /həʊl, *American* hoʊl/
holes, holing, holed

hole 'out
in golf, if someone holes out, they hit the ball into the hole

hole out *It took him another three shots to hole out.*

hole 'up [often passive]
to stay in a place and not leave it, for example because you are hiding from someone = HIDE

be holed up *She was holed up at her parents' home trying to avoid the media.*
hole up *We needed a place to hole up and get some rest.*

HOLLOW /'hɒləʊ, *American* 'hɑloʊ/
hollows, hollowing, hollowed

hollow 'out
to make a hole in something by removing what is inside it

hollow out sth *also* **hollow sth out**
Hollow out the tomatoes and fill them with the rice mixture. ♦ *He hollowed a piece of wood out and made it into a bowl.*

HOME /həʊm, *American* hoʊm/
homes, homing, homed

home 'in on
1 to aim at something and move quickly and directly to it

home in on sth *A large insect was homing in on his neck.*

2 to go straight to the most relevant part of a situation or the part of a situation that you are most interested in

home in on sth *Sometimes they homed in on the right conclusion with incredible speed.*

HONE /həʊn, *American* hoʊn/
hones, honing, honed

hone 'in on *same as* **home in on**

HOOK /hʊk/
hooks, hooking, hooked

hook 'into
1 to become connected to something such as a computer network or phone system

hook into sth *This system is designed to hook into the most popular operating systems.*

2 *American informal* to become closely involved in something, often in a way that makes it difficult to stop being involved

hook into sth *People are reluctant to hook into these long-term investments.*

hook 'through
to put your arm, finger, leg etc round something in order to hold it or bring it closer to you

hook sth through sth *She hooked her arm through mine.*

hook 'up ★
1 to connect two pieces of electrical or electronic equipment together, or to

connect a piece of equipment to a computer or power supply = CONNECT ≠ DISCONNECT

> **hook up sth** *First you have to hook up your speakers.* ♦ **+to** *He hooked up his tape recorder to the telephone.*

2 to connect two pieces of equipment, especially using a hook = COUPLE

> **hook sth up** *You just hook the car and the trailer up.*
> **hook up sth** *The train driver hooked up the two carriages.* ♦ **+to** *The thieves hooked up his new car to their vehicle and drove it away.*

3 *informal* if two people hook up, they start a relationship together or start doing something together = GET TOGETHER

> **hook up** *We must hook up again soon.* ♦ **+with** *While travelling, he hooked up with a group of American students.*

4 if you hook up to a place or to the Internet, or if you hook something up, you become connected to it through your computer = CONNECT

> **hook up sth to sth** *The government wants to hook up all classrooms to the Internet.*
> **hook up to sth** *I can hook up to the library from my computer.*

■ **'hook-up** noun [C] a connection between two electrical systems or pieces of equipment such as computers: *It's an older system with no hook-up facility.*

HOOVER /ˈhuːvə, *American* ˈhuvər/
hoovers, hoovering, hoovered

ˌhoover 'up *British*
to clean the dirt or dust from a carpet or floor with a vacuum cleaner

> **hoover up sth** *also* **hoover sth up** *We can hoover up any bits you drop.* ♦ *Let the dirt dry and hoover it up later.*

HORN /hɔːn, *American* hɔrn/
horns, horning, horned

ˌhorn 'in *American informal*
to try to become involved in something that other people do not want you to be involved in

> **horn in** *My little brother always horns in when I'm with my friends.* ♦ **+on** *Don't talk about the deal around Chuck, or he'll try to horn in on it.*

HORSE /hɔːs, *American* hɔrs/
horses, horsing, horsed

ˌhorse a'round (*also* ˌhorse a'bout
British) *informal old-fashioned*
to play in a very lively or rough way = FOOL AROUND

> **horse around** *We spent most of the day just horsing around.*

HOSE /həʊz, *American* hoʊz/
hoses, hosing, hosed

ˌhose 'down
1 to use a hose to clean something

> **hose down sth** *also* **hose sth down** *There was no water to hose down the horses.* ♦ *We need a room with a drain in the middle, so we can hose it down.*

2 *American mainly journalism* to try to stop people from believing something that may cause problems

> **hose down sth** *also* **hose sth down** *His assistant seems eager to hose down the rumours.*

HOT /hɒt, *American* hɑt/
hots, hotting, hotted

ˌhot 'up *British informal*
to become more lively or exciting = INTENSIFY

> **hot up** *The debate on electoral reform hotted up yesterday.*

HOUND /haʊnd/
hounds, hounding, hounded

ˌhound 'out
to force someone to leave a place or job by being unpleasant to them over a period of time

> **hound sb out** *He claims the media hounded him out of office.*

HOVER /ˈhɒvə, *American* ˈhɑvər/
hovers, hovering, hovered

'hover around
to be at or near a particular level without changing much

> **hover around sth** *Temperatures hovered around 10 degrees.*

'hover between
1 to stay between two levels without changing much

> **hover between sth and sth** *His marks have hovered between 50 and 60 percent.*

2 to change between two different states or situations so that you never know when it is going to change

> **hover between sth and sth** *Her mood hovered between euphoria and despair.*

HOWL /haʊl/
howls, howling, howled

,howl 'down [usually passive]
to stop someone from speaking or being heard by shouting loudly and angrily
= SHOUT DOWN, DROWN OUT
> **be howled down** *He was howled down even by members of his own party.*

HUDDLE /ˈhʌd(ə)l/
huddles, huddling, huddled

,huddle to'gether (*also* **,huddle 'up**)
to move close together in order to stay warm, feel safe, or talk
> **huddle together** *The night was cold and we huddled together for warmth.*

HUM /hʌm/
hums, humming, hummed

'hum with
if a place hums with activity, it is full of noise and activity
> **hum with sth** *The whole stadium was humming with excitement.*

HUNGER /ˈhʌŋɡə, American ˈhʌŋɡər/
hungers, hungering, hungered

'hunger after (*also* **'hunger for**) *mainly literary*
to want something very much
> **hunger for sth** *The current British champion clearly hungers after the US Open title.*

HUNKER /ˈhʌŋkə, American ˈhʌŋkər/
hunkers, hunkering, hunkered

,hunker 'down
1 to sit close to the ground on your heels with your knees bent up in front of you
> **hunker down** *They hunkered down around the fire.*
2 to wait for a difficult situation to end
> **hunker down** *Refugees are hunkering down in preparation for a long winter.*

HUNT /hʌnt/
hunts, hunting, hunted

,hunt 'down ★
1 [often passive] to try to find every member of a group, especially in order to arrest or kill them
> **be hunted down** *Those who protested were hunted down and killed.* ◆ *Most of the rebels were hunted down and killed.*

> **hunt down sb** *The army is dedicated to hunting down the terrorists.*
> **hunt sb down** *He wants to go after them. He wants to hunt them down.*
2 **hunt down** or **hunt out** to try to find a particular thing or person
> **hunt down sth** *They'll actually hunt down old books for you.* ◆ *August is a good time to hunt out bargains.*
> **hunt sth down** *He collects juke boxes and spends a lot of time hunting them down.*

,hunt 'up *American*
to find something or someone that is difficult to find
> **hunt up sb/sth** *also* **hunt sb/sth up** *Let me hunt up my notebook.*

HURL /hɜːl, American hɜrl/
hurls, hurling, hurled

'hurl at
to shout at someone in a very angry unfriendly way
> **hurl abuse/insults at sb** *A group of boys was hurling abuse at her.*

HURRY /ˈhʌri/
hurries, hurrying, hurried

,hurry 'along *same as* **hurry up**

,hurry 'on
1 to continue walking fast, often instead of stopping to do something
> **hurry on** *I stopped for a rest, but my friends hurried on.*
2 to continue talking, instead of pausing to let someone else talk
> **hurry on** *When he didn't reply, she hurried on.*

,hurry 'up ★★
1 to do something or move somewhere more quickly = BUCK UP ≠ SLOW DOWN
> **hurry up** *If we hurry up we'll be there before the others.* ◆ **+with** *She wished George would hurry up with her cup of tea.*
2 **hurry up** or **hurry along** to make someone do something more quickly or to make something happen sooner = COME ALONG, COME ON ≠ SLOW DOWN
> **hurry sb/sth up** *Try and hurry her up a bit or we'll be late.* ◆ *Certain drugs can hurry the healing process up.* ◆ *He took her hand to hurry her along.*
> **PHRASE hurry up!** used for telling someone to do something more quickly = BUCK UP ≠ SLOW DOWN: *Hurry up and finish your soup!*

HUSH /hʌʃ/
hushes, hushing, hushed

,hush 'up [often passive]
if someone in authority hushes something up, they try to prevent people knowing about it = COVER UP
be hushed up *There were rumours of suicide, which were hushed up.*
hush up sth *also* **hush sth up** *You can't hush up a murder.*

HYPE /haɪp/
hypes, hyping, hyped

,hype 'up *informal*
1 to make something sound more interesting or impressive than it is = TALK UP
hype sth up *also* **hype up sth** *They're trying to hype the event up but it's really nothing special.* ♦ **+into** *They tried to hype the show up into something it was never meant to be.*
2 [usually passive] to make someone very excited
be/get hyped up *I got really hyped up about the interview because I wanted the job so much.*
■ **,hyped 'up** **adj** *informal* feeling very excited and nervous: *By ten o'clock, the kids are completely hyped up.*

ICE /aɪs/
ices, icing, iced

,ice 'down *American*
to put ice on a part of your body that you have hurt in order to prevent it from swelling
ice down sth *also* **ice sth down** *Mom helped me to ice down my ankle.*

,ice 'over (*also* **,ice 'up**) [often passive]
to become covered with ice = FREEZE, FREEZE OVER ≠ THAW
be iced over *The pond was iced over for most of the winter.*
ice over *Drivers faced a new danger as roads iced over when floodwater froze.*

IDENTIFY /aɪˈdentɪfaɪ/
identifies, identifying, identified

id'entify as
to be a sign that shows who or what someone or something is
identify sb as sth *His red and gold jacket identified him as a steward.*

i'dentify with ★★★
1 to feel that you can understand and share someone else's feelings = EMPATHIZE WITH
identify with sb *He didn't seem to be able to identify with ordinary people and their aspirations.*
2 [often passive] to consider that someone or something is involved or connected with a particular group or opinion
be identified with sb/sth *The Americans were anxious not to become identified with anti-government forces.*
identify yourself with sb/sth *She has never really identified herself with the left.*
3 *formal* to think that something is the same as something else or is closely related to it
identify sth with sth *Most of these writers identify mind with consciousness.*

IDLE /ˈaɪd(ə)l/
idles, idling, idled

,idle a'way
to spend time relaxing and doing nothing important = WHILE AWAY
idle away sth *also* **idle sth away** *Tom idled away most of Monday in his office.* ♦ *We idled a few hours away playing pool.*

IMBUE /ɪmˈbjuː, American ɪmˈbju/
imbues, imbuing, imbued

im'bue with [usually passive] *formal*
if something is imbued with a particular quality or emotion, it is filled with that quality or emotion
be imbued with sth *His voice was imbued with a seriousness that Blanche had never heard before.*

IMMERSE /ɪˈmɜːs, American ɪˈmɜrs/
immerses, immersing, immersed

im'merse in [often passive]
to spend most of your time concentrating on something or working on something
be immersed in sth *David was deeply immersed in student politics.*

immerse yourself in sth *In these situations, it's not unusual for people to immerse themselves in their work.*

IMPACT /ɪmˈpækt/
impacts, impacting, impacted

imˈpact on (*also* **imˈpact upon** *formal*)
to have a serious or important effect or influence on someone or something, usually a negative one
impact on sb/sth *The failure of the transport system impacts daily on all our lives.*

IMPART /ɪmˈpɑːt, American ɪmˈpɑrt/
imparts, imparting, imparted

imˈpart to *formal*
to give something a particular quality
impart sth to sth *Cooking on charcoal imparts a distinctive smoky flavour to meat.*

IMPINGE /ɪmˈpɪndʒ/
impinges, impingeing, impinged

imˈpinge on (*also* **imˈpinge upon**) *formal*
to have an effect on something, especially in a negative way
impinge on sth *The new law will not impinge on the way companies conduct their business.*

IMPOSE /ɪmˈpəʊz, American ɪmˈpoʊz/
imposes, imposing, imposed

imˈpose on ★★★
1 to force people to accept something or deal with something
impose sth on sb/sth *They have imposed restrictions on all foreign trade.*
♦ *Teachers should not impose their views on their students.* ♦ *The new tax is imposing an unfair burden on employers.*
2 to make extra work for someone by asking them to do something that may not be convenient for them
impose on sb *Are you sure it's all right if I stay? I don't want to impose on you.*

IMPRESS /ɪmˈpres/
impresses, impressing, impressed

imˈpress on ★ (*also* **imˈpress upon** *formal*)
to try to make someone understand how important something is
impress sth on sb *They impressed the need for absolute secrecy on us.*

IMPRINT /ɪmˈprɪnt/
imprints, imprinting, imprinted

imˈprint on (*also* **imˈprint upon**) [often passive]
to make something have a strong and permanent influence on someone or something
be imprinted on your mind/ memory/brain *It was an extraordinary sight that will remain imprinted on my memory.*
imprint sth on/upon sth *Dave had tried to imprint his personality on the office.*

IMPROVE /ɪmˈpruːv, American ɪmˈpruv/
improves, improving, improved

imˈprove on ★★ (*also* **imˈprove upon** *formal*) [often passive]
to make something better than it was before, or to do something better than you did before
be improved on *These methods were adopted and improved on.*
improve on sth *We hope to improve on last year's performance.*

IMPUTE /ɪmˈpjuːt, American ɪmˈpjut/
imputes, imputing, imputed

imˈpute to *formal*
to say wrongly or unfairly that someone or something has a specific quality, especially a bad one, or that someone has done something wrong
impute sth to sb/sth *It is not our role to impute blame or guilt to anyone.* ♦ *Of course the critic can impute whatever meaning he chooses to the image.*

INCLINE /ɪnˈklaɪn/
inclines, inclining, inclined

inˈcline to *formal*
1 to tend to behave in a particular way or have a particular attitude or opinion
incline to do sth *He does incline to be rather nervous.*
incline to *We incline to the view that things are either totally good or totally bad.*
2 incline to or **incline towards** to slope in a particular direction, or to make something do this
incline to *The land inclines gradually downwards to the Simpson Desert.*

In has several different meanings when it is used as part of a phrasal verb. Some of these meanings are literal, but many are figurative.

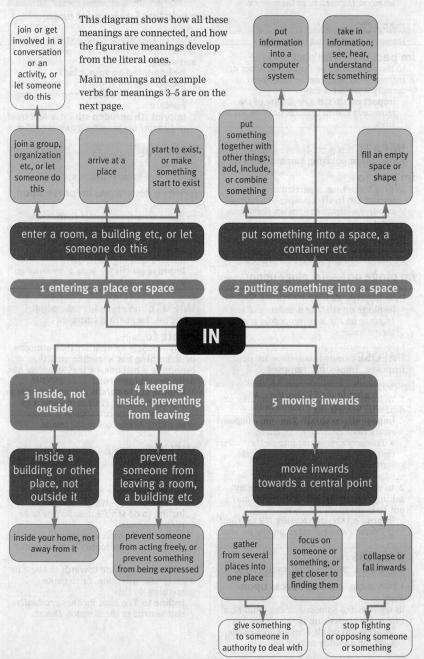

This diagram shows how all these meanings are connected, and how the figurative meanings develop from the literal ones.

Main meanings and example verbs for meanings 3–5 are on the next page.

join or get involved in a conversation or an activity, or let someone do this

put information into a computer system

take in information; see, hear, understand etc something

join a group, organization etc, or let someone do this

arrive at a place

start to exist, or make something start to exist

put something together with other things; add, include, or combine something

fill an empty space or shape

enter a room, a building etc, or let someone do this

put something into a space, a container etc

1 entering a place or space

2 putting something into a space

IN

3 inside, not outside

4 keeping inside, preventing from leaving

5 moving inwards

inside a building or other place, not outside it

prevent someone from leaving a room, a building etc

move inwards towards a central point

inside your home, not away from it

prevent someone from acting freely, or prevent something from being expressed

gather from several places into one place

focus on someone or something, or get closer to finding them

collapse or fall inwards

give something to someone in authority to deal with

stop fighting or opposing someone or something

Main meanings	Example verbs		
1 entering a place or space			
enter a room, a building etc, or let someone do this *Come in out of the cold.* ♦ *I'd invite you in, but the place is a mess.*	barge in breeze in burst in on call in come in	drop in go in invite in let in look in	pile in pop in show in take in walk in on
join a group, organization etc, or let someone do this *They voted to let him in the club.* ♦ *Eric fell in with a rough crowd at school.*	fall in with get in get in with	keep in with settle in	
join or get involved in a conversation or an activity, or let someone do this *'I know what you mean,' Sally chimed in.* ♦ *He didn't want anyone muscling in on his business.*	break in bring in butt in chime in chip in count in cut in deal in dive in	get in on go in for horn in join in jump in let in on listen in muck in muscle in	pitch in plunge in rope in rush in share in sit in on step in wade in weigh in
arrive at a place *The bus finally pulled in at 8 a.m.* ♦ *Sign in with the receptionist when you arrive.*	blow in book in check in clock in	draw in flood in fly in get in	pour in pull in roll in sign in
start to exist, or make something start to exist *The decade ushered in a number of technological advances.* ♦ *The new rules don't kick in until next year.*	bring in come in	kick in phase in	set in usher in
2 putting something into a space			
put something into a space, a container etc *You can plug in the TV over there.* ♦ *See if you can cram any more clothes in the suitcase.*	breathe in cram in hammer in	jam in pack in plug in	pump in put in squeeze in
put something together with other things; add, include, or combine something *Stir in a cup of milk.* ♦ *If you buy the TV now, we'll throw in the stand for free.*	add in blend in build in copy in factor in	fit in fold in include in mix in rub in	stir in throw in tie in with work in write in
put information into a computer system *Who types in all the data after it's compiled?* ♦ *Now punch in your personal identification number.*	key in	punch in	type in
take in information; see, hear, understand etc something *It took a few minutes for the news to sink in.* ♦ *They sat taking in the glorious sunset.*	drink in	sink in	take in
fill an empty space or shape *Fill in the blanks with the correct answers.* ♦ *I draw an outline, and the children colour it in.*	block in brick in	colour in fill in	ink in shade in

In has several different meanings when it is used as part of a phrasal verb. Some of these meanings are literal, but many are figurative.

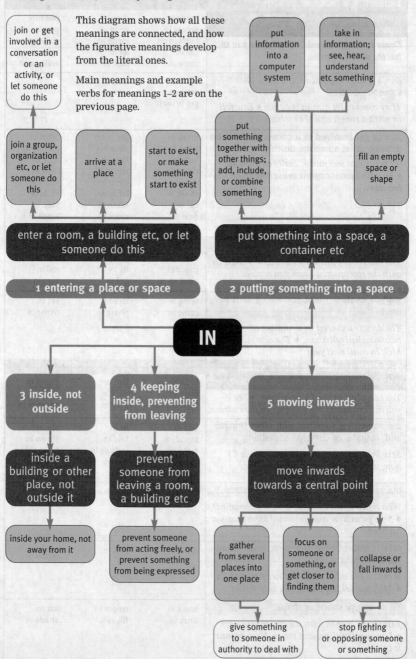

join or get involved in a conversation or an activity, or let someone do this

This diagram shows how all these meanings are connected, and how the figurative meanings develop from the literal ones.

Main meanings and example verbs for meanings 1–2 are on the previous page.

put information into a computer system

take in information; see, hear, understand etc something

join a group, organization etc, or let someone do this

arrive at a place

start to exist, or make something start to exist

put something together with other things; add, include, or combine something

fill an empty space or shape

enter a room, a building etc, or let someone do this

put something into a space, a container etc

1 entering a place or space

2 putting something into a space

IN

3 inside, not outside

4 keeping inside, preventing from leaving

5 moving inwards

inside a building or other place, not outside it

prevent someone from leaving a room, a building etc

move inwards towards a central point

inside your home, not away from it

prevent someone from acting freely, or prevent something from being expressed

gather from several places into one place

focus on someone or something, or get closer to finding them

collapse or fall inwards

give something to someone in authority to deal with

stop fighting or opposing someone or something

Main meanings	Example verbs		
3 inside, not outside			
inside a building or other place, not outside it	keep in	stay in	want in
*It was raining, so the kids had to **stay in** for break.*			
inside your home, not away from it	eat in	move in	stop in
*We usually just **eat in**. ◆ The nanny **lives in**.*	live in	order in	wait in
4 keeping inside, preventing from leaving			
prevent someone from leaving a room, a building etc	block in box in	fence in hem in	lock in snow in
*Someone parked behind me and **blocked me in**. ◆ They **lock** all the prisoners **in** at night.*			
prevent someone from acting freely, or prevent something from being expressed	box in hedge in hem in	hold in keep in	lock in rein in
*Tim knew he couldn't **hold in** his anger much longer. ◆ All the regulations are **hemming in** our business operations.*			
5 moving inwards			
move inwards towards a central point	close in crowd in	reel in	zoom in
*She felt as if the walls were **closing in** on her. ◆ And then he **reeled in** the biggest fish you've ever seen.*			
gather from several places into one place	bring in buy in gather in	get in haul in pull in	rake in roll in take in
*The charity event **brought in** $20,000. ◆ Farmers were in the fields **gathering in** their crops.*			
give something to someone in authority to deal with	cash in give in hand in	send in trade in	turn in write in
***Hand in** your homework before you go. ◆ Where can I **cash in** these chips?*			
focus on someone or something, or get closer to finding them	close in home in	move in on	zero in on
*Police are **closing in** on the gang leaders. ◆ The investigation has **zeroed in on** the issue of bribery.*			
collapse or fall inwards	bash in break in	cave in fall in	kick in smash in
*The roof **caved in** on top of them. ◆ Firefighters had to **kick in** the door.*			
stop fighting or opposing someone or something	cave in chuck in	give in jack in	pack in throw in
*Why don't you just **give in** and stop fighting. ◆ I may just **pack** my job **in** and travel.*			

INDULGE /ɪn'dʌldʒ/
indulges, indulging, indulged

in'dulge in ★★
to allow yourself to do or have something that you enjoy, sometimes something that is bad for you

indulge in sth *I occasionally indulge in a trip to a beauty parlour.* ♦ *The press is indulging in the usual speculation about the President's health.*

INFER /ɪn'fɜː, American ɪn'fɜr/
infers, inferring, inferred

in'fer from *formal*
to form an opinion about something that is based on information you already have

infer sth from sth *I could infer nothing at all from his expression.*
infer from sth that *David inferred from her appearance that she was very wealthy.*

INFEST /ɪn'fest/
infests, infesting, infested

be in'fested with
to be full of insects, animals etc that you do not want

be infested with sth *The whole house is infested with mice.* ♦ *When he was released, he was underweight and infested with lice.*

INFORM /ɪn'fɔːm, American ɪn'fɔrm/
informs, informing, informed

in'form on (*also* in'form against)
to secretly give information about someone to the police or someone in authority

inform on sb *The rule has always been that you don't inform on a friend.*

INFRINGE /ɪn'frɪndʒ/
infringes, infringing, infringed

in'fringe on (*also* in'fringe upon) *formal*
to limit or reduce the rights or freedom of a person, organization, or country

infringe on sth *The presence of so many foreign troops inevitably infringes on the country's sovereignty.*

INFUSE /ɪn'fjuːz, American ɪn'fjuz/
infuses, infusing, infused

in'fuse into
to add a particular quality to something in order to improve it

infuse sth into sth *The plan is to infuse new economic life into troubled cities.*

in'fuse with [often passive]
to give someone or something a particular quality

be infused with sth *Her paintings are infused with vitality.*
infuse sth with sth *The speech has infused the peace process with new hope.*

INHIBIT /ɪn'hɪbɪt/
inhibits, inhibiting, inhibited

in'hibit from *formal*
to make it difficult for someone to do something

inhibit sb from (doing) sth *The new tax rules may inhibit some people from working.*

INITIATE /ɪ'nɪʃieɪt/
initiates, initiating, initiated

i'nitiate into [usually passive]
1 if someone is initiated into a skill, subject, or activity, they are taught about it

be initiated into sth *Nicky was initiated into a world of robbery and violence.*

2 if someone is initiated into an organization or group, they become a member of it, often with a special ceremony

be initiated into sth *At the age of 30 they were initiated into the higher ranks of the Party.*

INJECT /ɪn'dʒekt/
injects, injecting, injected

in'ject into
1 to add something new and positive to something

inject sth into sth *Young designers are injecting new life into the fashion scene.* ♦ *She tried to inject some confidence into her voice.*

2 to provide more money for something

inject sth into sth *They may sell their house in order to inject cash into the business.*

INK /ɪŋk/
inks, inking, inked

,ink 'in
to finish a drawing of something using ink

ink in sth *also* **ink sth in** *I still have to ink in the characters' faces.*

INQUIRE /ɪnˈkwaɪə, *American* ɪnˈkwaɪr/
inquires, inquiring, inquired

in'quire after *British formal*
to ask someone about someone else,
especially about how they are or what
they are doing = ASK AFTER
inquire after sb *Rachel's mother was
inquiring after you.*

in'quire into
to ask questions and examine the answers
in order to find out the truth about
something = INVESTIGATE
inquire into sth *The committee inquired
into complaints made by several
prisoners.*

in'quire of *formal*
to ask someone something
inquire sth of sb *'Are you sure?' he
inquired of Rose anxiously.*

INSINUATE /ɪnˈsɪnjueɪt/
insinuates, insinuating, insinuated

in'sinuate into *formal*
to get yourself into a situation or position
that gives you some advantage, especially
by behaving in an insincere way
insinuate yourself into sth *She had
somehow managed to insinuate herself
into his favour.*

INSIST /ɪnˈsɪst/
insists, insisting, insisted

in'sist on ★★★ (*also* **in'sist upon**)
1 to say that you must have something
insist on sth *Some suppliers insist on
immediate payment.*
insist on doing sth *She insists on
walking me home.*
2 to keep doing something that annoys
people
insist on doing sth *Why do you insist on
leaving your dirty clothes all over the
floor?* ♦ *He will insist on whistling in the
shower!*

INSTALL /ɪnˈstɔːl, *American* ɪnˈstɔl/
installs, installing, installed

in'stall as [usually passive]
if someone is installed in an important job
or position, they are officially put in it
be installed as sth *She was installed as
the first woman chancellor of the
university.*

INSTIL /ɪnˈstɪl/
instils, instilling, instilled

in'stil in
to make someone have a particular feeling
or belief, especially a permanent one
instil sth in sb *How can we instil
confidence in our students?* ♦ *His parents
had instilled in him a lasting love of
music.*

INSTILL the American spelling
of **instil**

INSURE /ɪnˈʃʊə, *American* ɪnˈʃʊr/
insures, insuring, insured

in'sure against
to do something to stop something bad
from happening
insure against sth *There's no foolproof
way to insure against ill health while you
are abroad.*

INTEGRATE /ˈɪntɪgreɪt, *American*
ˈɪntəˌgreɪt/
integrates, integrating, integrated

'integrate into
to become or make someone become a full
member of a community or society
integrate sb into sth *These children can
be helped to integrate into mainstream
education.*
integrate into sth *It can be harder for
older people to integrate fully into a new
community.*

INTEREST /ˈɪntrəst/
interests, interesting, interested

'interest in
to make someone want to know about or
take part in something
interest sb in sth *We were hoping to
interest the buyer in our new line of
merchandise.*
PHRASE can/could I interest you in sth
used as a polite way of persuading
someone to do, try, or buy something:
*Can I interest you in a photograph of
your house?*

INTERFERE /ˌɪntəˈfɪə, *American*
ˌɪntərˈfɪr/
interferes, interfering, interfered

inter'fere with ★★★
1 to prevent something from happening
or developing in the correct way
interfere with sth *Mum says I can get a*

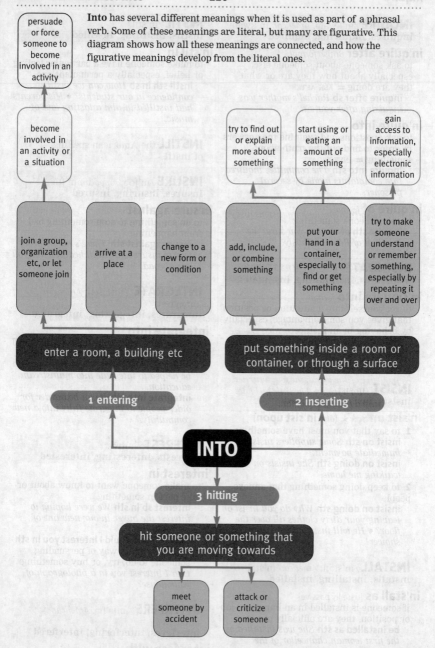

Into has several different meanings when it is used as part of a phrasal verb. Some of these meanings are literal, but many are figurative. This diagram shows how all these meanings are connected, and how the figurative meanings develop from the literal ones.

persuade or force someone to become involved in an activity

become involved in an activity or a situation

try to find out or explain more about something

start using or eating an amount of something

gain access to information, especially electronic information

join a group, organization etc, or let someone join

arrive at a place

change to a new form or condition

add, include, or combine something

put your hand in a container, especially to find or get something

try to make someone understand or remember something, especially by repeating it over and over

enter a room, a building etc

put something inside a room or container, or through a surface

1 entering

2 inserting

INTO

3 hitting

hit someone or something that you are moving towards

meet someone by accident

attack or criticize someone

Main meanings and example verbs for meanings 2 and 3 are on the next page.

Main meanings	Example verbs		
1 entering			
enter a room, a building etc *The girls all **crowded into** the kitchen.* ♦ *He's always **barging into** my office without knocking.*	barge into break into breeze into	burst into crowd into pile into	pop into see into show into
join a group, organization etc, or let someone join *Lara is hoping to **get into** medical school.* ♦ *Their son **married into** one of the wealthiest families in the county.*	get into let into	marry into	be received into
become involved in an activity or a situation *It's not easy to **break into** the acting business.* ♦ *Don't **rush into** any major decisions just yet.*	break into dive into enter into fall into fling into	get into launch into pitch into plunge into rush into	settle into tear into throw into wade into walk into
persuade or force someone to become involved in an activity *I'm sorry. I didn't mean to **drag you into** all of this.* ♦ *Lucy's going to try to **talk** Don **into** coming.*	bludgeon into bounce into charm into coax into drag into	dragoon into force into goad into press into push into	railroad into scare into shame into stampede into talk into
arrive at a place *The train was just **pulling into** the station when we arrived.* ♦ *We can't **check into** the hotel until 3 o'clock.*	check into draw into flood into	fly into get into pack into	pour into pull into roll into
change to a new form or condition *With a wave of the wand, the witch **turned** the prince **into** a frog.* ♦ *The little girl had **grown into** a beautiful woman.*	break into change into go into grow into	lapse into make into melt into morph into	sink into slip into translate into turn into

Into has several different meanings when it is used as part of a phrasal verb. Some of these meanings are literal, but many are figurative. This diagram shows how all these meanings are connected, and how the figurative meanings develop from the literal ones.

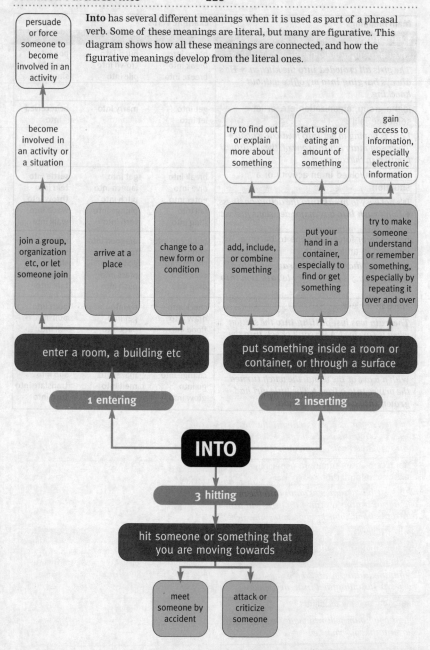

Main meanings and example verbs for meaning 1 are on the previous page.

Main meanings	Example verbs		
2 inserting			
put something inside a room or a container, or through a surface	bite into	plug into	ram into
	build into	pour into	slot into
*Alice **stuffed** her clothes **into** a suitcase and left.* ♦ *The collar is **biting into** the dog's neck.*	cram into	pump into	stuff into
	dig into	put into	thrust into
add, include, or combine something	blend into	fold into	plough into
	bring into	melt into	pump into
*They have **built** a number of safeguards **into** the system.* ♦ *All employees **pay into** a pension scheme.*	build into	merge into	put into
	dissolve into	mix into	stir into
	factor into	pay into	work into
	fit into	phase into	write into
put your hand in a container, especially to find or get something	delve into	dig into	dip into
*She **dug into** her purse, trying to find her lipstick.* ♦ ***Delving into** his pocket, he produced a large gold coin.*			
try to find out or explain more about something	delve into	go into	look into
	dig into	inquire into	nose into
*The committee will **look into** the allegations.* ♦ *I won't **go into** details right now.*			
start using or eating an amount of something	bite into	dig into	eat into
	break into	dip into	tuck into
*We had to **dip into** our savings to pay for the holiday.* ♦ *All these meetings are really **eating into** my time.*			
try to make someone understand or remember something, especially by repeating it over and over	din into	drum into	hammer into
	drill into		
*The government is trying to **drum** the 'no drugs' message **into** kids' heads.* ♦ *They **drill** it **into** you at school: no copying.*			
gain access to information, especially electronic information	hack into	key into	tap into
	hook into	log into	
*This system is designed to **hook into** the most popular operating system.* ♦ *PC users can **tap into** a wealth of information via the internet.*			
3 hitting			
hit someone or something that you are moving towards	bang into	cannon into	run into
	blunder into	crash into	smash into
*He **bumped into** the table on his way out.* ♦ *The car just **ploughed into** the crowd.*	bump into	plough into	walk into
meet someone by accident	bump into	run into	
*Guess who I **bumped into** today?* ♦ *I **ran into** Marge at the supermarket.*			
attack or criticize someone	lam into	light into	rip into
	lay into	pitch into	tear into
*Once we were alone, she **laid into** me.* ♦ *He spun round and **tore into** the other kid.*			

job if it doesn't interfere with my homework. ♦ *The defective gene interferes with normal body processes.*

2 [often passive] to do something to change something, especially to damage or spoil it, when you have no right to do this
= TAMPER WITH
    be interfered with *Problems arise when the system is interfered with.*
    interfere with sth *I saw him interfering with the smoke alarm.*

3 to persuade a witness to give false information in a court of law
    interfere with sb *Hebden's solicitor suggested she had interfered with the witness.*

4 to attack a child by touching them sexually = ABUSE
    interfere with sb *He had interfered with some of the boys in his care.*

INTERSPERSE /ˌɪntəˈspɜːs, *American* ˌɪntərˈspɜrs/
intersperses, interspersing, interspersed

be inter'spersed with
to be put in various places in or among something else
    be interspersed with sth *The text can be interspersed with full-page illustrations.*

INUNDATE /ˈɪnʌndeɪt, *American* ˈmənˌdeɪt/
inundates, inundating, inundated

be 'inundated with ★
to be given too much of something for you to deal with
    be inundated with sth *After the broadcast, the TV station was inundated with complaints.* ♦ *I've been inundated with emails recently.*

INURE /ɪˈnjʊr/
inures, inuring, inured

be i'nured to
to be so familiar with an unpleasant experience that you no longer become upset by it
    be inured to sth *We have become inured to the stinging insects here.*

INVALID /ˈɪnvəlɪd/
invalids, invaliding, invalided

be ,invalided 'out
to be forced to leave the armed forces because you are ill or injured
    be invalided out *It was because of his deafness that he was being invalided out.*

♦ **+of** *He was invalided out of the army and couldn't find work.*

INVEIGH /ɪnˈveɪ/
inveighs, inveighing, inveighed

in'veigh against *very formal*
to criticize someone or something very strongly
    inveigh against sth/sb *He inveighed passionately against the government's inaction.*

INVEIGLE /ɪnˈveɪg(ə)l, ɪnˈviːg(ə)l, *American* ɪnˈvɪg(ə)l/
inveigles, inveigling, inveigled

in'veigle into *formal*
to persuade someone to do something that they do not want to do by using clever or dishonest methods
    inveigle sb into (doing) sth *He had inveigled her into this situation.* ♦ *That way, we might inveigle him into signing a new agreement.*

INVEST /ɪnˈvest/
invests, investing, invested

in'vest in ★★★
1 to buy something, especially something that you need and will use a lot
    invest in sth *I think it's time I invested in a new computer.*

2 to spend a lot of something such as time or effort for a particular purpose
    invest sth in sth *We invest the major part of our lives in parenthood.*
    invest sth in doing sth *You have to be willing to invest a lot of time in taking care of elderly parents.*

3 to spend money on something in order to improve it or make it more successful
    invest in sth *This government believes in investing in education.* ♦ *The successful firms earn their success by investing in training.*
    invest sth in sth *The university has invested significant sums in the development of its computer systems.*

4 to put money into a company, for example by buying shares, because you expect it to be successful
    invest in sth *People seem more willing to invest in British companies.* ♦ *She refused to invest in businesses that gave political donations.*

in'vest with *formal*
1 to give something or someone a particular quality

invest sth/sb with sth *Nature has invested these animals with a capacity for not showing fear.*

2 [usually passive] to give a person or organization power, influence, or authority

be invested with sth *The Secret Service is invested with the authority to guard the president and his family.*

INVITE /ɪn'vaɪt/
invites, inviting, invited

in,vite a'long
to ask someone to go somewhere with you or do something with you = ASK ALONG

invite along sb *also* invite sb along *I don't mind you coming, but I didn't expect you to invite along half your family.*

in,vite a'round *same as* invite over

in,vite 'back

1 to invite someone to your house after you have been to their house = ASK BACK

invite sb back *We had them over for dinner a couple of times, but they never invited us back.*

2 to ask someone to come to your house after you have been somewhere with them = ASK BACK

invite sb back *I'd invite you back, but the kids will be asleep.*

in,vite 'in ★
to ask someone to come into your house, for example after you have been out with them = ASK IN

invite sb in *Did she invite you in for coffee?*

in,vite 'out ★ [often passive]
to invite someone to go somewhere such as a restaurant or cinema with you, often because you want to start a romantic or sexual relationship with them = ASK OUT

be invited out *She's been invited out by some man from the club.* ♦ +to *I was invited out to Sunday lunch by one of the teachers.*

invite sb out *He's invited me out next week.* ♦ +to *I'm thinking of inviting him out to the theatre.*

in,vite 'over (*also* in,vite a'round or in,vite 'round *British*)
to invite someone to your house, for example for a meal = ASK OVER

invite sb over *They had invited some friends over to watch the match.*

in,vite 'round *British same as* invite over

INVOLVE /ɪn'vɒlv, *American* ɪn'vɑlv/
involves, involving, involved

in'volve in ★★★

1 to put someone into a situation in which they must do something

involve sb in sth *This won't involve you in any extra work.*

involve sb in doing sth *Taking part in the campaign might involve you in getting arrested.*

2 to take part in something that other people are doing

involve yourself in sth *It's best not to involve yourself in other people's private affairs.*

IRON /'aɪən, *American* 'aɪrn/
irons, ironing, ironed

,iron 'out ★
to deal successfully with a disagreement or problem, especially by removing the last remaining difficulties = SORT OUT

iron out sth *They're meeting in Berlin to iron out the final details of the contract.*

iron sth out *The intention is to iron any minor hitches out in the early stages.*

♦ *There have been misunderstandings, and I want to iron them out now.*

ISSUE /'ɪʃuː, *American* 'ɪʃu, 'ɪsjuː/
issues, issuing, issued

,issue 'forth *formal*
if something issues forth from somewhere, it comes out of there

issue forth *Cheap electricity was soon issuing forth from nuclear reactors.*

'issue from *formal*
if something such as a sound or smell issues from a place, it comes out from there

issue from sth *Acrid black smoke issued from the burning factory.*

ITCH /ɪtʃ/
itches, itching, itched

be 'itching for
to want very much to do something immediately

be itching for sth *It was obvious she was itching for a fight.* ♦ *She's itching for a chance to show how good she is.*

J j

JAB /dʒæb/
jabs, jabbing, jabbed

'jab at
to push something with a sudden straight movement, usually with your finger, your elbow, or a narrow object
jab at sth *She kept jabbing at the letter as she spoke.*

JABBER /'dʒæbə, American 'dʒæbər/
jabbers, jabbering, jabbered

,jabber a'way
to talk very quickly, in an excited or nervous way
jabber away *Bill was jabbering away about his latest car, and I couldn't get away.*

JACK /dʒæk/
jacks, jacking, jacked

,jack a'round *American informal*
1 to waste time doing stupid things
jack around *Tell them to stop jacking around.*
2 to treat someone badly by not being direct or honest with them
jack sb around *Clinton has jacked this country around for too long.*

,jack 'in *British informal*
to stop doing something, especially a job, course of study etc = *formal* STOP
jack in sth *also* **jack sth in** *Did you know that Jenna's jacked in her college course?*

,jack 'off *American impolite*
if a man jacks off, he rubs his sexual organ in order to get sexual pleasure = *formal* MASTURBATE

,jack 'up
1 to increase the price, rate, or number of something by a large amount
= INCREASE, HIKE UP ≠ LOWER, SLASH
jack up sth *also* **jack sth up** *This would give them an excuse to jack up the price.*
♦ *He'll jack the rent up at the beginning of the year.*
2 to lift and support a heavy object, especially a car, using a piece of equipment called a jack that fits under the object ≠ LOWER

jack up sth *also* **jack sth up** *We can jack up the car on my drive.* ♦ *He managed to jack the van up at the side of the road.*
3 *informal* to put an illegal drug into your body using a needle = SHOOT UP
jack up *I caught her jacking up in the back of the car.*
PHRASE **be jacked up** *mainly American informal* to be very excited or nervous: *Your dad'll be all jacked up by now.*

JAM /dʒæm/
jams, jamming, jammed

'jam into (*also* 'jam in) [often passive]
to put too many people or things into a small space
be jammed into sth *Four men were jammed into the back of the car.*
jam in sth *also* **jam sth in** *The restaurant tries to jam in as many tables as possible.*
♦ *We might be able to jam another few people in.*

,jam 'on
PHRASE **jam on the brakes** or **jam the brakes on** to put your foot very suddenly and hard on the brake of a vehicle because you want to stop quickly: *I had to jam on the brakes to avoid hitting her.*

,jam 'up
if a machine, lock, window etc jams up, or if something jams it up, it stops moving or working normally
jam up *The photocopier has jammed up again.*
jam up sth *also* **jam sth up** *A crumpled sheet had jammed up the photocopier.*
♦ *The wire had snapped and jammed the lock up.*

JAR /dʒɑː, American dʒɑr/
jars, jarring, jarred

'jar on
if something unpleasant jars on you, it makes you feel uncomfortable or slightly annoyed
jar on sb/sth *Some of the expressions he used jarred on me.* ♦ *That noise really jars on the nerves.*

'jar with
to be unpleasant or not suitable in a particular place or situation
jar with sb/sth *His speech jarred with the informality of the occasion.*

JAZZ /dʒæz/
jazzes, jazzing, jazzed

jazz 'up *informal*
to make something more lively, exciting,
or interesting = LIVEN UP
jazz sth up *also* **jazz up sth** *It's a plain
old dress, but I'll find some way of
jazzing it up a bit.* ♦ *We're looking for
something to jazz up this room.*

■ **jazzed-'up** adj **1** jazzed-up music has
been changed to sound more like
popular music, especially jazz: *She
became famous for her unique brand of
jazzed-up pop.* **2** made more interesting
or lively: *If you're tired of chicken try
this jazzed-up recipe for fajitas.*

JERK /dʒɜːk, *American* dʒɜːrk/
jerks, jerking, jerked

jerk a'round *mainly American informal*
1 [usually passive] if someone jerks you
around, they treat you in an unfair or
dishonest way = MESS AROUND
be jerked around *We're not going to be
jerked around any more.*
2 to behave in a stupid way = MESS AROUND
jerk around *They spend most of their
time just jerking around.*

jerk 'off *mainly American impolite*
if a man jerks off, he rubs his sexual organ
in order to get sexual pleasure = JACK OFF;
formal MASTURBATE

JET /dʒet/
jets, jetting, jetted

jet 'off
to fly somewhere in a plane
jet off *They will be jetting off to Spain
this weekend.*

JIB /dʒɪb/
jibs, jibbing, jibbed

jib at
to be unwilling to do or accept something
jib at sth *Small struggling farms
naturally jib at paying large veterinary
bills.*

JOCKEY /'dʒɒki, *American* 'dʒɑːki/
jockeys, jockeying, jockeyed

jockey for
to try to gain an advantage over your
opponents, or to try to get something that
other people want
PHRASE **jockey for position** to try to get
into the best situation possible: *Several*
*candidates are already jockeying for
position.*

JOG /dʒɒg, *American* dʒɑːg/
jogs, jogging, jogged

jog a'long
to continue without changing, in a way
that is not interesting or exciting
jog along *Life was jogging along pretty
much as usual.*

JOIN /dʒɔɪn/
joins, joining, joined

join 'in ★★★
to do an activity with people who are
already doing it = PARTICIPATE, TAKE PART
join in *She laughed and Tom joined in.*
♦ **+with** *Everybody join in with the
chorus!*
join in sth *Pat didn't feel like joining in
the celebrations.*

join in

join 'up ★★
1 to become a member of the armed forces
= ENLIST ≠ QUIT
join up *He joined up right after leaving
school.*
2 to connect two things
join up sth *You need to join up these two
lines.*
join sth up *Join the two loose ends up.*
♦ *Take the two red cables and join them
up.*
3 to meet someone in order to work with
them or go and do something with them
= MEET UP
join up *I'm going to Germany first, but
we're planning to join up in Norway.*
♦ **+with** *They're about to join up with
the European research team.*

■ **'joined-up** adj PHRASE **joined-up
writing** joined-up writing is writing in
which the letters are joined to each

other: *He's practising his joined-up writing.*

joined-up thinking/government/policy etc a way of doing something in which all the separate parts work together in a sensible and effective way: *It's the perfect example of joined-up government.*

'join with ★ *formal*

to say or do something with other people
join with sb in doing sth *I'm sure everyone joins with me in wishing him a speedy recovery.*

JOLLY /'dʒɒli, *American* 'dʒɑli/
jollies, jollying, jollied

,jolly a'long *British informal*

to continue encouraging and persuading someone to do something
jolly sb along *It was my job to jolly people along.*

,jolly 'up *British informal*

to make an event or activity more lively and enjoyable
jolly sth up *also* **jolly up sth** *We're going to include a few games to jolly up the proceedings.* ♦ *We need something to jolly the party up a bit.*

JOSTLE /'dʒɒs(ə)l, *American* 'dʒɑs(ə)l/
jostles, jostling, jostled

'jostle for

to compete with someone for something
jostle for sth *In the run-up to the election the candidates were out jostling for votes in every state.* ♦ *Two companies in particular are jostling for position at the top of the table.*

JOT /dʒɒt, *American* dʒɑt/
jots, jotting, jotted

,jot 'down ★

to write something down in a quick informal way = WRITE DOWN
jot down sth *I'll jot down a few notes while you're talking, if that's OK.*
jot sth down *Just let me jot that number down.* ♦ *She told me the address and I jotted it down.*

JUICE /dʒuːs, *American* dʒus/
juices, juicing, juiced

,juice 'up [often passive] *informal*

to improve something by making it more interesting, attractive, or powerful = SEX UP
be juiced up *Certain scenes were juiced up for commercial purposes.*

juice up sth *also* **juice sth up** *An experienced screenwriter was asked to juice up the dialogue.* ♦ *It's essentially the same report, but someone has juiced the conclusions up.*

JUMBLE /'dʒʌmb(ə)l/
jumbles, jumbling, jumbled

,jumble 'up (*also* ,jumble to'gether)
[often passive]

to mix things in a confusing or untidy way
be/get jumbled up *These ideas are all jumbled up in his head.*
jumble sth up *also* **jumble up sth** *Be careful you don't jumble all my papers up.*

JUMP /dʒʌmp/
jumps, jumping, jumped

'jump at ★

to take an opportunity that is offered to you in a very enthusiastic way
jump at sth *I jumped at the chance to go with him.*

Nouns often used as objects with **jump at**

■ **chance, idea, offer, opportunity**

,jump 'in

1 to become involved in a situation very quickly = DIVE IN
jump in *Onlookers jumped in to break up the fight.*
2 to interrupt someone while they are talking = INTERRUPT
jump in *I'd just started talking when Kim jumped in.* ♦ **+with** *She always has to jump in with a few unhelpful comments.*

PHRASES **jump in at the deep end** to become involved in a very difficult situation: *I felt as if I'd really jumped in at the deep end.*
jump in with both feet to become involved in something without thinking carefully: *Don't go jumping in with both feet.*

'jump into

to become involved in a situation very quickly
jump into sth *He jumped headlong into organizing the event.*
PHRASE **jump into bed with sb** to have sex with someone that you have only met recently: *She wasn't the type to jump into bed with a total stranger.*

,jump 'off

PHRASE **jump off the page** if words or pictures jump off the page, they are the first thing you notice: *The words just jumped off the page at me.*

'jump on

1 *informal* to criticize someone severely
jump on sb *He jumps on me every time I get something wrong.*

2 [often passive] to attack someone physically
be jumped on *He was jumped on by a gang of teenagers.*
jump on sb *The door closed and someone jumped on him.*

jump 'out at

if something jumps out at you, you notice it immediately
jump out at sb *Of all the photos, one in particular jumps out at you.*

jump 'up

to stand up very quickly = LEAP UP
jump up *The phone rang and she jumped up to answer it.*

■ **'jumped-up** adj *British informal showing disapproval* thinking that you are more important than you are: *He wasn't going to take orders from a jumped-up schoolboy.*

JUT /dʒʌt/
juts, jutting, jutted

jut 'out

1 to be further forward than other things or than is normal = PROTRUDE
jut out *Her hip bones jutted out.*

2 to put your chin or lip further forward than normal because you are determined or angry
jut sth out *She jutted her lower lip out defiantly.*

Kk

KEEL /kiːl, *American* kil/
keels, keeling, keeled

keel 'over

1 *informal* if someone keels over, they fall, usually because they suddenly feel ill
= COLLAPSE
keel over *He was playing tennis one minute, and then he just keeled over.*

2 *informal* to suddenly stop working correctly = CRASH
keel over *My email system would keel over if I tried to send that much data.*

3 *informal* to become very ill, or to die
keel over *I'm surprised she hasn't keeled over by now, with all the strain she's under.*

4 if a ship keels over, it falls sideways
= CAPSIZE
keel over *Unless you balance her on the windward side, she'll keel over.*

KEEP /kiːp, *American* kip/
keeps, keeping, kept /kept/

keep 'at

to continue to work hard at something
= PERSEVERE WITH ≠ GIVE UP
keep at sth *You're doing fine – keep at it!*

keep a'way ★★

to avoid someone or something, or to make someone else do this
keep away *I've told him to keep away, but he won't listen.* ♦ **+from** *You should keep away from fried foods.*
keep sb/sth away *These candles keep the flies away.* ♦ *All this bad publicity is keeping customers away.* ♦ **+from** *You can't keep the kids away from the computer.*

■ **'keep-a,way** noun [U] *American* a children's game in which two people throw a ball to each other and a third person stands between them and tries to catch it: *They play the old games, like keep-away.* = *British* PIGGY-IN-THE-MIDDLE

keep 'back ★★

1	not say or show sth
2	not give the full amount of money
3	not move closer
4	prevent progress
5	keep part of sth for later
6	prevent yourself from laughing/crying

1 to not tell someone something, or to not show them how you feel = *formal* WITHHOLD
keep sth back *He said he was fine, but I knew he was keeping something back.* ♦ *What's she keeping back, I wonder?*

2 to keep part of an amount of money that belongs to someone or is owed to them
= RETAIN
keep back sth *He kept back £50 for himself.*
keep sth back *I normally keep a few pounds back for expenses.*

3 to not move towards someone or something, or to stop someone from doing this = HOLD BACK
keep back sb/sth *A barrier had been erected to keep back the crowds.*
keep sb/sth back *The stewards are*

instructed to keep people well back.
keep back *Police were warning people to keep back.*

4 to prevent someone from making progress = HOLD BACK, HINDER
keep sb back *It's only her lack of confidence that's keeping her back.*
keep back sb *It doesn't seem fair to keep back these brighter kids.*

5 to keep part of something so that you can use it later = RESERVE ≠ USE UP
keep back sth *Keep back some strawberries for decoration.*
keep sth back *Keep a few sticks back to light the fire with.*

6 if you keep back laughter or tears, you stop yourself laughing or crying = HOLD BACK
keep back sth *She struggled to keep back her tears.*
keep sth back *He couldn't keep a little chuckle back.*

keep 'down ★★

1	prevent sth from increasing
2	stop sb from achieving sth
3	keep food in your stomach
4	make less noise
5	control people

1 to control something and prevent it from increasing in size or number
keep sth down *We have to try and keep costs down.* ♦ *You can't eliminate waste altogether, but try to **keep** it **down to a minimum**.*
keep down sth *The cats help to keep down the rats.*

2 [often passive] to stop someone from achieving what they are capable of achieving = HOLD BACK
be kept down *She was being stifled at home and kept down at school.*
keep sb down *Even if you're intelligent, they still try to keep you down.*
keep down sb *The system is keeping down half the children in the school.*

3 to succeed in keeping food in your stomach although you feel as if you want to vomit
keep sth down *Let's see if she keeps that toast down.* ♦ *I'd eat something if I thought I could keep it down.*

4 to stop a noise that you are making from becoming too loud
keep sth down *I've asked them to keep their voices down.* ♦ *I'd be grateful if you'd **keep the noise down** a bit.* ♦ *Keep it down – I'm trying to sleep!*

5 [often passive] to control people in such a strict or cruel way that they have very little freedom or very few rights

be kept down *These immigrants were kept down for decades.*
keep sb down *The old way of ruling was to keep the people down.* ♦ *They were afraid of Christians and they kept them down.*

'keep from

1 to prevent someone from doing something, or to prevent something from happening = PREVENT FROM
keep sb/sth from (doing) sth *These worries kept her from sleeping properly.* ♦ *The troops withheld fire to keep the situation from escalating.* ♦ *Don't let me keep you from your work.*

2 to not tell someone something
keep sth from sb *I kept the news from him for a while.*

keep 'in

1 [often passive] *British* to make someone stay in a place such as a school or a hospital = *formal* DETAIN
be kept in *They were kept in after school as a punishment.*
keep sb in *If he takes her to hospital they might keep her in.*

2 to be enough to pay for something for someone
keep sb in sth *Her wage isn't enough to keep her family in even the basics.*

keep 'in with

to stay friendly with someone, especially someone who can help you
keep in with sb *It usually makes sense to keep in with your bosses!*

keep 'off ★★

1 to not touch something, or to prevent something from touching something else
keep sth off sth *Use a cloth to keep the flies off the food.*
keep sth off *Keep your hands off (=don't touch that), it's mine.*
keep off sth *Please keep off that sofa, your boots are dirty!*

2 [often passive] to not go onto a particular area of land
be kept off sth *Dogs must be kept off the beach.*
keep off sth *There were signs all over the park reminding us to **keep off the grass**.*

3 to avoid a particular thing, for example a type of food or a subject of conversation = AVOID
keep off sth *I'm trying to keep off fatty foods.*
keep sb off sth *Keep him off politics, for goodness sake.*

4 *British* if rain, sleet, or snow keeps off it

does not fall, although you expected it to
= HOLD OFF
> **keep off** *It's not sunny but at least the rain has kept off.*

,keep 'on ★★★

1 to continue doing something, especially in an annoying way = *formal* PERSIST IN
≠ GIVE UP
> **keep on doing sth** *My sister kept on asking me question after question.* ♦ *It won't do any good to keep on hassling him.*

2 [often passive] to continue to employ someone = *formal* RETAIN
> **be kept on** *Only highly skilled people were kept on after the merger.*
> **keep sb on** *If you work hard, they'll keep you on.* ♦ *She won't keep timewasters on.*
> **keep on sb** *I can't afford to keep on all the team.*

3 *informal* to continue talking about something in a way that annoys people
= HARP ON
> **keep on** *You'd think he was affected personally by it, the way he's keeping on.* ♦ **+about** *I don't know why you keep on about this.* ♦ **+at** *Lizzie's always keeping on at me to go for promotion.*

,keep 'out ★★

1 [often passive] to prevent someone or something from entering a place
= EXCLUDE ≠ ADMIT
> **be kept out** *Cars should be kept out of the city centre.*
> **keep sb/sth out** *Police officers were keeping people out.* ♦ *If customers arrive early, we keep them out until ten o'clock sharp.*
> **keep out sb/sth** *Make sure the trees don't keep out sunlight.* ♦ *The prices are high to keep out people the members would regard as undesirable.*

2 [usually in imperative] used on signs to tell people not to go into a place
> **keep out** *The sign said: Private: Keep Out.*

,keep 'out of

to not become involved with something
> **keep out of sth** *You keep out of this. It's none of your business.* ♦ *I warned her to keep out of it, but she wouldn't listen.*

'keep to ★★★

1 [often passive] to prevent an amount or number from passing a limit = LIMIT TO
> **be kept to sth** *Tasks should be kept to a manageable number.*
> **keep sth to sth** *You should keep your intake of alcohol to a minimum.*

2 to follow an agreement or a rule, by

doing what you should do or what you said you would do = OBEY
> **keep to sth** *Try to keep to a regular timetable of waking and sleeping.*
> ♦ *Always keep to the speed limit.*

Nouns often used as objects with **keep to 2**
■ **agreement, plan, rules, schedule, timetable**

3 to stay on a path, road etc when you are going somewhere = STICK TO
> **keep to sth** *You must keep to the path.*
> ♦ *They kept to the side of the field.*

4 to write or talk about the subject you have started to talk about, and not any other = STICK TO
> **keep to sth** *I wish he'd just keep to the point.*

'keep under [often passive]

to continuously watch or control someone or something
> **be kept under sth** *The prisoners are kept under constant surveillance.*
> **keep sb/sth under sth** *Keep that dog under control!*

,keep 'up ★★★

1	continue to do sth
2	be as fast as sb/sth
3	progress/learn as fast as sb/sth
4	continue to learn
5	keep pretending
6	continue to understand
7	prevent sb from going to bed
+	PHRASE
+	**upkeep** noun

1 to continue to do something = MAINTAIN
> **keep sth up** *We're on a winning streak – hopefully we can keep it up.*
> **keep up sth** *Keep up the good work* (=used to tell someone that they are doing something well). ♦ *The trade unions continued to keep up pressure for higher wages.*

2 to move at the same speed as someone or something = STAY BESIDE
> **keep up** *Try to keep up!* ♦ **+with** *He had to hurry to keep up with her.*

3 to make progress or learn at the same speed as other people or things
> **keep up** *By studying hard she managed to keep up.* ♦ **+with** *We always try to keep up with our competitors.*

4 to continue to learn about something or find out about something, so that you know the latest things that are happening
= STAY ABREAST ≠ LOSE TOUCH
> **keep up** *I keep up by reading trade journals and chatting to colleagues in the business.* ♦ **+with** *We try to keep up with what's happening.*

5 to continue to pretend that something is true

keep sth up *She tried to appear cheerful but couldn't keep it up.*

6 to continue to understand what people are saying

keep up *If a few words escape you, it can be impossible to keep up.* ♦ *I told you she's my sister, not my girlfriend. Keep up!* ♦ **+with** *I found myself unable to keep up with the conversation.*

7 to prevent someone from going to bed

keep sb up *It's late, I'd better not keep you up any longer.*

PHRASE keep up appearances to pretend that everything is good, for example with your marriage or your financial situation, even though you are having problems: *We were finding it increasingly hard to keep up appearances.*

■ **upkeep** /ˈʌpkiːp/ **noun** [singular/U] the process or cost of keeping a building or piece of land in good condition: *These costs relate to the upkeep of the castle.*

KEY /kiː, *American* ki/
keys, keying, keyed

key 'in
to put information into a computer or other electronic machine using the letters or numbers on a keyboard or control panel
= ENTER, TYPE IN
key in sth *also* **key sth in** *Now key in your password.* ♦ *Key your name in and press return.*

key 'into

1 to put information into a computer or other electronic machine using the letters or numbers on a keyboard or control panel

key sth into sth *First, key the code into the computer.*

2 [always passive] if someone is keyed into something, they understand it or like it

be/get keyed into sth *I started to get keyed into this album just after the birth of my first child.*

'key to [usually passive] *mainly American*
to change something so that it is suitable for a particular purpose

be keyed to sth *He said the peace process should not be keyed to disarmament.*

KICK /kɪk/
kicks, kicking, kicked

kick a'bout *British informal same as* **kick around**

'kick against (*also* **kick 'out against**)
to react against someone or something that you do not like but cannot change

kick against sb/sth *Katherine has an instinct for kicking against the establishment.*

kick a'round ★ (*also* **kick a'bout** *British*)
informal

1	discuss sth
2	treat sb badly
3	have no plans/intentions
4	have sth, but not know where
5	not take action about sth
6	kick/hit ball

1 to discuss an idea or suggestion with other people in an informal way

kick sth around *I just want to kick a few ideas around in today's meeting.*

kick around sth *I know the panel kicked around a lot of possible names before coming up with Marjorie Ferraro.*

2 [often passive] to treat someone in an unkind and unfair way

be kicked around *He was fed up with being kicked around by his managers.*

kick sb around *You can't just kick people around – you need to treat them with some respect.*

3 if people are kicking around, or kicking around a place, they are in that place without any definite plans

kick around sth *They'd been kicking around the park most of the day.*

kick around *I just kicked around in the town until her interview was finished.*

4 [always progressive] if something is kicking around, you have it but you are not sure exactly where it is **= BE KNOCKING AROUND**

be kicking around *I'm sure there are some paper clips kicking around somewhere.*

5 [always progressive] if ideas or suggestions are kicking around, they exist but no one is doing much about them

be kicking around *That idea has been kicking around for a while.*

6 to kick or hit a ball in a casual way, without showing much enthusiasm or seriousness

kick sth around *Some teenage boys were kicking a ball around in the back yard.*

,kick 'back *American informal*

1 to relax = CHILL OUT, RELAX

kick back *It was time to kick back and forget the worries of the day.*

2 to give someone some of the money that they have helped you to earn, usually dishonestly or illegally

kick back sth *also* **kick sth back** *They had to kick back as much as 10% of the money from the deal to the senator.*

■ **kickback** /'kɪkbæk/ **noun** [C/U] money paid illegally to another person in exchange for something they have done for you: *The governor denied accepting any kickbacks from the insurance industry.*

,kick 'in

1 to break a door or window open by kicking it

kick sth in *also* **kick in sth** *Police had to kick in the front door to gain access to the house.*

2 *informal* to start to have an effect = TAKE EFFECT

kick in *The medicine took some time to kick in.* ♦ *The new rules kicked in last year.*

3 *American* to give something, especially money, to something that other people are also giving something to = *formal* CONTRIBUTE

kick in sth *Sweden has kicked in about $10 million for the aid package.*

,kick 'off ★★

1 *informal* to begin, or to begin something = START, BEGIN ≠ END

kick off *The show kicks off this week in San Francisco.* ♦ **+with** *I'd like to kick off with a quick look at last month's sales figures.*

kick off sth *We kick off the tour with an hour at the Arc de Triomphe.*

kick sth off *I thought we'd kick the meeting off by saying a bit about our various research projects.*

2 when a football match kicks off, a player starts it by kicking the ball = START, BEGIN ≠ END

kick off *The game kicks off at 7.30.*

3 [often passive] *informal* to force someone to leave a place or activity = THROW OFF

be kicked off sth *He was kicked off the course for failing to hand in any work.*

kick sb off sth *They would kick you off the committee if they found out.*

4 to make your shoes come off by shaking your feet

kick off sth *Phyllis kicked off her sandals.*

kick sth off *He kicked his shoes off and*

put his feet up on the coffee table.

■ **kickoff** /'kɪkɒf/ **noun** **1** [C] the beginning of a game of football, when one player kicks the ball down the field: *At the kickoff, he's standing on the wing.* **2** [singular] the beginning of an event: *We arrived at the conference centre about an hour before the kickoff.* **3** [C] the starting time of a football match: *It's a 3 p.m. kickoff tomorrow.*

,kick 'out ★★ [often passive] *informal*

1 to force someone to leave a place or organization = THROW OUT

be kicked out *Any pupil who didn't obey the rules would be kicked out.* ♦ **+of sth** *My dad was kicked out of the club for hitting someone.*

kick sb out *He told me his wife had kicked him out.* ♦ **+of sth** *The army kicked the UN observers out of the country.*

2 to try to hit or attack someone suddenly and violently using your feet

kick out *He kicked out hard and knocked me off my feet.* ♦ **+at** *She tried to kick out wildly at her captors.*

,kick 'out against *same as* **kick against**

,kick 'over

1 if you kick something over, you make it fall onto its side by kicking it

kick over sth *also* **kick sth over** *They overturned tables and kicked over chairs.* ♦ *I accidentally kicked a tin of paint over and spoilt the carpet.*

2 *American* if an engine kicks over, it starts to work = TURN OVER

kick over *I turned the key but the engine didn't kick over.*

PHRASE **kick over the traces** to behave badly or do things that other people do not approve of: *I knew my parents wouldn't approve of my girlfriend. I suppose I was just kicking over the traces.*

,kick 'up ★

to make something go up into the air

kick up sth *The storm kicked up waves big enough to destroy whole villages.* ♦ *She seemed in a hurry, her boots kicking up dust.*

PHRASE **kick up a fuss/stink/row** *informal* to complain very angrily about someone or something: *The decision was changed after he kicked up a fuss.*

KID /kɪd/
kids, kidding, kidded

,kid a'round [usually progressive] to behave in a silly way = FOOL AROUND, MESS AROUND be **kidding around** *We didn't mean it: we were just kidding around.*

KILL /kɪl/
kills, killing, killed

kill 'off ★★

1 to destroy living things so that most or all of them are dead = DESTROY
kill off sth *Antibiotics may kill off beneficial bacteria too.*
kill sth off *Some experts argue this activity could kill the whole species off.*
♦ *Pollution is attacking the fish in the rivers, slowly killing them off.*

2 to stop, get rid of, or destroy something = PUT AN END TO
kill off sth *The BBC has decided to kill off some of its best-loved programmes.*
kill sth off *These two great countries are going to kill each other off.* ♦ *The party has survived many attempts to kill it off.*

3 [often passive] if a writer kills off a character in a television series or other story, the writer makes the character die = WRITE OUT
be/get killed off *She was killed off at the end of the second series.*
kill sb off *I knew they had plans to kill my character off.*
kill off sb *They wanted a dramatic ending where I kill off the central character.*

KIP /kɪp/
kips, kipping, kipped

kip 'down *British informal*
to sleep somewhere where you usually would not sleep, for example on a floor or sofa at someone else's house = DOSS DOWN
kip down *He could kip down on my floor.*

KISS /kɪs/
kisses, kissing, kissed

kiss a'way
to stop someone feeling sad, worried, or angry by kissing them to show that you are sympathetic
kiss away sth *also* **kiss sth away** *I held him like a child and kissed away his frown.* ♦ *Let me kiss those tears away.*

kiss 'off *American informal*

1 to get rid of something or someone
kiss off sth/sb *also* **kiss sth/sb off** *Some homeowners decided to kiss off the property.* ♦ *We're not going to kiss you off because of a few minor problems.*

2 to say or think that something or someone is not very good

kiss off sth/sb *also* **kiss sth/sb off** *Many voters had already kissed off the new President.* ♦ *+as sth He kissed the whole subject off as 'pseudo-science'.*

3 [often in imperative] used as a rude way of refusing to do something
kiss off *When they suggested another test, he told me to kiss off.*

4 [often in imperative] used as a rude way of telling someone to go away
kiss off *'Just kiss off!' he shouted.*

■ **'kiss-off** **noun** [singular] *informal* a rude way of telling someone that they are no longer wanted: *She finally gave her boyfriend the kiss-off.*

kiss 'up to *American informal*
showing disapproval to try to please a powerful person, because you want them to do something for you = SUCK UP TO
kiss up to sb *She spots the boss and starts kissing up to him.*

KIT /kɪt/
kits, kitting, kitted

kit 'out [usually passive] *British*
to give someone all the clothes and equipment necessary for a particular activity = EQUIP
be kitted out *He was kitted out for a day's hiking.* ♦ *+for We didn't feel we were properly kitted out for a day in the hills.*

KNACKER /'nækə, *American* 'nækər/
knackers, knackering, knackered

knacker 'out [often passive] *British very informal*
to make someone very tired
be knackered out *By the end of the day, we were all knackered out.*
knacker sb/yourself out *Why don't you stop now? You don't want to knacker yourself out.*

KNEEL /niːl, *American* nil/
kneels, kneeling, knelt /nelt/ or *American* **kneeled**

kneel 'down ★
to put one or both knees on the ground
kneel down *She knelt down beside the dog.* ♦ *I knelt down on the floor beside her.*

KNIT /nɪt/
knits, knitting, knitted

knit to'gether

1 if a broken bone knits together, its parts join together again
> **knit together** *The bones are knitting together nicely.*

2 if different styles, ideas, systems etc knit together, or if they are knitted together, they combine to form something new
> **knit together** *When two companies merge, it can take a long time for their different structures to knit together.*
> **knit sth together** *also* **knit together sth** *It would take decades to knit together this society which had been torn apart by civil war.*

KNOCK /nɒk, *American* nɑk/
knocks, knocking, knocked

Knock is often used with adverbs and prepositions when it means 'to hit something or someone': *She **knocked** her leg **against** the table.* ✦ *He **knocked** a couple of nails **into** the wall.* ✦ *The force of the wave nearly **knocked** him **over**.* These uses are not included here.

knock a'bout *same as* knock around

■ **knockabout** /'nɒkəˌbaʊt/ **noun 1** [C] an informal game with a ball: *John and I enjoy a knockabout after school.* **2** [C/U] a very lively argument, for example between politicians: *The two candidates could be relied on to provide some good knockabout for the TV cameras.* **3** [U] actions or stories that are silly or unlikely and are intended to make you laugh: *Younger viewers will love the comic characters and crazy knockabout.*

knock a'round (*also* ,knock a'bout)

1	hit sb a lot
2	discuss sth
3	spend time somewhere
4	spend time with sb
5	have sth, but not know where

1 *informal* to hit or kick someone a lot
> **knock sb around** *Her husband had been knocking her around.*

2 *British informal* to discuss ideas in an informal way = KICK AROUND
> **knock sth around** *also* **knock around sth** *We knocked that idea around for a few minutes.* ✦ *It gives us a chance to knock around some new theories.*

3 *informal* to spend time somewhere with no particular purpose

> **knock around sth** *I'd knocked around the Mediterranean for a few years after leaving university.*

4 if one person knocks around with another, or if two people knock around together, they spend time together because they are friends
> **knock around with sb** *Who was that lad you used to knock around with?*
> **knock around together** *We used to knock around together when we were young.*

5 [usually progressive] *British* if something is knocking around, it is in a place, although you do not know exactly where
= KICK AROUND
> **knock around** *I've got a knife knocking around somewhere.*

knock 'back ★ *informal*

1 to drink alcohol quickly or in large amounts = DOWN
> **knock sth back** *She poured herself a drink and knocked it back.*
> **knock back sth** *He's been knocking back whisky for a couple of hours.*

2 *British* to cause problems or delays = SET BACK
> **knock sb back** *One or two problems have knocked us back a couple of weeks.*

3 *British* to refuse to accept someone or something = REJECT
> **knock sb/sth back** *He's asked every girl in the school and they've all knocked him back.* ✦ *If you get an offer like that again, don't knock it back.*

4 *British* if something knocks you back a particular amount of money, it costs that much money = SET BACK
> **knock sb back sth** *How much did the repairs knock you back?* ✦ *That'll knock you back a few hundred pounds.*

knock 'down ★★

1	hurt sb with a vehicle
2	destroy a building/wall
3	reduce a price/amount
4	persuade sb to reduce a price
5	show that an idea etc is useless
+	**knockdown** adj, noun

1 [often passive] *British* to hit someone with a vehicle so that they are injured or killed = RUN OVER
> **be knocked down** *Sue was knocked down just yards from her home.*
> **knock sb down** *You idiot, you nearly knocked me down!*
> **knock down sb** *The bus left the road and knocked down two pedestrians.*

2 [often passive] to deliberately destroy a building or wall = DEMOLISH

be knocked down *Most of those houses have been knocked down.*
knock sth down *We could knock that wall down to make the room bigger.*
knock down sth *They start knocking down the old school next week.*

3 *informal* to reduce a price or amount = REDUCE ≠ PUT UP
knock sth down *They knocked the price of beer down over 20p a pint.*

4 to persuade someone to reduce the price of something = BEAT DOWN
knock sb down *I managed to knock him down a few pounds.* ♦ +to *We knocked them down to £120.*

5 [often passive] to show that something such as an idea or suggestion is not good or useful
be knocked down *It was a theory that was easily knocked down.*
knock sth down *I kept making suggestions and she kept knocking them down.*

■ **knockdown** /ˈnɒkdaʊn/ **adj** knockdown prices are very low: *They are prepared to sell the company at a knockdown price.*

■ **knockdown** /ˈnɒkdaʊn/ **noun** [C] a fall in a boxing match, after being hit: *The champion survived a knockdown in the tenth round.*

ˌknock ˈinto [usually passive] *British* to make two rooms into one larger room by knocking down the wall between them
be knocked into sth *Two of the downstairs rooms had been knocked into one.*

ˌknock ˈoff ★★ *informal*

1	reduce a price/amount
2	stop working
3	make sth carelessly
4	steal sth
5	rob a place
6	murder sb
7	have sex with sb
+	PHRASE
+	**knockoff** noun

1 to reduce a price or an amount = TAKE OFF
knock sth off sth *They might be willing to knock something off the price.* ♦ *Kelly knocked two seconds off her previous time.*
knock off sth *We can knock off 5% if you pay by cash.*
knock sth off *Ask them if they'll knock a few pounds off.*

2 if someone knocks off at a particular time, they finish working then = FINISH ≠ START
knock off *Do you want to knock off early tonight?*
knock off work *He usually knocks off work at 6.*

3 to produce something quickly and carelessly, especially a copy of something else
knock off sth *She thinks I can just knock off another story when I want to.*
knock sth off *I need to knock another chapter off this week.* ♦ *There's still some brickwork to do but a good builder should be able to knock it off in a few hours.*

4 *British* to steal something = STEAL
knock sth off *They knocked some TVs off from an electrical store.*
knock off sth *These boys can knock off anything you like.*

5 *British* to rob a place
knock off sth *They'd knocked off two banks the previous week.*

6 [often passive] *informal* to murder someone = BUMP OFF
be/get knocked off *He was worried about getting knocked off.*
knock sb off *One of Harry's guys knocked him off.*
knock off sb *He's the guy who knocked off his partner.*

7 *British offensive* to have sex with someone
knock sb off *He accused me of knocking off his wife.*
knock sb off *He's been knocking her off for months.*
PHRASE knock it off! *informal* used for telling someone to stop doing something: *Okay, you two. Knock it off, now!*

■ **knockoff** /ˈnɒkɒf/ **noun** [C] *informal* a bad or cheap copy of something: *She can tell the difference between designer jeans and knockoffs.*

knock off

,knock 'out ★★

1	make sb unconscious
2	defeat a player/team
3	destroy sth
4	impress sb
5	shock/upset sb
6	make sth carelessly
7	lose a quality
+	PHRASE

1 to make someone unconscious —*picture*
→ PASS OUT
knock sb out *He had eventually knocked the other man out.* ♦ *A roof tile fell on his head, knocking him out.* ♦ *She hit her head on the pavement when she fell and knocked herself out.*
knock out sb *He's the fighter who knocked out the world champion.*

2 [often passive] to make someone leave a competition by defeating them = DEFEAT
be/get knocked out *England had been knocked out of the World Cup again.*
knock sb out *They would have to play better than that to knock us out.* ♦ *They knocked our team out in the first round.*
knock out sb *They're the side that knocked out France.*

3 to destroy something or stop it working
knock out sth *It was our job to knock out the power station.*
knock sth out *A month without rain had knocked their entire crop out.*

4 *informal* to impress someone very much = IMPRESS, STUN
knock sb out *You'll knock them out in that dress.*

5 *informal* to make someone feel very shocked or upset = STUN
knock sb out *I read the report and it knocked me out.*

6 *informal* to produce something quickly or carelessly = BASH OUT, PRODUCE
knock out sth *I knocked out another letter to the company.*
knock sth out *You have to knock the report out in a couple of hours.* ♦ *If you need a new suit, we can knock one out for you in no time.*

7 [usually passive] if a quality is knocked out of someone, they lose that quality as a result of something that happens to them or something that someone does to them
be knocked out of sb *All the enthusiasm had been knocked out of him.*

> **PHRASE** **knock yourself out** *informal* to do a lot of work in order to achieve something: *Don't knock yourself out trying to achieve perfection.*

,knock 'over ★★

1 [often passive] *British* to hit someone with a vehicle = RUN OVER, KNOCK DOWN
be/get knocked over *Over 100 people are knocked over on Britain's roads every day.*
knock sb over *The truck nearly knocked us over.*

2 *American informal* to steal money or goods from a bank or business, especially using violence = ROB
knock over sth *He'd never knocked over a bank before.*

,knock to'gether

1 [usually passive] to make two rooms or buildings into one room or building by removing a wall that separates them
be knocked together *The two cottages had been knocked together.*

2 to produce something quickly and easily = THROW TOGETHER
knock together sth *also* **knock sth together** *While you get dressed, I'll knock together a quick dinner.* ♦ *It won't take long to knock an application together.*

,knock 'up

1 in games such as tennis, when players knock up, they practise hitting the ball to each other before the game starts
knock up *The players had just started knocking up when the rain came on.*

2 *British informal* to produce something quickly and easily
knock up sth *also* **knock sth up** *It doesn't take long to knock up some pasta.* ♦ *We knocked a basic shelter up using materials we found lying around.*

3 *British informal* to wake someone, usually in the middle of the night, by knocking on their door = WAKE UP, ROUSE
knock sb up *I'll knock you up around 6 o'clock.*

4 *offensive* to make a woman pregnant

■ **'knock-up** **noun** [C] *British* a period of practice before a match in tennis or a similar sport: *The day started with a gentle knock-up on the practice court.*

KNOW /nəʊ, *American* noʊ/
knows, knowing, knew /njuː, *American* nuː/, **known** /nəʊn, *American* noʊn/

'know as [usually passive]

if someone or something is known as something, they are given something as a name or title, although it is not their real name
be known as sth *Margaret Thatcher was known as 'The Iron Lady'.* ♦ *The US*

*residency permit is commonly known
as the 'green card'.*

be 'known for ★★★

to be well known because of a particular
feature or quality
be known for sth *France is a country
that is known for its wine and cheese.*
♦ *She is known for her bright and bubbly
personality.*

'know from

to recognize the difference between two
people or things
know sth/sb from sth/sb *Most people
wouldn't know it from real champagne.*

'know of ★★★

to know that someone exists and to know
who, what, or where they are
know of sth/sb *I know of someone who
might be able to help us.* ♦ *Do you know
of a good dress hire shop in the area?*
♦ *He hasn't got any secrets that I know
of.*
> **PHRASE** **not that I know of** *informal* used
> to say that you think something is not
> true, although you are not completely
> certain: *"Did she ever meet Mr Smith?"* –
> *'Not that I know of'.*

KNUCKLE /'nʌk(ə)l/
knuckles, knuckling, knuckled

,knuckle 'down *informal*

to start working hard, especially when
you should have done this earlier **=** WORK
HARD
knuckle down *You'll have to knuckle
down if you want to pass your
examinations.* ♦ **+to** *This year's students
seem much more inclined to knuckle
down to work.*

,knuckle 'under *informal*

to do what someone tells you to do **=** GIVE
IN
knuckle under *His club tried to
pressurize him into signing a new
contract but he refused to knuckle under.*

KOWTOW /kaʊ'taʊ, *American*
'kaʊ,taʊ/
kowtows, kowtowing, kowtowed

,kow'tow to *showing disapproval*

to try very hard to please someone,
treating them as though they are much
more important than you
kowtow to sb *He was a proud man who
kowtowed to nobody.* ♦ *Any country that
refused to kowtow to their demands was
treated as a hostile nation.*

LABOR the American spelling of
labour

LABOUR /'leɪbə, *American* 'leɪbər/
labours, labouring, laboured

'labour under

1 to find it difficult to make progress or
be successful because of something
labour under sth *Many countries labour
under a huge burden of debt they cannot
even begin to pay.*
2 to act as if something is true, even
though it is obvious to most other people
that it is not
labour under sth *Even after a decade,
she still seems to labour under the illusion
that she is party leader.*

LACE /leɪs/
laces, lacing, laced

,lace 'up

to tie shoes that have laces
lace up sth *also* **lace sth up** *Has he learnt
to lace up his shoes?* ♦ *When you've put
your gym shoes on I'll lace them up for
you.*

'lace with

1 [often passive] to put a small amount of
strong alcohol, a drug, or poison into a
drink or food, sometimes secretly
be laced with sth *She doesn't know that
the milk has been laced with poison.*
lace sth with sth *They lace their coffee
with brandy.*
2 [usually passive] if something is laced with
a particular quality, it has some of that
quality in all parts of it
be laced with sth *Each scene is laced
with romantic interest.*

LADLE /'leɪd(ə)l/
ladles, ladling, ladled

,ladle 'out

1 to serve something with a large deep
spoon with a long handle, called a ladle
ladle out sth *also* **ladle sth out** *I ladled
out some more casserole.* ♦ *They boil the
water over the fire and then ladle it out
into metal cups.*
2 to give large amounts of money, goods,

or information to someone without thinking carefully what it will be used for

ladle out sth *also* **ladle sth out** *She ladles out financial advice in her newspaper column.*

LAG /læg/
lags, lagging, lagged

,lag be'hind

1 to walk more slowly than the people you are with

lag behind *Come on, you two, stop lagging behind!*

2 to not be as successful or advanced as other organizations or groups = TRAIL BEHIND

lag behind sb *Their software tends to lag behind that of other producers.*

LAGER /'lɑːɡə, American 'lɑɡər/

be/get ,lagered 'up *British informal*

to be or become very drunk after drinking too much lager or beer

be lagered up *Most of the men are already well lagered up.*

LAM /læm/
lams, lamming, lammed

,lam 'into *British informal*

to strongly attack or criticize someone

lam into sb *As soon as I walked in, she lammed into me.*

LAND /lænd/
lands, landing, landed

'land in *informal*

to be in an unpleasant situation or place, or to cause someone to be in an unpleasant situation or place

land in sth *She landed in hospital with a broken leg.*

land sb in sth *His recklessness could land him in real trouble.*

PHRASE **land in sb's lap** if something good such as money or a job lands in someone's lap, it suddenly happens to them or is given to them without them having to make any effort: *What do you do when so much money suddenly lands in your lap?*

'land on *American informal*

to criticize someone severely = LAMBAST

land on sb *He really landed on me for being late.*

,land 'up *British informal*

to finally arrive at a place or in a situation after a series of events = FETCH UP

land up *We finally landed up at Tom's house.*

land up doing sth *How did you land up studying astronomy?*

'land with [often passive] *informal*

to give someone an unpleasant job that no one else wants to do = SADDLE WITH

be landed with sth *John was landed with the job of sorting Susan's files when she left.*

land sb with sth *She landed me with the job of telling her parents.*

LAP /læp/
laps, lapping, lapped

,lap 'up ★

1 to enjoy something and be keen to get more of it = ENJOY

lap sth up *The jokes were crude but the audience were lapping them up.* ◆ *Soon they were depending on me, and I lapped the situation up.*

lap up sth *The family is really lapping up this sunshine.*

2 if an animal laps up a drink, it drinks it gently with its tongue

lap up sth *Two little kittens were lapping up their milk.*

lap sth up *I put down a saucer of milk for the dog, and he lapped it up neatly.*

LAPSE /læps/
lapses, lapsing, lapsed

'lapse into

1 to gradually change to a quieter or less active state = SLIDE INTO

lapse into sth *A hypnotized person lapses into a kind of trance.* ◆ *Now it was her turn to lapse into thought.*

2 to change to a different, less usual, or less helpful way of speaking or behaving, often without realizing it

lapse into sth *The manual occasionally lapses into incomprehensible jargon.*

LARD /lɑːd, American lɑrd/
lards, larding, larded

be 'larded with *showing disapproval*

if a speech or text is larded with something, it contains a lot of extra things that are not welcome or necessary

be larded with sth *The entire chapter was larded with personal attacks on former colleagues.*

LARK /laːk, *American* lɑrk/
larks, larking, larked

ˌlark aˈbout (*also* ˌlark aˈround) *British*
old-fashioned
if young people or children lark about, they have fun by behaving in a silly playful way = FOOL AROUND
    lark about *The kids were all larking about in the water.*

LASH /læʃ/
lashes, lashing, lashed

ˈlash down *British*
to rain heavily = POUR DOWN
    lash down *It's been lashing down for an hour.*

ˌlash ˈinto
to criticize someone or something in a very angry way = LAY INTO
    lash into sb/sth *He lashed into my plan.*
    ♦ *He seemed to be lashing into her for no reason.*

ˌlash ˈout ★★
1 to try to hit or attack someone suddenly and violently = HIT OUT
    lash out *Catherine lashed out, her arm swinging wildly.* ♦ **+at** *Occasionally the patients will lash out at the nurses.*
2 to speak angrily to someone, or to criticize something angrily = HIT OUT
    lash out *If she thinks someone is criticizing her, she lashes out quite irrationally.* ♦ **+at** *They lashed out at the council's move to stop free parking.*
3 *British informal* to spend a lot of money on something = SPLASH OUT
    lash out *I decided to lash out and treat myself.* ♦ **+on** *We lashed out on the best seats.*
    lash out sth on sth *I can't believe you lashed out £70 on a new haircut!*

lash out

LAST /lɑːst, *American* læst/
lasts, lasting, lasted

ˌlast ˈout
1 to manage to stay alive for a particular period of time = SURVIVE
    last out sth *It doesn't look like she'll last out the night.*
    last out *You won't last out very long without food.*
2 *British* if a supply of money or food lasts out, it is enough for what people need = LAST
    last out *I doubt whether our money is going to last out.*

LATCH /lætʃ/
latches, latching, latched

ˌlatch ˈon *informal*
to suddenly understand or realize something = UNDERSTAND
    latch on *Sooner or later he's going to latch on.*

ˌlatch ˈonto *informal*
1 to go up to someone and spend time talking to them, even though they do not want to be with you
    latch onto sb *Two boys tried to latch onto us as we were leaving.*
2 to immediately become very interested in something that you discover = POUNCE ON
    latch onto sth *The media latched onto the rumour and reported it as fact.*
3 to get something, especially something good or useful
    latch onto sth *I've latched onto a source of cheap office supplies.*

LAUGH /lɑːf, *American* læf/
laughs, laughing, laughed

ˈlaugh at ★★★
1 to show that you think something is funny by laughing
    laugh at sth *People never laugh at my jokes.* ♦ *Audiences laughed at the way the two characters constantly argued with each other.*
2 to say unkind things about someone or something that are intended to make them seem silly = MAKE FUN OF
    laugh at sb/sth *The other kids laughed at his haircut.* ♦ *It seems the teacher was openly laughing at their mistakes.* ♦ *I always felt as though they were **laughing at me behind my back** (=saying unkind things about me when I was not listening).*

3 to behave in a way that shows you are not worried or frightened by something
laugh at sth *He's always been able to laugh at danger.*
PHRASE **laugh at yourself** to not be too serious or sensitive about yourself and the things you do: *It's important to be able to laugh at yourself.*

,laugh 'off ★ (*also* ,laugh a'way)
to joke about something to show that you think it is not important or serious
laugh off sth *They just laughed off the rumours about them getting married.*
laugh sth off *It was meant as a serious question, but she just laughed it off.*

Nouns often used as objects with **laugh off**

■ criticism, report, rumour, suggestion

LAUNCH /lɔːntʃ, *American* lɔntʃ/
launches, launching, launched

'launch into ★★
to start doing something or talking about something with a lot of enthusiasm and energy = EMBARK ON
launch into sth *He immediately launched into a detailed account of his trip.*

Nouns often used as objects with launch into

■ account, attack, description, explanation, story, tale, tirade

,launch 'out *British*
to start a new activity, especially one that involves some risk
launch out *They weren't brave enough to launch out on their own.* ♦ **+to do sth** *Before launching out to buy new materials, send for a catalogue from each company.*

LAVISH /ˈlævɪʃ/
lavishes, lavishing, lavished

'lavish on (*also* 'lavish upon)
to give someone a lot of something, for example money, love, or attention
lavish sth on sb *They lavished attention on their grandchildren.*

LAY /leɪ/
lays, laying, laid /leɪd/

Lay is often used with adverbs and prepositions when it means 'to put something or someone down in a careful way, especially so that they are lying flat': *Lay the baby in her cot and she might go to sleep.* ♦ *He had taken off his coat and laid it across the arm of the chair.* ♦ *We lay flowers on her grave once a month.* These uses are not included here.

,lay a'bout *British old-fashioned*
to attack someone by hitting them repeatedly = ATTACK
lay about sb *The woman began laying about him.* ♦ **+with** *He said that his captors had laid about him with whips.*

,lay a'side ★
1 to keep or save something, especially money, so that you can use it in the future = LAY BY
lay aside sth *For years my mother laid aside a small amount of money each week.*
lay sth aside *Make sure you lay a little money aside for the future.* ♦ *His grandmother had left him £10,000 and he has laid it aside for a time such as this.*
2 to not let yourself think about or be influenced by something so that you can achieve an aim = PUT ASIDE, SET ASIDE
lay aside sth *They agreed to lay aside their differences for the good of their families.*
lay sth aside *It's hard for him to lay all that jealousy aside.* ♦ *He had some doubts but he laid them aside.*
3 to put something down and to one side because you have finished with it or want to save it until another time
lay aside sth *'What do you want?' he said, laying aside his book.*
lay sth aside *She laid her newspaper aside and closed her eyes.* ♦ *Take some of the fruit and lay it aside for decoration.*

,lay be'fore
to offer something to someone in authority, for example a judge or senior politician, so that they can consider it and come to a decision on it = SET BEFORE
lay before sb *I have some more research to do before I'm ready to lay the case before the committee.*

,lay 'by
to keep or save something, especially money, so that you can use it in the future = LAY ASIDE

lay sth by *He had laid part of the money by.*

,lay 'down ★★★

1 to put something down to show you are not going to use it again, for example weapons or tools

lay down sth *The guerrillas have agreed to lay down their arms.* ♦ *Hundreds of workers laid down their tools and went on strike.*

2 [often passive] to state officially what someone must do or how they must do it
= SET DOWN, STIPULATE

be laid down *The procedure for dealing with these cases is laid down in the handbook.*
lay down sth *The government has laid down tough standards for water quality.* ♦ *+that The rules laid down that he could not directly intervene.*

> Nouns often used as objects with
> **lay down 2**
>
> ■ conditions, criteria, guidelines, principles, procedures, requirements, rules, standards

3 [usually passive] to form a layer of something such as soil or mud that gradually hardens and develops into rock

be laid down *In this area, deposits of sand are being laid down.*

4 *informal* a way of saying 'lie down' that many people think is incorrect

lay down *Come over here and lay down.*
PHRASES **lay down the law** to tell someone what to do or how to behave in a way that shows that you expect them to obey you completely: *With kids like that you have to lay down the law and let them see you're serious.*
lay down your life *formal* to die in order to help or save someone or something: *He was prepared to lay down his life for his country.*

'lay for *American informal*

to be hiding and waiting to attack someone
lay for sb *He scared off a mugger who was laying for him in the bushes.*

,lay 'in *old-fashioned*

to get and keep a supply of something such as food to use in the future = STORE

lay in sth *My friends had laid in a good stock of wine and beer.*

,lay 'into *informal*

1 to attack someone physically by hitting or kicking them repeatedly = ATTACK, HIT

lay into sb *They knocked me to the floor then started to lay into my friend.*

2 to criticize someone in an angry way
= CRITICIZE ≠ PRAISE

lay into sb *He laid into her with a string of insults.*

,lay 'off ★★

1 [often passive] to end someone's employment, especially temporarily, because there is not enough work for them
= DISMISS ≠ TAKE ON

be laid off *Half the workforce has already been laid off.*
lay off sb *They've had to cut back production and lay off workers.*

2 [usually in imperative] *informal* to stop doing something that is annoying someone
= STOP

lay off *Lay off! I'm trying to study.*
lay off doing sth *Just lay off complaining for a minute!*

3 *informal* to stop doing or using something, especially for a short period of time

lay off sth *I had to lay off the medication for a while to see if that was causing my headaches.*

■ **'lay-off** noun [C] **1** a situation in which an employer ends a worker's employment, especially temporarily, because there is not enough work for them: *The restructuring of the company is bound to result in some lay-offs.* **2** a period of time when you are not working or performing an activity such as a sport, usually because you are ill or injured: *It was difficult playing a full game after such a long lay-off.*

,lay 'on

1 [often passive] *British* to provide something such as food, entertainment, or a service, especially without charging for it
= PROVIDE

be laid on *Extra buses are being laid on for late-night shoppers.*
lay on sth *They laid on a special party to mark his 31 years of service.*

2 *informal* to tell something to someone, especially when you do not expect them to like it

lay sth on sb *Okay, I'm ready for the bad news, lay it on me.*
PHRASE **lay it on (a bit) thick** *informal* to make something such as your admiration for someone or their achievements seem greater or more important than it really is in order to impress someone: *Don't lay it on too thick, or they'll know you want something.*

lay 'out ★★★

1	make sth easy to use/look at
2	explain sth
3	arrange sth
4	spend money
5	hit sb
6	show a dead body
7	lie in a sunny place
+	**layout** noun; **outlay** noun

1 [often passive] to spread something out on a surface or arrange things so that they are ready to use or can be easily seen = DISPLAY
be laid out *A display of local history material was laid out on the table.*
lay sth out *Lay the map out so we can all see it.* ♦ *She unpacked her combs, brushes, and scissors and laid them out on the dressing table.*
lay out sth *She laid out the cups and saucers on the table.*

2 [often passive] to explain something carefully and clearly = SET OUT
be laid out *The problem is laid out in my letter.*
lay out sth *The documents lay out the principles clearly enough.*

3 [usually passive] to arrange something according to a detailed plan, for example rooms in a building, roads in a town, or areas on a piece of land
be laid out *The city was laid out with the government buildings on a hill.*
♦ *The brochure is beautifully laid out and illustrated.*

4 *informal* to spend an amount of money
lay out sth *They had already laid out a substantial amount.* ♦ **+for/on** *He'd already laid out a lot of money for the dress.*

5 *informal* to hit someone so hard that they fall to the ground and become unconscious = KNOCK OUT
lay sb out *Joe laid Ken out with one punch.*

6 [usually passive] to prepare a dead body so that people can come to see it before it is buried
be laid out *Relatives all filed upstairs to where the old man was laid out.*

7 *American informal* to lie outside in the sun, so that you get brown. This use is considered incorrect by many people.
lay out *We laid out on the roof and drank wine out of plastic cups.*

■ **layout** /ˈleɪaʊt/ **noun** [usually singular] **1** the way in which the different parts of something are arranged: *The user gradually becomes familiar with the layout of the keyboard.*

2 the way in which something such as a room, building, or city is arranged: *The layout of your house and garden can deter crime.* **3** the way in which the words and pictures on a page are arranged: *the layout of a business letter*

■ **outlay** /ˈaʊtleɪ/ **noun** [C/U] the amount of money that you must spend in order to buy something or to start a new business or project: *Horses are very expensive to keep, even after the initial outlay.*

lay 'over *American*
to stop somewhere for a short time during a long journey, especially between flights
lay over in sth *We laid over for 8 hours in Anchorage.*

■ **layover** /ˈleɪoʊvə/ **noun** [C] *American* a stop during a journey, especially during a flight: *After a brief layover in Manila, we flew home to San Francisco.*

lay 'to *technical*
if you lay a ship to, or if it lays to, it stops
lay sth to *The captain laid the ship to in Liverpool.*
lay to *We laid to as soon as we saw signs of the wreck.*

lay 'up ★ [usually passive]

1 to make someone stay in bed as a result of being ill or injured
be laid up *He's been laid up all week.*
♦ **+with** *I'm laid up with a bad back at the moment.*

2 to not use a vehicle or ship for a period of time, especially because it needs to be repaired
be laid up *The boats were laid up for the winter.*

LAZE /leɪz/
lazes, lazing, lazed

laze a'round (*also* **laze a'bout** *British*)
to relax and enjoy yourself, doing no work = CHILL OUT
laze around *Your children shouldn't be lazing around indoors on such a nice day.*

laze a'way
to spend time relaxing and enjoying yourself, doing no work
laze sth away *also* **laze away sth** *You can laze your days away doing nothing.*
♦ *We lazed away those long hot Mediterranean days.*

LEACH /liːtʃ, *American* litʃ/
leaches, leaching, leached

'leach into
if a substance, usually a harmful
substance, leaches into something such
as water or soil, it goes into it gradually
leach into sth *We want to prevent
harmful chemicals leaching into the
water supply.*

,leach 'out
if a substance, usually a harmful
substance, leaches out, it comes out of the
thing that it used to be part of
leach out *Chemicals in the cement leach
out and contaminate the water.*

LEAD /liːd, *American* lid/
leads, leading, led /led/

Lead is often used with adverbs and
prepositions when it means 'to show
someone the way to a place by going
there with them': *After showing us the
dining room, the estate agent **led** us **into**
the kitchen. ♦ She took the boy by the
hand and **led** him **from** the room.
♦ Dismounting, I **led** the horse **back to**
the stable.* These uses are not included
here.

'lead into
if something such as an idea or subject
leads into another, the second one is a
natural result of the first one
lead into sth *Discussion of a client's tax
affairs will lead naturally into
consideration of investment options.*

■ **lead-in** /'liːd ɪn/ **noun** [C] a
statement, action, or short piece of film
used for introducing something: *I'd like
to follow up a couple of points you made
in your lead-in to the programme.*

,lead 'off ★
to begin something by doing or saying
something = BEGIN ≠ END
lead off sth *The Prime Minister had
invited the President to lead off the press
conference. ♦ +with She led off the
afternoon with questions from the
audience.*
lead off *I'll lead off by introducing our
visitors.*

,lead 'on
to encourage someone to do something or
expect something, especially by lying to
them or promising them something that
they cannot have = ENTICE
lead sb on *I hope he's not just leading*

*her on, because I'd hate to see her get
hurt.*

'lead to ★★★
1 lead to or **lead on to** to begin a process
that causes something to happen
lead to sth *There is no doubt that stress
can lead to physical illness. ♦ We hope to
begin a process of negotiation leading to
a peaceful settlement.*

> Nouns often used as objects with **lead to 1**
>
> ■ (positive): emergence, growth,
> improvement, increase, rise
> (negative): breakdown, collapse, decline,
> decrease, demise, deterioration,
> downfall, drop, fall, loss

2 to make someone think something
lead sb to sth *The evidence leads me to
a different conclusion.*

,lead 'up to
1 if events, problems, actions etc lead up
to an important event, they happen one
after another in a way that makes it
possible for the event to happen
lead up to sth *The negotiations leading
up to the contract were very tough. ♦ The
book discusses the events leading up to
the incident.*
2 to happen or exist immediately before
something = *formal* PRECEDE
lead up to sth *In the weeks leading up
to graduation I did very little.*
3 to gradually direct a conversation
towards a particular subject, especially
one that is difficult or embarrassing
lead up to sth *I knew he was leading up
to something, but I had no idea what.*

■ **lead-up** /'liːd ʌp/ **noun** [singular] the
period that comes before an important
event: *the lead-up to the Olympic Games*

'lead with
1 to begin a speech, news broadcast, etc
with a particular story or subject
lead with sth *We'll lead with the Prime
Minister's visit to China.*
2 in the sport of boxing, to have a habit
of hitting with a particular hand
lead with sth *He leads with his right
hand.*

LEAF /liːf, *American* lif/
leafs, leafing, leafed

,leaf 'through
to turn the pages of a book or a pile of
papers quickly and without looking at
them carefully = LOOK THROUGH
leaf through sth *She sat leafing through
a newspaper, watching the door.*

LEAK /liːk, *American* liːk/
leaks, leaking, leaked

,leak 'out
if private or secret information leaks out,
it becomes known by the public = EMERGE
leak out *News leaked out that he was
leaving the show.*

LEAN /liːn, *American* lin/
leans, leaning, leaned /liːnd, *American*
lind/ or **leant** /lent/

,lean a'gainst
to put something at an angle against
something else for support, or to be put
against something else in this way
lean sth against sth *John leaned his
rake against the side of the barn.*
lean against sth *His bike was leaning
against the wall.*

'lean on
1 to depend on someone, especially when
you have problems = RELY ON, DEPEND ON
lean on sb *Everybody needs someone to
lean on in times of trouble.*
2 to keep pressing the horn of a car in a
determined way
lean on sth *The taxi driver was waiting
out front, leaning on the horn.*
3 *informal* to put pressure on someone to
make them do or say something
= PRESSURIZE
lean on sb *If the police lean on them,
they might give some more information.*
♦ **+to do sth** *The Prime Minister's been
leaning pretty heavily on her to resign.*

,lean to'wards
to be more likely to choose or support one
decision or course of action than another
lean towards (doing) sth *She is leaning
towards supporting military action.* ♦ *I
lean towards a radical approach.*

LEAP /liːp, *American* lip/
leaps, leaping, leaped or **leapt** /lept/

'leap at
to accept something quickly and in an
enthusiastic way = JUMP AT
leap at sth *Klein **leapt at the chance** to
appear in the show.* ♦ *When he offered
to show her round the recording studios,
she **leapt at the opportunity**.* ♦ *She
expected me to leap at the idea, but I'm
not that keen.*

,leap 'in
to do something immediately, and often
with enthusiasm, as soon as you have the
chance to do it = DIVE IN, JUMP IN

leap in *When they see a marketing
opportunity, companies leap in.* ♦ *It can
be dangerous to leap in without thinking
about it first.*

,leap 'off
PHRASE **leap off the page** if something that
is written leaps off the page, it is
immediately obvious or it immediately
gets your attention: *The solution to the
problem seemed to leap off the page.*

'leap on (*also* 'leap upon)
to be immediately very interested in
something or very keen to do or have
something = SEIZE ON
leap on sth *She found herself leaping on
the suggestion.* ♦ *Developing countries
often do not have the infrastructure to
leap upon trade opportunities that come
their way.*

,leap 'out at
if something leaps out at you, it is
immediately obvious or it immediately
gets your attention = JUMP OUT AT
leap out at sb *He looked through the list
of names but none leapt out at him.* ♦ *One
picture on the wall leapt out at him.*

,leap 'up
to move very quickly from a sitting
position into a standing position = JUMP
UP
leap up *He leapt up and poured her more
coffee.*

'leap upon *formal same as* **leap on**

LEAVE /liːv, *American* liv/
leaves, leaving, left /left/

,leave a'side ★★
to not talk about something because you
want to talk about something else instead
= PUT ASIDE
leave aside sth *Leaving aside the
financial implications, do you really
believe your proposal will solve our
problem?*
leave sth aside *We'll leave those
considerations aside for now.* ♦ *There
have been a few teething problems, but
leaving those aside, the project is a
success.*

,leave be'hind ★★★

1 go ahead of sb
2 make faster progress than sb/sth
3 ignore the past
4 not take sb/sth
5 forget to take sth

1 [often passive] to increase the distance by

which you are ahead of someone or something = OUTDISTANCE

> **be/get left behind** *The other climbers were fitter and more experienced and I was worried I'd get left behind.*
> **leave sb behind** *The Kenyan runner is leaving the rest of the field way behind.*

2 [often passive] to improve or progress much faster than someone or something else

> **be/get left behind** *While Japan flourishes, the rest of Asia gets left behind.*
> **leave sb/sth behind** *She's beginning to leave the rest of the class behind.*

3 to no longer be affected by something, especially an unpleasant or hurtful experience from your past = PUT BEHIND

> **leave sth behind you** *The best thing is to try and leave the past behind you.*
> **leave behind sth** *a young woman trying to leave behind a difficult adolescence*
> **leave sth behind** *She had not enjoyed living in France, and was glad to leave it all behind.*

4 to not take someone or something with you when you go somewhere

> **leave sth behind** *He had to leave his family behind in Chile.*

5 to forget to take someone or something with you = FORGET

> **leave sth behind** *It wasn't until she was halfway home that she realized that she'd left her purse behind.* ♦ *This is an expensive pen. Someone must have left it behind by mistake.*
> **leave behind sth** *She's left behind all the important papers.*

,leave 'in

to not remove something, especially from a piece of writing

> **leave sth in** *also* **leave in sth** *We decided to leave the scene in.* ♦ *I left in the chapter about my childhood.*

,leave 'off *British informal*

to stop doing something = STOP ≠ CARRY ON

> **leave off** *Just leave off, you two!*
> **leave off doing sth** *I wish he'd leave off moaning about everything!*

,leave 'out ★★★

to not include someone or something = OMIT ≠ INCLUDE

> **leave sth/sb out** *We decided to leave the chapter out of the book altogether.* ♦ *OK, that's the list of current members. Have I left anyone out?*
> **leave out sth/sb** *Tell me what happened, and don't leave out any details.*

> **be left out** *Although the economy is doing well, large sections of the population are still being left out.*
> **PHRASE** **leave it out** *British informal* used for telling someone to stop saying something: *I told him to leave it out, but he kept on teasing me.*

be ,left 'over ★★

1 if part of an amount of something such as money or food is left over, you still have some of it after you have used or eaten the rest of it

> **be left over** *There was some ham left over from lunch.* ♦ *Is there any money left over?*

2 to still exist from the past

> **be left over** *These attitudes are left over from the war.*

■ **leftover** /ˈleftəʊvə/ **adj** remaining after you have finished using the amount you want or need: *Is there any leftover paint?*

■ **leftovers** /ˈleftəʊvəz/ **noun** [plural] the food that remains at the end of a meal after you have finished eating: *We'll be having leftovers for supper.*

ˈleave to ★

1 to go away from someone in order to allow them to continue something that they were doing when you interrupted them

> **leave sb to sth** *We'll leave you to your book.* ♦ *I wanted them to go away and leave me to it.*

2 if you leave something to someone, you allow them to make a decision about it or be responsible for it = LEAVE UP TO

> **leave sth to sb** *I'll leave that decision to you.*
> **leave it to sb to do sth** *I left it to my wife to choose a colour for the bathroom.*

3 if you leave money, jewellery etc to someone, you ask for it to be given to them after you have died

> **leave sth to sb** *She left all her books to her grandchildren.*

,leave 'up to

if you leave something up to someone, you allow them to make a decision about it or be responsible for it = LEAVE TO

> **leave sth up to sb** *She left the choice of vehicle up to me.*
> **leave it up to sb to do sth** *We'll leave it up to you to decide how best to achieve this.*

LECH /letʃ/
leches, leching, leched

'lech after (also **'lech over**) *British informal*
showing disapproval

to look at or behave towards someone in a way that shows you are sexually interested in them

lech after sb *One older man was always leching after the new girls in the office.*

LEECH /liːtʃ, American litʃ/
leeches, leeching, leeched

'leech off *showing disapproval*

if someone leeches off someone else, they ask them for money and other things and make no effort to give anything back or pay for anything

leech off sb *You're far too old to leech off your parents!*

LEND /lend/
lends, lending, lent /lent/

'lend to

1 to give something to someone for a short time

lend sth to sb *I've lent my black dress to Teresa.* ◆ *If you ever want to use our caravan we'd be happy to lend it to you.* ≠ BORROW

2 to give something a particular quality

lend sth to sth *The grand piano lends a dramatic air to the dining room.*

LET /let/
lets, letting, let

Let is often used with adverbs and prepositions when it means 'to allow something to happen': *Open the windows and let some fresh air into the room.* ◆ *The holes at the bottom of the pot are designed to let the water out.* ◆ *There were gaps in the curtains that let the wind through.* These uses are not included here.

,let 'down ★★★

1	not do what people expect
2	work badly when other people work well
3	be a bad aspect/quality
4	let sth move down
5	make clothing longer
6	let air out of tyres
+	**letdown** noun

1 to make someone disappointed by not doing something that they are expecting you to do = DISAPPOINT

let sb down *I felt that I'd let my parents down.* ◆ *The families of the victims feel that the justice system has let them down.*
let down sb *The team felt that they had let down their fans.*

2 to work less hard or make more mistakes than the people you are working with

let sb down *She's a great player, and never lets her team down.* ◆ *I've got some great colleagues, and I don't want to let them down.*
let down sb *Any boy who misbehaves will be letting down the whole school.*

3 [often passive] to make someone or something less likely to be successful or effective

be let down *The whole system is let down by the poor quality of the graphics.*
let sth down *It's a nice car – the only thing that lets it down is its ugly interior.*

4 to allow someone or something to move to a lower position = LOWER

let sth down *Let the bucket down carefully into the well.*
let down sth *In the story, she lets down her hair and the prince climbs up it.*

5 to use the extra cloth in the hem (=bottom fold) of a piece of clothing to make it longer ≠ TAKE UP

let down sth *If you let down the hem, the skirt will be fine.*
let sth down *Your dress is a little short. Would you like me to let it down a bit?*

6 *British* to allow the air to go out of something such as a car tyre = DEFLATE ≠ INFLATE

let sth down *Someone's let my tyres down.*
let down sth *It'll take us ages to let down the paddling pool.*

■ **letdown** /'letdaʊn/ noun [singular] something that makes you feel disappointed because it is not as good as you expected: *The whole concert was a bit of a letdown.*

,let 'in ★★

1 to allow someone to enter a house, room etc = *formal* ADMIT ≠ KEEP OUT

let sb/yourself in *Don't let anybody in – I'll be back in 15 minutes.* ◆ *She took her key out of her bag and let herself in.*

2 *informal* to talk to someone about your problems and feelings = OPEN UP TO

let sb in *You've got to learn to let me in.*

,let 'in for *informal*

to put yourself in a situation that may be more difficult than you expect

let yourself in for sth *She didn't know what she was letting herself in for when* *she married John.* ♦ *He must have wondered what he'd let himself in for.*

,let 'in on

to tell someone a secret = MAKE AWARE OF ≠ KEEP FROM

> **let sb in on sth** *They were planning something, but they wouldn't let me in on it.* ♦ *If you promise not to tell, I'll let you in on a secret.*

,let 'into ★★

1 to allow someone to enter a house, room etc

> **let sb into sth** *They didn't let any customers into the shop until ten o'clock sharp.* ♦ *He took out a key and let himself into the building.*

2 *same as* **let in on**

,let 'off ★★

1	allow sb to avoid sth
2	not punish sb
3	let sb get out of a car etc
4	fire a gun
5	explode a bomb
6	produce heat etc
+	PHRASE

1 *British* to allow someone not to do something that they were expecting to have to do = EXCUSE

> **let sb off sth** *When we were in port, he let me off work and allowed me to go ashore.*
> **let sb off** *It was my turn to wash the dishes, but she let me off.*

2 [often passive] to give someone little or no punishment for something wrong that they have done ≠ PUNISH

> **be let off** *I was pulled over for speeding, but I was let off with a warning.*
> **let sb off** *I'll let you off this time, but don't let it happen again.* ♦ *They let her off lightly because she's only sixteen.*

3 to allow a passenger to get out of a car or off a bus

> **let sb off** *You can let me off at the corner.*

4 to fire a gun or bullet

> **let off sth** *They let off frequent bursts of fire into the air.*
> **let sth off** *He had a gun, and he let it off a couple of times to frighten passers-by.*

5 to make something such as a bomb explode = EXPLODE, DETONATE

> **let off sth** *Terrorists were letting off bombs all over Iraq.*
> **let sth off** *Some kids had been letting fireworks off in the street.*

6 to produce, heat, light, sound etc = EMIT

> **let off sth** *Don't store wine on top of the fridge, which lets off heat.*

> **PHRASE** **let off steam** to shout or do

something that allows you to get rid of anger or energy: *We went to the park so the kids could let off steam before bedtime.*

,let 'on *informal*

1 to talk about something that is intended to be a secret = ADMIT

> **let on** *He knows more than he lets on.* ♦ *No one in the office is letting on what really happened.* ♦ **+to** *How did she plan the surprise party without letting on to her husband?* ♦ **+(that)** *Don't let on that I told you.*

2 to say or show that you have particular feelings, especially unpleasant ones such as anger or jealousy = REVEAL

> **let on** *He was more annoyed than he let on.*

,let 'out ★★★

1	allow sb to leave
2	make a noise
3	make clothing wider
4	allow sb to use a place
5	when people leave a place
+	**let-out** noun; **outlet** noun

1 to allow a person or animal to leave a place

> **let sb/sth out** *Would you let the dog out please?* ♦ *We don't let the kids out after dark.*

2 if someone lets out a particular noise, they make it = *formal* EMIT

> **let out sth** *As he walked away, he let out a sigh of relief.* ♦ *One of the prisoners let out a cry of pain.*

> Nouns often used as objects with **let out 2**
>
> ■ **cry, gasp, groan, howl, roar, scream, shriek, sigh, wail, yell**

3 to use the extra cloth in a fold of a piece of clothing in order to make it wider ≠ TAKE IN

> **let sth out** *I'm going to have to let this skirt out.*
> **let out sth** *Ask her if she'll let out my dress.*

4 *British* to allow someone to use a room, building etc in exchange for money = RENT OUT

> **let out sth** *We could always let out the spare room.*
> **let sth out** *Some people are buying houses to let them out.* ♦ *You could always let the main building out and live in the flat.*

5 *American* when school, a film etc lets out, it ends and people leave

> **let out** *It's very busy around here when the school lets out.*

■ **'let-out** noun [singular] *British informal*
a way of avoiding doing something that
you had previously said you would do:
*They'd given themselves a let-out by
writing a hidden clause in the contract.*

■ **outlet** /'aʊtlet/ noun [C] **1** a shop or
place where a particular product is
sold: *Most of their sales were through
traditional retail outlets.* **2** a way of
expressing strong feelings that you
would normally not express: *Many
young people find music their best outlet
for creative expression.* **3** a way of
making good use of extra physical
energy: *What he needed was an outlet
for all his excess energy.* **4** a pipe or hole
through which gas or liquid flows out:
a hot water outlet **5** *mainly American* a
place on a wall where you can connect
equipment to the electricity supply: *Do
not poke any object into a power outlet.*

ˌlet 'past *same as* **let through**

ˌlet 'through (*also* **ˌlet 'past**)
to allow someone to go past you to the
place where they want to go
let sb through *We moved aside to let the
doctor through.* ♦ *Let me past – I can't
see!*

ˌlet 'up ★

1 if something bad or unpleasant lets up,
it slows down or stops = EASE UP
≠ INTENSIFY
let up *The icy wind never let up for a
moment.* ♦ *Things haven't let up at the
office: I'm still working over 60 hours a
week.*

2 [usually with a negative] to put less effort
into something, especially something you
have been doing with great determination
= EASE OFF
let up *Boy, you just never let up, do you?*
♦ **+on/in** *He said the US should never
let up on human rights issues.* ♦ *They
did not let up in their efforts to convince
the president she was wrong.*

■ **'let-up** noun [singular] a pause or
reduction in something, especially
something unpleasant: *There's been no
let-up in the fighting all week.*

LEVEL /'lev(ə)l/
levels, levelling, levelled

'level at

1 to point a weapon at someone
level sth at sb *The man levelled a
revolver at me menacingly.*

2 level at or **level against** [usually passive]
to criticize or accuse someone in public
be levelled at sb *Some serious*

allegations have been levelled at the
bank. ♦ *Several criticisms have been
levelled at the company's board of
directors.* ♦ *Accusations of corruption
have been levelled against the politician
for many years.*

ˌlevel 'off ★ (*also* **ˌlevel 'out**)

1 [often passive] to make something flat
= FLATTEN
be levelled off *The ground will have to
be levelled off before we can start
building.*
level sth off *Fill each pot with soil and
level it off with a trowel.* ♦ *They had to
stamp down the undergrowth and level
the area off with rocks.*
level off sth *Level off the mixture with
the back of a spoon.*

2 to stop sloping or moving up or down
level off *The plane will level off at
around 35,000 feet.* ♦ *The road levels off
as you get close to the village.*

3 to stop increasing or decreasing, and
remain the same = STABILIZE, PLATEAU,
FLATTEN OFF
level off *Oil prices should level off now
that the war is over.* ♦ *After a rapid
increase, unemployment is starting to
level out.*

ˌlevel 'out *same as* **level off**

ˌlevel 'up
to increase or improve something in order
to make it the same as other things of its
type
level up sth *also* **level sth up** *The
government is levelling up the tax on
beer and wine.* ♦ *Companies are tending
to level their prices up.*

'level with *informal*
to be honest with someone
level with sb *I've got to level with you
Bill, I don't like it.*

LIAISE /li'eɪz/
liaises, liaising, liaised

li'aise with ★★
if one person liaises with another, they
talk to each other and tell each other what
they are doing, so that they can work
together effectively
liaise with sb *Social workers are liaising
with the police to decide on the best way
to deal with these offenders.*

LIE /laɪ/
lies, **lying** /ˈlaɪɪŋ/, **lay** /leɪ/, **lain** /leɪn/

> **Lie** is often used with adverbs and prepositions when it means 'to be on a particular surface or in a particular place': *She was lying on the bed watching TV.* ♦ *His arm lay across his chest.* ♦ *The village lies in a deep valley.* These uses are not included here.

,lie a'head

if something lies ahead, especially something difficult or unpleasant, it is going to happen in the future and you will have to deal with it

> **lie ahead** *With major new construction work on the main road, months of delays lie ahead.* ♦ *We need to be ready for whatever problems lie ahead.*

,lie a'round (*also* ,lie a'bout *British*)

1 [always progressive] to have been left somewhere instead of being put in the correct place

> **be lying around** *Never leave cash or other valuables lying around.* ♦ *There were bottles of pills lying around the house.*

2 to spend a lot of time relaxing, often when you should be doing something

> **lie around** *We lay around all day playing cards and watching television.*
> **lie around sth** *She spends the days lying around the house.*

,lie 'back ★

to move from a sitting position into a position in which you are lying flat on a surface = *formal* RECLINE

> **lie back** *She lay back and closed her eyes.*

,lie be'hind

to be the real reason for a decision or action

> **lie behind sth** *We'd like to know what lay behind her decision to change her will.*

,lie 'down ★★★

to put yourself in a position in which your body is flat on a surface such as a bed, usually because you want to rest or go to sleep ≠ STAND UP —*picture* → STAY UP

> **lie down** *Lie down and relax.* ♦ *I'm going to go and lie down for a while.*
> **PHRASES** **lie down on the job** to not work as hard at something as you should do: *You could never accuse Bill of lying down on the job.*
> **not take sth lying down** to show that you will not accept unfair treatment by complaining about it or trying to change it: *I'm not going to take this lying down.*

■ '**lie-down**   noun   [singular] *British* a short rest when you lie on a bed: *Your mother's gone for a lie-down.*

,lie 'in *British*

to stay in bed in the morning for longer than usual = SLEEP IN—*picture* → STAY UP

> **lie in** *We usually lie in on Sundays.*

■ '**lie-in**   noun   [singular] *British* a time when you stay in bed longer than usual in the morning: *I haven't had a proper lie-in since I had my children.*

'lie with

1 if something such as responsibility or blame for something lies with someone, they are responsible for it or they should be blamed for it

> **lie with sb** *There is evidence to suggest that some blame lies with the police.*

2 if something such as power or a decision lies with someone, they have power or the right to make a decision

> **lie with sb** *Unfortunately, the decision doesn't lie with our department.*

3 *old-fashioned* to have sex with someone

LIFT /lɪft/
lifts, **lifting**, **lifted**

,lift 'off

when an aircraft or space vehicle lifts off, it goes up from the ground into the air

> **lift off** *The rocket finally lifted off at 0800 hours.*

■ '**lift-off**   noun   [C/U] **1** the time when a space vehicle goes up from the ground into the air: *The flight crew prepared the vehicle for lift-off.* **2** *mainly journalism* the time when something important or exciting will happen: *With only five days to lift-off, the tournament organizers were very busy.*

,lift 'up ★★

to move something to a higher position, usually by taking it in your hands

> **lift up sth** *He lifted up the heavy bags.*
> **lift sth up** *He was strong enough to lift a whole car up.* ♦ *There was a dirty old rug and when I lifted it up I found £100 underneath.*

■ **uplift** /ʌpˈlɪft/   verb   to make someone feel happier or more hopeful: *The building was so gracious and beautiful. It uplifted him, as it always did.*

■ **uplift** /ˈʌplɪft/   noun   [singular/U] **1** an increase in amount or value: *an uplift in the value of shares* **2** a sudden feeling of happiness: *It's the spiritual uplift you get from doing good.*

■ **uplifting** /ʌpˈlɪftɪŋ/ **adj** making you feel happier or more hopeful: *It's a very funny and quite uplifting romantic comedy.*

LIGHT /laɪt/
lights, lighting, lit /lɪt/

ˌlight ˈinto *informal*
to attack someone physically or with cruel words because you are angry with them
= ATTACK
light into sb *He used to light into them whenever he thought they weren't working hard enough.*

ˈlight on (*also* ˈlight upon)
1 *formal* to suddenly find something, see something, or think of something
light on sth *Suddenly she lit on a new way of approaching the problem.* ♦ *A flash of recognition crossed his face as he lit on her name.*
2 if a bird or insect lights on something, it lands on it when it stops flying = ALIGHT ON
light on sth *The bird lit on a branch just above my head.*

ˌlight ˈup ★★★

1	light a cigarette
2	make a light shine brightly
3	become colourful
4	begin to shine
5	look happy or excited

1 *informal* to light a cigarette ≠ PUT OUT
light up *As soon as they got off the plane, the smokers lit up.*
light up sth *He lit up his third cigar of the evening.*
2 [often passive] to make light shine brightly in a place or object = *formal* ILLUMINATE
be lit up *All the buildings are lit up at night.*
light up sth *Fireworks were lighting up the night sky.*
light sth up *Electricity flows through the wire and lights the bulb up.* ♦ *The sun shone through the roof of the hut, lighting it up.*
3 to become bright or light with colour
light up *There was a flash of lightning and the sky lit up.* ♦ *When you switch the ignition on, the dashboard lights up.*
4 if part of a machine lights up, it starts to shine ≠ GO OUT
light up *A warning signal lit up on the dashboard.*
5 if someone's face or eyes light up, they suddenly look very happy or excited
= BRIGHTEN
light up *Antony's eyes lit up when Keiko walked into the room.* ♦ **+with** *Her face lit up with pleasure when she saw what Joe had done.*

LIGHTEN /ˈlaɪt(ə)n/
lightens, lightening, lightened

ˌlighten ˈup
1 to make a situation or someone's mood more relaxed
lighten sth up *What can we do to lighten things up?* ♦ *Interviews can be very daunting, and we wanted to find a way of lightening them up a bit.*
2 *informal* to relax and become less serious
= LOOSEN UP
lighten up *I wish you two would lighten up a little.* ♦ *Lighten up, Sam. I was only joking!*

LIKEN /ˈlaɪkən/
likens, likening, likened

ˈliken to ★★ [often passive]
to say that someone or something is similar to someone or something else
be likened to sb/sth *He is often likened to Napoleon.* ♦ *His works have been likened to those of Beckett.*
liken sb/sth to sb/sth *He likens the Nineties to the Sixties.* ♦ *The article likens Hinton to Admiral Rickover.*

LIMBER /ˈlɪmbə, *American* ˈlɪmbər/
limbers, limbering, limbered

ˌlimber ˈup
to do gentle exercises that make your muscles stretch, usually in order to prepare for taking part in a sport = WARM UP
limber up *The athletes are at the trackside limbering up for the race.*
limber up sth *These exercises are for limbering up the muscles in your upper body.*

LINE /laɪn/
lines, lining, lined

ˌline ˈup ★★★

1	stand in line
2	put in row
3	organize
4	move sth to correct position
5	want to do sth

1 to stand in a line or row = QUEUE UP
line up *All children must line up when*

the whistle goes. ♦ **+to do sth** *We all lined up to buy tickets.* ♦ **+for** *The soldiers lined up for inspection.*

2 to put people or things in a row
line up sb/sth *He likes lining up his toy cars one behind the other.*
line sb/sth up *She lined the dolls up neatly on the shelf.* ♦ *They lined us up and led us into a tall building.*

3 [often passive] to organize or prepare things for an event or series of events
= ARRANGE
be lined up *We have a series of activities lined up to keep you entertained.*
line up sb/sth *My secretary has not yet lined up a replacement for him.* ♦ **+to do sth** *I have lined up decorators to paint the stairs and landing.* ♦ **+for** *Her father had already lined up a job for her.*

4 to move something so that it is in the correct position in relation to something else, especially so that it is level with it
line sth up *He lined the ball up and kicked it straight into the net.* ♦ **+with** *He looked through the sight of the gun and lined it up with the enemy tank.*
line up sth *Now line up the left-hand margin of your document and the tab stop.* ♦ **+with** *To test your eyesight, hold a pen in front of you and line up its tip with some distant object.*

5 [often progressive] if a group of people line up to do something, they all want to do it at the same time = QUEUE UP
line up *A growing number of her colleagues are lining up to demand her resignation.*

■ **'line-up** noun [C usually singular] **1** a team of players who play in a particular sports game: *The Scotland eleven is an impressive line-up.* **2** the people who will perform at an event: *Tonight's line-up includes Tom Jones and Jools Holland.* **3** a set of television or radio programmes that are broadcast one after another: *We had to compete with the BBC's Saturday night line-up.* **4** mainly American a line of people that the police use to find out if someone who saw a crime recognizes any of them: *Would you be able to pick him out of a line-up?* = British IDENTITY PARADE

,line 'up against
to compete against another team or player in sport
line up against sb *He'll line up against the former world champion in tomorrow's match.*

,line 'up with (*also* ,line 'up behind)
to compete in the same team as someone in sport
line up with sb *He fulfils a dream when he lines up with his childhood hero tonight at the Arms Park.*

LINGER /ˈlɪŋɡə, *American* ˈlɪŋɡər/
lingers, lingering, lingered

,linger 'on
1 to last or continue for longer than people expected
linger on *Ten years later, the memory still lingers on.* ♦ *Some childish ideas linger on in all of us.*
2 to be alive, although very ill, for a long time after you seemed likely to die
linger on *He did not want to linger on in pain and without dignity.*

'linger on
to continue looking at someone or something, especially because they are very attractive
linger on sb/sth *His eyes lingered on her face.*

'linger over
1 to stay somewhere longer than necessary, or to spend longer than necessary doing something, because you are enjoying it
linger over sth *The waiters encourage you to linger over your meal.*
2 to continue looking at someone or something, especially because they are very attractive
linger over sb/sth *The camera lingers over this touching scene.*

LINK /lɪŋk/
links, linking, linked

,link 'up ★★
1 to make a connection with something
link up *The two planes link up by means of a fuel pipe.* ♦ **+with** *The space shuttle will link up with the space station this afternoon.*
2 to connect one thing or person to another
link sb/sth up *We found apparently unrelated bits of information and tried to link them up.* ♦ **+with** *We advise small businesses and link them up with private investors.*
3 to join with someone in order to do something together
link up with sb/sth *We are interested in linking up with an overseas club.*
4 to connect computers or computer

systems so that electronic messages can be sent between them

link up to sth *All our computers link up to a central server.*

link up with sth *The Internet allows users to link up with people from anywhere in the world.*

■ **linkup** /ˈlɪŋkʌp/ **noun** [C] **1** a connection between machines or electronic equipment: *Viewers are able to see the events live, via a satellite linkup.* **2** an agreement between two companies to become closely related or to become business partners: *In 1961 he formed a linkup between Bryanston and an American company.*

LIQUOR /ˈlɪkə, American ˈlɪkər/
liquors, liquoring, liquored

be ˌliquored ˈup *American informal*
to have drunk too much alcohol = BE DRUNK

be liquored up *They were so liquored up they missed their train.*

LISTEN /ˈlɪs(ə)n/
listens, listening, listened

ˌlisten ˈin ★

1 to secretly listen to what someone says = EAVESDROP

listen in *Talk quietly, you never know who might be listening in.* ♦ **+on** *Rachel was listening in on our conversation.*

2 to listen to a radio programme = TUNE IN

listen in *If you like country music, remember to listen in at 8 o'clock tonight.* ♦ **+to** *Over a million people listened in to that broadcast.*

ˌlisten ˈout for (*also* **ˈlisten for**) *British*
to listen carefully to try and hear a sound that you are waiting for or hoping to hear

listen out for sth *I was listening out for their footsteps.* ♦ *Listen out for the children, will you?*

ˌlisten ˈup [always in imperative] *mainly American informal*
used for getting the attention of a noisy group of people = LISTEN, PAY ATTENTION

listen up *Hey, listen up everybody!*

LITTER /ˈlɪtə, American ˈlɪtər/
litters, littering, littered

be ˈlittered with ★★

1 if a place is littered with things, they are spread around there in an untidy way

be littered with sth *The room was littered with broken glass.*

2 *showing disapproval* if something is littered with bad things such as quarrels or mistakes, it includes many of them

be littered with sth *The report was littered with examples of bad English.* ♦ *The history of pop music is littered with disputes between songwriting partners.*

LIVE /lɪv/
lives, living, lived

ˈlive by
to behave according to a particular set of standards or beliefs

live by sth *We cannot expect children to live by our adult standards too early.* ♦ *He argued that even criminals have a code of ethics that they live by.*

PHRASE **live by your wits** to have no real job and make the money you need by being clever or dishonest: *On the street, you learn to live by your wits.*

ˌlive ˈdown [usually with a negative]
to make people forget about something embarrassing or silly that you have done

live sth down *also* **live down sth** *She was trying to live down her reputation as a 'difficult actress'.* ♦ *All the girls in my class are going except me! I'll never live it down!*

ˈlive for
to believe that someone or something is so important that they are your main reason for living

live for sth/sb *He lives for his work.* ♦ *She had lived for her son, and she found being without him unbearable.*

PHRASES **have something/nothing/everything to live for** to have a reason to want to stay alive: *When he lost his job, he felt he had nothing left to live for.* ♦ *Gregory was 21 and had everything to live for.*

live for the day when to want something to happen very much: *He lived for the day when he would be old enough to drive a car.*

live for the moment to enjoy the present time and not think about the future: *They lived for the moment and were completely happy.*

ˌlive ˈin *British*
to live at the place where you work or study ≠ LIVE OUT

live in *Their nanny lives in.* ♦ *A lot of students these days can't afford to live in.*

■ **live-in** /ˈlɪv ɪn/ **adj** [only before noun]
1 living in the house where you also work: *She's the only person I know with*

a live-in housekeeper. **2** not married to someone but living with them and having a sexual relationship with them: *How is he enjoying life with his live-in girlfriend?*

■ **'lived-in** /'lɪvd ɪn/ **adj** **1** a lived-in place looks comfortable and not new or completely tidy: *His flat had that **lived-in look** that I associate with single men.* **2** *informal* someone who has a lived-in face is rather old, but looks as if they have had an interesting life: *She has the lived-in face that all good character actors have.*

'live off ★★

1 to depend on someone or something for the money or food that you need
    live off sb/sth *He's 25 and still living off his parents.* ♦ *For the next five years, she lived off the proceeds of the sale of her house.*
2 to eat a particular kind of food, especially in order to stay alive = LIVE ON; *formal* SUBSIST ON
    live off sth *Left alone, teenagers will live off nothing but takeaway pizza.* ♦ *You sleep under the stars and live off whatever food you can find.*
    PHRASES **live off the fat of the land** *showing disapproval* to have a comfortable and enjoyable life without doing any work: *Rich merchants lived off the fat of the land.*
    live off the land to live on whatever food you can get by hunting, finding fruit, or growing vegetables: *This is a region where it's easy to live off the land.*

'live on ★★★

1 to have a particular amount of money to buy the things that you need to live = SURVIVE ON
    live on sth *I couldn't live on such a small amount of money.* ♦ *£50 a week is not enough to live on.*
2 to eat a particular kind of food, especially in order to stay alive = LIVE OFF; *formal* SUBSIST ON
    live on sth *These fish live on small sea creatures such as shrimp.* ♦ *They seem to live on nothing but hamburgers and fries.*
    PHRASE **be living on borrowed time**
1 to still be living after you were expected to die, but likely to die soon: *He's survived his third heart attack, but he knows he's living on borrowed time.*
2 to be likely to fail or stop existing soon: *The last remaining coal mines are now living on borrowed time.*

,live 'on

to continue to exist = SURVIVE
    live on *Her memory still lives on.* ♦ *His name lives on in the title of Lamplugh House.*

,live 'out

1 to spend the rest of your life in a particular place or situation
    live out sth *She wanted to live out the remaining weeks of her life at home.*
    ♦ **+in** *We imagined living out our days in happiness.*
2 *British* to not live at the place where you work or study ≠ LIVE IN
    live out *Universities do not have enough accommodation, so some students have to live out.*
    PHRASE **live out your dreams/fantasies** to do something that you have wanted to do, but thought that you would never be able to do: *The inheritance would allow her to live out her fantasies.* ♦ *Your wedding day is when you can live out your wildest dreams.*

,live 'through ★★

to experience a dangerous or unpleasant situation and still be alive after it
= SURVIVE, ENDURE
    live through sth *These are people who have lived through two world wars.*

'live together ★★

if two people live together, they are not married but live in the same house and have a sexual relationship = COHABIT
    live together *We've been living together for three years now.*

,live 'up

    PHRASE **live it up** *informal* to do enjoyable and exciting things that involve spending a lot of money: *I'm stuck at home with the kids and you're living it up with your friends!*

,live 'up to

to be as good as people expect it to be
= MATCH
    live up to sth *She certainly lived up to her reputation as a controversial speaker.* ♦ *University didn't quite live up to her expectations.* ♦ *Your brother was a great worker. You have a lot to live up to.*

'live with ★★★

1 to live in the same house and have a sexual relationship with someone you are not married to
    live with sb *How long have you been living with your boyfriend?*
2 to accept something unpleasant that

you cannot change = PUT UP WITH, TOLERATE
live with sth *How does she live with the guilt? ♦ He had learnt to live with her moodiness.*

3 if something lives with you, you keep remembering it or thinking about it
live with sb *The memory of that day would live with her forever.*
PHRASES **I can live with sth** used for saying that you can accept something: *It's a little less than I asked for, but I can live with that.*
live with yourself [usually with a negative or in questions] to continue to think that you are a good person, even after doing something bad: *I could never live with myself if I hit a child with my car. ♦ I don't know how she can live with herself after walking out on her kids.*

LIVEN /ˈlaɪv(ə)n/
livens, livening, livened

,liven 'up ★
1 to make something more interesting or exciting = SPICE UP ≠ TONE DOWN
liven sth up *What we needed was some music to liven things up. ♦ In order to liven their party up, she had ordered a stripper.*
liven up sth *The arrival of Tim certainly livened up the day. ♦ Visual aids are great for livening up boring presentations.*
♦ +with *You can liven up a plain shirt with a colourful scarf.*

2 to become more interesting or exciting
liven up *On April 25th things began to liven up.*

3 to make someone have more energy or enthusiasm than they had before
= ENERGIZE
liven sb up *Perhaps a walk in the park would liven us up.*

4 to have more energy or enthusiasm than you had before
liven up *Everyone seemed to liven up after they'd had something to eat.*

LOAD /ləʊd, American loʊd/
loads, loading, loaded

,load 'down [usually passive]
1 if you are loaded down with a lot of heavy things, you are carrying them
= WEIGH DOWN
be loaded down *I'd done most of the shopping the day before so I wasn't loaded down. ♦ +with The students were loaded down with rucksacks.*

2 if you are loaded down with responsibilities, problems, or work, you

have more than you can deal with = WEIGH DOWN
be loaded down with sth *He felt loaded down with the responsibility of government.*

,load 'up
1 to put a load onto or into something such as a vehicle or container = FILL UP ≠ UNLOAD
load up sth *also* **load sth up** *'I've got a lot of things to buy,' he said, loading up his trolley. ♦ I'll help you load the car up. ♦ +with She loaded her bag up with clothes and shoes.*

2 to give someone a lot of things to carry
load sb up with sth *She loaded him up with food and other treats and sent him on his way.*

3 to put information or a program into a computer
load up sth *also* **load sth up** *You can load up the software from a laptop.*

,load 'up on American
to buy a lot of something so that it is available when you need it = STOCK UP ON
load up on sth *Why are you loading up on canned food?*

LOAF /ləʊf, American loʊf/
loafs, loafing, loafed

,loaf a'round (also ,loaf a'bout British)
informal
to spend time doing nothing, usually when you should be working
loaf around *I just loafed around, eating and watching television.*
loaf around sth *All you do is loaf around the house all day!*

LOCK /lɒk, American lɑk/
locks, locking, locked

,lock a'way ★
1 [often passive] to put something in a place or container which you fasten with a lock
be locked away *Valuable items should be locked away.*
lock away sth *She had locked away her diaries in a trunk, and they had stayed there until her death.*
lock sth away *She took the key off her key ring and locked it away. ♦ We always lock all important documents away.*

2 [often passive] to put someone in prison, or in a hospital for mentally ill people
= PUT AWAY ≠ RELEASE
be locked away *After the murder he was locked away for 50 years.*
lock sb away *I was there when they*

arrested my brother and locked him away.

3 to go somewhere where you can be alone = SHUT AWAY

lock yourself away *James locked himself away in his bedroom.* ♦ *She locked herself away in a dance studio for a week to practise her routine.*

,lock 'in ★★★

1 to put someone in a room and lock the door so they cannot leave

lock sb in *I didn't mean to lock you in.*
lock yourself in *She went to her hotel room and locked herself in.*
lock sb in sth *I managed to lock him in the cellar until the police arrived.*
lock yourself in sth *He locks himself in his room for hours at a time.*

2 to get a financial benefit that lasts for a long time, for example by selling shares that have gone up in value before they can go back down

lock in profits/gains etc *The scheme locks in profits by paying yearly bonuses.*

3 [always passive] to be involved in a serious discussion or argument

be locked in sth *Union leaders and bosses were locked in negotiations.*

,lock 'in on *same as* lock onto

,lock 'into [often passive]

to involve someone or something in a system, plan etc in such a way that they cannot easily escape from it

be locked into sth *The currency is now locked into the European Monetary System.*
lock sb/sth into sth *Their strategy is to lock subscribers into long-term contracts.*
lock yourself into sth *Under this plan, you are locking yourself into another five years of mortgage payments.*

,lock 'onto (*also* ,lock 'in on)

if a missile, or a vehicle carrying missiles, locks onto something, it has found out its position and is preparing to destroy it

lock onto sth *The enemy planes had locked onto us.* ♦ *They had locked in on the target.*

,lock 'out ★

1 to prevent someone from coming into a room or building by locking the door = SHUT OUT

lock sb out *If her husband comes home drunk, she locks him out.* ♦ **+of** *He locked her out of the house after an argument.*
lock yourself out *I've locked myself out again – could I use your phone?* ♦ **+of** *That's the third time I've locked myself out of my hotel room.*

lock out sb *They barred the door to lock out any latecomers.*

2 if a company locks out its workers, it closes their place of work so that they cannot go to work until they agree to the employer's conditions

lock out sb *The mine owners locked out those miners who would not work for lower rates of pay.*
lock sb out *This is the first time any company has locked its workers out.* ♦ *The employers were threatening to lock us out.*

■ **lockout** /'lɒkaʊt/ **noun** [C] a situation in which a company refuses to allow workers to come to work until they accept the working conditions that the company is offering them: *There were threats of a lockout.*

,lock 'up ★★★

1 [often passive] to lock all the doors and windows of a building or vehicle so that no one can get in ≠ UNLOCK

be locked up *The house was all locked up.*
lock up sth *The last person to leave locks up the office.*
lock sth up *Someone attacked her when she was locking her car up.* ♦ *The office could easily be burgled if you don't lock it up.*
lock up *I locked up and went to bed.*

2 [often passive] to put something in a place or container that you fasten with a lock

be locked up *Make sure all harmful substances are securely locked up.*
lock up sth *Had he locked up his gun safely?*
lock sth up *The jewels are very valuable so we always lock them up after they have been worn.* ♦ *We lock any spare cash up in this box.*

3 [often passive] to put someone in prison or in a hospital for mentally ill people = PUT AWAY ≠ RELEASE

be locked up *He was locked up for 12 years for armed robbery.*
lock sb up *They're not going to lock you up just because you're depressed.*
lock up sb *To lock up young car thieves is taking action too late.*

4 [usually passive] to invest your money in something, so that it is not available for you to spend = TIE UP

be locked up *I don't have a lot of cash to spend because most of my money is locked up.* ♦ **+in** *There are vast sums of money locked up in pension funds.*

■ **lockup** /'lɒkʌp/ **noun 1** [C] British a garage that you can rent to keep a vehicle in, or to store goods in: *The equipment is kept in a lockup near the hotel.* **2** [U] a small prison in a village or town, where the police can keep a criminal for a short period of time: *The smaller stations don't even have one lockup.*

LOG /lɒg, *American* lɔg/
logs, logging, logged

log 'in (*also* log 'into) *same as* log on
■ **login** /'lɒgɪn/ **noun** **1** [C/U] the process of performing the necessary actions to start using a computer program or system: *Last login: Friday 16 March, 2004* **2** [C] your name, or another special word, that you type into a computer in order to be able to start using a program or system: *The program is verifying your login.*

log 'off (*also* log 'out)
to finish using a computer system, for example by typing a particular word = EXIT ≠ LOG ON
log off *If the system is running slowly, try logging off and logging on again.*
♦ **+of** *Make sure you log out of the system properly before you switch off.*

log 'on
log on or **log onto** or **log in** or **log into** to start using a computer system, for example by typing a particular word = GAIN ACCESS ≠ LOG OFF
log on *Can you log on for me?*
log onto sth *You need a password to log onto the company system.*
log in *I can't log in if I don't know the password.*
log into sth *How many users can log into the system at any given time?*

log 'out *same as* log off
■ **logout** /'lɒgaʊt/ **noun** [C/U] the process of performing the necessary actions to close a computer program or system: *Last logout: Monday January 5th, 2005*

LOLL /lɒl, *American* lɑl/
lolls, lolling, lolled

loll a'round (*also* loll a'bout *British*)
to sit, stand, or lie in a relaxed position
loll around *I spent the day lolling around on the sofa watching TV.*

LONG /lɒŋ, *American* lɔŋ/
longs, longing, longed

long for ★★
to want something very much = HANKER AFTER; *literary* YEARN FOR
long for sb/sth *It was freezing outside, and Marcia was longing for a hot drink.*
♦ *This was the excitement that she had secretly longed for.*
long for sb to do sth *I was tired and was longing for her to leave.*

LOOK /lʊk/
looks, looking, looked

look a'bout ★ *same as* look around 1

look a'cross
to look at someone or something that is some distance away, often on the opposite side of the room
look across *Marion looked across to see if her mother was still watching her.*
♦ **+at** *He looked across at the central desk.* ♦ *Cranston looked across at Simpson and nodded.*

look after ★★★
1 [often passive] to take care of someone or something and make certain that they have everything they need or that they are safe = TAKE CARE OF —*picture* → TAKE AFTER
be looked after *You could tell that the car had been well looked after.*
look after sb/sth *It's hard work looking after three children all day.* ♦ *They looked after the dog for us while we were away.* ♦ *Will you look after my bag for me?* ♦ *I hope you're looking after yourself.*
2 to be responsible for dealing with something = TAKE CARE OF
look after sth *They promised to look after the interests of disabled people.*
♦ *Who's looking after the department while you're away?*
PHRASES **be able to look after yourself**
to not need anyone else to take care of you: *I don't need you to fight my battles for me. I can look after myself.*
look after yourself *British informal* used for saying goodbye to someone you know well = TAKE CARE: *See you next week. Look after yourself!*

look a'head
to think about what is likely to happen, or to plan what you are going to do in the future = LOOK FORWARD
look ahead *Looking ahead, I think the company must develop some new services.*
♦ **+to** *Professional sportsmen have to*

look ahead to a time when they can no longer play sport for a living.

ˌlook aˈround ★★ (also ˌlook ˈround British)

1 **look around** or **look about** British to look at the area around you

look around *When you look around, all you see are fields.*

look around you *She stopped walking and slowly looked around her.*

2 to walk around a room, building, or place and see what is there

look around sth *Do you want to look around the school?* ♦ *Shall we go and look around the shops?*

look around *We were only in Paris for a couple of hours, so I didn't have time to look around.*

3 to try to find something that you want or need = SEARCH

look around *We've been looking around for a while now, but still haven't found a house we like.* ♦ **+for** *He was advised to start looking around for other work.*

ˈlook at ★★★

1	move your eyes to see sb/sth
2	think about sth carefully
3	read sth
4	examine sth
5	used for giving an example
+	PHRASES

1 to direct your eyes towards someone or something so that you can see them

look at sb/sth *He turned and looked at her.* ♦ *I couldn't stop looking at her purple hair.* ♦ *She couldn't see what he was looking at.*

2 to think about a situation or subject carefully, especially in order to make a decision = CONSIDER, EXAMINE

look at sth *We're looking at all the options carefully.*

look at how/why/where etc *You need to look at how you can spend less time working.*

3 to read something quickly

look at sth *Would you like me to look at your essay before you hand it in?*

4 if an expert looks at someone or something, they examine them and decide what to do

look at sb/sth *I'd like a skin specialist to look at that rash of yours.* ♦ *Could you look at my car, please – the gears are making a strange noise.* ♦ *The doctor will look at your baby and tell you if there is anything to worry about.*

5 [always in imperative] *informal* used for giving an example that proves that what you are saying is true

look at sb *Look at Helen. She's much happier now that she has a new job.* ♦ *You can recover from a broken marriage. Look at me.*

PHRASES **look at that** *informal* used for telling someone to look at something because it is surprising, unusual etc: *Look at that! Someone's taken my parking space!*

look at you *informal* **1** used for telling someone that you are surprised or impressed by them: *Look at you, all dressed up in a suit!* **2** used for telling someone that you are not impressed by them, especially in reply to a comment they have made about you or your behaviour: *Look at you! It's eleven o'clock and you're still in bed.*

not look twice at used for saying that you are not at all interested in someone or something: *I wouldn't look twice at someone like him.*

not much to look at *informal* not very attractive: *He's not much to look at but he's got a great personality.*

ˌlook aˈway ★★★

to direct your eyes away from someone or something so that you cannot see them

look away *Mrs Shottery looked away in embarrassment.*

ˌlook ˈback ★★★

to think about a time or event in the past = REMEMBER, RECALL

look back *Looking back, I think I made the right decision.* ♦ **+on** *Most people look back on their schooldays with fondness.* ♦ *Looking back on it, I've absolutely no idea why I said that.*

PHRASE **sb never looked back** used for saying that someone achieved something special and then became even more successful: *I took the art college offer and have never looked back.*

■ **ˈbackward-ˌlooking** adj not interested in new ideas or ways of doing things = REACTIONARY: *Their views were blatantly traditional and unashamedly backward-looking.* ♦ *He radically transformed a weak and backward-looking organization into an internationally renowned art school.*

ˌlook ˈdown ★★

to direct your eyes to the ground, especially because you are embarrassed or ashamed

look down *He blushed and looked down at the floor.*

look 'down on

to think that you are better or more important than someone else, or to think that they are not good enough for you
= SCORN ≠ LOOK UP TO

look down on sb *He looks down on anyone who didn't go to university.*
♦ *The worst mistake a manager can make is to look down on her staff.*

'look for ★★★ [usually progressive]

1 to hope to get something or someone that you want or need

look for sb/sth *He was looking for work as a builder.* ♦ *We are looking for a partner in a new business venture.* ♦ *The agency provides a list of things to look for when hiring a nanny.* ♦ *This is just the sort of opportunity I was looking for.*

2 to try to find someone or something
= SEARCH FOR

look for sb/sth *I'm looking for Jim. Have you seen him anywhere?* ♦ *We spent half the morning looking for the keys.*

3 to try to discover the facts about something in order to understand it

look for sth *The police were looking for clues as to the woman's identity.* ♦ *A team of explosives experts looked for signs of terrorist activity.*

Nouns often used as objects with **look for 3**

■ answer, cause, clue, evidence, explanation, motive, reason, sign, solution

PHRASE **be looking for trouble** *informal* behaving in a way that is likely to get you involved in an argument or fight: *He walked into the bar looking for trouble.*

look for (sense 2)

look 'forward to ★★★

to feel happy and excited about something that is going to happen = ANTICIPATE
≠ DREAD

look forward to sth *He had worked hard and was looking forward to his retirement.* ♦ *We're looking forward to the day when things will be a bit easier.*
look forward to doing sth *I'm really looking forward to working with you.*
♦ *She's looking forward to having more time to spend with the family.*

■ **'forward-,looking** adj looking at the future in a positive way and happy to try new ideas and methods: *The question now is whether Mr Clinton is going to be forward-looking.* ♦ *Forward-looking companies such as Sumitomo are introducing these systems.*

look 'in

to visit someone for a short time, often on your way to another place, especially if they are ill or may need help = POP IN

look in *I'll look in later and see if you need anything.* ♦ **+on** *Can you look in on Eileen and see if she needs anything from the supermarket?*

■ **'look-in** noun *British informal* PHRASE **get/have a look-in** [usually with a negative or in questions] to get an opportunity to take part in something or show how well you can do something: *Ordinary members of the party hardly got a look-in.*

look 'into ★★★

to try to discover the facts about something such as a problem or crime
= INVESTIGATE

look into sth *We're looking into the possibility of updating our computer network.* ♦ *I wrote a letter of complaint and the airline have promised to look into the matter.* ♦ *Detectives are looking into the circumstances surrounding the death of a man in Times Square.*

Nouns often used as objects with **look into**

■ allegations, case, circumstances, complaint, matter, possibility, problem, question

'look on

look on or **look upon** to think of someone or something in a particular way = THINK OF, REGARD AS

look on sb/sth as sth *We're not related but I look on him as a brother.* ♦ *I look on it as a challenge.*
look on sb/sth with sth *Thirty years ago, kids would have looked on such music with contempt.*

■ **onlooker** /ˈɒnˌlʊkə/ noun [C] someone who watches something happen but does not take part in it: *The* *incident attracted a crowd of amused onlookers.*

,look 'on ★★★

to watch an activity or event without taking part in it

look on *Phil looked on in disbelief as Maggie got up on the table and started to dance.* ♦ *This was humiliating enough without an audience looking on.*

,look 'out ★★ [always in imperative]

used for warning someone to be careful, especially because they are likely to have an accident

look out! *Look out, there's a car coming!*

■ **lookout** /'lʊkaʊt/ **noun** [C] **1** someone who is responsible for watching for danger and warning other people: *Smith acted as lookout and guide on our trip.* **2** a place that is suitable for watching whether someone or something is coming, especially in a dangerous situation: *At the top of the hill was a military lookout.*

,look 'out for ★★★

1 to look carefully at people or things around you in order to try to find a particular person or thing

look out for sb/sth *Mary said she was going to the concert too and would look out for us.* ♦ *She was excited about Greg's visit and spent most of the morning looking out for his car.* ♦ *We were told to look out for a blue van.*

2 to take care of someone and make sure that they are treated well = WATCH OUT FOR

look out for sb *I'm the oldest, and I always look out for my younger sisters.*

PHRASE **look out for yourself** or **look out for number one** to think only about yourself, and not worry or care about other people: *In this business, you have to look out for number one.*

,look 'out over

if a building or room looks out over something, you can see that thing in front of you when you look out of the window

look out over sth *My hotel room looked out over the bay.*

,look 'over

1 to look at someone or something that is some distance away, often on the opposite side of a room = LOOK ACROSS

look over *A man on the other side of the room looked over and waved.* ♦ **+at** *Johnson looked over at her, trying to catch her eye.*

2 to read through something, usually quickly = GO THROUGH

look over sth *He'd been looking over the leaflets he'd picked up earlier.* ♦ *If you're worried about your application, I'd be happy to look over it.*

3 to visit a place in order to examine it = INSPECT

look over sth *also* **look sth over** *An American inspection team had looked over the weapons sites in January.* ♦ *He was having a new house built, and he asked me to look it over for him.*

■ **overlook** /ˌəʊvə'lʊk/ **verb** [T] **1** to fail to notice or do something: *Accidents happen when safety checks are overlooked.* **2** to fail to consider someone or something, or to recognize success: *Sean Connery was once again overlooked in the New Year's Honours list.* **3** to have a view of something from above: *Our hotel overlooked the Temple of Luxor and the river.* **4** to choose to ignore a mistake, fault etc: *I'm prepared to overlook his indiscretions.*

,look 'round *British same as* **look around**

'look through ★★

1 to read something quickly, especially to find the information you need

look through sth *I've just been looking through your cookbooks for inspiration.*

2 to try to find something among a lot of other things = GO THROUGH

look through sth *I'll look through these files and see if I can find a copy of the letter.*

,look 'through

to not recognize, or to pretend not to recognize, someone that you know ≠ ACKNOWLEDGE

look through sb *I saw Angela this morning, but she looked right through me.*

'look to

1 to hope or expect to get help, advice etc from someone = DEPEND ON

look to sb for sth *As young children, we looked to our parents for guidance.*

look to sb to do sth *They're looking to me to help improve sales figures.*

2 to give all your attention to something

look to sth *The party needs to look to the future and forget its past problems.*

PHRASE **look to your laurels** to work hard in order to prevent someone from being more successful than you: *The reigning champion should look to her laurels.*

,look 'up ★★

1 to try to find a particular piece of

information by looking in a book or on a list, or by using a computer

look sth up *Have you looked any of these words up?* ♦ *I didn't know what 'loquacious' meant and had to look it up in a dictionary.*

look up sth *I'm trying to look up the phone numbers of all my old college friends.*

2 [usually progressive] if a situation is looking up, it is getting better = IMPROVE ≠ WORSEN

look up *She's had a terrible year, but things are looking up now.* ♦ **+for** *Finally, things are starting to look up for me.*

3 to go and see someone you know when you are visiting the place where they live = CALL ON

look sb up *Look me up next time you come to London.*

look up sb *It'll give me the chance to look up some old friends.*

4 to direct your eyes upwards so that you can see someone or something

look up *Jo looked up from her work, yawning.*

look up

'look upon *same as* **'look on**

,look 'up to
to admire and respect someone = ADMIRE ≠ LOOK DOWN ON

look up to sb *I always looked up to my older brother.* ♦ *He's a role model for other players to look up to.*

LOOM /luːm, *American* luːm/
looms, looming, loomed

,loom 'up
to appear as a large shape that is not clear, usually in a threatening way

loom up *Suddenly a huge truck loomed*

up ahead of us. ♦ **+out of** *A tall ship loomed up out of the fog.*

LOOP /luːp, *American* luːp/
loops, looping, looped

,loop a'round
to curl something long and thin around something

loop sth around sth *He looped a scarf around his neck.*

LOOSE /luːs, *American* luːs/
looses, loosing, loosed

,loose 'off
to fire something such as a bullet, missile, or arrow = FIRE

loose off sth *The policeman managed to loose off four shots.* ♦ **+at** *He loosed off an arrow at a squirrel.*

'loose on (*also* **'loose upon**) [usually passive] *literary*
to suddenly let something bad or unpleasant have its full effect on someone or something in an uncontrolled way

be loosed on sb/sth *Once good and evil are loosed on the world they cannot be called back.*

LOOSEN /ˈluːs(ə)n, *American* ˈluːs(ə)n/
loosens, loosening, loosened

,loosen 'up ★

1 to exercise your muscles, usually before doing physical activity = LIMBER UP, WARM UP

loosen up *You need to loosen up a bit before you start a workout.*

loosen up sth *This is a good exercise for loosening up your shoulders.*

loosen sth up *We always loosen the knees up first.* ♦ *It warms your muscles up and loosens them up too.*

2 *informal* to relax or become less serious, or to make someone relax or become less serious = LIGHTEN UP

loosen up *You need to loosen up – get rid of some inhibitions.*

loosen sb up *But the smile we had shared had loosened him up.*

loosen up sb *We find a glass of wine loosens up the most nervous of clients.*

LOP /lɒp, *American* lɑp/
lops, lopping, lopped

,lop 'off

1 to cut something off something else in one smooth movement

lop off sth *also* **lop sth off** *They lopped*

off more branches to help save the tree.
♦ *He had lopped his thumb off on a bacon slicer.*
lop sth off sth *She had lopped about six inches off my hair.*
2 to reduce something, especially by a large amount
lop sth off sth *The awful renovations had lopped £10,000 off the value of the house.* ♦ *The new rail link will lop an hour off journey times.*

LORD /lɔːd, American lɔrd/
lords, lording, lorded

'lord over *showing disapproval*
PHRASE **lord it over sb** to treat someone as if you think that you are much more important than they are, for example by telling them what to do: *He was the most unpopular man on the movie set – always turning up late, and lording it over everyone.*

LOSE /luːz, American luz/
loses, losing, lost /lɒst, American lɔst/

,lose 'in
1 [always passive] if you are lost in something that you are doing or thinking, you are giving so much attention to it that you do not notice other things around you
be lost in sth *He was soon lost in his memories of his schooldays.* ♦ *She smiled and was lost in thought for a moment.*
2 to give so much of your attention and energy to something that you do not think of or deal with anything else
lose yourself in sth *He escaped from life by losing himself in books.*

,lose 'out ★★
to not get a benefit that someone else is getting = MISS OUT
lose out *The proposal is likely to be opposed by the four countries which could lose out.* ♦ **+to** *If we don't act quickly, we'll lose out to another company.* ♦ **+on** *The report claims that Scotland is losing out on health funding.*

LOUNGE /laʊndʒ/
lounges, lounging, lounged

,lounge a'round (*also* ,lounge a'bout British)
to spend time relaxing or doing nothing in a place
lounge around *He showed me a photo of them lounging around in their house.*
lounge around sth *We spent the day lounging around the hotel pool.*

LOUSE /laʊs/
louses, lousing, loused

,louse 'up *American informal*
1 to spoil something = MESS UP
louse up sth *also* **louse sth up** *I don't want to louse up her chances of being happy.* ♦ *He doesn't need me lousing things up for him.*
2 to do something badly = MESS UP
louse up sth *also* **louse sth up** *I loused up the interview and didn't get the job.* ♦ *If he has to give a speech he'll only louse it up.*

LOVE /lʌv/
loves, loving, loved

be/get ,loved 'up
1 *informal* if someone is loved up, they are in a happy mood in which they like everybody, especially because they have been drinking or taking drugs
be/get loved up *She got all loved up on Ecstasy.*
2 *informal* if you are loved up, you are feeling full of love and emotion
be/get loved up *Which of these romantic songs gets you all loved up?*

LUCK /lʌk/
lucks, lucking, lucked

,luck 'into *American informal*
to find or achieve something good by chance
luck into sth *I lucked into a great apartment on the beach.*

,luck 'out *mainly American informal*
to be lucky
luck out *We lucked out and got the last two tickets.*

LULL /lʌl/
lulls, lulling, lulled

'lull into
to make someone feel relaxed or confident so that they are not prepared for something unpleasant that happens
lull sb into (doing) sth *They were trying to lull me into believing nothing was wrong.* ♦ *Their reports lulled us into a false sense of security* (=made us think that everything was fine when it was not).

LUMBER /ˈlʌmbə, *American* ˈlʌmbər/
lumbers, lumbering, lumbered

'lumber with [usually passive]
to give someone a job or responsibility
that they do not want = SADDLE WITH
be lumbered with sth *I'm sorry you've
been lumbered with driving me home.*

LUMP /lʌmp/
lumps, lumping, lumped

lump to'gether
to put people or things into the same
group, although they do not really belong
together
lump together sb/sth *also* **lump sb/sth
together** *They're lumping together all
of these children.*

LUST /lʌst/
lusts, lusting, lusted

'lust after (*also* **'lust for**)
1 to want to have sex with a particular
person
lust after sb *She had secretly lusted after
him for months.*
2 *often humorous* to want something very
much
lust after sth *The motor show was full
of young men lusting after fast cars.*

LUXURIATE /lʌgˈzjʊərieɪt, *American*
lʌgˈʒʊriˌeɪt/
luxuriates, luxuriating, luxuriated

lux'uriate in
to enjoy something that is very pleasant,
comfortable, or relaxing
luxuriate in sth *We sat on the river bank
and luxuriated in the cool breeze.*

M m

MAGIC /ˈmædʒɪk/
magics, magicking, magicked

magic a'way *British*
to make someone or something disappear
magic sth away *also* **magic away sth**
*This medicine will magic the pain away
in no time.* ♦ *Nothing can magic away
life's problems.*

magic 'up *British*
to make someone or something appear
magic up sth *also* **magic sth up** *Patricia
can magic up a delicious meal in five
minutes.*

MAIL /meɪl/
mails, mailing, mailed

'mail off *mainly American*
to send a letter, parcel etc by post
mail sth off *also* **mail off sth** *I wanted to
mail it off right away.* ♦ *She needs to
mail off this letter.*

'mail out
to send many copies of a letter,
advertisement etc by mail at one time
= SEND OUT
mail out sth *I mailed out 100 copies of
my CV.* ♦ **+to** *They mailed out
questionnaires to all of their customers.*
mail sth out *I asked John to mail the
leaflets out as soon as possible.*
■ **'mail-out** noun [C] a letter or
advertisement that is sent out to many
people at the same time: *Follow up your
mail-out with a phone call.*

MAJOR /ˈmeɪdʒə, *American* ˈmeɪdʒər/
majors, majoring, majored

'major in *mainly American*
to study something as your main subject
at a college or university
major in sth *She's majoring in physics.*

MAKE /meɪk/
makes, making, made /meɪd/

make 'after *British*
to chase someone = GO AFTER
make after sb *Hencke made after him.*

make a'way with
to escape with something that you have
stolen = MAKE OFF WITH
make away with sth *The burglars made
away with all their silverware.*

'make for ★★
1 to move towards a place = HEAD FOR
make for sth *He picked up his umbrella
and made for the door.* ♦ *When you hear
the signal, make straight for the exits.*
2 to help to make something possible
make for sth *The new computers make
for much greater productivity.* ♦ *Mutual
respect makes for a happy working
relationship.*
PHRASE **be made for each other** *informal*
if two people are made for each other,
they are perfect partners for each other

because they have similar personalities: *Everyone said that Jane and Danny were made for each other.*

'make into ★★ [often passive]

to change someone or something so that they become something else = TURN INTO

be made into sth *The story was made into a film two years ago.*

make sb/sth into sth *His first record made him into a star.* ♦ *They made a small local concern into a multi-million-pound business.*

'make of ★★★

1 to use chances and opportunities in order to be successful

make sth of sb/sth *I want to make something of my new life here.* ♦ *This job is whatever you make of it.* ♦ *It's a beautiful day today. Let's make the most of it (=enjoy it as much as we can).* ♦ *I hope he can make a success of his life.*

♦ *They're going to try to make a go of their marriage again (=make it successful).*

2 to understand someone, or the meaning of something, in a particular way

make sth of sb/sth *I don't know what to make of our new teacher.* ♦ *What do you make of this news?*

PHRASE **make something of it** *informal* to be prepared to fight or argue about something: *You want to make something of it, do you?* ♦ *She knew better than to try and make something of it.*

,make 'off

to leave quickly, especially after doing something wrong = RUN AWAY ≠ COME BACK

make off *The kids made off when they heard us coming.*

,make 'off with

to escape with something, especially something that you have stolen = MAKE AWAY WITH ≠ RETURN

make off with sth *They made off with our television and our stereo.*

,make 'out ★★★

1	see/hear/understand sth
2	write information on sth
3	know what sb is like
4	make people have a false opinion
5	pretend
6	used for saying whether sth succeeds
7	about sexual behaviour

1 to manage to see or hear someone or something, but only with difficulty = *formal* DISTINGUISH, DISCERN

make sth out *I can just make a few*

words out on this page.* ♦ *It sounded like French but I couldn't quite make it out.*

make out sth *Can you make out a face here on the photograph?*

make out what/who/where etc *I couldn't make out what he was saying.*

2 to write all the necessary information on a document such as a cheque = WRITE OUT

make out sth *She made out a cheque and handed it to me.*

make sth out *I can make a cheque out now.* ♦ *+to Who shall I make the cheque out to?* ♦ *I asked her to make it out to my wife.*

3 *informal* to understand someone's character = WORK OUT, UNDERSTAND

make sb out *I can't make her out.*

4 [often passive] to cause people to have a particular false opinion of someone or something

be made out to be sth *She's been made out in the press to be rather stupid and selfish.*

make sb/sth out to be sth *He made me out to be a liar.* ♦ *The letter made the hotel out to be some sort of castle.*

5 *informal* to pretend that something is true = PRETEND

make out (that) *He made out that he'd won the lottery.*

make out as if *She makes out as if she's not offended at all.*

6 *informal* to succeed or continue in a particular way = GET ON

make out *How is Frank making out in his new job?*

7 *American informal* to have sex, or to kiss and touch in a sexual way

make out *They were making out in the back of his car.*

,make 'over

1 to officially make someone else the owner of something

make sth over to sb *Before he died, he made his estate over to his wife.*

make over sth *He made over the farm when his son married.*

2 [usually passive] to change or improve the appearance of someone or something

be made over into sth *The old warehouse has been made over into apartments.*

■ **makeover** /ˈmeɪkˌəʊvə/ **noun** [C] a set of changes that make a person or thing look much better: *The offices are getting a much-needed makeover.*

'make towards

to go in the direction of someone or something

make towards sb/sth *I made towards the door, but he called me back.*

,make 'up ★★★

1	invent an explanation
2	invent a story/poem etc
3	form a whole thing
4	prepare sth
5	make an amount/number complete
6	become friends after arguing
7	do work you did not do before
8	make sth from cloth
9	decorate your face
+	PHRASES
+	**made-up** adj; **make-up** noun

1 to invent an explanation for something, especially in order to avoid being punished or embarrassed = INVENT
make up sth *He made up some excuse about the dog eating his homework.*
make sth up *There is no crisis. I made it up.* ♦ *He admitted he'd **made the whole thing up.***

2 to invent a story, poem etc = INVENT
make up sth *The children made up a little poem and wrote it in the card.*
make sth up *That was a good story. Did you make it up?* ♦ *The kids are making rhymes up using the rude words they learnt in the playground.*

3 [often passive] to combine together to form a whole = FORM, CONSTITUTE
be made up *The series explains how livings things are made up.* ♦ **+of** *The committee is made up of eight women and three men.*
make up sth *Women make up 40% of the workforce.*

4 to prepare or arrange something = PREPARE, PUT TOGETHER
make sth up *I'll get the pharmacist to make this prescription up for you.*
♦ *Don't worry about the kids' lunches – I've made them up already.*
make up sth *You can ask the florist to make up a bouquet with your own choice of flowers.* ♦ *Could you make up a list of all the things we need?*

5 to make an amount or a number complete ≠ DEDUCT
make up sth *I'm paying £500, and Dave is **making up the difference** (=paying the rest).*
make sth up *Unscrupulous producers make the missing few fluid ounces up with water.* ♦ *If you're a few pounds short, I'll make it up.*

6 to become friendly with someone again after having had an argument = BE RECONCILED ≠ FALL OUT
make up *Why don't you two forget your differences and make up?* ♦ *They argue a lot, but they always **kiss and make up**.*
♦ **+with** *Tom still hasn't made up with Alice.*

7 to work at different times from usual because you have not worked enough at the normal times
make up sth *Sorry I'm late; I'll make up the time tonight.*
make sth up *I'll have to make the hours up over the weekend.* ♦ *If work is slow during the day, she can always make it up in the evening.*

8 to produce something from cloth
make up sth *She bought some fabric to make up a jacket.* ♦ **+from** *You could make up some curtains from that material.*

9 [often passive] to put make-up such as powder and lipstick on someone's face
be made up *She's been made up to look about thirty years older.*
make sb/sth up *They made my face up to look like a clown.*
make up *She takes a long time to make up in the morning.*

PHRASES **make up a bed** to put sheets and covers on a bed so that it is ready for someone to sleep in: *I've still got the beds to make up.*
make up the numbers to be at an event so that there are enough people there: *They invited the girl next door to dinner, just to make up the numbers.*
make up your mind or **make your mind up** to make a decision: *I haven't made up my mind which bus to take.* ♦ *I wish he'd hurry up and make his mind up!*

make up (sense 6)

■ ,made-'up adj **1** imaginary or false: *a made-up story* **2** wearing make-up on your face: *her lightly made-up face*

■ 'make-up noun **1** [U] substances that people put on their faces, including

map 272 **mark**

their eyes and lips, in order to look attractive or change their appearance: *Some women wear no make-up at all.* ♦ *a make-up bag* **2** [singular] the people or things that combine to form something: *Does this group reflect the make-up of society as a whole?* ♦ *the strengths and weaknesses of his psychological make-up* **3** [C usually singular] the way that words and pictures are arranged on a page before a newspaper, magazine, or book is printed: *You can't add a single word without changing the page make-up.*

ˌmake 'up for ★★★

1 to take the place of something that has been lost or damaged, or to make a bad situation seem better
make up for sth *Nothing can make up for the loss of a child.* ♦ *He was stealing supplies from the office to make up for wages he had not been paid.*

2 if something good makes up for something bad, it makes the bad thing seem less of a problem
make up for sth *The good weather made up for the small campsite.*

3 to do something in order to make something bad that you did to someone seem less bad
make up for sth *I know I've been neglecting you but I'll make up for it.* ♦ *How are you going to make up for the way you've treated him?*
PHRASE make up for lost time 1 to enjoy experiences as much as possible because you have not experienced them before: *He's finally bought a computer and is making up for lost time.* **2** to work more quickly or at times when you do not usually work, because you have not been able to do the work before: *We're going to have to work harder next week to make up for lost time.*

ˌmake 'up to *informal old-fashioned*

to behave in a very friendly way towards someone, or to praise them, in order to get something for yourself = SUCK UP TO
make up to sb *She's always making up to the boss – it's really embarrassing.*
PHRASE make it up to sb to do something good that helps someone feel better after you did something bad to them: *I'm really sorry. I'll make it up to you.*

MAP /mæp/
maps, mapping, mapped

'map onto

to connect one thing to another thing, for

example as a way of understanding its meaning or structure
map sth onto sth *Can babies map these experiences onto their memories?*

ˌmap 'out ★★ [often passive]

to plan in detail how something will happen
be mapped out *Her own future had been mapped out for her by her parents.*
map out sth *She is mapping out a career path that will ensure she will never be poor.*

MARCH /mɑːtʃ, *American* mɑrtʃ/
marches, marching, marched

'march on

to walk along a road towards a place as part of a group of people protesting about something
march on sth *The day before, 50,000 demonstrators had marched on the Pentagon.*

ˌmarch 'on *mainly literary*

to continue to happen, develop, or make progress and be impossible to stop
march on *Time marches on.*

MARK /mɑːk, *American* mɑrk/
marks, marking, marked

'mark as ★ (*also* ˌmark 'down as *British*)

1 to decide that you think someone or something is a particular type of person or thing
mark sb/sth as sth *She immediately marked him as a troublemaker.* ♦ *He marked it as a place to come back to.*

2 to show that someone or something is a particular type of person or thing
mark sb/sth as sth *The glasses and the books marked him as a student.* ♦ *Huge neon signs mark this as a place of entertainment.*

ˌmark 'down ★

1 to write something in order to have a record of it = WRITE DOWN
mark down sth *As you go around the golf course, mark down your score.*
mark sth down *If you see something in the catalogue that you want to buy, mark its number down.* ♦ *When you want to discuss something, mark it down and we'll come back to it later.*
mark down how/where/why etc *Use this column to mark down how much each item costs.*

2 [usually passive] to reduce the price of something = REDUCE, DISCOUNT
be marked down *All our shoes have been*

marked down. ♦ **+by** *Room rates at the hotel have been marked down by 10%.*

3 to give a student a lower mark for their work because they have made a particular mistake or not done something in the way that they should have

mark sb down *A teacher can't mark you down just because they don't like you.* ♦ **+for** *They mark students down for poor spelling.*

4 [usually passive] to intend or plan that a particular thing should happen to someone or something

be marked down for sth *The museum has been marked down for closure.*

,mark 'down as *same as* **mark as**

,mark 'off

1 to mark the limits of an area using a line, fence, rope etc

mark off sth *also* **mark sth off** *Hedges are good for marking off special areas.* ♦ *Choose where your tennis court is going to be and mark it off.* ♦ *Each animal uses urine to mark his personal space off.* ♦ **+with** *They had marked the area off with official police tape.*

2 to mark something with a word, letter, or symbol in order to show that you have dealt with it

mark off sth *also* **mark sth off** *He marked off the names of all the suitable candidates.* ♦ *In the game of bingo, as they shout out your numbers, you mark them off.*

3 to show that someone or something is different from others = DISTINGUISH, SINGLE OUT

mark sb/sth off *It is the lizard's sheer size that marks it off.* ♦ **+from** *The tower marks it off from the other houses in the village.*

,mark 'out ★★

1 to show that someone or something is different from others = DISTINGUISH, SINGLE OUT

mark sb/sth out as sth *His talent has marked him out as one of the greatest runners ever.*

2 to show that someone or something will do something in the future

mark sb out for sth *It was the kind of singing voice that marks someone out for a professional career.*

3 [often passive] to show the shape of something by drawing or marking it on a surface

be marked out *The playing area should be clearly marked out.*

mark out sth *Use coloured pens to mark*

out your design. ♦ **+with** *First, mark out the shape of the pond with a spade.*

,mark 'up

1 [often passive] to increase the price of something, especially something that was bought for a lower price

be marked up *Foreign cars are often marked up by 40% for the American market.*

mark up sth *To make a 50% profit, you would mark up the cost by £300.*

2 to correct a piece of writing, or write notes or instructions on it, especially before it is published

mark up sth *also* **mark sth up** *It's easiest to mark up a printout of the figures.* ♦ *When you've marked the documents up, return them to my secretary.* ♦ *If you want changes in typeface, mark them up in green ink.*

■ **'mark-up** **noun** **1** [C] the amount of money that someone who sells goods adds to the price of the goods in order to make a profit: *There's a 200% mark-up on most wines.* **2** [U] instructions added to documents that tell a computer how to print or organize the information: *The program finds mark-up within the document.*

MARRY /'mæri, *American* 'meri/ **marries, marrying, married**

'marry into

to become a member of a family, religion, social group etc by becoming the husband or wife of someone who already belongs to it

marry into sth *Their seven daughters all married into prominent local families.* ♦ *He hoped his son would marry into money.*

,marry 'off

to find a husband or wife for someone

marry sb off *also* **marry off sb** *My mother's been trying to marry me off for years.* ♦ *He is desperate to marry off his daughters.* ♦ **+to** *They tried to marry their daughter off to a wealthy businessman.*

MARVEL /'mɑːv(ə)l, *American* 'mɑrv(ə)l/ **marvels, marvelling, marvelled**

'marvel at

to show or feel surprise or admiration

marvel at sth *I often marvel at the achievements of my predecessors.*

MASH /mæʃ/
mashes, mashing, mashed

‚mash 'up
to crush something, especially food, until it is smooth
mash up sth also **mash sth up** *Mash up the potatoes with a little milk.*

MASQUERADE /ˌmæskəˈreɪd/
masquerades, masquerading, masqueraded

masque'rade as
to pretend to be someone or something that you are not
masquerade as sb/sth *They were professional dealers masquerading as private buyers.*

MATCH /mætʃ/
matches, matching, matched

'match against (also **'match with**)
[usually passive]
to make a person or team compete against a particular opponent
be matched against sb *He is matched against the former champion in the first game.*

‚match 'up ★
1 if two things match up, they are the same or almost the same
match up *Information received from the two informants didn't match up.*
♦ **+with** *Her idea of a happy marriage did not match up with her husband's.*
2 to be as good as something or someone else
match up *While the rest of the band discovered a new passion for playing, Shaun just couldn't match up.* ♦ **+to** *The British sci-fi film has never matched up to its American counterpart.* ♦ *His performance did not **match up to expectations**.*
3 to find something or someone that forms the right combination with something or someone else
match up sb/sth *Match up the two halves of the sentences.* ♦ **+to** *You have to match up the inventor to the invention.*
match sb/sth up *There were four husbands and wives and you had to match them up.* ♦ **+with** *Contestants have to match the owners up with their dogs.*

'match with *same as* **match against**

MAX /mæks/
maxes, maxing, maxed

‚max 'out *informal*
1 to reach the limit of something, or to use all of a supply of something
max out sth also **max sth out** *I've maxed out all my credit cards.* ♦ *Once the computer has a controller for a cable modem, scanner, or some other gadget, you've maxed it out.*
2 to do something with as much energy as possible, or to have too much of something, so that you do not want to do or have it any more
max out *We maxed out after three hours of playing video games.* ♦ **+on** *I guess I maxed out on pizza last night!*

MEASURE /ˈmeʒə, American ˈmeʒər/
measures, measuring, measured

'measure against [often passive]
to form an opinion about how good or bad something is by comparing it with another person or thing
be measured against sb/sth *Measured against the success of their closest rivals, the team's performance looks poor.*
measure sb/sth against sb/sth *You can't fairly measure their performance against the performance of cars in the top group.*

'measure by
to form an opinion about how good or bad something is by considering one particular aspect of it
measure sb/sth by sth *They measure success by how much money you have.*

‚measure 'off
to measure a particular length, width, height etc, often at a point where something is to be cut
measure off sth also **measure sth off** *He took the fabric and measured off a couple of yards.*

‚measure 'out
to take a particular amount of something from a larger amount
measure out sth also **measure sth out** *Measure out half a cup of sugar.* ♦ *Take a bucket of water and measure two litres out.*

‚measure 'up ★
1 to be good enough ≠ FALL SHORT
measure up *The machines are being tried out to see how they measure up.*
♦ **+to** *Will he measure up to the challenges that lie ahead of him?*

♦ **+against** *How does the performance measure up against the best in the world?*

2 to measure something in preparation for making, building, or fitting something else

measure up sth *I measure up the boards and then Joe cuts them.*
measure sth up *He taught me how to measure the roof timbers up.* ♦ *Take the old sails and measure them up and write down the sizes.*

MEET /miːt, *American* mit/
meets, meeting, met /met/

,meet 'up ★★

1 to come together with someone, either unexpectedly or as planned
meet up *We usually meet up for a quick coffee in the morning.* ♦ **+with** *I met up with him outside the building.*

2 if roads, streets etc meet up, they join or cross each other = JOIN UP
meet up *The streets meet up at the next intersection.* ♦ **+with** *The track meets up with the main road ahead.*

'meet with ★★★

1 to have a formal meeting with someone
meet with sb *They're meeting with Russian leaders to try to end the crisis.*

2 to get a particular reaction or result
meet with sth *Experiments with the new drug have met with some success.* ♦ *They finally came to a decision that has met with general approval.*

Nouns often used as objects with meet with 2

■ **acclaim, approval, enthusiasm, success**

3 to unexpectedly experience trouble, danger, difficulty etc
meet with sth *She met with an unfortunate accident yesterday.*

Nouns often used as objects with meet with 3

■ **criticism, hostility, incredulity, opposition, protest, resistance, silence**

MELLOW /'meləʊ, *American* 'meloʊ/
mellows, mellowing, mellowed

,mellow 'out *informal*

to become more relaxed and calm
mellow out *He needs to mellow out a little.*

MELT /melt/
melts, melting, melted

,melt a'way ★

1 to disappear completely, usually gradually
melt away *I suddenly felt sorry for him and my anger melted away.* ♦ **+into** *The lioness and her cubs melted away into the jungle.*

2 if ice or snow melts away, it turns to water as it gets warmer
melt away *By morning, all the snow had melted away.*

,melt 'down [often passive]

to heat a metal until it becomes liquid, especially in order to make something new from it
be melted down *Statues had been melted down to provide bronze.*
melt down sth *also* **melt sth down** *In steelworks they melt down heavy bars of steel and pour them into moulds.*

'melt into

to gradually combine with something else, especially so that you can no longer see a difference
melt into sth *The reds and golds melted into each other as the sun set.* ♦ *I was trying to melt into the background when someone called my name.*

MERGE /mɜːdʒ, *American* mɜrdʒ/
merges, merging, merged

'merge into ★ (*also* 'merge with)

to combine with something else so that one thing is no longer clearly separate from the other
merge into sth *The hills merged into the dark sky behind them.* ♦ *Life and work seemed to merge with each other.*

MESS /mes/
messes, messing, messed

,mess a'round ★ (*also* ,mess a'bout *British*)

1 to behave in a silly way, especially when you should be working or paying attention to something = FOOL AROUND, MUCK AROUND
mess around *Stop messing around – I'm serious about this!*

2 to spend time doing things in a relaxed way
mess around *We spent the weekend messing around on John's boat.*

3 *British* to treat someone badly, especially

by changing your mind or not doing what
you promised

mess sb around *It looks like her
boyfriend's been messing her around
again.*

4 to waste time doing things that are not
important = FAFF ABOUT

mess around *There's no point in messing
around. Let's start now.*

PHRASE **not mess around** to do what
needs to be done immediately or in a
determined way: *The new coach
certainly didn't mess around – he got rid
of five players in the first week.*

,mess a'round with ★ (*also* **,mess
a'bout with** *British*)

1 to try to change or repair something,
especially when this is unnecessary or
unsuccessful

mess around with sth *He spends hours
messing around with that old motorbike.*

2 to have sex or a sexual relationship with
someone, especially when you should not
= FOOL AROUND WITH

mess around with sb *Diana's been
messing around with a married man.*

3 mess around with or **mess with** to make
someone angry or argue with them

mess around with sb *Don't mess around
with me!*

4 to become involved with something that
is dangerous = FOOL AROUND WITH

mess around with sth *A lot of the kids
had been messing around with drugs.*

,mess 'up ★★

1 to make a mistake or do something
badly

mess up sth *She says she completely
messed up the interview.*

mess sth up *I've really messed my French
test up.*

mess up *You messed up. Don't let it
happen again.* ♦ *He messed up big time
and never really got back on track.*

2 to make something dirty or untidy

mess up sth *They had managed to mess
up the whole office.*

mess sth up *The wind had messed his
hair up.*

3 *informal* to be the cause of someone's
physical, emotional, or mental problems

mess sb/sth up *Drugs really messed her
up.*

mess up sb/sth *The virus messed up my
body so badly that they told me I was
going to die.*

4 to damage or spoil something = RUIN

mess up sth *I'm not going to let him
mess up my life.*

mess sth up *I hope I haven't messed
things up for you.*

'mess with ★
same as **mess around with 3**

PHRASE **mess with sb's head** *informal* to
seriously upset someone or make them
confused: *Don't mess with my head; are
you kidding or not?*

METAMORPHOSE /ˌmetəˈmɔːfəʊz,
American ˌmetəˈmɔrˌfoʊz/
**metamorphoses, metamorphosing,
metamorphosed**

metamor'phose into *formal*
to change into something completely
different

metamorphose into sth *The skyline
metamorphosed into a sea of lights.*

METE /miːt, *American* mit/
metes, meting, meted

,mete 'out [often passive] *formal*
to give a punishment to someone = DEAL
OUT

be meted out *The building was the local
courthouse where justice was meted out.*
♦ **+to** *The same treatment should be
meted out to politicians who break the
rules.*

mete out sth *also* **mete sth out** *The
punishment they meted out was
degrading.*

MILITATE /ˈmɪlɪteɪt/
militates, militating, militated

,militate a'gainst *formal*
to make something more difficult to do or
less likely to happen

militate against sth *Their poor human
rights record militates against their
eventual entry to the EU.*

MILL /mɪl/
mills, milling, milled

,mill a'round (*also* **,mill a'bout** *British*)
informal
to move about a place in large numbers
as part of a crowd, without going in any
particular direction

mill around *A crowd of tourists were
milling around in the main square.*

mill around sth *Students were milling
around the library steps.*

MIND /maɪnd/
minds, minding, minded

mind 'out
PHRASE mind out! *British informal* used for telling someone to be careful, especially because they might hit something or something might hit them: *Mind out! There's a car coming.*

MINISTER /'mɪnɪstə, *American* 'mɪnɪstər/
ministers, ministering, ministered

'minister to *formal*
to help or look after someone, especially someone who is ill
minister to sb *Doctors ministered to the wounded.*

MINOR /'maɪnə, *American* 'maɪnər/
minors, minoring, minored

'minor in *American*
to study a particular subject at university or college in addition to your main subject
minor in sth *I thought you were going to minor in geography.*

MISS /mɪs/
misses, missing, missed

miss 'out ★★★
1 to miss an opportunity to do or have something
miss out *We will be repeating the questions later, so you won't miss out.* ♦ **+on** *He narrowly missed out on the world record.*
2 *British* to not include someone or something, usually by accident = OMIT ≠ INCLUDE
miss out sb/sth *You've missed out one important fact.*
miss sb/sth out *Have I missed anyone out?*

MIST /mɪst/
mists, misting, misted

mist 'over
1 if someone's eyes mist over, they begin to fill with tears = MIST ≠ CLEAR
mist over *Her eyes misted over as she talked about her dead husband.*
2 mist over or mist up *same as* steam up

MISTAKE /mɪ'steɪk/
mistakes, mistaking, mistook /mɪ'stʊk/, mistaken /mɪ'steɪkən/

mi'stake for ★★
to think that a person or thing is someone or something else
mistake sb/sth for sb/sth *The gunman had mistaken him for a drug dealer.*
♦ *It was such a good fake that you could easily mistake it for the real thing.*
♦ *There's no way he could have been mistaken for a terrorist.*

MIX /mɪks/
mixes, mixing, mixed

mix 'up ★★

1	think sb/sth is sb/sth else
2	put together without order
3	confuse sb
4	be involved in sth
5	spend time with sb
+	PHRASE
+	**mixed up** adj; **mix-up** noun

1 to think that one person or thing is another person or thing = CONFUSE
mix sb/sth up *They look so alike that it's easy to mix them up.* ♦ **+with** *I think I'm mixing him up with someone else.*
mix up sb/sth *I always mix up the words 'affect' and 'effect'.*
2 to put things together without any particular order = *informal* MUDDLE UP
mix sth up *I sorted all the papers and you've mixed them up again.*
mix up sth *Don't mix up your laundry with mine.*
3 [often passive] to make someone confused = CONFUSE
be/get mixed up *Hey slow down! I'm getting all mixed up.* ♦ **+with** *I got mixed up with the dates and went on the wrong day.*
mix sb up *All you're doing is mixing these kids up – they're not learning anything.*
4 [always passive] to be involved in something, especially something bad or embarrassing
be/get mixed up in sth *He seems to be mixed up in some kind of illegal trafficking.*
5 [always passive] *informal* to spend time with someone who has a bad influence on you
be/get mixed up with sb *How on earth did you get mixed up with someone like that?*

PHRASE mix it up (with sb) *mainly American informal* to get into a fight with someone: *He was grounded after mixing it up with one of the neighbour's kids.*

■ ,mixed 'up **adj** *informal* someone who is mixed up has a lot of emotional problems: *He's too mixed up to be in a position like this.*

■ 'mix-up **noun** [C] *informal* a mistake or problem that happens because someone is confused about details: *There was a mix-up and they lost my order.*

MOCK /mɒk, *American* mɑk/
mocks, mocking, mocked

,mock 'up
to make a simple copy of something that you will later make or do properly, in order to test it or show people what it will be like
mock up sth *also* **mock sth up** *I mocked up the toy with cardboard, to give them an idea of what it would look like.*

MODEL /'mɒd(ə)l, *American* 'mɑd(ə)l/
models, modelling, modelled

'model on (*also* 'model upon)
1 [usually passive] to deliberately copy something or do something in the same way as someone or something else
be modelled on sth *Their parliamentary system is closely modelled on the British system.*
2 to copy someone else because you admire them = STYLE AFTER
model yourself on sb *As a young actor, she tried to model herself on Meryl Streep.*

MOLD the American spelling of mould

MOLDER the American spelling of moulder

MONKEY /'mʌŋki/
monkeys, monkeying, monkeyed

,monkey a'round (*also* ,monkey a'bout *British*) *informal*
to behave in a silly way = FOOL AROUND
monkey around *Stop monkeying around and get on with your work!*

MOOCH /muːtʃ, *American* mutʃ/
mooches, mooching, mooched

,mooch a'round (*also* ,mooch a'bout *British*) *informal*

to spend time in a place without any particular purpose
mooch around sth *I'm just going to spend the day mooching around the shops.*
mooch around *What are you doing mooching around out there when dinner's on the table?*

MOON /muːn, *American* mun/
moons, mooning, mooned

,moon a'round (*also* ,moon a'bout)
British
to spend time doing nothing useful or important
moon around *He's just been mooning around all morning.*

'moon over
to spend time thinking about someone that you are attracted to instead of doing something useful
moon over sb *I spent much of that term mooning over a boy in Year 12.*

MOP /mɒp, *American* mɑp/
mops, mopping, mopped

,mop 'up ★★
1 to clean liquid or dirt from a surface using a mop, cloth etc = WIPE UP
mop up sth *Julie mopped up the water that had leaked from the radiator in the hallway.*
mop sth up *Can you mop that mess up at once?* ♦ **+with** *He mopped the milk up with a tissue.*
2 to remove any remaining members of an enemy army from an area after a victory
mop sb/sth up *The government had hoped to mop rebel resistance up in a few days.*
mop up sb/sth *Early on the morning of March 4th, they mopped up the remnants of the battalion.*
3 *informal* to finish something by dealing with a few final details
mop up sth *He stayed late to mop up the remaining tasks.*
mop sth up *We should be able to mop the rest of this up by the beginning of next week.*
4 *American* to win, or to succeed in doing something
mop up *I want you to go out there and mop up.*

MOPE /məʊp, *American* moʊp/
mopes, moping, moped

ˌmope aˈround (*also* ˌmope aˈbout *British*)

to spend time somewhere with no particular purpose, feeling bored or unhappy

mope around *Stop moping around and go and find yourself a job!*
mope around sth *She spent the weekend moping around the house.*

MORPH /mɔːf, *American* mɔrf/
morphs, morphing, morphed

ˌmorph ˈinto *informal*

to change into someone or something else

morph into sb/sth *She seems to be morphing into my mother!*

MOULD /məʊld/
moulds, moulding, moulded

ˌmould ˈinto

to give something a particular shape or form

mould sth into sth *Mould the dough into loaves.* ♦ *She moulded the clay into the shape of a head.*

MOULDER /ˈməʊldə/
moulders, mouldering, mouldered

ˌmoulder aˈway

to stay in the same position or place without developing or improving your situation

moulder away *At the time I was mouldering away in the office of a law firm.*

MOUNT /maʊnt/
mounts, mounting, mounted

ˌmount ˈup ★

to get much larger, especially by stages
= STACK UP

mount up *The costs are beginning to mount up.*

MOUTH /maʊð/
mouths, mouthing, mouthed

ˌmouth ˈoff *informal*

to give your opinions about something in a very annoying way, especially when you are complaining or criticizing something

mouth off *Keep mouthing off like that and you're going to get yourself into trouble.* ♦ **+about** *He's always mouthing off about the state of the roads.*

MOVE /muːv, *American* muv/
moves, moving, moved

Move is often used with adverbs and prepositions when it means 'to change position or go to a different place': *I moved along the bench to make room for him to sit down.* ♦ *She moved away from the open window so that she couldn't be seen.* ♦ *We'll be moving around a lot and you may not be able to reach us.* These uses are not included here.

ˌmove aˈlong ★

1 to leave a place when someone in authority tells you to, or to tell someone to leave a place = MOVE ON

move along *The police were telling us to move along.*
move sb along *A uniformed police officer moved people along if they tended to congregate.*
move along sb *Homeless people are forever getting moved along by the police.*

2 to progress or develop, or to make something progress or develop
= PROGRESS, MOVE ON

move along *The trial continues to move along.*
move sth along *It's up to the committee to move the process along.*

ˌmove aˈway

to stop living in one place and go to live in another

move away *'They've moved away,' said the old man in the yard. 'I don't know where to.'*

ˌmove aˈway from

to stop using a particular method, or to stop thinking in a particular way and start to do something in a different way

move away from sth *We're moving away from the idea that the longer you stay at your desk the more productive you are.*

ˌmove ˈin ★★★

1 to start living in a different house or flat ≠ MOVE OUT

move in *We're moving in next week.*

2 to start living in the same place as someone else —*picture* → ASK OUT

move in *She moved in a few weeks ago.* ♦ *Did you know they'd moved in together?* ♦ **+with** *He's moving in with his friends from college.*

3 to move closer to a person or place, for example in order to arrest or attack them
= CLOSE IN

move in *The troops moved in while the enemy was sleeping.*

,move 'in on

1 to try to control or get involved in something that someone else controlled before

move in on sth *A number of competitors are moving in on our sales territory.*

2 to get closer to a person or place, especially in order to arrest or attack them = CLOSE IN ON

move in on sb/sth *The police are beginning to move in on their principal suspects.*

,move 'into ★★★

1 to start living or operating a business in a place

move into sth *We're moving into new offices by the river.*

2 to begin a new business or new type of business

move into sth *They're planning to move into publishing.*

,move 'off ★

if a vehicle moves off, it starts to move = DRIVE OFF

move off *She jumped into a taxi which moved off immediately.*

,move 'on ★★★

1	leave a place
2	discuss/do sth new
3	change ideas
4	continue with your life
5	leave when ordered
6	progress/make sth progress

1 to leave one place and travel to another = LEAVE ≠ STAY PUT

move on *They stay for only a few days before moving on.*

2 to stop discussing or doing something and begin discussing or doing something different

move on *I'd like us to move on now.*
♦ **+to** *Let's move on to the next question.*

3 to change your ideas, attitudes, etc in a way that you think is better

move on *We like to think we've moved on as a society since the days of racial segregation.*

4 to start to continue with your life after you have dealt successfully with a bad experience

move on *It's been a nightmare, but now I just want to forget about it and move on.*

5 to leave a place when someone in authority tells you to, or to tell someone to leave a place = MOVE ALONG

move on *We moved on, as requested.*

move sb on *Police were aggressive in the*

way they moved the young people on.
move on sb *Soldiers moved on anyone who tried to stop and see what was happening.*

6 to progress or develop, or to make something progress or develop
= PROGRESS, MOVE ALONG

move on *Things have moved on since then.*

move sth on *We're trying hard to move everything on in the face of strong opposition.*

,move 'out ★★★

to permanently leave the place where you live or the place where you have your business = LEAVE ≠ MOVE IN

move out *The house has been sold, and we're moving out.*

,move 'over ★★

1 to change your position in order to make space for someone or something else

move over *She moved over to let me pass.*

2 to stop doing something in order to let someone else do it = STEP ASIDE

move over *They seem to expect older musicians to move over so that the younger ones can get a chance.*

3 to start to do something in a different way = CHANGE OVER

move over *Head office changed the invoicing system last month but most branches are still moving over.* ♦ **+to** *Most companies moved over to direct payments years ago.*

,move to'wards

to be taking action in order to achieve something, or to be starting to accept a particular situation = COME CLOSER TO

move towards sth *We seem to be moving towards greater integration.*

,move 'up ★★★

1 *British* to change your position in order to make space for someone or something

move up *Could everyone move up a bit, please?*

2 to go to a better job, higher class, higher level etc, or to make someone do this
= PROMOTE

move up *I don't think I'm ready to move up just yet.*

move sb up *This win has moved her up in the world rankings.* ♦ **+to** *They're moving him up to the position of manager.*

3 to increase to a higher level ≠ DROP

move up *Interest rates are slowly moving up again.*

move up

PHRASE move up in the world to
improve your social status, for example
by getting a better job: *She wanted to
move up in the world and have
something more than this little town
offered.*

MOW /məʊ, *American* moʊ/
mows, mowing, mowed, mown /məʊn,
American moʊn/

ˌmow ˈdown *informal*

1 to kill a lot of people quickly and
violently, especially by shooting them
mow sb down *also* **mow down sb** *A
gunman had mown down his entire
family at a wedding.*

2 [often passive] to kill someone by hitting
them with a car or other vehicle = KNOCK
DOWN, RUN OVER
be mown down *The infantry were mown
down by the advancing enemy tanks.*
mow down sb *also* **mow sb down** *The
driver came off the road and mowed
down two women waiting at a bus stop.*

MUCK /mʌk/
mucks, mucking, mucked

ˌmuck aˈround (*also* ˌmuck aˈbout)
British informal
to waste time, especially when you should
be doing something useful or paying
attention = MESS AROUND, FOOL AROUND
muck around *We just mucked around at
home all weekend.*

ˌmuck ˈin *British informal*
to join in an activity, especially in order
to help people to get a job done
muck in *If we all muck in, we'll be
finished in no time.* ♦ **+with** *Everybody
mucks in with the housework.*

ˌmuck ˈout
to clean a place or building where farm
animals live
muck out sth *It was always my job to
muck out the barn.*
muck out *Who's going to come and help
me muck out?*

ˌmuck ˈup *informal*

1 to not deal with something well or
skilfully so that you do not achieve what
you intended = MESS UP
muck up sth *also* **muck sth up** *I couldn't
take the risk of mucking up my chances.*
♦ *Don't give it to him to do. He'll only
muck it up again.*
muck up *This is the second time you've
mucked up and failed the exam.*

2 to spoil something or prevent it from
being successful = MESS UP, RUIN
muck up sth *also* **muck sth up** *Well that's
completely mucked up my evening.*

3 to make something dirty or untidy
= MESS UP
muck up sth *also* **muck sth up** *Don't
muck up the clean floor.*

MUDDLE /ˈmʌd(ə)l/
muddles, muddling, muddled

ˌmuddle aˈlong (*also* ˌmuddle ˈon)
to continue to live or do something
without having a clear idea of what you
want to achieve
muddle along *They're content to just
muddle along.*

ˌmuddle ˈthrough
to succeed in doing something despite
having no clear plan, method, or suitable
equipment
muddle through *The loan will allow
him to muddle through until he gets a
job.*

,muddle 'up

1 [usually passive] to put things into an untidy state or into the wrong order = MIX UP

> **be muddled up** *Now my papers are all muddled up.* ◆ **+with** *His business files were muddled up with his personal files.*

2 to think that someone or something is someone or something else as a result of a mistake = CONFUSE, MIX UP

> **muddle sb/sth up** *also* **muddle up sb/sth** *They're so alike it's easy to muddle them up.* ◆ *I always get 'its' and 'it's' muddled up.*

MUG /mʌg/
mugs, mugging, mugged

,mug 'up *British informal*

to quickly learn something or check that you know it, for example before an examination = LEARN

> **mug up sth** *also* **mug sth up** *He said I ought to mug up as much as I could about Italy before I went there.*
> **mug up** *I tried to mug up from an old textbook at the last minute.* ◆ **+on** *You'd better mug up on irregular verbs for tomorrow.*

MULL /mʌl/
mulls, mulling, mulled

,mull 'over

to think carefully about something over a period of time = CONSIDER, PONDER

> **mull over sth** *also* **mull sth over** *They'll need time to mull over the proposals.* ◆ *She sat at the window, mulling the whole thing over.*

MUSCLE /'mʌs(ə)l/
muscles, muscling, muscled

,muscle 'in

to use your power or influence to get involved in a situation in which you are not wanted = INTRUDE

> **muscle in** *They are trying to muscle in and take away our customers.* ◆ **+on** *We didn't appreciate the way he was trying to muscle in on our conversation.*

MUSE /mjuːz, American mjuz/
muses, musing, mused

'muse on (*also* 'muse upon) *literary*

to think about something in a slow careful way

> **muse on sth** *He started to muse on his relationship with his father.*

MUSS /mʌs/
musses, mussing, mussed

,muss 'up *mainly American*

to make something untidy, especially someone's hair

> **muss up sth** *also* **muss sth up** *Hey, stop that! You're mussing up my hair!*

MUSTER /'mʌstə, American 'mʌstər/
musters, mustering, mustered

,muster 'up

to try to produce as much of a feeling such as enthusiasm or determination as you can

> **muster up sth** *also* **muster sth up** *I tried to muster up all my courage.*

Nn

NAFF /næf/
naffs, naffing, naffed

,naff 'off [always in imperative] *British impolite*

used for telling someone rudely to go away

NAG /næg/
nags, nagging, nagged

'nag at

if a doubt, worry, or fear nags at you, you cannot stop thinking about it for very long

> **nag at sb** *The feeling that I shouldn't have given up nagged at me.*

NAIL /neɪl/
nails, nailing, nailed

,nail 'down

1 *informal* to definitely decide, arrange, or complete something = FINALIZE

> **nail sth down** *also* **nail down sth** *We're hoping to nail the agreement down some time this week..*

2 to fix something firmly in position with a nail or nails

> **nail sth down** *also* **nail down sth** *Can you nail that loose floorboard down?*

3 *informal* to make someone agree to something or tell you what they are going to do = PIN DOWN

> **nail sb down** *I'll try to nail Jim down about the date.*

LANGUAGE STUDY

Phrasal verbs can be challenging, and the aim of these pages is to help you to understand and use them correctly. You will find information on a range of topics that are especially relevant to phrasal verbs: how they are pronounced and where the stress falls (**Pronunciation and Phrasal Verbs**); how they combine with other words in a sentence (**The Syntactic Behaviour of Phrasal Verbs**); and what types of text they are typically used in (**Register and Phrasal Verbs**).

You can also read about the ways in which new phrasal verbs develop (**Metaphor and Phrasal Verbs**, '**New' Phrasal Verbs**) and the ways in which verbs, nouns, and adjectives combine with particles to make new word forms (**Phrasal Verbs and Other 'Phrasal' Vocabulary**). In addition to these topics we have included the most common problems experienced by learners using phrasal verbs (**Learners and Phrasal Verbs**).

These pages will give you a lot of useful information about how phrasal verbs behave. They will also show you how important phrasal verbs are in all types of English, and how much they contribute to the formation of new vocabulary. We hope that reading this section will show you some new aspects of phrasal verbs, and will give you confidence when you are using them.

Contents

THE SYNTACTIC BEHAVIOUR OF PHRASAL VERBS

Phrasal verbs are made up of a *verb* and a *particle*. A particle can be:

- an *adverb* (such as **out** or **away**): for example **go out, put away**

- a *preposition* (such as **with** or **from**): for example **deal with, shrink from**. Phrasal verbs with a preposition are sometimes called *prepositional verbs*.

Some phrasal verbs have two particles, both an adverb and a preposition: for example **get on with** or **stand up for**. Verbs with an adverb and preposition are sometimes called *phrasal-prepositional verbs*.

Like other verbs, phrasal verbs can be:

- transitive (followed by a noun or pronoun that is the object of the verb)

- intransitive (with no object)

- both transitive and intransitive

The most important thing to learn about the grammar of phrasal verbs is where to place the object. Should it go before or after the particle? What happens when there are two particles? And what happens if the object is a pronoun? In the dictionary, the way each verb behaves is shown by a combination of a *pattern* and an *example*. For example, the entry for the verb **bring along** gives the following information:

,bring a'long ★★

to take someone or something with you when you go somewhere = BRING

bring sb/sth along *Bring some friends along if you like.* ♦ *My mother is staying with me at the moment. Is it OK if I bring her along too?*
bring along sb/sth *They are expected to bring along enough school work to keep themselves busy.*

In this case, the patterns and examples show that you can place the object either before or after the particle. So you can say 'I'll bring some friends along' or 'I'll bring along some friends'. However, if the object of **bring along** is a pronoun it must *always* go between the verb and particle, so that you have to say 'Can I bring her along too?'.

The behaviour of intransitive phrasal verbs

Because they do not have objects, the behaviour of intransitive phrasal verbs is straightforward. The verb and particle always stay together:

*We've recorded a new album, and it's **coming out** in the spring.*

*I had the chance to change jobs, but I let it **slip by**.*

The behaviour of transitive phrasal verbs

Transitive phrasal verbs can be divided into four groups according to where the object goes in relation to the particle:

1 With most transitive phrasal verbs, the object can go *either* between the verb and the particle, *or* after the particle. These verbs are known as *separable* phrasal verbs:

*Just pack your bags and **load up** the car.*
*I'll **load** the car **up** while you lock the door.*
*Trim and **cut up** all the vegetables into fine slices.*
*She **cut** the cake **up** into twelve pieces.*

However, if the object is a pronoun (= a word such as **me, it, this,** or **them**), it *must* go between the verb and the particle, and it *cannot* go after the particle:

*You bring the car round and I'll **load** it **up**.*
~~You bring the car round and I'll **load** up it.~~
*Let's **cut** it **up** into twelve pieces.*
~~Let's **cut up** it into twelve pieces.~~

2 With a few transitive phrasal verbs, the object *must* go between the verb and the particle, whether it is a noun, a noun phrase, or a pronoun:

The two women are so similar that only

*their husbands can **tell** them **apart**.*
*I could hardly **tell** the two women **apart**.*
~~I could hardly tell apart the two women.~~

3   With some transitive phrasal verbs, the object *must* go after the particle or particles, whether it is a noun, a noun phrase, or a pronoun. This group includes all prepositional and phrasal-prepositional verbs:

*I **bumped into** your mother at the supermarket.*
*I **bumped into** her in the city centre.*
*He shouldn't be allowed to **get away with** such appalling behaviour.*
*They have repeatedly broken the law and **got away with** it.*

This group also includes a small number of phrasal verbs where the particle is an adverb, but verbs of this type *cannot* have a pronoun as an object:

*The victim wasn't able to **put up** much resistance.*
~~The victim wasn't able to put up it.~~

4   A small group of three-word phrasal verbs has two objects, one of which goes after the verb, the other after the particle or particles:

*She **played** one boy **off against** another.*
*That guy at the garage **did** me **out of** £50.*
*I've decided to **take** you **up on** that job offer.*

Phrasal verbs that are both transitive and intransitive

As with other verbs, some phrasal verbs can be both transitive and intransitive. When these verbs are intransitive, they behave like all other intransitive phrasal verbs:

*I'm not very good at **adding up** in my head.*
*I don't like children who **answer back**.*
*His hat **blew away** on the roller coaster.*

When they are transitive, they behave in one of the ways described above:

*Now **add up** the number of calories you have eaten.*
*If you **add** all that **up**, it comes to about three million.*

*We didn't dare **answer** the teacher **back**.*
*She switched on the fan to **blow away** the smoke.*

What decides the position of the object in separable phrasal verbs?

As we saw above, the objects of most transitive phrasal verbs can go either between the verb and the particle, or after the particle, with no difference in meaning or emphasis:

*He **picked** the phone **up** and dialled.*
*You can **pick up** the phone and give me a call.*
*Will you **turn** the television **off**, please?*
*It is now safe to **turn off** your computer.*
*Celia's immediate reaction was to **turn down** the offer.*
*Was it possible that he had actually wanted her to **turn** his offer **down**?*

However, the choice of whether to put the object before or after the particle is not always a completely free one. If the object contains information that the reader or listener already knows, it is more likely to come between the verb and the particle. But if the object presents *new* information, it is more likely to come after the particle. This is because we normally give more emphasis to new information than to information that is already known, and putting the object after the particle gives it a little more emphasis.

For example, consider these two sentences:

*Ann **slipped** the jacket **on** to see what it looked like.*
*She **slipped on** some flat sandals and made her way downstairs.*

In the first example, the jacket has been previously mentioned, so the object comes between the verb and the particle. In the second example, the object refers to something that has not been mentioned before (*some flat sandals*), so it comes after the particle.

If the object consists of more than three or four words, it usually goes after the particle, rather than between the verb and the particle:

*Officials are trying to **pin down** the cause of widespread power cuts in the western states.*
~~*Officials are trying to **pin** the cause of widespread power cuts in the western states **down**.*~~
*The doctors could **knock out** all of the pain that he's experiencing pretty easily.*
~~*The doctors could **knock** all of the pain that he's experiencing **out** pretty easily.*~~

This happens even when the object has already been referred to, as in the following example:

*If smog is hurting everybody everywhere, why not just **clean up** these smog-emitting power plants?*

Phrasal verbs in the passive

Most transitive phrasal verbs can be used in the passive, while a few are always or almost always used in the passive:

*Personal phone calls **are frowned on** at work.*
*First you **will be kitted out** with a safety helmet.*
*The brochure **is** beautifully **laid out** and illustrated.*

Even if the verb is normally 'separable', when it is in the passive the verb and the particle always stay together:

*I've **cleaned** the place **up** a bit.*
*The place **had been cleaned up**.*
*Will you **turn** the television **off**, please?*
*The television **had been turned off**.*

METAPHOR AND PHRASAL VERBS

The meanings of phrasal verbs are often difficult to remember, because they seem to have no connection with the words that they consist of (the verb and the particle). In fact many phrasal verbs are metaphorical, and if you understand the metaphors they use, it will be easier to understand and remember their meanings. These pages look at ways in which different phrasal verbs share similar metaphors.

What is a metaphor?

Look at these pairs of sentences: the phrasal verbs are shown in bold type.

- *The dog **dug up** an old bone.* ♦ *We **dug up** some interesting facts.*

- *Two planes were **shot down**.* ♦ *Each proposal was **shot down**.*

- *Burglars had **broken into** their house while they were away.* ♦ *She **broke into** his conversation.*

In each pair, the first phrasal verb has a literal meaning and refers to a physical action, while the second is metaphorical and describes an action that is similar in some way to the first. For example, when someone *digs up* information, they discover it, and the process seems similar to the way in which dogs find bones that have been buried in the ground.

Some phrasal verbs only have metaphorical meanings. For example, *to breeze in* means to enter a place confidently, without seeming to care what other people think: perhaps the attitude and action reminds us of the movement of a breeze (= a light wind). Similarly, *to rope someone in* means to persuade someone to do something that they do not really want to do: perhaps it reminds us of the way in which people use ropes to catch animals or to collect them together.

Adverbs, prepositions, and metaphor

A phrasal verb consists of a verb (like

dig, **shoot**, or **break**) and a particle (an adverb like **down** or **up**, or a preposition like **into**). When the *verb* part of a phrasal verb is used in a metaphorical way, this is usually quite obvious. But the *particles* may be used metaphorically too. This is less easy to recognize, but in fact there is often a clear connection between the literal meanings of the particle and its metaphorical uses. The sections below explain some of these connections.

In English, like many other languages, the basic, *literal* meanings of adverbs and prepositions refer to direction, position in space, distance, or extent.

- **up** literally describes movement towards a higher position

- **down** literally describes movement towards a lower position

- **ahead** literally describes a position in front of you (*the house is directly ahead*).

The *metaphorical* uses of these particles develop from these literal ones:

- **up** has metaphorical meanings to do with increases in size, number, or strength (*prices went up*)

- **down** has metaphorical meanings to do with decreases in size, number, or strength (*the children quietened down*)

- **ahead** metaphorically describes a point in the future (*many problems lies ahead of us*).

This dictionary has special pages on common particles (see Contents on page iii) that explain the meanings they have in phrasal verbs, including their metaphorical meanings.

Conceptual metaphors

Very often, the same metaphorical idea occurs in many different words and phrases, not just in phrasal verbs. For example, the idea of moving upwards or of being in a high position is found in many words that metaphorically describe increases in quantity (**go up, rise, climb, soar, peak** etc), and similarly with the opposite ideas (**go down, fall, drop, slump, dive**). These are called 'conceptual' metaphors, and they are the subject of *Metaphors We Live By* (1980) by George Lakoff and Mark Johnson. In this book, they demonstrate the importance of metaphor in relation to how we think and how we choose words to express our thoughts.

Sections 1 to 12 below explain some of the main conceptual metaphors that occur in groups of phrasal verbs.

Metaphor in English and other languages

Very few languages have phrasal verbs like English, but the same conceptual metaphors can be found in the vocabulary of other languages. In fact, some metaphors seem to occur in nearly all languages. One universal metaphor is the idea of 'up/high' and 'down/low' referring to quantities. Another conceptual metaphor that occurs with 'up/high' and 'down/low' refers to power and status: powerful, important people are thought of as being 'at the top' of an organization or society, while ordinary people without any power are 'at the bottom'. This idea also seems to occur in most languages.

Lakoff and Johnson believe that many conceptual metaphors originally developed because of basic human experiences, and that is why they occur in so many languages, even when the languages are not related. For example, the idea 'up/high' refers to large quantities because when more things are added to a pile, it becomes higher; and the idea 'up/high' refers to being powerful because if two people fight and one of them is physically on top of the other, that person usually wins.

Think whether your own language has words and expressions with similar metaphorical ideas to those that we describe in the following sections.

Explaining the metaphors

The metaphors in some phrasal verbs are difficult to explain, even when we

know a lot about how these meanings have developed. But in many cases, the metaphors form part of a system that *can* be explained. And some phrasal verbs that seem to have illogical meanings do in fact make sense. The following pairs of phrasal verbs have opposite meanings, as you would expect:

● **dress up** (= dress more formally than usual) / **dress down** (= dress more informally than usual)

● **pipe up** (= start talking) / **pipe down** (= stop talking)

But the following pairs – although they look like opposites – mean almost the same thing:

● **break up / break down**

● **wind up / wind down**

In fact, different meanings of **up** and **down** – and different metaphors – are involved here. The 'opposite' meanings are described in sections 1, 2, and 9 below, and they relate to the opposite ideas 'high' and 'low'. But **up** has another meaning to do with 'completion' (see section 3), while **down** has a meaning to do with 'ending' (see section 4): the ideas of 'completion' and 'ending' are quite similar, and so phrasal verbs with **up/down** may have similar meanings.

Use the sections listed below to see if you can explain other phrasal verb meanings.

Sets of metaphors

Each of the following sections deals with one common metaphorical idea, and the adverbs and prepositions that express this idea when they form part of a phrasal verb. There are other metaphors and other groups that we have not covered here. Use the special pages on common particles to see if you can find others: for example, are there other metaphors in phrasal verbs with **up** and **down**, **in** and **out**, or **on** and **off**? Look, too, for further examples of phrasal verbs that fit in with the metaphors below.

1 Increasing and decreasing: *down, out, up*

Up expresses ideas of increases in size, strength, or importance, while **down** expresses ideas of something becoming smaller, weaker, or less important.

*Fees have **gone up** again.* ♦ *She's doing some teaching in the evenings to **bump up** her income.* ♦ *The search operation has been **scaled down**.* ♦ *The government **played down** the threat to public health.*

Out expresses ideas of something becoming wider or fuller, covering a greater extent, or lasting for a longer time.

*Officers **fanned out** across the field.* ♦ *Her stories **flesh out** the world in which these historical characters lived.* ♦ *They had to **string** things **out** until the Duke arrived.*

2 Excitement, interest, and happiness: *down, up*

Some phrasal verbs with **up** refer to things becoming more exciting, lively, or interesting, or to people becoming happier. Phrasal verbs with **down** refer to things becoming quieter or calmer, or to people becoming more unhappy.

*Things are **looking up**.* ♦ ***Cheer up**!* ♦ *Their opponents said that they **sexed up** the report.* ♦ *This place needs **livening up**.* ♦ ***Calm down**!* ♦ *You need to **tone down** your argument.* ♦ *The endless wet weather was **getting** me **down**.*

3 Completeness: *up*

Up expresses an idea of completeness. For example, to *burn up* means to burn completely, and to *wind* something *up* means to bring it to a complete end.

*They **gobbled up** their dinner.* ♦ *Don't **use up** all the paper.* ♦ *The speaker had begun to **sum up**.* ♦ *All the shops had **closed up** for the night.*

4 Ending: *away, down, off, out*

When something ends, we can think of

it as gradually going farther away until it completely disappears. In phrasal verbs, **away, down, off,** and **out** all express ideas of something gradually ending.

*Her voice **faded away**.* ♦ *I suddenly felt sorry for him and my anger **melted away**.* ♦ *The wind **died down** during the night.* ♦ *The meeting **wound down**.* ♦ *The rain **eased off**.* ♦ *The effects of the drug **wore off**.* ♦ *The conversation soon **petered out**.* ♦ *The custom has almost **died out**.*

5 Time – past and future: *ahead, back, behind, forward*

Metaphors relating to time are often based on the idea that time is like a line that goes from the past to the future, with the past behind us and the future in front of us. Phrasal verbs with **ahead** and **forward** express ideas of the future, while phrasal verbs with **back** and **behind** express ideas of the past.

*What **lies ahead**?* ♦ *Let's **think ahead** to next season.* ♦ *I'm **looking forward** to seeing them again.* ♦ *I've **put** my watch **forward** one hour.* ♦ *The house **dates back** to the 16th century.* ♦ *Never **look back**, never have regrets.* ♦ *She was trying to **leave behind** a difficult adolescence.* ♦ ***Put** the whole episode **behind** you.*

6 Progress: *ahead, along, behind, on, through*

Making progress and achieving things is like being on a journey and moving towards your destination. Phrasal verbs with **along** describe the kind of progress that is being made, while phrasal verbs with **ahead** and **behind** express ideas of making good progress or poor progress.

*The building work was **coming along** nicely.* ♦ *They're content to just **muddle along**.* ♦ *He needs to **get ahead**.* ♦ *They are **pressing ahead** with the reforms.* ♦ *I've **fallen behind** with my work.* ♦ *We're **lagging behind** our competitors.*

Phrasal verbs with **through** describe

the process of achieving something or dealing with work.

*He has no ability to **carry through**. ♦ She **sailed through** her exams. ♦ I **ploughed through** the work.*

Phrasal verbs with **on** express the idea of continuing with an activity or task: **on** here has the same meaning as **onwards**.

*I can't **carry on**. ♦ They **kept on** until it was finished.*

7 Getting involved in an activity: *away, in, into, out*

We think of activities as if they have physical dimensions, like areas or spaces. In phrasal verbs, **in** and **into** express the idea of getting involved, while **away** and **out** express the idea of avoiding or ending an involvement.

*We **joined in** the fun. ♦ You're always trying to **muscle in**. ♦ I **flung** myself **into** my work. ♦ They **shied away** from commitment. ♦ You can't **walk away** from the relationship. ♦ The British forces **pulled out**. ♦ He **bowed out** gracefully.*

8 Problems: *around, aside, off, over, round*

We think of problems and difficulties as if they are physical objects that get in our way. Some phrasal verbs have meanings to do with ignoring problems or behaving as if they do not exist. The metaphorical idea is that we go around or over the things that are in our way, or we push them farther away.

*They **skirted around/round** the issue. ♦ We'll **work round** the problem somehow. ♦ He **brushed aside** my objections. ♦ We need to **put aside** our differences. ♦ I **laughed off** his criticisms. ♦ He couldn't **shake off** the allegations. ♦ They **glossed over** the question of who was going to pay for it. ♦ I tried to **smooth** things **over** between them.*

9 Power and weakness: *down, over, under, up*

When one person has power and controls another, we think of the first person as being in a higher position than the second. Some phrasal verbs with **over** and **up** express ideas of someone being in control, or becoming more powerful than someone else. Phrasal verbs with **down** and **under** express ideas of someone being forced into a weaker position, or of being controlled or restricted.

*He was **lording** it **over** me. ♦ The Emperor **ruled over** a vast area. ♦ They have **come up** in the world. ♦ She's been moved up to a more responsible job. ♦ The police **clamped down** on drinking in the streets. ♦ The rebellion was swiftly **put down**. ♦ Prisoners are **kept under** constant surveillance. ♦ We had to **knuckle under** and do what we were told.*

10 Relationships: *apart, off, together, up*

Relationships are like physical connections. Some phrasal verbs with **together** refer to a close relationship between two people or groups, while ones with **apart** refer to the ending of a relationship.

*We **got together** in our first year at college. ♦ The whole group **clubbed together** to buy him a present. ♦ They **drifted apart** over the years.*

Phrasal verbs with **up** refer to people forming a new relationship, or to a person joining a group.

*Two students from each class **pair up** to produce a short play. ♦ They feel that the international community is **ganging up** on them. ♦ He has been accused of **cosying up** to the new US president.*

However, some combinations with **up** and a verb meaning 'break' refer to the ending of a relationship.

*He's just **broken up** with his girlfriend. ♦ Her parents **split up** a few months ago.*

A few phrasal verbs with **off** refer to a new relationship between two people. The metaphorical idea is that the two people come together and become separate from a larger group.

*All our friends seemed to be **pairing off**.* ♦ *They tried to **marry** their daughter **off** to a wealthy businessman.*

11 Communication: *across, between, forth, in, into, out, over, through*

We think of communication between two people as a connection between them, with information passing from one to the other, often across a large space.

*I don't know how to **put** it **across**.* ♦ *I don't seem to be able to **get through** to them.* ♦ *The message **came over** clearly.* ♦ *Something **passed between** them.*

When one person says something, their words seem to leave them physically. When they are told something, the message or information seems to enter them.

*She **poured out** her problems.* ♦ *I **blurted out** his name.* ♦ *Dave was*

holding forth on the subject of politics. ♦ *She had to repeat her words several times before they finally **sank in**.* ♦ *My parents **drummed** its importance **into** us.*

12 Information and knowledge: *into, out, up*

We think of things that are not yet known, or that other people may not want us to know, as if they are in a container, or covered or buried. Phrasal verbs with **into** describe the process of trying to find information from someone or something.

*I wrote a letter of complaint, and the airline has promised to **look into** the matter.* ♦ *She **delved into** his past.* ♦ *You don't want them **nosing into** your finances.*

Some phrasal verbs with **out** and **up** express ideas of revealing secrets or finding information, as if they are uncovered or brought to the surface.

*She tried not to tell them, but in the end she **let** it **out**.* ♦ *I **wormed** the information **out of** him.* ♦ *We **dug up** some interesting facts.* ♦ *They **raked up** some scandal from his university days.*

PHRASAL VERBS AND OTHER 'PHRASAL' VOCABULARY

This article explains the various ways in which verb-forms and particles can combine to form other words. It shows that these combinations not only produce phrasal verbs, but are a central feature of word formation in English, and help to explain a wide range of vocabulary items. The aims of this article are to show that:

● understanding phrasal verbs provides a key to a large amount of *other* English vocabulary

● contrary to popular belief, many other languages also have vocabulary that is very similar to English phrasal verbs.

From phrasal verbs to phrasal nouns and phrasal adjectives

The term 'phrasal verb' is familiar from English language coursebooks and syllabuses. But the process of combining a verb and a particle generates not only phrasal verbs but also 'phrasal nouns' and 'phrasal adjectives', though these terms are not in general use. For example, as well as the phrasal verb **hand out**, there is also the 'phrasal noun' **handout**, and as well as the phrasal verb **speak out**, there is also the 'phrasal adjective' **outspoken**.

These combinations have the following characteristics:

1 The order can be either verb+particle or particle+verb:

verbs	nouns	adjectives
set up, upset	set-up, upset	upset, upsetting
stand up	stand-up	stand-up, upstanding
come in	income	incoming
set off, offset	offset	offset
hang over, overhang	hangover, overhang	hungover, overhanging

2 They can be spelled as one word, two separate words, or with a hyphen. There are no definite spelling rules, but in most cases you can follow these guidelines:

combination	used to form	written as	examples
verb+ particle	phrasal verbs	two words	make up, look over
particle+ verb	verbs	one word	downgrade, overlook
verb+ particle	nouns	one word or hyphenated	make-up, makeover, carry-on, carryout, check-up, checkout
particle+ verb	nouns	one word	downgrading, input, onset
verb+ particle	adjectives	hyphenated	jazzed-up, made-up, watered-down
particle+ verb	adjectives	one word or hyphenated	ongoing, off-putting

3 Adjectives may be formed from either present or past participles:

outstanding (but not ~~outstood~~)
outspoken (but not ~~outspeaking~~)

4 Adverbs may be formed from phrasal adjectives ending with –ing:

outstandingly
overwhelmingly

As a result of all these types of word formation, there are sometimes quite large 'word families' – of verbs, nouns, adjectives, and adverbs – that are based on different combinations of the same verb and particle. Within each word family, there may be substantial differences of meaning. For example:

The **set+up** word family:

● **set up** *phrasal verb* = to start an organization, business etc

● **upset** *verb* = to make someone unhappy

● **set-up** *noun* = the way that something is organized

● **upset** *noun* = an unexpected defeat

● **upset** *adjective* = feeling unhappy

● **upsetting** *adjective* = making you feel unhappy

Other types of 'phrasal' vocabulary in English

English vocabulary includes words from many different languages, but the two main sources are *Germanic* words, and words that come from *Latin* and *French*. The words listed here are closely related in meaning but are different in origin:

Germanic	Latin/French
dog	canine
house	domestic
come	arrive
tooth	dentist
unhappy	miserable
unsettling	disturbing
watchful	observant

Phrasal verbs, and the nouns and adjectives derived from them, are generally thought of as part of the Germanic component of English vocabulary, but in fact we find very similar combinations in vocabulary that is derived from Latin and French too. In this case the order is particle+verb, and the spelling is always a single word.

Words formed from *gress*

The Latin element **gress**, meaning 'step' or 'walk', appears in many English words, such as:

verbs	nouns	adjectives
progress	progress, progression	progressive
	congress	congressional
	egress	
regress	regression	regressive
digress	digression	
transgress	transgression	

The Latin element *pro* has the meaning of 'forward, ahead, in front'. When we **progress**, we move forward or **get on** (here **on** has the meaning 'ahead, along', which can also be seen in the phrasal verb **go on**, meaning 'continue'). In the same way:

- a **congress** is an event where people **come together** (*con* = together)

- an **egress** is a way of **going out** (*e* is a reduced form of *ex* = out)

- to **regress** is to **go backwards** (*re* = back, again)

- if we **digress**, we **stray from** the metaphorical path we are following in a discussion or a description (*di* is a form of *dis* = aside, apart)

- a **transgression** is a situation in which someone **steps beyond** the limits of what is permitted or acceptable (*trans* = through, across, beyond)

Words formed from *pose* or *pone*

Similarly, the Latin elements **pose** and **pone**, meaning 'to put' or 'to yield', appear in many English words:

verbs	nouns	adjectives
compose compound compost	composer composition composure component compote compost compound	composed compound composite
depose deposit	deposition deposit	deposed
expose	exposure exposition	exposed
oppose	opposite opposition	opposite opposed

- *Com* is an alternative form of *con* (= together). So a **composer** is simply someone who **puts together** notes of music – though in a particularly skilful way, of course. Someone who is able to keep their **composure** (= to remain calm) will give the impression of being 'together' rather than 'all over the place'.

- *De* is 'down', so to **deposit** or **depose** is to **put down**, literally or metaphorically.

- If something or someone is **exposed**, they are **put out** and made visible, or deprived of shelter.

- *Op* is an alternative form of *ob* and means 'towards', 'against', so when you **oppose** someone you position yourself against them.

Vocabulary pairs with different origins

There are many cases where a Germanic phrasal verb, noun, or adjective has an exact equivalent word whose origins are Latin/French. For example:

Germanic word	Latin / French equivalent	Meaning elements
foretell	predict	*pre* = before, ahead *dict* = to say
put forward	propose	*pro* = forward *pose* = to put
come between	intervene	*inter* = between *ven* = to come
drive out	expel	*ex* = out *pel* = to drive
look down (on someone)	despise	*de* = down *spise* = to look
forerunner	precursor	*pre* = before, ahead *curs* = to run
lead-in	introduction	*intro* = inwards *duct* = to lead
downcast	dejected	*de* = down *ject* = to throw

If learners can recognize

● the original meanings of particles and the verbs they combine with

● the metaphorically extended meanings of these particles and verbs

● the meanings that are generated by combining them

then they are more likely to understand the meanings of phrasal verbs, phrasal nouns, and phrasal adjectives. The way the meaning has developed is clear in some cases, and less clear in others, but in general, the meanings of these items are not as random or illogical as is often supposed.

Phrasal vocabulary in other languages

Exactly the same principles apply in other Germanic, Romance, and Slavonic languages. Most obviously, Romance languages (such as French, Spanish, and Italian) have words almost identical to English ones like **compose, introduction**, etc. In the other Germanic languages there are forms like:

German/ Swedish	English	Meaning elements
durchdenken (German)	think through	*durch* = through *denken* = to think
ausdrücken (German)	express	*aus / ex* = out *drücken* = to press
überschreiten (German)	cross pass exceed	*über* = over *schreiten* = to stride
ge upp (Swedish)	give up	*ge* = to give *upp* = up
ta efter (Swedish)	imitate copy	*ta* = to take *efter* = after
förse (Swedish)	provide	*för / pro* = before *se / vide* = to see

In these languages, just as in English, there are also nouns and adjectives derived from such verbs.

In Slavonic languages, too, the same principle operates:

Polish/ Russian	English	Meaning elements
odwołać (Polish)	call off	*od* = off, from *wołać* = to call
wpaść (Polish)	drop in	*w* = in *paść* = to drop
перейти (Russian)	cross exceed	пере = across, through идти = to go
выставить (Russian)	exhibit	вы / *ex* = out ставить = to put, set

Speakers of all such languages can benefit from being shown that 'phrasal verbs' are not by any means – as is often thought – a unique feature of English. And once students understand how phrasal verbs produce other combinations they will have the key to many English word families.

REGISTER AND PHRASAL VERBS

Introduction: are phrasal verbs 'informal'?

Phrasal verbs can cause anxiety for learners and teachers alike. Apart from resolving the problems of *meaning* and *grammar*, there is the difficult question of when it is *appropriate* to use them. Many articles written as guides for using phrasal verbs claim that they should be used mainly in speaking rather than writing, and in informal rather than formal situations and texts. It is often said that, in formal contexts, single-word equivalents are more appropriate than phrasal verbs. This advice may sometimes be useful but it is an oversimplification, and if it is followed too closely, it can sometimes lead to unnatural or over-formal language.

In fact, there are many situations – even in quite formal texts – when a phrasal verb is the most natural-sounding way of expressing a particular idea, so learners should be encouraged to use phrasal verbs as and when they are most appropriate.

Phrasal verbs can be found in all types of text. Take the example below:

1a *Issues **brought up** by the President of the College and by the Board of Regents shall be addressed by the Faculty Senate and, if necessary, by the Association as* … (from a college constitution document)

1b *Answering the big questions **raised** by the war.* (from an online book review)

Sentence 1a is an extract from a very formal written text. The writers of this document could have chosen to use **raised** in place of **brought up**, but clearly the phrasal verb is natural and acceptable in this context. On the other hand, sentence 1b is from an online book review – a much less formal register – and in this case the writer chose to use **raise** rather than **bring up**. This is probably because the combination 'raise+question' is a strong collocation, whereas 'bring up+question' is a rather rare combination. Phrasal verbs are used across all types of text, even where the writer or speaker has the option of choosing a single-word alternative. Although phrasal verbs tend to enter the language through casual speech, in most cases they progressively become accepted across a wider range of texts, until they reach even the most technical or conservative of text types.

Some corpus-based statistics

In order to illustrate this point, consider the following statistics (based on the evidence of a large language corpus) showing the frequency of the phrasal verb **give up** across different text types; the figures show the approximate number of times this verb is used per million words of text:

text type	per million words
academic prose	10
fiction	30
newspapers	30
conversation	25

So although **give up** is clearly less common in academic writing, it is by no means always avoided. Learners should appreciate that it is possible to use phrasal verbs in formal contexts, and that they limit themselves unnaturally by accepting the idea that they should use phrasal verbs in informal chat, for example, but not in academic writing or in a presentation to business colleagues. Most of the verbs in this dictionary (apart from those that are marked as *informal, very informal, impolite,* or *offensive*) can be found in *all* types of text, and their use in English is widespread and prevalent. Writers of legal documents and scientific papers may still opt for **tolerate** in preference to **put up with**, or **decelerate** rather than **slow down**, but even these extremely formal texts will contain some phrasal verbs.

A similar search in the corpus shows that the single-word verb **tolerate** is more common than **put up with** in academic texts, with around 16 occurrences per million words of text, compared with 3 for **put up with**. But with **decelerate** and **slow down**, the figures are different, showing that **decelerate** is simply a rare and rather specialized term, with fewer than 0.5 occurrences per million words in *all* registers. By contrast, the equivalent phrasal verb **slow down** registers about 10 occurrences per million in academic texts.

Below are some examples of texts that include **slow down**, showing that this common phrasal verb appears even in very formal texts:

*Once dormant, however, their metabolism **slows down** so much that the pineal is virtually switched off.* (from a zoology textbook)

*The current structure would need to be searched to establish whether or not the required paths exist, which would **slow down** the building algorithm.* (from a computer science textbook)

*The second WHO review of its 'Health for All' policy concludes that 'the implementation of strategies to achieve those aims has in many cases **slowed down'**.* (from a medical journal)

There are many situations in which a phrasal verb may be more appropriate than a single-word verb. Often there are subtle differences in meaning. The meaning of one will rarely cover *exactly* the same semantic ground as the other. In the case of the **slow down / decelerate** pair, we find that **slow down** can comfortably be used in a much wider range of contexts:

2a   *He was highly agitated and speaking too fast so I asked him to slow down.*

2b   ~~He was highly agitated and speaking too fast so I asked him to decelerate.~~

Decelerate provides an alternative to **slow down** only in certain specialized contexts, and this explains its comparative rarity. The learner who ignores **slow down** in formal registers will be left searching for another expression for some time.

When a phrasal verb is the best choice

The idea that phrasal verbs should be avoided in formal registers perhaps reflects a belief that the phrasal verb is somehow an 'imperfect' alternative to the single-word verb. But this is a misconception. Phrasal verbs are not just an informal version of 'purer' English. In many cases they fill important lexical gaps: that is, they express concepts for which there is no obvious single-word equivalent. In such cases, there really is no natural way of saying something other than through a phrasal verb – and choosing a single-word equivalent risks sounding stilted or pompous. Compare:

3a   *It was going to be a special night so she decided to **don** her new Old Skool Vans.*

3b   *She **put on** her new Nikes.*

In 3a the use of the verb **don** is either slightly affected, or is used in order to emphasize the *special* nature of the night referred to. But in most contexts, **put on** is a much more natural choice.

There is a large number of phrasal verbs that native speakers use in all registers including formal and technical. The Macmillan Defining Vocabulary – a list of the 2,500 English words used for writing the dictionary definitions – includes the following 16 phrasal verbs:

consist of, deal with, get up (= get out of bed), **give up, grow up, happen to, leave out, look for, make up** (= invent), **pick up, put down** (= put something on the floor etc), **put on** (= get dressed), **slow down, stick out, take off** (= remove clothes), and **wake up**

These words are included in the Defining Vocabulary because they are the most usual and natural ways of expressing these ideas. Compare some of the one-word equivalents to these very common phrasal verbs:

phrasal verb	one-word equivalent
leave out	omit
look for	seek
put on	don
stamp out	eradicate
stick out	protrude

Most of these single-word verbs are much less common than the phrasal verbs. **Put on** is 20 times more frequent than the rather literary word **don**. **Protrude** is only about half as frequent as **stick out**, and it is used mostly in technical contexts and occasionally in fictional descriptions.

Learning phrasal verbs is very much a part of learning English and not just something a learner does to sound 'authentic' or to be able to talk to native speakers. Phrasal verbs are found in all types of text and are essential for expressing many ideas in natural English. Learners and teachers alike should study them in context and get to know the collocational patterns they most commonly occur in, just as they do for other vocabulary. Understanding when it is appropriate to use a phrasal verb instead of a single-word verb, and knowing which gaps in the language are best covered by phrasal verbs, are two keys to writing and speaking natural English. A good dictionary and a lot of exposure to phrasal verbs will make it easy.

LEARNERS AND PHRASAL VERBS

Introduction

It is well known that phrasal verbs are a challenging area of English-language learning and teaching. In this section, we will identify – and offer some solutions for – the main problems that learners experience when they try to use phrasal verbs in their own speech and writing. We will focus on combinations of high-frequency verbs, with which learners ought to be familiar (such as **go**, **take**, **put**, and **give**), with:

- adverbial particles such as **up**, **in**, **out**, **off**, **down**, and **through**

- prepositional particles such as **at**, **for**, **to**, and **with**

There are two types of evidence that help with understanding the kinds of problem that learners have when they use phrasal verbs. These are:

- experimental data, such as translation tests or multiple-choice tests in which learners have to select the most appropriate verb (phrasal verb or single-word verb) to fill in a gap in a sentence

- computer learner corpora, which are electronic collections of spoken or written texts produced by learners (such as essays or transcribed conversations)

On the basis of this evidence, we can identify a number of issues that seem to cause problems for many learners.

Phrasal verbs formed with adverbial particles

The following main problems have been highlighted in relation to phrasal verbs of this type:

1 avoidance
2 style deficiency
3 semantic confusion
4 lack of collocational awareness
5 using 'idiosyncratic' phrasal verbs
6 syntactic errors

The following sections are essentially based on data from the International Corpus of Learner English (ICLE) and from the Louvain International Database of Spoken English Interlanguage (LINDSEI). The ICLE and LINDSEI projects are based at the Centre for English Corpus Linguistics, Université catholique de Louvain (http://fltr.ucl.ac.be). ICLE is made up of formal argumentative essays written by upper-intermediate and advanced EFL learners from a variety of mother-tongue backgrounds. ICLE's spoken counterpart LINDSEI consists of informal interviews between students and native speakers of English.

1 Avoidance

The evidence suggests that learners who lack phrasal verbs in their mother tongue (such as French-speaking or Spanish-speaking students) tend to avoid using phrasal verbs in English. This does not mean that they do not use phrasal verbs at all, but rather that they use fewer phrasal verbs and more single-word verbs than native-speakers of English performing similar tasks.

Learners who do have phrasal verbs in their mother tongue, on the other hand, do not avoid using these in English. In fact, Dutch-speaking and German-speaking EFL learners tend to use more phrasal verbs than native speakers in written discourse.

2 Style deficiency

Learner corpus research has shown that EFL learners tend to be 'stylistically deficient': that is, they appear to be largely unaware of the differences between informal speech and formal writing. Their formal writing sometimes contains speech-like features, whereas their informal spoken language often sounds rather formal and bookish. Learners' use of phrasal verbs is no exception to this.

Phrasal verbs are often presented as characteristic of informal spoken

English. Although this is an oversimplification (phrasal verbs can be found even in the most formal types of text), it is nevertheless true that native speakers of English use approximately half as many phrasal verbs in formal writing as in informal speech.

EFL learners, on the other hand, have a tendency to use more phrasal verbs in formal writing than in informal speech. What is more, learners can also be seen to use phrasal verbs that are not typically associated with formal writing. Consider the following examples from learners' formal essays:

- *The state in its turn is responsible for its citizens' well-being and must **help out** when needed.*

- *... many people are constantly **getting away from** tradition, religion and moral values.*

- *The Swedish well-meaning immigration policy is sometimes stopping people from **getting into** the society.*

Besides style deficiency, one of the possible reasons why learners tend to use more phrasal verbs in writing than in speech is that a writing task usually gives learners more time to plan and encode their messages, and actually consider the possibility of using a group of verbs that they are generally not very comfortable with or confident about using.

In some cases, learners' over-reliance on phrasal verbs in formal writing can be directly traced to the influence of their mother tongue, and more specifically to the fact that in some Germanic languages (for example Dutch, German, and Swedish), phrasal verbs are not marked for style and can be used equally in informal speech and formal writing.

3 Semantic confusion

By far the most common errors made by learners when using phrasal verbs are *semantic* errors, reflecting an incomplete understanding of the

meaning of phrasal verbs. All the sentences shown here are taken from the ICLE or LINDSEI data, and in each case a correct or more appropriate word is shown in brackets:

Learners confuse phrasal verbs and single-word verbs whose meanings are related:

- *He has to **find out** (discover) new means to fight against them.*
- *Students couldn't **put on** (wear) a scarf in winter.*
- *He will **find out** (find) that the number of conventional families decreases.*
- *Procedures must be taken in order not to let the disease **spread out**. (spread)*
- *The impulse to **build up** (build) also **springs up** (springs) from the need ...*
- *... because infants **grow up** (grow up) surrounded by them.*
- *because sometimes he's like an actor: he **dresses** (dresses up) as different people*

Learners use the right verb but the wrong particle:

- *They **fill up** (fill in) many forms.*
- *It is a task which must be **carried on** (carried out) using the brain.*
- *Sect members are told to refrain from talking to their parents and to **keep out** (keep away) from their friends.*

Learners use the right particle but the wrong verb:

- *We tried to **come back to** (go back to) Los Angeles.*
- *Saddam Hussein had the power to **shut off** (turn off) the heat in millions of homes.*

4 Lack of collocational awareness

Studies have shown that learners lack 'collocational awareness': that is, they tend to be unaware of the preferred relationships that exist between some words. Some words belong together with other words and occur more naturally with these words rather than with that of other words with the same meaning.

For example, if you are using a camera,

you do not *make* **a picture** but you *take* **a picture**. You do not say that 'scientists *made* **an experiment**', but 'they *conducted* or *carried out* **an experiment**'. Learners tend not to be aware of these special relationships, which means that they often combine words that do not normally occur in each other's company.

Consider the following examples involving phrasal verbs:

- *Even the majority of teachers also* ***cut down*** *pupil's creativity either in their lessons or in their exams.*
- *Religion was also a means of* ***calming down*** *eventual revolts and unrests.*
- *... teaching them moral values and preparing them to* ***set up*** *their own families.*

Native speakers of English would normally talk about *stifling* **creativity**, *quelling* **revolts/unrests**, and *starting* **a family**.

5 Using idiosyncratic phrasal verbs

Learners sometimes use phrasal verbs that do not actually exist in English, either because they mix up verbs, because they use the wrong verb or particle, or possibly also because they feel the need to create a new phrasal verb by combining a verb and a particle to cover a gap in the language.

- *These differences need to be* ***levelled down.*** *(ironed out)*
- *People who decide to marry are usually more responsible and they can trust each other more because they know that in case of problems they do not just* ***split apart.*** *(split up)*

6 Syntactic errors

The evidence shows that learners sometimes make syntactic errors involving transitive phrasal verbs being used intransitively, and vice versa:

- *The state should help parents to* ***grow up*** *better generations.*

- *He or she begins to look for another love,* ***splitting up*** *the relationship.*

Compare:

'I ***grew up*** in the countryside' (intransitive) and '***Bringing up*** children (= helping them to grow up) is not always easy' (transitive).
'Jane and Shane have ***split up***' (intransitive) vs. 'They've ***ended*** their relationship' (transitive).

Phrasal verbs formed with prepositional particles

Phrasal verbs with prepositional particles (also called prepositional verbs) are a particularly frequent source of errors, even at an upper-intermediate and advanced level. The major sources of error include:

1 The influence of the learner's mother tongue

The learner is unaware that a verb is a prepositional verb in English, as it is not a prepositional verb in his/her mother tongue:

- *I would also like to* ***comment*** (comment on) *the second part of the title* (written by a French-speaking learner: in French you 'comment something')
- *We don't have enough money to* ***pay*** (pay for) *a flight* (Spanish-speaking learner: in Spanish you 'pay something you buy')
- *I am used to using computers or* ***listening*** *the radio* (Italian-speaking learner: in Italian you 'listen something or someone')

The verb is a prepositional verb in English *and* in the learner's mother tongue, but the prepositional particles differ and are not direct translational equivalents:

- *While the others ... tried to* ***participate to*** (participate in) *our discussions* (Italian-speaking learner: in Italian you 'participate at something')
- *Athletes that have the honour to* ***participate at*** (participate in) *these Olympic Games* (German-speaking learner: in German you 'participate at something'.)
- *And that means to* ***concentrate*** *more*

in the national policy than in the European one (Spanish-speaking learner: in Spanish you 'concentrate in something'.)

● *It depends of (our) mental image of the matter* (French-speaking learner: in French 'something depends of' something else.)

The learner is unaware that, although a verb is a prepositional verb in his/her mother tongue, it is not a prepositional verb in English:

● *And at the same time he is courting to (courting) a lady* (Spanish-speaking learner: the equivalent Spanish verb is a prepositional verb.)

2 Intralingual confusion

Sometimes an English verb can take more than one prepositional particle (with different meanings), and the learner confuses the two:

● *The group ... consists in (consists of) five students (= is made up of five students).*
● *Religious alienation consisted of (consisted in) the idea that religion send out the man outside of the real ... (= has this idea as its most important or only aspect)*
● *Only a few years back I felt that very few people seemed to care for (care about) the world we live in and the future our children will live in. (= be interested in it and think it is important)*

An English verb is not a prepositional verb (it is not followed by a prepositional particle) but the derived noun *is* used with a preposition. For example, you *discuss* something but you have a *discussion about* something; you *doubt* something but you have *doubts about* something; you *contact* someone but you are *in contact with* someone.

● *A general feeling of emptiness prompted some students to doubt about (doubt) the value of their university degrees.*
● *Shaw doubts about (doubts) the existence of miracles and saints.*
● *Children, in fact, must be trained to discuss about (discuss) violent events*

as well as about the happy ones they experience.
● *Recently in the* Financial Times, *the journalist, Joe Rogaly, discussed about (discussed) the possibility of making gun ownership illegal in every nation ...*
● *For years they have been discussing about (discussing) it.*
● *We must contact with (contact) people in other countries.*

An English verb is used both as a prepositional verb *and* as a verb that does not require the use of a preposition. The two forms have different meanings, and learners sometimes confuse them:

● *You go to the university, attend to (attend = go to) classes but you don't learn anything about real world.*
● *Once, a shop assistant refused to attend (attend to = serve) her.*
● *Some society doesn't approve (approve of = think it is right or suitable etc.) a single unmarried woman with a child.* (Compare: *Parliament approved the budget* = accepted it officially)
● *In such cases, lying cannot be approved (approved of) and regarded as right.*

An English verb is used as a prepositional verb, but learners fail to realize that the particle 'to' is a preposition and not the infinitive particle:

● *She had consented to marry (consented to marrying) him only after he had conducted a thorough search ...*
● *However, last year the Queen finally consented to pay (consented to paying) taxes and she will open Buckingham Palace to visitors.*
● *So when women prove their skills, men object to appreciate (object to appreciating) them and give (giving) them their due.*
● *While they wouldn't object to have (object to having) an 'ex-burglar' work for them ...*

3 Style deficiency

Learners sometimes use, in *formal* writing, prepositional verbs that are not typically associated with this type of text:

● *Their communities ought to organize*

*meetings to **talk about** (discuss) the epidemic.*

- *But the English version of the Treaty **talked about** (mentioned) land ownership.*

- *The problem that I am interested in and I want to **speak about** (discuss) is the death penalty.*

Practical applications: suggestions for teaching

In view of all the evidence of the difficulties that phrasal verbs can cause for learners, it is quite clear that these verbs ought to be treated as 'chunks' – together with their syntactic, contextual, and collocational features – rather than in isolation. Providing learners with *lists* of phrasal verbs to learn by heart ought to be a thing of the past.

Corpus-based studies of phrasal verbs clearly show the need for a *contextualized* approach based on (semi-)authentic texts, as this will enable teachers to draw learners' attention to:

- whether or not certain phrasal verbs

are more typical of speech or of writing
- the syntactic environment of phrasal verbs
- the words that phrasal verbs tend to combine with

Dealing with phrasal verbs *as they crop up* in spoken and written texts (rather than giving learners lists of phrasal verbs with the same verb or the same particle) will also help learners not to feel overwhelmed or unnecessarily confused.

The learners' *mother tongue* should also be taken into consideration when teaching phrasal verbs. In particular:

- .if the learners' first language (L1) does not contain phrasal verbs with adverbial particles, teachers should devote more time to verbs of this type so that the learners become familiar with the phenomenon
- if the learners' L1 *does* contain phrasal verbs with adverbial particles, teachers should raise learners' awareness of any *stylistic* differences between phrasal verbs in the L1 and in English
- it is important to raise learners' awareness of any differences between verbs with prepositional particles in their L1, and similar combinations in English.

PRONUNCIATION AND PHRASAL VERBS

This article describes the various ways in which the *Macmillan Phrasal Verbs Plus* dictionary deals with pronunciation and stress. It also explains some simple rules that will help you to pronounce phrasal verbs confidently when they form part of a sentence.

What the dictionary shows

This dictionary shows the pronunciation and stress pattern of each 'base' verb using the IPA (International Phonetic Alphabet). See the key on the inside back cover.

witness /ˈwɪtnəs/
straighten /ˈstreɪt(ə)n
characterize /ˈkærɪktəraɪz, *American* ˈkerəktə,raɪz/

In most cases, a single pronunciation is given, and this can be used in all varieties of English. But where a verb is pronounced differently in British and American English, both pronunciations are shown, with the British version first and the American version second:

attune /əˈtjuːn, *American* əˈtun/

When a verb ends with the letter 'r', the usual pronunciation rules apply: in British English the 'r' is not normally pronounced, *unless* it is followed by a vowel sound. So the 'r' in **hanker** is pronounced in the phrasal verb **hanker after** /ˈhæŋkər ˌɑːftə/ but not in the phrasal verb **hanker for** /ˈhæŋkə fɔː/. In American English, the 'r' is *always* pronounced.

The stress pattern for each individual phrasal verb is shown using the symbol / ˈ / to show *primary* stress and the symbol / ˌ / to show *secondary* stress. For example:

ˌplay aˈround
ˈplay at
ˌplay ˈdown
ˌplay ˈoff against
ˈplay on
ˌplay ˈup

ˌplay ˈup to
ˈplay with

Getting the stress right

The main pronunciation question with phrasal verbs concerns the placement and distribution of stress on the verb, the particle and the other words in the sentence. Here are some guidelines to help you.

Stress patterns: two main types

With a few exceptions, phrasal verbs have either one stress

ˈmake for

or two stresses

ˌmake ˈoff

Phrasal verbs with one stress have the main stress on the verb, and no stress on the particle:

| ˈmake for | **ˈMake for** the door! |
| ˈlook at | We're **ˈlooking at** all the ˌoptions. |

Phrasal verbs with two stresses have the *primary* stress on the particle and a *secondary* stress on the verb.

| ˌmake ˈoff | They **ˌmade ˈoff** when the police arrived. |
| ˌtake aˈpart | You could try **ˌtaking** it **aˈpart**. |

Sometimes the same phrasal verb can have different stresses depending on its meaning. The dictionary treats these cases as separate phrasal verbs:

| ˈlive on | The animals **ˈlive on** bamboo shoots. |
| ˌlive ˈon | Long after her death, her memory ˌlives ˈon. |

Phrasal verbs with one stress

The single stress is on the first word, which is the verb. The second word, which is the particle, has no stress,

| ˈmake of | What do you **ˈmake of** it? |
| ˈcare for | Would you ˌcare for some tea? |

a'gree with   *I a'gree with you*

In the majority of phrasal verbs of this type, the particle is a *preposition* like *at, for, from, of,* or *to*. These particles often have both a *strong* form, such as

at /æt/ *from* /frɒm/ *of* /ɒv/

and a *weak* form, such as

at /ət/ *from* /frəm/ *of* /əv/

It is usually the weak form that is used in phrasal verbs with one stress.

However, if the particle comes at the end of a phrase, the strong form would be used, though still unstressed

¦What would you 'care for?
¦What are you 'looking at?

The speaker might also choose to stress the particle in order to convey a particular meaning, for example an emphasis, or contrast, or correction

I saw him ¦speaking to the 'president. Yes, and later he spoke 'for the president.

In this case the speaker is following the normal rules of stress placement in discourse.

Phrasal verbs with two stresses

These phrasal verbs have both a *primary* and a *secondary* stress. The primary stress is on the second word, the particle. The secondary stress is on the first word, the verb. The majority of phrasal verbs are like this.

¦make 'out
¦turn 'on

These phrasal verbs are 'separable': that is, the verb and the particle can be separated, with the object of the verb coming between them. Separable phrasal verbs can be used in three possible ways, and this affects where the stress falls. The dictionary tells you which of these three ways you can use for a particular phrasal verb.

1 *When the object is a pronoun*
When the object of a separable phrasal verb is a pronoun, it must come between the verb and the particle:

Can you ¦make it 'out?
¦Turn it 'on.

2 *When the object is a noun coming between the verb and particle*
In this case, the stress will usually be on the noun rather than on the particle:

Can you ¦make the 'writing out?
¦Turn the 'light on.

3 *When the object is a noun coming after the verb and particle*
If the noun is important for the speaker's meaning, then it will be stressed and the stress on the particle may be lost:

Can you ¦make out the 'writing?
¦Turn on the 'light.

Three-part phrasal verbs

Some phrasal verbs have an extra preposition after the particle. These are stressed in the same way as phrasal verbs with two stresses, so the verb carries a secondary stress and the first particle carries the main stress. The third word is unstressed:

¦make 'up for	*I'll ¦make 'up for it.*
¦take 'up on	*Can I ¦take you 'up on this?*
¦put 'up with	*I don't know why she ¦puts 'up with it.*

However, if the word following the preposition is a noun, the speaker might choose to stress it, and then the particle could either reduce or retain its stress, without significant difference in meaning:

I'll ¦make 'up for the mistake.	or	*I'll ¦make up for the mis'take.*
I'll ¦take you 'up on your ¦offer.	or	*I'll ¦take you up on your 'offer.*
She ¦puts 'up with a 'lot.	or	*She ¦puts up with a 'lot.*

Citation form and discourse

The term *citation form* refers to the pronunciation and stress pattern that is shown in a dictionary entry. This information is accurate when the phrasal verb is spoken in isolation, and even when a phrasal verb is used in context, it is still likely to follow the stress pattern of its citation form. But it is also possible that in connected speech the speaker may choose to place the stress differently in order to convey a particular meaning. In such cases the normal rules of stress shift apply.

Nouns and adjectives formed from phrasal verbs: rules for stress

It is common in English for nouns and adjectives to be formed from verbs. For example:

verb	noun	adjective
protect	protection	protective
act	action	active
mean	meaning	meaningful

The same is true for phrasal verbs, and the dictionary includes many nouns and adjectives that are formed from phrasal verbs. These are shown at the end of a phrasal verb entry. For example, the entry for the verb **black out** also shows the related noun **blackout**.

The majority of phrasal verbs are stressed on their *second* word (the particle), but nouns formed from those verbs usually have the stress on the *first* part of the word:

verb	noun
ˌlet 'down	'letdown
ˌprint 'out	'printout
ˌturn 'off	'turn-off
ˌbreak 'in	'break-in

Even when the word order is reversed, and the second word in the verb becomes the first in the noun, the noun still has the stress on the first syllable:

verb	noun
ˌturn 'down	'downturn
ˌcry 'out	'outcry
ˌbreak 'out	'outbreak
ˌturn 'up	'upturn

This pattern follows the general rule for

pairs of two-syllable nouns and verbs in English, which is that the verb is usually stressed on the second syllable while the noun is usually stressed on the first. For example:

verb	noun
in'crease	'increase
per'mit	'permit
pre'sent	'present
re'cord	'record

For adjectives formed from phrasal verbs, the rules are less straightforward. Some adjectives are stressed on the second element, especially those where the verb is in its past participle form. When these adjectives come at the end of a phrase, their stress pattern usually follows the 'citation form':

*My shoes are **worn** 'out.*
*The place looks really **run** 'down.*
*The area is quite **built** 'up.*
*The warehouse was completely **burnt** 'out.*

However, when the adjective comes before a noun or noun phrase, then the noun is usually stressed, and the two words of the adjective may be equally but less stressed:

***worn-out** 'shoes*
*a really **run-down** 'place*
*a **built-up** 'area*
*a **burnt-out** 'warehouse*

Other adjectives have the stress on the first element, especially those where the verb is in its present participle form:

*She is the '**outgoing** president.*
*This is an '**ongoing** problem.*
*Watch out for '**oncoming** traffic.*

However, if the adjective comes at the end of a sentence or phrase, the speaker may put the stress on the second element. This allows the speaker to leave a longer space between the two stresses:

*The ˌproblem is on'**going**.*

'NEW' PHRASAL VERBS

How new words develop

In English, very few 'new' words are *completely* new. The vast majority include at least one component that we are already familiar with. A very common way of giving a name to a new concept is simply to combine two existing words into a new phrase. Some recent examples are:

text message
speed dating
self-build

As well as new combinations of words, parts of existing words are sometimes merged together to form new words. For example:

digibox (digital + box)
movieoke (movie + karaoke)

Very often, too, we simply find new ways of using words that already exist. For example, because of the widespread use of computers, nouns and verbs such as the ones below have acquired completely new senses – some of which are now used more frequently than the original meanings:

window, mouse, virus, bug, web, surf

New phrasal verbs

New verbs and adjectives are much less frequent than new nouns. So all these trends in the development of new words suggest that completely new phrasal verbs are likely to be quite rare in English, and that any 'new' phrasal verbs that we do find will in most cases be formed *either* from new combinations of existing verbs and particles, *or* through existing phrasal verbs acquiring new meanings.

For instance, until recently, the phrasal verb **bump** someone **off** had only one meaning: an informal way of saying 'to murder someone'. But we now see this verb being used in a new way, in examples like these:

*An error message appeared and I was **bumped off** the Net.*

*There's a problem with a virus and you get **bumped off** after a few minutes of being online.*

This use of **bump off** refers to the situation where the connection between a person's computer and the Internet is unexpectedly broken. A new sense of the phrasal verb has been born, so the dictionary entry now shows two meanings:

ˌbump ˈoff *informal*
1 [often passive] to murder someone = DO IN, KILL
    be bumped off *He was scared of being bumped off.*
    bump off sb *also* **bump sb off** *He's the guy who bumped off the professor.* ♦ *She paid someone to bump him off.*
2 [usually passive] if you are bumped off a computer system, you can no longer use the Internet because the connection with your computer is suddenly broken
    be/get bumped off *If you don't have the right software installed, you may be bumped off the system.* ♦ *I got bumped off my connection while I was trying to reserve a flight.*

Creative uses of phrasal verbs

Many new combinations of verbs and particles arise from a creative use of English, when a speaker wants to find a verb that will express their thoughts at a particular moment.

A common way of doing this is by manipulating one of the components of the phrasal verb – either the *verb* or the *particle*.

Creative use of the verb component

In 2003, the celebrity cook Delia Smith was quoted as saying that she was

'all reciped out ...'

when she announced her intention to retire from TV cookery programmes. You will not find an entry in any dictionary for the phrase **be reciped out**: writers and speakers often use words in creative ways, but dictionaries do not generally describe these individual creative acts.

Nevertheless, we understand what Delia means, because the expression she has created follows a pattern that we are already familiar with. By saying she is *reciped out*, she is expressing the idea of 'having done something so much that you don't want to do it any more'. She means, in other words, that she has used up all her ideas for new recipes.

We understand this because it reminds us of many existing phrasal verbs that express similar ideas, for example:

tire someone **out** (= make them feel exhausted)

and its derived form

tired out (= very tired)

And similarly:

worn out   (from **wear** someone **out**)
burnt out   (from **burn** yourself **out**)

Because we are already familiar with phrases like these, we can make a mental association between the idea of being exhausted and the use of the particle **out**, especially in the pattern:

-ed (past participle) + **out**

This enables us to create new expressions by using **out** with a 'new' verb form, usually one that has been formed from a *noun* (such as **recipe**). Here are some other examples:

partied out   ('tired of going to parties, because you have been to so many')
conferenced out   ('tired of going to conferences')
barbecued out   ('tired of eating barbecue food')

Sometimes adjectives are used to create new phrasal verbs. For example the recent phrasal verb

vague something **up**

means 'to make something seem less clear or detailed', as in this example:

*I **vagued up** certain parts of the story.*

Another example from informal spoken English is the new phrasal verb

big something **up**.

This means 'to recommend something in an enthusiastic way', as in:

*I know I sound like I'm **bigging** it **up**, but it was a great piece of music.*

It is also used in the form **big it up**, to mean 'to enjoy yourself in a social situation, often by spending lots of money', as in:

*We took a trip to a local club where the lads were really **bigging it up**.*

Creative use of the particle component

As well as the verb element in a phrasal verb, the *particle* element can be changed to create new meanings. A common way of doing this is to change the particle to create a phrasal verb that has an opposite meaning to an existing one. For example, the phrasal verb

dumb something **down**

is a disapproving way of saying 'to make something simpler and easier to understand', and it implies this leads to a loss of quality. People now sometimes use the 'new' verb 'to **dumb** something *up*' to describe the process of making something appear *more* complicated or more intellectual.

The particle plays a very important role here. In order to make sense of this phrasal verb, we have to remember that **up** is the opposite of **down**, and therefore that **dumb up** must mean the opposite of **dumb down** – despite the use of the word *dumb* (='stupid') as the verb.

To give another example, the recent phrasal verb **sex** something **up** means 'to change something in order to make it seem more interesting, exciting, or important'. It is used in sentences like this:

*He deliberately **sexed up** the report so that they would pay more attention to his ideas.*

Some speakers and writers now use the expression 'to **sex** something **down**' to refer to the process of making something seem *less* interesting or exciting.

The same process can occur in nouns that are derived from phrasal verbs. For example the derived noun

hand-me-down (from **hand** something **down**)

refers to clothing that is passed on from an older brother or sister to a younger member of the family:

All her clothes were hand-me-downs.

The antonym (opposite) **hand-me-up** is now sometimes used to refer to something that a younger person gives to an *older* person because they no longer use it or because they have something better to replace it.

Particle meanings and 'new' phrasal verb structures

Writers and speakers often create 'new' phrasal verbs and derived nouns and adjectives that depend on associating a particular 'meaning' with the particle. The special particle entries in this dictionary (for words such as **up**, **back**, and **out**) are designed to explain the various ways in which the particle contributes to the meaning of a phrasal verb. So these entries will help you to understand any new combinations that you come across.

Here are a few examples of particles that are often used in this way, with a description of their 'meanings' and some examples of the new phrasal verb structures they have produced:

OFF

This particle is often used to express the idea of removing something (as in phrasal verbs like **cut off** and **cross**

off). For example, in the context of removing someone from a job or position, we sometimes find the new verb **bin** someone/something **off**:

*He was given the chairman's job when Arthur **was binned off** for missing too many meetings.*

OUT

As we have seen, this particle is used creatively to express the idea of having done something so much that you don't want to do it any more. This explains 'new' verbs and adjectives like **reciped out** and **partied out**. It is sometimes also used (as in verbs like **find out** and **hunt out**) to suggest the idea of discovering information by means of a thorough search. For example:

*I had **Googled out** a relevant website.*

means 'I managed to find it by using the Google search engine'.

UP

This particle is often used creatively in two ways:
• Improving, making something seem more sophisticated, attractive, interesting, or exciting. This meaning is reflected in phrasal verbs like **jazz up** and **dress up**, and has been used to create 'new' phrasal verbs like **sex up** and **big up**. Another example of the same idea is **tech up**, which produces the adjective **teched-up** (meaning 'provided with computers, Internet access etc':

*Our schools are rapidly becoming **teched-up** centres of learning.*

• Preparing for something by gathering things or people together. This meaning is reflected in phrasal verbs like **stock up**.

Following patterns like *let's get stocked up for the winter*, new combinations often occur in the structure *get -ed up*, as in the example **get lawyered up**:

*We need to **get lawyered up** if we want to claim our money back.*

,nail 'up

1 to use nails to fasten a door or window firmly shut

nail sth up also **nail up sth** Someone had nailed up the door to the cellar.

2 to fix something to a wall with a nail or nails

nail sth up also **nail up sth** I'll get my hammer and nail the picture up for you.

NAME /neɪm/
names, naming, named

,name 'after ★★★ (also ,name 'for American)

to give someone or something the same name as someone or something else
= CALL AFTER

name sb/sth after sb/sth We decided to name him after his grandfather. ♦ The prize is named for the late Mexican writer Juan Rulfo.

NARROW /'nærəʊ, American 'neroʊ/
narrows, narrowing, narrowed

,narrow 'down ★

to reduce the number of possibilities or choices

narrow down sth We're working to narrow down the list of possible suspects.
narrow sth down They managed to narrow the number of candidates down a bit. ♦ +to That narrowed it down to just two possibilities.

NIBBLE /'nɪb(ə)l/
nibbles, nibbling, nibbled

,nibble a'way at

to reduce the total amount of something by gradually using small amounts of it

nibble away at sth Beware of hidden costs that can nibble away at your budget.

NOD /nɒd, American nɑd/
nods, nodding, nodded

,nod 'off informal

to go to sleep, especially when you do not intend to **= DOZE OFF ≠ WAKE UP**

nod off I must have nodded off in front of the TV.

NOSE /nəʊz, American noʊz/
noses, nosing, nosed

,nose a'round (also ,nose a'bout British)

showing disapproval

to look around a place and try to find out information about someone or something, usually information that people do not want you to have

nose around A few kids were nosing around outside.
nose around sth We've had reporters nosing around the school already.

'nose into showing disapproval

to try to find out information about something

nose into sth I don't want them nosing into my finances.

,nose 'out showing disapproval

to find out information, especially something that someone does not want you to know

nose out sth also **nose sth out** We've managed to nose out a few things that I'm sure he wouldn't want to be made public.

NOTCH /nɒtʃ, American nɑtʃ/
notches, notching, notched

,notch 'up ★ informal

to win or achieve something **= CLOCK UP**
notch up sth The company notched up over £10 million in profits last year.
notch sth up They'd had several easy victories so far, and they've just notched another one up.

Nouns often used as objects with **notch up**

■ gains, record, success, triumph, victory, win

NOTE /nəʊt, American noʊt/
notes, noting, noted

,note 'down ★

to write down something, especially so that you can refer to it later **= WRITE DOWN**
note sth down She quickly noted the car's number down.
note down sth I noted down all the names of the speakers.

NUMBER /'nʌmbə, American 'nʌmbər/
numbers, numbering, numbered

'number among formal

to be part of a particular group or include someone or something among a particular group

number sb/sth among sb/sth I number him among my friends.
number among sb/sth He numbers among America's top authors.

be ,numbered 'off

if people in a group are numbered off, each person is given a number that is used for referring to them

be numbered off The children stand in a line and are numbered off.

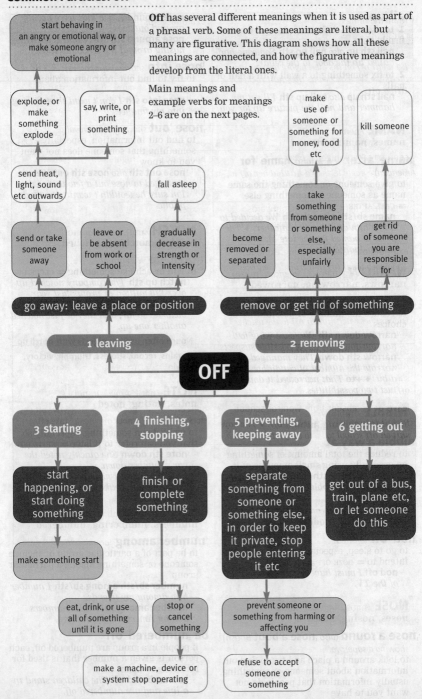

start behaving in an angry or emotional way, or make someone angry or emotional

Off has several different meanings when it is used as part of a phrasal verb. Some of these meanings are literal, but many are figurative. This diagram shows how all these meanings are connected, and how the figurative meanings develop from the literal ones.

Main meanings and example verbs for meanings 2–6 are on the next pages.

explode, or make something explode

say, write, or print something

make use of someone or something for money, food etc

kill someone

send heat, light, sound etc outwards

fall asleep

take something from someone or something else, especially unfairly

get rid of someone you are responsible for

send or take someone away

leave or be absent from work or school

gradually decrease in strength or intensity

become removed or separated

go away: leave a place or position

remove or get rid of something

1 leaving

2 removing

OFF

3 starting

4 finishing, stopping

5 preventing, keeping away

6 getting out

start happening, or start doing something

finish or complete something

separate something from someone or something else, in order to keep it private, stop people entering it etc

get out of a bus, train, plane etc, or let someone do this

make something start

eat, drink, or use all of something until it is gone

stop or cancel something

prevent someone or something from harming or affecting you

make a machine, device or system stop operating

refuse to accept someone or something

Main meanings	Example verbs		
1 leaving			
go away: leave a place or position	back off	lift off	shoot off
*Ed **went off** on his own before anyone was awake.* ♦ *We watched as the giant rocket **lifted off**.*	blast off	make off	shove off
	branch off	make off with	slope off
	clear off	move off	start off
	dash off	peel off	strike off
	drive off	push off	take off
	go off	run off	turn off
	go off with	run off with	veer off
	head off	set off	walk off with
send or take someone away	bundle off	frighten off	see off
*Before we knew it, they'd **hauled** her **off** to jail.* ♦ *Aunt Mimi **saw** us **off** at the station.*	cart off	haul off	send off
	chase off	pack off	spirit off
	drive off	scare off	wave off
send heat, light, sound etc outwards	give off	let off	throw off
*The chemical **gives off** an orange glow as it burns.*			
explode, or make something explode	fire off	let off	set off
*The bomb **went off** in a crowded marketplace.* ♦ *Kids were **setting off** fireworks by the river.*	go off	loose off	
start behaving in an angry or emotional way, or make someone angry or emotional	hack off	set off	tee off
*Did you hear her **mouth off** to the teacher?* ♦ *You never know what's going to **set** Rob **off**.*	mouth off	sound off	tick off
say, write, or print something	dash off	rattle off	run off
*Andrea quickly **rattled off** a list of everyone she had invited.* ♦ *Do you want me to **print off** a copy for you?*	print off	reel off	toss off
leave or be absent from work or school	bunk off	get off	skive off
*Rich is **taking** next Thursday **off**.* ♦ *The boys **skived off** school to go to the football match.*	clock off	knock off	take off
gradually decrease in strength or intensity	cool off	ease off	tail off
*New orders have **fallen off** in the last few months.* ♦ *The effects of the drug soon **wore off**.*	die off	fall off	taper off
	drop off	level off	trail off
	dry off	slack off	wear off
fall asleep	doze off	drop off	go off
*I must have **nodded off** during the lecture.* ♦ *Were you able to **get** the children **off** to sleep?*	drift off	get off	nod off

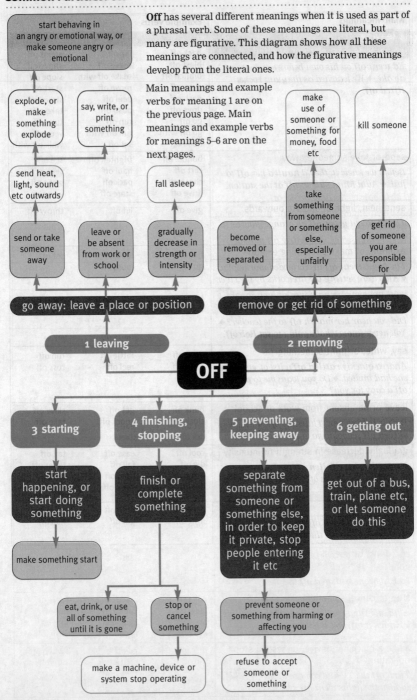

Off has several different meanings when it is used as part of a phrasal verb. Some of these meanings are literal, but many are figurative. This diagram shows how all these meanings are connected, and how the figurative meanings develop from the literal ones.

Main meanings and example verbs for meaning 1 are on the previous page. Main meanings and example verbs for meanings 5–6 are on the next pages.

start behaving in an angry or emotional way, or make someone angry or emotional

explode, or make something explode

say, write, or print something

make use of someone or something for money, food etc

kill someone

send heat, light, sound etc outwards

fall asleep

send or take someone away

leave or be absent from work or school

gradually decrease in strength or intensity

become removed or separated

take something from someone or something else, especially unfairly

get rid of someone you are responsible for

go away: leave a place or position

remove or get rid of something

1 leaving

2 removing

OFF

3 starting

4 finishing, stopping

5 preventing, keeping away

6 getting out

start happening, or start doing something

finish or complete something

separate something from someone or something else, in order to keep it private, stop people entering it etc

get out of a bus, train, plane etc, or let someone do this

make something start

eat, drink, or use all of something until it is gone

stop or cancel something

prevent someone or something from harming or affecting you

make a machine, device or system stop operating

refuse to accept someone or something

Main meanings	Example verbs		
2 removing			
remove or get rid of something *Let me **wipe** that smudge **off** your cheek.* ♦ *I'd already **crossed** several items **off** the list.*	auction off break off burn off cast off chop off cross off cut off fall off fling off get off hack off	help off with kick off kill off lop off palm off peel off sell off shave off slip off slough off soak off	steam off strip off sweat off take off tear off throw off walk off wash off wipe off write off work off
become removed or separated *The handle of the mug **broke off**.*	break off come off	drop off fall off	peel off wash off
take something from someone or something else, especially unfairly *They're accused of **skimming off** most of the profits.*	cream off draw off	rake off rip off	siphon off skim off
make use of someone or something for money, food etc *He's been **sponging off** his family for years.* ♦ *People in those days knew how to **live off** the land.*	feed off	live off	sponge off
get rid of someone you are responsible for *The company **laid off** 700 workers.*	lay off	marry off	pay off pension off
kill someone *He hired two men to **bump off** his wife.* ♦ *Snipers **picked off** soldiers from the rooftops.*	bump off finish off	kill off knock off	pick off polish off
3 starting			
start happening, or start doing something *The game **started off** badly.*	get off kick off	lead off start off	tee off
make something start *His killing **sparked off** a riot.*	kick off set off	spark off start off	touch off trigger off
4 finishing, stopping			
finish or complete something *The party **went off** without any problems.* ♦ *We're going to **round off** the trip with a visit to Buckingham Palace.*	bring off carry off come off	finish off go off log off	ring off round off sign off
ear, drink, or use all of something until it is gone *I see someone **finished off** the pie.*	finish off	polish off	
stop or cancel something *John and Cindy have **called off** the wedding.* ♦ ***Knock** it **off**, or I'll tell Dad.*	beg off blow off break off call off	cry off cut off knock off lay off	leave off put off rain off write off
make a machine, device, or system stop operating ***Turn off** the TV and come to dinner.* ♦ *All of a sudden the lights **went off**.*	flick off flip off	go off shut off	switch off turn off

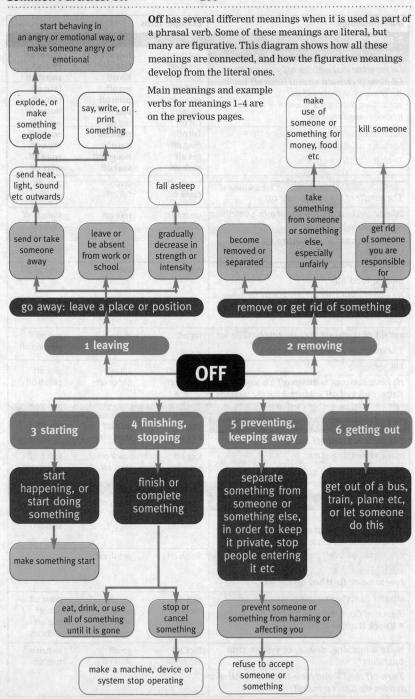

Off has several different meanings when it is used as part of a phrasal verb. Some of these meanings are literal, but many are figurative. This diagram shows how all these meanings are connected, and how the figurative meanings develop from the literal ones.

Main meanings and example verbs for meanings 1–4 are on the previous pages.

start behaving in an angry or emotional way, or make someone angry or emotional

explode, or make something explode

say, write, or print something

send heat, light, sound etc outwards

fall asleep

make use of someone or something for money, food etc

kill someone

take something from someone or something else, especially unfairly

get rid of someone you are responsible for

send or take someone away

leave or be absent from work or school

gradually decrease in strength or intensity

become removed or separated

go away: leave a place or position

remove or get rid of something

1 leaving

2 removing

OFF

3 starting

4 finishing, stopping

5 preventing, keeping away

6 getting out

start happening, or start doing something

finish or complete something

separate something from someone or something else, in order to keep it private, stop people entering it etc

get out of a bus, train, plane etc, or let someone do this

make something start

eat, drink, or use all of something until it is gone

stop or cancel something

prevent someone or something from harming or affecting you

make a machine, device or system stop operating

refuse to accept someone or something

Main meanings	Example verbs		
5 preventing, keeping away			
separate something from someone or something else, in order to keep it private, stop people entering it etc	block off	divide off	screen off
	close off	fence off	seal off
	cone off	hive off	section off
*We're going to **fence off** part of the back garden for the dogs.* ♦ *Several of the galleries had been **cordoned off**.*	cordon off	mark off	shut off
	curtain off	partition off	spin off
	cut off	rope off	wall off
prevent someone or something from harming or affecting you	beat off	frighten off	scare off
	buy off	head off	stave off
*I'm still **fighting off** a cold.* ♦ *She carries a weapon to **ward off** attackers.*	fend off	hold off	ward off
	fight off	keep off	warn off
refuse to accept someone or something	brush off	put off	shrug off
*Cole just **laughed off** the mistakes.* ♦ *She's an expert at **brushing off** criticism.*	laugh off	shake off	throw off
6 getting out			
get out of a bus, train, plane etc, or let someone do this	come off	get off	put off
	drop off	let off	
*You can **let** me **off** at the next corner.* ♦ *People kept **coming off** the plane.*			

On has several different meanings when it is used as part of a phrasal verb. Some of these meanings are literal, but many are figurative. This diagram shows how all these meanings are connected, and how the figurative meanings develop from the literal ones.

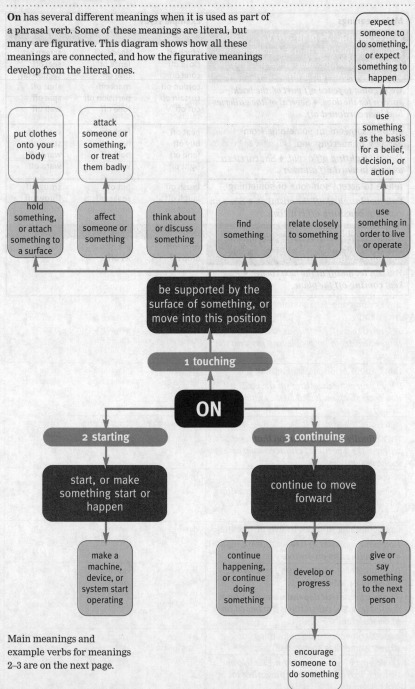

Main meanings and example verbs for meanings 2–3 are on the next page.

Main meanings	Example verbs		
1 touching			
be supported by the surface of something, or move into this position *The bus driver waited until we had **got on**.* ♦ *Everyone applauded when Forster **came on**.*	come on	get on	go on
hold something, or attach something to a surface **Hang on** – *the road gets bumpy here.* ♦ *We'll **slap on** a little paint, and it'll look as good as new.*	add on build on cling on	dab on hang on hold on	put on slap on tack on
put clothes onto your body *You're going to buy it without **trying it on**?* ♦ *Can I **help** you **on with** your coat?*	fling on have on help on with	pop on pull on put on	slip on throw on try on
affect someone or something *Martha simply **dotes on** her grandchildren.* ♦ *Both candidates are clearly **playing on** voters' fears.*	cheat on dawn on descend on dote on encroach on fall on grass on heap on	impress on impinge on inform on pin on play on prevail on put on rat on	sit on spring on spy on tell on train on turn on weigh on work on
attack someone or something, or treat them badly *It seemed that all his friends had **turned on** him.* ♦ *Watch out for people who **prey on** the elderly.*	beat on dump on fall on jump on	pick on pounce on prey on round on	set on start on turn on
think about or discuss something *There's no point **dwelling on** the past.* ♦ *Why don't you **sleep on** it and let me know tomorrow.*	chew on decide on dwell on	elaborate on enlarge on expand on	reflect on sleep on touch on
find something *We've finally **hit on** a solution that we think will work.* ♦ *The hikers **chanced** on a cottage in the woods.*	chance on come on	happen on hit on	strike on stumble on
relate closely to something *Her behaviour **borders on** criminal at times.* ♦ *Police found information **bearing on** the court case.*	bear on	border on	verge on
use something in order to live or operate *How am I supposed to **live on** $1,000 a month?* ♦ *The radio **runs on** ordinary batteries.*	depend on feed on	live on rely on	run on
use something as the basis for a belief, decision, or action *The exact date will **depend on** when Kim is available.* ♦ *The calculations are **based on** historical trends.*	act on base on build on depend on	draw on hang on hinge on model on	pattern on pivot on trade on turn on
expect someone to do something, or expect something to happen *Don't worry – you can **rely on** Eric to come through in a crisis.* ♦ *We're **planning on** at least 40 guests.*	bank on bargain on bet on	count on depend on plan on	reckon on rely on wait on

On has several different meanings when it is used as part of a phrasal verb. Some of these meanings are literal, but many are figurative. This diagram shows how all these meanings are connected, and how the figurative meanings develop from the literal ones.

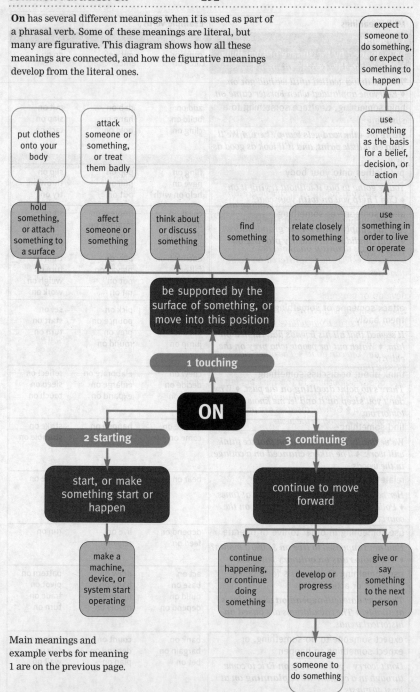

- put clothes onto your body
- attack someone or something, or treat them badly
- expect someone to do something, or expect something to happen
- use something as the basis for a belief, decision, or action

- hold something, or attach something to a surface
- affect someone or something
- think about or discuss something
- find something
- relate closely to something
- use something in order to live or operate

be supported by the surface of something, or move into this position

1 touching

ON

2 starting

3 continuing

start, or make something start or happen

continue to move forward

- make a machine, device, or system start operating

- continue happening, or continue doing something
- develop or progress
- give or say something to the next person

- encourage someone to do something

Main meanings and example verbs for meaning 1 are on the previous page.

Main meanings	Example verbs		
2 starting			
start, or make something start or happen *His heart attack was **brought on** by stress.* ♦ *After leaving college, Lucy **embarked on** an acting career.*	bring on catch on clock on	cotton on embark on latch on	log on sign on start on
make a machine, device, or system start operating *Could you **turn on** the lamp?* ♦ *The lights **came on** all by themselves.*	come on flick on	go on jam on	switch on turn on
3 continuing			
continue to move forward *We **pressed on**, hoping to arrive before dark.* ♦ *They stayed only a day before **moving on**.*	carry on go on	move on plod on	press on push on
continue happening, or continue doing something *She's always **droning on** about her boyfriend.* ♦ *They have **soldiered on** despite obstacles.*	bang on carry on drag on drone on hang on hold on	keep on linger on live on play on plod on press on	push on ramble on soldier on stay on struggle on wear on
develop or progress *How is your father **getting on**?* ♦ *Society's attitudes towards women have **moved on**.*	get on	march on	move on
encourage someone to do something ***Come on**! You can do it!* ♦ *The other kids kept **egging** him **on**.*	cheer on egg on	goad on lead on	spur on urge on
give or say something to the next person *You should probably **hand on** the information.* ♦ *Genetic diseases are **passed on** from one generation to the next.*	hand on	pass on	sell on

O o

OBJECT /əb'dʒekt, American ab'dʒekt/
objects, objecting, objected

ob'ject to ★★★
to not approve of something, or to disagree
strongly with it
object to sth *I really object to the way
she never asks my opinion.* ♦ *There's
nothing in the report that they could
really object to.*

OCCUR /ə'kɜː, American ə'kɜr/
occurs, occurring, occurred

oc'cur to ★★★ [never passive]
if a thought or idea occurs to you, you
suddenly and unexpectedly start to think
about it = COME TO
occur to sb *The thought of giving up
never occurred to me.* ♦ **+that** *It suddenly
occurred to her that Joe was afraid of
being alone.* ♦ **+to do sth** *It didn't occur
to her to ask how he'd found her.*

OFFEND /ə'fend/
offends, offending, offended

of'fend against *formal*
to do something that is against a set of
principles, a law, or a rule
offend against sth *The new proposals
offend against the very idea of
democracy.*

OFFER /'ɒfə, American 'ɔfər, 'ɑfər/
offers, offering, offered

offer 'up ★
1 to give thanks, praise, etc to God or a
god
offer up thanks/praise/ prayers etc
*They offered up thanks for the ship's safe
return.* ♦ **+to** *Lord, we offer up our
prayers to you.*
2 to provide something that is intended
to impress someone or make them feel
pleased or satisfied
offer up sth *The friendly staff offer up a
real taste of Southwest America.*
offer sth up *We are offering a
programme up that has something to
appeal to all voters, young and old.*

OFFSET /'ɒf,set, American ,ɔf'set,
'ɔf,set/
offsets, offsetting, offset

'offset against
to be able to balance one thing against
another, so that there is no advantage or
disadvantage = SET AGAINST, SET OFF
AGAINST
offset sth against sth *You can offset
most of your travel expenses against tax.*

OPEN /'əʊpən, American 'oʊpən/
opens, opening, opened

open 'into
if a room or door opens into another room,
you can get directly from one room to the
other
open into sth *The door opened into a
dark passage.*

open 'off
if a room or door opens off another room,
you can get directly from one room to the
other
open off sth *Two formal reception rooms
opened off the hall.*

open 'onto
if a door opens onto something, that is the
room or space that is outside it
open onto sth *The kitchen door opens
onto a patio.*

open 'out ★★
1 if a path, passage, valley etc opens out,
it becomes wider at the end or joins an
open space
open out *The cottage was at that point
where the valley suddenly opens out.*
♦ **+into** *The alleyway opened out into a
courtyard behind the houses.*
2 if something opens out, or if you open
it out, it opens from a folded position so
that you can see its shape = OPEN UP,
SPREAD OUT, UNFOLD ≠ FOLD UP
open out *The buds on the trees were
starting to open out.*
open sth out *She opened the map out on
the table.*
open out sth *He opened out the folded
newspaper to read the rest of the article.*
3 if a discussion opens out, or if you open
it out, it becomes more general or starts
to include more subjects = BROADEN, OPEN
UP, WIDEN
open out sth *He tried to open out the
conversation.*
open sth out *No attempt to open the
discussion out succeeded.*
open out *Slowly the debate began to
open out and become more interesting.*

'open to

to make something available for people to see, take part in, or visit

open sth to sb/sth *We decided to open the grounds to the public last year.* ♦ *I think they should open the competition to younger participants.*

open 'up ★★★

1	open sth locked
2	make travel/trade easier
3	create new opportunities
4	make people seem different
5	discussion: become more general
6	talk about your feelings
7	shoot a gun
8	when doctors cut sb's body
9	become available to use/visit
10	become open from a folded position
+	PHRASE

1 to open a locked door, container, or building = OPEN ≠ LOCK UP

open up sth *He opens up the shop every morning.*
open sth up *When they opened the safe up, all there was inside was a sealed letter.*

2 to make it easier to travel or do business in a country

open up sth *The building of canals opened up the interior of the country.*
open sth up *The government of this isolated nation refuses to do anything to open their territory up.*
open up *The state has opened up significantly in the last ten years.* ♦ **+to** *China is opening up to foreign investment.*

3 to create a new opportunity or possibility

open up sth *Going freelance opens up all sorts of possibilities to you.*
open up *New markets are opening up every day.*

4 to create a difference between the people or groups involved in something

open up sth *The issue of Europe has opened up deep divisions within the party.*
♦ *United have opened up a 6-point lead over their nearest rivals.*
open sth up *The controversy has opened a rift up between members of the various churches.*

5 if a discussion opens up, or if you open it up, it becomes more general or starts to include more subjects = BROADEN, OPEN OUT, WIDEN

open up sth *He tried to open up the conversation to include the new people in the group.*

open up *I think the discussion needs to open up a bit.*

6 to talk more about your personal feelings and experiences

open up *It might help if we could persuade him to open up a little more.*
♦ **+to** *It's taken a few months, but Katy is finally starting to open up to me.*

7 to start shooting a gun, or to start being fired = OPEN FIRE

open up *The helicopters narrowly escaped being hit when enemy guns opened up as they flew in.* ♦ **+on** *He opened up on the crowd with an automatic rifle.*

8 *informal* to cut into someone's body for medical reasons

open sb up *I think we're going to have to open you up and take a look inside, I'm afraid.*

9 if a new business, building etc opens up, or if someone opens it up, it becomes available for people to use for the first time

open up sth *Donald wants to retire and open up a bookshop.*
open up *Two new cinemas are opening up in town.*

10 if something opens up or you open it up, it opens from a folded position so that you can see its shape = UNFOLD, OPEN OUT, SPREAD OUT ≠ FOLD UP

open up *The rose buds are beginning to open up.*
open up sth *I opened up a folding chair for my grandmother.*
open sth up *She opened her umbrella up at the first drops of rain.*

PHRASE **open up!** *informal* used to order someone to open their door: *Open up! It's the police.*

OPPOSE /əˈpəʊz, American əˈpoʊz/
opposes, opposing, opposed

be op'posed to ★

to think that something should not happen or should not be done

be opposed to sth *He was bitterly opposed to the war.*
be opposed to doing sth *Some residents were opposed to naming the school after Martin Luther King.*

OPT /ɒpt, American ɑpt/
opts, opting, opted

'opt for ★★★

to make a choice or decision from a range of possibilities = CHOOSE

opt for sth *Most people these days opt for holidays abroad.*

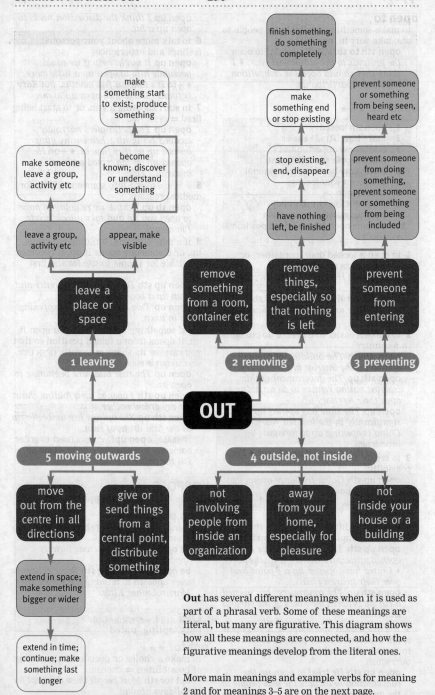

finish something, do something completely

make something end or stop existing

make something start to exist; produce something

stop existing, end, disappear

prevent someone or something from being seen, heard etc

make someone leave a group, activity etc

become known; discover or understand something

have nothing left, be finished

prevent someone from doing something, prevent someone or something from being included

leave a group, activity etc

appear, make visible

leave a place or space

remove something from a room, container etc

remove things, especially so that nothing is left

prevent someone from entering

1 leaving

2 removing

3 preventing

OUT

5 moving outwards

4 outside, not inside

move out from the centre in all directions

give or send things from a central point, distribute something

not involving people from inside an organization

away from your home, especially for pleasure

not inside your house or a building

extend in space; make something bigger or wider

extend in time; continue; make something last longer

Out has several different meanings when it is used as part of a phrasal verb. Some of these meanings are literal, but many are figurative. This diagram shows how all these meanings are connected, and how the figurative meanings develop from the literal ones.

More main meanings and example verbs for meaning 2 and for meanings 3–5 are on the next page.

Main meanings	Example verbs		
1 leaving			
leave a place or space *All the pans **fell out** when I opened the cupboard.* ♦ *He **stormed out** and slammed the door.*	bail out break out bust out check out clear out clock out come out drive out fall out	fly out get out go out move out pile out pop out pour out pull out set out	ship out show out sign out spill out of start out step out storm out strike out turn out
leave a group, activity etc *Shelley **dropped out** of college after just three months.*	back out bail out bottle out	bow out drop out log out	opt out pull out want out
make someone leave a group, activity etc *Briggs was **forced out** of the party.*	boot out buy out chuck out drum out	ease out elbow out freeze out hound out	kick out throw out turf out vote out
appear, make visible *The sun **came out** from behind a cloud.* ♦ *The window went up and a man's head **poked out**.*	come out fish out hatch out	jut out poke out stand out	stick out take out whip out
make something exist, produce something *They're **bringing out** a new computer game next week.* ♦ *She **tapped out** the rhythm with her feet.*	bang out bring out burst out	churn out crank out roll out	rush out trot out turn out
become known; discover or understand something *We **found out** that she was lying.* ♦ *It **turned out** that he was not a qualified doctor at all.*	come out dig out ferret out	figure out find out slip out	sound out turn out work out
2 removing			
remove something from a room, container etc *She opened the door to **let out** the cat.* ♦ *I'm going to **throw out** these old magazines.*	chuck out clear out kick out	let out pull out push out	put out throw out toss out
remove things, especially so that nothing is left *I couldn't **wash out** the stain.* ♦ *He **emptied out** the bag onto the table.*	cross out cut out edit out empty out filter out	flush out rinse out scrub out strip out	tear out wash out weed out wipe out
have nothing left, be finished *After two days, all the food **ran out**.* ♦ *Tickets for the show **sold out** in less than an hour.*	run out	sell out	
stop existing, end, disappear *The fire **burned out** after a few hours.* ♦ *It's an old custom that has almost **died out**.*	burn out conk out die out	fade out fizzle out give out	go out peg out peter out

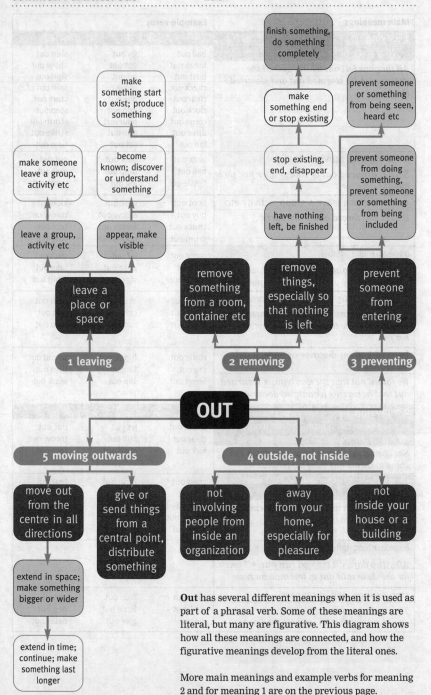

finish something,
do something
completely

make
something start
to exist; produce
something

make
something end
or stop existing

prevent someone
or something
from being seen,
heard etc

make someone
leave a group,
activity etc

become
known; discover
or understand
something

stop existing,
end, disappear

prevent someone
from doing
something,
prevent someone
or something
from being
included

leave a group,
activity etc

appear, make
visible

have nothing
left, be finished

leave a
place or
space

remove
something
from a room,
container etc

remove
things,
especially so
that nothing
is left

prevent
someone
from
entering

1 leaving

2 removing

3 preventing

OUT

5 moving outwards

4 outside, not inside

move out
from the
centre in all
directions

give or
send things
from a
central point,
distribute
something

not
involving
people from
inside an
organization

away
from your
home,
especially for
pleasure

not
inside your
house or a
building

extend in space;
make something
bigger or wider

extend in time;
continue; make
something last
longer

Out has several different meanings when it is used as part of a phrasal verb. Some of these meanings are literal, but many are figurative. This diagram shows how all these meanings are connected, and how the figurative meanings develop from the literal ones.

More main meanings and example verbs for meaning 2 and for meaning 1 are on the previous page.

Main meanings	Example verbs		
make something end or stop existing *The new law will **stamp out** drug trafficking.* ♦ *I tried to **blot out** the painful memory.*	blot out blow out cancel out	phase out root out snuff out	stamp out stub out wipe out
finish something, do something completely *Did you **carry out** all my instructions?* ♦ *You have to **fill out** a long application form.*	carry out clean out copy out	dry out fill out hear out	kit out thrash out tire out

3 preventing

prevent someone from entering *Police stood at the gates to **keep out** the protesters.*	keep out	lock out	shut out
prevent someone from doing something, prevent someone or something from being included *I tried to **talk** her **out of** it.*	argue out of coax out of	leave out rule out	talk out of weed out
prevent someone or something from being seen, heard etc. *A big cloud **blocked out** the sun.* ♦ *The traffic noise **drowned out** our conversation.*	block out	blot out	drown out

4 outside, not inside

not inside your house or a building *She **stayed out** all night without telling her parents.*	board out camp out get out	hide out move out	sleep out stay out
away from your home, especially for pleasure *How often do you **eat out**?* ♦ *Why don't you **ask** her **out** to a movie?*	ask out dine out	eat out invite out	take out
not involving people from inside an organization *The job was **farmed out** to a specialist agency.* ♦ *We **contract out** all the cleaning work.*	contract out farm out		hire out

5 moving outwards

move out from the centre in all directions *The group **spread out** and began their search.*	branch out	fan out	spread out
extend in space; make something bigger or wider *We **spread out** the map on the floor.* ♦ *I **stretched out** my arm to get a book.*	broaden out bulk out fill out	flare out hollow out open out	roll out spread out stretch out
extend in time; continue; make something last longer *They **dragged out** the negotiations for several days.* ♦ *We managed to **hold out** till the police arrived.*	drag out draw out hold out	last out ride out sit out	stick out string out wait out
give or send things from a central point, distribute something *We **sent out** invitations to all our friends.*	deal out dish out dole out	give out hand out measure out	parcel out send out share out

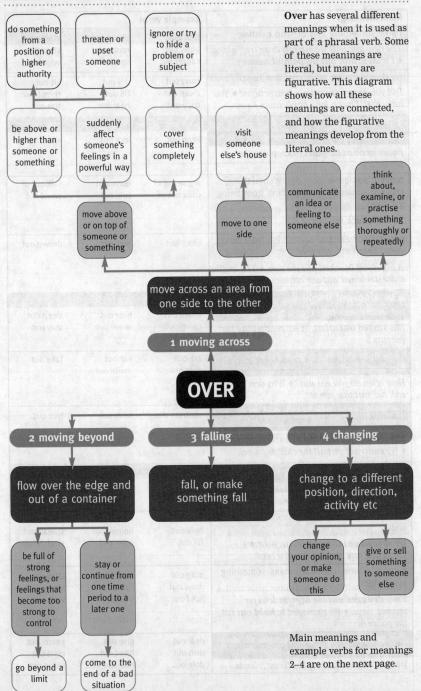

Over has several different meanings when it is used as part of a phrasal verb. Some of these meanings are literal, but many are figurative. This diagram shows how all these meanings are connected, and how the figurative meanings develop from the literal ones.

do something from a position of higher authority

threaten or upset someone

ignore or try to hide a problem or subject

be above or higher than someone or something

suddenly affect someone's feelings in a powerful way

cover something completely

visit someone else's house

communicate an idea or feeling to someone else

think about, examine, or practise something thoroughly or repeatedly

move above or on top of someone or something

move to one side

move across an area from one side to the other

1 moving across

OVER

2 moving beyond

3 falling

4 changing

flow over the edge and out of a container

fall, or make something fall

change to a different position, direction, activity etc

be full of strong feelings, or feelings that become too strong to control

stay or continue from one time period to a later one

change your opinion, or make someone do this

give or sell something to someone else

go beyond a limit

come to the end of a bad situation

Main meanings and example verbs for meanings 2–4 are on the next page.

Main meanings	Example verbs		
1 moving across			
move across an area from one side to the other *He **called** the waiter **over** to complain.* ♦ *Myra went **over** to greet them as soon as they came in.*	call over	go over	look over
move above or on top of someone or something *Our cat was **run over** by a car.* ♦ *A wind was **passing over** the plains.*	pass over	run over	
be above or higher than someone or something *She **bent over** him to look at his work.* ♦ *Larkin **towers over** the other players.*	bend over	stand over	tower over
do something from a position of higher authority *Judge Davis will **preside over** the hearing.* ♦ *Soldiers are now **watching over** the village.*	preside over	rule over	watch over
threaten or upset someone *Threats of layoffs are still **hanging over** workers.* ♦ *Jake is the kind of person to **hold** your past **over** you.*	hang over	hold over	
suddenly affect someone's feelings in a powerful way *A feeling of desperation **swept over** Kevin.*	bowl over	come over	sweep over
cover something completely *The wound will heal **over** in a few days.* ♦ *All the windows had been **boarded over**.*	board over cloud over freeze over	grass over glaze over heal over	ice over pave over roof over
ignore or try to hide a problem or subject *The report **skates over** a few major issues.* ♦ *Both men have tried to **gloss over** their differences.*	gloss over	pass over	skate over
move to one side *A policeman **pulled** me **over** for speeding.* ♦ ***Move over** – there's not enough room for us.*	move over	pull over	
visit someone else's house ***Come over** and watch the game with me.* ♦ *We're **having** the Dunbars **over** on Thursday.*	ask over come over	have over	invite over	pop over stop over
communicate an idea or feeling to someone else *I think she **put** her message **over** quite well.* ♦ *It's important to **come over** as self-confident.*	come over	get over	put over
think about, examine, or practise something thoroughly or repeatedly *I've **gone over** it a thousand times in my head, but I still don't understand why he left.* ♦ *Could you help me **run over** my lines for the play?*	agonize over brood over check over go over	mull over pore over puzzle over rake over	run over sweat over talk over think over

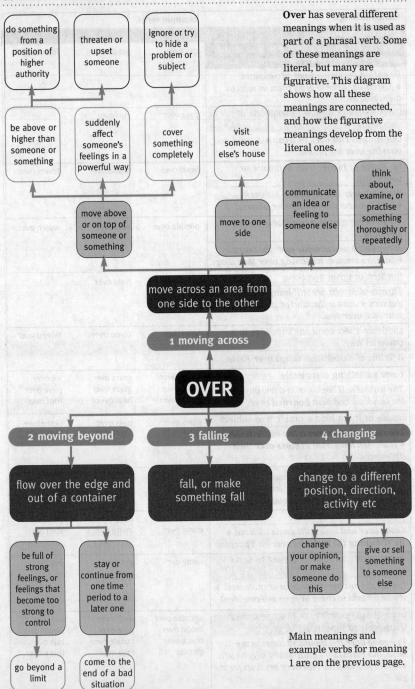

Over has several different meanings when it is used as part of a phrasal verb. Some of these meanings are literal, but many are figurative. This diagram shows how all these meanings are connected, and how the figurative meanings develop from the literal ones.

do something from a position of higher authority

threaten or upset someone

ignore or try to hide a problem or subject

be above or higher than someone or something

suddenly affect someone's feelings in a powerful way

cover something completely

visit someone else's house

communicate an idea or feeling to someone else

think about, examine, or practise something thoroughly or repeatedly

move above or on top of someone or something

move to one side

move across an area from one side to the other

1 moving across

OVER

2 moving beyond

3 falling

4 changing

flow over the edge and out of a container

fall, or make something fall

change to a different position, direction, activity etc

be full of strong feelings, or feelings that become too strong to control

stay or continue from one time period to a later one

change your opinion, or make someone do this

give or sell something to someone else

go beyond a limit

come to the end of a bad situation

Main meanings and example verbs for meaning 1 are on the previous page.

Main meanings	Example verbs		
2 moving beyond			
flow over the edge and out of a container	boil over	spill over	run over
*Don't let the milk **boil over**. ♦ Following the rains, the river **ran over** its banks.*	brim over		
be full of strong feelings, or feelings that become too strong to control	boil over	brim over	bubble over with
*Katie and Lil were **bubbling over with** excitement. ♦ Tensions finally **boiled over** and the riots began.*			
go beyond a limit	run over	spill over	
*The meeting **ran over** by 30 minutes. ♦ Fighting has **spilled over** into surrounding areas.*			
stay or continue from one time period to a later one	carry over	lay over	stay over
*Why don't you **stay over** and drive back tomorrow? ♦ Discussion was **held over** until the next meeting.*	hold over	sleep over	stop over
come to the end of a bad situation	blow over	get over	tide over
*I just can't wait to **get** the whole project **over** with. ♦ Could you lend me some money to **tide** me **over** till payday?*			
3 falling			
fall, or make something fall	blow over	keel over	push over
*Strong winds **blew over** the old school house. ♦ She started to sway and then **fell over**.*	double over	kick over	tip over
	fall over	knock over	topple over
4 changing			
change to a different position, direction, activity etc	change over	make over	switch over
*We're **switching over** to a new computer system at work next week. ♦ **Turn over** your test when you've finished.*	go over to	swap over	turn over
give or sell something to someone else	fork over	hand over	sign over
*As part of the agreement, he **signed** the house **over** to his ex-wife. ♦ **Hand over** the money and no one will get hurt.*	give over to	make over	turn over
change your opinion, or make someone do this	cross over	go over to	win over
*I'm surprised that Higgins **went over** to the other side. ♦ Mark can **win** anyone **over** with his charm.*			

,opt 'in (also **,opt 'into**)

to decide that you want to do something or be involved in something

opt in *Members are given the choice to opt in.*

opt into sth *The British government was reluctant to opt into such a system.*

,opt 'out ★★

to decide not to take part in something, or to stop taking part in it = BOW OUT

opt out *I'd said I would do it and it was too late to opt out.* ♦ **+of** *The firm opted out of the company car scheme last year.*

ORDER /'ɔːdə, *American* 'ɔrdər/
orders, ordering, ordered

,order a'round (also **,order a'bout** *British*)

to keep telling someone what to do as if you have authority over them, in a way that annoys people

order sb around *Who do you think you are, ordering me around like that?*

,order 'in *American*

to order food from a restaurant and ask for it to be delivered to you = ORDER OUT

order in *We were too tired to cook, so we ordered in.*

order in sth also **order sth in** *I ordered in pizza for dinner.* ♦ *We usually ordered something in from the deli.*

,order 'off

in sport, to tell a player that they must leave the field because they have broken the rules = SEND OFF

order sb off *The referee had no option but to order him off.*

,order 'out *American*

to order food from a restaurant and ask for it to be delivered to you = ORDER IN

order out *We got back late and decided to order out.*

,order 'up

1 to tell someone to do something, provide something, or deliver something

order up sth also **order sth up** *The Pentagon ordered up cruise missile attacks.* ♦ *We ordered up FBI reports on the men.*

2 in a hotel, to choose food or drinks and ask for them to be delivered to your room

order up sth also **order sth up** *I decided to order up breakfast.*

OSCILLATE /'ɒsɪleɪt, *American* 'ɑsɪˌleɪt/
oscillates, oscillating, oscillated

'oscillate between

to continuously change your feelings, opinions, or decisions from one extreme position to another

oscillate between sth and sth *He oscillated between optimism and despair.*

OVERCOME /ˌəʊvə'kʌm, *American* ˌoʊvər'kʌm/
overcomes, overcoming, overcame /ˌəʊvə'keɪm, *American* ˌoʊvər'keɪm/,
overcome

be over'come with ★ [usually passive]

1 to make someone feel a very strong emotion

be overcome with sth *The entire family was overcome with grief.*

Nouns often used as objects with **be overcome with 1**

■ curiosity, emotion, gratitude, grief, joy, remorse, shame, shyness

2 to make someone very weak, ill, or unconscious

be overcome with sth *The two men tried to escape but were overcome with fumes.*

OWE /əʊ/
owes, owing, owed

'owe to

1 to have something only because someone or something has helped you to get it

owe sth to sb/sth *The company owes its success to its excellent training programme.* ♦ *I owe everything to my partner Claire.*

2 to think that you should do something for someone, especially because they deserve it

owe sth to sb *I should stay here really. I feel I owe that much to my mother.*
♦ **+to do sth** *They owe it to their children to try and save the marriage.*

OWN /əʊn/
owns, owning, owned

'own to *literary*

to admit that something bad about yourself is true

own to sth *She owned to occasional feelings of jealousy.*

,own 'up ★

to admit that you have done something

bad or embarrassing = CONFESS; *informal* FESS UP

own up *Dan could have made this whole thing go away simply by owning up.* ♦ *Come on, own up! It was you who drank all the beer, wasn't it?* ♦ **+to** *Two local students later owned up to the prank.*

own up

Pp

PACE /peɪs/
paces, pacing, paced

pace 'out (*also* pace 'off)
to measure a distance by counting the number of steps that you need to walk from one end of something to the other
pace out sth *also* **pace sth out** *I had already paced out the dimensions of my new home.*

PACK /pæk/
packs, packing, packed

pack a'way ★
1 to put something back into the container where it is stored, after you have finished using it
pack away sth *We packed away the picnic things and started up the engine.*
pack sth away *Pack your books away and come to the front of the class.*

2 *informal* to eat a large quantity of food
pack sth away *She can really pack it away.*
pack away sth *He had packed away a large pizza but was still hungry.*

pack 'in ★★

1	attract a big audience
2	stop doing sth
3	put a lot of people/things in sth
4	do a lot of activities
5	end a romantic/sexual relationship
+	PHRASE

1 *informal* to attract very large audiences
pack sb in *The play was still **packing them in** after several weeks.*
pack in sb *The show is expected to pack in huge audiences in its short run.*

2 *British informal* to stop doing something, especially a job = PACK UP, GIVE UP
pack in sth *A year ago, she packed in her job to join the band.*
pack sth in *I'd love to pack this job in but I can't.*

3 to fill something with a lot of people or things = CRAM IN
pack sb/sth in *The more people they can pack in, the more money they make.*
pack in sb/sth *These hotels pack in as many guests as they can in tiny rooms.*

4 to fill a period of time with a lot of activities = CRAM IN
pack in sth *He packed in an amazing amount in such a short life.*
pack sth in *We were only in Paris for a few days, so we had to pack a lot in during that time.*

5 *British informal* to end a sexual or romantic relationship with someone = CHUCK, DITCH
pack in sb *Apparently he's packed in his new girlfriend already.*
pack sb in *I'm thinking of packing him in.*

> **PHRASE pack it in** *British informal* used for telling someone to stop doing something that is annoying you: *Pack it in, you lot.*

pack 'into
1 to go into a place in large numbers
pack into sth *At least 150,000 people packed into Manezh Square.*

2 to fit a lot of activities into a period of time = CRAM INTO
pack sth into sth *The festival offers 16 different shows, all packed into one weekend.*

pack 'off [often passive] *informal*
to send someone away somewhere suddenly
be packed off *The best thing would be for him to be packed off back where he came from.* ♦ **+to** *To avoid family disgrace, Frank was packed off to India.*
pack sb off *also* **pack off sb** *'Is John still*

pack up

staying with you?' 'No, we packed him off home yesterday.'

be ˌpacked ˈout
to be very crowded
> **be packed out** *The hall was packed out by the time we got there.*

ˌpack ˈup ★★
1 to put things into a bag, case, or box so that you can take or send them somewhere = PACK
> **pack up sth** *He simply packed up his belongings and moved out on Tuesday.*
> **pack sth up** *We were still packing everything up for the removal men when they arrived.*

2 *British informal* if a machine or piece of equipment packs up, it stops working
> **pack up** *The camera had packed up.*

3 *informal* to finish work for the day by putting work or equipment away
> **pack up** *The workmen have already packed up and left.*

4 *British informal* to stop doing something, especially a job = PACK IN, GIVE UP
> **pack up sth** *Do you think he's going to pack up this job too?*
> **pack sth up** *He's threatening to pack it all up and go off around the world.*

PAD /pæd/
pads, padding, padded

ˌpad ˈout
to put unnecessary information into something in order to make it longer
> **pad sth out** *also* **pad out sth** *Try not to pad your report out with irrelevant statistics.*

ˌpad ˈup
if someone playing the game of cricket pads up, they put special thick soft covers

on their legs in order to protect them before they start hitting the ball
> **pad up** *He had already padded up and was waiting in the pavilion.*

PAGE /peɪdʒ/
pages, paging, paged

ˌpage ˈdown
to press a key on a computer that brings up the next page of a document on the screen
> **page down** *I quickly paged down till I found his name.*

ˈpage through *mainly American*
to turn the pages of a book, newspaper, or magazine quickly without reading or looking at it carefully = LEAF THROUGH
> **page through sth** *She sat in the waiting room, casually paging through glossy magazines.*

ˌpage ˈup
to press a key on a computer that brings up the previous page of a document on the screen
> **page up** *She then paged up to the beginning of the document again.*

PAIR /peə, American per/
pairs, pairing, paired

ˌpair ˈoff
to start a sexual or romantic relationship with someone, or to bring two people together because you want them to have a relationship with each other
> **pair off** *All our friends seemed to be pairing off.*
> **pair sb off** *also* **pair off sb** *He suspected that she had paired off Damien and Clare in her mind.* ♦ **+with** *They paired me off with a gorgeous man.*

,pair 'up

to form a pair or make two people form a
pair = TEAM UP

pair up *Two students from each class
pair up to produce a short play.* ♦ **+with**
*I paired up with Jimmy to help with the
search.*

pair sb up *also* **pair up sb** *The
organization has paired up writers and
artists, commissioning essays dedicated
to particular works of art.*

PAL /pæl/
pals, palling, palled

,pal a'round (*also* ,pal a'bout *British*)
informal

to spend time with a friend

pal around *The two boys palled around
the whole summer.* ♦ **+with** *Who's she
been palling around with?*

,pal 'up *British old-fashioned*

to become someone's friend

pal up *We palled up shortly after we first
met.* ♦ **+with** *He had palled up with a
boy from another school.*

PALM /pɑːm, *American* pɑlm, pɑm/
palms, palming, palmed

,palm 'off *informal*

to get rid of something that you do not
want, by persuading someone else to take
or buy it from you

palm off sth *also* **palm sth off** *If you want
to palm off that old Playstation, try your
local youth club.* ♦ **+on/onto** *I managed
to palm off all my old college books on
my little sister.*

,palm 'off as

to try to trick someone by making them
believe that something is something else,
usually something much better than it
really is = PASS OFF AS

palm sth off as sth *They tried to palm
them off as real diamonds.*

,palm 'off with *showing disapproval*

to give someone an explanation or excuse
that is not true or is not satisfactory, but
which you hope they will accept

palm sb off with sth *He tried to palm us
off with some story about his mother
being sick.*

PAN /pæn/
pans, panning, panned

,pan 'out *informal*

if a situation pans out in a particular way,
it develops in that way = TURN OUT

pan out *Let's see how things pan out
before we decide.*

PANDER /'pændə, *American* 'pændər/
panders, pandering, pandered

'pander to

to do or say what someone wants in order
to please them, even though you know it
is not right = INDULGE ≠ RESIST

pander to sb/sth *The government was
accused of pandering to racial prejudice.*

PAPER /'peɪpə, *American* 'peɪpər/
papers, papering, papered

,paper 'over

to try to hide a problem or disagreement
instead of finding a satisfactory solution
to it = CONCEAL ≠ HIGHLIGHT

paper over sth *It's no use trying to paper
over the differences between them.* ♦ *The
government tried desperately to **paper
over the cracks** in their policy.*

PARACHUTE /'pærəʃuːt, *American*
'perəˌʃut/
parachutes, parachuting, parachuted

,parachute 'in

1 to send people or goods to a place using
planes and parachutes (=large pieces of
cloth used for jumping from planes)

parachute sb/sth in *also* **parachute in
sb/sth** *The CIA has parachuted in a
number of agents.*

2 to suddenly put someone in a new job
or role when people do not expect it and
so are annoyed by it

parachute sb in *They had to parachute
her in to tackle the crisis.*

PARCEL /'pɑːs(ə)l, *American* 'pɑrs(ə)l/
parcels, parcelling, parcelled

,parcel 'off

to divide something into smaller parts that
are easier to sell

parcel off sth *also* **parcel sth off** *They're
parcelling off most of the company's
assets.*

,parcel 'out

to share something among several people
= DISTRIBUTE

parcel out sth *also* **parcel sth out** *We try
to parcel out the responsibility evenly
between the students.*

,parcel 'up *British*

to prepare something for sending by post
by wrapping it in paper or putting it in a

box or special envelope = WRAP UP
≠ UNWRAP

parcel up sth also **parcel sth up** *She quickly parcelled up the magazines and took them to the post office.*

PARE /peə, *American* per/
pares, paring, pared

,pare a'way (*also* **,pare 'off**) [often passive]
to reduce something, or to remove some parts of something, for example parts that are not wanted

be pared away *Only two pieces of information were essential. The rest could be pared away.*

pare away sth *People see these changes as government paring away their rights.*

,pare 'down (*also* **,pare 'back**) [usually passive]
to reduce the total number or amount of something ≠ INCREASE

be pared down *The list has been pared down from 9 teams to 4.*

PARLAY /'pɑːli, *American* 'pɑrleɪ/
parlays, parlaying, parlayed

'parlay into *American*
to use something that you have in order to get something much better or much more valuable

parlay sth into sth *She parlayed a single television appearance into a whole career.*

PART /pɑːt, *American* pɑrt/
parts, parting, parted

be 'parted from
to be prevented from being with someone you want to be with or something you want to have

be parted from sb/sth *Being parted from his family made him feel homesick.*

'part with ★★
to give something to someone although you would prefer to keep it

part with sth *I don't want to part with any of my books.*

PARTAKE /pɑː'teɪk, *American* pɑr'teɪk/
partakes, partaking, partook /pɑː'tʊk, *American* pɑr'tʊk/, **partaken** /pɑː'teɪk(ə)n, *American* pɑr'teɪk(ə)n/

par'take of

1 *old-fashioned* to take or be given something to eat or drink

partake of sth *Would you care to partake of some refreshments before your journey?*

2 partake of or **partake in** *formal* to be involved in an activity

partake of sth *Some guests were partaking of exercise classes.*

3 *formal* to have some of a particular quality

partake of sth *An instructor is supposed to partake of the very spirit of the art.*

PARTITION /pɑː'tɪʃ(ə)n, *American* pɑr'tɪʃ(ə)n/
partitions, partitioning, partitioned

par,tition 'off [usually passive]
to separate an area from the rest of a room with a wall, screen, or piece of glass

be partitioned off *A section at the back of the warehouse was partitioned off.*

♦ **+from** *The foreman's office was partitioned off from the shop floor.*

PARTNER /'pɑːtnə, *American* 'pɑrtnər/
partners, partnering, partnered

,partner 'up (*also* **,partner 'off** *British*) *informal*
to join with someone in order to work together, dance together etc

partner up *We start by partnering up.*

♦ **+with** *Please partner up with another student before we begin the game.*

PASS /pɑːs, *American* pæs/
passes, passing, passed

Pass is often used with adverbs and prepositions when it means 'to move in a particular direction or to a particular place or position': *Two large birds* **passed over** *our heads.* ♦ *We* **passed through** *the gates of the old city.* ♦ *At this point the road* **passes under** *a bridge.* These uses are not included here.

,pass a'round ★ (*also* **,pass 'round** *British*) [often passive]
to give something to one person in a group, who gives it to someone else, who then gives it to someone else etc

be passed around *The photos were passed around for each of them to have a look at.*

pass sth around *Waiters were passing trays of sandwiches around.*

pass around sth *It was the kind of party where people sit on the floor and pass around a bottle.*

PHRASE **pass the hat around** *informal* to collect money from people in a group for a particular purpose: *We're going to pass the hat around later, to buy some beer.*

'pass as *same as* **pass for**

,pass a'way ★

to die. This word is used to avoid saying 'die' when you think that this might upset someone = DIE, PASS ON

pass away *He passed away in his sleep at the age of eighty-four.*

,pass be'tween

if things such as words, looks, or feelings pass between people, they talk to each other or communicate with each other in some way

pass between sb *Hardly a word passed between them for the next hour.* ♦ *Sparks of sexual tension were passing between them.*

,pass 'by ★★

1 to go past someone or something without stopping = GO BY

pass by *Three buses passed by, but none of them was the right one.*

pass by sb/sth *I was just passing by her place, so I thought I'd call in and see her.* ♦ *A car slowly passed by the front of the house.*

2 if something passes you by, you do not notice it

pass sb by *Did you tell me about that? Sorry, it completely passed me by.*

3 if something passes you by, it happens, but you get no advantage from it

pass sb by *Sometimes I feel that **life is just passing me by**.*

■ **bypass** /'baɪpɑːs/ **noun** [C] **1** a road that goes round a town or city so that you can avoid going through its centre: *the Newbury bypass* **2** a medical operation to make someone's blood flow past a blocked or damaged part of their heart rather than through it: *He underwent a triple heart bypass operation last March.* **3** a tube that allows gas or liquid to flow around something rather than through it: *Oil is kept away from the heated plate by means of this bypass.*

■ **bypass** /'baɪpɑːs/ verb [T] **1** to avoid dealing with someone or something, especially because you think you can achieve something more quickly without using them: *I bypassed the lawyers and filed the documents myself.* **2** to avoid the centre of a town or city by using a road that goes round it: *I took the road that bypassed the city altogether.* **3** to perform a medical operation to make someone's blood flow past a blocked or damaged part of their heart rather than through it: *an operation to bypass the damaged artery*

■ **,passer-'by** **noun** [C] someone who is walking past a place, especially when an accident or violent event occurs: *A passer-by called the police.*

,pass 'down ★ [usually passive]

to give knowledge, or to teach skills to your children or to younger people = HAND DOWN

be passed down *These traditional stories have been passed down from parent to child over many generations.*

'pass for ★ (*also* **'pass as**)

to be accepted, wrongly, as being a particular type of person or thing

pass for sb/sth *He's nearly forty, but he could pass for twenty-five.* ♦ *This kind of name-calling passes for political debate these days.*

'pass from

1 to change from one state to another

pass from sth to sth *At this temperature, the mixture passes from a solid to a liquid state.*

2 to stop being owned or controlled by one person and start being owned or controlled by another

pass from sb to sb *The estate has passed from father to son for generations.*

,pass 'off *British*

if an event passes off in a particular way, it happens in that way

pass off *The protest march passed off without any serious trouble.*

,pass 'off as ★

to make people believe that a person or thing is someone or something else = PALM OFF AS

pass sb/sth off as sb/sth *The watches are fakes, but they tried to pass them off as genuine Rolexes.*

pass yourself off as sb *He put on an old blue suit, intending to pass himself off as a businessman.*

,pass 'on ★★★

1	give sth that sb gave you
2	give sb an illness
3	give your children a disease
4	tell sb sth
5	die
+	PHRASE

1 to give someone something that someone else has given you = HAND ON

pass sth on *When you've read this message, please pass it on.* ♦ **+to** *I'll pass these clothes on to my nephew when my lads have outgrown them.*

pass on sth *Please pass on the booklet to*

pass out/black out

knock out

come round/come to

put someone under/go under

verbs to do with being conscious or unconscious

your classmates when you've finished reading it.

2 to give someone an infectious illness = SPREAD

pass on sth *There is a period when there is virtually no chance of the infection being passed on.* ♦ **+to** *I took the day off work because I didn't want to pass on my flu to everyone in the office.*

pass sth on *There's always the danger that people who are unaware they have the disease will pass it on.* ♦ **+to** *In an environment like a school, it's easy for one person to pass their germs on to another.*

3 [usually passive] to give something such as a disease to your children through your genes = HAND DOWN

be passed on *The virus is passed on from the parent to the unborn child.*

4 to tell someone something, often something that someone else has told you = *formal* CONVEY

pass on sth *I passed on as many details as I could remember.*

5 to die. This word is used to avoid saying 'die' when you think that this might upset someone = PASS AWAY, DIE

pass on *Her husband passed on last year.*

PHRASE **pass on the torch to sb** to let

someone else do the work that you were doing or support the ideas that you supported: *The torch has been passed on to the new generation.*

pass 'on to

1 if a business passes on its costs to you, it adds them to the price that you pay for its goods or services

pass sth on to sb *The retailer is forced to pass these extra costs on to the customer.*

2 to arrange for a customer to speak to someone else who can give them the information or service that they have asked you for, because you cannot provide it for them

pass sb on to sb *I'll pass you on to our claims department.*

pass 'out ★★

1 to suddenly become unconscious, for example because you are too hot = FAINT

pass out *People everywhere were passing out from the heat.*

2 [often passive] to give something to each member of a group = HAND OUT, DISTRIBUTE

be passed out *The hall was silent as the examination papers were passed out.*

pass out sth *He was passing out leaflets at the factory gate.*

pass sth out *Will you pass these out among the class?*

3 *British* to officially complete a course at a military or a police college = GRADUATE

pass out *Some of our finest cadets are passing out this summer.*

,pass 'over ★★

1 [often passive] to not give someone a better job, choosing instead someone who is younger or who has less experience

be passed over *Bill was upset about being passed over for the marketing job.*

pass sb over *That's the third time they've passed me over.*

2 [often passive] to deliberately ignore or not mention a problem or subject = IGNORE

be passed over *I mentioned that you were unhappy with your salary, but it was passed over.*

pass over sth *They quickly pass over that unfortunate period in the club's history.*

3 to move over the top of something or someone below you without stopping

pass over sb/sth *The noise of the planes passing over us was deafening.*

,pass 'round *British same as* pass around

,pass 'through

1 to go to a place for only a short period of time before continuing a journey

pass through *It's a hotel used mainly by people passing through.*

2 to go through a place on your way to somewhere else = CROSS

pass through sth *I was just passing through London on my way home and I thought I'd call in and see you.*

3 to experience something, often something difficult or unpleasant = UNDERGO

pass through sth *She argues that society is passing through a crisis in morals.*

'pass to ★

if money or property passes to you, it becomes yours, usually after someone has died

pass to sb *The house will eventually pass to my grandchildren.* ♦ *The property passed to her husband on marriage.*

,pass 'up *informal*

to not take advantage of an opportunity

pass up sth *also* **pass sth up** *I can't believe you passed up the chance to do a parachute jump.* ♦ *I had an invitation to the concert but regretfully I had to pass it up.*

PAT /pæt/
pats, patting, patted

,pat 'down [often passive] *mainly American*

to touch someone's clothes in order to check whether they are carrying something such as a weapon or illegal drugs, for example at an airport = FRISK

be patted down *People wearing leather jackets are usually patted down.*

pat sb down *A woman was brought over to pat me down.*

PATCH /pætʃ/
patches, patching, patched

,patch 'through *mainly American*

to allow someone speaking to you on a phone or radio to speak to someone else

patch sb through *I'm just patching you through now.*

,patch to'gether

to make something quickly and often carelessly by putting together various objects or ideas

patch together sth *also* **patch sth together** *We managed to patch together an impromptu evening's entertainment.*

♦ *We had to patch a new political party together in a few days.*

,patch 'up ★

1 to become friends with someone again after a disagreement

patch up sth *The meeting was intended to patch up relations between the two sides.*

patch sth up *Isn't it time you two **patched it up**?* ♦ *Apparently, they've since **patched things up** with their father.*

Nouns often used as objects with
patch up 1

■ differences, quarrel, relations, relationship, rift, things

2 to repair something, often quickly and not very well = MEND

patch up sth *The road needs to be resurfaced, not just patched up.*

patch sth up *I'll just have to patch these old jeans up.*

3 to give basic medical treatment to someone who is injured

patch sb up *The nurses managed to patch her up temporarily.*

patch sb up *It was our job to patch up the troops and send them back to the front.*

PATTERN /ˈpæt(ə)n, *American* ˈpætərn/
patterns, patterning, patterned

be ˈpatterned on (*also* **be ˈpatterned after**)

if something is patterned on something else, it is made so that it is similar to something else

be patterned on sth *Some of these modern housing developments are patterned on 19th-century villages.*

PAVE /peɪv/
paves, paving, paved

ˌpave ˈover [usually passive]

to cover an area of ground with a hard surface, using bricks, blocks of stone etc

be paved over *Many of the region's orchards have been paved over.*

PAW /pɔː, *American* pɔ/
paws, pawing, pawed

ˈpaw at

1 if an animal paws at something, it touches it several times with its foot

paw at sth *The cat kept pawing at the door.*

2 *informal* to touch someone, usually in a rough or sexual way that they do not like

paw at sb *Fans and photographers paw at them as they push their way through.*

PAWN /pɔːn, *American* pɔn/
pawns, pawning, pawned

ˌpawn ˈoff *American informal*

to persuade someone to buy or accept something that you do not want, especially something of low quality

pawn off sth *also* **pawn sth off** *I managed to pawn off all of the old stock.*

ˌpawn ˈoff as

to pretend that someone or something is good when they are not in order to deceive someone else

pawn sb/sth off as sb/sth *They tried to pawn him off as some sort of expert.* ♦ *She's pawning this off as a great opportunity for us.*

PAY /peɪ/
pays, paying, paid /peɪd/

ˌpay ˈback ★★

1 to give someone the same amount of money that you borrowed from them

= REPAY

pay sb back *I'll be able to pay you back next week.*

pay back sb *Don't forget we have to pay back my parents first.*

pay sth back *I don't think we can afford to pay the full amount back now.*

pay back sth *We wanted to pay back everything we'd borrowed.*

pay sb sth back *She'll pay us the rest back when she gets her wages.*

2 to do something bad to someone because they have done something bad to you

= GET BACK AT

pay sb back *She couldn't forget what they'd done and was determined to pay them back.* ♦ **+for** *She knew how to pay them back for the trouble they had caused.*

■ ˈback pay noun [U] money that is owed to someone who works for a company but who has not been paid yet: *They owe me hundreds of pounds in back pay.*

■ payback /ˈpeɪbæk/ noun [singular/U]
1 a result of doing something: *The no-smoking policy offers a payback of improved employee health.* **2** a bad or unpleasant thing that someone does to you after you have done something bad or unpleasant to them: *It's simply payback for the way they defeated us.* ♦ *The Lions are hoping that today's game is payback time.* **3** payment that you make to someone who has lent you money: *We argued for a longer payback period.*

ˌpay ˈdown *American*

to pay an amount of money you owe in small amounts over a long period of time

pay down sth *Should we use the surplus to cut taxes or to pay down the national debt?*

ˌpay ˈin

to put money into your bank account

= DEPOSIT ≠ WITHDRAW

pay sth in *also* **pay in sth** *I'd like to pay these two cheques in.* ♦ *She paid in two very large amounts last week.*

ˌpay ˈinto ★★

1 *British* to put money into your bank account

pay sth into sth *You can pay cash into any one of our three hundred branches.*

2 to invest money in something such as an insurance policy or a pension fund so that you will receive money in the future

pay into sth *She pays into the employees' pension scheme.*

pay sth into sth *They've paid several thousand pounds into this fund over the years.*

pay off ★★★

1	bring some benefit
2	give back the money you borrowed
3	stop employing sb
4	pay sb to do sth bad
5	pay sb not to tell sth
+	**payoff** noun

1 if something that you do pays off, it brings you some benefit
pay off *All those weeks of studying will pay off when you take the exam.*

2 [often passive] to give someone all the money that you have borrowed from them to buy something
be paid off *Only another six months and the house will be paid off.*
pay sth off *It'll take another six months to pay the car off.*
pay off sth *Most people have paid off their house by now.*

3 [often passive] to stop employing a worker and give them any money that they are owed = LAY OFF
be paid off *Over 1,000 workers will be paid off if this factory closes.*
pay sb off *They've paid half the workforce off already.*
pay off sb *We're paying off all our casual staff.*

4 [usually passive] to give someone money so that they will do something bad or dishonest for you = BRIBE
be paid off *There were suspicions that officials had been paid off.*

5 to give someone money so that they will not do something that will cause you problems, especially by telling people about something bad that you have done = BUY OFF
pay sb off *They threatened to tell reporters about him unless he paid them off.*
pay off sb *It emerged that they had paid off officials.*

■ **payoff** /'peɪɒf/ noun [C] **1** the benefit you get from doing something: *There is a positive payoff in terms of professional development.* **2** a final payment that you make to someone when they stop working for you: *He got a big cash payoff.* **3** a payment that you make to someone as part of an agreement so that they do not cause trouble for you: *His ex-wife pocketed a £20 million payoff after 26 years of marriage.* **4** a payment that you make to someone so that they will do something bad or dishonest for you: *the payoffs which he received for helping them to obtain the licences*

pay out ★★★

1 to spend or pay money, especially a lot of money = SHELL OUT
pay out sth *We've paid out thousands of pounds in health insurance over the years.*
pay sth out *People don't want to pay that much out in one go.*

2 to provide money from an amount invested over a period of time
pay out *It'll be a few years before our investments start paying out.*
pay out sth *The policy won't pay out enough to cover our expenses.*

3 to gradually let a rope become straight and long so that it no longer forms a series of circles
pay out sth *They paid out the rope swiftly and were towed to the quay.*
pay sth out *Pay the rope out slowly.*

■ **payout** /'peɪaʊt/ noun [C] a large amount of money paid to someone, for example by an insurance company or as a prize in a competition: *Policyholders are receiving tax-free payouts.*

pay up ★

to pay money that you owe, especially when you are unwilling to pay = *American* ANTE UP, COUGH UP
pay up *We're waiting for the insurance company to pay up.*

PEAL /piːl, *American* pil/
peals, pealing, pealed

peal out

if bells peal out when they are rung on a special occasion, they make a loud sound
peal out *Church bells pealed out across the English countryside.*

PECK /pek/
pecks, pecking, pecked

peck at

1 to eat only a small amount of a meal, without much interest = PICK AT
peck at sth *Debbie just pecked at her food.*

2 when a bird pecks at something, it moves its beak quickly forward to hit or bite it
peck at sth *The birds pecked at the insect-infested tree.*

PEE /piː, American piː/
pees, peeing, peed

pee 'down [usually progressive] British
impolite
if it is peeing down, a lot of rain is falling
= POUR DOWN

PEEL /piːl, American piːl/
peels, peeling, peeled

peel 'off ★★

1	remove clothing
2	remove from surface
3	fall off surface
4	start moving
5	remove banknotes

1 to remove a tight or wet piece of
clothing
peel off sth *The kids peeled off their wet
clothes.*
peel sth off *Madeline takes the stocking
by its top and peels it off slowly.*
2 to remove something from the surface
of something else, especially by taking
one end or side and pulling it
peel sth off *She peeled the wrapper off
slowly.*
peel off sth *Peel off the outer skin under
running water.*
3 to fall off a surface in small flat pieces
peel off *On my shoulders the skin was
peeling off.*
4 peel off or **peel away** to start moving in
a different direction from the people or
vehicles that you are with
peel off *One by one the aircraft started
to peel off.*
5 to remove some banknotes from a pile
that you are holding
peel off sth *Leroy peeled off six fifty-
dollar bills.*
peel sth off *He whispers in Dad's ear
and Dad peels another note off.*

peel 'out *mainly American informal*
if you peel out, or if a car peels out, you
suddenly make it start moving very
quickly so that it makes a lot of noise
peel out *A black car peeled out behind
me.* ♦ **+of** *She peeled out of the car park.*

PEG /peg/
pegs, pegging, pegged

peg 'as [usually passive] *informal*
to think that someone is a particular type
of person or has particular qualities
be pegged as sb *We had him pegged
from the start as a liar and a fraud.*

peg at
to keep prices, salaries, or the amount of
something at a particular level
peg sth at sth *OPEC oil producers
pegged the cartel's output at 26.6 million
barrels per day.*

peg a'way British informal
to keep doing something in a determined
way, especially when it is boring or
difficult
peg away *To succeed, you have to keep
pegging away.* ♦ **+at** *I don't know how
people peg away at such a dull job.*

peg 'back
1 to control something so that it does not
increase above a particular level
peg back sth *also* **peg sth back**
*Government measures to peg back
inflation have caused a recession.*
♦ *Employers are constantly striving to
peg wages back.*
2 [usually passive] in sport, to prevent an
opponent from winning
be pegged back *They took the lead early
but were pegged back by an equalizer
from Johnny Jameson.*

peg 'out British
1 *informal* to die = DIE
peg out *The old guy just pegged out on
the spot.*
2 *informal* to fall down or have to go to bed
because you are very tired
peg out *By five o'clock I was ready to
peg out.*
3 to fasten wet clothes, sheets etc on a
line outside to dry using pegs (=small
plastic or wooden pins)
peg out sth *also* **peg sth out** *John was
pegging out the washing.*
4 [usually passive] to fix the ropes that
support a tent, into the ground with pegs
be pegged out *All the ropes were firmly
pegged out.*

peg 'to [usually passive]
to control the level of something in
relation to something else
be pegged to sth *The country's peso is
pegged to the dollar.*

PELT /pelt/
pelts, pelting, pelted

pelt 'down [usually progressive]
if it is pelting down, a lot of rain is falling
= POUR DOWN
be pelting down *It's absolutely pelting
down outside.*

PEN /pen/
pens, penning, penned

pen 'in

1 pen in or pen up to put an animal in a small area with a fence around it in order to keep it there
pen sth in *We penned the sheep in for the night.*

2 to make it impossible for someone to get out of a place = BLOCK
pen sb in *A van was parked behind me, penning me in.*

3 [usually passive] to make someone feel that they cannot escape from a situation = TRAP
be/feel penned in *She began to feel penned in.*

PENCIL /'pens(ə)l/
pencils, pencilling, pencilled

pencil 'in [often passive]
to arrange for something to happen or for someone to do something, knowing that it may have to be changed later
be pencilled in *One match has already been organized, and they have another six pencilled in.* ♦ **+for** *The meeting has been pencilled in for the beginning of June.*
pencil sb/sth in *'I think tomorrow's OK for me.' 'Shall I pencil you in then?'*
♦ **+for** *Pencil me in for lunch on Friday.*

PENSION /'penʃ(ə)n/
pensions, pensioning, pensioned

pension 'off

1 to force someone to stop working and give them a pension
pension sb off *also* **pension off sb**
They're pensioning Helen off this year.
♦ *We may consider pensioning off everyone over 55.*

2 [usually passive] British to get rid of a piece of equipment because it is old
be pensioned off *Old coal-fired stations will be pensioned off.*

PEP /pep/
peps, pepping, pepped

pep 'up informal
to make someone or something more active and lively = LIVEN UP
pep sb/sth up *also* **pep up sb/sth** *A short break would pep you up.* ♦ *We need to look at ways of pepping up the economy.*

PEPPER /'pepə, American 'pepər/
peppers, peppering, peppered

be 'peppered with

1 to have things in many different places all over the surface
be peppered with sth *His chin was peppered with stubble.*

2 if something such as a speech or piece of writing is peppered with something, it has a lot of examples of it
be peppered with sth *The letter was peppered with spelling mistakes.*

PERCH /pɜːtʃ, American pɜrtʃ/
perches, perching, perched

'perch on

1 [often passive] if you perch on something, or are perched on it, you sit on something that is narrow or small, and usually high, especially for a short time
be perched on sth *Sophie was perched on the arm of the couch.*
perch on sth *Rob came over to perch on the corner of her desk.*

2 [usually passive] to put something on a narrow surface that is usually high
be perched on sth *Heavy black glasses were perched on the bridge of his nose.*
♦ *The villa is perched on a cliff above Monte Carlo.*

PERK /pɜːk, American pɜrk/
perks, perking, perked

perk 'up ★

1 if someone perks up, or if something perks them up, they begin to feel happier or more lively = LIVEN UP
perk up *Sue perked up when she heard the news.*
perk sb up *A change of scenery will perk you up.*

2 to become more interesting or exciting, or to make something more interesting or exciting = LIVEN UP
perk sth up *Some chilli sauce will perk the dish up.*
perk up *After a slow first act, the performance began to perk up.*

PERMIT /pə'mɪt, American pər'mɪt/
permits, permitting, permitted

per'mit of very formal
to make something possible = ALLOW
permit of sth *The results of the test permit of no other interpretation.*

PERTAIN /pə'teɪn, *American* pər'teɪn/
pertains, pertaining, pertained

per'tain to *formal*
to be directly related to something
= RELATE TO
pertain to sth *They are trying to gather all the facts pertaining to this situation.*

PETER /'pi:tə, *American* 'pitər/
peters, petering, petered

peter 'out ★
to gradually become smaller or weaker before coming to an end or disappearing completely = FIZZLE OUT
peter out *The narrow trail petered out before long.* ♦ *The conversation soon petered out.*

PHASE /feɪz/
phases, phasing, phased

phase 'in [usually passive]
to gradually start using something
be phased in *The new regulations can be phased in over a number of months.*

phase 'out ★★ [usually passive]
to gradually stop using something
be phased out *Over the following three years, national currencies were phased out.*

PHONE /fəʊn, *American* foʊn/
phones, phoning, phoned

phone 'back ★
to phone someone again later, for example because you were away when they phoned you earlier or because you were too busy to speak to them before = RING BACK, CALL BACK
phone sb back *I've got someone at the door. I'll phone you back.* ♦ *I told her you'd phone her back when you got home.*
phone back *She's not in at the moment. Can you phone back later?*

'phone for
to phone someone in order to ask for something to be sent to you or someone to come to you
phone for sb/sth *We immediately phoned for a doctor.*

phone 'in
1 to phone the place where you work in order to leave a message = CALL IN
phone in *Another reporter phoned in later with the story.* ♦ *Kevin's just phoned in sick (=phoned to say that he is sick), so he won't be at the meeting.*

2 to phone a radio or television programme with a question or comment
= CALL IN
phone in *Hundreds were phoning in to say they agreed.*

■ **'phone-in** noun [C] *British* a radio or television programme that people phone with their questions or comments. The usual American word is **call-in**: *The character presents a radio phone-in.*

phone 'round *British*
to phone several people in order to ask them something
phone round sb *It's normal for companies to phone round their big customers and try to persuade them to invest.*
phone round *I knew I could get a better deal if I phoned round a bit.*

phone 'through
to give someone a particular piece of information using the phone
phone sth through *also* **phone through sth** *I phoned my order through last week.* ♦ *You can phone through your credit card number when you get home, if you don't have it now.* ♦ **+to** *Just get the car's registration number, and phone it through to the police.*

phone 'up ★★
to phone someone = PHONE, RING, CALL, TELEPHONE
phone up sb *He phoned up the editor and told her what he thought of her.*
phone sb up *Why don't you phone her up and ask her?*

PICK /pɪk/
picks, picking, picked

'pick at
1 to eat only small amounts of a meal because you do not feel hungry
pick at sth *Most of the time he just picks at his food.*

2 to keep pulling something with your nails
pick at sth *He picked at a loose thread on his coat.*

3 *American* to keep criticizing someone or something in an angry way
pick at sb/sth *Like any family we pick at each other a little.* ♦ *She's driving me crazy, picking at every little thing I do.* ♦ **+for** *They picked at him for relatively minor mistakes.*

pick 'off
1 to shoot people, animals, or aircraft one

by one by aiming at them carefully from a distance

pick sb/sth off *also* **pick off sb/sth** *A sniper in a nearby tree was picking them off one by one.* ♦ *I picked off half a dozen enemy soldiers.*

2 to attract people or things, often the best people or things

pick off sb/sth *The new superstores pick off customers heading for the town centres.*

'pick on ★★

to keep treating someone badly or unfairly, especially by criticizing them = GET AT

pick on sb *Why do you always pick on me?*

> PHRASE **pick on sb your own size** *informal* used for telling someone to stop criticizing or attacking someone who is smaller or weaker than them: *We didn't want the war. We thought America should have picked on someone their own size.*

,pick 'out ★★★

1	choose sb/sth
2	recognize sb/sth
3	manage to see sb/sth
4	shine a light on sb/sth
5	use colour to make sth easy to see

1 to choose one person or thing from a group = CHOOSE, SELECT

pick out sb/sth *Have you picked out a dress for the party?*

pick sb/sth out *Just go to the wardrobe and pick a shirt out.* ♦ *I wondered why she'd picked me out.*

2 to recognize someone or something from a group = SPOT

pick out sb/sth *You can pick out liars by the nervous way they act.*

pick sb/sth out *Could you pick him out for us from this line of suspects?*

3 to see someone or something when they are difficult to see = SPOT

pick out sb/sth *The yellow coat makes her easier to pick out in a crowd.*

pick sb/sth out *We painted the sign orange so drivers can pick it out at night.*

4 to shine a light on someone or something so that they are easy to see

pick out sb/sth *The spotlight picked out a woman in the crowd.*

5 [usually passive] to make something easy to see by painting it, or by making it in a different colour from the things that surround it = HIGHLIGHT

be picked out *The symbol of a flame was picked out in yellow and red.*

,pick 'over

1 to examine a collection of things carefully so that you can decide which ones you want

pick over sth *Birds were picking over the rubbish washed up on the beach.*

2 to talk about something in detail, especially the unpleasant or embarrassing aspects of it

pick over sth *They spent ages picking over the flaws in his character.*

> PHRASE **pick over the bones (of sth)** to examine something very carefully in order to find anything of value and keep it for yourself: *There wasn't much left of the estate after the lawyers had finished picking over the bones.*

,pick 'through

to search through a collection of things in order to find something

pick through sth *They are picking through the ruins, searching for survivors.*

,pick 'up ★★★

1	lift sb/sth
2	take sb in a vehicle
3	learn/do sth new
4	notice sth
5	start sth after a pause
6	improve
7	take sth in your hands
8	put things in a tidy place
9	take sb in your vehicle
10	get an illness
11	buy sth
12	receive an electronic signal
13	wind: become stronger
14	earn money
15	win a prize
16	arrest sb
17	try to start a sexual relationship
18	make a place tidy
+	PHRASES
+	**pick-me-up** noun; **pickup** noun, adj

1 to lift someone or something up from a surface ≠ PUT DOWN

pick sb/sth up *He picked the phone up and dialled.*

pick up sb/sth *She rushes to pick up the baby as soon as it starts to cry.*

2 to go and meet someone or get something that you have arranged to take somewhere, usually in a vehicle = COLLECT

pick sb/sth up *Will you pick me up after the party?*

pick up sb/sth *I need to pick up my bags before we leave.*

3 to learn a new skill or start a habit without intending to = LEARN

pick up sth *She picked up a few German*

phrases while staying in Berlin.
pick sth up I don't want her picking these habits up.

4 to notice a smell or sound, or to notice that someone or something is present
pick up sth The dogs must have picked up his scent.
pick sth up The cameras picked the car up again as it came round the corner.

5 to start something again, from the point where you stopped
pick up sth We'll pick up this conversation when I come back.
pick up He seems to think that we can get back together and just **pick up where we left off**.

6 to improve = IMPROVE ≠ DETERIORATE
pick up They won't let him home until his health has picked up a bit. ♦ After a few quiet months, business was beginning to pick up again.

7 to lift something up and take it away with you
pick up sth Pick up a leaflet from your doctor.
pick sth up I picked this up for you on my way home.

8 to lift things up and put them in the place where they are kept in order to make a place tidy
pick sth up I've already asked them to pick their toys up.
pick up sth I am constantly picking up the things the children leave lying around. ♦ You could start by picking up all these papers.

9 if you pick up someone who is waiting by the road, you stop your car and take them somewhere in it
pick up sb We picked up a hitchhiker on the way.
pick sb up I stopped to pick her up.

10 informal to get an illness = CATCH
pick up sth Most tourists are worried that they'll pick up a nasty stomach bug.
pick sth up Patients are picking these infections up in hospital. ♦ In a crowded classroom, kids pick everything up.

11 informal to buy something, especially something you find unexpectedly and that costs very little
pick up sth There's a market where you can pick up some amazing bargains.
pick sth up We picked a few bottles up for ourselves. ♦ I picked this up for you at the airport.

12 informal to receive an electronic signal on a radio or similar piece of equipment = RECEIVE
pick up sth/sb I don't think this thing can pick up foreign stations.

pick sth/sb up On a short-wave radio, you can sometimes pick police broadcasts up. ♦ Do you think the ship can pick us up at that distance?

13 if the wind picks up, it increases or becomes stronger ≠ DROP
pick up By this time a stiff breeze had picked up.

14 informal to earn an amount of money = EARN
pick up sth These are the huge salaries that professional athletes pick up.
pick sth up I'd like to be picking his salary up at the end of the month!

15 informal to win something such as a prize = WIN
pick up sth He's tipped to pick up another Oscar this year.
pick sth up The winner will pick a cheque up for £1,000.

16 [often passive] informal to arrest someone and take them away in a car
be picked up He was picked up in the early hours of Thursday morning.
pick sb up The police picked him up at the airport.

17 informal to start talking to someone because you want to have sex with them
pick up sb She went home with some man she picked up in a bar.
pick sb up We watched him trying to pick women up.

18 American to make a place clean and tidy = TIDY UP
pick up sth I told you to pick up your room.

PHRASES **pick up the ball and run with it** to take responsibility for getting something done, especially after someone else has tried and failed: Britain has put the process in place, but the rest of Europe hasn't picked up the ball and run with it.

pick up the bill/tab informal to pay for something: Her father picks up the tab for her expensive lifestyle.

pick up the pieces to try to return to a normal life after a difficult experience: Victims are left trying to pick up the pieces.

pick up speed if something picks up speed, it starts to move faster: The plane picked up speed as we taxied down the runway.

pick up the threads (of sth) to return to a situation that existed before something went wrong: They're doing their best to pick up the threads of their shattered lives.

■ **'pick-me-up** noun [C] something such as a drink that makes you feel

be picked up (sense 16)

more lively: *He went into the bar for a pick-me-up.*

■ **pickup** /ˈpɪkʌp/ **noun** **1** [C] a truck with an open back and low sides: *The boys ride in the back of the pickup.* **2** [C] a stranger that you meet with the purpose of having a short sexual relationship with them: *He's just her latest pickup.* **3** [U] *American* the power of a vehicle to accelerate (=go faster) quickly: *It's a little car, but it has a lot of pickup.* **4** [singular] an improvement or increase in something: *The survey showed a pickup in corporate confidence.* **5** [C] the part of a record player that touches the record and sends the sound to the speakers: *The problem always was that the pickup was very sensitive to movement.* **6** [C] a place or time at which people, goods, or other things are collected: *They make deliveries in the mornings and pickups in the afternoons.*

■ **pickup** /ˈpɪkʌp/ **adj** *American* a pickup game is played by a group of people who do not always know each other, but suddenly decide that they want to play together: *a pickup game of basketball*

ˌpick ˈup after
to make a place tidy after someone else has made a mess there = CLEAR UP AFTER
 pick up after sb *I'm fed up with having to pick up after you and your friends.*

ˌpick ˈup on
1 to talk in more detail about something that someone has mentioned
 pick up on sth *I'd just like to pick up on a couple of points that you made.*

2 to react to something that has happened or that you have noticed = REGISTER
 pick up on sth *She had expected Dan to pick up on her insult.*

3 to notice something that is not very obvious = NOTICE ≠ MISS
 pick up on sth *This is something you would expect a skilled negotiator to pick up on.*

4 to correct someone who has made a mistake, or to criticize them for doing something wrong = PULL UP ON
 pick sb up on sth *She's always picking me up on my grammar.*

ˌpick ˈup with
to start meeting or spending time with someone who you have not seen for a while
 pick up with sb *He picked up with Jill as though the years had changed nothing.*

PIDDLE /ˈpɪd(ə)l/
piddles, piddling, piddled

ˌpiddle aˈround (*also* ˌpiddle aˈbout
British) *informal*
to spend time doing things that are not important = FIDDLE AROUND
 piddle around *I wish you'd stop piddling around.*

ˌpiddle aˈway *very informal*
to waste time, energy, or money
 piddle away sth *also* **piddle sth away** *I piddled away the days until the weekend.*
 ♦ *She'd already piddled half the money away.*

PIECE /piːs, *American* piːs/
pieces, piecing, pieced

ˌpiece toˈgether
1 to learn the truth about something by considering all the separate bits of information that you have
 piece together sth *also* **piece sth together** *Detectives are still piecing together the circumstances surrounding the incident.* ♦ *You can piece his ideas together from reading the mass of articles he wrote.*

2 to make something by combining separate bits = ASSEMBLE ≠ TAKE APART
 piece together sth *also* **piece sth together** *The rugs are constructed by piecing together strips of fabric.* ♦ *Our job is piecing the fragments together.*

PIG /pɪg/
pigs, pigging, pigged

be ˌpigged ˈoff *British informal*
to feel very annoyed or upset
 be pigged off *He admits he was pigged off by the whole experience.*

,pig 'out *informal*

to eat an extremely large amount of food, much more than you need

pig out *She felt like pigging out for once.*
♦ **+on** *kids pigging out on junk food and soda*

PILE /paɪl/
piles, piling, piled

,pile 'in (*also* **,pile 'into**)

to enter a place in large numbers, especially in a way that is not organized

pile in *They opened the doors and all fifteen of us piled in.*
pile into sth *Four huge men piled into the back of the car.*

,pile 'on ★

1 to increase something by a large amount, or to do it a lot = HEAP ON

pile on sth *Ten minutes into the film, the director piles on the action.* ♦ *The UN is* **piling on the pressure** *and the two sides may both have to withdraw.*

2 if someone piles on weight, or if it piles on, their weight increases suddenly and by a large amount

pile on *In spite of my efforts, the weight continued to pile on.*
pile on sth *I always* **pile on the pounds** *over Christmas.*

PHRASES **pile it on** *British informal* to talk about something, often about the way you feel, in a way that makes it seem more extreme than it really is: *I know he must be upset, but he does tend to pile it on a bit.*

pile on the agony *British* **1** to make a bad situation much worse for someone: *This latest announcement just piles on the agony for investors.* **2** to enjoy making a situation much worse than it is: *They see a weakness in a child and they start piling on the agony.*

,pile 'out *informal*

to leave a place in large numbers, especially in a way that is not organized

pile out *Someone opened a door and we all piled out.* ♦ **+of** *People began piling out of the house.*

,pile 'up ★★

1 [often passive] to put a large number of things on top of each other = STACK UP ≠ SCATTER

be piled up *Newspapers and magazines were piled up on the floor.*
pile sth up *You can pile the boxes up over there.*
pile up sth *They'd been piling up their dirty plates and leaving them.*

2 if something piles up, or if someone piles it up, the amount of it increases a lot = ACCUMULATE

pile up *All the time the bills were piling up.*
pile up sth *These policies could be piling up financial trouble for future governments.*

■ **'pile-up** noun [C] **1** an accident in which several vehicles crash into each other: *a six-car pile-up* **2** a situation in which there are a lot of things that need to be dealt with at the same time: *a massive pile-up of data*

PILOT /'paɪlət/
pilots, piloting, piloted

,pilot 'through

1 to give someone advice or instructions that help them to do something

pilot sb through sth *Our advisers are here to pilot members through the new procedure.*

2 to make sure that something such as a new law is introduced or accepted

pilot through sth *also* **pilot sth through** *How will they pilot through this new philosophy?*
pilot sth through sth *She was personally responsible for piloting this measure through Parliament.*

PIN /pɪn/
pins, pinning, pinned

,pin 'down ★★

1 to understand or describe something exactly = IDENTIFY

pin down sth *Officials are trying to pin down the cause of the power failure.*
pin sth down *We use satellite tracking to pin the exact location down.*

2 to force someone to make a decision about something = NAIL DOWN

pin sb down *We finally pinned him down and got him to agree to a meeting.*

3 to hold someone firmly on the ground so that they cannot move = HOLD DOWN

pin sb down *He flipped me over and pinned me down.*

4 [often passive] to keep soldiers in a place so that they cannot move

be pinned down *The Allied armies had been pinned down by the Germans.*
pin sb down *We managed to pin them down in the woods.*

'pin on

to blame someone for something, or to accuse someone of doing something, often when they are not responsible for it

pin sth on sb *He has managed to pin the blame on the previous government.* ♦ *The police can't pin anything on him.*

> PHRASE **pin your hopes/faith on sb/sth** to hope very much that someone or something will succeed when everyone or everything else has failed: *It wasn't wise to pin your hopes on one possible solution.*

,pin 'up ★

1 to fix something such as a picture to a wall

pin sth up *Have you pinned the notices up?*

pin up sth *I'll pin up the details for everyone to see.*

2 to make the lower edge of a piece of clothing shorter by using pins

pin up sth *You could help me to pin up this dress.*

pin sth up *Before I sew it, I need to pin it up.*

■ **'pin-up** noun [C] *informal* **1** someone who is sexually attractive, and appears in photographs that people hang on their walls: *He's become something of a pin-up for middle-aged women.* **2** a photograph hanging on a wall showing someone who is sexually attractive, especially someone wearing very few clothes: *The garage walls are covered with pin-ups.*

PINE /paɪn/
pines, pining, pined

,pine a'way

to feel very sad because you cannot be with the person you love, so that you become weak and ill and sometimes even die

pine away *The dog pined away when its owner died.*

'pine for

1 to feel very sad because you cannot be with the person you love

pine for sb *She spent the days pining for him.*

2 to want something very much, especially something that you used to have, and feel sad because you no longer have it

pine for sth *He was pining for some excitement in his life.*

PIPE /paɪp/
pipes, piping, piped

,pipe 'down [usually in imperative] *informal*
used for telling someone to stop talking or to make less noise

pipe down *You sit there wishing the people over the fence would pipe down.* ♦ *Pipe down, you two!*

,pipe 'up

to join a conversation, for example by interrupting or speaking for the first time = SPEAK UP

pipe up *The man at the back piped up.*

PISS /pɪs/
pisses, pissing, pissed

,piss a'bout (*also* ,piss a'round) *British impolite*

1 to behave in a silly way that annoys other people = MESS AROUND

2 to waste time by doing things that are silly or not important = MESS AROUND

3 to treat someone in an unfair way, for example by wasting their time = MESS AROUND

,piss a'way *British impolite*

to waste time, energy, or money

'piss down [usually progressive] *British impolite*

if it is pissing down, a lot of rain is falling = POUR DOWN

,piss 'off *impolite*

1 *British* to leave a place, usually because you no longer want to be there

2 to annoy someone very much = ANNOY

3 [always in imperative] *offensive* used for telling someone to go away or for saying 'no' in an angry way

PIT /pɪt/
pits, pitting, pitted

,pit a'gainst

1 [often passive] to make someone compete or fight against someone else = SET AGAINST

be pitted against sb/sth *Venus Williams will be pitted against her sister in tomorrow's game.*

pit sb/sth against sb/sth *He realized he would have to pit his best troops against the enemy.*

2 if you pit your skill, knowledge, or ability against someone, you use all of it in order to deal successfully or compete with them

pit sth against sb *Small businesses are having to pit their wits against the giant companies.*

pit 'out *American informal*
if you pit out, you sweat so much that the clothing under your arms becomes wet
pit out *I was sitting there in the middle of this meeting, feeling myself pitting out.*

PITCH /pɪtʃ/
pitches, pitching, pitched

pitch a'gainst [usually passive] *informal*
to make someone compete or fight against someone else
be pitched against sb *He was pitched against Kennedy in the battle for the party leadership.*

pitch 'at (*also* **pitch to'wards**) [often passive]
to design something so that a particular group of people will like it or buy it
be pitched at sb *Most of these shows are pitched at viewers under 25.*
pitch sth at sb *They create habits by pitching these products at children.*

'pitch for
to try to get something that several other people or organizations are competing for
pitch for sth *Several companies are pitching for this account.*

pitch 'in *informal*
1 to join with other people in doing a job
pitch in *If we all pitch in, we can finish today.*
2 to give your opinion, ideas etc during a conversation
pitch in *If you have a suggestion to make, just pitch in.* ♦ **+with** *My brother pitched in with an offer to lend us some money.*

pitch 'into *informal*
1 to put someone in a new situation, especially when they were not expecting it
pitch sb into sth *The incident had pitched him into the national headlines.*
2 to start attacking or criticizing someone
pitch into sb *And then the others starting pitching into him.*

pitch 'out [usually passive] *informal*
to force someone to leave a place, organization etc = TURF OUT
be pitched out *She's likely to be pitched out if sales figures don't improve soon.*
♦ **+of** *He was pitched out of office last year after a series of blunders.*

pitch 'up *informal*
to arrive, especially late or in an unusual way
pitch up *They pitched up in some old car that looked as if it should be on a scrap heap.*

PIVOT /'pɪvət/
pivots, pivoting, pivoted

'pivot on
to depend on or be based on a particular thing
pivot on sth *The health of the company pivoted on the success of this one album.*

PLAGUE /pleɪg/
plagues, plaguing, plagued

be 'plagued with
if you are plagued with something unpleasant, it happens often or it causes a lot of problems
be plagued with sth *The east coast has been plagued with blizzards for most of this month.* ♦ *Although plagued with failing eyesight, he continues to lecture.*

PLAN /plæn/
plans, planning, planned

plan a'head ★
to think carefully about what is likely to happen in the future and prepare for it
plan ahead *The most successful companies are always planning ahead.*

'plan for [usually passive]
to make plans for something to happen at a particular time or place
be planned for sth *The shopping centre that is planned for this site may take years to build.*

'plan on
to intend to do something, or to expect something to happen
plan on (doing) sth *We are planning on going to Australia this year.* ♦ *We hadn't planned on so many people coming.*

plan 'out
to think carefully about a series of actions that you need to take in order to achieve something
plan out sth *also* **plan sth out** *Get a map before you start your journey and plan out a route.* ♦ *I knew exactly what I was going to say in the interview. I'd planned it all out.*

PLANT /plɑːnt, American plænt/
plants, planting, planted

plant 'out
to take a young plant that is growing in a container and put it in the ground to grow
= BED OUT
plant out sth also **plant sth out** I want to plant out these geraniums today. ♦ You can plant them out when there is no danger of frost.

plant 'over [often passive]
to grow plants or trees over an area of ground so that it is covered with them
be planted over with sth The shelters were planted over with vegetation for camouflage.
plant over sth They are planting over the beach areas.

plant 'up
to put trees, plants, or seeds in soil in a container or in the ground
plant up sth also **plant sth up** There were enough plants to plant up four hanging baskets. ♦ I've nearly finished planting the borders up.

PLASTER /'plɑːstə, American 'plæstər/
plasters, plastering, plastered

plaster 'over
to cover a hole or area of a wall or ceiling by spreading plaster (=a substance that forms a smooth hard surface) over it
plaster over sth I'll need to plaster over these cracks.

plaster 'with [often passive]
1 to cover a surface or a place with labels, advertisements, pictures etc
be plastered with sth She had a battered old suitcase that was plastered with labels.
plaster sth with sth The first thing they do is plaster the walls with posters.
2 if you plaster someone with a substance, you spread a lot of it on their body
be plastered with sth She came downstairs, her face plastered with cream.
plaster sb/sth with sth We plastered our neck and shoulders with suncream.
♦ The men plaster themselves with oil.

PLAY /pleɪ/
plays, playing, played

play a'bout British
to behave in a silly way, especially when you should be doing something else
= PLAY AROUND, FOOL AROUND

play about Stop playing about and get on with your homework.

play a'long
to pretend to agree with someone or something, especially in order to get what you want or to avoid an argument
play along They threatened to hurt me if I didn't play along. ♦ **+with** Just play along with what he wants. It's easier.

play a'round
1 informal if someone who is married or has a partner plays around, they have sexual relationships with other people
play around He was the kind of man who played around. ♦ **+with** He had played around with other women.
2 to behave in a silly way, especially when you should be doing something else
= PLAY ABOUT
play around They're always playing around when they should be working.

play a'round with
to think about all the different possible ways of doing something before you make a decision
play around with sth They played around with lots of different schemes before opting for this one.

play at ★
1 showing disapproval to do something without being very serious about it
play at doing sth I think she's just playing at running a business.
play at sth These countries are really just playing at democracy.
2 if children play at something, they pretend to be someone else or to be involved in a particular type of situation
play at sth A child playing at shopping, for example, will display early skills with numbers.
PHRASE **what is sb playing at?** used when you think that someone is behaving in a stupid or dishonest way: What does he think he's playing at, making the children lie for him?

play 'back ★
to play a message or video that has been recorded in order to listen to it or watch it
play back sth Play back the phone message.
play sth back Let's play that last sequence back.

■ **playback** /'pleɪbæk/ **noun** [C/U] the use of a machine to show pictures or play sounds that were recorded earlier: We recorded the show for later playback.

play 'down ★★

to try to make a problem or difficult situation seem less serious or important than it is = DOWNPLAY, MINIMIZE ≠ PLAY UP, EXAGGERATE

play down sth *At first the government played down the threat to public health.*
play sth down *Local people are deliberately playing the incident down.*

Nouns often used as objects with **play down**

■ **extent, fears, importance, risk, significance, threat**

■ **downplay** /daʊnˈpleɪ/ *verb* [T] to deliberately make a situation seem less serious or important than it is: *The senator is downplaying the significance of the issue.*

play 'off

if two or more teams or players who have the same number of points in a competition play off, they play a game or games to see who is the winner

play off *The 16 finalists will play off to see who will win the championship.*

■ **'play-off** noun [C] an extra game that is played to decide the winner after a game or series of games ends with an equal score: *Ipswich won the play-off 3–2.*

play 'off against

if you play someone off against someone else, you try to cause an argument between them because you think that this will give you more power or control in a situation

play sb off against sb *The third person tries playing the other two off against each other.*

'play on

1 *showing disapproval* to use a situation or emotions such as fear or worry in order to get what you want

play on sth *She plays on the fact that people feel sorry for her.*

2 *mainly literary* if light plays on something, it shines on it

play on sth *The evening sun played on his handsome face.* ♦ *Moonlight played on the surface of the lake.*

play 'on

to continue to play a game, often after someone has been injured or has broken the rules

play on *We played on in spite of the rain.* ♦ *The referee told us to play on.*

play 'out ★

1 to develop or end in a particular way
play out *They disagreed violently, and*

no one knew how the situation would play out.

2 if you play out a situation, you pretend that it is really happening

play out sth *Children often play out quite violent scenes.*

play sth out *Her role in the family was to be peacemaker, and she played it out dutifully.*

3 to continue to play until the end of a particular period

play out sth *She played out her career in America.* ♦ *It looks like he'll play out the season in the reserves.*

4 [always passive] if an event or situation is played out in a particular way, it happens in that way

be played out *His career as a writer was played out against a background of alcoholism.*

play 'up ★★

1 *British informal* if children play up, or if they play someone up, they behave badly in a way that they think is funny so that the person looking after them finds them hard to control = MISBEHAVE

play up *I don't want you boys playing up again like yesterday.*
play sb up *I'm exhausted! The children have been really playing me up this afternoon.*

2 to try to persuade people to believe that something is more important than it is = TALK UP ≠ PLAY DOWN

play up sth *The newspapers have really played up our poor election results.*
play sth up *We tried to play that aspect of his character up.*

3 *informal* to fail to work or operate properly

play up *The printer's playing up again.*

4 *informal* to cause difficulties or pain for someone = BOTHER

play sb up *My back's been playing me up all day.*
play up *In bad weather her arthritis always played up.*

play 'up to

to behave in a very friendly or polite way to someone because you want them to like you or do something for you = FLATTER

play up to sb *He took great pains to play up to Joan's mother.*

'play with

1 to keep touching something, especially because you are bored = TOY WITH
play with sth *Stop playing with your hair!*

2 if you play with words or ideas, you use them in a clever or funny way play with sth *In this work she plays with narrative continuity in a fascinating way.*   **PHRASE** **play with yourself** *informal* to rub your sexual organs in order to get sexual pleasure

PLOD /plɒd, *American* plɑd/
plods, plodding, plodded

plod a'long (*also* plod 'on)

1 to walk with slow heavy steps
plod along *James was plodding along towards the rear.* ♦ *The horse shook its head and plodded on.*

2 to progress at a slow steady rate
plod along *I want an exciting career. I don't want to plod along in the same job for years.* ♦ **+with** *He's still plodding along with his novel.*

plod a'way

to keep working fairly hard doing something that is boring or that never changes
plod away *She had been plodding away at her research for years.*

plod 'on *same as* plod along

PLONK /plɒŋk, *American* plɑŋk/
plonks, plonking, plonked

plonk 'down *informal*

1 to sit or lie down on something in a careless or noisy way
plonk yourself down *She plonked herself firmly down on the bed.*

2 to put something down in a careless or noisy way
plonk sth down *also* **plonk down sth** *Mike plonked the grocery bags down on the table.*

PLOP /plɒp, *American* plɑp/
plops, plopping, plopped

plop 'down *informal*

to sit down somewhere heavily, especially as if you are tired = FLOP DOWN
plop yourself down *He plopped himself down and kicked off his shoes.* ♦ **+on** *He plopped himself down on the nearest chair.*
plop down *She plopped down by the edge of the swimming pool.*

PLOUGH /plaʊ/
ploughs, ploughing, ploughed

plough a'head

to continue to do something that may involve problems or that other people are opposing

plough ahead *Their decision to plough ahead before safety checks had been made was strongly criticized.* ♦ **+with** *Fortunately my family decided to plough ahead with the plan.*

plough 'back [often passive]

to put any profits made by your business back into it in order to make it more successful
be ploughed back *All that money ought to have been ploughed back.*
plough back sth into sth *also* **plough sth back into sth** *The group has ploughed back £31 million into the business over the past six months.* ♦ *To him, paying taxes was a waste of money, when you could plough that money back into the company.*

plough 'into ★

1 to crash into someone or something with force, especially because you are moving or driving carelessly or too fast
= CRASH INTO
plough into sth *Luckily no one was hurt when their car ploughed into a tree.*

2 to invest a lot of money in something in order to improve it or make it successful
plough sth into sth *Last year the government ploughed more than £80 million into road repairs.*

plough 'on

to continue doing something that takes a lot of effort or is likely to cause you problems
plough on *Rather than plough on regardless, we have decided to suspend the project.* ♦ *He ignored her laughter and ploughed on (=carried on speaking) in a determined way.* ♦ **+with** *He ploughed on with his work until the early evening.*

plough through ★

1 to read or deal with something that takes a long time and is difficult or boring
= WADE THROUGH
plough through sth *Bob was the only one to plough through all three volumes.* ♦ *She has mountains of paperwork to plough through every week.*

2 to crash through something or through a group of people with force, especially because you are moving or driving carelessly or too fast
plough through sth/sth *The car mounted the grass verge and ploughed through the safety barrier.*

‚plough 'up

1 to turn over the grass surface of a field with a plough in order to use the field for growing crops

plough up sth *also* **plough sth up** *They were ploughing up one of the fields near the river.* ♦ *They're going to plough that field up and plant corn there.*

2 to damage the surface of the ground by walking or driving over it too much
= CHURN UP

plough up sth *also* **plough sth up** *The kids had ploughed up the lawn with their bikes.*

PLOW the American spelling of **plough**

PLUCK /plʌk/
plucks, plucking, plucked

'pluck at
to pull something gently and quickly several times

pluck at sth *Annabel was plucking at his sleeve with her fingertips.*

'pluck from [often passive]
to take someone quickly from a particular place or situation

be plucked from sth *Princess Diana was very young when she **was plucked from obscurity**.*

pluck sb from sth *The blast plucked her from her feet and threw her across the floor.*

PLUG /plʌg/
plugs, plugging, plugged

‚plug a'way
to continue doing something in a determined way despite difficulties

plug away *I'll just keep plugging away and try to get it finished by tonight.*
♦ **+at** *We were impressed at how the kids plugged away at their assignments.*

'plug for American
to support or encourage someone

plug for sb/sth *Their parents will all be there plugging for the team.*

‚plug 'in ★★

1 to connect a piece of equipment to an electricity supply or to another piece of equipment ≠ UNPLUG

plug sth in *Then I realized I hadn't plugged the TV in.*
plug in sth *I forgot to plug in the kettle.*

2 to be connected to an electricity supply or to another piece of equipment

plug in *Can you see where it plugs in?*

■ 'plug-in [adj] a plug-in piece of equipment gets power by being connected to an electricity supply by means of a plug: *We only had a small plug-in heater.*

‚plug 'into ★

1 to connect a piece of equipment to an electricity supply or to another piece of equipment

plug sth into sth *First plug the keyboard into your computer.*

2 to be connected to an electricity supply or to another piece of equipment

plug into sth *The hairdryer plugs into this socket on the wall.*

3 to become connected or involved with someone or something and get some benefit from them

plug into sth *With this latest book, she is clearly hoping to plug into the international market.*

4 if you plug into a larger computer system, your computer becomes connected to it and you can get information from it

plug into sth *I plug into the company's system when I want to download my files.*

‚plug 'up
to fill a hole with a substance or piece of material so that nothing can get through it

plug up sth *also* **plug sth up** *He'd tried to plug up every hole in the stonework.*
♦ *They used cement to plug the well up.*

PLUMB /plʌm/
plumbs, plumbing, plumbed

‚plumb 'in British
to connect a piece of equipment such as a washing machine to the water pipes in a room so that water can flow to and from it

plumb in sth *also* **plumb sth in** *I plumbed in the washing machine myself.* ♦ *If there's a problem with your new dishwasher, contact the person who plumbed it in.*

PLUMP /plʌmp/
plumps, plumping, plumped

‚plump 'down
to sit down quickly and heavily

plump down *She plumped down on the bed.*
plump yourself down *He bustled into the room and plumped himself down beside Jenny.*

'plump for *informal*

to choose someone or something after being unable to decide what to do = GO FOR, CHOOSE

plump for sth *I think I'll plump for the chocolate cake this time.*

'plump 'out

to become fatter

plump out *She's plumped out a bit since I last saw her.*

'plump 'up

to hit something such as a pillow or cushion gently in order to make it return to its full shape

plump up sth *also* **plump sth up** *She started to plump up the cushions.* ♦ *He plumped my pillow up and tried to make me more comfortable.*

PLUNGE /plʌndʒ/
plunges, plunging, plunged

'plunge 'in

1 to suddenly start doing something with energy and enthusiasm, but sometimes without thinking about it first

plunge in *Your help may not be appreciated at first, but plunge in anyway.*

2 to quickly push something a long way into something else

plunge sth in *Luke plunged the needle in deep.*

3 to quickly jump or dive into water

plunge in *He plunged in at the deep end.*

'plunge 'into

1 to suddenly start doing something with energy or enthusiasm

plunge into sth *This was not the time to be plunging into some new business venture.*

2 to quickly push something a long way into something else

plunge sth into sth *He plunged his arm into the sack once more.* ♦ *Plunge the sliced onions into boiling water.*

3 [often passive] to suddenly put someone or something in a particular state or situation

be plunged into sth *The city was plunged into total darkness when the entire electrical system failed.*

plunge sb/sth into sth *The death of his friend had plunged him into an even greater depression.*

4 to suddenly get into a particular state or situation

plunge into sth *The country is plunging into recession once more.*

PLUNK /plʌŋk/
plunks, plunking, plunked

plunk 'down *American informal*

to pay a particular amount of money for something, especially when it is expensive

plunk down sth for sth *When I plunk down $3000 for a computer, I expect it to work.*

PLY /plaɪ/
plies, plying, plied

'ply with

to keep giving someone a lot of presents, food, or drinks, especially in order to make them do something

ply sb with sth *They plied me with food and drink until I could barely move.*

PHRASE **ply sb with questions** to keep asking someone questions: *Hannah plied him with questions about his childhood.*

POINT /pɔɪnt/
points, pointing, pointed

point 'out ★★★

1 to show someone who a person is or where something is = *formal* INDICATE

point out sb/sth *He pointed out the best beaches on the map.*

point sb/sth out *I'll point Adam out when he arrives.* ♦ **+to** *The captain pointed the dolphins out to his passengers.*

2 to tell someone something that they need to know

point sth out *Thank you for pointing that out.*

point out sth *It can be helpful if someone points out your mistakes.*

point out (that) *He pointed out that we had two hours of free time before dinner.* ♦ **+to** *She pointed out to me that we were miles from our destination and it was quickly getting dark.*

'point to ★★★

to show that something exists or is true

point to sth *The evidence clearly points to her guilt.* ♦ *Statistics point to the fact that more and more children are overweight.*

point 'up *formal*

to emphasize something = EMPHASIZE, HIGHLIGHT

point up sth *also* **point sth up** *Her research points up the difficulty of finding a solution.*

POKE /pəʊk, *American* poʊk/
pokes, poking, poked

poke a'long *American informal*
to move slowly, especially when others
are moving faster
poke along *If you don't stop poking
along we'll be late.*

poke a'round (*also* **poke a'bout** *British*)
1 to try to find something, especially by
moving other things
poke around *I'll poke around in the
refrigerator and see what I can find for
supper.*
2 to try to get information, especially
when other people do not want you to
poke around sth *Police poked around
the neighbourhood, searching for clues.*
♦ **+in** *Politicians are always poking
around in each other's private lives.*

'poke at
to push something quickly with your
finger or a pointed object
poke at sth *He poked at his dinner with
his fork.* ♦ *Don't go poking at the
animals – they might bite you.*

poke 'out
if something pokes out of something, you
can see it because part of it is coming out
of a hole or opening or it is not covered
poke out *The window went up and a
bald head poked out.* ♦ **+of/from** *You
could see his wallet poking out of the
back pocket of his jeans.*

poke 'through
if something pokes through something, it
appears from underneath a surface
poke through *You'll have to dig up all
the weeds that are poking through.*
poke through sth *Her toes were poking
through her socks.*

POLISH /'pɒlɪʃ, *American* 'pɑlɪʃ/
polishes, polishing, polished

polish 'off ★ *informal*
1 to eat or drink something until it is
finished
polish sth off *It won't take the kids long
to polish the cake off.*
polish off sth *They had polished off two
bottles of wine.*
2 to defeat or kill someone = FINISH OFF
polish sb off *The climb up to the front
door nearly polished me off.*

polish 'up
1 to improve your skills in something,

especially something that you used to be
able to do well
polish up sth *also* **polish sth up** *I could
do the job if I spent some time polishing
up my Spanish.*
2 to make something better, especially to
improve the way that people think about
you
polish up sth *also* **polish sth up** *It's time
that the company **polished up its act**.*
♦ *China is trying to polish up its image
abroad.*

PONCE /pɒns, *American* pɑns/
ponces, poncing, ponced

ponce a'bout (*also* **ponce a'round**)
British very informal
to waste time, especially by appearing to
be busy or popular, when you should be
working or paying attention to something
ponce about *If they hadn't ponced about
all week, the job could be finished by now.*

'ponce off *British very informal*
to get something you want by asking
someone else for it instead of providing it
or paying for it yourself = BUM OFF,
SCROUNGE OFF
ponce sth off sb *You're not poncing any
more money off me!*
ponce off sb *It's about time he stopped
poncing off his parents.*

PONY /'pəʊni, *American* 'poʊni/
ponies, ponying, ponied

pony 'up *American informal*
to pay for something
pony up *How will members of the public
feel about having to pony up for this?*
pony up sth *They ponied up $4.1 million
for the Bush campaign.*

POOP /puːp, *American* pup/
poops, pooping, pooped

poop 'out *American informal*
to stop doing something because it is too
difficult for you or because you are too
tired
poop out *It was your fault we lost! You
pooped out!*

POOTLE /'puːt(ə)l, *American* 'put(ə)l/
pootles, pootling, pootled

pootle a'bout (*also* **pootle a'round**)
British
to spend time doing things that you enjoy
but that are not important
pootle about *He spent a lot of time*

pootling about with a video camera.

pootle a'long *British*
to move along slowly and in a relaxed way, especially in a car
pootle along *I was just pootling along enjoying the scenery when a man appeared in the road.*

POP /pɒp, *American* pɑp/
pops, popping, popped

pop 'in ★★ (*also* pop 'into) *informal*
to go somewhere quickly or for a short time = POP ROUND
pop in *I'll pop in this afternoon and bring you your shopping.* ♦ *I often pop into the bank in my lunch hour.* ♦ **+to do sth** *I thought I'd just pop in to say hello.* ♦ **+with** *She popped in with my birthday present earlier.*

pop 'off *British informal*
to die
pop off *When the old lady finally popped off they found she'd left two wills.*

pop 'on [usually in imperative] *informal*
to put on an item of clothing or something such as a pair of glasses or a wig
pop sth on *Could you pop your glasses on again please?* ♦ **+over** *Just pop the sweater on over your T-shirt.*

pop 'out ★ *informal*
1 to leave a room or other place quickly or for a short time
pop out *Sarah's not here. She just popped out.* ♦ **+to do sth** *I'm just popping out to post a letter.* ♦ **+to** *Do you mind if I pop out to the shops?*
2 if words pop out, you say them suddenly without thinking first about what they mean
pop out *I didn't mean to say that – it just popped out.*

pop 'over *British informal*
to visit a friend or relative at their house for a short time = VISIT
pop over *I've got the photos from the wedding – I'll pop over and show you tomorrow.*

pop 'round *informal*
to visit someone or go somewhere quickly or for a short time = POP IN
pop round *Can you pop round later? I need to speak to you.* ♦ **+to do sth** *I'll pop round to see you after school.* ♦ **+with** *I'll ask Dan to pop round with your card.*

pop 'up ★★ *informal*
to appear very quickly or suddenly = BOB UP
pop up *The daffodils and tulips are popping up everywhere.* ♦ *We see this issue popping up again and again.* ♦ *After a long absence, he popped up in Aberdeen in May.*

■ **pop-up** adj **1** a pop-up book or card has pictures inside that have been cut out so that they stand up when you open the pages **2** a pop-up toaster pushes the pieces of bread up when they are ready to eat **3** used for describing something that appears suddenly on a computer screen when you click the mouse or press a particular key: *How can I get rid of all these pop-up ads?*

PORE /pɔː, *American* pɔr/
pores, poring, pored

pore over
to examine or read something very carefully and in a lot of detail = EXAMINE
pore over sth *I've just left Ben poring over computer printouts with an engineer.*

PORTION /'pɔːʃ(ə)n, *American* 'pɔrʃ(ə)n/
portions, portioning, portioned

portion 'out
to divide something among several people = APPORTION
portion out sth *also* **portion sth out** *The board will have to portion out the corporation's multi-million-dollar budget among the separate business units.*

PORTRAY /pɔːˈtreɪ, *American* pɔrˈtreɪ/
portrays, portraying, portrayed

por'tray as ★★ [often passive]
to show or describe someone or something in a particular way
be portrayed as sth *Fathers in sitcoms are often portrayed as incompetent.* ♦ *It is wrong that we should be portrayed as money-grabbers.*
portray sb/sth as sth *Opponents portray the president as weak and ineffectual.*

POSE /pəʊz, *American* poʊz/
poses, posing, posed

pose as
to pretend to be a particular person or type of person in order to trick people
pose as sth *Police officers posing as customers were sold some of the stolen*

items. ♦ *Police are hunting for a man who posed as a care worker to gain entry into old people's homes.*

POSSESS /pə'zes/
possesses, possessing, possessed

be po'ssessed of *formal*
to have a particular quality, ability, knowledge etc: *He is possessed of a quite extraordinary intelligence.*

POST /pəust, *American* poust/
posts, posting, posted

post 'off *British*
to send a letter or package to someone in the mail = POST, MAIL
post off sth *also* **post sth off** *I posted off my order form yesterday.* ♦ *She nagged me until I wrote a letter and posted it off.*

post 'up
to put information or a message where the public can see it, for example on a wall
post up sth *also* **post sth up** *The headteacher posted up a list of prize-winners.* ♦ *We'll post the exam results up as soon as we get them.*

POT /pɒt, *American* pɑt/
pots, potting, potted

pot 'on [often passive] *British*
to move a plant into a larger container because it has grown bigger
be potted on *The new plants should be planted in small pots then potted on as they grow.*
pot on sth *Use this compost if you are potting on young houseplants.*

POTTER /'pɒtə, *American* 'pɑtər/
potters, pottering, pottered

potter a'round (*also* potter a'bout *British*)
to do things in a slow and enjoyable way
potter around *I just spent the rest of the day pottering around in the studio.*
potter around sth *She was pottering around the apartment when the phone rang.*

POUNCE /paʊns/
pounces, pouncing, pounced

'pounce on (*also* 'pounce upon *formal*)
1 to quickly jump on or hold someone or something = LATCH ONTO, SEIZE
pounce on sb/sth *They pounced on their suspect.*

2 to react to something quickly, especially by criticizing someone or something
pounce on sb/sth *White House aides pounced on the remark.*

POUND /paʊnd/
pounds, pounding, pounded

pound 'out *informal*
1 if you pound out a song, you play it loudly by hitting your instrument very hard
pound out sth *also* **pound sth out** *Everyone sang as Mary pounded out the family favourites on the piano.*

2 *American* to produce something in a very short period of time = CHURN OUT
pound out sth *also* **pound sth out** *Some of these writers pound out three books a year.*

POUR /pɔː, *American* pɔr/
pours, pouring, poured

'pour down
to rain very hard
pour down *The rain poured down in torrents.* ♦ *You can't go outside now. It's pouring down!*

pour 'in ★★
1 to arrive somewhere quickly in a large group or in large amounts
pour in *The doors opened and a crowd of people poured in.* ♦ *Complaints have been pouring in about last night's show.*

2 to flow into a place quickly and in large amounts
pour in *The door was forced open and flood water poured in.*

'pour into
1 to arrive somewhere in a large group or in large amounts
pour into sth *Donations have been pouring into the appeals office.*

2 to flow into a place quickly and in large amounts
pour into sth *Smoke was pouring into the room.*

3 to give a lot of effort, money, or help to someone or something
pour sth into sth *They've already poured a lot of time and money into this project.*
♦ *After the accident, he poured all his energy into learning to walk again.*

pour 'out ★★
1 to put some drink into a glass or cup from another container
pour out sth *She poured out the rest of the tea and handed it to me.*

pour sth out *Would you pour some water out for me, please?*

2 to tell someone everything that you are feeling

pour out sth *She began pouring out her fears about the future.*

pour sth out *Once he had started, he couldn't stop pouring his feelings out.*
♦ **+to** *She longed to pour her troubles out to someone.* ♦ *I rang my best friend and poured my heart out to him.*

> Nouns often used as objects with
> pour out 2
>
> ■ fears, heart, love, problems, story, troubles

3 to leave somewhere quickly in a large group or in large amounts = STREAM OUT

pour out *The aircraft landed and the passengers poured out.* ♦ **+of** *Workers poured out of the factory train.*

4 to flow out of a place continuously and in large amounts

pour out *The valve broke and water came pouring out.* ♦ **+of** *Crude oil poured out of the tanker.*

■ **outpouring** /'aʊtpɔːrɪŋ/ **noun** [C/U]
1 the act of expressing a strong emotion: *There was an extraordinary outpouring of grief following her death.* **2** a sudden production of something in large amounts, especially books, poems, music etc: *What followed was a huge outpouring of anti-Communist art.*

POWER /'paʊə, *American* 'paʊər/
powers, powering, powered

power 'up
to switch on a computer or other piece of electrical equipment = START UP

power up sth *also* **power sth up** *Power up your computer and we'll start.*

PRACTISE /'præktɪs/
practises, practising, practised

'practise on (*also* **'practise upon**) *British*
to do something bad or unpleasant to someone

practise sth on sb *We can't let him practise this emotional blackmail on us.*

PREDISPOSE /ˌpriːdɪs'pəʊz, *American* ˌprɪdɪs'poʊz/
predisposes, predisposing, predisposed

predis'pose to *formal*
1 **predispose to** or **predispose towards** to make someone likely to think, feel, or behave in a particular way

predispose sb to sth *Is there a set of economic conditions that predisposes a nation to revolution?*

2 [often passive] to make someone likely to suffer from a particular illness or condition

be predisposed to sth *Some people seem to be predisposed to depression.*

predispose sb to sth *a mutation that predisposes some people to lung cancer*

PREFACE /'prefəs/
prefaces, prefacing, prefaced

'preface with [often passive] *formal*
to say, do, or write something before you say, do, or write the most important part

be prefaced with sth *His speech was prefaced with a short explanation.*

preface sth with sth *She prefaced her remarks with a few words of thanks to the organizers.*

PREJUDICE /'predʒʊdɪs, *American* 'predʒədɪs/
prejudices, prejudicing, prejudiced

'prejudice against
to make someone form a bad opinion about someone or something before they have enough information to know what they are really like

prejudice sb against sb *His ex-wife's testimony might prejudice the jurors against him.*

PRESIDE /prɪ'zaɪd/
presides, presiding, presided

pre'side over
to be in a position of power while important changes or events are happening

preside over sth *He presided over the worst season in the team's history.*

PRESS /pres/
presses, pressing, pressed

press a'head ★
to continue doing something in a determined way, despite difficulties, opposition, or interruptions = PRESS ON, WEIGH ON

press ahead *They pressed ahead regardless of objections.* ♦ **+with** *We shall press ahead with our plans for reform.*

'press for
to try in a determined way to get something

press for sth *The committee also agreed*

to press for changes in the current financing system.
press sb for sth *The more she pressed him for an explanation, the more he refused to speak.*

ˌpress ˈforward
to continue doing something in a determined way, despite difficulties
press forward with sth *The government says it will press forward with vital reforms.*

ˌpress ˈin
to move closer to something in a threatening way
press in on sb *The crowd was pressing in on him all the time.*

ˌpress ˈinto [often passive]
to try in a determined way to make someone do something or tell you something
be pressed into (doing) sth *She was pressed into giving the manager's son a job.*
press sb into (doing) sth *His ambitious parents pressed him into staying on at university.*

ˌpress ˈon ★★
1 to continue with a journey, even though there are obstacles or delays
press on *We pressed on, hoping to arrive before dark.*
2 to continue doing something in a determined way, despite difficulties
= PRESS AHEAD
press on *Mr. Scott ignored the comment and pressed on.* ♦ **+with** *It was very difficult to press on with the rehearsal.*
3 to try in a determined way to give someone something, especially something that they do not really want = FORCE ON
press sth on sb *It's not fair to keep pressing chocolates on her when she's trying to diet.* ♦ *What I like about Tim is that he doesn't try to press his opinions on other people.*
4 if a problem or unpleasant feeling presses on you, it makes you upset or worried
press on sb *There were too many thoughts pressing on her.*

PRESUME /prɪˈzjuːm, *American* prɪˈzuːm/
presumes, presuming, presumed

preˈsume on (*also* **preˈsume upon** *formal*)
to expect more than you should get or more than you have a right to, especially

in your relationships with other people
presume on sth *She knew he looked on her as his role model, but was determined not to presume on that.* ♦ *I will not **presume upon** your **friendship** any further.*

PREVAIL /prɪˈveɪl/
prevails, prevailing, prevailed

preˈvail on (*also* **preˈvail upon**) *formal*
to ask or persuade someone to do something = PERSUADE
prevail on sb to do sth *She had prevailed on Dorothy to come and reason with them.* ♦ *They might be prevailed upon to come with us.*

PREY /preɪ/
preys, preying, preyed

ˈprey on ★ (*also* **ˈprey upon**)
1 to harm someone who is weak or cannot defend themselves
prey on sb *The gang has been preying on foreign tourists.*
2 to hunt another creature in order to eat it
prey on sth *The lake is full of predators that prey on eggs and chicks.*
PHRASE **prey on sb's mind** if something preys on your mind, you think and worry about it all the time: *The criticism preyed on my mind.*

PRICK /prɪk/
pricks, pricking, pricked

ˌprick ˈout *British*
to remove a small young plant from a pot and put it into the ground or into a bigger pot
prick out sth *also* **prick sth out** *She watched him pricking out the seedlings.*

PRIDE /praɪd/
prides, priding, prided

ˈpride yourself on
to feel proud about an achievement, skill, or special quality that you have
pride yourself on (doing) sth *We pride ourselves on the quality and thoroughness of our work.* ♦ *She prided herself on being fair and honest with all her students.*

PRINT /prɪnt/
prints, printing, printed

print 'out ★★ (also print 'off)
to produce a copy of a computer document from a printer

print out sth *Should I print out that graph now?* ♦ *Can you print off a few copies of this document for me?*
print sth out *He spellchecked the document and printed it out.*

■ **printout** /'prɪntaʊt/   **noun** [C/U] paper printed with information from a computer file: *I asked for a printout of the document.*

PRIZE /praɪz/
prizes, prizing, prized

prize a'part
to force two things apart

prize sth apart *I had to prize the dog's jaws apart to give him the medicine.*

prize 'out of
to persuade someone to tell you something they do not want to tell you = PRY OUT OF

prize sth out of sb *In the end I had to prize the names out of him.*

PROCEED /prə'siːd, American prə'sid/
proceeds, proceeding, proceeded

pro'ceed against *legal*
to begin a case against someone in a court of law

proceed against sb *There was never enough evidence to proceed against him.*

pro'ceed from *formal*
to have a particular cause or origin

proceed from sth *Growth proceeds from a small crystal nucleus.* ♦ *He has that confidence that proceeds from really knowing what he is talking about.*

pro'ceed with ★★ *formal*
to do something that you have planned to do or thought about doing

proceed with sth *The police decided not to proceed with the case.* ♦ *If you decide not to proceed with the transaction, please let us know within 14 days.*

PROFIT /'prɒfɪt, American 'prɑfɪt/
profits, profiting, profited

'profit from ★★ (also 'profit by) *formal*
1 to get an advantage from a situation

profit from sth *She hopes to profit from the experience.* ♦ *Did he try to profit by the information he received?*

2 to make a profit from something = CASH IN ON

profit from sth *They were accused of profiting from the sale of state assets.*

PROJECT /prə'dʒekt/
projects, projecting, projected

pro,ject 'onto
to imagine an emotion that you feel is also being felt by someone else, especially without realizing that you are doing this

project sth onto sb *It's not me who's unhappy, it's her! She's projecting her problems onto me.*

PRONOUNCE /prə'naʊns/
pronounces, pronouncing, pronounced

pro'nounce against *legal*
to give a judgment against someone or something in a court of law

pronounce against sb/sth *The judge pronounced against the previous conviction, saying there was no firm evidence whatsoever.*

pro'nounce for *legal*
to give a judgment in favour of someone or something in a court of law

pronounce for sb/sth *Would the court pronounce for the prisoners' extradition from the UK?*

pro'nounce on (also pro'nounce upon)
to give your opinion on something, especially in a formal way

pronounce on sth *It is too early to pronounce on the success or failure of the project.*

PROP /prɒp, American prɑp/
props, propping, propped

prop 'up ★★
1 [often passive] to stop something from falling by putting something under it or against it

be propped up *A large handwritten notice was propped up by the door.*
♦ **+against** *A piece of wood was propped up against the wall.*
prop sth up *Prop the baby up in a bouncy chair.* ♦ **+with** *She turned on one side, propping her head up with her elbow.*
prop up sth *The fire had damaged the beams that prop up the roof.*

2 to help a government, system, organization etc to continue to exist, especially by providing financial or military support = SHORE UP

prop up sth *This new initiative is a*

desperate attempt to prop up the economy.
prop sth up *The company was in deep trouble and he used his own money to prop it up.*

PROVIDE /prə'vaɪd/
provides, providing, provided

pro'vide against *formal*
to make arrangements to prevent or deal with something bad that might happen
provide against sth *It is essential to provide against future attacks.* ♦ *There are some circumstances that human care can't provide against.*

pro'vide for ★★★
1 to look after someone by making money in order to buy the things that they need
provide for sb *She has always provided for her children.*

2 if a law or agreement provides for something, it states that something can or must happen = STIPULATE
provide for sth *The bill provides for the establishment of a consumer protection board.*

> **Nouns often used as subjects with provide for 2**
> ■ agreement, clause, law, legislation, scheme, statute, treaty

3 to make it possible for something to happen in the future = ALLOW FOR
provide for sth *The budget provides for a salary increase after one year.* ♦ *Private health insurance does not always provide for emergency treatment.*

PRY /praɪ/
pries, prying, pried

pry 'out of (*also* 'pry from)
to get information from someone with a lot of effort or difficulty = PRIZE OUT OF
pry sth out of sb *We managed to pry the secret code out of him.*

PSYCH /saɪk/
psychs, psyching, psyched

psych 'out *informal*
to talk or behave very confidently in order to make someone that you are competing against feel nervous and less likely to succeed
psych sb out *also* **psych out sb** *Don't worry – he's just trying to psych you out.* ♦ *It is a common tactic for a player to try and psych out his opponent before a game.*

psych 'up [often passive] *informal*
to try to make yourself or someone else feel mentally ready for something
be/get psyched up *Before the game everyone gets psyched up and starts shouting.* ♦ **+for** *I was psyched up for my first TV interview.*
psych yourself up *How do singers psych themselves up before a performance?* ♦ **+to do sth** *I was psyching myself up to ask her out to dinner.*

PUCKER /'pʌkə, *American* 'pʌkər/
puckers, puckering, puckered

pucker 'up
to squeeze your lips together and out before you kiss someone or when someone is going to kiss you
pucker up sth *Expecting a kiss, Katy puckered up her lips.*
pucker up *She puckered up and planted a large kiss on Sam's cheek.*

PUFF /pʌf/
puffs, puffing, puffed

puff a'way
to smoke a cigarette, pipe etc for a period of time
puff away *She didn't smoke, but she watched the others puff away.* ♦ **+on/at** *I left him still puffing away at his pipe.*

puff 'out
1 if air or smoke puffs out, or if you puff it out, it comes out in small amounts that disappear quickly
puff out sth *also* **puff sth out** *He puffed out a cloud of smoke from his cigar.* ♦ *He drew a breath, then puffed it out.*
puff out *Steam puffed out from the pie crust.*

2 to fill something, for example your cheeks, with air so that it looks bigger
puff out sth *also* **puff sth out** *The dove cooed and puffed out the feathers on his breast.* ♦ *She puffed her cheeks out and strutted around pretending to be fat.*

puff 'up
1 if something puffs up, or if you puff it up, it looks bigger, usually because it has air in it
puff up *When the cookies puff up and turn brown they are ready.*
puff up sth *also* **puff sth up** *She tried to puff up her hair a bit.* ♦ *I always puff the pillows up when I make the bed.*

2 to swell because of an injury or illness
puff up *The next day his face had really puffed up.*

■ ˌpuffed ˈup adj **1** behaving as though you are especially good in some way, and people should admire you: *They arrange luxury transport for puffed-up executives.* **2** a part of the body that is puffed up is swollen: *His eye was black and puffed up.*

PUKE /pjuːk, *American* pjuk/
pukes, puking, puked

ˌpuke ˈup *very informal*
if you puke up, food comes up from your stomach and out through your mouth, usually because you are ill = THROW UP; *formal* VOMIT
    puke up *She puked up during class today.*

PULL /pʊl/
pulls, pulling, pulled

Pull is often used with adverbs and prepositions when it means 'to move someone or something towards you using your hands': *The guide **pulled** gently **at** my sleeve.* ♦ *Help me **pull** the sofa **away** from the wall.* ♦ *I climbed into bed and **pulled** the covers **over** my head.* These uses are not included here.

ˌpull aˈhead
1 to get in front of someone by moving faster than they do
    pull ahead *When the dog pulls ahead, the leash tightens and causes the animal discomfort.*
2 to start to make progress faster than someone, especially when you have previously been making progress at the same rate = PULL AWAY
    pull ahead *The Labour Party was level with the Conservative Party and threatening to pull ahead.* ♦ **+of** *She hated it when I started pulling ahead of her.*

ˌpull aˈpart
to separate two people or animals that are fighting
    pull sb apart *When the boys started fighting no one tried to pull them apart.*

ˌpull aˈside
to take someone away from a group of people in order to talk to them on their own
    pull sb aside *He pulled Paula aside and began to whisper to her.*

ˌpull aˈway ★★
1 if a vehicle or driver pulls away, they start to move

    pull away *Pulling away in her car, Vicky waved.*
2 to start to make progress faster than someone, especially when you have previously been making progress at the same rate = PULL AHEAD
    pull away *The scores were level, then our team pulled away.* ♦ **+from** *He appears to be pulling away from his rivals in the election campaign.*
3 *British* to get in front of someone by moving faster than they do = PULL AHEAD
    pull away *Sullivan pulled away in the final lap.*
4 to move your body away from someone who is trying to hold you or touch you = PULL BACK
    pull away *She tried to take his hand but he pulled away.* ♦ **+from** *When he tried to kiss her, she pulled away from him.*

ˌpull ˈback ★★★
1 if soldiers pull back, or if someone pulls them back, they move back towards their own land = WITHDRAW
    pull back *Our tank and infantry forces pulled back to regroup.*
    pull back sth *They had to pull back some units to stem the advance on the capital.*
2 to decide not to do something that you had planned to do
    pull back *She seemed keen to move in with him at first, but pulled back when they started having arguments.* ♦ **+from sth** *The company has pulled back from its initial moves into the hotel market.* ♦ **+from doing sth** *The government has pulled back from sending the navy there.*
3 to move your body away from someone who is holding you or touching you = PULL AWAY
    pull back *Why do you always pull back when I try to kiss you?* ♦ **+from** *Jim pulled back from her with a hurt expression.*
4 *British mainly journalism* to score a goal when your team is losing in a soccer match
    pull sth back *Tully pulled one back for United after 40 minutes.*
    pull back sth *Will England be able to pull back another goal?*

ˌpull ˈdown ★★
1 [often passive] to destroy a building, especially because it is very old or dangerous = KNOCK DOWN, DEMOLISH
    be pulled down *The group of old buildings had to be pulled down.*
    pull sth down *They are planning to pull the prison down and build a new one.*
    pull down sth *They are pulling down*

historic buildings to make way for cheap housing.

2 *American* to earn a particular amount of money = BRING IN, PULL IN

pull down sth *She pulls down over $1 million a year in salary.*

'pull for

to encourage someone or something to succeed

pull for sb/sth *I was pleased with our teamwork, with everyone pulling for each other.*

ˌpull 'in ★★

1	train: arrive in a station
2	earn money
3	attract a big audience
4	arrest sb
5	stop by the side of the road
6	when a lot of people vote

1 pull in or **pull into** if a train pulls in, it arrives at a station = ARRIVE

pull in *The train from London was just pulling in.*

pull into sth *He jumped off the train as soon as it pulled into the station.*

2 to earn a particular amount of money = *American* PULL DOWN

pull in sth *She's pulling in a six-figure salary.*

pull sth in *I don't think she'll be pulling that much money in.*

3 if a performer or a performance pulls in an audience, a large number of people come to watch them = ATTRACT, DRAW

pull in sth *The programme pulled in 3.6 million viewers.*

pull sth in *She's still pulling the crowds in after eighteen years.*

4 *informal* if the police pull someone in, they arrest them = ARREST

pull sb in *There's not enough evidence to pull her in.*

5 pull in or **pull into** if a vehicle or driver pulls in, they stop by the side of the road = PULL OVER, STOP

pull in *Can you just pull in here please?* ♦ *We pulled in by the side of the road.*

pull into sth *The car pulled into the car park and four men got out.*

6 if a politician pulls in votes, a lot of people vote for him or her

pull in sth *The Green Party candidate pulled in quite a few votes.*

pull sth in *We needed to pull another few thousand votes in quickly.*

ˌpull 'off ★★

1	succeed in doing sth
2	leave road
3	transfer information
4	remove clothes
5	sports: remove player

1 to succeed in doing something that is difficult

pull off sth *Sandy managed to pull off a surprise party for her husband.*

pull sth off *They nearly managed to get the loan but just failed to pull it off.*

2 if a vehicle or driver pulls off a road, they leave it, especially before stopping

pull off sth *If you get tired, pull off the motorway and have a rest.*

3 *informal* to take information from one computer and put it onto another = DOWNLOAD

pull sth off sth *You can pull the files you need off the Internet.*

4 to take off clothes, especially quickly = TAKE OFF ≠ PUT ON

pull sth off *She pulled the dress off over her head.*

pull off sth *She pulled off her clothes and left them in a heap.*

5 [often passive] to decide that someone should no longer take part in something such as a sports game

be pulled off *Rooney was pulled off just minutes after the game started.*

pull sb off *The England manager clearly decided it was time to pull off his star player.*

ˌpull 'on ★★

1 to put on clothes, especially quickly = PUT ON ≠ TAKE OFF

pull on sth *Emily pulled on her gloves as she walked.*

pull sth on *'We need to leave now,' she said, pulling her coat on.*

2 to take a gun or knife out of a pocket and be ready to use it to attack someone

pull sth on sb *I hadn't been expecting him to pull a gun on me.*

3 to suck smoke from a cigarette, cigar, or pipe into your mouth or lungs

pull on a cigarette/cigar/pipe *She pulled on her cigarette, staring into space.*

ˌpull 'out ★★

1 to stop being involved in an activity, event, or situation = STOP, WITHDRAW

pull out *Three players were forced to pull out because of injury.* ♦ **+of** *The firm is pulling out of the personal computer business.*

2 if soldiers pull out of a place, or if

someone pulls them out, they leave
= WITHDRAW

pull out of sth *Troops are beginning to pull out of the capital.*

pull sth out *If they pulled their troops out tomorrow, what would happen?*

3 if a train pulls out, it leaves a station
= LEAVE

pull out *He stood on the platform and watched her train pull out.* ♦ **+of** *As the train pulled out of the station, she realized she'd left her suitcase in the waiting room.*

4 if a vehicle or driver pulls out, they move onto a road or onto a part of a road where the traffic is moving faster

pull out *She just pulled out in front of me without any warning.*

PHRASE **pull out all the stops** to make a big effort so that something happens or is successful: *Staff at the Children's Hospital pulled out all the stops to make sure patients had a happy Christmas Day.*

ˌpull ˈover ★

1 if a vehicle or driver pulls over, they stop by the side of the road = PULL IN

pull over *At a parade of shops, the car suddenly pulled over.*

2 [often passive] if the police pull a vehicle over, they order its driver to stop at the side of the road

be pulled over *He was pulled over by the police because he was driving too fast.*

pull sb over *Police pulled the motorist over and asked to see his driving licence.*

ˌpull ˈround

to start to get better after being ill or in a bad situation

pull round *He was just beginning to pull round after his operation.* ♦ *In the past few months we've seen the company pull round.*

ˌpull ˈthrough

1 to manage to stay alive after you have been very sick or very badly injured
= SURVIVE

pull through *Don't worry, your dad's going to pull through.*

2 to succeed in a very difficult situation, or to help someone do this

pull through *We need to work together if we are going to pull through.*

pull sb through *He said the support of his fans had pulled him through.*

ˌpull toˈgether ★★

1 if people pull together, they work together to achieve something = UNITE

pull together *If we all pull together, we can get this done tonight.*

2 to combine different things so that they form a single unit

pull together sth *The report pulls together information from several offices.*

pull sth together *A musical is a good way for her to pull her talents together.*

PHRASE **pull yourself together** to control your emotions and behave calmly after being upset, angry, or shocked: *Come on Jane, pull yourself together.*

ˌpull ˈunder

to move something or someone so that they are under the water in a river, sea, lake etc

pull sb/sth under *There are dangerous currents that can pull you under.*

ˌpull ˈup ★★★

1	of plants: remove from ground
2	driver/vehicle: stop
3	criticize sb
4	make sth stop
5	move your seat near sb

1 to use force to remove a plant and its roots from the ground

pull sth up *She was pulling up the weeds.*

2 if a vehicle or driver pulls up, they stop

pull up *Their taxi pulled up outside the church.*

3 to criticize someone about something they are not doing well

pull sb up on sth *My teachers are always pulling me up on my spelling.*

4 if something pulls you up, you suddenly stop what you are doing or saying

pull sb up *The anger in his voice pulled me up sharply.*

5 to move a seat near to where someone is sitting, and sit on it

pull up a chair/stool/seat etc *Come in John. Pull up a seat and have some food.*

PHRASES **pull sb up short** to make someone unexpectedly stop in surprise and think: *The question pulled Rory up short.*

pull your socks up used for telling someone that they have not done a job well enough and must do better: *You'll have to pull your socks up if you want to pass these exams.*

■ **'pull-up** noun [C] an exercise in which you hold a bar that is above your head and pull yourself up off the ground: *I did some press-ups and pull-ups.*

PUMP /pʌmp/
pumps, pumping, pumped

ˌpump aˈway
to remove liquid or gas from something using a pump
pump away sth *also* **pump sth away** *The equipment is used to pump away sewage.*
♦ *A special machine shreds the waste and pumps it away.*

ˌpump ˈin (*also* ˌpump ˈinto)
1 to force liquid or gas into a place
pump in sth *also* **pump sth in** *Pumping in carbon dioxide failed to put out the fire.* ♦ *They pumped clean air into the building.*
2 to invest a lot of money, effort etc in something
pump sth in sth *The whole area looks better now that the government has pumped a lot of money in local housing.*

ˌpump ˈout
1 to force liquid or gas out of a place
= *formal* EMIT
pump out sth *also* **pump sth out** *Huge generators were pumping out black smoke.* ♦ *The Victorians had the idea of pumping raw sewage out to sea.*
2 to produce a lot of something = CHURN OUT
pump sth out *also* **pump out sth** *The machine pumps radio waves out into space.* ♦ *They get paid too much for pumping out work like that.*

ˌpump ˈup ★★
1 to fill something with air using a pump
= INFLATE ≠ DEFLATE
pump up sth *I need to pump up my bicycle tyres.*
pump sth up *It took half an hour just to pump the airbed up.* ♦ *If you take the tyre from a child's bicycle, you could pump it up in a few seconds.*
2 *informal* to make something increase by a large amount = BOOST
pump up sth *They have cut prices in an attempt to pump up sales.*
pump sth up *They pump their fees up if they know you're rich.* ♦ *If demand for these goods is falling, prices drop to pump it up.*
3 [usually passive] *informal* to make someone feel excited and enthusiastic = REV UP
be/get pumped up *The coach's job is to get everyone pumped up for the game.*

■ ˌpumped ˈup **adj** *informal* very excited or enthusiastic about something: *The crowd is tense and the players are pumped up.*

PUNCH /pʌntʃ/
punches, punching, punched

ˌpunch ˈin
1 to enter information into a machine by pressing keys or buttons = ENTER
punch in sth *also* **punch sth in** *If you punch in the wrong code, the alarm sounds.* ♦ *I'll punch those details in now.*
2 *American* to record the time you arrive at work by putting a card into a machine = CLOCK IN
punch in *Laura punched in at 7.30 am.*

ˌpunch ˈout *American*
to record the time that you leave work by putting a card into a machine = CLOCK OFF
punch out *He punched out early and went home.*
⬛ **PHRASE** **punch sb's lights out** *informal* to hit someone so hard that they fall and cannot get up: *The guy was threatening to punch my lights out.*

ˌpunch ˈup
to make information appear on something such as the screen of a computer or the screen of the till in a shop, by pressing keys or buttons
punch up sth *also* **punch sth up** *He punched up a price, but it was the wrong price.* ♦ *You punch the words 'Stock Check' up on the screen.*

PURGE /pɜːdʒ, *American* pɜrdʒ/
purges, purging, purged

ˈpurge of [usually passive] *mainly literary*
to remove an unpleasant feeling or an unpleasant aspect of something
be purged of sth *He was purged of all his fears and fell into a peaceful sleep.*

PUSH /pʊʃ/
pushes, pushing, pushed

Push is often used with adverbs and prepositions when it means 'to move someone or something away from you, or from their previous position, using part of your body, especially your hands': *He was pushing a trolley around the supermarket.* ♦ *Rebecca pushed her handkerchief into her pocket.* ♦ *She pushed him out of the room and slammed the door shut.* These uses are not included here.

ˌpush aˈbout *British same as* push around

ˌpush aˈhead (*also* ˌpush ˈforward)
to continue trying to achieve something in spite of opposition or difficulties

push ahead *They are insisting on pushing ahead in the face of massive opposition.* ♦ **+with** *The company is pushing ahead with plans to expand production.*

push a'round (*also* **push a'bout** *British*) *informal*

to keep telling someone what to do in an unfair and unpleasant way = BOSS AROUND
push sb around *I wouldn't try to push her around if I were you. She just won't take it.*

push a'side

to refuse to think about something unpleasant
push sth aside *also* **push aside sth** *She pushed her doubts aside and carried on.* ♦ *You learn to push aside the fear of being hurt.*

push a'way

to show that you do not want someone's help or attention
push sb away *I feel as though you're always pushing me away.*

push 'back [often passive]

to arrange a later time for something = PUT BACK
be pushed back *The deadline has been pushed back a few days.*
push sth back *Couldn't we push the date back a couple of weeks?* ♦ **+to/until** *Can I push back our meeting to 27 May?*
PHRASE **push back the limits/frontiers** to discover new things about something or a better way of doing it: *We're pushing back the frontiers of technology.*

push 'by

to push someone as you go past them, in a rude way = PUSH PAST
push by sb/sth *She pushed by him and out of the door.*
push by *He burnt my hand with his cigarette as he pushed by.*

push for ★

1 to try hard to get or achieve something = PRESS FOR
push for sth *They continue to push for more pay.* ♦ *We are pushing for a ban on all nuclear testing.*

2 to try to make someone give you something or do something for you
push sb for sth *He's pushing us for a decision by tomorrow.*

push 'forward

1 *same as* **push ahead**

2 to move nearer a place in a determined way, or in spite of opposition or difficulties

push forward *John pushed forward into the dark entrance of the cave.*

3 to try to make people recognize someone's qualities or abilities
push sb forward *You see competitive and ambitious parents pushing their children forward.*
push yourself forward *Nicola was never one to miss out on a chance to push herself forward.*

push 'in *British*

to stand in front of people who have been waiting longer than you in a queue, in a way that is unfair
push in *We were all waiting patiently for a taxi, but he just pushed in.*

push 'into

to strongly encourage or force someone to do something
push sb into (doing) sth *She claims that the police pushed her into giving evidence.* ♦ *I'm glad my husband pushed me into the purchase.*

push 'off

1 *informal* to leave a place = GO AWAY, CLEAR OFF
push off *If there's nothing else, I'll push off then.*

2 if a person or boat pushes off, or if you push a boat off, you sail away from the land
push off *I dragged the boat down to the water and pushed off.*
push sth off *We pushed the little boat off and rowed for Wildcat Island.*

3 [often in imperative] *informal* used for telling someone rudely to go away
push off *Tell them to push off and leave you alone.*

push 'on

1 to continue a journey, especially after stopping for a period of time = PRESS ON
push on *It's getting late. We'd better be pushing on.* ♦ **+towards** *Next day we pushed on towards London.*

2 to continue doing something, especially when you do not have much time = PRESS ON
push on *There's a lot to do, so let's push on.*

push 'over

to push someone or something hard so that they fall from a standing position
push sb/sth over *also* **push over sth/sb** *She pushed me over in the playground.* ♦ *He pushed over the lamp.*

■ **pushover** /ˈpʊʃˌəʊvə/ **noun** [C]
1 someone who is easy to influence or

persuade, or an opponent who is easy to defeat: *Colonel Moore was a kind and sympathetic man, but no pushover.*
2 something that is easy to achieve: *Saturday's game will be no pushover.*

ˌpush ˈpast ★

to push someone as you go past them, in a rude way = PUSH BY
push past sb/sth *A man pushed past her and knocked her bag out of her hand.*
push past *She started to push past, but I caught her arm.*

ˌpush ˈthrough ★

to succeed in getting a law, agreement etc accepted quickly although a lot of people oppose it = RUSH THROUGH
push sth through sth *He is determined to push the bill through Parliament.*
push through sth *We're hoping to push through a raft of new legislation.*
push sth through *We'll do everything we can to push the amendment through.*

ˌpush ˈto

to close a door or window by pushing it = SHUT, CLOSE
push sth to *Can you push the door to, please?*

ˌpush ˈtowards

to make someone do something or try to do something
push sb towards (doing) sth *His treatment at work pushed him towards resignation.* ♦ *Pressing economic priorities pushed the country towards cutting defence spending.*

ˌpush ˈup

to make something increase = DRIVE UP
push up sth *also* **push sth up** *Inflation is pushing up costs.* ♦ *There will be very few new sites, which will push land prices up.*

■ **pushup** /ˈpʊʃʌp/ **noun** [C] *mainly American* an exercise in which you lie flat on your stomach and use your arms to push yourself up: *How many pushups can you do?*

PUSSYFOOT /ˈpʊsifʊt/
pussyfoots, pussyfooting, pussyfooted

ˌpussyfoot aˈround *informal*

to avoid doing or saying anything definite because you are not sure what to do or you do not want to offend anyone
pussyfoot around *Stop pussyfooting around and make a decision!*

PUT /pʊt/
puts, putting, put

Put is often used with adverbs and prepositions when it means 'to move something to a particular position, especially using your hands': *Did I put my wallet in your bag?* ♦ *She put her hand on Cliff's arm.* ♦ *She put her suitcase up on the luggage rack.* These uses are not included here.

ˌput aˈbout

1 put about or **put around** [often passive] *British informal* to tell a lot of people something, especially something that is not true = SPREAD
be put about *This was just one of the stories that had been put about.*
put sth about *also* **put about sth** *I don't know who's been putting these rumours about, but they're not true.* ♦ **+that** *Clare's been putting it about that I'm pregnant.*

2 if a ship puts about, it turns and sails in the opposite direction = TURN ROUND
put about *Davies wanted to put about and stay away from the shore.*
PHRASE **put yourself about** or **put it about** *British informal* to have sex with a lot of different people: *Like all young men, he puts himself about.*

ˌput aˈbove

to treat one thing or person as being more important than another thing or person
put sb/sth above sb/sth *Many men put their careers above that of their partners.* ♦ *Soldiers are supposed to put country above personal interests.*

ˌput aˈcross ★★ (*also* ˌput ˈover)

to explain an idea, belief etc in a way that is easy to understand = CONVEY, GET ACROSS; *formal* COMMUNICATE
put across sth *Television can be a useful way of putting across health messages.*
put sth across *A lot depends on how you put your message across.* ♦ *They have interesting things to say but they're not putting them across.*
put yourself across *Emily puts herself across very well.*

ˌput aˈround (*also* ˌput ˈround *British*)

[often passive] *informal*
to tell a lot of people something, especially something that is not true = SPREAD
be put around *Among the stories being put around was one that I was being paid a million dollars a show.*
put sth around *also* **put around sth** *The papers started putting these rumours*

around. ♦ *She had put around the rumour that the factory was closing down.* ♦ **+that** *Someone was **putting it around** that we were getting divorced.*

put a'side ★★

1 to not allow yourself to be affected by a problem, argument etc so that you can achieve something more important = DISREGARD

put aside sth *Laura put aside her concerns and got on with the job.* ♦ *Both sides need to **put aside their differences** and continue the peace talks.*

put sth aside *You have to be prepared to put your own ambitions aside.*

2 same as **put away** 4

3 to keep something so it can be used or taken away later = RESERVE, SET ASIDE

put aside sth *Put aside half the coriander to use as a garnish.*

put sth aside *Take a little of the lemon juice and put it aside for the sauce.* ♦ *The shop offered to put the dress aside while I went to the bank.*

4 to keep a period of time free so that you can use it for a particular purpose = SET ASIDE

put aside sth *I put aside a day at the end of each month for doing the business accounts.*

put sth aside *Put a little time aside each day so that you can simply relax.*

put at ★ [often passive]

to calculate the cost, amount, size etc of something

be put at sth *The cost of repairing the damage was put at £100,000.*

put sth at sth *A recent estimate puts the cost at around £3 million.*

put a'way ★★★

1	store sth in its usual place
2	eat/drink sth
3	put sb in prison
4	save money
5	score a goal
6	kill sb

1 to put something in the place where you usually keep it when you are not using it

put sth away *He put the notebook away and stood up.* ♦ *Take these towels and put them away.*

put away sth *Put away your toys now.*

2 informal to eat or drink a lot of something = formal CONSUME

put away sth *They put away vast quantities of beer between them.*

put sth away *She put half the potatoes away herself.* ♦ *Don't give him any more*

whisky – *he's been putting it away all day.*

3 [often passive] informal to put someone in a prison = SEND DOWN

be put away *He ought to be put away for a very long time.*

put sb away *They could put him away for ten years.*

4 put away or **put aside** or **put by** to save an amount of money so that you can buy or pay for something in the future = SET ASIDE

put away sth *Try and put away a little each month.*

put sth away *People aren't putting enough money away for their retirement.* ♦ *We can't afford to put that much away.*

5 informal to score a goal by kicking or hitting the ball into the net, especially in football = SCORE

put sth away *He put that one away with the confidence of a true professional.*

6 American very informal to kill someone = BUMP OFF; formal KILL

put sb away *He wouldn't have the nerve to put someone away.*

put 'back ★★★

1 to put something in the place where it was before it was moved = formal REPLACE

put sth back *Put the books back where you found them.* ♦ *If you take money from the savings account, put it back when you get paid.*

put back sth *Remember to put back anything you borrow.*

2 to change the time or date of an event so that it happens later than originally planned = PUT BACK; formal POSTPONE

put sth back *We've put the trip back until June now.* ♦ *If the date of the next meeting doesn't suit you, we could put it back a few weeks.*

put back sth *One option is to put back the wedding.*

3 to change the time of a clock or watch to an earlier time ≠ PUT FORWARD

put sth back *Don't forget to put your watch back an hour.* ♦ *If you're wearing a watch, put it back four hours.*

put back sth *It's this weekend that we put back the clocks.*

4 to make something happen more slowly or at a later time than it should happen = formal DELAY

put back sth *The fire has put back the opening of the theatre by several months.*

put sth/sb back *These problems are putting publication back by at least two months.* ♦ *Lack of progress in the early stages has put us back several weeks.*

'put be'fore [often passive]

if a plan, idea etc is put before someone, they think about it and decide whether to accept it

be put before sb *The bill is expected to be put before Parliament next month.*
put sth before sb *Members put their suggestions before a committee of judges.*

put be'hind ★

if you put something behind you, you try to forget about it and not let it affect what you do in the future

put sth behind sb *Why can't you put your past behind you?* ♦ *We're trying to put the whole episode behind us and get on with our lives.*

put 'by *same as* put away 4

put 'down ★★★

1	put sth on a surface
2	criticize sb publicly
3	kill an old animal
4	write sth
5	write sb's name on a list
6	pay only part of the cost now
7	let a passenger get out
8	when a plane lands
9	put a baby in bed
10	ask officials to consider sth
11	stop a protest using force
+	PHRASES
+	**put-down** noun

1 to put something that you are holding onto a surface, especially the floor = SET DOWN ≠ PICK UP

put down sth *Emma put down her bag and went upstairs.*
put sth down *Put the gun down, John.* ♦ *If the box is too heavy, just put it down for a while.*

2 to criticize someone, especially when other people are there, in a way that makes them feel stupid = DISPARAGE

put sb down *He's always trying to put me down.* ♦ *She's the kind of manager who puts the staff down in front of customers.*
put down sb *It's not my style to put down other players.*
put yourself down *You're a good student. Don't put yourself down.*

3 [often passive] to kill an animal using a drug because it is very old, ill, or dangerous

be put down *In the end the cat had to be put down.*
put sth down *We didn't want to put him down, but it was probably for the best.*
put down sth *You don't want to put down an animal that is basically healthy.*

4 to write something on a piece of paper = SET DOWN

put sth down *I put my name down on the list.* ♦ *If you want to give any extra information, put it down in this box here.*
put down sth *Put down your email address and we'll be in touch.*

5 to write someone's name on a list, especially so that they can take part in something = SIGN UP

put sb/sth down *You don't mind if I put your name down, do you?* ♦ **+to do sth** *She put me down to help with the food.*

6 to pay part of the cost of something and agree to pay the rest later

put down sth *We've put down a deposit on a new car.*
put sth down *You can put £100 down now and pay the rest next month.* ♦ *If £10 is all you have, you can still put it down as a deposit.*

7 *British* to stop a car, bus etc and let someone get out of it = LET OFF, SET DOWN ≠ PICK UP

put sb down *Can put me down by the library?*
put down sb *The driver won't put down passengers where there's no bus stop.*

8 if a plane puts down, or if someone puts it down, it lands = LAND

put down *There didn't seem to be anywhere to put down.*
put sth down *The pilot was confident he could put the plane down on the beach.*

9 to put a baby in a bed so that it can go to sleep

put sb down *I usually put the baby down for a couple of hours in the afternoon.*

10 *British* to officially ask a parliament or committee to consider something and make a decision on it = *formal* TABLE

put down sth *The government put down numerous amendments to the Bill.*

11 to use force to stop a riot or an attempt by people to take power away from a government or leader = *formal* QUELL, SUPPRESS

put down sth *He used tanks to put down an armed uprising last June.*
put sth down *It's my job to put this rebellion down.*

> **Nouns often used as objects with put down 11**
>
> ■ **insurrection, rebellion, revolt, riot, uprising**

PHRASES **sb can't put sth down** used for saying that a book is very interesting or exciting: *I couldn't put her latest book down.*

put the phone down to put the telephone receiver back onto its base after you have finished talking to someone = HANG UP ≠ PICK UP: *As soon as I heard her voice, I put the phone down.*
put the phone down on sb to end a telephone conversation with someone before they have finished speaking = HANG UP: *Whenever I call, he puts the phone down on me.*

■ **'put-down** noun [C] a comment intended to criticize someone and make them feel stupid: *She was searching for a suitably vicious put-down.*

put 'down as
to think that someone is a particular type of person
put sb down as sth *I'm surprised she was nervous. I'd always put her down as being very confident.*

put 'down for
1 to write someone's name on a list so that they can take part in an activity or become a member of an institution or organization = SIGN UP FOR
put sb/sth down for sth *It's the sort of school you have to put them down for at birth.* ♦ *I've put my name down for the trip to Paris.*
2 to write on a list that someone agrees to give or take something
put sb down for sth *I'll put you down for £20 then.* ♦ *Can you put me down for one of the puppies?*

put 'down to
to think that something is the cause of something else = *formal* ATTRIBUTE TO
put sth down to sth *I put his irritability down to tiredness.*
  PHRASE **put sth down to experience** to decide not to be upset or affected by an unpleasant experience, but try to avoid it happening again in the future: *Don't worry about it. Just put it down to experience.*

put 'forth
1 [often passive] *formal same as* **put forward 1**
2 *literary* if a plant or tree puts forth leaves, roots etc, they start to grow on it
put forth sth *We admired the tree's ability to put forth new branches.*

put 'forward ★★★
1 [often passive] **put forward** or **put forth** to suggest something or offer an idea, opinion, reason etc, especially so that people can discuss it and make a decision = SUGGEST
be put forward *He rejected all the proposals put forward by the committee.*

put sth forward *You can put the idea forward at the next meeting.*
put forward sth *Planners put forward proposals to build a road right through an area of national park.*

> Nouns often used as objects with
> **put forward 1**
> ■ **argument, hypothesis, idea, plan, proposal, recommendation, suggestion**

2 [often passive] to change the time or date of an event so that it happens earlier than originally planned = BRING FORWARD ≠ PUT BACK; *formal* POSTPONE
be put forward *The meeting has been put forward to Monday.*
put sth forward *We can always put the deadline forward if that will help.*
3 to change the time of a clock or watch to a later time ≠ PUT BACK
put sth forward *I've put all the clocks forward an hour.*
4 to officially suggest that someone should be considered for a particular job or position = PROPOSE
put sb forward *I'll introduce you and put you forward.* ♦ *We're looking for a new team leader and someone has put your name forward.* ♦ **+to do sth** *I've thought about putting myself forward to chair the meeting.* ♦ **+as** *He put me forward as head of publicity.*

put 'in ★★★

1	give time/effort
2	make equipment ready to use
3	request/offer sth officially
4	interrupt sb
5	invest money
6	elect sb
7	give sb trust/responsibility
8	ship: stop at a port
9	choose sb for a job
+	PHRASE
+	**input** noun, verb

1 to spend a particular amount of time doing something, or to make a particular amount of effort in order to do something = DEVOTE
put in sth *Wendy has been putting in more hours at the office recently.*
put sth in *They must have put a lot of work in to achieve such an interesting exhibition.*
2 [often passive] to fix something such as equipment in the place where it will be used and make it ready to use = INSTALL, FIT ≠ TAKE OUT
be put in *We're having a burglar alarm put in.*
put sth in *They're coming to put the new kitchen in next week.* ♦ *If you can't afford*

central heating now, you could always
put it in next year.
put in sth *There isn't the space to put in
a shower room.*

3 to make an official request, claim, offer
etc ≠ WITHDRAW
put in sth *He put in a bid of $1 million
for the company.*
put sth in *If you've lost money over this,
why don't you put a claim in?*

> Nouns often used as objects with **put in 3**
>
> ■ **application, bid, claim, offer, plea, request**

4 to say something that interrupts
someone who is speaking = INTERRUPT
put in sth *'Why don't you ask them?' he
suddenly put in.*

5 to invest money in a business or an
account
put in sth *To start up the business, they
each put in £50,000.*
put sth in *Each partner puts £50,000 in
now, and a further £20,000 later.* ♦ *We
can't put that amount in at this stage.*

6 [often passive] to elect a politician to a
parliament, or to elect a political party to
govern a country = VOTE IN, ELECT
be put in *Labour had been put in with a
large majority.*
put sb in *You put them in, so you have
to live with the consequences.* ♦ *A
disaffected electorate put Labour in after
fifteen years.*
put in sb *I don't believe people will put
in another Conservative government this
decade.*

7 to give something such as your trust or
responsibility for your safety to someone
or something
put sth in sb/sth *You have to put your
faith in the pilot when you're flying.*
♦ *They had put all their hopes in him.*
♦ *You do realize you're **putting your life
in his hands**?*

8 if a ship puts in, it stops at a port = DOCK
≠ PUT OUT
put in *I suggested putting in for the night.*

9 to choose someone for a job or position,
especially an important one = APPOINT
put sb in *They put in a new manager to
try and improve sales.*
put sb in sth *Are you happy to put him
in such a senior post?*

> **PHRASE** **put in an appearance** to go
> somewhere for a short time, especially
> because you feel you should go there: *I
> thought the head of section would have
> at least put in an appearance.*

■ **input** /ˈɪmpʊt/ **noun** **1** [C/U] help in
the form of ideas, advice, or
information, used in a process or in
making a decision: *Teachers have*

considerable input into the school's
decision-making process. **2** [C/U]
information that is put into a computer
or a piece of electronic equipment using
another machine such as a keyboard or
microphone: *The program accepts input
from a variety of sources.* **3** [U] electrical
power that is put into a machine: *an
input socket* **4** [C/U] information that
your brain receives from your eyes,
ears, or nerves: *acoustic input* **5** [C] the
connection on a computer or piece of
electronic equipment where
information enters it from another
machine: *The cable was plugged into the
wrong input.*

■ **input** /ˈɪmpʊt/ **verb** [T] to put
information into a computer or a piece
of electronic equipment

ˌput ˈin for

1 to officially ask for something = APPLY
FOR
put in for sth *We've put in for a grant to
repair the building.*

2 *British* to arrange for someone or
something to take part in a competition
or examination = ENTER
put sb in for sth *They've put him in for
the entrance exam.*

ˌput ˈinto ★★

1	improve sth
2	give time/effort
3	invest money
4	ship: stop at a port
5	choose sb for a job

1 to improve something by adding a
particular quality to it
put sth into sth *I want to put some
excitement back into my life.* ♦ *Try and
put some enthusiasm into your work.*

2 to spend a particular amount of time
doing something, or to make a particular
amount of effort in order to do something
put sth into sth *I put a lot of effort into
the project.*
put sth into doing sth *When I think of
all the hours I put into getting it exactly
right!*

3 to invest money in a business or an
account = INVEST
put sth into sth *How much are you
prepared to put into the business?*

4 if a ship puts into a place, it stops there
put into sth *We would put into Cuxhaven
for a day or two.*

5 to choose someone for a job or position,
especially an important one = APPOINT TO
put sb into sth *I had some doubts about
putting him into such a dangerous job.*

ˌput ˈoff ★★★

1	make sb not want/like sth
2	delay sth you do not want to do
3	make sth happen later
4	arrange to see sb later
5	prevent sb from concentrating
6	let a passenger get off
+	PHRASE
+	off-putting adj

1 to make someone not want to do something, or to make someone not like someone or something
put sb off *Lack of parking space was putting potential customers off.*
♦ *Robert's attitude towards women really puts me off.*
put sb off sb/sth *My parents put me off the idea of religion for ever.*
put sb off doing sth *All this rain really puts you off going out after work.*

2 to delay doing something, especially because you do not want to do it = DELAY; *formal* POSTPONE
put off sth *I was trying to put off the moment when I would have to leave.*
put sth off *You can't put the decision off any longer.* ♦ *I've got a job to do. I've been putting it off long enough.*
put off doing sth *He was glad to have an excuse to put off telling her the news.*

3 to change the time or date of something so that it happens later than originally planned, especially because of a problem = *formal* POSTPONE
put sth off *They had to put the wedding off because the bride's mother had an accident.* ♦ *About the meeting: can we put it off for a few days?*
put off doing sth *I'll put off going to Scotland until you're well enough to look after yourself again.*

4 [often passive] to tell someone that you cannot see them or do something until a later time
be put off *I'm not willing to be put off any longer.*
put sb off *We'll have to put George off if your mother's coming on Thursday.*

5 to prevent someone from concentrating on something so that they have difficulty doing it = *formal* DISTRACT
put sb off *Stop laughing – you'll put her off.*

6 to stop a car, bus etc and let someone get out of it = LET OFF, DROP OFF ≠ PICK UP
put sb off *I'll put you off by the bus stop.*
♦ *The driver is instructed to put children off inside the gate.*
put off sb *I don't put off any more passengers until I reach Waterloo.*
PHRASE **put sb off their stride/stroke**

[often passive] to stop someone from thinking clearly or doing something confidently = *formal* DISTRACT: *He was determined not to be put off his stroke by her presence.*

■ **'off-ˌputting** adj **1** used for describing something that you want to avoid because it is unpleasant and not attractive: *It tasted OK but the smell was a bit off-putting.* **2** used for describing something that stops you concentrating on what you are doing: *I prefer films that have been dubbed into English. Subtitles are so off-putting.*

ˌput ˈon ★★★

1	start wearing wear clothes/jewellery
2	make equipment start working
3	spread a substance on sth
4	get sth ready to watch or listen to
5	organize an event
6	pretend to have feelings/attitudes
7	become fatter
8	start to cook
9	make sth affect sb/sth
10	increase the cost/value of sth
11	risk money on a guess
12	allow sb to speak on the phone
13	give people transport
14	give sb medical treatment
15	make sb do sth
16	record the money to be paid later
17	show your skills
18	make sb responsible for sth
19	make sb believe sth false
+	put-on adj, noun

1 to dress yourself with a piece of clothing or jewellery ≠ TAKE OFF
put on sth *Dorothy put on her coat and went out.*
put sth on *Kim had forgotten to put his watch on.* ♦ *If you have a rain jacket, put it on.*

2 to make a machine or piece of electrical equipment start working, especially by pressing a switch = SWITCH ON, TURN ON
put sth on *Can you put the light on, please?* ♦ *Shall I put the kettle on?*
put on sth *Put on the heater if you're cold.*

3 to spread a substance on a surface, for example to rub cream on your skin = *formal* APPLY ≠ TAKE OFF
put on sth *Melanie was putting on her makeup in front of the mirror.*
put sth on *Don't put so much hair gel on.* ♦ *With gloss paint, you have to put it on thinly.*

4 to put a video, CD etc in a piece of equipment so that you can watch it or listen to it

put on

try on

take off

dress up

do up

verbs to do with wearing clothes

put sth on *I'm going to put my new CD on.* ♦ *If you want to watch a DVD for a while, put it on now.*
put on sth *Shall we put on some music?*

5 to organize an event, show, performance etc = STAGE
put on sth *We're putting on a concert to raise money for cancer charities.*
put sth on *There was the possibility that we wouldn't be putting a performance on at all.* ♦ *We did Hamlet last year, and we'll be putting it on again in the spring.*

6 to pretend to have a particular feeling or a particular way of speaking or behaving
put on sth *Stop putting on that funny voice!* ♦ *I think he was just **putting on an act** to get sympathy.*
put it on *She's not really upset – she's just **putting it on**.*

7 if you put on weight, you get fatter = GAIN ≠ LOSE
put sth on *She put a lot of **weight on** after the children were born.* ♦ *You lose a few pounds, then put them all back on over Christmas.*
put on sth *I've put on five pounds in the last month.*

8 to start cooking something
put sth on *I'll put the vegetables on in a minute.* ♦ *Don't worry about the meat. I've already put it on.*
put on sth *What time should I put on the potatoes?*

9 [often passive] to make something affect someone or something
be put on sb/sth *I feel that too much responsibility is put on teachers.*
put sth on sb *Advertising aimed at children **puts** a lot of **pressure on** parents.*

10 *British* to add an amount of money to the cost or value of something
put sth on sth *The government is putting 2p on the price of petrol.*

11 to risk a particular amount of money by trying to guess the result of a race or competition
put sth on sb/sth *I put £5 on The Whitkirk Wanderer to win the Grand National.*

12 to pass the phone to someone so that they can speak to the person you have been talking to
put sb on *Wait a minute, Vicky – I'll put Joe on.*

13 to provide a bus, train etc for people to use = LAY ON
put on sth *They're going to put on extra buses to take fans to the concert.*

put sth on *The best thing would be to put a coach on for everyone coming from Glasgow.* ♦ *There's no train service to St Andrews, and no plans to put one on.*

14 [often passive] to say what medical treatment someone should have

be put on sth *I was put on a low-fat diet.*
put sb on sth *The doctor put him on a course of antibiotics.*

15 to make a rule or law that stops or limits something

put sth on sth *They've put a ban on smoking in restaurants.*

16 to record something in an account so that someone can pay for it later ≠ TAKE OFF

put sth on sth *Can you put the drinks on my bill, please?* ♦ *We put the meal on expenses.*

17 to show a particular level of skill or ability in doing something, especially in a competition

put on sth *We put on a fantastic performance against a much more experienced side.*

18 [often passive] to make someone responsible for dealing with something = *formal* ASSIGN ≠ TAKE OFF

be put on sth *I was put on cleaning duties.*
put sb on sth *They put new recruits on toilet duty.*

19 *mainly American informal* to try to make someone believe something that is not true = HAVE ON; *formal* DECEIVE

put sb on *Don't believe that! He's putting you on!*

■ **'put-on** adj pretended, not real: *a put-on Russian accent*

■ **'put-on** noun [C usually singular] an attempt to make someone believe something that is not true: *It sounds like a put-on to me.*

put 'onto
to tell someone about someone or something that would be useful to them

put sb onto sb/sth *Jan put me onto a great hairdresser in the centre of town.*

put 'out ★★★

1	stop sth burning
2	machine: stop working
3	offer sth to people
4	create problems by asking for help
5	put sth outside
6	give people information
7	publish sth
8	defeat
9	make sb unconscious
10	make a number incorrect
11	broadcast sth
12	injure your back/shoulder etc
13	move a hand etc away from your body
14	ship: leave a port
15	have sex
+	PHRASES
+	**output** noun, verb; **put out** adj

1 [often passive] to make something stop burning = *formal* EXTINGUISH

be put out *Has the fire been put out yet?*
put out sth *It took firefighters three hours to put out the blaze.*
put sth out *Please put that cigarette out.*
♦ *The fire raged for several hours and it took four appliances to put it out.*

put out

2 to make a machine or piece of electrical equipment stop working = TURN OFF ≠ TURN ON

put out sth *I must have forgotten to put out the lamp.*
put sth out *Tara put the light out and went to sleep.*

3 to put something in a place where someone will see it, so that they can use it or have it

put out sth *I put out food for the birds in cold weather.*
put sth out *I took the sign and put it out at the front, by the pavement.*

4 [usually with a negative or in questions] to cause problems or difficulties for someone

by asking them to do something for you
= *formal* INCONVENIENCE

put sb out *It would be lovely to stay with you, but I don't want to put you out.*
put yourself out *I don't see why I should put myself out for him.*

5 to put something outside your house
put sth out *We usually put the cat out at night.* ♦ *Don't forget to **put the rubbish out** (=so that it can be collected and taken away).*
put out sth *Don't forget to put out the bin.* ♦ *He found her in the back yard, **putting out the washing** (=hanging clothes outside to dry after she had washed them).*

6 to produce information for people to read, watch, or hear = *formal* ISSUE
put out sth *Police have put out a warning about an escaped prisoner.*
put sth out *The band put a statement out denying rumours of a split.*

7 to publish a book, magazine, or newspaper, or to produce a video or CD for sale = PUBLISH, RELEASE, BRING OUT
put out sth *The company has put out several new titles this year.*
put sth out *They'll be putting her memoirs out in the spring.*

8 [often passive] to defeat a player or team in a game or competition so that they can no longer take part in it = DEFEAT, KNOCK OUT
be put out *He was put out in the first round at Wimbledon.*
put sb out *She's the player who put the champion out last year.* ♦ *France will probably put them out in the next round.*
put out sb *She's already put out last year's runner-up.*

9 to make someone unconscious before a medical operation
put sb out *We'll put you out before we do the extraction.*

10 to affect numbers or calculations in a way that makes them incorrect
put sth out *A mistake with the decimal point could put the figure out tenfold.*

11 [often passive] to broadcast a programme on television or radio = SHOW, BROADCAST
be put out *The programme wouldn't have been put out by a less liberal station.*
put sth out *It was decided not to put the programme out before the news.* ♦ *If we wait another month, we'll be putting it out after the election.*
put out sth *In my view they put out an awful lot of programmes that aren't worth watching.*

12 to injure your back, knee etc by

stretching or twisting it too much or by moving a bone out of its position
put your back/shoulder etc out *You'll put your back out lifting the table like that.*

13 to move your hand, arm, or foot away from your body
put your hand/arm/foot etc out *She put her hand out to stop herself from falling.*

14 if a ship puts out, it sails away from a port = SET SAIL ≠ PUT IN
put out *We were preparing to put out.* ♦ *+to The ship never actually put out to sea.*

15 *very informal* if someone puts out, they have sex with someone, usually someone that they do not know very well
put out *Was she the kind of girl who put out?*

PHRASES **put out feelers** to begin to find out what people think about something you are hoping to do: *I've put out a few feelers and the response has been positive so far.*
put the word out *informal* to tell people about something: *Can you put the word out that the meeting has been cancelled?*

■ **output** /ˈaʊtpʊt/ **noun** [C/U] **1** the amount of something that a person, organization, system etc produces: *Industrial output increased by four per cent last year.* **2** the information shown on a screen or printed on paper by a computer: *graphics output* **3** the electricity or power produced by a piece of equipment or an engine: *variations in the output of power*

■ **output** /ˈaʊtpʊt/ **verb** [T] to produce information from a computer, for example by showing it on a screen or printing it: *These programs are ideal for outputting images.*

■ ˌput ˈout **adj** [never before noun] annoyed, offended, or upset by something that someone has said or done: *She agreed but she seemed a little put out.*

ˌput ˈover *same as* put across

PHRASE **put one over on sb** *informal* to trick someone into believing something that is not true: *The programme-makers are putting one over on a gullible audience.*

ˌput ˈpast

PHRASE **I wouldn't put it past him/her/them etc** used for saying that you would not be surprised if someone did something, even though it is extreme or unusual: *I wouldn't put it past him to fake his own death.*

,put 'round British same as **put around**

,put 'through ★★

1	give sb an unpleasant experience
2	test sb/sth
3	allow sb to speak on the phone
4	make sth accepted/approved
5	pay for sb's education
+	PHRASE
+	**throughput** noun

1 [often passive] to make someone do or experience something difficult or unpleasant = formal SUBJECT TO

be put through sth Children shouldn't be put through the ordeal of giving evidence in court.

put sb through sth She put him through a lot while they were still married. ♦ He's put me through hell (=caused me a lot of very unpleasant experiences) during the last year. ♦ They really put the young soldiers through it (=make their lives very unpleasant) during the first few weeks.

2 [often passive] to test someone or something in order to make sure everything is working correctly

be put through sth He was put through a series of tests to discover what was wrong with him. ♦ The drug has been put through several trials.

put sb/sth through sth We have to put each new design through a series of rigorous tests. ♦ We put all candidates through the government's vetting procedure before they're called for interview.

3 if you put a person or a call through, you connect someone to the person they want to speak to on the phone = CONNECT

put sth through The switchboard operator refused to put the call through.

put sb through Hold the line a moment and I'll put you through. ♦ +to Can you put me through to the accounts department, please?

4 [often passive] to make it certain that something is accepted, approved, or successfully completed

be put through sth A string of similar measures had already been put through Parliament.

put through sth Their huge majority means they can put through virtually any legislation they want.

put sth through It won't be easy to put these changes through.

5 to pay for someone to be a student at a school, university, or college

put sb through school/university/ college etc Parents on average incomes

are wondering how they're going to put their children through university.

PHRASE **put sb through the wringer** [usually passive] to make someone suffer an unpleasant experience: The young princes have already been put through the wringer over revelations in the press.

■ **throughput** /ˈθruːpʊt/ noun
[singular/U] the amount of work, people, or things that a system deals with in a particular period: The mark of a good network is excellent data throughput.

'put to ★★★

1 to formally suggest something to a group of people so they can discuss it or vote on it

put sth to sb I put the resolution to the meeting.

2 to ask someone a question, especially in public

put sth to sb Let me put a different question to you. ♦ The questions they put to me were quite difficult to answer.

3 to suggest something to someone, especially something that they might not want to hear

put sth to sb I'm not quite sure how to put it to her. ♦ +that I put it to him that their relationship might not be as good as he thought.

PHRASES **put sb to trouble/bother/ inconvenience** to cause problems or difficulties for someone by making them do something for you: You don't have to give me a lift. I don't want to put you to any trouble.

put sth to a/the vote to ask people to vote on a proposal: Despite pressure, the chairperson refused to put the issue to the vote.

,put to'gether ★★★

1 [often passive] to produce or organize something by combining several different things

be put together The exhibition has been put together by a group of young artists.

put together sth Initially, they simply put together a series of guidelines.

put sth together He can put an amazing meal together from things you've got lying in your fridge. ♦ If she wants the report by Monday, I'll put it together over the weekend.

2 to make something by joining all its parts = ASSEMBLE

put sth together Will you help me put this desk together? ♦ The instructions claim you can put it together in around an hour.

put together sth *We spent the morning putting together flat-pack furniture.*

3 [often passive] to choose people or things to form a team or group = ASSEMBLE

be put together *A team of experts has been put together to examine the effects of global warming.*

put sth together *Can they put a decent team together without buying new talent?*

put together sb/sth *We've put together a group of ordinary people to see how they cope.*

PHRASE **more than sb/sth put together** used for saying that someone or something is better or bigger than the whole of a group of other people or things: *He knows more about computers than the rest of them put together.*

‚put to'wards

to give a particular amount of money to a collection in order to buy something

put sth towards sth *We each put £5 towards her leaving present.* ♦ *If there's money left over, we put it towards our holiday.*

‚put 'under (*also* ‚put 'out)

to make someone unconscious before a medical operation by giving them a drug = ANAESTHETIZE ≠ BRING ROUND —*picture* → PASS OUT

put sb under *You'll have to fast for 24 hours before we put you under.*

‚put 'up ★★★

1	build a wall etc
2	increase the value of sth
3	give money
4	raise sth
5	suggest sb for a position
6	try to achieve/prevent sth
7	make a picture available to see
8	put a shelf on a wall
9	let sb stay in your house
10	stay somewhere for a short time
11	show your ability
+	PHRASES

1 to build something such as a wall, fence, or house = *formal* ERECT ≠ PULL DOWN

put up sth *Grants were available to help with the cost of putting up new school buildings.*

put sth up *John was in the garden putting a fence up.* ♦ *The thing I don't like about the tent is putting it up.*

2 to increase the value or price of something = RAISE

put up sth *Several of the banks have decided to put up their interest rates.*

put sth up *We've had to put our fees up twice this year.* ♦ *Instead of keeping prices low, the shops are putting them up.*

3 to provide a large amount of money for something

put up sth *The family has put up £15,000 towards the cost of the child's medical treatment.*

put sth up *A reward has been offered, with the police putting the money up.*

4 to raise something, especially so that it is ready to use

put sth up *I was soaked before I could put my umbrella up.* ♦ *The coat has a hood, but putting it up is a little awkward.*

put up sth *Put up your hood or you'll catch cold.*

5 to suggest that someone should be elected to a particular position

put up sb *In all, 60 political parties put up candidates.*

put sb up *My colleagues have put me up for the position of chairman.*

6 to make a particular effort in order to achieve or prevent something

put up sth *Menzies' counsel put up a spirited defence of his client.* ♦ *The victim was able to put up little resistance.* ♦ *Residents have put up a fight against plans to build a new road.*

7 to fix a picture or notice onto an upright structure such as a wall = STICK UP

put up sth *She put up a notice about the school trip to Italy.*

put sth up *I put a few posters up to make the room look less bare.* ♦ *We're not putting these up in the living room, are we?*

8 to fix a shelf or cupboard onto a wall

put up sth *She put up some bookshelves in the study.*

put sth up *It would take me all day to put one cupboard up.* ♦ *If there are extra shelves, you could put them up over here.*

9 to let someone stay in your house

put sb up *Could you put me up for the night when I come to London?* ♦ *I don't think we can put the whole family up.*

put up sb *We could put up a couple more people.*

10 *old-fashioned* to stay for a short time in a place that is not your home = STAY

put up *Why don't we put up here for the night?*

11 *British* to show a particular level of skill or ability in doing something, especially in a competition = PUT ON

put up sth *Liverpool put up a marvellous performance throughout the game.*

PHRASES **put up a good/poor show** to do something well or badly: *If you're*

*paid to give a talk, people don't expect
you to put up a poor show.*

put up or shut up *informal* used for
telling someone that they should either
deal with something or stop talking
about doing it: *He challenged dissenters
within the party to put up or shut up.*

put up the shutters to close a shop or
business at the end of the day, or to
close it permanently: *More than 70,000
shopkeepers have been forced to put up
the shutters in the past year.*

put up your hand to raise your arm to
show that you want to ask or answer a
question, or so that someone can count
you: *If you have a question, put up your
hand.*

put up (sense 4)

'put upon (*also* **'put on**) [usually passive]
British
to make someone do something for you
that you should not expect them to do but
which they do out of kindness
be put upon *His eagerness to please
ensured that he was always put upon.*

put 'up to
to encourage someone to do something
stupid or wrong = *formal* INDUCE
put sb up to sth *One of the older boys
must have put him up to it.*

put 'up with ★★★
to accept unpleasant behaviour by
someone or an annoying situation
without complaining, even though you do
not like it = STAND, TOLERATE —*picture* →
TAKE AFTER
put up with sb/sth *How has Jan put up
with him for so long?* ♦ *I don't see why
you should have to put up with sexual
harassment.*

PUTTER an American spelling of
potter

PUZZLE /'pʌz(ə)l/
puzzles, puzzling, puzzled

'puzzle about *same as* **puzzle over**

'puzzle 'out
to solve a confusing or complicated
problem by thinking carefully about it
= WORK OUT
puzzle sth out *also* **puzzle out sth** *That's
all he told us, and we were left to puzzle
the whole thing out for ourselves.*
♦ **+ who/what/why etc** *She seemed to be
trying to puzzle out who the caller might
be.*

'puzzle over (*also* **'puzzle about**)
to think hard about someone or something
for a long time and try to understand
them = *formal* PONDER
puzzle over sb/sth *I've puzzled over this
question for a while, and I'm still not
sure what the right answer is.*

Qq

QUARREL /'kwɒrəl, *American* 'kwɔrəl/
quarrels, quarrelling, quarrelled

'quarrel with [usually with a negative]
to think that someone or something is
wrong = ARGUE WITH, DISAGREE WITH
quarrel with sb/sth *Few people would
quarrel with the aims of these proposals.*
♦ *I won't quarrel with you on that point.*

QUEUE /kjuː, *American* kju/
queues, queuing *or* **queueing, queued**

queue 'up
to stand in a line of people, waiting to do
something or get something = LINE UP
queue up *Hundreds of people were
queuing up outside.* ♦ **+for** *a long line of
fans queuing up for tickets* ♦ **+to do sth**
*Some people had queued up all night to
get in.*

QUIETEN /'kwaɪət(ə)n/
quietens, quietening, quietened

,quieten 'down ★ (*also* **,quiet 'down**)
to make someone calmer or quieter, or to
become calmer or quieter = CALM DOWN
    quieten sb down *He waved his arms to
quieten them down.*
    quieten down sb *John is sent out front
to quieten down the audience.*
    quieten down *We'll wait till things
quieten down before we go out.*

Rr

RABBIT /'ræbɪt/
rabbits, rabbiting, rabbited

,rabbit 'on British informal
to talk about something for a long time so
that people feel bored or annoyed
= RATTLE ON
    rabbit on *What's Elizabeth rabbiting on
about?*

RACK /ræk/
racks, racking, racked

,rack 'up informal
1 to get a large number or amount of
something = COLLECT
    rack up sth *also* **rack sth up** *The film
racked up five Oscar nominations.*
2 to get a large amount of sales or profits
= MAKE
    rack up sth *also* **rack sth up** *Last year,
they racked up profits of more than
£3 million.*
3 in sports, to get a large number of points
or goals = SCORE
    rack up sth *also* **rack sth up** *Leonardsen
racked up his tenth goal of the season.*

RAFFLE /'ræf(ə)l/
raffles, raffling, raffled

,raffle 'off
to offer something as a prize in a raffle
(=a competition that you win if the
number on your ticket matches the ticket
chosen from a container)
    raffle off sth *also* **raffle sth off** *We raffle
off all the items that have been donated.*

RAG /ræg/
rags, ragging, ragged

'rag on American informal
to say things in order to embarrass
someone, usually in a friendly way
    rag on sb *The boys enjoyed ragging on
each other.*

RAGE /reɪdʒ/
rages, raging, raged

'rage at (*also* **'rage against**) mainly literary
to shout angrily at someone
    rage at sb *I could hear one of the
customers raging at him.*

RAIL /reɪl/
rails, railing, railed

'rail against (*also* **'rail at**) formal
to express strong anger about something
that you think is wrong or unfair
    rail against sth *His articles rail against
the decline of culture in American
society.*

RAILROAD /'reɪlrəʊd, American
'reɪlˌroʊd/
railroads, railroading, railroaded

'railroad into [often passive]
to force someone to do something that they
do not really want to do
    be railroaded into (doing) sth *We were
railroaded into accepting the deal.*
    railroad sb into (doing) sth *They weren't
going to railroad us into signing.*

,railroad 'through
if people in authority railroad something
through, they use pressure to make other
people accept or approve it
    railroad sth through *They hope to
railroad the treaty through before June.*
    railroad sth through sth *The prime
minister was accused of trying to
railroad the bill through parliament.*

RAIN /reɪn/
rains, raining, rained

,rain 'down
1 to fall in large amounts from the air
    rain down *Sparks from the fire rained
down.* ♦ **+on** *They fled as debris from the
explosion rained down on the square.*
2 to hit someone continuously and
violently
    rain down *Bullets rained down from the
upstairs windows.* ♦ **+on** *I felt kicks and*

blows raining down on me from all directions.

be ˌrained 'off (*also* be ˌrained 'out American)

if an event is rained off, it is cancelled because there is too much rain

be rained off *Saturday's match was rained off.*

RAKE /reɪk/
rakes, raking, raked

ˌrake 'in *informal*

showing disapproval to earn a lot of money

rake in sth *also* **rake sth in** *She raked in over $500,000 last year.* ♦ *A lot of computer engineers nowadays are raking it in.*

ˌrake 'off *informal*

to take a part of the profits from something, especially in an unfair or dishonest way

rake off sth *also* **rake sth off** *Agents continue to rake off 10% of everything their clients bring in.*

■ **'rake-off** noun [C] *informal* a part of the profits from a business activity, especially when someone obtains it in an unfair or dishonest way: *Five per cent of a million pounds is an impressive rake-off.*

ˌrake 'over *British*

to continue to talk about something unpleasant that other people no longer want to talk or think about

rake over sth *There's no point in raking over the past.*

ˌrake 'through *informal*

to search a place quickly for something

rake through sth *He raked through his pockets, trying to find a pen.*

ˌrake 'up *informal*

to mention something unpleasant that happened in the past and that other people do not want to talk about = MENTION

rake up sth *also* **rake sth up** *Newspaper journalists are always raking up scandalous stories.* ♦ *There was a danger he would rake that whole episode up again.*

RALLY /'ræli/
rallies, rallying, rallied

ˌrally 'round (*also* ˌrally a'round)

informal

if a group of people rally round someone, they work together to help them in a difficult situation

rally round *Friends and neighbours rallied round to help.*

rally round sb *The other team members rallied round Blasco, angry at the way he had been treated.*

RAM /ræm/
rams, ramming, rammed

ˌram 'into

to push something into a place with great force

ram sth into sth *Angrily Pam rammed her keys into the lock.*

RAMBLE /'ræmb(ə)l/
rambles, rambling, rambled

ˌramble 'on *informal*

to talk or write about something for a long time in a way that is boring or annoying

= WAFFLE ON

ramble on *We all wished he'd stop rambling on.*

RAMP /ræmp/
ramps, ramping, ramped

ˌramp 'up

to increase something such as a rate or level, especially the rate at which goods are produced = INCREASE

ramp up sth *also* **ramp sth up** *We've had to ramp up production to meet demand.* ♦ *He ramps the speed up as he comes out of the bend.*

RANGE /reɪndʒ/
ranges, ranging, ranged

be 'ranged against

if a group of people are ranged against something or someone, they all oppose it or them

be ranged against sb/sth *She has some formidable opponents ranged against her.*

RANK /ræŋk/
ranks, ranking, ranked

'rank among

1 to put someone or something into a position according to their success, importance, size etc

rank sb/sth among sth *Nomura is now ranked third among the world's information services companies.*

2 rank among or **rank as** to be good, bad, important, unimportant etc compared with other similar things

rank among sth *Flying still ranks*

among the safest forms of travel. ♦ *This must rank as one of the most violent fights ever seen on television.*

RAP /ræp/
raps, rapping, rapped

,rap 'out *literary*
to say something loudly and quickly
= BARK OUT
rap out a command, order etc *The major rapped out his orders.*

RAT /ræt/
rats, ratting, ratted

'rat on *informal*
1 to tell someone in authority about something that someone has done wrong
= *formal* BETRAY
rat on sb *We might be poor, but we don't rat on our friends.*
2 *British* to not do something that you promised to do = GO BACK ON ≠ STICK TO
rat on sth *I can't back someone who rats on his promises.*

RATCHET /'rætʃɪt/
ratchets, ratcheting, ratcheted

,ratchet 'up
to increase something by small amounts over a period of time = INCREASE
ratchet up sth *also* **ratchet sth up** *We are taking steps to ratchet up our profit margin.* ♦ *Gas companies have been ratcheting costs up.*

RATE /reɪt/
rates, rating, rated

'rate as ★
1 [often passive] to consider someone or something to have reached a particular standard or to have a particular quality, especially a very high one
be rated as sth *She is rated as one of the best young writers of her generation.*
rate sb/sth as sth *I still don't rate him as a world-class player.*
2 to be considered to have a particular quality
rate as sth *The exhibition must rate as the most successful ever held.*

RATION /'ræʃ(ə)n/
rations, rationing, rationed

,ration 'out [usually passive]
to divide something among people so that each one gets a small amount
be rationed out *Time spent using the*

computer had to be strictly rationed out.

'ration to [often passive]
to allow someone to have only a small amount of something
be rationed to sth *I was rationed to half an hour of television.*
ration sb to sth *The kitchen staff rationed us to one biscuit each per day.*
ration yourself to sth *I've rationed myself to one bar of chocolate a week.*

RATTLE /'ræt(ə)l/
rattles, rattling, rattled

'rattle a,round
to live or work in a place in which you have a lot more space than you need
rattle around *The house was much too big. We just rattled around in it.*
rattle around sth *Now there's just me rattling around a house meant for a large family.*

,rattle 'off
to say something quickly, especially something you have learnt from memory
= REEL OFF
rattle off sth *also* **rattle sth off** *She rattles off a list of movies that her father directed.* ♦ *When asked for the names of kings and queens, he rattles them off with ease.*

,rattle 'on *informal*
to talk quickly and for a long time about things that are not important or interesting = RABBIT ON
rattle on *I can hear him still rattling on in the next room.* ♦ **+about** *He rattles on about nothing in particular.*

,rattle 'out *British*
to produce a series of quick loud words or sharp noises
rattle out sth *also* **rattle sth out** *He rattled out a series of questions.* ♦ *She rattled more books out in two years than I did in a twenty-year career.*

,rattle 'through *British informal*
to do or say something quickly because you want to finish it as soon as you can
rattle through sth *I rattled through the first two questions in ten minutes.*

,rattle 'up *British informal*
to score a particular amount very quickly in a game or competition
rattle up sth *also* **rattle sth up** *France rattled up 10 goals in the first round of the competition.*

letter, read back what you have written.

RAVE /reɪv/
raves, raving, raved

'rave about (*also* 'rave over)
to talk or write about someone or something in a very enthusiastic way
rave about sb/sth *The critics are raving about her performance.*

,rave 'up
PHRASE **rave it up** *old-fashioned* to enjoy yourself drinking and dancing with other people

REACH /riːtʃ, *American* ritʃ/
reaches, reaching, reached

,reach 'out ★★
to stretch out your arm to try to touch or hold something
reach out *She reached out and touched his face.* ◆ **+for** *Crowds of little children were reaching out for scraps.*
reach out your hand/arm *Reach out your arm and I'll try to pull you through.*

■ **outreach** /'aʊtriːtʃ/ **noun** [U] the practice of providing help and advice to people in a community before they have to ask for it: *agencies involved in outreach to refugees*

,reach 'out to ★
1 to offer help to someone
reach out to sb *We are reaching out to the most vulnerable members of the community.*
2 to ask someone for help
reach out to sb *She urged him to reach out to his family.*

REACT /riˈækt/
reacts, reacting, reacted

re'act against
to do the opposite of what people or rules say you should do, because you disagree with them
react against sth *It's not surprising that he reacted against such a strict upbringing.*

READ /riːd, *American* rid/
reads, reading, read /red/

,read 'back
to read something that you wrote down earlier or something that someone has just read to you, usually to check that you have understood it correctly
read sth back *also* **read back sth** *I wrote down everything she said then read it back later.* ◆ *When you have typed a*

'read for
1 if an actor reads for a part in a play, film etc, they act some of the part in front of the people who are deciding which actors to choose = AUDITION
read for sth *A number of actors will be reading for the part.*
2 *British old-fashioned* to study for a particular degree
read for sth *She's reading for a degree in Classics.*

,read 'into [often passive]
to find an extra meaning in someone's words or actions that is not obvious or that does not exist
be read into sth *A lot can be read into his reaction.*
read sth into sth *I think you're reading too much into a casual remark.*

,read 'off
to read the measurement on a piece of equipment or graph
read off sth *also* **read sth off** *Hold the tape measure tightly and read off the length.* ◆ *He looked at the thermometer and read the temperature off.*

,read 'out ★★★
to say aloud the words that you are reading so that people can hear them
read out sth *He read out the list of names.*
read sth out *Will you read the letter out?* ◆ *Find the passage and read it out.*

■ **read-out** /'riːd aʊt/ **noun** [C] a record of information produced by a computer or other piece of electronic equipment, shown on a screen or printed on paper: *The meter gives a digital read-out of the amount of water you have used.*

,read 'through ★★ (*also* ,read 'over)
to read all of a document, book etc in order to check or correct it
read sth through *Read the contract through carefully before you sign.* ◆ *Just read it through before you print it.*
read through sth *We read through your script, and we're delighted with it.*

,read 'up on (*also* ,read 'up about)
to get information on a subject by reading a lot about it
read up on sth *I need to read up on my American history.*

REAR /rɪə, American rɪr/
rears, rearing, reared

'rear on [usually passive]
if you are reared on a particular kind of food, music, books etc, your parents feed it to you, play it to you, read it to you etc a lot when you are a child = BRING UP ON
be reared on sb/sth *As the son of a miner, I was reared on stories of coal and coalmines.* ♦ *He had been reared on the Beatles and knew all their hits.*

rear 'up ★
if a horse rears up, it suddenly stands up on its back legs and lifts its front legs into the air
rear up *My horse reared up and then promptly cleared a low wall.*

REASON /'riːz(ə)n, American 'riz(ə)n/
reasons, reasoning, reasoned

reason 'out
to find a successful way of dealing with something by thinking about it
reason sth out *also* **reason out sth** *When you encounter a problem, you try to reason it out.*

'reason with
to try to persuade someone to do something or agree with something by explaining why you think it is sensible
reason with sb *It's no use trying to reason with people like that.*

REBOUND /rɪ'baʊnd/
rebounds, rebounding, rebounded

re'bound on (*also* **re'bound upon** *formal*)
if something bad that you try to do to someone rebounds on you, it harms you instead of them = BACKFIRE ON
rebound on sb *I think Nicole's tricks are rebounding on her.*

RECEIVE /rɪ'siːv, American rɪ'siv/
receives, receiving, received

re'ceive into [often passive]
to officially accept someone into a group
be received into sth *Over a thousand people were received into the congregation that day.*
receive sb into sth *Father Peter received her into the League and was most kind to her.*

RECKON /'rekən/
reckons, reckoning, reckoned

'reckon on [often with a negative]
to expect something to happen and plan for it
reckon on (doing) sth *Jenny hadn't reckoned on having twins!* ♦ *We hadn't reckoned on such fierce opposition.*

'reckon with ★
to consider something important when you are making plans and so be prepared for it
reckon with sth *Napoleon had not reckoned with the severity of the Russian winter.*
PHRASES a force to be reckoned with someone or something that could be difficult to compete with or argue with: *The new women's movement in the country is fast becoming a force to be reckoned with.*
have sb/sth to reckon with to be forced to deal with someone or something: *If he threatens you again, he'll have me to reckon with.*

reckon with'out
to not consider or include something in your plans and so not be prepared for it
reckon without sth *I expected to be there by ten, but I'd reckoned without the heavy traffic on the highway.*

RECONCILE /'rekənsaɪl/
reconciles, reconciling, reconciled

'reconcile to [often passive]
to make someone accept a situation that they do not like
be reconciled to sth *She was never really reconciled to her partner's death.*
reconcile yourself to sth *It might take some time to reconcile yourself to the idea that he won't be coming back.*

REDUCE /rɪ'djuːs, American rɪ'dus/
reduces, reducing, reduced

re'duce to ★★★

1 [usually passive] to make something change into a different form by destroying it or crushing it
be reduced to sth *The fruit is reduced to a pulp and then mixed with sugar.* ♦ *This beautiful forest has been reduced to a wasteland.* ♦ *The building was **reduced to rubble** by the explosion.*

2 [often passive] to force someone into an unpleasant state or situation
be reduced to doing sth *Mandy was reduced to stammering out an apology.*

be reduced to sth *The majority of the population had been reduced to a state of extreme poverty.*
reduce sb to sth *Stress had reduced him to a nervous wreck.*
PHRASE **reduce sb to tears/silence** to upset or shock someone so much that they cry or are unable to speak: *The voices just reduce you to tears.* ◆ *Never before had the class been reduced to silence.*

REEK /ri:k, *American* rik/
reeks, reeking, reeked

'reek of

1 to have a strong unpleasant smell = STINK OF
reek of sth *The boat reeked of fish.*
2 *literary* if something reeks of something, it makes you think that something unpleasant is involved
reek of sth *The whole place reeked of desolation and neglect.*

REEL /ri:l, *American* ril/
reels, reeling, reeled

,reel 'back

to move backwards quickly, especially after someone has hit you
reel back *She reeled back as though she had been slapped across the face.*

,reel 'in

1 to bring a fish towards you by turning the handle on the reel of your fishing rod in order to make the strong string become shorter
reel in *I gently reeled in and carefully removed the hook.*
reel in sth *also* **reel sth in** *He reeled in a large trout.*
2 to achieve something easily
reel in sth *also* **reel sth in** *The show continues to reel in audiences of over 20 million.*

,reel 'off

to say a list of things quickly and without much effort = RECITE
reel off sth *also* **reel sth off** *Lloyd reeled off the names of all the past winners.*
◆ *She reeled these facts off in a bored voice.*

,reel 'out

to make something such as rope become straighter by removing it from an object shaped like a wheel that it was wrapped around
reel out sth *also* **reel sth out** *The electricians reeled out more cable.* ◆ *Reel*

the hose out so it reaches the top of the garden.*

REFER /rɪˈfɜ:, *American* rɪˈfɜr/
refers, referring, referred

reˈfer to ★★★

1 to mention someone or something when you are speaking or writing = ALLUDE TO
refer to sb/sth *She referred to the subject several times during her speech.* ◆ *Jack was careful not to refer to the woman by name.* ◆ *I would like to refer back to something I said in my introduction* (=mention it again). ◆ **+as** *Even as a boy he referred to his father as Steve.*
2 to describe something or be about something
refer to sth *These notes refer to the case of a teenage murderer.* ◆ *The term 'groupware' refers to software designed to be used by several computer users at once.*
3 [often passive] to send someone to another person or place in order to get help, information, or advice
be referred to sb/sth *Her case was referred to the Court of Appeal.*
refer sb to sb/sth *The doctor referred me to a skin specialist.*
4 to look at a book, map etc for information
refer to sth *Please refer to our website for more details.*

REFLECT /rɪˈflekt/
reflects, reflecting, reflected

reˈflect on ★★★ (*also* reˈflect upon)

1 to think carefully and seriously about something that has happened
reflect on sth *Josie reflected on how easily she could have been killed.*
2 to give people a particular opinion about someone or something
reflect on sb/sth *The affair reflected very badly on the administration.* ◆ *We hope her latest success will reflect well on the school.*

REFRAIN /rɪˈfreɪn/
refrains, refraining, refrained

reˈfrain from ★★ *formal*

to not do something, especially when someone has asked you or told you not to do it = ABSTAIN FROM
refrain from doing sth *Please refrain from smoking in this area.*
refrain from sth *They agreed to refrain from any action that might put the peace process at risk.*

REGALE /rɪ'geɪl/
regales, regaling, regaled

re'gale with
to entertain someone with stories
regale sb with sth *At dinner Grandpa regaled us with tales of his youth.*

REIN /reɪn/
reins, reining, reined

,rein 'in (*also* ,rein 'back)
1 to limit or control something that has developed too much or continued for too long
rein in sth *also* **rein sth in** *France has asked its EU partners to rein in their criticism of nuclear testing.*
2 to make a horse stop or go more slowly by pulling the reins (=long narrow pieces of leather fastened to its head)
rein in *Philip reined in and came to ride beside her.*
rein sth in *also* **rein in sth** *As they rounded the final bend and the house came into view, the man reined in his horse.*

REJOICE /rɪ'dʒɔɪs/
rejoices, rejoicing, rejoiced

re'joice in
to be very happy about something
rejoice in sth *At the moment we're just rejoicing in the fact that we're alive.*
PHRASE **rejoice in the name/title of sth**
British humorous to have a strange and funny name or title: *One of their leaders rejoiced in the name of Erik Bloodaxe.*

RELAPSE /rɪ'læps/
relapses, relapsing, relapsed

re'lapse into
to return to a previous state or way of behaving
relapse into sth *Annie shook her head and relapsed into silence again.*

RELATE /rɪ'leɪt/
relates, relating, related

re'late to ★★★
1 to be about something, or to be connected with something = *formal* APPERTAIN TO, PERTAIN TO
relate to sth *We're only interested in events that relate directly to the murder.* ♦ *We need to see figures relating to the last six months.*
2 to be able to understand a situation or the way that someone feels and thinks

relate to sb/sth *Martin had always found it easier to relate to women.* ♦ *The show deals with scientific subjects in a way that ordinary people can relate to.*

RELEGATE /'reləgeɪt/
relegates, relegating, relegated

'relegate to [often passive]
to move someone or something to a less important position
be relegated to sth *It looked as if I'd been relegated to second best.*
relegate sb/sth to sth *They've relegated us to a dark little office in the basement.*

RELIEVE /rɪ'liːv, American rɪ'lɪv/
relieves, relieving, relieved

re'lieve of ★
1 to take a responsibility or obligation from someone so that they do not have to deal with it or do it
relieve sb of sth *Someone should relieve him of at least some of the responsibility.*
2 *formal* to make someone leave their job, usually because they have done something wrong
relieve sb of sth *I'm afraid we have had to relieve her of her position.*
3 *humorous* to steal something from someone
relieve sb of sth *It was a clever attempt to relieve him of his fortune.*

RELY /rɪ'laɪ/
relies, relying, relied

re'ly on ★★★
1 to trust someone or something to do something for you = DEPEND ON
rely on sb/sth *My brother can help. At least we can rely on him.* ♦ *Sometimes you just have to rely on your own judgment.* ♦ **+to do sth** *Can we rely on him to support us?*
2 to need something in order to continue living, existing, or operating = DEPEND ON
rely on sth *The industry relies heavily on government subsidies.* ♦ **+to do sth** *The museum relies on voluntary donations to keep open.*

REMEMBER /rɪ'membə, American rɪ'membər/
remembers, remembering, remembered

re'member to
PHRASE **remember me to sb** *formal* used for asking someone to mention you to a person you have not seen for a long time

as a greeting: *Remember me to your parents.*

REMIND /rɪ'maɪnd/
reminds, reminding, reminded

re'mind of ★★★

1 to make someone remember something that happened in the past
remind sb of sb/sth *That song always reminds me of our holiday in Mexico.*
2 to be very similar to someone or something else
remind sb of sb/sth *She was tall and dark, and reminded me of my cousin Sarah.* ♦ *It's a strange taste – it reminds me of melons.*

REMONSTRATE /'remənstreɪt/
remonstrates, remonstrating, remonstrated

'remonstrate with *formal*

to argue with, complain to, or criticize someone
remonstrate with sb *I attempted to remonstrate with the officials.*

RENDER /'rendə, *American* 'rendər/
renders, rendering, rendered

,render 'down

to heat solid fat in order to make it liquid, or to boil bones and pieces of meat in order to produce fat that can be used for cooking
render down sth *also* **render sth down** *The cattle feed is made by rendering down the remains of sheep.*

'render into *formal*

to translate something into another language
render sth into German/Spanish etc *That's quite a difficult idea to render into English.*

RENEGE /rɪ'neɪg, rɪ'niːg, *American* rɪ'neg, rɪ'nɪg/
reneges, reneging, reneged

re'nege on *formal*

to not do something that you promised or agreed to do
renege on sth *Their refusal to sign effectively meant they had **reneged on** the agreement.* ♦ *He apparently had little compunction about **reneging on** his promises.*

RENT /rent/
rents, renting, rented

,rent 'out

to allow a house, room, office etc that you own to be used by someone who pays you regularly for using it = HIRE OUT, LET OUT
rent out sth *also* **rent sth out** *Liz Martin used to rent out her cottage next door to her home.* ♦ *All the rooms are rented out to students.*

REPAIR /rɪ'peə, *American* rɪ'per/
repairs, repairing, repaired

re'pair to *formal*

to move to a particular room or place
repair to sth *It was time for us to repair to our quarters.*

REPEAT /rɪ'piːt, *American* rɪ'pit/
repeats, repeating, repeated

re'peat on

if food that you have eaten repeats on you, it causes you to make noises for a long time afterwards by making air come up from your stomach and out through your mouth
repeat on sb *Cucumber always repeats on me.*

REPORT /rɪ'pɔːt, *American* rɪ'pɔrt/
reports, reporting, reported

re,port 'back ★★

to tell or send someone information that you have discovered
report back *I want you to find out everything you can and report back on Monday.* ♦ **+to** *He promised to investigate it and then report back to the committee.* ♦ **+with** *Investigators will report back with their findings in January.*

re,port 'in

to go somewhere or talk to someone by telephone in order to let them know that you are ready to start working or that you are in a particular place
report in *Fire officers have to report in when they arrive back at the fire station.* ♦ **+to** *When you arrive in Rome, report in to Mr Cura.*

re'port to

if you report to someone at work, they are directly in charge of you
report to sb *Kramer **reports directly to** the chief executive.*

RESIDE /rɪˈzaɪd/
resides, residing, resided

reˈside in *formal*
to exist in or consist of something
reside in sth *Its appeal resides in its simplicity.*

RESIGN /rɪˈzaɪn/
resigns, resigning, resigned

reˈsign yourself to ★
to accept that something unpleasant must happen and that you cannot change it
resign yourself to sth *He has resigned himself to the fact that he will lose his job.*
resign yourself to doing sth *In the end we had to resign ourselves to living in suburbia.*

RESONATE /ˈrezəneɪt/
resonates, resonating, resonated

ˈresonate with
1 to produce or be filled with a deep clear sound that continues for a long time
resonate with sth *The hall resonated with music.*
2 to produce an emotional effect on someone
resonate with sb *This issue has resonated with voters more than any other.*

RESORT /rɪˈzɔːt, American rɪˈzɔrt/
resorts, resorting, resorted

reˈsort to ★★★
to do something extreme or unpleasant in order to deal with a difficult situation
= TURN TO
resort to sth *I think we can solve this problem without resorting to legal action.*
resort to doing sth *The senator would never resort to using underhand tactics against an opponent.*

Nouns often used as objects with **resort to**

■ measures, methods, tactics, the use of, violence

REST /rest/
rests, resting, rested

ˈrest on ★★ (*also* ˈrest upon)
1 to be based on something = HINGE ON
rest on sth *The theory rests on the assumption that there are enough jobs for everyone.*

Nouns often used as objects with **rest on 1**

■ argument, assumption, belief, foundation, idea, premise, principle, proposition

2 if your eyes rest on someone or something, you start to look at that person or thing for a period of time
rest on sth *Her eyes rested on his face for a moment.*

ˌrest ˈup *informal*
to spend a period of time relaxing or sleeping after doing something tiring
rest up *I just need to rest up for a few days.*

ˈrest with ★
if a decision or responsibility rests with someone, they must take that decision or they have that responsibility
rest with sb *The matter now rests with the medical committee.* ♦ *Responsibility for child care rests with social services.*

RESTORE /rɪˈstɔː, American rɪˈstɔr/
restores, restoring, restored

reˈstore to ★★ [often passive]
to cause someone or something to be in a particular condition or situation again, especially a good one
be restored to sth *The garden had been restored to its former glory.* ♦ *It won't be long before she's fully restored to health.*
restore sb/sth to sth *If we are to restore the country to prosperity we must all work together.*

RESULT /rɪˈzʌlt/
results, resulting, resulted

reˈsult in ★★★
to cause or produce something
result in sth *A sudden change in temperature will inevitably result in rain.* ♦ *The crash resulted in the deaths of 14 passengers.*

Nouns often used as objects with **result in**

■ (positive) creation, formation, improvement, increase, saving, victory; (negative) collapse, damage, death, decrease, destruction, dismissal, fall, injury, loss, reduction

RETAIL /ˈriːteɪl, American ˈriteɪl/
retails, retailing, retailed

ˈretail at (*also* ˈretail for)
to be sold directly to the public for their own use
retail at sth *It retails for around £250.*

RETURN /rɪˈtɜːn, *American* rɪˈtɜrn/
returns, returning, returned

reˈturn to ★★★

1 to go back to a place where you were earlier, or to come back from a place where you have just been = COME BACK TO
return to sth *Be careful. We want you to return to base in one piece.*

2 to go back to a previous state or way of behaving
return to sth *Once the holidays were over, our lives returned to normal.*

3 to go back to a subject that has already been mentioned = COME BACK TO
return to sth *I'd like to return to what David was saying earlier.*

4 to go back to an activity after an interruption
return to sth *She looked up momentarily but then returned to her reading. ♦ He won't be able to return to work for at least two weeks.*

REV /rev/
revs, revving, revved

ˌrev ˈup

1 to press the accelerator of a vehicle with your foot when the vehicle is not moving in order to make the engine work faster
rev up *They sit at the lights, revving up.*

2 *informal* to become or make something become faster, more active, or stronger
= PUMP UP
rev up sth *also* **rev sth up** *The presidential candidates are now revving up their campaigns.*
rev up *Media attention on the Balkans was revving up in America. ♦ +for The students were revving up for another outbreak of violence.*

REVEL /ˈrev(ə)l/
revels, revelling, revelled

ˈrevel in ★

to enjoy something very much, especially something that most people would not like or approve of = GLORY IN
revel in sth *She told the story with a wicked smile, revelling in the embarrassment of her listeners. ♦ For a while, I revelled in the routine normality of cooking and cleaning.*

REVENGE /rɪˈvendʒ/
revenges, revenging, revenged

reˈvenge yourself on (*also* be reˈvenged on) *formal*

to hurt or punish someone because they have hurt you or someone else
revenge yourself on sb *It was a cunning plot to revenge himself on his old enemy.*
be revenged on sb *Nico swore he would be revenged on his father's killer.*

REVERT /rɪˈvɜːt, *American* rɪˈvɜrt/
reverts, reverting, reverted

reˈvert to ★★

1 to return to a previous state or way of behaving, often one that is not good
revert to sth *If you revert to your old eating habits, you'll gain weight again. ♦ The house reverted to its former state of disrepair.*

2 to start talking about something that you were talking about earlier
revert to sth *Sensing her uneasiness, Joseph reverted to their discussion about the weather.*

3 *legal* if property reverts to its previous owner, it is returned to that owner
revert to sb *The house will revert to her family on her or her husband's death.*
PHRASE **revert to type** *showing disapproval* to start behaving in your usual way again after seeming to change and improve: *Once he's had a girlfriend for a week or two, he reverts to type and starts chasing other girls.*

REVOLVE /rɪˈvɒlv, *American* rɪˈvɑlv/
revolves, revolving, revolved

reˈvolve around

to have something as a very important aspect
revolve around sth *Sicilian life revolves around good food.*
PHRASE **think the world revolves around you** *showing disapproval* to think that other people and things are not as important as you are: *Clare was a spoilt child of wealthy parents who thought the world revolved around her.*

RID /rɪd/
rids, ridding, rid

ˈrid of ★

to stop a person or thing from being affected by someone or something annoying, unpleasant, or harmful by removing them

rid sb/sth of sb/sth *Our aim is to rid the world of nuclear weapons.*
rid **yourself** of sb/sth *You'd do well to rid yourself of those romantic notions.*

RIDDLE /'rɪd(ə)l/
riddles, riddling, riddled

'riddle with

1 [often passive] to make a lot of holes in someone or something, especially with bullets
be riddled with sth *The oak beams were infested with woodworm and riddled with holes.*
riddle sb/sth with sth *Gunfire riddled the facade of the building with bullets.*
2 [usually passive] to make something full of a lot of people or things that are bad or not wanted
be riddled with sb/sth *The organization was riddled with spies.* ♦ *The team produced another disappointing performance riddled with errors.*

RIDE /raɪd/
rides, riding, rode /rəʊd, *American* roʊd/, ridden /'rɪd(ə)n/

'ride on [usually progressive]
to depend on something for success
ride on sth *I feel as though my whole future is riding on this interview.*

'ride 'out
to get to the end of a difficult or dangerous period or situation without any serious problems = ENDURE
ride out sth *also* ride sth out *We hope to ride out this recession better than last time.* ♦ *The ship rode out the storm without sustaining any permanent damage.* ♦ *When the crisis finally came, they were able to ride it out.*

'ride 'up
if a piece of clothing rides up, it gradually moves upwards on your body ≠ FALL DOWN
ride up *My slip keeps riding up.*

RIFLE /'raɪf(ə)l/
rifles, rifling, rifled

'rifle through
to search quickly through something such as a drawer or pile of papers in order to find or steal something
rifle through sth *I caught her rifling through my private letters.*

RIG /rɪg/
rigs, rigging, rigged

'rig 'out [often passive] *informal*
to give someone a particular type of clothing to wear, especially unusual clothing
be rigged out *She was rigged out in a cowgirl outfit.*
rig **yourself** out *I'm not going to rig myself out in that ridiculous thing!*

■ 'rig-out noun [C] *British informal old-fashioned* a set of clothes, especially if they are unusual: *Have you seen Ian's rig-out?*

'rig 'up
to make something quickly out of whatever you can find = IMPROVISE
rig up sth *also* rig sth up *They rigged up a shelter using a sheet and some branches.*

RING /rɪŋ/
rings, ringing, rang /ræŋ/, rung /rʌŋ/

'ring a'round *same as* ring round

'ring 'back ★ *British*

1 to phone someone again = PHONE BACK, CALL BACK
ring back *I'll ring back later.*
2 to phone someone who phoned you earlier = PHONE BACK, CALL BACK
ring sb back *Can you ask him to ring me back when he gets home?*

'ring 'in *British*
to phone a place, especially the place where you work or a television or radio station = PHONE IN, CALL IN
ring in *I'd better ring in and tell him I'll be late.* ♦ *John's rung in sick (=phoned work to say that he is ill) again.* ♦ +to do sth *Hundreds of people rang in to complain about his remarks.*
PHRASE ring in the New Year to ring bells to celebrate the beginning of a new year: *At midnight they listened to the church bells ringing in the New Year.*

■ 'ring-in noun [C] *Australian informal* someone or something that takes the place of another person or thing, especially in order to trick someone: *The guy must have been a ring-in.*

'ring 'off ★ *British*
to finish a phone call = HANG UP
ring off *He rang off before she had a chance to reply.*

,ring 'out ★ *mainly literary*
to produce a loud clear sound
ring out *Rob's laughter rang out in the large room.*

,ring 'round (*also* **,ring a'round**)
to phone several people, companies etc in order to arrange something or to get information = PHONE AROUND
ring round sb/sth *I'll ring round some of my friends and see if they can help.*

,ring 'through *British*
to phone from one part of a building to another = PHONE THROUGH
ring through *Reception rang through and said there was someone waiting to see me.*

,ring 'up ★★★
1 *British* to phone a person or place = CALL, PHONE, CALL UP, PHONE UP, RING
ring up *She rang up yesterday to make an appointment.*
ring up sb/sth *I'll ring up the theatre and see when the show finishes.*
ring sb/sth up *Don't forget to ring me up when you get there.*
2 to record a payment of money by pressing buttons on a cash register, for example in a shop
ring up sth *She rang up our purchases quickly and we left.*
ring sth up *He rang the bill up and handed me my change.*
3 to make or lose a particular amount of money in sales, profits, or losses in a period of time
ring up sth *The bank rang up about £600 million in trading losses.*

RINSE /rɪns/
rinses, rinsing, rinsed

,rinse 'out ★
1 to wash the inside of something quickly, especially in water
rinse out sth *also* **rinse sth out** *Mary rinsed out the cup and put it away.*
2 to put something into clean water after you have washed it with soap
rinse out sth *also* **rinse sth out** *Steve rinsed the T-shirt out and hung it up to dry.*

RIP /rɪp/
rips, ripping, ripped

,rip a'part
to destroy something completely = TEAR APART
rip sth apart *The allegations are likely to rip the administration apart.* ♦ *The*

explosion ripped the bus apart.

'rip at
to tear something quickly and with a lot of force, especially while attacking it
rip at sth *The dog went wild, ripping at the child's flesh.*

,rip 'into *informal*
to attack or criticize someone very severely
rip into sb *She had publicly ripped into him on a television chat show.*

,rip 'off ★★ [often passive] *informal*
1 to steal something = STEAL
be/get ripped off *Cars get ripped off all the time round here.*
rip sth off *He's always ripping my ideas off and using them in his show.*
rip off sth *The bank clerk was said to have made a small fortune ripping off clients.*
2 to cheat someone, especially by charging them too much money for something = FLEECE
be/get ripped off *Tourists are worried they'll get ripped off.*
rip off sb *This government is ripping off the country.*
rip sb off *The big banks stand accused of ripping their customers off.*
■ **'rip-off** noun [C usually singular]
informal something that is more expensive than it should be: *Our meal in town was a complete rip-off.* ♦ *rip-off prices*

'rip through
if something such as a fire, storm, or bomb rips though a place, it damages or destroys the place very quickly
rip through sth *The explosion ripped though her home.*

,rip 'up ★
1 to tear something into small pieces = TEAR UP
rip up sth *I ripped up all the letters she'd sent me.*
rip sth up *He ripped the cheque up into tiny pieces.*
2 *informal* to decide that something such as a plan or an agreement is useless and stop using it = TEAR UP
rip up sth *Channel bosses have ripped up their schedules in a bid to beat plunging ratings.*
rip sth up *Jones had to rip the blueprint up and go back to the drawing board.*
♦ *They took her ideas and unceremoniously ripped them up.*
PHRASE **rip up the rulebook** to completely stop following the rules

about how something should be done, especially in order to find a better way of doing it: *We have to just rip up the rulebook and start again.*

RISE /raɪz/
rises, rising, rose /rəʊz, American roʊz/, risen /ˈrɪz(ə)n/

ˌrise aˈbove
1 to deal well with a difficult or unpleasant situation
   rise above sth *Cara did her best to rise above the shocking news.*
2 to be better than other things of the same type = OUTDO
   rise above sth *This book clearly rises above the thousands of its competitors.*
3 to be morally good enough not to do something bad, especially something that most other people do
   rise above sth *He was able to rise above the prejudices of his generation.*

ˌrise aˈgainst
to protest or fight against a government or leader = REBEL AGAINST
   rise against sb/sth *The Yugoslav people were urged to rise against Milosevic.*

ˈrise to
to react to something in the way that someone wants you to, especially by becoming angry
   rise to sth *He's just trying to provoke you. Don't rise to it.*
   PHRASES rise to the bait to react to something in the way that someone wants you to: *I was too tired to rise to the bait, so I said nothing.*
   rise to the challenge/occasion to deal successfully with a difficult problem or situation, especially one that means you have to work harder than usual: *He had never done any building before but he rose to the challenge and built his own house.* ♦ *Athletes have to be able to rise to the occasion.*

ˌrise ˈup ★
1 to move upwards or into a higher position
   rise up *The crows rose up in alarm at the sound of the shotgun.*
2 *literary* to stand after you have been sitting, lying, or on your knees
   rise up *The choir rose up together and began to sing.*
3 if a building or natural feature rises up somewhere, it is tall or high and can be seen clearly
   rise up *Lush green hillsides rose up ahead of us.*

4 to protest and fight against a government or leader = REBEL
   rise up *The peasants rose up in revolt against the landowner.*

ROB /rɒb, American rɑb/
robs, robbing, robbed

ˈrob of ★★ [often passive]
1 to take away something that someone feels they have a right to, or stop them from doing something that they would normally be able to do
   be robbed of sth *I felt I had been robbed of what was rightfully mine.*
   rob sb of sth *His remark temporarily robbed her of her powers of speech.*
2 to take money or property illegally from a person or place, often using threats or violence
   be robbed of sth *Daniel was robbed of his car and briefcase.*
   rob sb of sth *The intruder has robbed her of her life savings.*

ROLL /rəʊl, American roʊl/
rolls, rolling, rolled

ˌroll aˈround British informal
if a time of year or regular event rolls around, it happens again
   roll around *By the time summer rolled around, Jamie had learned to swim.*

ˌroll ˈback ★
1 to remove or reduce the influence of something
   roll back sth *You can't roll back all the reforms of the last ten years.*
   roll sth back *The party promised to roll government back from areas where it has no useful role to play.*
2 [usually passive] *American* to reduce something such as a price or salary
   be rolled back *Eventually prices were rolled back to prewar levels.*

ˌroll ˈdown
1 if you roll a car window down, you turn a handle or push a button so that the window goes down
   roll sth down *Rolling the passenger window down, she stuck her head out and yelled to me.*
2 if you roll down your sleeves or the legs of your trousers, you make them longer by removing any folds in them
   roll down sth *also* **roll sth down** *Mark rolled down his sleeves when it started to get cold.*

,roll 'in

1 to arrive in large numbers or amounts
roll in *Money started rolling in and the business grew and grew.*

2 to arrive in a relaxed way despite being late = BREEZE IN ≠ LEAVE
roll in *Susan rolled in half an hour after the rehearsal had begun.*

,roll 'out ★

1 to make a substance flat and thin by pushing something heavy across it
roll out *Roll out the pizza dough on a well-floured surface.*

2 to introduce a new product or service = INTRODUCE
roll out sth *Australia will roll out the prototype of its new jet fighter in January.*
roll sth out *The company will roll its broadband service out gradually over the coming months.*

3 to make something that is wrapped around itself become flat = UNROLL
roll out sth *She rolled out the document on the table.*
roll sth out *He rolled the carpet out gradually, cutting and trimming as he worked his way around the room.*
PHRASE roll out the red carpet for sb to give special treatment to an important visitor: *China rolled out the red carpet for him and his team.*

,roll 'over ★★

1	change your position when lying down
2	not defend yourself
3	offer a prize that was not won before
4	let sb pay money later
5	invest money
+	**rollover** noun

1 to change the position of your body when you are lying down, for example from lying on your back to lying on your side
roll over *He rolled over and opened his eyes.*

2 [usually with a negative or in questions] *informal* to be easily defeated because you do not defend yourself
roll over *You don't expect me to just roll over and let them walk all over me, do you?*

3 [often passive] *British* if a lottery or other game with a money prize rolls over, or if it is rolled over, no one wins the prize that week and it is added to the prize for the next week
be rolled over *The £5.5 million is rolled over to next week.*

roll over *There are no winners tonight, so this week's jackpot rolls over.*

4 *business* to agree that an amount of money that someone owes can be paid back at a later date
roll sth over *They said we could roll it over until January next year.*
roll over sth *They want to ensure South Africa cannot roll over its debt.*

5 *business* if you roll over money that you have invested, you invest it in something similar
roll over sth *Investors were willing to roll over their original stake.*
roll sth over *I was persuaded to roll the money over.* ♦ *The agreement was that we would take any profit and roll it over.*

■ **rollover** /ˈrəʊləʊvə/ **noun 1** [C] *British* a situation in which no one wins the prize money from a lottery competition and it is added on to the money for the next competition: *No tickets matched the six winning lottery numbers, resulting in a rollover.* **2** [C/U] an occasion when a vehicle turns over while it is moving: *Accidents involving rollovers can cause internal injuries.*

,roll 'up ★★

1 to fold something or wrap it around itself so that it forms a tube or ball
roll up sth *Rolling up the magazine, he took a swipe at the bluebottle.*
roll sth up *She rolled her scarf up and put it into her bag.*

2 [often passive] if you roll your sleeves or the legs of your trousers up, you fold the cloth several times until they are shorter = TURN UP
be rolled up *The sleeves of his shirt were rolled up to the elbow.*
roll sth up *Roll your sleeves up or they'll get wet.*
roll up sth *He rolled up his trouser legs and went for a paddle.*

3 if you roll a car window up, you turn a handle or push a button so that the window goes up
roll sth up *The breeze was blowing her hair into her eyes, so she rolled the window up.*

4 *informal* to arrive somewhere late or at a time when you were not expected = APPEAR, TURN UP ≠ LEAVE
roll up *They eventually rolled up at lunchtime.*
PHRASE roll up! *British* used for getting people's attention when you want to tell them to come and watch something or take part in something: *Roll up, roll up for a fun-packed day of family entertainment.*

- ■ **'rolled-up** `adj` something that is rolled up has been folded or wrapped around itself so that it forms a tube: *She hit him playfully with her rolled-up newspaper.*

- ■ **'roll-up** `noun` [C] *British informal* a cigarette that you make yourself: *He's sitting on the floor smoking a roll-up.*

ROMP /rɒmp, *American* rɑmp/
romps, romping, romped

,romp a'head (*also* ,romp a'way)
to win or increase quickly and easily
romp ahead *The bank has seen its shares romp ahead recently.*

,romp 'through *informal*
to do something quickly and easily
romp through sth *He romped through the opening set of his match with the 22-year-old Swede.*

ROOF /ruːf, *American* ruf/
roofs, roofing, roofed

,roof 'over [often passive]
to cover an area with a roof
be roofed over *The stadium will be roofed over.*
roof sth over *also* **roof over sth** *If you roof the terrace over, you can still use it when it's raining.*

ROOT /ruːt, *American* rut/
roots, rooting, rooted

,root a'round
to put your hand deep into a place and push things around in order to try and find something
root around *He rooted around in his coat pocket and brought out her address.*

'root for *informal*
to support someone in a game, competition etc
root for sb *I'm sure you'll win. Everyone's rooting for you.*

be 'rooted in ★★
if one thing is rooted in another, the second thing started because of the first thing
be rooted in sth *Our instinctive reactions are rooted in our past experiences.*

,root 'out
to find something bad or illegal and get rid of it = ERADICATE
root out sth *also* **root sth out** *The president vowed to root out corruption.*

,root 'through
to search a place or group of things by putting your hand deep into it and pushing things around
root through sth *He rooted through the bins like a tramp.*

,root 'up [often passive]
to pull a plant out of the ground, including its roots = UPROOT
be rooted up *Half of his prize plants had been rooted up and scattered on the lawn.*
root up sth *also* **root sth up** *We'll need to root up these weeds before they become established.*

ROPE /rəʊp, *American* roʊp/
ropes, roping, roped

,rope 'in [often passive] *informal*
to persuade someone to do something that they do not really want to do
be/get roped in *I get roped in to help whenever I visit them.*
rope sb in *also* **rope in sb** *Judy, see if you can rope in your little brothers.*

,rope 'off [often passive]
to enclose an area using ropes, usually because of danger
be roped off *The path was roped off on either side.*
rope off sth *Last night police roped off the area of the find and were searching the undergrowth.*

,rope 'up [often passive]
to tie people together with ropes, or to be tied together with ropes, especially people who are climbing
be roped up *The drop was very steep, so I was relieved to be roped up.*
rope up *We stopped at the foot of the ridge and roped up.*

ROT /rɒt, *American* rɑt/
rots, rotting, rotted

,rot a'way
1 to decay by a gradual natural process, or to make something decay in this way
rot away *The window frames had completely rotted away.*
rot away sth *The salt put on the roads in winter is rotting away all the concrete.*
2 to be in a physical or mental condition that is gradually getting worse
rot away *Those who were convicted were sent to rot away in prison.*

ROUGH /rʌf/
roughs, roughing, roughed

,rough 'out
to produce a drawing or piece of writing without including all the details = DRAFT
rough out sth also **rough sth out** *I've roughed out a few sketches for you.*

,rough 'up *informal old-fashioned*
to physically attack someone = BEAT UP
rough sb up also **rough up sb** *They roughed us up and took away our equipment.*

ROUND /raʊnd/
rounds, rounding, rounded

,round 'down
to reduce a number to the nearest whole number, or the nearest number ending in zero
round sth down also **round down sth** *The total came to £10.04, but she rounded it down to £10.*

,round 'off ★★
1 to end something in a satisfactory way
round sth off *McCann rounded things off with a glorious goal minutes from the end.*
round off sth *Mr Orme rounded off the evening by buying everyone a drink.*
♦ **+with** *They rounded off their six-match tour with a brilliant victory yesterday.*
2 to make an angle or surface curved and smooth
round off sth *Use a sharp knife to round off the edges.*
round sth off *I picked up the file and continued rounding the corners off.*
3 to change a number to the nearest whole number, or the nearest number ending in zero
round sth off *Well that comes to 169, so let's round it off to 170.*
round off sth *Round off the numbers to three decimal places.*

'round on (*also* 'round upon) *British*
to react angrily towards someone = TURN ON
round on sb *He rounded on critics who have been calling for his resignation.*

,round 'out
to make something more thorough or complete
round out sth also **round sth out** *Her book rounds out our understanding of this amazing man.*

,round 'up ★★
1 [often passive] to find and arrest people = PULL IN
be rounded up *Dozens of political activists have been rounded up for questioning.*
round sb up *Orders were given to round as many of the demonstrators up as possible.*
round up sb *Police have orders to round up the troublemakers.*
2 to bring animals or people together in one place for a particular purpose
round up sb/sth *I used to help round up the cows at milking time.*
round sb/sth up *Round the rest of the kids up and we'll go back indoors.*
3 to increase a number to the nearest whole number, or the nearest number ending in zero
round sth up *If you round all the numbers up, you'll skew the total.*
round up sth *They rounded up the figure from 0.3871 to 0.39.*

■ '**round-up** noun [C] **1** a summary of something, especially the most important parts of the news: *Let's get a round-up of the day's sport.* **2** an occasion when animals or people are forced to gather together in one place: *a round-up of suspects*

'round upon *same as* round on

RUB /rʌb/
rubs, rubbing, rubbed

,rub a'gainst
to move backwards and forwards on something while pressing against it
rub against sth *The cat rubbed against my knee.* ♦ *Her thighs were so fat they rubbed against each other as she walked.*

,rub a'long *British informal*
to live or work with someone in a friendly way
rub along *We rub along pretty well most of the time.*

,rub 'down
1 to dry someone's body by rubbing it with a towel = DRY
rub sb down also **rub down sb** *My sister had the job of rubbing down the younger kids.*
rub yourself down *I rubbed myself down with a dry towel.*
2 to clean a horse by rubbing its hair and skin with a brush
rub sth down also **rub down sth** *The horses had been sweating a lot so we had to rub them down.*

3 to rub a surface in order to make it smooth or dry, or in order to prepare it for painting etc

rub down sth *also* **rub sth down** *For a natural worn look, lightly rub down the varnish when hard with fine steel wool.*

■ **rubdown** /'rʌbdaʊn/ *noun* [C] **1** a rub with a cloth to dry a person or an animal: *Each horse gets a good rubdown and some water.* **2** the process of rubbing a surface to make it dry or smooth: *Give the paintwork a rubdown between coats.* **3** *mainly American* a treatment in which you rub someone's body to help them relax: *The men have a sauna and a rubdown.*

,**rub 'in** ★

to mix something such as butter or fat into another substance such as flour, using your fingers

rub in sth *Place the flour in a bowl and rub in the butter.*

rub sth in *You need to rub the fat in until the mixture resembles breadcrumbs.*

PHRASE **rub it in** to remind someone of something stupid or embarrassing that they did: *Ok, I know I messed up, but there's no need to keep rubbing it in.*

,**rub 'off**

if a quality that someone has rubs off, it begins to affect another person so that they begin to have that quality too

rub off *I think her appreciation of decent music must have rubbed off.* ♦ **+on** *Hopefully his dedication will rub off on the rest of the team.*

,**rub 'out** ★

1 *British* to use a rubber to remove something that you have written or drawn in pencil, especially because you have made a mistake = ERASE

rub out sth *Let me rub out the entire thing and start all over again.*

rub sth out *I immediately rubbed the words out and tried again.*

2 to remove writing or drawing from a blackboard, whiteboard etc so that the surface is clean

rub sth out *She would write up equations on the board, get them wrong, and rub them out.*

rub out sth *He grabbed the duster and quickly rubbed out what someone had put on the blackboard.*

3 *American informal* to kill someone = TAKE OUT, KILL

rub out sb *He threatened to rub out anyone who opposed him.*

rub sb out *The boss gave the order to rub Jackson out.*

RUCK /rʌk/
rucks, rucking, rucked

,**ruck 'up** [often passive]

if a piece of cloth or clothing rucks up, or if you ruck it up, it is pulled upwards and forms untidy folds

be rucked up *The curtains were rucked up.*

ruck up *Her skirt had rucked up at the back.*

RULE /ruːl, *American* rul/
rules, ruling, ruled

,**rule 'in** [usually passive]

to decide that something is a possibility or that it will definitely happen ≠ RULE OUT, EXCLUDE

be ruled in *Nothing has been ruled in and nothing has been ruled out.*

,**rule 'out** ★★★ [often passive]

to stop considering something as a possibility = EXCLUDE ≠ RULE IN

be ruled out *Police said arson could not be ruled out.*

rule out sth *The president has ruled out the use of American troops.*

rule sth out *The possibility crossed my mind, but the facts rule it out.*

,**rule 'out of**

to make it impossible for someone to take part in something, especially a game or competition

rule sb out of sth *A shoulder injury ruled him out of the World Cup.* ♦ *I had a serious shoulder injury that ruled me out of the game for six weeks.*

'**rule over**

to govern a country, area, or its people with complete power, for example as a king or queen

rule over sth/sb *At that time, the Emperor ruled over a vast area, including most of Europe and North Africa.*

RUMBLE /'rʌmb(ə)l/
rumbles, rumbling, rumbled

,**rumble 'on** *British*

to continue to cause trouble or arguments

rumble on *They have allowed the misunderstanding to rumble on.*

RUN /rʌn/
runs, running, ran /ræn/, **run**

Run is often used with adverbs and prepositions when it means 'to move quickly using your legs and feet': *A cat* **ran across** *the road in front of me.* ♦ *I heard voices downstairs and* **ran down** *to see who it was.* ♦ *As soon as the rain started, we* **ran under** *a tree for shelter.* These uses are not included here.

,run a'bout *British same as* **run around**

■ **runabout** /'rʌnəˌbaʊt/ **noun** [C] *informal* **1** a small car used for making short journeys: *It's the perfect little runabout for the city.* **2** *British* a period of sports training: *We warm up with a ten-minute runabout.*

,run a'bout with *British same as* **run around with**

,run a'cross

to find something or meet someone by chance = COME ACROSS
run across sb/sth *I ran across the letter while I was going through the drawers.* ♦ *We work in the same part of town, so I run across him from time to time.*

,run 'after ★★

1 to chase someone or something = *formal* PURSUE
run after sb/sth *Velluci ran after the car waving his fists.* ♦ *He was faster than the other player running after the ball.*

2 *informal* to try to make someone notice you because you are sexually attracted to them
run after sb *There are always plenty of guys running after her.*

,run a'long [usually in imperative] *old-fashioned*

used for telling children to go away
run along *Run along now, you two.*

,run a'round (*also* **,run a'bout** *British or* **,run 'round** *British*)

to be very busy doing a lot of different things
run around *I've been running around all day.*

,run a'round after (*also* **,run 'round after** *British*)

to do a lot of things for someone, often things that you expect people to do for themselves
run around after sb *I spend my days running around after the kids.*

,run a'round with (*also* **,run a'bout with** *British*) *informal*

to spend a lot of time with someone, especially someone who other people do not approve of = ASSOCIATE WITH
run around with sb *She didn't like her*

son running around with those kids from next door.

,run a'way ★★★

1 to escape from someone or something
= MAKE OFF
run away *They ran away when they saw the police coming.*

2 to secretly leave your home or your family, because you are not happy there
run away *He ran away and left his wife and children.* ♦ **+from** *When I was 13, I ran away from home.*

■ **runaway** /'rʌnəˌweɪ/ **adj** **1** a runaway vehicle or animal is moving fast without anyone controlling it: *She was hit by a runaway truck.* **2** increasing more quickly than expected: *The play was a runaway success.* **3** a runaway person has left their home or escaped from somewhere: *The police are dealing with more runaway children.*

■ **runaway** /'rʌnəˌweɪ/ **noun** [C] someone who has left their home or escaped from somewhere: *One of the runaways was her son.*

,run a'way from

to try to avoid dealing with a difficult or unpleasant situation
run away from sth *You can't keep running away from the problem.*

,run a'way with ★

1 to secretly leave your home or your family with someone so that you can live together
run away with sb *She ran away with her teacher when she was only sixteen.*

2 *informal* to win a competition, game, or prize very easily
run away with sth *They ran away with the match in the second half.*

PHRASES **let your feelings/emotions run away with you** to fail to control your feelings, so that you say or do something stupid: *I was in danger of letting my emotions run away with me.* **run away with the idea/impression that** to believe that something is true when it is not: *I wouldn't want him to run away with the impression that I don't care.*

,run 'by

to tell someone your ideas so that they can give you their opinion
run sth by sb *Can I run a few ideas by you?* ♦ *Run that by me again* (=repeat what you just said).

,run 'down ★★

1	injure/kill sb with a car
2	criticize sb
3	machine/clock etc: stop working
4	business etc: become smaller
5	read a list quickly
6	find sb/sth after searching
+	**rundown** noun; **run-down** adj

1 [often passive] to hit someone with your car and injure or kill them = KNOCK DOWN, RUN OVER

be/get run down *She got run down outside the school.*

run sb down *The thief deliberately ran her down.*

2 to criticize someone or something, especially in an unfair way

run sb/sth down *You're always running me down!* ♦ *He tries to make himself look better by running other people down.* ♦ *She's a great worker. Why does she run herself down?*

run down sb/sth *She tends to run down every other department.*

3 if something such as a machine runs down, or if you run it down, it gradually stops working because it has no power

run sth down *Switch your headlights off, or you'll run the battery down.*

run down sth *We start running down the printing press ready for the weekend shutdown.*

run down *The battery on his hearing aid had run down.*

4 *British* if a business or organization runs down, or if someone runs it down, it gradually becomes smaller

run sth down *They've been running the factory down for the last five years.*

run down sth *They seemed to be deliberately running down the business.*

run down *The decision was taken to let the steel industry run down.*

5 to quickly read everything on a list = RUN THROUGH

run down sth *I'll just run down the list and see if we've forgotten anything.*

6 to finally find someone or something after searching for them for a long time

run sb/sth down *Police eventually ran him down in woods north of the city.*

■ **rundown** /ˈrʌndaʊn/ **noun** [C usually singular] a short report: *Can you give us a **rundown** of the main points?*

■ ,**run-'down** **adj** **1** so tired that you do not feel well: *If you're run-down you're more likely to get colds and flu.* **2** in bad condition because no one has spent money on repairs: *a run-down farmhouse*

,run 'in

1 to drive a new vehicle slowly for a period of time so that you do not damage the engine

run sth in *I haven't had the car for long. I'm still running it in.*

2 *informal old-fashioned* to find a criminal and take them to a police station = ARREST

run sb in *The police ran him in after a chase.*

■ '**run-in** **noun** [C] **1** *informal* an argument: *She's had another run-in with her boss.* **2** *British* the period of time before an important competition: *the run-in to the Olympic Games*

,run 'into ★★★

1 to meet someone when you did not expect to = COME ACROSS, BUMP INTO

run into sb *I ran into your mother the other day.* ♦ *Guess who I ran into this morning?*

2 to hit someone or something by accident while you are driving = COLLIDE WITH

run into sb/sth *You can see where the truck ran into me (=hit my car).* ♦ *Three people were killed when their car ran into the side of a train.*

3 to reach a particular amount or number

run into (the) millions/hundreds/ thousands etc *Flood damages could run into millions.* ♦ *Their expenses are already running into the thousands.*

4 to start to have problems = *formal* ENCOUNTER

run into sth *Our project **ran into difficulties** when we lost our sponsor.* ♦ *Yet another travel firm has **run into trouble**.* ♦ *If you **run into problems** loading the software, contact our help desk.*

PHRASE **run into a brick wall** to reach a point in a process where there are problems that seem impossible to solve: *When it came to talking about money, we ran into a brick wall.*

,run 'off ★★★

1	leave suddenly
2	print sth
3	write sth
4	flow out or away
5	force sb to leave
+	PHRASE
+	**runoff** noun

1 to suddenly leave, especially leave the place where you live or leave the person you live with

run off *Their dad ran off when they were little.*

2 to quickly print a copy of something

run off sth *Would you mind running off some more copies of the agenda?*
run sth off *I need to run a few more copies off.* ♦ *If you want extra handouts, my secretary will run them off for you.*

3 to quickly and easily write something such as a poem or speech
run off sth *James can just run off a poem for any occasion.*
run sth off *I had to run the new speech off on the train.* ♦ *You have about an hour to run one off.*

4 if a liquid runs off, or if it runs off something, it flows away from or out of it
run off *This channel allows excess water to run off.*
run off sth *The slope means rainwater runs off the roof.*

5 *American very informal* to force someone to leave a place
run sb off *He's still there unless Dad's run him off.*
PHRASE run off at the mouth *American informal* to talk too much: *He should think before he starts running off at the mouth.*

run off (sense 2)

■ **runoff** /ˈrʌnɒf/ **noun 1** [U] a flow of water or chemicals from one place to another, especially when this damages the environment: *The problems are caused by the runoff of agricultural chemicals.* **2** [C] a second election or competition that is organized when the first one does not have a winner: *Neither candidate won a clear majority, forcing a runoff.*

ˌrun ˈoff with ★ *informal*

1 to secretly leave your home with someone in order to marry them or have a sexual relationship with them —*picture* → ASK OUT
run off with sb *They said Phil had run off with his wife's best friend.*

2 to steal something or take it without permission
run off with sth *It was the night before he ran off with my car.*

ˌrun ˈon ★★★

1 to continue for longer than expected or planned = GO ON
run on *I hope this meeting doesn't run on too long.* ♦ *Her speeches do tend to run on sometimes.*

2 to use a particular type of fuel
run on sth *They're working on an engine that runs on water.*

3 *mainly American* to talk for a long time about something in a way that is boring
run on *Bobby ran on for hours about her relationship problems.*

ˌrun ˈout ★★★

1 to use all of something so that you do not have any left
run out *I bought more beer so we wouldn't run out.* ♦ **+of** *Some hospitals are running out of blood supplies.* ♦ *The negotiations dragged on, and we were beginning to run out of patience.*

2 if something runs out, you do not have any more of it left
run out *They returned home from South Africa when their money ran out.* ♦ *What will the world do when supplies of oil run out?*

3 if an official agreement or document runs out, it stops being legal at a certain date = END
run out *My contract runs out next July.* ♦ *When does your passport run out?*

4 [often passive] in the sport of cricket, to end a player's innings by throwing the ball at the wicket which the player is running towards, and hit it before the player arrives
run sb out *He had a habit of running his team-mates out.*
PHRASES run out of steam to lose energy, enthusiasm, or importance: *After its initial success the fundraising venture seemed to be running out of steam.*
time is running out if time is running out, you do not have long to do something: *We have to save the hostages, but time is running out.*

ˌrun ˈout on

to suddenly leave your wife, husband, or partner = WALK OUT ON
run out on sb *Jane's husband ran out on her when their children were still young.*

run out

,run 'over ★★

1	injure/kill sb with a car
2	practise a performance
3	explain sth again
4	think about sth a lot
5	continue for longer
6	when there is too much liquid

1 [often passive] to hit someone or something with a vehicle and injure or kill them = KNOCK DOWN
be/get run over *Keeley was run over by a car outside her house.*
run sb over *The guy nearly ran me over.*

2 to practise what you are going to say in a speech, performance etc = REHEARSE, RUN THROUGH
run over sth *Do you want me to run over your lines with you?*

3 to explain something again so that someone understands
run over sth *Would you run over the sequence of events again?*

4 to think a lot about something such as a decision or experience = GO OVER
run over sth *She keeps **running over** the incident again and again **in her mind**.*

run over

5 to continue for longer than planned
= OVERRUN
run over *Sorry I'm late – the meeting ran over.*

6 if a container runs over, there is so much liquid in it that some liquid comes out over the top of the container
= OVERFLOW
run over *The bath had run over and water was coming through the ceiling.*

,run 'round British same as run around

,run 'through ★★★

1	explain/read sth
2	practise a performance
3	when everyone in a group feels sth
4	when a quality is in many parts
5	spend a lot of money
6	kill sb with a sword
+	**run-through** noun

1 to explain or read something quickly
run through sth *I'll just run through the names and make sure everyone's here.*
♦ *Do you want me to run through the details with you?*

2 to practise something so that it is correct for a performance or test
= REHEARSE, RUN OVER
run through sth *Let's just run through the piece one more time.*

3 if a feeling runs through a group of people, they all feel it
run through sb/sth *Panic ran through the crowd as a shot was heard.*

4 if a quality or idea runs through something, you can find it in many parts of that thing
run through sth *The theme of jealousy runs through a lot of her work.* ♦ *There was a lot of bitterness running through their conversation.*

5 to spend or use a lot of money in a short period of time = GO THROUGH ≠ CONSERVE
run through sth *The project ran through £50 million in the first year.*

6 *literary* to push a sword through someone's body = SPEAR
run sb through *The hero's sword ran him through.*

■ **'run-through** noun [C] a practice performance of a ceremony, play, or concert: *We're going to have one final run-through before Saturday night.*

'run to ★★

1 to ask someone for help, especially when you should not need their help
run to sb *You can't go running to your parents every time you have a problem.*

2 to reach a particular amount, especially a large amount

run to sth *The cost of repairs ran to £300.* ♦ *The interview transcripts run to over 120 pages.*

3 [usually with a negative] *British* to have enough money to buy a particular thing

run to sth *I don't think we can run to a new television at the moment.*

run 'up ★★

1 if you run up a bill or debt, you owe a lot of money

run up sth *My son ran up a huge phone bill.*

run sth up *How did they manage to run this much debt up in two months?*

> Nouns often used as objects with **run up 1**
>
> ■ bill, debt, deficit, losses, overdraft

2 to make something very quickly, especially something that you sew

run up sth *I can run up a pair of curtains in a day.*

run sth up *She ran this waistcoat up for me herself.* ♦ *If she needs a new dress, she expects me to run one up for her.*

3 to raise a flag to the top of a pole

run up sth *Every morning, they run up the colours.*

run sth up *It was Peter's turn to run the flag up.* ♦ *We tie the flag on and run it up.*

■ **'run-up** noun a run that someone makes before jumping, throwing a ball etc: *The bowler started his run-up.*
  PHRASE the run-up to sth the period of time just before an important event: *The government are vulnerable all the time, but especially in the run-up to a general election.*

run 'up against

1 if you run up against problems, difficulties etc, you have to deal with them

run up against sth *We ran up against a few problems finding enough money.*

2 to compete against a particular opponent

run up against sb *Everything depends on who they run up against in the next round.*

RUSH /rʌʃ/
rushes, rushing, rushed

rush a'round (*also* **rush a'bout** *British*)
to try to do a lot of things or go to a lot of places in a short period of time = DASH AROUND

rush around *I've been rushing around shopping all day.* ♦ *All that hard work*

and rushing about tires you out.

rush 'into ★
to do something without first thinking carefully about it

rush into sth *Try not to rush into a decision you may later regret.* ♦ *I swore to myself I wouldn't rush headlong into another romance.*

rush 'off ★
to leave, especially soon after arriving
= DASH OFF

rush off *I'll have to rush off. I've got another class.*

rush 'out
to quickly produce something and make it available for people to buy

rush out sth *also* **rush sth out** *The publishers rushed out a paperback edition of the book.* ♦ *There was the feeling that they'd rushed the album out before it was ready.*

rush 'round *same as* **rush around**

rush 'through [often passive]
to deal with official or legal business more quickly than usual

be rushed through sth *The legislation had been rushed through parliament.*

rush sth through *We needed to rush this rule-change through.*

RUST /rʌst/
rusts, rusting, rusted

rust a'way
if a metal object rusts away, a rough red substance forms on its surface and destroys it

rust away *There were holes where the iron had rusted away.*

rust 'up
if a metal object rusts up, a rough red substance forms on its surface and damages it

rust up *The spokes on the bike's wheels had rusted up.*

RUSTLE /ˈrʌs(ə)l/
rustles, rustling, rustled

rustle 'up *informal*
to quickly produce something such as a meal using whatever is available
= PREPARE

rustle up sth *also* **rustle sth up** *I'll see if I can rustle up some lunch.* ♦ *If you're hungry, I'm sure we can rustle something up.*

S s

SACK /sæk/
sacks, sacking, sacked

,sack 'out *American informal*
to go to sleep = CRASH OUT
    sack out *The kids had sacked out on the
    floor while watching television.*

SADDLE /'sæd(ə)l/
saddles, saddling, saddled

,saddle 'up
to get a horse ready for riding by putting
a leather seat on it
    saddle up *I told the men to saddle up.*
    saddle up sth *also* **saddle sth up** *We
    saddled up our horses.* ♦ *Saddle the colt
    up and we'll see how he likes it.*

'saddle with [often passive]
to give someone something that is difficult
or unpleasant to deal with = LUMBER WITH
    be saddled with sth *The company was
    saddled with a huge debt last year.*
    saddle sb with sth *We didn't want to
    saddle you with a job like that.*

SAFEGUARD /'seɪfgɑːd, *American*
'seɪfˌgɑrd/
safeguards, safeguarding,
safeguarded

'safeguard against
to do something that prevents something
bad from happening
    safeguard against sth *The rules are
    there to safeguard against an abuse of
    power.*

SAIL /seɪl/
sails, sailing, sailed

'sail ,through
1 to deal with something very easily, with
no problems = DO WELL, DO WELL IN ≠ FAIL
    sail through sth *She sailed through the
    first interview.*
2 to make fast and easy progress, with no
delays
    sail through sth *The bill sailed through
    the Senate on a 9 to 5 vote.*

SALLY /'sæli/
sallies, sallying, sallied

,sally 'forth
to leave a place in order to do something,
especially in a way that shows confidence
and energy
    sally forth *Every afternoon she sallied
    forth to do the shopping.*

SALT /sɔːlt, *American* sɔlt/
salts, salting, salted

,salt a'way [usually passive]
to save money for the future, often hiding
it illegally = HOARD ≠ FRITTER AWAY
    be salted away *Most of the money leaves
    the country and is salted away in Swiss
    bank accounts.*

SAND /sænd/
sands, sanding, sanded

,sand 'down
to make wood very smooth by rubbing it
with a special rough paper = SAND
    sand sth down *also* **sand down sth** *Sand
    old wood down before you repaint it.* ♦ *I
    sanded down the edges to round them off.*

SANDWICH /'sæn(d)wɪdʒ, *American*
'sændwɪtʃ/
sandwiches, sandwiching,
sandwiched

be 'sandwiched between
1 to be in a small or tight space between
two things that are larger
    be sandwiched between sth and sth
    *The tiny kingdom was sandwiched
    between Austria and Czechoslovakia.*
2 to face a difficult choice between two
duties or responsibilities
    be sandwiched between sth *Many
    women are sandwiched between the
    needs of children and parents.*
3 to have a layer of a different substance
on either side
    be sandwiched between sth *Mattresses
    consist of metal springs sandwiched
    between padding.*

,sandwich to'gether
to put two things together, especially with
a layer of something in between
    sandwich sth together *also* **sandwich
    together sth** *Use a little cream to
    sandwich the cakes together.* ♦ *He
    sandwiched together two pieces of glass.*

SAVE /seɪv/
saves, saving, saved

'save on
1 to spend less money on something than you would normally
save on sth *Using eco-friendly lightbulbs will help you save on electricity bills.*
2 to avoid using something, or to use less of it
save on sth *Keep your showers short to save on water.*

,save 'up ★★
1 to regularly put money in a bank or invest it so that you can use it later
save up *The wedding is not until next year. We need some time to save up.*
♦ **+for** *I'm saving up for a new car.*
save up sth *I've already saved up £100.*
2 to collect a set of things and save them for a particular purpose
save up sth *You save up the tokens to get a prize.*
save sth up *We've been saving these cards up for you.* ♦ *If you have any bottle tops, save them up for school.*

SAVOR the American spelling of **savour**

SAVOUR /'seɪvə, *American* 'seɪvər/
savours, savouring, savoured

'savour of *formal*
to seem to have a small amount of an unpleasant quality = SMACK OF
savour of sth *He disapproved of anything that savoured of discrimination.*

SAW /sɔː, *American* sɔ/
saws, sawing, sawn /sɔːn, *American* sɔn/ or sawed

,saw 'down
to cut through something such as a tree with a saw in order to make it fall to the ground
saw down sth *also* **saw sth down** *I needed some help sawing down a tree.*
♦ *Our neighbour complained that the trees were too tall, and asked us to saw them down.*

,saw 'off
to remove something by cutting through it with a saw or knife
saw off sth *also* **saw sth off** *He sawed off a piece of meat from the bone.* ♦ *She had sawn her finger off by accident.*

,saw 'up
to cut something into several pieces using a saw or knife
saw up sth *also* **saw sth up** *They were busy sawing up the logs into two-foot lengths.* ♦ *The next job is sawing this timber up into boards.*

SAY /seɪ/
says /sez/, said /sed/

'say about
to show indirectly what someone or something is like
say sth about sth/sb *Your clothes say a lot about you.* ♦ *This incident says something about the way the company is run.* ♦ *What does your hairstyle say about you?*

'say to [usually with a negative]
to seem pleasant to someone, or to have a particular meaning for someone
say sth to sb *This music says nothing to me.*

SCALE /skeɪl/
scales, scaling, scaled

,scale 'down ★ (*also* ,scale 'back) [often passive]
to make something smaller in size, amount etc than it used to be = REDUCE ≠ SCALE UP
be scaled down *The search operation has been scaled down.*
scale down sth *We're scaling down our peacekeeping force.*

■ **'scaled-down** adj [only before noun]
made smaller in size, amount etc than before: *a scaled-down workforce*

,scale 'up
to make something larger in size, amount etc than it used to be = INCREASE ≠ SCALE DOWN
scale up sth *also* **scale sth up** *An order this size means scaling up our production capacity.*

SCAN /skæn/
scans, scanning, scanned

,scan 'in
to copy words or pictures from a book or document into a computer document using a scanner (=piece of equipment that photographs the words or pictures)
scan sth in *also* **scan in sth** *We can scan the images in later.* ♦ *I scanned in the company's logo.*

SCAR /skɑː, *American* skɑr/
scars, scarring, scarred

‚scar 'over
if an injury scars over, it forms a permanent mark as it becomes better
scar over *There was a ridge of flesh where the wound had scarred over.*

SCARE /skeə, *American* sker/
scares, scaring, scared

‚scare a'way (*also* ‚scare 'off)
1 to make someone feel so frightened or worried that they do not do something they had planned to do
scare sb away *also* **scare away sb** *Higher fees will only scare some parents away.*
♦ *The city's high murder rate has scared away tourists.* ♦ *He was very fond of Janet, but her wish to be a mother scared him away.*
2 [often passive] to make a person or animal so frightened that they go away
scare sb away *also* **scare away sb** *The noise must have scared the children away.* ♦ *The police started shooting and scared them away.* ♦ *The scandal could scare away potential investors.*

'scare ‚into [often passive]
to make someone feel so worried or frightened that they do something
be scared into doing sth *Many people have been scared into buying organic food.*
scare sb into doing sth *They're looking to scare customers into taking out insurance.*

‚scare 'off *same as* scare away

‚scare 'up *American informal*
to make something using the few things that are available
scare up sth *also* **scare sth up** *Dad went into the kitchen to try to scare up a meal.*

SCARF /skɑːf, *American* skɑrf/
scarfs, scarfing, scarfed

‚scarf 'down *American informal*
to eat something fast
scarf down sth *also* **scarf sth down** *Back in the kitchen I scarfed down a bowl of cereal.*

SCHEDULE /ˈʃedjuːl, *American* ˈskedʒul, ˈskedʒəl/
schedules, scheduling, scheduled

'schedule for [often passive]
to plan for something to happen at a particular time
be scheduled for sth *Another round of talks is scheduled for next year.*
schedule sth for sth *They have scheduled the factory for completion in 2012.*

SCHOOL /skuːl, *American* skul/
schools, schooling, schooled

'school in [usually passive]
to teach or train someone in a particular subject or skill
be schooled in sth *He had been well schooled in the art of diplomacy.*

SCOOP /skuːp, *American* skup/
scoops, scooping, scooped

‚scoop 'out
to remove the inside part of something, usually a fruit or vegetable, using a spoon or your hands
scoop out sth *also* **scoop sth out** *Cut the potatoes in half and scoop out each half with a spoon.* ♦ *Take a large tomato and scoop the middle out.*

‚scoop 'up ★
1 to lift something or someone quickly with your hands or arms
scoop sb/sth up *He scooped the ball up and dived over the line for a try.* ♦ *The child flung her arms around him as he knelt down to scoop her up.*
scoop up sb/sth *Ralph scooped up a handful of dirt.*
2 *informal* to get something, usually something good or valuable, for example by buying it
scoop up sth *People arriving early scooped up fantastic bargains.*
scoop sth up *You have to scoop these opportunities up while they're there.*

SCOOT /skuːt, *American* skut/
scoots, scooting, scooted

‚scoot 'over *American*
if someone sitting down scoots over, they move to a different position, for example to make space for someone else to sit down
= MOVE UP
scoot over *She scooted over and whispered in my ear.* ♦ *If I scoot over a little, there's room for you.*

SCOPE /skəʊp, *American* skoʊp/
scopes, scoping, scoped

,scope 'out *American informal*
to examine someone or something
carefully
> **scope out sth** *also* **scope sth out** *We need to scope out the competition first.*

SCORE /skɔː, *American* skɔr/
scores, scoring, scored

'score off
to gain an advantage over someone,
especially by saying something clever or
funny that makes them seem stupid
> **score off sb** *Why does she constantly try to score off her sister?*

,score 'out (*also* **,score 'through**)
to draw a line through written words
= CROSS OUT
> **score out sth** *also* **score sth out** *Score out the guests' names as they arrive.*

,score 'through *same as* **score out**

SCOUR /'skaʊə, *American* skaʊr/
scours, scouring, scoured

,scour 'out
if one thing scours out another, the first
thing forms a passage or hole in the other
by moving continuously over it
> **scour out sth** *also* **scour sth out** *The water had scoured out the bed of the stream.*

SCOUT /skaʊt/
scouts, scouting, scouted

,scout a'round
to try to find something by searching in
several places = SEARCH
> **scout around** *I needed a flat, so I scouted around near the station.* ♦ **+for** *We scouted around for firewood.*
> **scout around sth** *When looking for new talent, they tend to scout around the lower divisions.*

,scout 'out
to try to find something
> **scout out sth** *also* **scout sth out** *He asked her to scout out job opportunities for him while she was in London.*

,scout 'round
to try to find something by searching in
several places = SEARCH
> **scout round** *There are still some bargains available if you're prepared to scout round.* ♦ **+for** *I scouted round for a place to stay.*

> **scout round sth** *I found the ring whilst scouting round an antiques fair.*

SCRABBLE /'skræb(ə)l/
scrabbles, scrabbling, scrabbled

,scrabble a'round (*also* **,scrabble a'bout**)
to try to find something that you cannot
see by searching with your hands or
fingers
> **scrabble around** *We scrabbled around on the ground.* ♦ **+for** *He scrabbled around in his pocket for the key.*

'scrabble at
to make a lot of small quick movements
with your fingers on something,
especially when you are trying to find
something you cannot see
> **scrabble at sth** *She scrabbled at the earth with her fingers.*

SCRAMBLE /'skræmb(ə)l/
scrambles, scrambling, scrambled

'scramble ,for
to hurry or try very hard to get something,
often competing with other people
> **scramble for sth** *Companies are scrambling for skilled workers.*

SCRAPE /skreɪp/
scrapes, scraping, scraped

,scrape a'long *same as* **scrape by**

,scrape 'back [usually passive] *British*
to tie your hair tightly so that it does not
touch your face
> **be scraped back** *She wears her fair hair scraped back.*

,scrape 'by (*also* **,scrape a'long**)
to have enough money to pay for the
things you really need in order to live,
but no more = GET BY
> **scrape by** *We did what we could to scrape by.* ♦ **+on** *She just manages to scrape by on her wage.*

,scrape 'in (*also* **,scrape 'into**) *British*
to achieve a position by a very small
number of votes or points
> **scrape in** *The new candidate scraped in by a tiny one-vote margin.*
> **scrape into sth** *The team scraped into the final with a 2–1 win.*

,scrape 'out
1 to rub a sharp edge or tool against the
side of a container to remove something
from it
> **scrape out sth** *also* **scrape sth out** *She*

lets me scrape out the bowl when she makes a cake. ♦ They had to scrape the drain out until it was clear.

2 to remove something from a container or object by rubbing a sharp edge or tool against it

scrape sth out also **scrape out sth** *First, scrape the seeds out.* ♦ *an operation in which the surgeon scrapes out the contents of the uterus*

,scrape 'through

to just succeed in doing something, but not in a very impressive way = SQUEAK THROUGH

scrape through sth *He just managed to scrape through the entrance exam.*
scrape through *The London team scraped through by a two-point margin.*

,scrape to'gether (also ,scrape 'up)

to succeed in getting enough of something, especially money, by making a lot of effort = COLLECT

scrape together sth also **scrape sth together** *They have trouble even scraping together their rent.* ♦ *I'm sure we can scrape a few more pounds together.*

SCRATCH /skrætʃ/
scratches, scratching, scratched

,scratch a'round

to try to find something by looking everywhere, even in places you would prefer not to look in

scratch around *Some dogs were scratching around near the bins.* ♦ **+for** *We scratched around for a place to shelter.*

,scratch 'off

to remove something from a surface using your fingernails

scratch off sth also **scratch sth off** *You have to scratch off the silver panel to reveal your prize.* ♦ *Don't scratch the paint off.*
scratch sth off sth *He had accidentally scratched the scab off his knee.*

,scratch 'out [usually passive]

to remove a word from a sentence or something from a list by drawing a line through it = CROSS OUT

be scratched out *Some of the names on the list had been scratched out.*

SCREAM /skriːm, American skrim/
screams, screaming, screamed

,scream 'out at (also ,scream 'at) informal

if something bad or ugly screams out at you, you cannot avoid noticing it

scream out at sb *The grammatical mistakes just scream out at you.* ♦ *He's wearing a pink and orange shirt that just screams at you.*

SCREEN /skriːn, American skrin/
screens, screening, screened

'screen for

to test someone to find out if they have a particular illness

screen sb for sth *He recommends screening pregnant women for diabetes.*

,screen 'off [usually passive]

to separate one part of a room from another, for example to make it more private

be screened off *Part of the hall had been screened off as a waiting room.*

■ ,off-'screen **adj** , **adv** in the real life of an actor: *their off-screen romance* ♦ *Off-screen, she's a hard-headed businesswoman.*

,screen 'out

1 to prevent something that is dangerous or unsuitable from coming in

screen out sth also **screen sth out** *Cycle masks are designed to screen out pollutants.* ♦ *A good program can screen these options out.*

2 to refuse to accept someone who is not suitable for something, for example a job

screen out sb also **screen sb out** *The tests are used to screen out poor applicants.*

SCREW /skruː, American skru/
screws, screwing, screwed

,screw a'round informal

1 impolite showing disapproval to have a lot of sexual relationships, instead of having one regular partner

screw around *I don't screw around.*

2 mainly American to waste time in silly or useless activities

screw around *I pay him all this money and all he does is screw around.*

3 mainly American to treat someone badly, for example by changing arrangements or agreements or by wasting their time

screw sb around *We felt the company was screwing us around.*

,screw 'out of informal

to unfairly prevent someone from having something that they should get

screw sb out of sth *They tried to screw me out of royalty payments.*

¡screw 'over *American impolite*
to cheat someone, especially by getting
money from them in a dishonest way
  screw sb over *People seeing this will
  think the administration is screwing
  them over.*

¡screw 'up ★★

1	twist or squeeze sth
2	close your eyes
3	show you dislike sth with your face
4	make a big mistake
5	spoil an event/situation
6	upset sb
+	PHRASE
+	**screwed up** adj

1 [often passive] to make something into a
smaller shape by squeezing or twisting it,
especially a piece of paper = SCRUNCH UP
  be screwed up *Several pages had been
  screwed up and tossed in the basket.*
  screw sth up *I screwed the letter up and
  threw it in the bin.* ♦ *She grabbed the
  note and screwed it up.*

2 if you screw up your eyes, you close
them tightly
  screw up your eyes *He screwed up his
  eyes, trying to peer through the fog.*
  screw your eyes up *She screwed her eyes
  up tightly against the glare of the lights.*

3 if you screw up your face, you pull your
forehead down and push your mouth and
nose up, usually to show that you dislike
something
  screw up your face *He screwed up his
  face in distaste.*
  screw your face up *Whenever she
  screwed her face up like that it meant
  she had some kind of confession to make.*

4 *very informal* to make a serious mistake
  screw up *I really screwed up this time,
  didn't I?*

5 *very informal* to spoil an event or
situation, especially by making a big
mistake
  screw up sth *He made a bad decision
  that screwed up his entire life.*
  screw sth up *We suspected she would
  screw things up.* ♦ *This is a really
  important interview. I don't want to
  screw it up.*

6 *informal* to make someone feel so upset
or confused that their whole personality
is affected, often permanently = MESS UP
  screw sb up *Divorce doesn't have to screw
  your children up.* ♦ *Her father's suicide
  screwed her up.*

  **PHRASE screw up the courage/nerve to
  do sth** to prepare mentally for doing
  something difficult or doing something
  that you are nervous about: *I'm trying*

*to screw up enough nerve to ask her
out.*

screw up (sense 3)

■ **¡screwed 'up** adj *informal* **1** feeling
very upset, unhappy, or confused,
especially as a result of a bad
experience: *After his wife left him, he
was completely screwed up for a while.*
2 a plan that is screwed up is spoiled:
*The whole event was screwed up when
the sponsors pulled out.*

SCRIBBLE /ˈskrɪb(ə)l/
scribbles, scribbling, scribbled

¡scribble 'down
to write something quickly and carelessly
  scribble sth down *also* **scribble down sth**
  *I scribbled the numbers down as they
  were read out.* ♦ *I just had time to scribble
  down the address.*

SCROLL /skrəʊl, American skroʊl/
scrolls, scrolling, scrolled

¡scroll 'down
to move information up a computer screen
in order to read it
  scroll down *Can you scroll down a bit
  further?*
  scroll down sth *Scroll down the page
  and see if you can see her name.*

¡scroll 'up
to move information down a computer
screen in order to read it
  scroll up *Use the mouse or the arrow keys
  to scroll up and down.*
  scroll up sth *If you scroll up your screen
  you will see the title of the document.*

SCROUNGE /skraʊndʒ/
scrounges, scrounging, scrounged

¡scrounge a'round *American*
to try to get something you want by asking

people or by looking for it in different places

scrounge around for sth *He's been scrounging around for a new tv set.*

,scrounge 'up *American informal*
to get something with difficulty, usually by asking other people to give it to you
scrounge up sth *also* **scrounge sth up** *We sent someone to Saigon to scrounge up building materials.*

SCRUB /skrʌb/
scrubs, scrubbing, scrubbed

,scrub 'in *American*
if a doctor or nurse scrubs in, they wash their hands and arms thoroughly before doing a medical operation = SCRUB UP
scrub in *Another surgeon offered to scrub in and assist.*

,scrub 'off
to remove something from a surface by washing it hard, especially with a brush
scrub off sth *also* **scrub sth off** *How long will it take to scrub off all that graffiti?* ♦ *She used a brush to scrub the mud off.*
scrub sth off sth *She quickly scrubbed the tears off her cheeks.*

,scrub 'out
to clean the inside of something thoroughly
scrub out sth *also* **scrub sth out** *We finished scrubbing out the inside of all the cupboards.* ♦ *We cleaned the basin and scrubbed the old bath out.*

,scrub 'up *British*
if a doctor or nurse scrubs up, they wash their hands and arms thoroughly before doing a medical operation = SCRUB IN
scrub up *Dr Graham was already scrubbing up at the washbasin in the corner.*
PHRASE **scrub up well** *humorous* if someone scrubs up well, they look attractive when they are clean and wearing nice clothes: *I imagine he scrubs up pretty well.*

SCRUM /skrʌm/
scrums, scrumming, scrummed

,scrum 'down
in rugby, if players scrum down, they join together in a circle and all try to get the ball
scrum down *They scrummed down and France won the ball.*

SCRUNCH /skrʌntʃ/
scrunches, scrunching, scrunched

,scrunch 'up
1 to press or squeeze something into a smaller shape, especially a piece of paper = SCREW UP
scrunch up sth *also* **scrunch sth up** *He scrunched up the letter and stuffed it in his pocket.* ♦ *I saw her scrunch the piece of paper up and throw it in the fire.*
2 *American* if people scrunch up, they move closer to each other, usually in order to make room for more people
scrunch up *It would help if you all scrunched up a little.*

SEAL /si:l, American sil/
seals, sealing, sealed

,seal 'in
to prevent the flavour, smell, or juice of a food from getting out
seal in sth *also* **seal sth in** *The tomatoes are then heated to seal in the juices.* ♦ *Chemicals are added to food such as meat and bread to seal the water in.*

,seal 'off ★ [often passive]
to prevent people from entering an area or a building = CLOSE OFF
be sealed off *The area around the park was sealed off.*
seal off sth *Police sealed off the area so that the investigations could begin.*

,seal 'up [often passive]
to close a container or space by covering it with something so that air or other substances cannot get in or out
be sealed up *The jars were sealed up with wax.*
seal sth up *We sealed up the windows and doors with tape.*

SEARCH /sɜ:tʃ, American sɜrtʃ/
searches, searching, searched

'search for
to try to find something or someone by looking carefully
search for sb/sth *Police are still searching for the missing child.* ♦ *They lifted the floorboards to search for money.*

,search 'out
to work hard in order to find something = SEEK OUT
search out sth *also* **search sth out** *People need to search out the treatments that work best for them.* ♦ *No one offered support. I had to search that out.*

,search 'through

to try to find something or someone by looking amongst a group of things = GO THROUGH

search through sth *'I've got his number somewhere', she said, searching through her address book.* ♦ **+for** *He searched through his pockets for change.*

SECOND /sɪˈkɒnd, *American* sɪˈkɑnd/
seconds, seconding, seconded

,be se'conded to

to be sent somewhere to work there for a short time

be seconded to sth *She's been seconded to the Foreign Office.*

SECTION /ˈsekʃ(ə)n/
sections, sectioning, sectioned

,section 'off [usually passive]

to separate one area from the other areas that surround it

be sectioned off *Part of the balcony had been sectioned off.*

SEE /siː, *American* si/
sees, seeing, saw /sɔː, *American* sɔ/,
seen /siːn, *American* sin/

'see about ★

to deal with or organize something

see about sth *I should go and see about this job.*

see about doing sth *Can you see about getting us a ride home?*

PHRASES we'll (soon) see about that *informal* used for saying that you are not going to let someone do something they are intending to do: *He thinks he's coming on holiday with us, but we'll see about that.*

we'll have to see about that *informal* used for saying that you are not able or willing to decide about something now: *My husband would like a lot of children, but we'll have to see about that.*

,see a'round

1 to notice someone often in places you go to regularly

see sb around *I've never actually met her, but I've seen her around.*

2 *British* to examine a place by walking around it = SEE ROUND

see around sth *What a beautiful house! I'd love to see around it.*

'see as [often passive]

to consider someone or something in a particular way

be seen as sth *This was seen as an attempt to fool the voters.*

see sb/sth as sth *He seems to see me as a threat.*

,see 'in

1 to welcome a visitor to a building and take them to where they want to go = SHOW IN ≠ SEE OUT

see sb in *The ambassador waited on the steps to see the visiting dignitaries in.*

2 to see the inside of a building through a window or open door

see in *People can see in from the street.*

PHRASES see in the New Year to celebrate the beginning of a new year by staying awake until midnight: *We wanted to see in the New Year together.*

not know what sb sees in sb *informal* to not understand why one person finds another person attractive or likes them: *I don't know what you see in him, I think he's boring.*

'see into ★

PHRASES see into sb's mind/soul to be able to tell what someone is thinking or what someone is really like: *I wish I could see into his mind and find out what he thinks of me.*

see into the future to be able to tell what will happen in the future: *If we had known what was going to happen we might have done things differently, but you can't see into the future.*

,see 'off ★★

1 to go somewhere such as a station or airport with someone in order to say goodbye to them ≠ WELCOME

see sb off *Anne saw Terry off at the station.*

2 to make someone go away or leave a place, especially by chasing them

see off sb *My parents soon saw off any boys who were interested in me.*

see sb off *The dog would see most burglars off.* ♦ *If I catch him again I'll see him off.*

3 to deal successfully with someone or something, especially by defeating them easily

see off sb/sth *The England team saw off a tired-looking Poland 3–1.*

see sb/sth off *Will they be able to see this challenge off?* ♦ *We saw them off easily.*

Nouns often used as objects with **see off 3**
■ challenge, competitor, enemy, opposition, rival, threat

see off

,see 'out ★

1 to go with someone to the door when they are leaving in order to say goodbye to them = SHOW OUT ≠ SEE IN

see sb out *My secretary will see you out.*
♦ *Don't bother, I'll see myself out.*

2 to continue to the end of a period of time or an activity

see out sth *He will see out the year remaining on his contract.*

see sth out *She saw the rest of the season out on the substitute's bench.* ♦ *Once you start a performance, you have to see it out even if it isn't going well.*

3 if something sees you out, it lasts longer than the time you live

see sb out *These are good strong shoes and they'll probably see me out.*

PHRASE **see out the Old Year** to celebrate the end of a year by staying up until after midnight: *It was depressing to watch all these people seeing out the old year.*

,see 'over

to walk around a place or building and look at what is there

see over sth *I wonder if they'd let me see over the place.*

,see 'round *British*

to examine a place by walking around it = SEE AROUND

see round sth *Have you ever seen round this place properly?*

,see 'through ★★

1 to recognize that something is not true and not be tricked by it

see through sth *We can all see through your little game, Adam.*

2 to realize what someone is really like or what they are really doing and not be tricked by them

see through sb *I'm not fooled that easily. I can see right through you.*

3 to continue doing something until it is finished, especially something unpleasant or difficult ≠ GIVE UP

see sth through *Having come this far, she was determined to see things through.*
♦ *Having started on a course of action, he usually sees it through.*

4 to make it possible for someone to continue to the end of something, especially something unpleasant or difficult = LAST THROUGH

see sb through sth *They had enough food to see them through the winter.*

■ **'see-through** **adj** made of cloth or plastic that you can see through = TRANSPARENT: *a see-through blouse*

'see to ★★★ [often passive]

to deal with or take charge of someone or something = ATTEND TO

get sth seen to *You'd better take her to hospital and get her ankle seen to.*

see to sth *You try to get some sleep, I'll see to the children's breakfast.* ♦ *I should have seen to it that she was told.*

SEEK /siːk, *American* sik/
seeks, seeking, sought /sɔːt, *American* sɑt/

,seek 'out ★★

to find someone or something by looking for them in a determined way = SEARCH OUT

seek out sth/sb *Corbett resolved to seek out the truth.*

seek sth/sb out *My officers have sought him out.* ♦ *Famous people often seek each other out.*

SEEP /siːp, *American* sip/
seeps, seeping, seeped

,seep a'way

to gradually become less or disappear

seep away *Their supply of food gradually began to seep away.* ♦ *She could tell his strength was seeping away.*

SEGUE /'segweɪ/
segues, seguing, segued

,segue 'into

to change smoothly from one song or subject of conversation to another without stopping

segue into sth *The songs segue into each other with no gaps in between.*

SEIZE /siːz, American siz/
seizes, seizing, seized

'seize on [often passive]
to use something in an enthusiastic way in order to gain an advantage = SEIZE UPON
be seized on *Her comments were seized on as evidence that she is not reliable.*
seize on sth *Companies were quick to seize on the possibilities offered by new technology.*

,seize 'up
to suddenly stop moving or working properly
seize up *Her back seized up painfully after she'd lifted the box.* ♦ *If you don't add oil, the engine will eventually seize up.*

'seize upon [often passive]
to use something in an enthusiastic way in order to gain an advantage = SEIZE ON
be seized upon *Even the most unlikely incident was seized upon as a diversion from the monotony of the work.*
seize upon sth *She seized upon the chance to promote her views on television.*

SELL /sel/
sells, selling, sold /səʊld, American soʊld/

,sell 'off ★★★
to sell something quickly and for a low price, usually because you need money = American CLOSE OUT
sell off sth *The company will have to sell off assets to avoid bankruptcy.*
sell sth off *She's started selling her jewellery off bit by bit.* ♦ *He buys houses, renovates them, then sells them off again.*

■ **'sell-off** noun [C] **1** *British* a situation in which a business or part of a business is sold: *Employees are hoping that the sell-off will not go ahead.*
2 *business American* a situation in which a lot of stocks are sold at the same time, making prices go down: *Share prices in Hong Kong were knocked by Tokyo's late sell-off.*

,sell 'on
to sell something to someone after buying it from someone else
sell sth on *They buy it at a low price and sell it on for a huge profit.*

'sell on [often passive] American informal
to persuade someone to do or have something
sell sb on (doing) sth *I don't think I've*
sold her on spending Christmas with my parents.
be sold on (doing) sth *I'm not completely sold on that idea.*

,sell 'out ★★
1 if a shop sells out of something, it sells all that it has so that there is no more available
sell out *I went to get some bread, but the shop had sold out.* ♦ **+of** *On a hot day, we can sell out of ice cream in an hour.*

2 if goods sell out, all of them have been sold and there are none left = RUN OUT
sell out *The tickets had sold out within a few hours.*

3 *informal* to do something that shows you no longer have the same moral principles you used to have
sell out *As you get older, you are more inclined to sell out.* ♦ **+to** *Some fans thought she'd sold out to mainstream pop music.*

4 **sell out** or **sell up** *American* to deliberately sell all the goods in your business, especially because you are closing the business permanently
sell out *The idea of selling out and retiring was looking more attractive.*

■ **'sell-out** noun [singular] **1** a performance, sports event etc for which all the tickets are sold: *The band's last three tours have been sell-outs.* **2** *informal* a situation in which someone does something that is the opposite of what they had promised or that seems to be against their principles: *Many people saw the prime minister's decision as a sell-out.*

,sell 'up ★ British
to sell your house or business because you want to live somewhere else or do something else
sell up *We're selling up and moving to the Western Isles.*

SEND /send/
sends, sending, sent /sent/

Send is often used with adverbs and prepositions when it means 'to arrange for something to be delivered to someone': *She sent a letter to the manager.* ♦ *It could take hours to send a message across town.* ♦ *We'll send your bags up to your room later.* These uses are not included here.

,send a'way [often passive]
to order someone to leave a place = TURN AWAY

be sent away *His lawyer was sent away by the security guards.*
send sb away *We knocked on the door but they sent us away.*

,send a'way for

to write to a person or organization asking them to send something to you = SEND OFF FOR
send away for sth *I've sent away for details of their cruises.*

,send 'back ★ [often passive]

to return something that is not satisfactory = RETURN
be sent back *Any faulty or broken items can be sent back.*
send sth back *If you're not happy with it, you can always send it back.*
send back sth *We will send back your proof of address within 14 days.*

,send 'down [usually passive] British

1 *informal* to send someone to prison = PUT AWAY ≠ RELEASE
be sent down *He's been sent down for five years for forgery.*

2 *old-fashioned* to order someone to leave a university because they have behaved badly
be sent down *She could have been thrown off the course, or even sent down.*

'send for ★★★

1 to ask for someone to come to you = SUMMON
send for sb *I think we should send for a doctor.* ♦ *Wait here until they send for you.*

2 to arrange for something to come to you or be delivered to you = REQUEST
send for sth *In the end we had to send for an ambulance.* ♦ *I've sent for a copy of their catalogue.*

,send 'in ★★★

1 [often passive] to arrange for people or equipment to go to a place
be sent in *Government forces were sent in to fight the rebellion.*
send in sb *In these cases, we usually send in a team of experts.*
send sb in *They don't want to send troops in just yet.* ♦ *The tanks are in position. We must send them in.*

2 to send a letter or document to an organization
send sth in *Send your entry forms in by December 21.* ♦ *If you know the answer to the question, send it in.* ♦ **+to** *Keep sending your letters and suggestions in to us.*
send in sth *And you can send in a picture of your pet.*

,send 'off ★★★

1 [often passive] to post something to someone = POST, MAIL; *formal* DISPATCH
send sth off *I want to send this application off today.* ♦ *I've written the letter but I haven't sent if off yet.*
send off sth *They probably haven't even sent off your order yet.*

2 to arrange for someone to go somewhere = *formal* DISPATCH
send sb off *They sent us off with a bottle of water and an apple.* ♦ **+to** *We've sent the children off to the zoo for the afternoon.*

3 [often passive] *British* to tell a sports player officially to leave the sports field because they have done something that is not allowed by the rules
be sent off *He was sent off for arguing with the referee.*
send sb off *I'd send him off for a tackle like that.*

send off (sense 3)

■ **sendoff** /'sendɒf/ **noun** [C] *informal* a party or celebration to say goodbye to someone who is leaving a place: *We wanted to give her a good sendoff from work.*

,send 'off for

to write to a person or organization asking them to send something to you = SEND AWAY FOR
send off for sth *I've sent off for details about the offer.*

,send 'out ★★★

1 to send a lot of copies of the same document to a large number of people = MAIL OUT
send out sth *We sent out 300 invitations to our gallery opening.*
send sth out *I haven't had time to send the thank-you cards out.* ♦ *We're preparing the information packs now and will be sending them out soon.*

2 to send something such as light, signals, or smoke into the atmosphere = EMIT

send out sth *The factory sends out toxic gases into the surrounding countryside.*
send sth out *The captain sent a distress call out after his vessel hit an unidentified object.*

3 to send someone to a place for a particular purpose

send out sb *During the drought the government sent out teams to distribute bottled water.*
send sb out *Police sent a search party out to look for the missing climbers.*

,send 'out for *informal*

to order something and ask for it to be delivered to you

send out for sth *I don't feel like cooking – let's send out for a pizza.*

,send 'up ★ *informal*

1 to make someone seem silly by pretending to speak or behave like them = LAMPOON

send sb up *He sends the prime minister up brilliantly.* ♦ *It's nice to see politicians sending themselves up occasionally.*

2 [usually passive] *American* to send someone to prison

be sent up *He was sent up for 10 years.*

■ **'send-up** noun [C] *informal* a way of talking or behaving in which you copy the way that someone else talks or behaves in a humorous way: *a hilarious send-up of the American president*

SEPARATE /'sepəreɪt/
separates, separating, separated

,separate 'out

1 to divide something into different parts or groups = SPLIT UP

separate out sth *also* **separate sth out** *The material is processed to separate out the impurities.* ♦ *I separated the letters out into two piles.* ♦ **+from** *Residents are being asked to separate out ordinary waste from recyclable materials.*

2 to become divided into different parts or groups

separate out *The silicon makes the aluminium separate out harmlessly.*

,separate 'out from (*also* ,separate 'from)

to be the quality or detail that makes someone or something different from other people or things

separate sb/sth out from sb/sth *also* **separate out sb/sth from sb/sth** *What separates him out from other world leaders?* ♦ *It is our ability to think that*

separates us from other creatures sharing our planet . ♦ *Two factors separate out the German middle class from its counterparts in other countries.*

SERVE /sɜːv, *American* sɜrv/
serves, serving, served

'serve as ★★★

to be used for a particular purpose = ACT AS

serve as sth *The directors decided that the building would serve as their headquarters.*

'serve on *same as* serve with

,serve 'out

1 to continue doing something until you are officially allowed to stop doing it

serve out sth *also* **serve sth out** *We want you to serve out your full contract.* ♦ *He has repeatedly said that he will serve out his term as president.*

2 *British same as* serve up 2

,serve 'up ★★

1 *informal* to provide something

serve up sth *The teams served up some highly entertaining football this afternoon.*

2 **serve up** or **serve out** to put food onto a plate for someone = SERVE

serve up sth *Aunt Edie served up a lovely roast leg of lamb for dinner.*
serve sth up *I'll help you serve the food up.*

'serve with (*also* 'serve on) [often passive]

to officially give someone a legal document that orders them to do something

be served with sth *She was served with a summons to appear in court.*
serve sb with sth *Lawyers immediately served him with a writ.*

SET /set/
sets, setting, set

Set is often used with adverbs and prepositions when it means 'to put someone or something in a particular position': *She knocked, entered, and set the tray down beside the bed.* ♦ *He set the baby on the floor to play.* ♦ *The house was set back a short distance from the main road.* These uses are not included here.

'set about ★★★

1 to begin doing something, especially in a determined or enthusiastic way = BEGIN

set about sth *She set about the problem with her usual energy.* ♦ *I had set about the daunting task of reading the complete*

works of Shakespeare that summer.
set about doing sth *He set about resolving the problem of finding somewhere to live.*

2 *old-fashioned* to hit or kick someone many times = ATTACK, LAY INTO
set about sb *Three boys set about Ben and beat him up.* ♦ **+with** *A couple of teenage boys set about him with baseball bats.*

,set a'gainst ★★

1 [often passive] to compare one thing with another or to consider it in relation to something else = OFFSET AGAINST, SET OFF AGAINST
be set against sth *The advantages of the new system must be set against its disadvantages.*
set sth against sth *To call it a remarkable sight is to set it against today's standards.*

2 to cause two people or groups to fight each other although they were in a friendly relationship before = PIT AGAINST
set sb against sb *It was a bitter industrial dispute that had set worker against worker.*

3 [often passive] *British* to state officially that an amount of money is a cost to your business in order to pay less tax = SET OFF AGAINST, WRITE OFF AGAINST
be set against sth *Your expenses can be set against tax.*
set sth against sth *The system allowed people to set 100 percent of a restaurant bill against tax as a business expense.*

,set a'part

1 to be the aspect or quality that makes someone or something different and special = DISTINGUISH
set sb/sth apart *The standard of skill in his players have always set his teams apart.* ♦ **+from** *Graf's natural athleticism set her apart from other tennis players.*

2 [often passive] to keep something separate in order to use it for a particular purpose
be set apart *A whole floor of deluxe rooms had been specially set apart.*
♦ **+for** *Several acres of public land have been set apart for recreation.*

,set a'side ★★★

1 to keep or save something from a larger amount or supply in order to use it later for a particular purpose = RESERVE
set aside sth *I set aside a third of my salary every month.* ♦ **+for** *Have you set aside some money for your child's education?* ♦ *Set aside some of the fruit for decorating the cake.*

set sth aside *Set some time aside every day when you can be alone.* ♦ **+for** *It is important to set a room aside for studying.*

2 to not let a particular feeling, opinion, or belief influence you, in order to achieve something more important = PUT ASIDE
set aside sth *They agreed to set aside their differences and work together for peace.*
set sth aside *Try to set negative thoughts aside.*

3 to officially state that a particular legal decision will no longer be followed = OVERTURN
set aside sth *The Supreme Court has set aside the lower court's ruling.*
set sth aside *In the end, the judge set this earlier conviction aside.*

■ **'set-a,side** **noun** [U] *British* **1** a system in which the European Union pays farmers not to grow crops in particular areas, in order to control prices or the amount of crops grown: *There are complaints about the unfairness and madness of set-aside.* **2** land not used for crops according to this system: *Over half the farm is set-aside.*

,set 'back ★★

1 to delay the progress of someone or something = *British* KNOCK BACK
set sb/sth back *The injury set me back a lot.*
set sth back sth *The spending cuts have set the research project back several years.*

2 *informal* to cost someone a particular amount of money, especially a large amount
set sb back sth *Dry-cleaning will set you back around £20.*

■ **setback** /'setbæk/ **noun** [C] a problem that delays or stops progress or makes a situation worse: *Falling share prices may be another **setback** for the troubled economy.*

,set 'down ★★★

1 to write something on a piece of paper so that it will not be forgotten and can be looked at later = PUT DOWN
set sth down *She set all these events down in her diary.*
set down sth *Why don't you set down your thoughts on paper.*

2 [often passive] *formal* to state officially how something should be done = LAY DOWN
be set down *These conditions were set down by the United Nations.* ♦ *The rules are set down by the sports governing body.*

set down sth *Who sets down the guidelines for development?*

3 *British formal* to stop a vehicle so that a passenger can get out = PUT DOWN

set sb down *I'll set you down at the West Gate.*

set down sth *The buses set down their passengers at the entrance to the theme park.*

,set 'down as

to consider something in a particular way

set sth down as sth *He set the whole experience down as a failure.*

,set 'forth

1 *literary* to start a journey, especially one that is long or difficult = SET OFF, SET OUT, START OUT, LEAVE

set forth *We set forth shortly after breakfast.* ♦ **+on** *Once these preparations had been made, they set forth on their voyage.*

2 *formal* to explain or describe something in a clear and detailed way, especially in writing = SET OUT, PUT FORWARD

set forth sth *This memorandum sets forth basic departmental policies.*

,set 'in

if something unpleasant sets in, it starts to happen and have an effect, and is not likely to stop for a long time = COME TO STAY

set in *Let's get inside – the rain's set in for the day.* ♦ *Shortly after the business started, a long economic downturn set in.*

,set 'off ★★★

1	begin a journey
2	make sth start working
3	make sth explode
4	make sth happen accidentally
5	make sb/sth look attractive
6	make sb laugh/cry/talk a lot
+	**offset** adv, noun, verb

1 to start a journey or start going somewhere = LEAVE, SET OUT, START OUT; *literary* SET FORTH

set off *We set off early the next morning.* ♦ **+for** *We packed our bags and set off for the coast.* ♦ **+on** *We were just setting off on our holiday when we realized we'd forgotten the tent.*

2 to make something start operating, especially by accident

set off sth *Jeff pushed open the front door, which set off the burglar alarm.* ♦ *They were fighting and accidentally set off a fire extinguisher.*

set sth off *That noise is the fire alarm. I bet someone has set it off by accident.*

3 to make something explode = DETONATE, EXPLODE, LET OFF

set off sth *Terrorists breached tight security to set off a bomb.*

set sth off *Some kids were setting fireworks off in the street.*

4 to cause a situation or a series of events to happen, especially without intending to = UNLEASH

set off sth *He fears that the election could set off mass protests.*

set sth off *Are there any clues as to what set this violence off?* ♦ *We wanted to avoid a confrontation, but a careless comment could easily have set one off.*

5 [usually passive] to make someone or something look more attractive by being clearly different from them

set sth off *The stained glass sets the windows off beautifully.*

set off sth *A feather-trimmed hat set off her plain blue dress.*

6 to make someone start to laugh, cry, or talk a lot

set sb off *Just mentioning her father's death could set her off again.*

■ **offset** /ˈɒfset/ **adv** not straight, or not in a straight line: *The row of seats was slightly offset to the left.*

■ **offset** /ˈɒfset/ **noun** **1** [U] a method of printing in which ink is put onto paper from another surface **2** [C] something that balances the effect of something else, so that there is no advantage or disadvantage: *tax offsets*

■ **offset** /ɒfˈset/ **verb** [often passive] to balance the effect of something, with the result that there is no advantage or disadvantage: *Falling sales in Thailand were offset by strong performances in other markets.*

set off (sense 3)

ˌset ˈoff aˌgainst

1 *British* to state officially that an amount of money is a cost to your business in order to pay less tax = SET AGAINST, WRITE OFF AGAINST

> **set sth off against sth** *You can set claims for expenses off against taxes.*

2 to compare one thing with another or to consider one thing in relation to another = OFFSET AGAINST, SET AGAINST

> **set sth off against sth** *You need to set the quality of the facilities off against the cost of using them.*

ˈset on

1 *British* to tell a person or animal to attack another person or animal

> **set sb/sth on sb/sth** *Leave now or I'll set the dogs on you.*

2 *same as* **set upon**

ˌset ˈout ★★★

1 to start a journey = LEAVE, SET OFF, START OUT; *literary* SET FORTH

> **set out** *After a three-day rest, the travellers set out again.* ♦ **+on** *The soldiers set out on their march to the capital.*

2 to explain, describe, or arrange something in a clear and detailed way, especially in writing = DISPLAY, PUT FORWARD, SET FORTH

> **set out sth** *In his report he sets out his plans for the department.*
> **set sth out** *You'll find I've set everything out in my memo.*

Nouns often used as objects with **set out 2**

■ agenda, aims, conditions, criteria, objectives, options, plans, principles, proposals, policy, reasons, strategy, terms

3 to put something where it can be seen or used = LAY OUT

> **set out sth** *Traders set out their goods on long tables.*
> **set sth out** *She set her clothes out neatly on the bed.*

4 to start doing or working on something in order to achieve a goal

> **+on** *When we set out on this project, we knew it would be difficult.* ♦ **+to do sth** *Are you suggesting that he deliberately set out to sabotage your work?*

ˌset ˈto *old-fashioned*

to start doing something in a determined or enthusiastic way

> **set to** *After the party we all set to and cleared everything up.*

■ **ˈset-to** noun [C] *informal* a quick argument or fight: *He had a set-to with a sheepdog.*

ˌset ˈup ★★★

1	start a business etc
2	organize or plan sth
3	build sth
4	make equipment ready to use
5	make sth happen
6	make sb feel good
7	make people blame sb wrongly
8	give sb money for a business/house
9	help people start a relationship
10	make a noise
+	PHRASES
+	**set-up** noun; **upset** adj, noun, verb

1 to start something such as a business, organization, or institution = ESTABLISH

> **set up sth** *The group plans to set up an import business.* ♦ *Rebels have set up an independent state within the country.*
> **set sth up** *It was decided to set a joint commission up to expand economic cooperation between the two nations.*

2 to organize or plan something such as an event or system = ORGANIZE

> **set up sth** *Ask your secretary to set up a meeting for Thursday.* ♦ *There are plans to set up a regional library system.*
> **set sth up** *How do you go about setting the assignments up?*

3 to build a structure or put it in a particular place = ERECT

> **set up sth** *Police have set up an emergency medical unit outside the building.*
> **set sth up** *We need to set roadblocks up at all these points.*

4 to put equipment together or arrange it so that it is ready for use

> **set up** *They played some music while the band were setting up.*
> **set sth up** *It's difficult for one person to set a tent up on their own.* ♦ *He set his camera up in the middle of the lounge.*
> **set up sth** *The kids are setting up the volleyball net.* ♦ *Will you be able to set up my PC?*

5 to make something start to happen = CAUSE, INITIATE

> **set up sth** *Their negligence set up a chain reaction that resulted in extensive damage.*
> **set sth up** *It was a very unfortunate sequence of events and the agency was to blame for setting it up.*

6 *British* to make someone feel good, healthy, or lively

> **set sb up** *I think a relaxing holiday would set you up nicely.* ♦ **+for** *Eat something hot to set you up for the journey.*

7 *informal* to arrange a situation so that

someone is blamed for doing something, especially something illegal = *British* FIT UP, FRAME

> **set sb up** *She claims she's innocent and someone set her up.*

8 to make it possible for someone to start a business or have a home, especially by paying for it = ESTABLISH

> **set sb up** *She wanted to start her own business, so she got her parents to set her up.* ♦ **+in** *Sam was a privileged kid whose father set him up in business.* ♦ *Her parents set her up in her own flat when she left college.* ♦ **+as** *He decided to set himself up as a nutritionalist.*

9 to arrange for two people you know to go out together because you think they might be attracted to each other

> **set sb up** *You're a friend of Joe's, aren't you? Any chance of setting me up?* ♦ **+with** *I think we should set Ryan up with my cousin.*

10 to start to make a lot of noise

> **set up sth** *The kids set up a terrible racket with their music.*

> PHRASES **set up camp 1** if a group of people set up camp somewhere, they put up their tents there and stay there for a while: *They found a dry spot and set up camp for the night.* **2** to put your possessions or equipment in a particular place so you can live, work, or spend a lot of time there: *She set up camp in the kitchen while they painted the bedroom.*

> **set sb up for life** to provide someone with enough money so that they do not have to work for the rest of their life: *A lump sum of £400,000 can set you up for life.*

> **set up house/home** to begin living in a particular place or with a particular person: *After graduation, we decided to set up house together.*

> **set up shop** to start a business: *His father set up shop as a photographer in 1900.*

■ **'set-up** noun [C] **1** the way a particular group of people or things is organized: *The club's present set-up is inefficient and costly.* **2** an organization: *It's quite an efficient set-up they're running.* **3** *informal* a situation in which someone cheats or tricks you, especially by making you appear guilty when you are not: *She appeared to be the victim of a set-up.*

■ **upset** /ʌpˈset/ adj **1** very sad, worried, or angry about something: *They felt too upset to talk about the incident.* **2** if your stomach is upset, you have an illness that is affecting your stomach, usually caused by something

that you have eaten or drunk: *Phone and tell them you've got an upset stomach.*

■ **upset** /ˈʌpset/ noun **1** [C] an occasion when someone defeats an opponent who is considered to be better than them: *It was one of the biggest upsets of the tournament.* **2** [C] an illness that affects your stomach, usually caused by something that you have eaten or drunk: *a stomach upset* **3** [C/U] a feeling of sadness, worry or anger: *He regretted the upset that the conversation had caused.*

■ **upset** /ʌpˈset/ verb **1** to make someone feel sad, worried, or angry: *I'm sorry, I didn't mean to upset you.* ♦ *People were upset by Hansen's rude remarks.* **2** to spoil something such as a plan: *I'm sorry if I've upset your plans for this evening.* **3** to make something stop working in the normal way: *A new policy on taxation would upset the political balance of the country.* **4** to knock something over accidentally = SPILL: *She leaned forward and upset a glass of water all over the table.* **5** to defeat an opponent who is considered to be better than you: *Sweden came close to upsetting Brazil during their match in Stockholm.*

ˌset 'up as
to put someone in a position of power

> **set sb up as sth** *There was a plan to set him up as party leader.*

> PHRASE **set yourself up as sth** to claim to be something you are not: *He sets himself up as some kind of a financial expert.*

'set upon (*also* **'set on**) [often passive]
to attack someone or something

> **be set upon** *He was set upon by a group of youths.*

> **set upon sb/sth** *A gang set upon him as he played in the park.*

SETTLE /ˈset(ə)l/
settles, settling, settled

ˌsettle 'back ★

1 to lean back in a chair or bed, especially when you are preparing to enjoy something

> **settle back** *She leaned forward from her chair then settled back again.* ♦ **+in/into** *He settled back in his chair with his feet on the table.* ♦ **+to do sth** *We settled back to watch the late night movie.*

2 to become used to a situation that you have been away from for a while

settle back *Children usually settle back quite quickly after the long school holiday.* ♦ **+into** *The sooner you settle back into your old routine the better.*

,settle 'down ★★★

1 to become calm after being upset, nervous or excited = QUIETEN DOWN
settle down *Settle down children, it's time to go to sleep.* ♦ *It was hard to settle down and work after the excitement of the morning.*

2 to make someone calm after they have been upset, nervous, or excited = QUIETEN DOWN
settle sb down *She fed the baby and settled him down.*
settle down sb *The teacher settled down her class after playtime.*

3 to begin to live a quieter life by getting married or staying permanently in a place
settle down *Are you ever going to settle down and get married?*

4 to make yourself comfortable in a place, especially in order to do something that will take a lot of time or effort
settle down *I settled down in front of the television for the evening.* ♦ **+to do sth** *She took a seat and settled down to wait.*
settle yourself down *He settled himself down at the table and said, 'Now, let's have a chat'.*

'settle for ★★★

to accept someone or something that is not exactly what you wanted because you cannot have what you wanted = AGREE TO
settle for sb/sth *Injuries and illness forced the team to settle for third place.* ♦ *Why* **settle for second best** *when you can have something better?*

,settle 'in ★ (also ,settle 'into)

1 to become familiar with a new way of life, place, or job, or to make someone do this = SHAKE DOWN
settle in *She seems to have settled in quickly at her new school.*
settle into sth *He soon settled into the routine of college life.* ♦ *How are you settling into your new home?*
settle sb in *His new colleagues did their best to settle him in quickly.*
settle sb into sth *After settling the children into their hotel, the team took them out to the cinema.*

2 to make yourself comfortable in a place because you are going to stay there for a long time
settle in *This will be your room. I'll leave you to settle in.* ♦ **+for** *We found our seats and settled in for the journey.*

settle into sth *We settled into our tent.*

'settle on ★

1 to make a decision between two or more people or things after not being certain which to choose = DECIDE ON ≠ REJECT
settle on sb/sth *The band has still not settled on a name.* ♦ **+to do sth** *Stone settled on Val Kilmer to take on the lead role in the film.*

2 *British formal* to arrange to give someone money or property in a legal and official way
settle sth on sb *If you were planning to give some money to your grandchildren, now would be a good time to settle it on them.*

3 if your eyes settle on someone or something, you begin to look at them
settle on sb/sth *'Is there anything else you want to tell me?', he said, his eyes settling on my pregnant belly.*

'settle to *British*

to start doing something or thinking about something with all your attention
settle to sth *I can't seem to settle to anything today.* ♦ *She settled to the task of finding a school for her young son.*

,settle 'up

1 to pay all of an amount of money that you owe to a particular person or company
settle up *He went to the hotel reception to settle up and check out.* ♦ **+with** *Let's settle up with the waiter and get out of here.*

2 to agree how much each person or group should pay = SQUARE UP
settle up *I'll pay – we can settle up later.*

SEW /səʊ, *American* soʊ/
sews, sewing, sewed, sewn /səʊn, *American* soʊn/

,sew 'up

1 to repair something such as a hole in a piece of cloth by sewing it = STITCH UP
sew sth up *also* **sew up sth** *She was sewing the holes in her socks up.* ♦ *They had to sew up all the tears in the boat's sails.*

2 [usually passive] *informal* to achieve something by dealing successfully with it, or by making certain you are going to win
get/have sth sewn up *We've got the deal sewn up now.* ♦ *They seem to have the contest all sewn up.*

SEX /seks/

,sex 'up *informal*
to change something in order to make it
seem more interesting, exciting or
important
> **sex up sth** *also* **sex sth up** *They brought
> in an advertising agency to try to sex up
> the city's image.* ♦ *She was accused of
> sexing the report up in order to justify
> the President's decision.*

SHACK /ʃæk/
shacks, shacking, shacked

,shack 'up *informal*
1 to live or stay in a place for a short time
> **shack up** *You can shack up here for a
> while if you like.* ♦ **+with** *He shacked up
> with my sister while he was looking for
> his own place.*

2 [often passive] *showing disapproval* to start
living with another person as sexual
partners without being married
> **be shacked up** *They've been shacked up
> together for six months now.*
> **shack up** *Didn't you know – John and
> Kate have shacked up together!* ♦ **+ with**
> *She's shacked up with her boyfriend and
> they're sharing a flat.*

SHADE /ʃeɪd/
shades, shading, shaded

,shade 'in
to make an area of a picture or drawing
darker than the other areas
> **shade in sth** *also* **shade sth in** *I'd like you
> to shade in all the triangles.* ♦ *He drew
> the shadow then shaded it in.*

'shade into
if one thing shades into another thing, it
is difficult to know where one ends and
the other begins, or when something stops
being one thing and becomes the other
> **shade into sth** *After a while, each year
> began to shade into the next.* ♦ *Sometimes,
> self-consciousness can shade into actual
> fear.*

SHAG /ʃæg/
shags, shagging, shagged

be ,shagged 'out *British informal*
to be extremely tired

SHAKE /ʃeɪk/
shakes, shaking, shook /ʃʊk/**, shaken**
/'ʃeɪkən/

,shake 'down
1 *informal* if something shakes down, it
becomes more organized or effective after
people have got used to it
> **shake down** *Let's wait and see how
> everything shakes down.*

2 *British informal* to become familiar with a
new job or place to live = SETTLE IN
> **shake down** *The coach asked the fans to
> be patient until the team shook down.*
> ♦ *He seemed to shake down quite quickly
> at his new school.*

3 *mainly American informal* to get money
from someone by threatening them
> **shake down sb** *Police are watching for
> gangs who shake down unsuspecting
> tourists.* ♦ **+for** *He had been shaking
> down younger children for their dinner
> money.*

4 *American informal* to search a person or a
place very carefully
> **shake down sb/sth** *also* **shake sb/sth
> down** *The police would shake down
> anyone they thought was acting
> suspiciously.* ♦ *He managed to shake the
> place down without interruption.*

■ **shakedown** /'ʃeɪkdaʊn/ **noun** [C]
informal **1** *British* a place used as a
temporary bed: *Can you give me a
shakedown, Watson?* **2** a test of
something new, for example a new
system, vehicle, or machine: *The
accident happened during a shakedown
race last season.* **3** *mainly American* a
situation in which someone uses threats
to force someone else to give them
money: *He was operating some form of
local shakedown.* **4** *American* a situation
in which someone searches a place
thoroughly: *They carried out an
organized shakedown of fast-food places.*

,shake 'off ★★
1 to get rid of something bad such as a
problem, illness, or fear = THROW OFF
> **shake off sth** *I haven't been able to shake
> off this cold for weeks.*
> **shake sth off** *They called him boring
> and it took many years for him to shake
> that label off.*

2 to escape from someone who is
following or chasing you = THROW OFF;
formal ELUDE
> **shake off sb** *I tried to shake off whoever
> was following me.*
> **shake sb off** *However fast I ran, I just
> couldn't shake him off.*

,shake 'out

1 to shake a cloth, sheet, piece of clothing etc so that dust and dirt fall off
shake sth out also **shake out sth** *He shook his sandy socks out and put them in his bag.* ♦ *Shake out the rug before you fold it up.*

2 to remove dust or dirt from a cloth, sheet, piece of clothing etc by shaking it
shake sth out *He removed the tablecloth and shook all the bits out.* ♦ **+of** *The housekeeper should have shaken the dust out of the rug.*

■ **'shake-out** noun [C] *informal* a major change in an industry that causes some companies to close or a lot of people to lose their jobs: *We were cast aside in the national shake-out.*

,shake 'up ★

1 to upset or frighten someone by shocking or surprising them
shake sb up *The accident really shook her up.*
shake up sb *A series of robberies has shaken up residents of the neighbourhood.*

2 to make changes in the way a company is organized so that it is more effective or successful = TRANSFORM
shake up sth *A new manager was brought in to shake up the company.*
shake sth up *I hired you because I thought you might shake the place up a bit.*

■ **'shake-up** noun [C] an important change in the way something such as a department or company is organized: *We need a radical shake-up of the whole system.*

SHAME /ʃeɪm/
shames, shaming, shamed

'shame into

to make someone feel so guilty or embarrassed that they do what you want
shame sb into (doing) sth *She was trying to shame me into visiting my grandmother.* ♦ *News reports of starving children had shamed her into action.*

SHAPE /ʃeɪp/
shapes, shaping, shaped

'shape into

to form something into a particular shape
shape sth into sth *First, shape the clay into a round ball.*

,shape 'up

1 to develop
shape up *Investors are waiting to see how the market shapes up before they make a decision.* ♦ **+as** *Education is shaping up as the hottest issue on the agenda.*

2 to improve your behaviour or your work
shape up *The new boss has warned Roger to shape up.*

3 to make yourself slim or physically fit
shape up *These exercises will help you to shape up for the holidays!*

SHARE /ʃeə, American ʃer/
shares, sharing, shared

,share 'out ★★

to divide something among several people or groups = *formal* APPORTION, DISTRIBUTE
share out sth *We shared out the money so we each had enough to buy a meal.*
share sth out *We bought a pizza and shared it out.* ♦ **+between/among** *They share the work out between them.*

■ **'share-out** noun [C] *British* an act of dividing something between people: *Some members are opposed to the idea of a share-out.*

SHARPEN /'ʃɑːpən, American 'ʃɑrpən/
sharpens, sharpening, sharpened

,sharpen 'up

to improve or make something improve
sharpen up *You need to sharpen up or you'll get sacked.*
sharpen sth up also **sharpen up sth** *Students will be helped to sharpen up their reading skills.*

SHAVE /ʃeɪv/
shaving, shaved, shaved or **shaven**

,shave 'off

1 to cut hair from part of your body using a razor or a shaver
shave off sth also **shave sth off** *You've shaved off your beard.* ♦ *Do you think I should shave my moustache off?*

2 to cut thin pieces from the surface of something
shave off sth also **shave sth off** *She shaved off some slices of Parmesan cheese for the salad.*

3 to reduce something such as a time or a price by a very small amount
shave sth off sth *He managed to shave nearly a second off the world record.*

SHEAR /ʃɪə, American ʃɪr/
shears, shearing, sheared, shorn
/ʃɔːn, American ʃɔrn/ or **sheared**

,shear 'off
if part of something shears off, or if you shear it off, it is suddenly removed by being broken or cut
   shear off *The aircraft's wings sheared off as it crashed between the skyscrapers.*
   shear off sth *also* **shear sth off** *His plane sheared off the tops of the trees.* ◆ *He sheared his finger off in a bacon slicer.*

SHEER /ʃɪə, American ʃɪr/
sheers, sheering, sheered

,sheer 'off (*also* ,sheer a'way)
to change direction very suddenly
   sheer off *The car sheered off to the left.* ◆ *The railway line sheered away into the distance.*

SHELL /ʃel/
shells, shelling, shelled

,shell 'out ★ *informal*
to spend a lot of money on something
= PAY
   shell out sth *How did you get them to shell out all that money?* ◆ **+on** *Students shell out hundreds of pounds on books for college.* ◆ **+for** *I shelled out £30 for a ticket to a show that was terrible.*
   shell out for sth *I'm not shelling out for another hotel room.*

SHIELD /ʃiːld, American ʃild/
shields, shielding, shielded

'shield from ★
1 to protect something, usually from being hit, touched, or seen
   shield sth from sth *He tried to shield his eyes from the sun.* ◆ *A huge wall shields the young plants from the light.*
2 to protect someone from something unpleasant
   shield sb from sth *He wanted to shield his family from involvement in his disgrace.*

SHIN /ʃɪn/
shins, shinning, shinned

'shin up *British informal*
to climb up a tree, rope etc quickly, using your hands and legs = *American* SHINNY UP
   shin up sth *I watched him shin up the old lime tree.*

SHINE /ʃaɪn/
shines, shining, shone /ʃɒn, American ʃoun/

,shine 'through
if a good feeling or quality shines through, it is very noticeable
   shine through *Perlman's musical talents shone through at an early age.*

SHINNY /'ʃɪni/
shinnies, shinnying, shinnied

'shinny up *American informal*
to climb up a tree, rope, etc quickly, using your hands and legs = *British* SHIN UP
   shinny up sth *He shinnied up the ladder into the hayloft.*

SHIP /ʃɪp/
ships, shipping, shipped

,ship 'in [often passive]
1 to bring goods into a place, especially by ship
   be shipped in *Some materials had to be shipped in from England.*
   ship in sth *also* **ship sth in** *We ship most of our supplies in from the mainland.*
2 to bring people to a place for a particular purpose, usually in large numbers
   ship in sb *also* **ship sb in** *It is the time when the major political parties ship in their famous supporters.*

,ship 'off [often passive] *informal*
to send someone somewhere, usually when they do not want to go
   be shipped off *I was expelled from boarding school and shipped off home the same day.* ◆ **+to** *We were shipped off to our grandparents' for the summer.*
   ship sb off *When war broke out he shipped his children off abroad immediately.* ◆ **+to do sth** *She shipped her daughter off to live with her father in New York.*

,ship 'out
1 [often passive] to move goods or people away from a place
   be shipped out *Thousands of tons of steel were shipped out from the docks.*
   ship sb/sth out *also* **ship out sb/sth** *We order everything in England then ship it out.* ◆ *Long Island ships out nearly all its household refuse.*
2 to leave a place
   ship out *The situation looked bad and tourists were shipping out.*

SHIT /ʃɪt/
shits, shitting, shit or shat /ʃæt/

'shit on *impolite*
to treat someone in an extremely unfair way

SHOOT /ʃuːt, *American* ʃʊt/
shoots, shooting, shot /ʃɒt, *American* ʃɑt/

'shoot at
to aim something at a target, suddenly or with a lot of force

shoot sth at sb/sth *He shot the ball at the back of the net.* ♦ *If you shoot enough bullets at a target, one of them will hit it.* ♦ *He **shot a glance at** (=looked quickly at) Molly to see what her reaction was.*

shoot 'down ★★
1 to shoot an enemy aircraft out of the sky

shoot down sth *US pilots shot down a fighter jet.*
shoot sth down *If they find an aircraft in the no-fly zone, they will shoot it down.*

2 to kill someone with a gun
shoot sb down *He took out his gun and one by one he shot them down.*

3 to refuse even to consider something such as an idea or a plan = REJECT
shoot sth down *Whatever proposition was put forward, he shot it down on principle.* ♦ *Each proposal was **shot down in flames**.*

'shoot for *mainly American informal*
to try to achieve a particular thing
shoot for sth *We're shooting for a December deadline, if all goes as planned.*

shoot 'off *informal*
to leave a place quickly or suddenly = DASH OFF

shoot off *He had to shoot off quickly after the meeting.*

  PHRASE **shoot your mouth off** *informal*
to annoy people by talking too much, especially in a proud way about your achievements or possessions: *He's always shooting his mouth off about how good he is at football.*

shoot 'out
to quickly and suddenly move forward your arm or something that you are holding

shoot out sth *also* **shoot sth out** *He shot out a hand and grabbed her arm.* ♦ *She shot her arm out and tried to grab the letter from him.*

shoot 'through *informal*
to leave a place, especially to avoid something that you have to do
shoot through *You can't shoot through every time things aren't going well for you.*

be shot 'through with
to contain a lot of something
be shot through with sth *His argument is shot through with inconsistency.* ♦ *At that time, the industry was shot through with inefficiency.*

shoot 'up ★★

1	increase quickly
2	damage sth with guns
3	about illegal drugs
4	appear
5	become taller

1 to increase quickly by a large amount = SOAR ≠ PLUMMET
shoot up *Oil prices have shot up in the last six months.* ♦ *+by Since 1950 pesticide use has shot up by 170%.*

2 *mainly American* to damage or destroy something by shooting bullets into it
shoot up sth/sb *They shot up his car as a warning.*
shoot sth/sb up *If anyone gets in their way, the villains shoot them up with no questions asked.*

3 *informal* to put an illegal drug into your body with a needle
shoot up *Drug addicts had been shooting up in the shop doorway.*
shoot up sth *He couldn't bear the thought of his daughter shooting up drugs.*

4 to appear suddenly
shoot up *There were fast-food restaurants shooting up all over town.*

5 to grow taller very quickly
shoot up *She's shot up since the last time we saw her.*

SHOP /ʃɒp, *American* ʃɑp/
shops, shopping, shopped

shop a'round ★★
1 to go to several shops before you decide what particular thing to buy
shop around *When buying a new car, it's important to shop around.* ♦ *+for I'm shopping around for a new winter coat.*

2 to consider several possibilities before making a choice about something you want
shop around *If your boyfriend lets you down, shop around and get another one.*

♦ **+for** *I'm shopping around for a new babysitter.*

SHORE /ʃɔː, *American* ʃɔr/
shores, shoring, shored

,shore 'up

1 to give support or help to something that is having problems or is likely to fail = PROP UP

shore up sth *also* **shore sth up** *He called for action to shore up the ailing university.* ♦ *She shored her loan application up with a guarantee from her father.*

2 to support something such as a wall in order to prevent it from falling = PROP UP

shore up sth *also* **shore sth up** *If something isn't done to shore up those cliffs, they will fall into the sea.* ♦ *We need something to shore the roof up.*

SHOUT /ʃaʊt/
shouts, shouting, shouted

'shout about *British*

to show that you are happy or proud of something

shout about sth *He does a lot for charity but he doesn't shout about it.* ♦ *We want to give our fans something to shout about.*

'shout at

to use a loud voice when you are angry at someone or something, especially when you are criticizing them = YELL AT

shout at sb/sth *She's always shouting at her kids.* ♦ *I walked into the room to find him shouting at the TV screen.*

,shout 'down [often passive]

to shout while someone is speaking so that people cannot hear what they have to say, usually because you disagree with them = HOWL DOWN

be shouted down *The minister was shouted down as he tried to justify the government's decision.*

shout sb down *The audience tried to shout him down, but he carried on speaking.*

,shout 'out ★

to say something suddenly in a very loud voice = CALL OUT

shout out *I wanted to shout out and stop her but she was already gone.*

shout out sth *An officer was shouting out orders.*

shout sth out *Stop shouting the answers out!*

SHOVE /ʃʌv/
shoves, shoving, shoved

,shove a'round (*also* ,shove a'bout *British*) *informal*

to treat someone badly and in an unfair way, especially by giving them orders

shove sb around *Well, they won't be able to shove me around any longer.*

,shove 'off

1 [always in imperative] *informal* used for telling someone to go away or leave you alone because you are angry or annoyed with them

shove off *Tell your annoying friends to shove off.*

2 if a boat shoves off, it moves away from the land into the water

,shove 'over (*also* ,shove 'up) *British* *informal*

to move in order to make more room for someone else, for example on a seat by moving your body closer to the person sitting next to you

shove over *He told her to shove over so he could get in bed with her.* ♦ *If he shoved up a bit there'd be room for us all to sit down.*

SHOW /ʃəʊ, *American* ʃoʊ/
shows, showing, showed, shown /ʃəʊn, *American* ʃoʊn/

,show a'round (*also* ,show 'round *British*)

to take someone around a place for the first time, so that they can see all parts of it = TAKE AROUND

show sb around *I'll get someone to show you around.*

show sb around sth *They sent someone to show me around the new offices.*

,show 'in (*also* ,show 'into)

to take someone into a room where they are going to meet other people

show sb in *When she arrives, show her in right away.*

show sb into sth *He showed me into his office and asked me to sit down.*

,show 'off ★★★

1 *showing disapproval* to behave in a way that is intended to attract people's attention and make them admire you

show off *The children start showing off the minute anyone comes to visit.* ♦ *He's just showing off because his friends are here.*

2 to show people something you are very proud of so they will admire it

show off sth *Young musicians will get the chance to show off their musical skills.*
show sth off *He invited us over just so that he could show his new house off.*
♦ **+to** *She likes showing her children off to her friends.*

3 to make something look very impressive or attractive = DISPLAY
show off sth *The skirt was very tight-fitting, showing off her slim figure.*
show sth off *Does the picture show the subject off to the best advantage?*

■ **showoff** /'ʃəʊɒf/ **noun** [C] *informal showing disapproval* someone who tries to get attention and praise from other people by showing how clever they are: *He's a top-class player, if something of a showoff.*

show off

,show 'out

to take someone to the door by which they leave a place
show sb out *Ask someone in the office to show you out.* ♦ **+of** *He couldn't wait to show me out of the building.*

,show 'over *British*

to take someone around a place in order to show them how interesting or attractive it is
show sb over sth *She was busy showing some important guests over the factory.*

,show 'round *British same as* show around

'show to

to lead someone somewhere, for example because they do not know where to go
show sb to sth *The waiter showed us to our table.* ♦ *James will show you to your room.*

,show 'up ★★★

1 *informal* to arrive in a place where people are expecting you = APPEAR, TURN UP
show up *I'll be very surprised if they show up on time.*

2 to behave in a way that makes someone you are with feel embarrassed
= EMBARRASS
show sb up *You're always showing me up in front of my friends.*
show up sb *Kids often show up their parents without intending to.*
show yourself up *You'll only show yourself up if you don't prepare properly for your interview.*

3 if something shows up, it is clear enough for people to see it = STAND OUT
show up *The writing didn't show up very well on yellow paper.*

4 to make it possible to see something
≠ HIDE
show up sth *The clear skies showed up the stars quite clearly.*
show sth up *I want a sofa that doesn't show the dirt up.*

,show 'up as *(also ,show 'up for)*

to show what someone or something is really like, when this is not very good
show sb/sth up as sth *The interview showed him up as an ignorant fool.*
♦ *This sort of behaviour shows them up for what they really are.*

,show 'through

if a feeling or quality shows through, people know it is there even though you may be trying to hide it
show through *Although he seemed outwardly cheerful, a deep sense of sadness showed through.*

SHOWER /'ʃaʊə, *American* 'ʃaʊr/
showers, showering, showered

,shower 'down on *(also ,shower 'down upon)*

to fall on someone or something, usually in lots of very small pieces
shower down on sb/sth *Confetti showered down on the happy couple.*

'shower on *(also 'shower upon)*

to give a large number of things or a large amount of something to someone
shower sth on sb *He showered gifts on his children, but gave them no attention.*
♦ *A lot of praise has been showered on her by the public.*

'shower with

to give a large number of things or a large amount of something to someone
shower sb with sth *He showered her with expensive gifts.* ♦ *I couldn't understand why she was showering me with compliments.*

SHRINK /ʃrɪŋk/
shrinks, shrinking, shrank /ʃræŋk/ **or shrunk** /ʃrʌŋk/, **shrunk** /ʃrʌŋk/

'shrink from ★
to not be willing to do something difficult or deal with something unpleasant
= RECOIL FROM
> **shrink from sth** *Anne doesn't shrink from her responsibilities.*
> **shrink from doing sth** *He shrank from telling his secrets to anyone.*

SHRIVEL /'ʃrɪv(ə)l/
shrivels, shrivelling, shrivelled

'shrivel 'up
1 if something such as a plant shrivels up, it becomes smaller and thinner than usual and it does not look fresh and healthy
> **shrivel up** *The leaves had shrivelled up in the summer heat.*

2 to make something smaller and thinner than usual
> **shrivel up** *The fierce heat had shrivelled up the meat.*

3 to become weaker or smaller in amount
> **shrivel up** *Funding for the project eventually shrivelled up.*

SHROUD /ʃraʊd/
shrouds, shrouding, shrouded

'shroud in [often passive] *literary*
to cover or hide something with something else
> **be shrouded in sth** *The house was shrouded in darkness.*
> **shroud sth in sth** *The explosion shrouded nearby buildings in a cloud of dust.*

SHRUG /ʃrʌg/
shrugs, shrugging, shrugged

,shrug 'off ★★
1 **shrug off** or **shrug aside** to show that something does not worry or upset you
= DISMISS
> **shrug off sth** *They've clearly shrugged off the disappointment of last week's defeat.*
> **shrug sth off** *If anyone criticizes his work he just shrugs it off.*

2 to deal with something easily and successfully
> **shrug off sth** *She won't shrug off this latest attack quite so well.*
> **shrug sth off** *Healthy people don't often*

get ill, and when they do, they're usually strong enough to shrug it off.

3 to remove clothes by shaking them off your body
> **shrug off sth** *He walked into the room, shrugging off his coat.*
> **shrug sth off** *He shrugged his bathrobe off and began to dress.*

SHUCK /ʃʌk/
shucks, shucking, shucked

,shuck 'off *American informal*
1 to take a piece of clothing off
> **shuck off sth** *also* **shuck sth off** *He shucked off his coat and sat down.*

2 to get rid of something
> **shuck off sth** *also* **shuck sth off** *These countries have now shucked off communism.*

SHUDDER /'ʃʌdə, American 'ʃʌdər/
shudders, shuddering, shuddered

'shudder at
to be shocked by something
> **shudder at sth** *They would have shuddered at the thought of what we're doing now.*

SHUFFLE /'ʃʌf(ə)l/
shuffles, shuffling, shuffled

'shuffle through
to look for something in a group or pile of things
> **shuffle through sth** *He sat there, shuffling through the papers on his desk.*

SHUT /ʃʌt/
shuts, shutting, shut

,shut a'way
to put someone in a place where they are kept apart from other people = LOCK AWAY
> **shut sb away** *Edmund's parents shut him away as a child.* ♦ *Prisoners are shut away with no chance of escape.*
> **shut yourself away** *Don't shut yourself away all day in your room.*

,shut 'down ★★
1 if a shop, school, factory, or business shuts down, or if someone shuts it down, it closes, usually permanently = CLOSE DOWN
> **shut down** *Factories are shutting down all over the northeast.*
> **shut down sth** *In 1986, they shut down the mine.*
> **shut sth down** *We should be building more hospitals, not shutting them down.*

2 if a machine or computer shuts down, or if someone shuts it down, it stops operating

shut down *All the computers at the university shut down for 65 minutes this morning.*
shut down sth *They decided to shut down the nuclear reactor.*
shut sth down *We can back up the database without shutting it down.*

3 *informal* to stop someone from doing something, especially to stop a player from having the freedom to move around or play well

shut sb/sth down *Tonight we shut the other team down completely.*

,shut 'in

to put a person or animal in a place that they cannot leave = CONFINE

shut sb/sth in *She pushed them into the kitchen and shut them in.*
shut sb/sth in sth *You can't shut animals in the house all day.*
shut yourself in sth *He shut himself in his room all evening.*

,shut 'off ★

1 if a machine shuts off, or if someone shuts it off, it stops working = SWITCH OFF ≠ TURN ON

shut off *The engines shut off automatically if there is a fire.*
shut off sth *How do I shut off this car alarm?*
shut sth off *I shut the machine off and silence returned to the room.*

2 to stop the flow of something, usually water or electricity = TURN OFF

shut off sth *Did you shut off the water?*
shut sth off *Make sure you shut the gas off if you suspect a leak.*

3 if a person or community is shut off, or if they shut themselves off, they do not see or meet other people very often = CUT OFF

shut yourself off *She shut herself off, and spent all her time reading.*
be shut off *Regions that were shut off from the sea by high mountains had very little contact with trading ships.* ♦ **+from** *Bob was shut off from the rest of the team.*

,shut 'out ★★

1 if you shut something out, you stop yourself from seeing it, hearing it, or thinking about it = BLOCK OUT

shut out sth *He closed the door to shut out the sound of the rain.*
shut sth out *The thought was so painful to me that I tried to shut it out.* ♦ **+of** *I tried to shut the incident out of my mind.*

2 to not allow someone to enter a particular place = LOCK OUT ≠ LET IN

shut sb out *He shut me out and wouldn't let me back in the room.* ♦ **+of** *Joe's shut me out of the house.*

3 *American* in sports, to win and not allow the other team to score any points

shut out sb *In hockey last night, the Rangers shut out the Hawks 3–0.*
shut sb out *We kept pushing forward but they succeeded in shutting us out.*

■ **'shut-out** noun [C] *American* in sport, a match in which one team does not score any points: *The Sun Devils shocked Nebraska in a 19–0 shutout.*

,shut 'out of [often passive]

to not allow someone to do something or be involved in something

be shut out of sth *For years, women were shut out of the top ranks of the industry.*
shut sb out of sth *You can't shut your children out of decisions that affect them.*

,shut 'up ★★★

1 [often in imperative] *impolite* to stop talking or making a noise = BE QUIET

shut up *Oh, just shut up! I've had enough of this.* ♦ *Why don't you shut up?*
♦ **+about** *I wish he'd shut up about his holiday.*

2 *impolite* to make someone stop talking or making a noise = SILENCE

shut sb up *Can't you shut the kids up for just five minutes? ♦ You can't shut her up when she starts talking about her work.*
♦ *I think she agreed just to shut him up.*

3 to close a building so that people cannot enter or leave it = CLOSE, CLOSE UP ≠ OPEN UP

shut up sth *He shut up the shop at 5.30pm.*
shut sth up *We shut the office up early that evening and went out to a bar.*

4 if you shut yourself up somewhere, you stay in a room, house etc for a specific purpose

shut yourself up *Many students shut themselves up in their rooms to study.*
PHRASE **shut up shop** *informal* to close a business, either permanently or at the end of the working day: *Many traders have shut up shop and moved away as a result of the recession.*

SHY /ʃaɪ/
shies, shying, shied

,shy a'way

to avoid someone or be unwilling to do something, because you are nervous, afraid, or not confident

shy away *The reason why buyers are shying away is fear of the unknown.*
♦ **+from** *So far the government has shied away from taking any action.*

SICK /sɪk/
sicks, sicking, sicked

‚sick 'up *British informal*
if you sick up food you have eaten, it comes out of your stomach through your mouth = *formal* VOMIT
sick up sth *also* **sick sth up** *The baby had sicked up most of its feed.* ♦ *He took a swig of the cleaning fluid by mistake, but sicked it up again.*

SICKEN /'sɪkən/
sickens, sickening, sickened

'sicken for [always progressive] *British informal*
if you are sickening for a particular illness, you are about to get it
be sickening for sth *I think I must be sickening for a cold.* ♦ *You're not looking well. I hope you're not **sickening for something.***

'sicken of *mainly literary*
to become bored with something
sicken of sth *He had begun to sicken of his superstar lifestyle.*

SIDE /saɪd/
sides, siding, sided

'side with ★
to agree with one particular person and support them in an argument = BACK
≠ OPPOSE
side with sb *She always sided with my brother.*

SIDLE /'saɪd(ə)l/
sidles, sidling, sidled

‚sidle 'up
to move slowly towards someone or something, usually because you are nervous or do not want to be noticed
sidle up *The pony sidled up and took the lump of sugar from her hand.* ♦ **+to** *I saw Ron sidle up to her and whisper something in her ear.*

SIFT /sɪft/
sifts, sifting, sifted

‚sift 'out
to remove one part of something
sift out sth *also* **sift sth out** *We get a different impression of the economy if we*
sift out the figures for imports. ♦ *Some of the applicants are sifted out immediately.*

'sift through
to examine information, documents etc in order to find something
sift through sth *He spent hours sifting through all the documents relating to the case.* ♦ *Detectives had to sift through a vast quantity of information until they found what they were looking for.*

SIGN /saɪn/
signs, signing, signed

‚sign a'way
if you sign away property or a right, you agree that it no longer belongs to you by officially signing your name on a legal document
sign away sth *also* **sign sth away** *Without knowing it, she had signed away all rights over her child.*

'sign for
1 if you sign for a parcel or letter, you show that you have received it by signing your name on a document
sign for sth *Could you sign for this package please?*
2 *British* if you sign for a sports club, you join it by signing a contract
sign for sth *The 23-year-old striker is expected to sign for Manchester United.*

‚sign 'in
to write your name or someone else's name on an list as a record of when you or they arrived at a place ≠ SIGN OUT
sign in *All visitors must sign in at the front desk.*
sign sb in *He's signed you in and is waiting for you inside.*

‚sign 'off ★

1	end a broadcast
2	end a letter
3	end Internet conversation
4	officially approve sth
5	give sb doctor's note

1 to end a broadcast on television or radio
sign off *It's time for me to sign off now.*
2 to end a letter or email in a particular way
sign off *How do you usually sign off when you're writing to your bank manager?* ♦ **+with** *She signed off with a row of Xs as usual.*
3 to end a conversation by radio or on the Internet
sign off *I'm signing off now. Bye!*

4 *business* to officially approve of something or officially agree that something has been completed in a satisfactory way by signing your name

sign sth off *You don't do any overtime until somebody's signed it off and authorized it.*

sign off sth *What did the auditors think they were doing when they signed off the accounts?*

5 *British* to give someone a medical certificate saying that they are sick and unable to work

sign sb off *The doctor said I was still too weak, and signed me off for another month.* ♦ *The tribunal heard that Mawdsley had been signed off work for depression.*

,sign 'off on *mainly American*

to officially agree to something

sign off on sth *White House officials said the president has signed off on the policy.*

,sign 'on ★

1 to write your name or a secret word in order to use a computer **= LOG ON**

sign on *You need your password to sign on.*

2 to employ someone to do a job **= RECRUIT, SIGN UP ≠ FIRE;** *British informal* **SACK**

sign on sb *We've signed on three new security guards.*

sign sb on *They signed someone on last week.*

3 *British* to apply to receive money from the government when you do not have a job by regularly signing your name on an official form in order to say that you are looking for work

sign on *She used to go and sign on every Monday.*

sign on sth *I've never had to sign on the dole, fortunately.*

4 to agree to do something or to take part in something

sign on *Companies have signed on as business partners with high schools across the country.* ♦ *+to We're hopeful that they will sign on to this plan.*

,sign 'out

1 to write your name or someone else's name on a list as a record of when you or they leave a place **≠ SIGN IN**

sign out *Please sign out when you leave.*

sign sb out *I'll sign both of us out.*

2 if you sign out an object or vehicle, you write your name on an official list to show that you have borrowed or hired it

sign out sth *also* **sign sth out** *I'll sign out a laptop for the weekend.*

,sign 'over

to officially give your property to someone by writing your name on a legal document

sign over sth *also* **sign sth over** *He's nervous about signing over the whole farm.* ♦ *+to Her dad signed the car over to her.*

,sign 'up ★★

1 to join a course or organization **= JOIN UP**

sign up *It's a voluntary course – students only sign up if they want to.* ♦ *+for She's decided to sign up for music school.*

2 to put someone's name on an official list for something

sign sb up *They've signed me up without even asking me.* ♦ *+to do sth They've signed me up to do voluntary work next month.*

3 to officially employ someone to work for an organization **= RECRUIT, SIGN ON ≠ FIRE;** *British informal* **SACK**

sign up sb *We have signed up two new players.*

sign sb up *A major record company immediately signed him up.*

4 to agree to do something

sign up *Do you think I'd have signed up if I'd known what was really involved?* ♦ *+for Hey! I never signed up for a full-time child care role!*

'sign with

if you sign with a sports club, you join it by signing a contract

sign with sb/sth *He has an offer to sign with the Phoenix Suns.*

SILT /sɪlt/
silts, silting, silted

,silt 'up

if a river or other area of water silts up, it gradually fills up with silt (=small pieces of stone, grains of sand etc), often stopping the flow of the water or making it difficult to travel on

silt up *Experiments were done to find out how the canals silted up over long periods of time.*

SIMMER /'sɪmə, *American* 'sɪmər/
simmers, simmering, simmered

,simmer 'down

to become calm after being excited or angry

simmer down *Give him a couple of days to simmer down and we'll ask him again.*

SING /sɪŋ/
sings, singing, sang /sæŋ/, **sung** /sʌŋ/

,sing a'long
to sing a song with someone who is already singing

sing along *If you know the words, sing along.* ♦ **+with** *She started singing along with the song on the radio.*

■ **singalong** /'sɪŋəˌlɒŋ/ **noun** [C] an informal occasion on which people sing songs together for fun: *After a few drinks, there's the usual singalong.*

,sing 'out
1 *literary* to say something in a loud clear voice = CALL OUT

sing out sth *'Uncle Charlie,' Jo sang out.*
2 to sing with a louder voice = SING UP

sing out *They were all singing out loud now.*

sing sth out *Let's sing that tune out!*

,sing 'up *British*
to sing with a louder voice = SING OUT

sing up *Sing up everyone!*

SINGLE /'sɪŋg(ə)l/
singles, singling, singled

,single 'out ★★
to choose one person from a group for special attention, praise, or criticism = PICK OUT

single sb out *He was irritated that fate seemed to have singled him out yet again.*
single out sb *I don't want to single out anyone in particular – you all need to make some improvements.* ♦ **+for** *Katie was often singled out for punishment.*
♦ **+as** *Who would you single out as the most promising student of the year?*

SINK /sɪŋk/
sinks, sinking, sank /sæŋk/, **sunk** /sʌŋk/

,sink 'back
to move or fall back, especially because you are tired

sink back *She sank back in her chair.*

,sink 'down
to move or fall downwards, especially so that you are sitting or lying

sink down *With a groan she sank down.*
♦ *He went into the lounge and sank down into a chair.*

,sink 'in ★★ (*also* **sink 'into**)
if a piece of news, new information etc sinks in, you finally begin to understand and accept it = GO IN

sink in *She had to repeat her words several times before they finally sank in.*
♦ *Asked what it felt like to win $2.5m, Trudi said, 'It hasn't really sunk in yet'.*
sink into sth *When will it sink into her thick skull that he's not interested in her?*

Nouns often used as subjects with **sink in**

■ **meaning, message, news, significance, truth, words**

'sink to *showing disapproval*
to do something bad that you would not usually do

sink to (doing) sth *How could you sink to stealing money from your own mother?*

SIPHON /'saɪf(ə)n/
siphons, siphoning, siphoned

,siphon 'off
1 to move liquid from one container to another through a tube = DRAW OFF

siphon off sth *also* **siphon sth off** *Siphon off all excess liquid.*
2 to move money from one bank account to another, especially illegally or dishonestly

siphon off sth *also* **siphon sth off** *They had siphoned off millions of pounds into their personal accounts.*

SIT /sɪt/
sits, sitting, sat /sæt/

Sit is often used with adverbs and prepositions when it means 'to be in a position in which the lower part of your body rests on a seat or on the ground, while the upper part of your body is upright': *Six of us were **sitting around** the table talking.* ♦ *I was **sitting at** my computer when the phone rang.* ♦ *Matt **sat on** a park bench, eating his lunch.* These uses are not included here.

,sit a'round ★★ (*also* ,sit 'round *British*)
to spend time in a lazy way, doing nothing important

sit around *Are we going to sit around all night, or shall we go out?*
sit around sth *Since Dad lost his job he just sits around the house all day.*

,sit 'back ★★★
to relax and stop making the effort to do or change something

sit back *I can't afford to sit back with the tournament coming up.*

,sit 'by

to make no effort to stop something bad
from happening
  sit by *Are we just going to **sit by** and
  watch them take over the company?*

,sit 'down ★★★

to lower your body into a sitting position
  = BE SEATED ≠ STAND UP
  sit down *We were tired so we decided to
  sit down for a while.* ♦ *Please, sit down
  and make yourselves comfortable.*
  PHRASE sit yourself down *informal* to
  make yourself comfortable in a chair:
  *Why don't you sit yourself down? We'll
  do the dishes.*

  ■ **'sit-down** adj **1** a sit-down meal is
  served to people who are sitting down
  2 a sit-down protest is one in which
  people sit down in order to stop a
  business from operating until they get
  what they want

'sit for

to be a model for an artist or photographer
  sit for sb *I'd love to paint you. Would
  you sit for me?*

,sit 'in

if people sit in, they all sit down in a
public place and refuse to move as a
protest against something
  sit in *They decided to sit in until their
  demands were met.*

  ■ **'sit-in** noun [C] a protest in which
  people sit down in order to stop a
  business from operating until they get
  what they want: *Some workers are
  threatening a sit-in.*

,sit 'in for

to take the place of someone temporarily
  = STAND IN FOR
  sit in for sb *I'll be sitting in for the
  secretary at the meeting tonight.*

,sit 'in on

to go to a meeting or a class although you
are not directly involved in it
  sit in on sth *Do you mind if I sit in on
  your class this afternoon?*

'sit on

to delay dealing with something
  sit on sth *They've been sitting on my
  application for over a month now.*

,sit 'out ★

1 to stop taking part in something such
as a game or dance for a short time
  sit out sth *I'm tired, so I think I'll sit out
  the next dance.*
  sit sth out *Do you mind if I sit this one
  out?*

2 to stay until the end of something,
especially something unpleasant
  sit sth out *I know it's boring, but we're
  just going to have to sit it out.*
  sit out sth *They sat out the war in the
  country, far away from the fighting.*

'sit over

to have a meal or a drink in a relaxed
pleasant way
  sit over sth *They sat over their coffee,
  chatting intimately.*

,sit 'round *British* same as **sit around**

'sit through ★

to stay until the end of something,
especially something you are not enjoying
  sit through sth *If I have to sit through
  one more boring meeting, I think I'll
  scream.*

,sit 'up ★★★

1 to go from a lying position to a sitting
position, or to help someone do this
  sit up *Would you like to sit up and read
  for a while?*
  sit sb up *We sat her up in a chair.*

2 to sit straight and not bend or lean
  sit up *You've got to stop slouching and
  sit up straight.*

3 to suddenly notice something and
realize that it is important or serious
  sit up *The action was designed to **make
  the authorities sit up**.* ♦ *If these figures
  don't make them **sit up and listen**,
  nothing will.*

4 *British* to go to bed later than usual
  sit up *We sat up very late talking last
  night.*

  ■ **'sit-up** noun [C] an exercise in which
  you lie on your back with your knees
  bent and raise your upper body then lie
  back down: *I did the usual press-ups
  and sit-ups.*

SIZE /saɪz/
sizes, sizing, sized

,size 'up

to form an opinion about someone or
something by thinking carefully about
them or it = ASSESS
  size up sb/sth *also* **size sb/sth up** *He
  sized up the situation and immediately
  decided what to do.* ♦ *They were sizing
  each other up, waiting to see who would
  make the first move.*

SKATE /skeɪt/
skates, skating, skated

‚skate 'over (also ‚skate a'round or ‚skate 'round British)
to avoid talking or writing about of a difficult or embarrassing subject or situation in a detailed way = SKIM OVER ≠ DWELL ON
skate over sth *The report seems to have skated over all the things people really want to know about.*

SKETCH /sketʃ/
sketches, sketching, sketched

‚sketch 'in
to add more information or details to something
sketch in sth *also* **sketch sth in** *We need to sketch in a few more details before presenting the plan.*

‚sketch 'out
to make a general plan or give a general description of something, with only a few details
sketch out sth *also* **sketch sth out** *I've sketched out a rough proposal.*

SKIM /skɪm/
skims, skimming, skimmed

‚skim 'off
to remove a substance that is floating on the surface of a liquid
skim sth off *Skim the fat off the soup.*

‚skim 'through
to read something quickly and not very carefully
skim through sth *Would you skim through the report and check for spelling mistakes?*

SKIMP /skɪmp/
skimps, skimping, skimped

'skimp on
1 to not use or provide enough of something
skimp on sth *The dessert was good but they had skimped on the chocolate sauce.*
2 to not spend enough money on something
skimp on sth *Don't skimp on grass seed – it's worth paying more for the better varieties.*

SKIP /skɪp/
skips, skipping, skipped

‚skip 'out American
to leave a place quickly, usually because you do not want to be noticed or want to avoid paying money
skip out *They skipped out and left us to pay the bill.* ♦ **+on** *They skipped out on us without paying.*

SKIRT /skɜːt, American skɜrt/
skirts, skirting, skirted

‚skirt a'round
1 to go around the edge of a place or thing
skirt around sth *If we skirt around the field we can avoid the mud.*
2 to avoid talking or writing about something unpleasant or embarrassing
skirt around sth *As usual, he just skirted around the subject.*

SKIVE /skaɪv/
skives, skiving, skived

‚skive 'off British informal
to not go to school or work when you should be there
skive off *She said she was ill but I knew she was skiving off.*
skive off sth *We always used to skive off PE lessons if we could.*

SLACK /slæk/
slacks, slacking, slacked

‚slack 'off
1 to get weaker, less violent, or less active
= EASE OFF ≠ INTENSIFY
slack off *The rain seemed to be slacking off.*
2 to stop working as hard as you should be working or as hard as you have been working
slack off *This really isn't the time to start slacking off. You've got exams next week.*

SLACKEN /'slækən/
slackens, slackening, slackened

‚slacken 'off
to become slower or less active, or make something slower or less active
slacken off *When you're in the lead, don't slacken off.*
slacken off sth *also* **slacken sth off** *He slackened off his pace a little.*

SLAG /slæg/
slags, slagging, slagged

,slag 'off *British informal*
to criticize someone or something unfairly
slag sb/sth off *also* **slag off sb/sth** *I don't know why she goes out with him – she's always slagging him off.* ♦ *Apart from slagging off the food, the accommodation and the people, he hasn't said much about the place.*

SLAM /slæm/
slams, slamming, slammed

,slam 'out
to leave a place quickly and angrily
slam out *They argued again and she slammed out, leaving him to sulk on his own.* ♦ **+of** *He slammed out of the room.*

SLAP /slæp/
slaps, slapping, slapped

,slap a'round (*also* ,slap a'bout *British*)
informal
to hit or be violent towards someone, especially regularly and over a long period of time
slap sb around *Her husband slaps her around.*

,slap 'down [often passive]
to unfairly criticize or disagree with someone, or make them feel that what they are saying is stupid or useless
be/get slapped down *As soon as I say anything in meetings I get slapped down.*
slap sb down *also* **slap down sb** *If you slap people down too much you'll never get any good ideas out of them.*

'slap on *informal*
1 to order that something should be done immediately, especially as a punishment
slap sth on sth *The court has slapped a ban on the video.*
2 to add something as an extra cost
slap sth on sth *They've slapped another 10 pence on a packet of cigarettes.*
3 to put something, especially something liquid, onto a surface in a careless way
slap on sth *also* **slap sth on** *Just slap on a few coats of paint and the place will look fine.* ♦ *Give me a second to slap a bit of make-up on.*

SLASH /slæʃ/
slashes, slashing, slashed

'slash through
1 to move somewhere in a violent way that causes a lot of damage
slash through sth *Tornadoes slashed through the area.* ♦ *The rotors slashed through the roof of the building.*
2 to try to cut or hit something by making several swinging movements
slash through sth *They slashed through the undergrowth with sticks.*

SLATE /sleɪt/
slates, slating, slated

be 'slated for [usually passive]
to be expected to happen at a particular time or to be done, especially at a particular time
be slated for sth *The meeting is slated for next Tuesday.* ♦ *Almost 35 percent of state enterprises were slated for privatization.*

SLAVE /sleɪv/
slaves, slaving, slaved

,slave a'way
to work very hard
slave away *I've been slaving away all day while you've been out enjoying yourself.*

SLEEP /sliːp, American slip/
sleeps, sleeping, slept /slept/

,sleep a'round *informal showing disapproval*
to have a lot of different sexual partners
sleep around *If you sleep around, you increase your risk of HIV infection.*

,sleep 'in
to continue sleeping after the time you usually get up = LIE IN, OVERSLEEP —*picture* → STAY UP
sleep in *The whole family sleeps in on Sundays.*

,sleep 'off
to get rid of an unpleasant or uncomfortable feeling by sleeping, especially after eating or drinking too much
sleep off sth *also* **sleep sth off** *The day after the wedding, I'll still be sleeping off the champagne.* ♦ *You should just leave him to sleep it off.*

'sleep on
PHRASE **sleep on it** to wait to make a decision until the next day, after you

have rested and had more time to think:
Let me sleep on it and I'll give you an answer tomorrow.

,sleep 'out

to sleep outside
sleep out *Most people who sleep out do it because they are homeless.*

,sleep 'over

to sleep at someone else's house for one night
sleep over *Mum, can Billy sleep over on Saturday?*

■ **oversleep** /ˌəʊvəˈsliːp/ **verb** [I] to wake up later than you intended to

■ **sleepover** /ˈsliːpəʊvə/ [C] **noun** a children's party at which the guests stay the night at one person's house

,sleep 'through

1 to remain sleeping and not be woken by something
sleep through sth *'Did you hear the storm last night?' 'No, I must have slept through it.'*

2 to continue sleeping for a long time
—*picture →* STAY UP
sleep through *I was so tired I slept through until noon.* ♦ *Is your baby sleeping through yet (=not waking up in the night)?*

'sleep together ★

if two people sleep together, they have sex
sleep together *Do you think they're sleeping together?*

'sleep with ★★

to have sex with someone, especially someone you are not married to or in a relationship with
sleep with sb *I only slept with him once.*

SLICE /slaɪs/
slices, slicing, sliced

,slice 'off

to remove something by cutting it with a sharp knife or blade
slice off sth *also* **slice sth off** *He accidentally sliced off the tip of his finger.*

,slice 'up

to cut something into several flat thin pieces
slice up sth *also* **slice sth up** *He sliced up the loaf of bread and buttered each piece.*
♦ *Slice the meat up thinly.*

SLICK /slɪk/
slicks, slicking, slicked

,slick 'back [often passive]

to move your hair back from your face and make it flat and shiny by putting something such as oil or water on it.
be slicked back *His long white hair was slicked back with gel.*
slick sth back *also* **slick back sth** *He came running in to wash his hands and slick his hair back.*

,slick 'down [often passive]

to make hair flat and shiny by putting something such as water or oil on it
be slicked down *His long wispy hair had been combed back and slicked down with something to make it neat.*
slick sth down *also* **slick down sth** *He spent hours slicking his hair down.*
♦ *Gel was used to slick down the front sections of the hair.*

SLIM /slɪm/
slims, slimming, slimmed

,slim 'down

1 to deliberately reduce your body weight, for example in order to become healthier
slim down *He's slimmed down since he had his heart attack.* ♦ **+to** *Angie has slimmed down to an astonishing 120 pounds.*

2 if you slim down an organization, or if it slims down, you reduce the number of people working in it ≠ EXPAND
slim down sth *also* **slim sth down** *We expect to have to slim down his workforce in the near future.* ♦ *The company was slimmed down drastically last year, but still the shareholders aren't happy.*
slim down *The advertising industry has slimmed down in recent years.*

SLINK /slɪŋk/
slinks, slinking, slunk /slʌŋk/

,slink a'way (also ,slink 'off)

to leave a place slowly and quietly so that people will not notice you = SLOPE OFF
slink away *The man turned and slunk away, disappearing into the crowd.*

SLIP /slɪp/
slips, slipping, slipped

Slip is often used with adverbs and prepositions when it means 'to go somewhere, especially quickly and quietly without people noticing you or stopping you': *Sarah **slipped into** the room and carefully shut the door behind her.* ♦ *The members of the band **slipped out** through a back door to avoid the crowd of waiting fans.* ♦ *Several people managed to **slip past** the guards and get into the the building.* These uses are not included here.

,slip a'way ★★

1 slip away or **slip off** to leave quietly or secretly
slip away *We managed to slip away early.*

2 if something such as power or an opportunity slips away, you no longer have it
slip away *Organizers felt support for the project slowly slipping away.* ♦ **+from** *He could feel victory slipping away from his grasp.*

,slip 'by

1 if time slips by, it seems to pass quickly
slip by *The months and years slipped by, and I still didn't hear from him.*

2 if an opportunity slips by, it happens but you do not use it or gain an advantage from it
slip by *I did have the chance to change jobs once, but I let it slip by.*

,slip 'down

1 to fall down to a lower level on a scale that measures how good something is
slip down sth *The report shows that our universities are slipping down the international league table in scientific research.*

2 if an alcoholic drink slips down, it tastes good and that you enjoy drinking it
slip down *This wine slips down very nicely with a bowl of pasta.*

,slip 'in

to mention something quickly and in a way that is not too obvious when you are talking or writing about something else
slip in sth *also* **slip sth in** *He managed to slip in a few comments about his rich father.* ♦ *The author slips a tiny clue in early in the book, hoping that readers will miss it.*

,slip 'into ★★★

1 to mention something quickly and in a way that is not too obvious in a conversation or piece of writing about something else
slip sth into sth *That was rather a strange thing to slip into the conversation.*

2 to quickly put on a piece of clothing
slip into sth *Give me a moment to slip into something more comfortable.*

3 to gradually start to be in a bad state or situation
slip into sth *She felt herself slip into unconsciousness.* ♦ *The country is slipping into recession.*

,slip 'off ★

1 to take a piece of clothing off quickly
slip off sth *He quickly slipped off his jacket and sat down at the table.*
slip sth off *Slip your shirt off and I'll listen to your heart.*

2 *same as* **slip away 1**

,slip 'on

to put clothes on
slip sth on *also* **slip on sth** *Ann slipped the jacket on to see what it looked like.*

■ **'slip-on** noun [C] a shoe that you do not need to fasten: *a pair of gents' slip-ons*

,slip 'out ★

if something, especially a secret, slips out, you say it without intending to
slip out *I know you asked me not to tell him, but it just slipped out.*

,slip 'out of

to take clothes off quickly
slip out of sth *I'm going to slip out of this uniform as soon as we get home.*

,slip 'over

if you slip over, your feet slide accidentally and you lose your balance or fall over
slip over *I turned to run but slipped over.* ♦ **+on** *Be careful not to slip over on the ice.*

,slip 'through

if something such as a mistake or an illegal action slips through or slips through something, it is not noticed by a system that is intended to stop it
slip through *I think we picked up most of the errors, but one or two might have slipped through.*
slip through sth *Too many drugs consignments manage to slip through customs each year.*

PHRASES slip through your fingers if

something such as an opportunity slips through your fingers, you do not use it or get an advantage from it while you can: *We let the award slip through our fingers again.*

slip through the net/cracks to not be protected or noticed by a system, especially a system that is intended to protect or help people: *Thousands of the poorest families slip through the welfare net.*

ˌslip 'up ★ *informal*

to make a small careless mistake
slip up *This time be extra careful. We can't afford to slip up again.*

■ **'slip-up** noun [C] *informal* a small careless mistake: *It was a slip-up that anyone could have made.*

SLOB /slɒb, *American* slɑb/
slobs, slobbing, slobbed

ˌslob aˈround (*also* ˌslob aˈbout *British*)
informal
to spend time in a lazy way, not doing very much
slob around *I spent the weekend slobbing around.*

SLOBBER /'slɒbə, *American* 'slɑbər/
slobbers, slobbering, slobbered

'slobber over *informal*

to show that you like or are sexually attracted to someone in a very obvious way that other people think is silly or embarrassing
slobber over sb *He's always slobbering over her in public.*

SLOG /slɒg, *American* slɑg/
slogs, slogging, slogged

ˌslog aˈway

to work hard and for a long time at something that is difficult or boring
slog away *Most of the night was spent slogging away at the report.*

ˌslog 'out

PHRASES **slog your guts out** *informal* to work very hard: *I've been slogging my guts out to get this report finished in time.*
slog it out *informal* to argue or fight about something until someone wins = SLUG IT OUT: *The two men slogged it out until only Harrison was left standing.*

SLOPE /sləʊp, *American* sloʊp/
slopes, sloping, sloped

ˌslope aˈway

if something such as land or a road slopes away, it gets lower as it continues farther away from a high point
slope away *At the back of the house the land slopes away.* ♦ *The road sloped away towards the crossroads.*

ˌslope 'off *British informal*

to leave somewhere quietly or secretly, especially in order to avoid being noticed
= SLINK AWAY
slope off *The men sloped off, looking ashamed of themselves.*

SLOSH /slɒʃ, *American* slɑʃ/
sloshes, sloshing, sloshed

ˌslosh aˈround [usually progressive]
informal
if money is sloshing around, a lot of it is available or people are spending a lot of it
be sloshing around *There's so much money sloshing around in professional tennis these days.*

SLOT /slɒt, *American* slɑt/
slots, slotting, slotted

ˌslot 'in

1 to fit closely into a narrow space or fit something into a narrow space
slot in *The last tile slotted in neatly.*
slot sth in *also* **slot in sth** *Slotted in among the novels on the shelf was a book on English grammar.*

2 to arrange a time for someone or something between other things you have to do = FIT IN
slot sb/sth in *also* **slot in sb/sth** *We could slot you in just before our ten o'clock meeting.* ♦ *I could probably slot in one more client.*

3 to fit well with a group of people or a way of life = FIT IN
slot in *The new members of the team slotted in easily.*

'slot into

1 to fit something into a narrow space
slot sth into sth *She slotted another tape into the VCR.*

2 to fit well with a group of people or a way of life = FIT IN
slot into sth *She slotted straight back into the military lifestyle.*
PHRASE **slot into place** if something slots into place, you suddenly

understand it = FALL INTO PLACE: *I didn't understand everything at the time, but later it all slotted into place.*

ˌslot to'gether

to fit together exactly, or fit things together exactly

slot together *They slot together like pieces of a jigsaw puzzle.*
slot sth together *also* **slot together sth** *The wardrobe parts can be slotted together easily.* ♦ *Construction crews are slotting together the huge concrete sections at the rate of three a day.*

SLOUGH /slʌf/
sloughs, sloughing, sloughed

ˌslough 'off

1 *literary* to get rid of something you do not want = CAST OFF
slough off sth *also* **slough sth off** *People think you can just slough off depression and pull your socks up.*
2 *technical* if an animal such as a snake sloughs off its skin, it removes its outer layer of skin = SHED
slough off sth *also* **slough sth off** *Snakes slough off their dead skins.*

SLOW /sləʊ, American sloʊ/
slows, slowing, slowed

ˌslow 'down ★★★ (also ˌslow 'up)

1 if someone slows down, or if something slows them down, they become less active or effective
slow down *For me, holidays are a time to slow down and relax with my family.*
slow sb down *This cold is really slowing me down.*
2 to reduce the level, amount, or rate of something = HOLD UP ≠ SPEED UP
slow down sth *Opposition by business leaders is slowing down the pace of reform.*
slow sth down *The effect of big interest rate rises was to slow the economy down.*
3 to move more slowly, especially in a vehicle, or make something move more slowly = *formal* DECELERATE ≠ SPEED UP
slow down *Slow down! You're driving too fast.* ♦ *You should always slow down if there are children in the area.*
slow sth down *I slowed the car down as we approached the scene.*
slow down sth *This narrowing of the arteries can slow down the flow of the blood to your heart.*

■ **slowdown** /'sləʊdaʊn/ **noun**
[C usually singular] **1** a period when there is less activity: *an economic slowdown*

♦ *a slowdown in industrial activity*
2 *American* a situation in which workers protest about something by working more slowly than usual: *There was an organized slowdown for three days.*

SLUG /slʌg/
slugs, slugging, slugged

ˌslug 'out

PHRASE **slug it out** *informal* to argue or fight about something until someone wins: *Rebels and government forces have been slugging it out in the west of the country for months now.*

SMACK /smæk/
smacks, smacking, smacked

'smack of

to be a sign of something bad = SAVOUR OF
smack of sth *Going out with him smacks of desperation.* ♦ *The whole affair smacked of a government cover-up.*

SMARTEN /'smɑːt(ə)n, American 'smɑrt(ə)n/
smartens, smartening, smartened

ˌsmarten 'up

1 to make yourself look tidy and clean = SPRUCE UP
smarten up *You need to smarten up a bit if you're going to an interview.*
smarten yourself up *'Smarten yourself up. Get your belt on straight', said the sergeant.*
2 *American informal* to stop yourself from making bad decisions = *informal* WISE UP
smarten up *It's time you smartened up.*
3 to improve the appearance of something, for example by cleaning or painting it = BRIGHTEN UP, SPRUCE UP
smarten up sth *also* **smarten sth up** *A fresh coat of paint can really smarten up a room.* ♦ *I tried to smarten this old chair up with some new pillows.*

SMASH /smæʃ/
smashes, smashing, smashed

ˌsmash 'down

to make something fall down and break into pieces by hitting it very hard
smash down sth *also* **smash sth down** *The police had to smash down the door.*

ˌsmash 'in [often passive] *informal*

to cause a lot of damage to something by hitting it violently
be smashed in *The front of the car was all smashed in.*

smash sth in *also* **smash in sth** *Vandals had smashed in all the windows.*

PHRASE **smash sb's face/head in** *informal* to hit someone hard in the face, seriously injuring them: *He was threatening to smash my face in.*

'smash into

to hit something very hard while moving fast, causing injury or damage, or make something do this

smash into sth *His car smashed into a tree.*

smash sth into sth *She smashed her new motorcycle into a wall.*

,smash 'up ★ *informal*

to destroy something completely by violently breaking it into many pieces
= WRECK

smash sth up *She got angry and started smashing things up.*

smash up sth *The bands was renowned for smashing up the hotels they stayed in.*

■ 'smash-up **noun** [C] *informal* an accident that happens when a moving vehicle hits something, causing damage: *Her leg was shattered in a smash-up.*

SMELL /smel/
smells, smelling, smelled or smelt /smelt/

'smell of

to have a particular smell

smell of sth *It smells of disinfectant in here.* ♦ *I always smell of cigarette smoke when I get back from the pub.*

,smell 'out

1 to be able to tell where someone or something is by using your ability to smell things = SNIFF OUT

smell out sb/sth *also* **smell sb/sth out** *These dogs can smell out drugs from 100 metres away.*

2 to be able to tell what someone or something is really like, when it is not obvious = DETECT

smell out sb/sth *also* **smell sb/sth out** *He had the ability to smell out weakness in others and use it to his advantage.*

,smell 'up *American*

to cause a person or place to have an unpleasant smell = STINK OUT

smell up sb/sth *also* **smell sb/sth up** *That burnt fish is smelling up the whole house.*

SMILE /smail/
smiles, smiling, smiled

'smile on

if something such as good luck or success smiles on you, you have a lot of good luck or are successful

smile on sb *Fortune smiled on the couple once again.*

SMOKE /sməʊk, *American* smoʊk/
smokes, smoking, smoked

,smoke 'out

1 to force a person, animal, or insect to leave the place where they have been hiding by filling it with smoke

smoke sb/sth out *also* **smoke out sb/sth** *She was badly stung while trying to smoke the bees out.*

2 to find out who has been involved in secret and illegal activities = FLUSH OUT

smoke sb out *also* **smoke out sb** *Police say it is getting easier to smoke out people who visit banned websites.*

SMOOTH /smuːð, *American* smuð/
smooths, smoothing, smoothed

,smooth a'way *same as* **smooth out**

,smooth 'down

to move your hand across the surface of something until it is flat and even

smooth down sth *also* **smooth sth down** *He smoothed down his hair with his hand.* ♦ *She smoothed her dress down and walked over to the reception desk.*

,smooth 'out (*also* ,smooth a'way)

to get rid of problems or disagreements

smooth sth out *also* **smooth out sth** *If she had a problem, her husband always smoothed things out for her.* ♦ *They stayed up half the night trying to smooth out their differences.*

,smooth 'over

to make a problem seem less serious
= EASE ≠ STIR UP

smooth over sth *also* **smooth sth over** *He's trying to smooth over differences between the two leaders.*

SNACK /snæk/
snacks, snacking, snacked

'snack on

to eat a small amount of food between meals

snack on sth *He was snacking on a bar of chocolate.*

SNAP /snæp/
snaps, snapping, snapped

,snap 'back *American informal*
to quickly become better after being ill or
in a difficult situation = BOUNCE BACK
> **snap back** *The economy has snapped
back after two disappointing years.*

,snap 'out
to say something quickly, especially an
order or a rude comment
> **snap out sth** *also* **snap sth out** *He
snapped out an order to his servant.*
> **PHRASE snap out of it** used to tell
someone to stop being unhappy or
upset: *She needs to snap out of it and get
her life back together.*

,snap 'to
> **PHRASE snap to it** [usually in imperative] used
for telling someone to start working or
to start working harder or faster: *Come
on, snap to it! We've got a lot to do before
the end of the day.*

,snap 'up ★★
1 [often passive] to buy something as soon
as it becomes available = POUNCE ON
> **be snapped up** *By 10 o'clock most of the
best bargains had been snapped up.*
> **snap sth up** *Anyone would snap it up at
that price.*
> **snap up sth** *They've snapped up a 10%
share in the company.*
2 to immediately take advantage of an
opportunity = GRAB
> **snap sth up** *I'd snap his offer up if I
were you.*
> **snap up sth** *The team snapped up every
chance that came their way.*

SNARL /snɑːl, *American* snɑrl/
snarls, snarling, snarled

,snarl 'up
to make something such as traffic unable
to move —*picture* → BACK UP
> **snarl up sth** *also* **snarl sth up** *An accident
snarled up the traffic for hours.*

■ **'snarl-up** noun [C] a situation in
which traffic coming from several
different directions is prevented from
moving: *There's the usual snarl-up
around the Arc de Triomphe.*

SNEAK /sniːk, *American* snik/
sneaks, sneaking, sneaked /sniːkt,
American snikd/

'sneak on *British*
old-fashioned to tell someone in authority
about something bad that someone has
done, especially because you want to cause
problems for them = *informal* SNITCH ON,
GRASS UP
> **sneak on sb** *Someone must have sneaked
on you.*

,sneak 'up
to get very close to someone before they
notice you = CREEP UP
> **sneak up** *He has this annoying habit of
sneaking up behind you.* ♦ **+on** *Don't
sneak up on me like that!*

,sneak 'up on
if something sneaks up on you, it happens
when you are not expecting it = CREEP UP
ON
> **sneak up on sb** *Christmas seems to have
sneaked up on us again.*

SNEEZE /sniːz, *American* sniz/
sneezes, sneezing, sneezed

'sneeze at
> **PHRASE not to be sneezed at** *informal* very
good, or good enough to consider
having: *Six goals is not to be sneezed
at.*

SNIFF /snɪf/
sniffs, sniffing, sniffed

,sniff a'round (*also* **,sniff 'round** *British*)
1 *showing disapproval* to try to find out
information
> **sniff around** *We've got to stop any more
media people sniffing around.*
> **sniff around sth** *Military police have
been sniffing around the bars.*
2 *informal* to show that you are sexually
interested in someone
> **sniff around** *She always got loads of
boys sniffing around.*
> **sniff around sb** *They broke up quite a
while ago, but he's still sniffing around
her.*

,sniff 'out
1 *informal* to discover something,
especially something that was previously
hidden or not known = DISCOVER
> **sniff out sth** *also* **sniff sth out** *Record
companies are keen to sniff out new
bands.*
2 if an animal such as a dog sniffs out

something, it finds it by using its ability to smell things

> **sniff out sth** *also* **sniff sth out** *A police tracker dog sniffed out 400 pounds of cocaine.*

SNIPE /snaɪp/
snipes, sniping, sniped

'snipe at *showing disapproval*
to criticize someone or make unkind comments about them

> **snipe at sb** *She spends the whole time sniping at other team members, but never really contributes anything herself.*

SNOOP /snuːp, American snup/
snoops, snooping, snooped

,snoop a'round *showing disapproval*
to look around a place in order to try and find information about someone's private business

> **snoop around** *If old Frank comes snooping around, just tell him to mind his own business.*
> **snoop around sth** *There was a suspicious-looking woman snooping around the office.*

'snoop on *showing disapproval*
to watch someone secretly so that you know everything they do

> **snoop on sb** *Some employers use special software to snoop on staff and the emails they send.*

SNOW /snəʊ, American snoʊ/
snows, snowing, snowed

be ,snowed 'in (*also* be ,snowed 'up)
to be unable to leave a place because a lot of snow has fallen there: *We were snowed in for three days.*

be ,snowed 'under
to have too much work to deal with: *I'm absolutely snowed under at the office.*

be ,snowed 'up *same as* be snowed in

SNUFF /snʌf/
snuffs, snuffing, snuffed

,snuff 'out
1 [often passive] to make something end quickly, especially by using force

> **be snuffed out** *It's tragic to see such a young life snuffed out.*
> **snuff out sth** *Richie Daly's visit had snuffed out that hope.*

2 to make a flame stop burning by squeezing it with your fingers or covering it closely with something

> **snuff out sth** *also* **snuff sth out** *She laid down her book and snuffed out the candle.* ♦ *I had already snuffed my bedside candle out.*

SNUGGLE /'snʌg(ə)l/
snuggles, snuggling, snuggled

,snuggle 'down
to put yourself into a warm, comfortable position by sliding your body down under the covers on a bed

> **snuggle down** *She snuggled down under the quilt again, but sleep still eluded her.*

,snuggle 'up
to sit or lie with your body resting against someone else's because you want to feel warm and comfortable = CUDDLE UP

> **snuggle up** *Let's snuggle up by the fire.*
> ♦ **+to** *He came over and sleepily snuggled up to her.*

SOAK /səʊk, American soʊk/
soaks, soaking, soaked

,soak 'in ★
1 soak in or soak into if a liquid soaks in, it goes into the surface or substance that it touches, so that you can no longer see it

> **soak in** *Put some cleaning foam on the carpet and wait for it to soak in.*
> **soak into sth** *Sweat was soaking into his shirt.*

2 if you soak in the atmosphere in a place, you spend time there so that you can experience and enjoy it

> **soak in sth** *We soaked in the charming 17th century ambiance of the place.*

,soak 'through
if a liquid soaks through something, it passes through it

> **soak through sth** *The rain was starting to soak through the sides of the tent.*
> **soak through** *If the bandage isn't thick enough the blood will just soak through.*
> **PHRASE** **be soaked through** to be completely wet: *She only had a thin jacket on and she was soaked through.*
> ♦ *She had been crying so much her handkerchief was soaked through.*

,soak 'up ★★
1 if a dry or soft substance soaks up a liquid, the liquid goes into it = SOP UP

> **soak up sth** *Use paper towels to soak up the oil.*
> **soak sth up** *My sponge wasn't big enough to soak all the juice up.* ♦ *If you*

spill red wine on your carpet, pour some salt on it to soak it up.

2 *informal* to spend time experiencing, listening to, or feeling something enjoyable

soak up sth *Visit the market to soak up the local atmosphere.* ♦ *We're having a great time **soaking up the sun**.*

soak sth up *Relax and allow yourself to soak this luxury up.* ♦ *There's plenty of local culture and we've been soaking it up.*

3 *informal* to use a lot of something such as money or time

soak up sth *That old car really soaks up the petrol.*

soak sth up *A winter heating bill would soon soak the rest of the money up.* ♦ *If there is any free time, other visits are arranged to soak it up.*

SOBER /ˈsəʊbə, American ˈsoʊbər/
sobers, sobering, sobered

,sober 'up
1 to become sober after being drunk
sober up *I had sobered up by then.*

2 to make someone become sober after they were drunk
sober sb up *also* **sober up sb** *The news seemed to sober him up instantly.* ♦ *We need some trick to sober up guests who have indulged too much.*

SOCK /sɒk, American sak/
socks, socking, socked

,sock 'to *informal*
PHRASE **sock it to sb** to say or do something to someone in a very strong and direct way: *The singer's sexy new look is designed to sock it to her critics.*

SOD /sɒd, American sad/
sods, sodding, sodded

,sod 'off [often in imperative] *British impolite*
1 to go away
sod off *OK, I'll just sod off then.* ♦ *Sod off, will you!*

2 used as an angry way of saying 'no' or of showing that you do not believe what someone has just said
sod off *'You'll lend me the money, won't you?' 'Sod off!'* ♦ *'His dad was a famous footballer, apparently'. 'Sod off! No chance!'*

SOFTEN /ˈsɒf(ə)n, American ˈsɔf(ə)n/
softens, softening, softened

,soften 'up
1 to make someone more likely to do what you want by being nice to them
soften sb up *also* **soften up sb** *His strategy was to soften them up with compliments.* ♦ *The question was how to soften up the dissenters.*

2 *informal* to hurt or threaten someone to make it more likely that they will do what you want or tell you something
soften up sb *also* **soften sb up** *He had men working for him whose job was softening up reluctant customers.* ♦ *They paid him a visit and softened him up.*

SOLDIER /ˈsəʊldʒə, American ˈsoʊldʒər/
soldiers, soldiering, soldiered

,soldier 'on
to continue to do something even though it is difficult or unpleasant = PERSEVERE
≠ GIVE UP
soldier on *We'll just have to soldier on till we finish the job.*

SOP /sɒp, American sɑp/
sops, sopping, sopped

,sop 'up
to remove liquid from a surface using a cloth or soft paper that the liquid goes into = SOAK UP
sop up sth *also* **sop sth up** *We put paper towels on the floor to sop up the worst of the mess.* ♦ *He used a piece of garlic bread to sop the sauce up.*

SORT /sɔːt, American sɔrt/
sorts, sorting, sorted

,sort 'out ★★★

1	make arrangements
2	deal with sth successfully
3	organize things
4	find out sth
5	provide sth
6	punish sb
+	PHRASES
+	**sort-out** noun

1 [often passive] *British* to make arrangements for something to happen, or decide how it will happen
be/get sorted out *Danny's organizing the food and the music's already sorted out.*
sort out sth *So who's sorting out the travel arrangements?*
sort sth out *If Bob deals with the New*

York office, I'll sort things out at this end.

sort out who/how etc *Have we sorted out who's sitting where?* ♦ *We needed to sort out how we're going to move the boat across land.*

2 [often passive] to do what is necessary to deal with a problem, disagreement, or difficult situation successfully

be sorted out *This matter could be sorted out if they would just try to be reasonable.* ♦ *We need to get this affair sorted out as soon as possible.*

sort sth out *A good lawyer will know how to sort this mess out.* ♦ *If we just get them to talk, I'm sure we can sort something out.*

sort out sth *He knew that speaking to friends wouldn't help sort out his love life.*

3 to get rid of things you do not need and arrange things that you do need in a neat way

sort out sth *I need to sort out the mess on my desk.*

sort sth out *I've managed to sort her papers out.* ♦ *I took his pile of receipts and invoices and spent a couple of hours sorting them out.*

4 to find out information that allows you to understand something = RESOLVE

sort out why/how etc *Investigators are still trying to sort out why the accident happened.* ♦ *The government should try to sort out who is to blame for the outbreak.*

5 *British informal* to provide something for someone

sort sb out *If you need a new water bottle, I can sort you out.*

sort sth out for sb *We'll sort out more suitable clothes for you.*

sort sb out with sth *The personnel staff will sort you out with a place to stay.*

sort sb out sth *We'll go down to the garage and sort you out a decent car.*

6 *British informal* to make someone stop causing problems for you, for example by talking to them or punishing them = DEAL WITH

sort sb out *Don't worry about him. I'll sort him out for you.*

sort out sb *We had to sort out some idiots who were hassling the old folks on the estate.*

PHRASES **sort itself out** if a bad situation sorts itself out, it ends without anyone taking action to deal with it: *Problems like these don't just sort themselves out.*

sort yourself out *British* to make yourself a more organized or sensible person so

that you can deal effectively with a situation: *Come back and see me when you've sorted yourself out.* ♦ *She needs to get herself sorted out before she starts applying for jobs.*

■ **'sort-out** noun [singular] *British informal* the process of getting rid of things you do not need and arranging things that you do need tidily: *I'm having a sort-out of the kids' clothes.*

,sort 'through

to look at a lot of things in order to find what you want or need

sort through sth *She sorted through the papers on her desk.*

SOUND /saʊnd/
sounds, sounding, sounded

,sound 'off

1 to express your opinions loudly, especially in an unreasonable way = HOLD FORTH

sound off *He's just sounding off at the moment – he'll calm down soon.* ♦ **+about** *Maria's always sounding off about politics.*

2 *American* if soldiers sound off, they count loudly together as part of a military exercise, for example while marching

sound off *The sergeant gives the order to sound off.*

,sound 'out ★

to try to find out someone's opinions, ideas, feelings etc by talking to them

sound out sb *Candidates will be sounding out voters during the months before the election.*

sound sb out *We need to find a way of sounding members out.* ♦ *I sounded them out on how their teams were likely to respond.*

SOUP /suːp, *American* sup/
soups, souping, souped

,soup 'up *informal*

to change something to make it faster, more powerful or more effective = BOOST

soup sth up *also* **soup up sth** *Young men souped their vehicles up and raced along the roads around Los Angeles.* ♦ *They've souped up their anti-virus software.*

■ **,souped-'up** adj [only before noun] made faster or more powerful or effective: *It's really a souped-up version of the old model.*

SPACE /speɪs/
spaces, spacing, spaced

ˌspace 'out

1 to arrange objects, events, activities etc so that they are not too close together, or so that they are a particular time or distance apart
space sth out *also* **space out sth** *Space bean plants out three inches apart.* ♦ *Try to space out your treats so that there's always something to look forward to.*
2 *American informal* to not pay attention to someone or something because you are thinking, tired, bored etc
space out *Say that again please – I spaced out for a minute.*

■ ˌspaced 'out **adj** not paying attention or not reacting properly: *Some of them looked spaced out on drugs.*

SPARK /spɑːk, American spɑrk/
sparks, sparking, sparked

ˌspark 'off ★

1 to make something happen, especially something involving violence or angry feelings = TRIGGER OFF
spark off sth *The trial sparked off widespread rioting in London.*
spark sth off *Let's look at the circumstances that sparked these events off.*
2 to make someone feel, think of, or remember something = TRIGGER OFF
spark off sth *Your article sparked off happy memories for me.*
spark sth off *I think I knew what had sparked this reverie off.* ♦ *The tears came without my knowing what had sparked them off.*

SPATTER /'spætə, American 'spætər/
spatters, spattering, spattered

'spatter with [usually passive]

to cover a surface with a lot of small drops of a liquid
be spattered with sth *The walls were spattered with blood.*

SPEAK /spiːk, American spik/
speaks, speaking, spoke /spəʊk, American spouk/, spoken /'spəʊkən, American 'spoʊkən/

'speak for ★★★

to represent the feelings or opinions of another person or group of people = SPEAK ON BEHALF OF
speak for sb/sth *I know I speak for us*

all when I say how sorry I am for this mistake. ♦ *I can't speak for other women in the group, but I was deeply offended by the remark.*

PHRASES **be spoken for**

1 if someone is spoken for, they are married or in a relationship with someone and therefore not available to start a relationship with someone else: *Don't look at him. He's spoken for.*
2 if something is spoken for, someone is using it or has claimed it and it is therefore not available to use: *I'm sorry. This seat's spoken for.*
speak for itself if something speaks for itself, it is obvious to people and you do not have to mention it or explain it: *The quality of the writing speaks for itself.*
speak for yourself 1 to give your opinion about something when you know that other people will disagree: *Speaking for myself, I'd say the event was a complete success.* ♦ *I am speaking not only for myself, but for everyone who has ever suffered this kind of discrimination.* **2** [always in imperative] used for telling someone that you do not agree with what they have said: 'We all hate it here.' 'Speak for yourself. I'm having a great time.'

'speak of *literary*

to seem to prove that something exists or something is true
speak of sth *Her extensive library spoke of her love of reading.*

ˌspeak 'out ★★

to state your opinion firmly and publicly about something, especially in order to protest against or defend something = BE FRANK, SPEAK UP
speak out *Don't be afraid to speak out if you feel you are not being treated fairly.* ♦ *He had always spoken out in favour of gay rights.*

■ **outspoken** /aʊt'spəʊkən/ **adj** an outspoken person states their opinion honestly, even if other people do not like it: *an outspoken critic of the government*

'speak to

to tell someone that you do not approve of something they have done and they must change their behaviour = REPRIMAND
speak to sb *I'm going to have to speak to her if this goes on any longer.*
♦ **+about** *You really ought to speak to him about coming late to class.*

,speak 'up ★★

1 to talk louder
speak up *You have to speak up. The people in the back can't hear you.*

2 to say what you think instead of saying nothing = SPEAK OUT
speak up *If anyone has a better idea, please speak up.*

,speak 'up for

to say something in support of someone or something = SUPPORT
speak up for sb/sth *In the end there was no-one who was prepared to speak up for her.*

SPEED /spiːd, *American* spid/
speeds, speeding, sped /sped/ **or speeded**

,speed 'off

to leave a place very quickly, especially in a vehicle
speed off *He jumped into the car and sped off.*

,speed 'up ★★★

1 to move faster or do something faster
= *formal* ACCELERATE ≠ SLOW DOWN
speed up *You see drivers speeding up when they should be slowing down.* ♦ *Is the expansion of the universe speeding up or slowing down?*

2 to make something move faster or happen faster ≠ SLOW DOWN
speed up sth *We're introducing new procedures to speed up the application process.*
speed sth up *I'll appreciate anything you can do to speed the building work up.*
♦ *We're hoping the changes will help speed things up a bit.*

SPELL /spel/
spells, spelling, spelt, spelt /spelt/ **or spelled**

,spell 'out ★★★

1 *informal* to say or explain something very clearly because someone has not understood something
spell sth out *It's frustrating when you have to spell everything out for them.*
♦ *Do I have to spell it out? This work is not up to standard.*
spell out sth *Can you spell out exactly why you took that decision?*

2 to say or write the letters of a word in the correct order
spell out sth *Children are encouraged to spell out each word aloud.*
spell sth out *Spell the word out in your head.* ♦ *If you're having difficulty saying a word, it often helps to spell it out.*

SPEW /spjuː, *American* spju/
spews, spewing, spewed

,spew 'out

to flow out or make something flow out with a lot of force
spew out sth *also* **spew sth out** *Every car spews out black exhaust fumes.* ♦ *Our factories spew all these gases out every day.*

,spew 'up *informal*

if someone spews up, food from their stomach comes out through their mouth, for example because they are ill
spew up *He spent the whole night spewing up.*
spew sth up *also* **spew up sth** *She spewed her breakfast up this morning.* ♦ *Then they spew up everything they've drunk.*

SPICE /spaɪs/
spices, spicing, spiced

,spice 'up

1 to make something more interesting or exciting = PEP UP
spice up sth *also* **spice sth up** *Spice up your life with an all-inclusive trip to Las Vegas!* ♦ *As a junior reporter you learn to spice stories up with a romantic interest where possible.*

2 to give food a stronger taste by adding things such as spices
spice up sth *also* **spice sth up** *You can spice up potatoes by adding a little garlic and nutmeg.* ♦ *I like to spice the sauce up with a teaspoon of brandy.*

SPILL /spɪl/
spills, spilling, spilled **or spilt** /spɪlt/

,spill 'out of

if people spill out of a place, a lot of them leave at the same time
spill out of sth *Crowds were spilling out of the bars and restaurants.*

,spill 'over

1 if a liquid spills over, it accidentally falls over the edge of its container, usually because the container is too full
= OVERFLOW
spill over *My hands shook so much that my coffee spilled over.*
spill over sth *The river spilled over its banks, causing widespread flooding.*

2 to spread to other areas
spill over *The protests have spilled over to affect other parts of the city.* ♦ *+to/into*

The new housing developments soon spilled over into the more rural areas.

■ **overspill** /ˈəʊvəspɪl/ **noun** [U] **1** the people who begin to live and work in places just outside a crowded city, making it bigger: *This seemed to be the answer to the problem of London's overspill.* **2** used generally about people or things that cannot fit into a crowded place: *an overspill car park*

■ **spillover** /ˈspɪləʊvə/ **noun** [singular] an effect that spreads to more people or things than originally intended: *We would have to limit the political spillover from such a move.*

SPIN /spɪn/
spins, spinning, span /spæn/, **spun** /spʌn/

ˌspin aˈround *same as* **spin round**

ˌspin ˈoff
1 [usually passive] to create something new based on something else that already exists
be spun off from sth *A whole new series was spun off from the original movie.*
2 to make part of a company into a new independent company
spin off sth *also* **spin sth off** *The company plans to spin off its manufacturing operation.* ♦ *It seemed feasible to spin the holiday side of the business off completely.*

■ **ˈspin-off** **noun** [C] **1** something good that happens unexpectedly as a result of something else: *The aim was a higher volume of business, and any benefits to staff were a spin-off.* **2** a new product, service, television programme etc that is based on another one that already exists: *She played a supporting role in the movie and starred in the TV spin-off.*

ˌspin ˈout
to make something last for a long time, usually longer than is good or necessary
= DRAG OUT
spin sth out *also* **spin out sth** *I tried to spin things out until you arrived.*

ˌspin ˈround ★ (*also* **ˌspin aˈround**)
1 to turn your head or body quickly to face the opposite direction, or turn someone quickly so that they face you
spin round *He spun round in surprise.*
spin sb round *He put a hand on the boy's shoulder and spun him round.*
2 to turn round and round, or make something turn round and round
spin round *He watched the wheel spinning round.* ♦ *She stared at the ceiling, which seemed to be spinning round.*
spin sth round *She spins the globe round with her hand.*
3 if thoughts spin round in your head, you keep thinking about different things in a nervous and uncontrolled way
spin round *She needed a diversion from the thoughts spinning round in her head.*

SPIRIT /ˈspɪrɪt/
spirits, spiriting, spirited

ˌspirit aˈway (*also* **ˌspirit ˈoff**) [usually passive]
to take someone or something away suddenly but without being noticed
be spirited away *Protesters were spirited away before they could cause a disruption.*

SPIT /spɪt/
spits, spitting, spat, spat /spæt/

ˈspit at
to force liquid out of your mouth in the direction of someone else, as an insult
spit at sb *That kid just spat at me!*

ˌspit ˈout *informal*
1 to force something out of your mouth
spit sth out *also* **spit out sth** *Babies are always spitting their food out.* ♦ *She spits out everything we give her to drink.*
2 to say something quickly and angrily
spit sth out *also* **spit out sth** *'Is that it – money?' She spat the word out.* ♦ *He paced about the room spitting out threats.*
PHRASE **spit it out!** used for telling someone to say something when they are too nervous or embarrassed to say it: *What happened here? Spit it out!*

ˌspit ˈup *American informal*
if a baby or animal spits up, or if it spits something up, a small amount of food from its stomach comes out of its mouth
spit up *Do the babies spit up much?*
spit sth up *also* **spit up sth** *She tends to spit her food up.* ♦ *You expect the younger ones to spit up a little milk.*

SPLASH /splæʃ/
splashes, splashing, splashed

ˌsplash aˈbout *British same as* **splash around**

'splash across (*also* **'splash over**) [usually passive]
if a news story or photograph is splashed across something, especially a newspaper, it is put in a position where it is very easy to see
be splashed across sth *You'd better co-operate if you don't want the story splashed across the front pages of the tabloids.*

'splash a'round (*also* **'splash a'bout** *British*)
to move around noisily in water
splash around *I left the kids splashing around in the pool.*

'splash 'down
when a space vehicle splashes down, it lands in the sea after being in space
splash down *They'll be splashing down in the Pacific.*

- **splashdown** /ˈsplæʃdaʊn/ **noun** [C]
an occasion when a space vehicle lands in the sea after being in space: *We expect splashdown to be at around 2.30 this afternoon.*

'splash 'out on ★ *British informal*
to spend a lot of money, especially on nice things for yourself
splash out *I'd just like to be able to splash out and enjoy myself occasionally.*
splash out on sth *He's just splashed out on a brand new car.*
splash out sth on sth *We'd just splashed out a small fortune on moving house.*
splash sth out on sth *We wouldn't splash that much out on a TV.*

splash out

'splash on (*also* **'splash onto**)
to put a liquid on a surface in a careless way
splash on sth *also* **splash sth on** *I'll just splash on a bit of perfume and I'll be*

ready. ♦ *They splashed as much paint as possible onto the boards.*

'splash over *same as* **splash across**

SPLIT /splɪt/
splits, splitting, split

'split 'off
to separate yourself from a larger group, organisation etc = BREAK AWAY
split off *A group of senior managers split off and formed their own company.*
♦ **+from sth** *Military sources said the plane had split off from the others during a training flight.*

'split 'up ★★
1 to end a marriage or romantic relationship = PART —*picture* → ASK OUT
split up *Her parents split up a few months ago.* ♦ **+with** *He's splitting up with his wife.*
split sb up *She didn't want anything to split her parents up.*
split up sb *How could such a trivial incident split up such a devoted couple?*
2 [often passive] to separate someone from the person or people they were with = PART, SEPARATE
be split up *If you get split up for any reason, call me immediately.*
split sb up *I had to split them up because they wouldn't stop messing around.*
split up sb *Confusion over which train to catch had split up our party.*
3 to divide into groups or parts, or divide people or things into groups or parts = DIVIDE
split up *She told the class to split up into four groups.*
split sth up *We split the money up between us.* ♦ *Take the coins and split them up into silver and copper.*
split up sth *The decision was taken to split up the programme into three one-week courses.*

SPOIL /spɔɪl/
spoils, spoiling, spoiled or **spoilt** /spɔɪlt/

'spoil for
PHRASE **be spoiling for a fight** to want to fight or argue with someone: *It seems that the music industry is spoiling for a fight.*

SPONGE /spʌndʒ/
sponges, sponging, sponged

ˌsponge ˈdown
to wash something or someone with a piece of a soft substance called a sponge, which sucks up water
> **sponge sth/sb down** also **sponge down sth/sb** *She sponged the child down at the sink.* ♦ *I'll have to sponge down these trousers.*

ˈsponge off *informal*
to ask for money and other things from friends or relatives and make no effort to give anything back or pay for anything yourself
> **sponge off sb** *Since he left college he's been sponging off his parents.*

SPRAY /spreɪ/
sprays, spraying, sprayed

ˈspray with
to shoot a large number of bullets at something
> **spray sth with sth** *Two gunmen were spraying the convoy with automatic gunfire.*

SPREAD /spred/
spreads, spreading, spread

ˈspread across *same as* **spread over**

ˌspread ˈout ★★★

1	gradually cover larger area
2	unfold or arrange on a surface
3	cover wide area below you
4	be in different areas
5	affect large area
6	divide into parts or stages
7	stretch out fingers, toes

1 if people in a group spread out, or if they spread themselves out, they move away from one another so that they cover a large area = FAN OUT
> **spread out** *Let's spread out more and search the whole field.*
> **spread yourselves out** *The police spread themselves out so that they surrounded the whole building.*

2 to open something that is folded so that it covers a surface, or separate things that were together and put them separately on a surface = LAY OUT
> **spread sth out** *We spread our picnic out on the grass.* ♦ *Davies took down a chart and spread it out on the table.*
> **spread out sth** *Spread out the map so we can all see it.*

3 [often passive] to cover a large area of land that you can see in front of you
= EXTEND
> **be spread out** *She gazed at the lights of the sprawling city spread out below her.*
> **spread out** *The suburbs of Athens spread out below us as far as we could see.*

4 [usually passive] to be present in many parts of a large area
> **be spread out** *The peacekeeping forces are now spread out over most of the country.*

5 to gradually affect or cover a larger area
> **spread out** *These vibrations spread out in all directions like a series of waves.* ♦ *Eventually the rioting spread out beyond the city centre.*

6 [usually passive] to make something happen at several times over a long period, rather than all at once
> **be spread out** *The students felt the course would be better if it was spread out over two years instead of one.*

7 to stretch out your arms, fingers, toes etc so that they are wide apart
> **spread sth out** *He spread out his toes in the soft sand and wriggled them.* ♦ *She rushed towards me, her arms spread out in welcome.*

ˈspread over (*also* ˈspread across)

1 [often passive] to divide an amount of money that you must pay into smaller parts and pay each amount separately over a period of time
> **be spread over sth** *The payments can be spread over 18 months.*
> **spread sth over sth** *Can we spread the repayment over several months?*

2 [always passive] to be present in many parts of a large area
> **be spread over sth** *Indonesia is a nation of over 200m people spread over 17,000 islands.*

SPRING /sprɪŋ/
springs, springing, sprang /spræŋ/, **sprung** /sprʌŋ/

ˌspring ˈback

1 to move your body backwards quickly and with a lot of energy
> **spring back** *From this position, you can spring back if you are attacked.*

2 if something that you pull or stretch springs back, it quickly returns to its original position or shape when you stop pulling or stretching it
> **spring back** *The metal springs back into shape.*

'spring for *American informal*

to pay for someone else's share of something

spring for sth *I'll spring for dinner tonight.*

'spring from ★★

to come from a particular place, family, or situation

spring from sb/sth *Hugh's interest in languages sprang from his upbringing in Spain.*

PHRASE **where did sb/sth spring from?** or **where has sb/sth sprung from?** used for showing that you are surprised that something exists, or that someone is present, because they were not there a short time ago: *Is that Ricky? Where did he spring from?* ♦ *I wondered where all these new shops had sprung from.*

'spring on

to tell someone something that they do not expect

spring sth on sb *They just sprang it on me at the office meeting.*

,spring 'up ★★

to appear or be produced suddenly and quickly = APPEAR

spring up *In southern California new Internet companies were springing up every day.*

SPRINKLE /'sprɪŋk(ə)l/
sprinkles, sprinkling, sprinkled

'sprinkle with ★

1 to shake small amounts of a liquid, powder etc over the surface of something
sprinkle sth with sth *Sprinkle the chicken with soy sauce.*

2 [always passive] to exist on or in something in a lot of separate small amounts
be sprinkled with sth *It's a touching and tragic story sprinkled with humour.*
♦ *Her dark brown hair was **liberally sprinkled** with grey (=she had a lot of grey hairs).*

SPROUT /spraʊt/
sprouts, sprouting, sprouted

,sprout 'up

if things sprout up somewhere, they appear there or increase in number suddenly and very quickly
sprout up *New businesses began to sprout up across the country.* ♦ *Anti-government posters are sprouting up along a nearby wall.*

SPRUCE /spruːs, *American* sprus/
spruces, sprucing, spruced

,spruce 'up [often passive]

to improve the appearance of someone or something = SMARTEN UP

be spruced up *The Convention Center had been spruced up for the occasion.*
spruce sth up *also* **spruce up sth** *Spruce your room up with a few pot plants.*
♦ *We spent the weekend trying to spruce up the garden.*

SPUR /spɜː, *American* spɜr/
spurs, spurring, spurred

,spur 'on

to encourage someone to do something
spur sb on *also* **spur on sb** *His comments spurred me on to success.* ♦ *We need plenty of supporters to spur on our team.*

SPY /spaɪ/
spies, spying, spied

'spy on ★ (*also* 'spy upon *formal*)

1 to watch someone secretly so that you know everything they do
spy on sb *Managers feel it is their duty to spy on the workforce.*

2 to secretly find out what an enemy country, government etc is doing or planning
spy on sb/sth *They were accused of spying on Soviet military installations.*

,spy 'out *formal*

1 to notice someone or something = NOTICE
spy out sb/sth *He quickly spied out the waiter.*

2 to look around an area in order to find something = DISCOVER
spy out sth *I've already spied out a decent-looking restaurant.*

'spy upon *same as* spy on

SQUARE /skweə, *American* skwer/
squares, squaring, squared

,square a'way [usually passive] *American*

to do the things necessary to complete something
be squared away *The project should be squared away in the spring.*

,square 'off

1 to make something such as an edge or corner straight
square off sth *also* **square sth off** *He squared off the front of the shelves.* ♦ *We*

lined the boards up and squared the ends off.

2 *American* if two people or groups square off, they prepare to start competing or fighting with each other = *British* SQUARE UP

square off *These commercial giants are squaring off like ageing warriors.*

,square 'up

1 if two people square up or square something up, one pays what they owe so that both people are equal = SETTLE UP

square up *Don't worry about it now. We can square up later.*

square up sth *also* **square sth up** *They agreed to square up any expenses once they got home.* ♦ *We can square any discrepancies up later.*

2 *British* if two people or groups square up, they prepare to start competing or fighting with each other = *American* SQUARE OFF

square up *In the meadow flanking the lane, two hares were squaring up.* ♦ **+to** *The two teams are squaring up to each other.*

,square 'up to

to start to deal with something or someone in a brave and determined way

square up to sth/sb *They squared up admirably to a very difficult situation.*

'square with ★

1 if one idea, opinion, explanation etc squares with another, they both seem good or reasonable

square with sth *Her story doesn't quite square with what the first witness said.*

square sth with sth *It was difficult to square this behaviour with his religious beliefs.*

2 to get permission from someone to do something

square sth with sb *I'll have to square it with the manager first.*

SQUAT /skwɒt, *American* skwɑt/
squats, squatting, squatted

,squat 'down

to bend your knees and lower yourself towards the ground so that you balance on your feet

squat down *Iris squatted down behind the wall.*

SQUEAK /skwiːk, *American* skwik/
squeaks, squeaking, squeaked

,squeak 'by *American informal*

to manage to achieve something or defeat someone after almost failing or losing

squeak by *With 588 votes, I just squeaked by.*

squeak by sb/sth *The Cats had squeaked by their first two opponents.*

'squeak through

to only just be successful, or only just be accepted = SCRAPE THROUGH

squeak through *The legislation is likely to squeak through.*

squeak through sth *She barely squeaked through her exams.*

SQUEEZE /skwiːz, *American* skwiz/
squeezes, squeezing, squeezed

,squeeze 'in

to be able to do something or see someone, even though you do not have much time

squeeze sth/sb in *also* **squeeze in sth/sb** *The doctor will be able to squeeze you in this afternoon.* ♦ *I can squeeze in a meeting early tomorrow morning.*

,squeeze 'out ★

1 [often passive] if one thing squeezes out another, the first one becomes so important or successful, or it takes up so much time, that the other cannot succeed or continue = FORCE OUT

be squeezed out *The longer you work, the more your family life is being squeezed out.* ♦ **+of** *Music instruction is slowly being squeezed out of the curriculum.*

squeeze out sb/sth *The company tried hard to squeeze out competitors and raise prices.*

squeeze sb/sth out *Supermarkets become successful by squeezing smaller shops out.*

2 to make someone tell you something even though they do not want to = WRING, EXTRACT

squeeze sth out of sb *They made one final attempt to squeeze concessions out of us.*

SQUIRREL /'skwɪrəl/
squirrels, squirrelling, squirrelled

,squirrel a'way

to put something away in a secret place, especially money and especially over a long period of time

squirrel away sth *also* **squirrel sth away**

Over the years she had squirrelled away over $30,000. ♦ *By saving a little each week, you'll have squirrelled a fair amount away by the end of the year.*

STACK /stæk/
stacks, stacking, stacked

ˌstack 'up ★

1 to increase continuously = MOUNT UP
stack up *The evidence against her is stacking up all the time.*

2 [often passive] to arrange things so that they are on top of each other in a pile
be stacked up *The books had been stacked up in neat piles.*
stack sth up *You can stack the boxes up in that corner.*
stack up sth *I found Jimmy stacking up chairs in the hall.*

3 to fly above or below other planes while waiting to land
stack up *High winds forced planes to stack up over Heathrow Airport.*

4 *informal* to show how good or bad you are when compared to someone or something else
stack up *OK, let's see how you guys stack up.* ♦ **+against** *Teachers will know how they stack up against national standards.*

stack up (sense 2)

STAKE /steɪk/
stakes, staking, staked

'stake on

1 to risk losing or damaging something important if you do not succeed in doing, getting or achieving something
stake sth on sth *I'd staked my whole future on this marriage.* ♦ *The government has staked its reputation on reducing the deficit.*

2 to risk losing money by betting on the result of a race, game, competition etc
stake sth on sth *If they get a good tip, some punters are willing to stake a month's wages on it.*

ˌstake 'out

1 to explain your opinion clearly and defend it in a determined way
stake out sth *also* **stake sth out** *Political leaders are busy staking out their positions on this issue.* ♦ *The honest thing to do is to stake your view out openly.*

2 to stay outside a building and watch it, especially because something exciting or illegal is happening
stake out sth *also* **stake sth out** *The police are staking out his home in case he returns.* ♦ *We've been staking the factory out for a few days.*

3 to mark an area with fences or posts to show that it belongs to someone
stake out sth *also* **stake sth out** *The settlers would arrive in a place and immediately stake out their territory.*

■ ˌstaked 'out adj waiting outside a building and watching it, especially because something exciting or illegal is happening: *I have dozens of reporters staked out on my lawn.*

■ **stakeout** /ˈsteɪkaʊt/ noun [C] an act of watching a place secretly over a period of time in order to catch a criminal or find out whether there is any illegal activity there

STAMMER /ˈstæmə, *American* ˈstæmər/
stammers, stammering, stammered

ˌstammer 'out

to say something with great difficulty, especially because you are very nervous or frightened
stammer out sth *also* **stammer sth out** *The boy managed to stammer out a description of his attacker.* ♦ *She eventually stammered the words out.*

STAMP /stæmp/
stamps, stamping, stamped

'stamp on

1 *British* to stop something by taking determined action = CRACK DOWN ON
stamp on sth *The referees will stamp on any sign of violence on the field.*

2 *British* to use unfair or cruel methods to stop someone from doing something
stamp on sb *They will stamp on anyone who gets in their way.*

,stamp 'out ★★

1 [often passive] to end something bad or unpleasant by taking strong and determined action = *formal* ERADICATE
> **be stamped out** *Those sloppy standards had been stamped out by the time I arrived.*
> **stamp out sth** *It is our duty to stamp out any abuses of political power.*
> **stamp sth out** *We will not flinch from stamping such behaviour out completely.*

2 to make a fire stop burning by stamping on it (=putting your feet down hard on it) = *formal* EXTINGUISH
> **stamp out sth** *He stamped out the flames before they could spread.*
> **stamp sth out** *'What shall we do about the fire?' 'Better stamp it out before the girls see it'.*

3 to press the shape of an object out of a substance such as clay or plastic using a tool or machine
> **stamp out sth** *Once crowned king, he began stamping out coins with his name on.*
> **stamp sth out** *Of course, the Vikings would have stamped these coins out by hand.*

4 to produce an object or a particular type of person easily and in large quantities
> **stamp out sb/sth** *The Brazilians seem able to stamp out players of amazing ability year after year.*

STAMPEDE /stæm'piːd, *American* ˌstæm'piːd/
stampedes, stampeding, stampeded

stam'pede into

to force someone into doing something without giving them the chance to think about it
> **stampede sb into sth** *Don't let them stampede you into anything you might regret.*

STAND /stænd/
stands, standing, stood /stʊd/

Stand is often used with adverbs and prepositions when it means 'to have your body in an upright position supported by your feet': *He blushed whenever Mrs Carter was standing nearby.* ♦ *A man stood in the doorway, sheltering from the rain.* ♦ *He stood on the balcony and addressed the expectant crowd below.* These uses are not included here.

,stand a'bout *British same as* **stand around**

,stand a'gainst *British*

1 to oppose someone or something, especially in a brave or determined way
> **stand against sb/sth** *We must stand against the evil forces that are threatening our country.*

2 to compete against a particular person in an election
> **stand against sb** *He stood against her in the party elections of 2003.*

,stand a'part

1 to not involve yourself in something or with someone
> **stand apart** *It's difficult to stand apart when so many people are suffering.*
> ♦ **+from** *Some seem able to stand apart from the drama while others are in tears.*

2 if one person or thing stands apart, they are much better than all others
> **stand apart** *As a blues musician, he stands apart.* ♦ **+from** *It stands apart from all other visitor attractions in the region.*

,stand a'round ★ (*also* ,stand a'bout *British*)

to stand somewhere and do nothing, often when you should be doing something
> **stand around** *A group of construction workers were standing around outside the site.* ♦ *They left us standing around in the lobby for over two hours.*

,stand a'side ★★

1 to move to one side in order to let someone go past you
> **stand aside** *They quickly stood aside to let me pass.*

2 *British* to not involve yourself in a situation, especially one that you should be trying to prevent = STAND BY
> **stand aside** *You can't just stand aside and let your colleagues be treated like that!*

3 to stop doing your job and let someone else do it instead = STAND DOWN, STEP DOWN, RESIGN
> **stand aside** *The trade secretary has been asked to stand aside in favour of her deputy.*

,stand 'back ★★

1 to move away from something or stand at a distance from something, especially something dangerous
> **stand back** *Stand back all of you – this could be dangerous.* ♦ **+from** *The children were told to stand well back from the fire.*

2 to not let yourself be influenced by your

feelings about a situation so that you can think about it more clearly

stand back *I forced myself to stand back and assess the situation.*

,stand 'back from

if a building stands back from a road, it is a short distance away from it

stand back from sth *The house stands about 20 yards back from the main street.*

,stand be'tween

to prevent someone from gaining or achieving something = COME BETWEEN

stand between sb and sth *Only one person stood between her and the presidency.*

,stand 'by ★★★

1 [often progressive] to be ready to do something

stand by *A boat will be standing by in case of emergency.* ♦ **+to do sth** *Stand by to start the engine when I say.*

2 to not do anything about something when you should do something = STAND ASIDE

stand by *We can't just stand by and watch her die.*

3 to be loyal to someone who is in a difficult situation = SUPPORT, STICK BY ≠ ABANDON

stand by sb *We knew they would stand by us no matter what we'd done.*

4 to continue to have an opinion or belief even though other people have doubts about it or disagree with you

stand by sth *The doctors are standing by their claim that they are not at fault.* ♦ *We're standing by our decision not to allow him to play.*

■ **bystander** /'baɪstændə/ **noun** [C] someone who is in a particular place by chance when an accident or an unusual event happens but who is not directly connected with it: *Three innocent bystanders were wounded in the explosion.*

■ **standby** /'stændbaɪ/ **adj** a standby plane ticket is a cheap one that you buy just before the flight is ready to leave if there are still seats available: *These are the risks when you take a standby ticket.* **PHRASE** **on standby 1** available to be used if it is needed in a particular situation: *The troops are on standby and can return at a moment's notice.* **2** ready to get on a plane if there is a seat left when it is about to take off: *Our flight was overbooked so we were put on standby for the next one.* **3** used about a piece of electrical equipment, for example a

television, that is switched on but not in use: *People are being encouraged to save electricity by not leaving their electrical appliances on standby.*

■ **standby** /'stændbaɪ/ **noun** [C] someone or something that is always available to be used if it is needed in a particular situation: *a standby diesel generator*

,stand 'down ★★

1 to leave a job or position, especially an important one = RESIGN, STAND ASIDE, STEP DOWN

stand down *They are calling on the governor to stand down.* ♦ **+as** *She'll be standing down as president at the end of the year.*

2 to leave the witness box in a court of law after you have answered lawyers' questions

stand down *Thank you. You may now stand down.*

'stand for ★★★

1 if a letter, an abbreviation, or a symbol stands for something, that is what it means or represents = REPRESENT

stand for sth *The letters ETA stand for Estimated Time of Arrival.* ♦ *What does 'eg' stand for?*

2 [usually with a negative] to be willing to accept something that someone does = PUT UP WITH; *formal* TOLERATE

stand for sth *I'm not going to stand for any of this nonsense any longer.* ♦ *No one makes a fool of me. I won't stand for it!*

3 if someone stands for a particular principle, they believe that principle is important

stand for sth *I hate them and everything they stand for.*

4 *British* to try to get chosen in an election for a particular position or to become a member of a particular institution = *mainly American* RUN FOR

stand for sth *Malcolm McLaren once stood for Mayor of London.* ♦ *She is intending to stand for parliament.*

,stand 'in

to do someone else's job temporarily while they are not available to do it = FILL IN

stand in *Lorraine was ready to stand in if Helen got sick.* ♦ **+for** *I'll be standing in for Peter while he's away.*

■ **'stand-in noun** [C] **1** someone or something that takes the place of another person or thing for a short time, especially in order to do their job while they are not available: *He's not the* *manager. He's just a stand-in.* **2** someone who takes the place of the main actor in a particular scene of a film, especially a dangerous scene: *She refused to let a stand-in do the scene.*

‚stand 'out ★★★

1 to be easy to see or notice because of being different = SHOW UP, STICK OUT

stand out *I don't want to do anything that might make me stand out.* ♦ *Her bright clothes always make her stand out in a crowd.* ♦ **+against** *His turquoise tie stood out against his black suit.* ♦ **+from** *Their battered old car stood out from all the rest.*

2 to be much more impressive or important than other people or things

stand out *All the entries were good, but one in particular stands out.* ♦ *It stands out in my mind as the most exciting day of my career.* ♦ **+as** *Germany stands out as the leader in environmental reporting.*

■ **outstanding** /aʊtˈstændɪŋ/ **adj** **1** extremely good or impressive: *a visit to an area of outstanding natural beauty* **2** a job or action that is outstanding has not yet been completed or dealt with: *Some tasks are still outstanding.* **3** an amount of money that is outstanding has not yet been paid: *All your outstanding debts must be settled now.*

■ **standout** /ˈstændaʊt/ **noun** [C] *American informal* someone or something that you notice because they are much better than anyone or anything else: *Everyone else is fine, but Ellen Burstyn as Beth's mother is a standout.*

■ **standout** /ˈstændaʊt/ **adj** [only before noun] *American informal* noticeable because of being much better than anyone or anything else: *a standout performance*

‚stand 'out against *British*

to oppose something publicly and in a determined way

stand out against sth *They are not ashamed to stand out against injustice.*

‚stand 'out for *British*

to refuse to accept less than you are asking for = HOLD OUT FOR

stand out for sth *We are standing out for a fair reward for our hard work.*

‚stand 'over

to stand close to someone and watch them while they are doing something, usually in order to make sure they are doing it correctly

stand over sb *I'm fed up with him standing over me while I work.*

stand out

‚stand 'up ★★★

1	make your body upright
2	have your body upright
3	react to severe conditions
4	still be true/correct
5	fail to meet sb
+	PHRASE
+	**stand-up** adj, noun; **upstanding** adj

1 to put your body into an upright position from a sitting or lying position = *formal* RISE ≠ SIT DOWN

stand up *A man at the back of the hall stood up.* ♦ *She stood up and wandered over to the window.* ♦ **+to do sth** *I stood up to open the window.*

2 to have your body in an upright position supported by your feet

stand up *You have the chair. I don't mind standing up.* ♦ *Stand up straight and take your hands out of your pockets.*

3 to react in a particular way to severe conditions or treatment = HOLD UP

stand up *I wasn't sure how well the house would stand up in a storm.* ♦ **+to** *She was confident her witness would stand up well to detailed questioning.*

4 [usually with a negative] to still seem true or correct after being examined carefully

stand up *I'm afraid his alibi doesn't stand up.* ♦ *We all knew her story wouldn't stand up in court.*

5 [often passive] to not come to meet someone you have arranged to meet, especially someone you are having or starting a romantic relationship with

be stood up *She's been stood up again.* ♦ *I'm sick of being stood up by him!*

stand sb up *Did she stand you up again?*

PHRASE **stand up and be counted** to state or show publicly that you support someone or something, especially when something bad could happen to you as a result: *Thankfully, plenty of his friends* were willing to stand up and be counted.

■ **'stand-up** adj **1** consisting of one person standing in front of an audience and entertaining them by telling jokes: *stand-up comedians* **2** *British* noisy and sometimes violent: *a stand-up fight* **3** *American* loyal and able to be trusted: *He's a stand-up kind of guy.*

■ **'stand-up** noun **1** [U] an activity in which one person stands in front of an audience and entertains them by telling jokes: *A lot of comedians hate doing stand-up.* **2** [C] someone whose job is to stand in front of an audience and entertain them by telling jokes: *He started out as a stand-up.*

■ **upstanding** /ˌʌpˈstændɪŋ/ adj *formal* honest and deserving respect: *He was a fine, upstanding young man.*
   PHRASE **be upstanding** *British formal* used as a way of asking people to stand up during an official ceremony or in a court of law: *Please be upstanding for the bride and groom.*

ˌstand 'up for ★★

to defend someone or something that is being criticized or attacked = DEFEND
   stand up for sth/sb *You've got to stand up for what you believe in.* ♦ *The only crime they've ever committed is to stand up for their rights.* ♦ *If your friends won't stand up for you, who will?*
   stand up for yourself *I learned how to stand up for myself early on in life.*

ˌstand 'up to

to not allow yourself to be treated badly, especially by someone in authority = FACE
   stand up to sb *Nobody thought he would be brave enough to stand up to her.*

stand up to

STARE /steə, *American* ster/
stares, staring, stared

ˌstare 'down (*also* ˌstare 'out)

to look at someone for so long that you force them to look away
   stare sb down *also* **stare down sb** *She was trying to stare me down.* ♦ *It's not a good idea to stare down the judges.*

START /stɑːt, *American* stɑrt/
starts, starting, started

ˌstart 'back ★

1 to begin returning to a place
   start back *It's time we were starting back.* ♦ **+to/towards** *The rest of us had started back to Oxford.* ♦ *She had started back towards the house.*

2 to make a sudden and nervous movement away from someone or something that has frightened you
   start back *She started back in fright.*

3 to begin studying or working again after a break
   start back *She starts back at work on Monday.* ♦ *I want to start back as soon as I'm fit.*

4 if school, university etc starts back, classes begin again after a break
   start back *When do the schools start back?*

'start for *old-fashioned*

to begin a journey to a place
   start for sth *Tomorrow I start for Bristol.*

ˌstart 'in *American informal*

to begin talking in a boring or annoying way, usually complaining or criticizing someone or something
   start in *She was waiting for me and started in again.* ♦ **+on** *Then she starts in on the dangers of marriage.*

ˌstart 'off ★★★

1 to make something begin
   start off sth *We don't want to start off a riot.*
   start sth off *I always start the show off with a song.* ♦ **+by** *If it's going to be a long interview, I start it off by making my guest feel comfortable.*

2 to start, especially in a particular way or by doing a particular thing = BEGIN ≠ FINISH
   start off *She started off well but slowed down halfway through the race.* ♦ **+with** *Let's start off with some questions from the audience.*

3 to begin moving, or begin a journey

start off *There are one or two things to bear in mind before you start off.* ♦ **+for** *He started off for the station at a brisk pace.*

4 *informal* to make someone behave in a silly or emotional way

start sb off *Take care what you say or you'll start her off again.*

PHRASE start off on the wrong foot to immediately establish a bad relationship with someone when you first meet them or first start working with them: *We seemed to have started off on the wrong foot.*

'start on ★★

1 to begin doing or dealing with something

start on sth *We could have breakfast before we start on the painting.* ♦ *She ate all the cakes, then started on the chocolates.*

2 *informal* to begin to criticize or complain about someone or something

start on sb *Don't start on me!* ♦ **+about** *She started on about this dog barking in the street.*

,start 'out ★★

1 to begin as one thing before developing into something else

start out *When she first started out she sang in a church choir.* ♦ **+as** *Some businesses start out as hobbies.*

2 to begin a trip = SET OUT, START OFF

start out *We started out at five o'clock and got there at eight.*

3 to intend to do or be something = SET OUT, INTEND

start out to do sth *She didn't start out to be a model.*

,start 'over *American*

1 to begin doing something again from the beginning

start over *She counted all the envelopes, put them back in the box, then started over.*

2 to begin a new career or way of life

start over *I'm getting a little bit too old to start over.*

,start 'up ★★★

1 to start a new business, organization or project = SET UP; *formal* ESTABLISH

start up *The agency helps over 1,000 companies start up each year.*

start up sth *She left the company last year to start up her own business.*

start sth up *One week I contacted a few people and we started the charity up the following week.* ♦ *There are many good*

ideas for research projects but nobody has started them up.

2 to switch on a machine or engine, especially a motor vehicle

start up sth *She got into the car and started up the engine.*

start sth up *I showed him how to start the truck up and get it into gear.* ♦ *She was an old wreck of a car but I never had any trouble starting her up.*

■ **'start-up** noun **1** [singular] the process of starting a business or other activity: *An outside team is brought in to manage the start-up.* **2** [C] a business or company that has just started: *She's the brains behind the Massachusetts-based Internet start-up.*

STARVE /stɑːv, *American* stɑrv/
starves, starving, starved

'starve for [often progressive]
if you are starving for something or you are starved for something, you want it very much because you have not had it for a long time

be starving for sth *They talked as if they were starving for talk.*

be starved for sth *Soldiers were always starved for news of home.*

be 'starved of
to have very little of something that you need or want very much:

be starved of sth *These children are starved of affection.* ♦ *China is starved of oil.*

,starve 'out
to force people to leave a place by preventing them from getting enough food

starve sb out *also* **starve out sb** *If we can't flush them out, we'll starve them out.* ♦ *The idea was to starve out the enemy.*

STASH /stæʃ/
stashes, stashing, stashed

,stash a'way [often passive] *informal*
to keep money or something valuable in a safe place, where other people cannot find it

have sth stashed away *Police suspect that Barnes has about $5 million stashed away in various accounts.*

stash sth away *She gathered up her jewellery and stashed it away under the bed.*

STAVE /steɪv/
staves, staving, staved or stove /stoʊv/, staved

stave 'in [usually passive]
to seriously damage something by crushing it or breaking it from the outside
be staved in *The side of the car was staved in from the accident.*

stave 'off
to stop something bad from happening or stop it from affecting you = FEND OFF
stave off sth *also* **stave sth off** *We're still trying to stave off a trade war with the US.* ♦ *High running costs are a danger, but a good manager can stave that off.* ♦ *They ate grass and berries to try and stave off their hunger.*

STAY /steɪ/
stays, staying, stayed

stay a'head
to remain in a better position or situation than others
stay ahead *Our economy needs to grow if we are to stay ahead.*

stay a'round
to continue to stay with a person or at a place
stay around *How long do you think Jason will stay around this time?*

stay a'way ★
1 to not go to a place = STOP AWAY
stay away *So far, customers have stayed away.*
2 to not meet someone, talk to someone, or have a relationship with someone
stay away *My dad told him to stay away.* ♦ **+from** *I want you to stay away from my son.*

stay a'way from
to avoid mentioning something or avoid becoming involved in something
stay away from sth *We stayed away from the subject of politics.* ♦ *I want to stay away from any arrangement to look after her kids.*

stay 'back
1 to remain somewhere after everyone else has left = STAY BEHIND
stay back *I stayed back and let the others go home.*
2 to not move forwards, or not move towards something, usually something dangerous or unpleasant
stay back *I warned them to stay back.* ♦ *Most defenders are happier staying back.*

stay be'hind ★
to remain somewhere after everyone else has left = STAY BACK
stay behind *Tony stayed behind and helped John clean up the kitchen.*

stay 'down
1 to remain under water
stay down *Even with breathing apparatus, you couldn't stay down for an hour.*
2 if food that you have eaten stays down, it stays in your stomach and you are not sick
stay down *She had a piece of toast and that stayed down.*

stay 'in ★
to stay at home, or to stay indoors, instead of going out = STOP IN
stay in *I think I'd rather stay in tonight.*

stay 'off ★

1	avoid sth
2	not go to work/school
3	not mention sth
4	avoid place
5	not become heavier

1 to avoid eating a particular food, avoid drinking a particular drink, or avoid using illegal drugs
stay off sth *The best advice is to stay off alcohol altogether.*
2 *British* to not go to work or school because you are ill
stay off *She stayed off for another two days.*
stay off sth *I daren't stay off work.*
3 to avoid mentioning something
stay off sth *My main concern was to stay off the subject of religion.*
4 to avoid going to a particular place
stay off sth *We decided to stay off the motorway.* ♦ *You won't get into trouble if you stay off the streets.*
5 if weight that you have lost from your body stays off, you do not become heavier again
stay off *Let's make sure those pounds stay off.*

stay 'on ★★
to stay in a job, at school, at a place etc longer than you had intended to or longer than you have to = REMAIN, STOP ON
stay on *James promised to stay on for six months after his contract was up.* ♦ **+after** *I used to stay on after school to help the teacher clear up.*

stay up

sleep through

sleep in/lie in

lie down

get up

verbs to do with sleeping

,stay 'out

to not return to your home, especially
when it is late = *British informal* STOP OUT
stay out *Please don't stay out all night
again!* ♦ *She used to stay out late night
after night.*

,stay 'out of

to avoid becoming involved in something
stay out of sth *They had promised to
stay out of political affairs.* ♦ *I was
determined to stay out of trouble.*

,stay 'over

to sleep in someone's house as a guest for
one night = STOP OVER
stay over *It's getting late. Do you want
to stay over?*

,stay to'gether ★

if two people stay together, they continue
to live together or to have a relationship
with each other
stay together *They decided to stay
together for the sake of the children.*

,stay 'up ★★

to not go to bed at your usual time = *British
informal* STOP UP
stay up *Josh could stay up all night
without getting tired.*

,stay 'with

to continue doing something although it
is difficult or although other people have
stopped doing it = STICK WITH
stay with sth *How many students stay
with the course?* ♦ *Kids who become
involved in the sport tend to stay with it
into adulthood.*

STEAL /stiːl, *American* stil/
steals, stealing, stole /stəʊl, *American*
stoʊl/, **stolen** /'stəʊlən, *American*
'stoʊlən/

,steal a'way (*also* ,steal 'off)

to leave a place quietly and secretly
steal away *Some people say she stole
away in the dead of night.*

,steal 'over

1 if a feelings steals over you, you
gradually begin to feel it
steal over sb *I felt a warm deep pleasure
steal over me.*

2 if an expression steals over someone's
face, they gradually begin to have that
expression on their face
steal over sth *A grim expression stole
over his face.*

ˌsteal 'up

to move towards someone quietly and slowly, because you do not want them to see or hear you = CREEP UP

steal up *I didn't notice him stealing up silently behind me.* ♦ **+on** *He stole up on her silently in the dark.*

STEAM /stiːm, *American* stiːm/
steams, steaming, steamed

ˌsteam 'off

to remove something from a surface using steam

steam off sth *also* **steam sth off** *People used to steam off the stamps.* ♦ *We tried steaming the paint off.*

ˌsteam 'open

to use steam in order to separate two edges of an envelope that have been stuck together, so that you do not have to tear the paper in order to open it

steam sth open *also* **steam open sth** *Someone had steamed open the envelope.*

ˌsteam 'up [often passive]

to cover something with steam or become covered with steam = MIST UP

be/get steamed up *My glasses were getting steamed up.*

steam up sth *also* **steam sth up** *The hot bathwater had steamed the mirror up.*

steam up *The car windows had all steamed up.*

■ ˌsteamed-'up *adj* **1** *informal* angry or upset about something: *There's no point getting all steamed up about it.* **2** covered with steam: *I peered through the steamed-up windows.*

STEEP /stiːp, *American* stiːp/
steeps, steeping, steeped

be 'steeped in

to have a lot of a particular quality or thing

be steeped in sth *The region is steeped in history.*

STEER /stɪə, *American* stɪr/
steers, steering, steered

ˌsteer a'way from

to try to influence someone or something so that they avoid or do not get involved in something

steer sb/sth away from sth *She always tried to steer her kids away from crime.* ♦ *I could see that Jim was attempting to steer the conversation away from religion.*

ˌsteer to'wards

to influence someone or something so that they do what you want them to do or so that they develop in the way you want them to

steer sb/sth towards sth *We need to think of more ways to steer students towards higher education.*

STEM /stem/
stems, stemming, stemmed

'stem from

to be caused by someone or something = ARISE FROM

stem from sb/sth *His popularity stemmed from the fact that he was born in the area.* ♦ *Many of her problems stem from her family.*

STEP /step/
steps, stepping, stepped

Step is often used with adverbs and prepositions when it means 'to move a short distance, especially by putting one foot in front of the other': *Step back or you'll get hit by the ball.* ♦ *Carl stepped from the taxi, pulling up his collar against the rain.* ♦ *I sneaked out early the next morning, stepping carefully over the sleeping bodies in the living room.* These uses are not included here.

ˌstep a'side

to leave a position or job, especially so that someone else can take your place = MOVE OVER

step aside *The manager announced he is stepping aside.* ♦ **+for** *Older, more experienced workers are not necessarily going to step aside for younger people.*

ˌstep 'back ★

to stop what you are doing for a short time in order to think carefully about it

step back *Let's step back and have another look at this.*

ˌstep 'down ★★

to leave your job, especially an important job = STAND ASIDE ≠ STAY ON

step down *The chairman was forced to step down because of ill health.* ♦ **+as** *Sandra stepped down as treasurer.*

ˌstep 'forward

to offer to help or do something for someone = COME FORWARD, VOLUNTEER

step forward *Ron stepped forward and offered to change the tyre.* ♦ *We're urging as many people as possible to step forward.*

,step 'in ★★

to become involved in a discussion or argument, especially in order to make it stop = INTERVENE

step in *Many people feel it's time for the government to step in and resolve the dispute.*

'step on

PHRASE **step on it** *informal* used to tell someone to go faster, especially in a car: *Step on it, will you. I'm in a hurry.*

,step 'out

to leave a place for a short time = GO OUT

step out *I'm sorry, Karen's just stepped out for a second.*

,step 'up ★★

1 to increase something = INCREASE, INTENSIFY

step up sth *The president has stepped up the pressure on the groups to come to an agreement.*

step sth up *Today police stepped their search up in the hope of still finding possible witnesses.*

Nouns often used as objects with **step up 1**

■ attack, campaign, efforts, fight, pace, pressure, production, search, security

2 to move forwards to a place where an official event is happening

step up *She stepped up to receive her prize.*

PHRASE **step up (to the plate)** *American* to offer to help someone or take responsibility for something: *Women have been waiting for decades for men to step up to the plate and share the workload of parenting.*

STEREOTYPE /'steriətaɪp/
stereotypes, stereotyping, stereotyped

'stereotype as [usually passive] *showing disapproval*

to say or think that someone has a particular character or behaves in a particular way because this is what a lot of people think someone of their race, class, sex etc is usually like

be stereotyped as sth *Feminists are sometimes stereotyped as aggressive and unattractive.*

STICK /stɪk/
sticks, sticking, stuck /stʌk/

Stick is often used with adverbs and prepositions when it means 'to fix one thing to another, especially using a sticky substance such as glue', or 'to put something somewhere quickly and without taking much care': *We stuck the articles in a scrapbook.* ♦ *She was busy sticking posters on her bedroom wall.* ♦ *Ned stuck his head around the kitchen door and said goodbye.* ♦ *Here, take this book and stick it back on the shelf for me.* These uses are not included here.

,stick a'round *informal*

to stay in a place for longer than you originally intended, especially in order to wait for something to happen = LINGER ≠ LEAVE

stick around *If you stick around a bit longer you might see some action!*

'stick at *British*

to continue to work at something difficult or unpleasant in a determined way = KEEP AT, PERSEVERE WITH ≠ GIVE UP

stick at sth *Just stick at it and I'm sure it'll get easier.*

PHRASE **stick at nothing** *informal* to do whatever is necessary, even something illegal or cruel, in order to achieve your aim: *He'll stick at nothing to get what he wants.*

'stick by

1 to continue to support someone who is in a difficult situation = STAND BY

stick by sb *My mother has stuck by me throughout all this.*

2 to do something that you promised or decided that you would do

stick by sth *The head teacher is sticking by his decision to resign.*

,stick 'down *informal*

to write something quickly and without taking much care

stick sth down *also* **stick down sth** *Just stick your details down on a piece of paper and I'll get back to you.*

,get stuck 'in *British informal*

to start to do something with a lot of energy or enthusiasm

get stuck in *Pull on a pair of gloves and get stuck in.*

'stick ,on

1 *informal* to say that someone is responsible for something bad

stick sth on sb *Don't try and stick the blame for this mess on me.*

2 [always passive] to think that someone or something is extremely good or attractive
be stuck on sb/sth *He still seems stuck on the idea of going to Florida.*

,stick 'out ★★★

1 to continue further than the end of a surface or the main part of an object
= PROTRUDE
stick out *Your hair's all sticking out at the back.* ♦ **+of** *A magazine was sticking out of his coat pocket.* ♦ **+from** *A pair of feet stuck out from under the blanket.*
♦ **+through** *His bony elbows stuck out through holes in his jacket.*

2 to push or stretch something forwards or away from you, especially a part of your body
stick sth out *He stuck his chest out proudly as he stepped onto the stage.*
stick out sth *Ben stuck out his tongue at the little girl.* ♦ **+of** *She stuck her arm out of the car window and waved.*
♦ **+from** *Alice stuck her head out from under the duvet.*

3 to be easy to notice or remember because of being unusual or different
= STAND OUT
stick out *Of all my memories of her, one in particular sticks out.* ♦ **+of** *One face in particular stuck out of the crowd.*

4 to continue doing something difficult or unpleasant to the end ≠ GIVE UP
stick out sth *Try to stick out the treatment for a few more weeks.*
stick sth out *It was a tough course, but most of us stuck it out.*
PHRASES **stick your neck out** to take a risk by saying or doing something that could be wrong or could make other people react angrily: *I'm going to stick my neck out here and say it's possible that Gary's to blame for all this.*
stick out like a sore thumb to be very different from everyone or everything else: *You stick out like a sore thumb in that uniform.*
stick out a mile *informal* to be very obvious: *It sticks out a mile that she's in love with him.*

,stick 'out for *informal*

to be determined to get what you want or need, and not be willing to accept anything less = HOLD OUT FOR
stick out for sth *The workers are sticking out for a 6% pay rise.*

stick out

'stick to ★★★

1	do what you promised to do
2	obey rules/instructions
3	continue doing/using sth
4	deal with one thing only
5	not leave a path/road etc
6	stay close to sb
7	not change your opinion/decision
+	PHRASE

1 to do something that you promised or decided you would do, or that you believe you should do = KEEP TO
stick to sth *We said we'd give her the cash, and we must stick to our agreement.* ♦ *A lot of people have trouble sticking to a diet.*

2 to obey rules or instructions = FOLLOW
stick to sth *He always sticks precisely to the recipe.* ♦ *If everyone sticks to the rules, we shouldn't have any problems.*

3 to continue to do or use one particular thing and not change it or stop it for any period of time = KEEP TO ≠ ABANDON
stick to sth *I think we should stick to our original plan.*

4 to talk about, write about, or deal with one particular thing only
stick to sth *Writers should stick to what they know about.* ♦ *I do wish you'd stick to the point.* ♦ *I don't care what you think. Just stick to the facts.*

5 to continue to follow a particular path, road etc, especially in order to avoid danger or getting lost = KEEP TO
stick to sth *Remember to stick to the tracks – some of the land around here is mined.*

6 to stay very close to someone and follow them wherever they go
stick to sb *Moore stuck close to the race leader until the last lap.* ♦ *I want you to find him and stick to him. Don't let him out of your sight.*

7 to refuse to change what you originally said

stick to sth *I've told you everything I know and I'm sticking to it.* ♦ *Despite widespread ridicule, she's **sticking to her story**.*

PHRASE **stick to your guns** *informal* to refuse to change what you are saying or doing despite the opposition or criticism of other people

,stick to'gether ★ *informal*

if people stick together, they support each other, especially when other people are opposing or attacking them ≠ SPLIT UP

stick together *We're a team and we're sticking together.*

,stick 'up ★★

1 to continue upwards further than the end of a surface or the main part of an object ≠ HANG DOWN

stick up *His hair was sticking up and he needed a shave.* ♦ *The oil rig stuck up out of the darkness.*

2 *informal* to raise something upwards, especially your arm or hand

stick sth up *Stick your hands up if you agree.*

stick up sth *Joe stuck up his arm immediately to volunteer.*

3 *mainly American informal* to steal money or goods from a person or place using a gun = ROB, HOLD UP

stick up sb/sth *They tried to stick up a local bank.*

stick sb/sth up *The attempt to stick the gas station up went badly wrong.*

PHRASE **stick 'em up** *informal* if someone with a gun tells you to stick 'em up, they are ordering you to raise your arms above your head, usually because they are going to steal money or goods from you

■ **'stick-up** noun [C] *mainly American informal* an occasion when someone tries to steal money from a bank, shop etc by threatening people with a gun: *A man with a gun carried out an old-fashioned stick-up.*

,stick 'up for ★ *informal*

to speak in support of a person or an idea, belief, or plan, especially when no one else will = SUPPORT, DEFEND

stick up for sb/sth *I hope you'll always stick up for your beliefs.* ♦ *I don't need any help, thanks. I can stick up for myself.*

'stick with ★★ *informal*

1 to stay close to someone and go with them wherever they go, especially so that they can help or protect you

stick with sb *Stick with me and you'll be all right.*

2 to continue to do or use something, and not change it

stick with sth *They're going to stick with the same team as last Saturday.* ♦ *We had a tough time for a few years, but we stuck with it.*

3 if something sticks with you, you continue to remember it clearly = STAY WITH

stick with sb *It was a moment that has stuck with me for years.*

STING /stɪŋ/
stings, stinging, stung /stʌŋ/, **stung**

'sting for [often passive] *informal*

to make you pay more than you should for something

be stung for sth *Millions of homeowners could be stung for more council tax because of a Government blunder.*

sting sb for sth *How much did they sting you for, then?*

STINK /stɪŋk/
stinks, stinking, stank /stæŋk/ **or stunk** /stʌŋk/, **stunk**

'stink up (*also* **'stink out**) *informal*

to fill a place with a very unpleasant smell

stink up sth *also* **stink sth up** *I've had enough of them stinking up the place with their cigars!* ♦ *I'm not having that dog of yours stinking my car out.*

STINT /stɪnt/
stints, stinting, stinted

'stint on

PHRASE **not stint on sth** *informal* to use enough, or more than enough, of

stick up

something = BE SPARING WITH: *Mike certainly doesn't stint on the wine in his cooking.*

STIR /stɜː, *American* stɜr/
stirs, stirring, stirred

,stir 'in ★
to add something to a liquid or substance and mix it
stir in sth *Brown the meat for 3 minutes; then stir in the sauce.*
stir sth in *Melt the butter, stirring the flour in and adding milk.*

'stir into
1 to mix something into a liquid or substance
stir sth into sth *Stir the cream into the soup.*
2 [often passive] to make someone or something react in a particular way
be stirred into sth *The insects were stirred into motion by the growing heat of the sun.*
stir sb into sth *The news is sure to stir local residents into action.*

,stir 'up ★★
1 to make someone feel a particular bad emotion such as anger = AROUSE
stir up sth *He was accused of stirring up racial hatred.*
stir sth up *It was the proposed development that had stirred all this anger up in the local community.* ♦ *If there was a hint of trouble, you could be sure who had stirred it up.*

> Nouns often used as objects with **stir up 1**
>
> ■ animosity, controversy, emotions, feelings, hatred, resentment, trouble

2 to make someone think about or remember something = CALL UP
stir up sth *The sight of the school stirred up a lot of memories.*
stir sth up *Meeting him again stirred thoughts up that I had hoped I had forgotten.*
3 to make someone feel something such as interest, enthusiasm, hope = AROUSE
stir up sth *The scandal certainly stirred up interest in the business.*
stir sth up *His mysterious remarks certainly stirred our curiosity up.*
4 to make water or dust move around
stir up sth *Winds over 35 knots have stirred up very rough seas.*
stir sth up *In winter, the storms stir the water up, and nutrients are brought up from the bottom.*

PHRASE stir up a hornets' nest to create a situation that makes a lot of people

angry or upset: *You certainly stirred up a hornets' nest with that article you wrote.*

STITCH /stɪtʃ/
stitches, stitching, stitched

,stitch 'up
1 to repair a piece of cloth that has been torn by sewing it = SEW UP
stitch up sth *also* **stitch sth up** *You ought to stitch up that hole in your jeans.*
2 to join someone's skin together after it has been cut = SEW UP
stitch sth up *also* **stitch up sth** *Doctors stitched up the wound.*
3 [often passive] *British informal* to arrange a situation so that someone is blamed for something they did not do = FRAME; *British informal* FIT UP
be stitched up *I think I've been stitched up.*
stitch sb up *also* **stitch up sb** *You stitched me up good and proper!*
4 *informal* to arrange an agreement or deal
stitch up sth *also* **stitch sth up** *He's stitched up a major deal with one of the European banks.*
■ **'stitch-up** noun [C] *informal* a situation in which someone is blamed for something they did not do: *The police know this is a stitch-up.*

STOCK /stɒk, *American* stɑk/
stocks, stocking, stocked

,stock 'up
to provide yourself with things that you will need, or to store things that you will need in a particular place
stock up *We'll need to stock up before winter.* ♦ *All the cupboards are pretty well stocked up.* ♦ **+on** *Make sure you stock up on fuel.* ♦ **+with** *We stocked up with canned and dried food.*
stock sth up with sth *also* **stock up sth with sth** *Stock your fridge up with healthy snacks.*

STOKE /stəʊk, *American* stoʊk/
stokes, stoking, stoked

,stoke 'up
1 to add fuel to a fire
stoke up sth *also* **stoke sth up** *He fetched some more coal and stoked the fire up.*
2 to make a feeling stronger
stoke up sth *also* **stoke sth up** *She relied on hype and headlines to stoke up interest in her and her music.*

stock up

STOOP /stuːp, *American* stup/
stoops, stooping, stooped

,stoop 'down
to bend the top half of your body
downwards
stoop down *I stooped down so that I
could hear what he was saying.*

STOP /stɒp, *American* stɑp/
stops, stopping, stopped

'stop at
PHRASE **stop at nothing** to do whatever is
necessary, even something illegal or
cruel, in order to achieve your aim
= STICK AT NOTHING: *She would stop at
nothing to get her own way.*

,stop a'way *British informal*
to avoid going to a place = STAY AWAY
stop away *A lot of fans stopped away.*

,stop 'back
to return somewhere later
stop back *Please stop back later, and I'll
have this ready.*

,stop 'by
to visit a person or place for a short time
stop by *I was passing, so I though I'd
stop by.*
stop by sth *I would sometimes stop by
his shop on the way home.*

,stop 'in *British informal*
to stay at home = STAY IN
stop in *Let's just stop in tonight. I'm
really tired.*

,stop 'off ★
to visit somewhere before continuing to
another place
stop off *We stopped off in town on the
way to Jenni's house.* ♦ **+at** *Could you
stop off at the supermarket and get some
bread?*

,stop 'on *British informal*
to stay in a place after the time when you
usually leave, or after other people have
left = STAY ON
stop on *I might stop on for a day or two.*

,stop 'out *British informal*
to not come home at night = STAY OUT
stop out *He stopped out all night again.*
■ **'stop-out** **noun** [C] *humorous* someone
who stays out late at night: *Where have
you been, you dirty stop-out?*

,stop 'over
1 to stay somewhere for a short time
during a long journey, especially between
flights = LAY OVER
stop over *We stopped over in New York
on our way to Seattle.*
2 *British informal* to spend the night at
someone's house = STAY OVER
stop over *Do you want to stop over
tonight?*
■ **stopover** /'stɒp,əʊvə/ **noun** [C] a
stop during a journey, especially during
a flight: *There's a twelve-hour stopover
in Seoul.*

,stop 'up
1 to block something such as a pipe or a
hole so that water or another substance
cannot go through it = PLUG
stop up sth *also* **stop sth up** *We need to
stop up that hole.*
2 if a sink or bath stops up, water will not
go out of it because the pipes are blocked
stop up *The kitchen sink's always
stopping up.*
3 *British informal* to not go to bed at your
usual time = STAY UP
stop up *I stopped up to watch the late
film last night.*

STORE /stɔː, *American* stɔr/
stores, storing, stored

,store a'way
to put something in a safe place until you
need it
store away sth *also* **store sth away** *She
had stored away most of his old clothes.*

,store 'up ★
1 to keep a lot of something so that you
can use it later
store up sth *Many animals store up food
for the winter.*
store sth up *A car battery stores energy
up.*
2 to remember something, especially so
that you can refer to or use it later
store up sth *I had stored up a few
questions to ask her about the job.*

store sth up *She had stored all his unkind remarks up to use against him when the opportunity presented itself.*

3 to do something that will cause problems in the future
store up problems/trouble/difficulties etc *People who don't exercise are storing up health problems for themselves.*

STORM /stɔːm, *American* stɔrm/
storms, storming, stormed

ˌstorm ˈoff
to leave a person or place quickly because you are angry or upset
storm off *There's no point in storming off – you should have tried to talk to him about it.*

ˌstorm ˈout ★
to leave a room or building quickly because you are angry or upset
storm out *I was so furious I just swore at her and stormed out. ♦ +of He stormed out of the meeting, saying he would not negotiate with terrorists.*

STOW /stəʊ, *American* stoʊ/
stows, stowing, stowed

ˌstow aˈway
1 to hide in a vehicle, ship, or plane in order to travel without permission and without paying
stow away *Legend has it that he stowed away in a cargo ship.*

2 to put something somewhere while you are not using it
stow sth away *also* **stow away sth** *She stowed the shoes away in a box under the bed.*

■ **stowaway** /'stəʊəˌweɪ/ **noun** [C]
someone who hides on a ship, plane or other vehicle so that they can travel without permission and without paying: *Stowaways are a big worry for truck drivers.*

STRAIGHTEN /'streɪt(ə)n/
straightens, straightening, straightened

ˌstraighten ˈout ★
1 to make something straight ≠ BEND
straighten out sth *They're planning to straighten out some of the worst bends in the road.*
straighten sth out *She tried to straighten her leg out, crying in pain.*

2 to deal with a problem or a confused situation = PUT RIGHT ≠ CONFUSE
straighten out sth *A team of accountants*

was brought in to straighten out the firm's finances.
straighten sth out *These are difficult situations, and it takes time to straighten them out.*

3 to help someone with problems to improve their behaviour
straighten out sb *He spent years trying to straighten out his drug-addict brother.*
straighten sb out *She had hoped for a while that Seth could straighten Joey out.*

ˌstraighten ˈup ★★
1 to stand up straight
straighten up *Straighten up slowly and take a deep breath.*

2 to make something tidy = NEATEN
straighten up sth *Sarah, can you straighten up your room please?*
straighten sth up *Straighten your tie up – you look a mess!*

STRAIN /streɪn/
strains, straining, strained

ˈstrain at
to pull at something very hard
strain at sth *The elephants strained at their ropes.*
PHRASE be straining at the leash to be impatient to do something: *The opportunities for profit were everywhere and small companies were straining at the leash.*

STRAP /stræp/
straps, strapping, strapped

ˌstrap ˈup
to wrap a piece of cloth tightly round something, especially a part of your body that has been injured
strap up sth *also* **strap sth up** *He strapped up her injured ankle.*

STRETCH /stretʃ/
stretches, stretching, stretched

ˌstretch aˈway ★
if an area of land stretches away, it continues for a long distance ahead of you
stretch away *Below them the garden stretched away. ♦ The darkness stretched away in every direction.*

ˌstretch ˈout ★★★
1 to lie down, usually in order to relax or sleep
stretch out *There wasn't enough room to stretch out, so I didn't get much rest. ♦ +on Porter stretched out on his bunk, hands clasped behind his head.*
be stretched out *Hundreds of people*

were stretched out on sun loungers.
stretch yourself out *She sat down on the sofa and then stretched herself out.*

2 to move your arm or leg away from your body, for example in order to reach something
stretch out sth *I stretched out a hand to touch her face.*
stretch sth out *He stretched his arms out, appealing to her to come to him.*

STREW /struː, *American* struː/
strews, strewing, strewn /struːn, *American* struːn/ or **strewed** /struːd, *American* struːd/

be 'strewn with

1 to be covered with things that are spread around in a careless or untidy way
be strewn with sth *One room was strewn with children's toys.*

2 to contain a lot of something
be strewn with sth *His career was strewn with misfortune.*

STRIKE /straɪk/
strikes, striking, struck /strʌk/

Strike is often used with adverbs and prepositions when it means 'to hit against or crash into someone or something': *The ball **struck** her **in** the left shoulder.* ♦ *A fight broke out and someone was **struck on** the head.* ♦ *James was **struck with** a stick.* These uses are not included here.

'strike as ★★

if someone or something strikes you as something, that is what you think or feel about them
strike sb as sth *Doesn't it strike you as strange that he didn't call that night?*
♦ *She actually strikes me as quite a shy person.*
strike sb as being sth *Some of their ideas strike me as being a little simplistic.*

'strike at ★

1 to try to hit someone or something with your hand or a weapon
strike at sb/sth *He struck at me several times but I managed to dodge the blows.*

2 to make a sudden violent or illegal attack on someone or something
strike at sb/sth *The rebels struck at government camps that night.*

3 to try to hit or kick something such as a ball with your hand, foot, or a piece of sports equipment
strike at sth *He struck wildly at the ball and missed completely.*

4 to be likely to seriously damage or destroy something important
strike at the heart/foundation/roots of sth *Such atrocities strike at the very heart of democracy.*

,strike 'back

to attack, harm, or criticize someone who has attacked, harmed, or criticized you
= RETALIATE
strike back *The most vulnerable are also those least able to strike back.* ♦ **+at** *The bombing was apparently carried out to strike back at the occupying forces.*
♦ **+against** *They threatened to strike back against their captors.* ♦ **+with** *Faced with the accusations, the senator struck back with a blistering attack on his critics.*

,strike 'down

1 [usually passive] to make someone die or become so ill that they can no longer live a normal life = AFFLICT
be struck down *As a tiny baby she was struck down by polio.* ♦ **+with** *In the early 1980s, many of the local people were struck down with a mysterious illness.*

2 to hit someone with enough force to make them fall down
strike sb down *also* **strike down sb** *Someone struck him down from behind.*

3 *American* if a judge or court strikes down a law, they officially end it
strike down sth *also* **strike sth down** *Another federal appeals court struck down the Ohio law.*

'strike from

to officially remove something from a document or record
strike sth from sth *'Strike that from the court record', the judge ordered.*

,strike 'off ★

1 [often passive] to remove something from a list or record = DELETE FROM ≠ INCLUDE IN
be struck off sth *My name has been struck off the guest list.*
strike off sth *We can strike off that topic from today's agenda – it's been settled.*
strike sth off *You can't simply strike dairy products off the shopping list.*

2 to go in a particular direction in a way that shows energy or determination
= HEAD OFF
strike off *I think they struck off in that direction.* ♦ **+across** *They struck off across the desert without supplies.*
♦ **+through** *Startled by the noise, he had struck off through the woods.*

3 [always passive] *British* if someone such as a doctor or lawyer is struck off, they are

no longer allowed to work in their profession because they have done something wrong or are no longer considered capable of doing it properly
be struck off *Patients were calling for him to be struck off.*

'strike on (*also* 'strike upon)

1 to find or think of something suddenly, unexpectedly, or by accident
strike on sth *I think I've struck on a solution to our problem.*

2 [always passive] *British informal* if you are struck on someone or something, you like them
be struck on sb *I'm not particularly struck on him.*

,strike 'out ★★

1	do sth new or different
2	hit/attack sb
3	criticize sb/sth
4	go in a particular direction
5	be unsuccessful
6	remove words from sth
7	when sb misses the ball in baseball
8	when you defeat sb in baseball

1 to start doing something new or different, especially in order to become more independent
strike out *O'Connor quit his job and decided to **strike out on his own**.* ◆ **+for** *It was an opportunity to strike out for independence.*

2 to try to hit or attack someone or something = HIT OUT
strike out *She struck out blindly but missed her target.* ◆ **+at** *Without warning, he struck out at Holmes with his right hand.*

3 to criticize someone or something, especially in a speech, interview, or article = HIT OUT, LASH OUT
strike out *Feeling threatened, she struck out, accusing him bitterly of everything she could think of.* ◆ **+at** *He struck out at supporters of the bill in his speech yesterday.*

4 to walk or swim in a particular direction in a way that shows energy or determination
strike out *We decided to strike out on foot.* ◆ **+for** *Rostov surfaced, then struck out for the nearest shore.* ◆ **+across** *She slid into the water and struck out across the lake.*

5 **strike out** or **strike through** *mainly American informal* to be unsuccessful in trying to do something = FAIL
strike out *It looks like we've struck out again.*

6 to remove words from a document, for example by drawing a line through them = CROSS OUT, STRIKE THROUGH
strike sth out *I think you should strike the last sentence out.*
strike out sth *Strike out lines 5 to 18.*

7 in baseball, if the person trying to hit the ball strikes out, they miss the ball three times and so end their turn at trying to hit it
strike out *When Edmonds struck out, they cheered even louder.*

8 in baseball, if the person throwing the ball strikes someone out, they throw three balls that that person is unable to hit so that their turn at trying to hit it ends
strike sb out *Brown struck him out to end Sunday's game.*
strike out sb *Carson struck out 11 San Francisco hitters Saturday.*

,strike 'through *same as* strike out 5

,strike 'up ★

1 to start to play or sing a piece of music
strike up sth *We could hear the band striking up the bridal march.*
strike up *The musicians struck up and people began to dance.* ◆ **+with** *They struck up with Happy Birthday to You.*

2 if a piece of music strikes up, someone starts playing it = BEGIN
strike up *The bridal march struck up and everyone turned to look to the back of the church.*

3 to start something such as a relationship or conversation with someone in an informal way
strike up a friendship/conversation etc *The bartender tried to strike up a conversation.* ◆ *Anna had struck up a friendship with a girl she met at night school.*

Nouns often used as objects with
strike up 3

■ acquaintance, conversation, friendship, partnership, rapport, relationship

'strike upon *same as* strike on

STRING /strɪŋ/
strings, stringing, strung /strʌŋ/

,string a'long

to make someone continue to believe something that is not true for a long time, especially something about what you intend to do = DECEIVE
string sb along *She's just stringing you along – she won't marry you.*

,string 'out

1 to make something last longer than was intended or longer than is necessary

= PROLONG

string sth out *also* **string out sth** *They had to string things out until the Duke arrived.* ♦ *They seem to be stringing out the dispute just for the sake of it.*

2 [usually passive] to arrange something in a long line

be strung out *The South Isles are strung out in a line from Mainland to South Ronaldsay.*

3 [always passive] *informal* to be very nervous and unable to relax

be strung out *When I called he was so strung out he could hardly talk.*

4 [always passive] *informal* to be under the influence of drugs or alcohol

be strung out *When I was strung out, I'd have done almost anything.* ♦ *+on They spent the whole weekend strung out on cocaine and booze.*

,string to'gether

to arrange a group of things into a series

string sth together *also* **string together sth** *He was so drunk he could hardly string a sentence together.*

,string 'up *informal*

to kill someone by hanging them

string sb up *also* **string up sb** *The only answer is to string them all up!*

STRIP /strip/
strips, stripping, stripped

,strip a'way

1 to remove a layer that covers something

strip away sth *also* **strip sth away** *Take care when stripping away old paint.*

2 to remove the things that hide what someone or something is really like

strip away sth *also* **strip sth away** *If you strip away the fancy language, these policies are just the same as the old ones.* ♦ *Strip all the bravado away and you're left with a very frightened man.*

,strip 'down

1 to remove all or most of your clothes

strip down *He was told to go into the cubicle and strip down for his examination.* ♦ *+to He stripped down to his underwear.*

2 to take something such as a machine apart

strip down sth *also* **strip sth down** *She completely stripped down the engine.*

strip down

'strip from [often passive]

to remove something from something else, especially using force

be stripped from sth *Much of the religious content was stripped from the speech.*

strip sth from sth *She stripped the suede gloves from her hands.*

'strip of [often passive]

to take something away from someone, especially something such as authority, status or a right

be stripped of sth *He was stripped of his rank and thrown out of the army.*

strip sb of sth *The new regime stripped women of the few rights they previously had.*

,strip 'off ★★

1 to take off all your clothes

strip off *We stripped off and dived into the lake.*

2 to take off some of your clothes

strip off sth *He stripped off his shirt and jumped in.*

strip sth off *She stripped her sweater off, and then her jeans.*

3 to remove a layer or cover from something

strip sth off sth *Men were stripping bark off the trees.*

,strip 'out

1 to remove part of something, especially something that is not wanted or needed

strip out sth *also* **strip sth out** *Even when you strip out the 40% charge, it's still expensive.* ♦ *The government wants water companies to strip these chemicals out.*

2 [often passive] to make a building completely empty by removing everything inside it

be stripped out *The bathroom has been stripped out.*

strip sth out *also* strip out sth *A developer has stripped the place out.*

STRUGGLE /'strʌg(ə)l/
struggles, struggling, struggled

,struggle 'on
to continue doing something that you find very difficult
struggle on *The government managed to struggle on with its tiny majority.*

STUB /stʌb/
stubs, stubbing, stubbed

,stub 'out
to press a cigarette hard against a surface to make it stop burning
stub sth out *also* stub out sth *Bernard stubbed out the cigarette and got to his feet.*

STUFF /stʌf/
stuffs, stuffing, stuffed

'stuff into
to push something soft into a container or space
stuff sth into sth *Alice stuffed her clothes into a suitcase and left.*

STUMBLE /'stʌmb(ə)l/
stumbles, stumbling, stumbled

'stumble across ★ (*also* 'stumble on or 'stumble upon)
to find something or meet someone by accident = COME ACROSS, COME ON, COME UPON
stumble across sth *We stumbled across him in the library.* ◆ *A journalist finally stumbled on the truth.*

'stumble into
to become involved in something by accident
stumble into sth *He claims he stumbled into acting.*

'stumble on *same as* stumble across

STUMP /stʌmp/
stumps, stumping, stumped

be 'stumped for
to not know what to say or how to react or to explain something
be stumped for sth *When she asked if I wanted to be her date I was **stumped for words**.* ◆ *She was stumped for a reply to such an unusual question.*

,stump 'up *British*
to give money, usually when you do not want to give it = COME UP WITH ≠ WITHHOLD
stump up sth *also* stump sth up *Their insurance company eventually stumped up £15,000.*

STYLE /staɪl/
styles, styling, styled

'style after (*also* 'style on)
to copy the style that someone or something has = MODEL ON
style yourself after sb/sth *She has styled herself after Marilyn Monroe.*

SUBJECT /səb'dʒekt/
subjects, subjecting, subjected

sub'ject to [often passive]
to make someone experience something unpleasant
be subjected to sth *We were subjected to a series of extremely intrusive questions.*
subject sb to sth *Her husband subjected her to years of abuse.*

SUBMIT /səb'mɪt/
submits, submitting, submitted

sub'mit to ★★
1 to accept that someone is more powerful than you and therefore do what they tell you to do
submit to sb/sth *He thinks everyone should be prepared to submit to his will.*
2 to allow something to happen or be done to you, especially something unpleasant
submit to sth *He reluctantly submitted to what he feared would be a painful course of treatment.*
submit yourself to sth *I wasn't going to submit myself to any further embarrassment.*
3 to agree to obey a rule, law etc
submit to sth *As a member of the Union, you must submit to its rules.*

SUBSCRIBE /səb'skraɪb/
subscribes, subscribing, subscribed

sub'scribe to ★★
1 to agree with an idea = ADHERE TO
subscribe to sth *Weir subscribes to the view that children benefit from being independent.*

2 to pay money in order to regularly receive a newspaper or magazine, be a member of a group or organization, or receive a regular service
subscribe to sth *We subscribe to all the main medical journals.* ◆ *Patrick*

subscribes to a number of Internet newsgroups.

SUBSTITUTE /'sʌbstɪtjuːt, *American* 'sʌbstɪˌtut/
substitutes, substituting, substituted

'substitute for
1 to use something new or different instead of what is normally used
substitute sth for sth *You can substitute chicken for beef if you don't like red meat.*
♦ *The objective is to substitute real democratic politics for conflict and violence.*
2 to do someone else's job for a short period of time
substitute for sb *Mark will substitute for me tomorrow.*
3 to remove one thing and put something else in its place
substitute sth for sth *Police investigators substituted Palmer's bag for a similar one, and then followed him to his hideout.*

SUBSUME /səb'sjuːm, *American* səb'sum/
subsumes, subsuming, subsumed

be sub'sumed under *formal*
to be included in a larger and more important group
be subsumed under sth *Individual departments have been subsumed under a general faculty.*

SUCCEED /sək'siːd, *American* sək'sid/
succeeds, succeeding, succeeded

suc'ceed as [often passive]
to replace someone in an important or powerful position or job
be succeeded as sth *She was succeeded as party leader in 1990.*
succeed sb as sth *Anderson is expected to succeed Leech as CEO.*

suc'ceed in ★★
to achieve something that you planned to do or attempted to do
succeed in sth *They succeeded in the second task.*
succeed in doing sth *We finally succeeded in getting Marjorie up the stairs.*

SUCK /sʌk/
sucks, sucking, sucked

,suck 'in
1 [usually passive] *informal* to gradually involve someone in something bad in a way that they cannot control = DRAG IN ≠ EXCLUDE
be/get sucked in *I didn't want to get involved in their argument, but somehow I got sucked in.*
2 to hold your stomach in with your muscles so that it does not look big = HOLD IN
suck your stomach/belly/tummy etc in *Suck your stomach in as far as it will go, and then release.*

,suck 'into [usually passive] *informal*
to involve someone in something bad in a way that they cannot control = BE DRAGGED INTO ≠ BE EXCLUDED FROM
be/get sucked into sth *Like many unemployed people, Teresa got sucked into a spiral of debts.* ♦ *Would America be sucked into an unwanted war?*

,suck 'off *impolite*
to use your mouth on a man's penis in order to give him sexual pleasure

,suck 'up *informal showing disapproval* to be very nice to someone in authority so that they will treat you well = INGRATIATE YOURSELF
suck up *It's obvious you're sucking up.*
♦ +**to** *Kristen is already sucking up to the new boss.*
PHRASE **suck it up** *American informal* used for telling someone not to complain about something because it will not change: *I know it's painful but you've got to suck it up and play through it.*

SUFFER /'sʌfə, *American* 'sʌfər/
suffers, suffering, suffered

'suffer from ★★★
to have a particular illness or physical problem
suffer from sth *He suffers from asthma.*
♦ *If you are always tired, you may be suffering from anaemia.*

SUIT /suːt, *American* sut/
suits, suiting, suited

be 'suited to ★★★
to be right for a particular purpose or situation, because of having all the qualities that are needed
be suited to sth *She is ideally suited to the job.* ♦ *We want schooling that is suited*

to the needs of the local community.

Adverbs often used with **be suited to**

- **admirably, best, eminently, ideally, perfectly, well**

,**suit 'up** *American*
to get ready for an activity by putting on a uniform or special clothes
> **suit up** *The players were in the locker room suiting up.*

SUM /sʌm/
sums, summing, summed

,**sum 'up** ★★★
1 to give a summary of something
= SUMMARIZE
> **sum up** *I'll sum up briefly and then we'll take questions.*
> **sum up sth** *Summing up the discussion, he said that all parties would consider how best to resolve the problem.*
> **sum sth up** *How would you sum your conversation up?*

2 if a statement sums someone or something up, it shows what they are like
= REPRESENT
> **sum sb/sth up** *That remark just about sums him up.*
> **sum up sb/sth** *Her reply seemed to sum up the attitude of all the refugees.*

3 to make a judgment about what someone or something is like
> **sum sb/sth up** *I'd already summed him up, and I knew he'd be difficult to work with.*
> **sum up sb/sth** *An experienced person will be able to sum up the situation very quickly.*

4 if a judge sums up a case, they give a summary of all the evidence that has been given
> **sum up sth** *The judge will sum up the evidence tomorrow.*
> **sum up** *When summing up, the judge said he had taken into account the fact that the defendant had no previous convictions.*

- **summing-up** /ˌsʌmɪŋ ˈʌp/ **noun** [C]
1 a statement made by a lawyer or judge that gives a summary of the evidence in a case: *This point was made in the judge's summing-up.* **2** a statement in which someone gives a short account of something: *He remembered Gina's summing-up of Eleanor's character.*

SUMMON /ˈsʌmən/
summons, summoning, summoned

,**summon 'up**
to manage to produce a quality or a reaction that helps you deal with a difficult situation
> **summon sth up** *also* **summon up sth** *He couldn't summon the strength up to carry on fighting.* ♦ *She could barely summon up a smile.*

SUP /sʌp/
sups, supping, supped

,**sup 'up** *British informal*
to finish drinking something
> **sup up** *They supped up and left the pub.*

SURGE /sɜːdʒ, *American* sɜrdʒ/
surges, surging, surged

,**surge 'through**
if a feeling surges through you, you feel it very strongly and suddenly
> **surge through sb** *A fresh wave of anger surged through her.*

,**surge 'up**
if a feeling or emotion surges up, you start to feel it very strongly
> **surge up** *An uncontrollable anger surged up within him.*

SURROUND /səˈraʊnd/
surrounds, surrounding, surrounded

sur'round with ★
to always be close to or spend time with particular people or things
> **surround yourself with sb/sth** *He surrounds himself with an entourage of loyal followers.* ♦ *We all tend to surround ourselves with people who share our beliefs and make us feel comfortable.*

SUSS /sʌs/
susses, sussing, sussed

,**suss 'out** *British informal*
to understand a situation or the reason why someone does something
> **suss sb/sth out** *also* **suss out sb/sth** *I've just sussed out the reason he's being so difficult.*

SWALLOW /ˈswɒləʊ, American ˈswɑloʊ/
swallows, swallowing, swallowed

swallow down

1 to swallow food or drink, so that it goes into your stomach
swallow sth down also **swallow down sth** She always swallowed the medicine down like a good girl. ♦ He swallowed down more wine.

2 to prevent yourself from expressing a feeling, or to try not to let it become strong
swallow down sth also **swallow sth down** She swallowed down the fear she felt. ♦ Paige swallowed down the sense of having lost something important.

swallow up ★★

1 [often passive] if a company or country swallows up a smaller company or country, the smaller one becomes part of the larger one
be swallowed up The company was swallowed up in a corporate merger.
swallow up sth also **swallow sth up** A large corporation can swallow up its smaller competitors.

2 to use a lot of something such as money, time, or effort
swallow up sth Campaigning swallows up a lot of time without guaranteeing success.
swallow sth up Dealing with emails can easily swallow that time up. ♦ There'd been a pound or two left over but shopping for tea had swallowed it up.

3 [often passive] literary to destroy something completely or make it disappear
be swallowed up The whole building was swallowed up by the flames.
swallow up sth I watched the traffic swallow up the departing taxi.

SWAN /swɒn, American swɑn/
swans, swanning, swanned

swan around British informal showing disapproval to go from place to place in a relaxed and careless way, without paying attention to your work or responsibilities
swan around All she does all day is swan around.
swan around sth Why am I stuck in the office while everyone else is swanning around the south of France?

swan off British informal showing disapproval
to leave somewhere in a relaxed and careless way, without paying attention to your work or responsibilities

swan off You can't just swan off whenever you feel like it. ♦ **+to** He was not happy with the idea of me swanning off to London without him.

SWAP /swɒp, American swɑp/
swaps, swapping, swapped

swap for ★★

to replace one person or thing with another
swap sb/sth for sb/sth He swapped his skis for a pair with sharper edges. ♦ We're going to swap him for a smaller dog. ♦ I wouldn't swap you for anything.

swap over

if two people swap over, or if you swap two people or things over, each one does what the other was doing before, or each one is used for what the other was being used for before
swap over Let's swap over: I'll drive and you can navigate.
swap sb/sth over also **swap over sb/sth** Drew called a team meeting and said he was going to swap us two over.

SWARM /swɔːm, American swɔrm/
swarms, swarming, swarmed

swarm with [usually progressive]

if a place is swarming with people, insects, or animals, it is full of them
be swarming with sb/sth The room was hot and stuffy, and swarming with flies. ♦ The courtroom steps were swarming with photographers.

SWATHE /sweɪð/
swathes, swathing, swathed

swathe in [usually passive] literary

to completely cover someone or something with something
be swathed in sth The moon was swathed in mist. ♦ Her head was swathed in a bandage.

SWEAR /sweə, American swer/
swears, swearing, swore /swɔː, American swɔr/, sworn /swɔːn, American swɔrn/

swear by informal

to believe that something is effective
= TRUST
swear by sth My father swears by whisky as a cure for a cold. ♦ He always has a massage after a race. Top runners swear by it.

ˌswear 'in [usually passive]

to make someone give a formal promise
in a law court or at an official ceremony
before they start doing a particular job
= INAUGURATE ≠ DISCHARGE
  be sworn in *The new government was
  sworn in on November 1st.* ♦ **+as** *He was
  sworn in as president.*

ˌswear 'off

to promise to stop doing or using
something
  swear off sth *The headache I got was
  almost enough to make me swear off
  wine forever.*

'swear to

1 [often with a negative] to be completely
certain of something
  swear to sth *I can't swear to it, but I
  think I saw Joan yesterday.* ♦ *Those
  pictures were originals. He would swear
  to that.*
2 to make someone promise something
  swear sb to sth *He had sworn me to
  secrecy about his new job.*
  swear yourself to sth *She decided to
  swear herself to celibacy until she got
  married.*

SWEAT /swet/
sweats, sweating, sweated

ˌsweat 'off

1 to get rid of body weight by doing
physical activity that needs a lot of effort
and makes you sweat (=produce liquid on
the surface of your skin)
  sweat off sth *also* **sweat sth off** *You
  could try to sweat off a few pounds in
  the gym.*
2 **sweat off** or **sweat out** to get rid of an
illness by sweating (=producing a lot of
liquid on the surface of your skin)
  sweat sth off *If you have a temperature
  it may be better to sweat it off.*

ˌsweat 'out

PHRASE **sweat it out** to wait for something
that you are worried or nervous about
to end ≠ GIVE UP ON: *You're just going to
have to wait and sweat it out.*

'sweat over *informal*

to use a lot of effort or energy doing
something
  sweat over sth *I've sweated over this for
  six months.*

SWEEP /swi:p, *American* swip/
sweeps, sweeping, swept /swept/

ˌsweep a'long [often passive]

if something sweeps you along, you
become very involved in it because you
are so excited about it
  be swept along *She allowed herself to
  be swept along by her friend's excitement.*
  ♦ *It is difficult not to be swept along by
  the romance of the early days of a
  relationship.*
  sweep sb along *She has produced a story
  that sweeps the reader along from one
  exciting event to the next.*

ˌsweep a'side ★

to ignore someone or their ideas or
suggestions, or to refuse to consider them
= DISMISS ≠ CONSIDER
  sweep aside sb/sth *He swept aside all
  her objections.*
  sweep sb/sth aside *She simply swept his
  resistance aside, and carried on with her
  plan.*

ˌsweep a'way ★★

1 to destroy or completely remove
something
  sweep sth away *Many people died when
  floods swept their homes away.*
  sweep away sth *Your reassurances have
  swept away any doubts I had.*
2 **sweep away** or **sweep up** [usually passive]
to involve someone completely in a story,
situation, emotions etc = CARRY AWAY
  be/get swept away *I got quite swept
  away with the spirit of the moment.*

ˌsweep 'back

to put your hair into a style that keeps it
away from your face
  sweep sth back *also* **sweep back sth** *She
  swept her hair back into a bun.* ♦ *Her
  hair was swept back from her face.*

ˌsweep 'out

to make the floor of a room or place clean
by using a brush with a long handle
  sweep out sth *also* **sweep sth out** *We
  swept out each room in the house.* ♦ *I
  was given the job of sweeping the
  basement out.*

ˌsweep 'over

to suddenly affect someone very strongly
  sweep over sb *A wave of tiredness swept
  over her.* ♦ *I could see relief sweeping over
  him.*

ˌsweep 'up ★

1 to clean and remove dirt, glass, dust etc
from a floor or the ground using a brush

sweep up *You need to sweep up before you mop the floor.*
sweep up sth *Would you sweep up the broken glass?*
sweep sth up *I'll help you sweep this rubbish up.*
2 *same as* **sweep away 2**

SWEETEN /ˈswiːt(ə)n, *American* ˈswit(ə)n/
sweetens, sweetening, sweetened

,**sweeten 'up**
to be especially nice to someone so that they will agree to something you want them to agree to
sweeten sb up *also* **sweeten up sb** *He bought his wife flowers to sweeten her up.* ♦ *He sweetened up his staff with a free meal before asking them to work more hours.*

SWELL /swel/
swells, swelling, swelled, swollen /ˈswəʊlən, *American* ˈswoʊlən/

,**swell 'up** ★
if a part of your body swells up, it becomes larger than normal, especially because of liquid forming inside
swell up *Her ankles swell up in the heat.* ♦ *My eye swelled up within minutes of him hitting me.*

SWILL /swɪl/
swills, swilling, swilled

,**swill 'down**
1 to drink a large amount of something, especially alcohol, in an enthusiastic way
swill sth down *also* **swill down sth** *He just swilled down his beer and walked out.*
2 to make a place or surface clean by pouring water over it
swill sth down *also* **swill down sth** *A tiled floor is easy to swill down.*

,**swill 'out**
to make a place or container clean by pouring water into it or onto it
swill sth out *also* **swill out sth** *She swilled the pan out in the sink.*

SWIM /swɪm/
swims, swimming, swam /swæm/, **swum** /swʌm/

'**swim in** (*also* '**swim with**) [usually progressive]
if food is swimming in a liquid, there is more liquid than there should be

be swimming in sth *The food was swimming in grease.*

SWING /swɪŋ/
swings, swinging, swung /swʌŋ/

,**swing a'round** (*also* ,**swing 'round** *British*)
to turn your body or head with a smooth curving movement so that you are facing in a different direction
swing around *She swung around and grabbed his arm.*

'**swing at**
to try to hit someone or something by making a smooth curving movement with your hand, a weapon, or a piece of sports equipment
swing at sb/sth *Dan swung at Michael, catching him on the chin.* ♦ +**with** *Mrs Shaw swung at the youth with her bag.*

,**swing 'by** *mainly American informal*
to make a short visit to a person or place
swing by *Just swing by on your way home, okay?*
swing by sth *I'll try and swing by your office later.*

,**swing 'round** *British same as* **swing around**

,**swing 'through** *American informal*
to visit a place for a short time on your way to another place
swing through sth *We're going to swing through Nashville on our way to the reunion.*

SWITCH /swɪtʃ/
switches, switching, switched

,**switch a'round** (*also* ,**switch 'round** *British*)
to move two people or things so that each one is in the position that the other one was in before
switch sb/sth around *Someone could have switched the cakes around without us noticing.*

,**switch 'off** ★★★
1 if you switch off something such as a light or a machine, you make it stop working, especially by pressing or moving a switch = TURN OFF ≠ SWITCH ON
switch sth off *Make sure you switch all the lights off before you go to bed.* ♦ *Let's switch the TV off and have a conversation instead.*
switch off sth *I parked the car and switched off the engine.*
2 if something such as a light or a

machine switches off, it stops working
= GO OFF, TURN OFF
> **switch off** *The heating switches off when it reaches a certain temperature.* ♦ *I set the light to switch off at 10.30 every night.*

3 *informal* to stop listening to someone or stop thinking about something
> **switch off** *When he starts talking about football I just switch off.* ♦ *I work so hard it's sometimes difficult to switch off.*

,switch 'on ★★★

1 if you switch on something such as a light or a machine, you make it start working, especially by pressing or moving a switch = TURN ON, PUT ON ≠ SWITCH OFF
> **switch on sth** *Don't switch on the light.* ♦ *Every time you switch on the television there's a new reality show on.*
> **switch sth on** *I forgot to switch the answering machine on.*

2 if something such as a light or a machine switches on, it starts working
= COME ON, GO ON, TURN ON ≠ SWITCH OFF
> **switch on** *The air conditioning switches on automatically when you close the door.*

■ **,switched-'on** **adj** *informal old-fashioned* someone who is switched on knows about fashionable new ideas, methods etc: *This will be obvious to any switched-on teenager.*

,switch 'over

1 to stop doing one thing and start doing another
> **switch over** *If I decide to change my course, when could I switch over?* ♦ **+to** *He played baseball for ten years before switching over to coaching.*

2 *British* to start watching or listening to a different television or radio programme by pressing a switch on your television or radio
> **switch over** *Stop switching over when I'm in the middle of watching something!* ♦ **+to** *Can't we switch over to Channel 4?*

■ **switchover** /'swɪtʃˌəʊvə/ **noun** [C] *American informal* a change from one method, system, or activity to another: *the **switchover to** a new currency* ♦ *the formal **switchover from** British to Chinese rule*

,switch 'round *British same as* switch around

SWIVEL /'swɪv(ə)l/
swivels, swivelling, swivelled

,swivel a'round (*also* ,swivel 'round *British*)

if someone or something swivels around,

or if you swivel them around, they turn round on a fixed point and face in a different direction = WHEEL AROUND
> **swivel sth around** *Helen swivelled her chair around to get a better look.*
> **swivel around** *She swivelled around and glared angrily at him.*

SWOT /swɒt, *American* swɑt/
swots, swotting, swotted

,swot 'up *British informal*

to study something very hard, especially for an examination
> **swot up sth** *also* **swot sth up** *I've got to swot up the French Revolution for tomorrow's test.*
> **swot up** *I've forgotten all my Spanish. I'll have to swot up before the interview.*
> ♦ **+on** *They spent their evenings swotting up on useless facts.*

SYMPATHIZE /'sɪmpəθaɪz/
sympathizes, sympathizing, sympathized

'sympathize with

1 to understand someone's problems and feel sorry for them = FEEL FOR
> **sympathize with sb/sth** *We sympathize deeply with the families of the victims.* ♦ *I sympathize with teachers, because they have a very hard job.* ♦ *I really sympathized with her distress.*

2 to approve of and support someone or something
> **sympathize with sb/sth** *Many people admit they sympathize with the rebels' demands.*

SYNCHRONIZE /'sɪŋkrənaɪz/
synchronizes, synchronizing, synchronized

'synchronize with

to make two or more things happen or move at the same time or speed
> **synchronize sth with sth** *An editing unit is used to synchronize sound with images.*

T t

TACK /tæk/
tacks, tacking, tacked

,tack 'on [often passive]
to add something extra, especially something that does not seem to belong to the rest = TAG ON

be tacked on *The final clause of the contract was tacked on as an afterthought.*

tack on sth *also* **tack sth on** *They had converted the garage into a workshop and tacked on a conservatory.*

TACKLE /'tæk(ə)l/
tackles, tackling, tackled

'tackle about
to ask someone questions in a very direct way, because you disagree with them and want them to explain their opinions or behaviour

tackle sb about sth *I decided I was going to tackle him about his comments.*

TAG /tæg/
tags, tagging, tagged

,tag a'long
to go somewhere with someone else although you are not needed = COME ALONG

tag along *When Charlie goes on a business trip, I often tag along.*

,tag a,long be'hind
to walk behind someone you are with, although you are not needed

tag along behind sb *The little boy tagged along behind her.*

,tag 'on [usually passive]
to add something extra, especially something that does not seem to belong to the rest = TACK ON

be tagged on *This information was tagged on at the end.*

TAIL /teɪl/
tails, tailing, tailed

,tail a'way *same as* tail off

,tail 'back *British*
if traffic tails back, there is a long line of traffic that is not moving

tail back *Traffic tailed back for twelve miles.*

■ **tailback** /'teɪlbæk/ **noun** [C] **1** *British* a long line of traffic that is moving very slowly or not moving at all: *There's a six-mile tailback on the southbound M6.* **2** *American* a football player whose position is farthest behind the front line of players: *She had brother who played tailback for Washington.*

,tail 'off ★ (*also* ,tail a'way)

1 if someone's voice tails off, it becomes quieter until you cannot hear it at all

tail off *Her voice tailed off as she began to read the letter.*

2 to become weaker or smaller, often before disappearing completely = DWINDLE ≠ BUILD UP

tail off *Unemployment seems to be tailing off.* ♦ *Any improvement begins to tail off after a certain amount of time.*

■ **'tail-off noun** [C] the process of slowly becoming smaller in amount: *a tail-off in profits*

TAILOR /'teɪlə, *American* 'teɪlər/
tailors, tailoring, tailored

'tailor for (*also* 'tailor to)
to make or change something especially for a particular person or purpose

tailor sth for sb/sth *This computer software is specially tailored for schools.* ♦ *All our courses can be tailored to the needs of individuals.*

TAKE /teɪk/
takes, taking, took /tʊk/, taken /'teɪkən/

Take is often used with adverbs and prepositions when it means 'to move someone or something from one place to another': *Our guide **took** us **around** the cathedral.* ♦ *We **took** the plants **into** the greenhouse.* ♦ *The cat had to be **taken to** the vet.* These uses are not included here.

be ,taken a'back ★★
to be shocked or surprised, especially by something that someone says or does

be taken aback *Bill was taken aback by the girl's directness.*

,take 'after ★ [never progressive]
to look or behave like an older relative = RESEMBLE ≠ DIFFER FROM

take after sb *In looks she takes after her father.* ♦ *Who do you take after, your mother or your father?*

fall out

look after

put up with

take after

verbs to do with the family

take a'gainst *informal*

to begin to dislike someone, often without having a good reason

take against sb *Martin took against her almost straight away.*

take a'long ★★

to take someone or something with you when you go somewhere

take sb/sth along *Take your brother along with you.*

take along sb/sth *I took along my binoculars in case we saw any dolphins.*

take a'part ★

1 to separate an object into pieces
= DISMANTLE ≠ PUT TOGETHER

take sth apart *If you take your watch apart, you might not be able to put it together again.*

take apart sth *How do you take apart an armchair to fix a loose spring?*

2 *mainly journalism* to beat someone very easily in a game or sport = THRASH

take sb/sth apart *If you don't prepare properly, your opponent will take you apart.*

3 to criticize a person or an idea very severely = CRITICIZE ≠ PRAISE

take sb/sth apart *The moment he made a mistake, the press started taking him apart.* ♦ *Why do you have to take everything I say apart?*

take as ★★

to react to or think about someone or something in a particular way

take sth as sth *I don't know whether I should take what he said as a compliment or an insult!* ♦ *We can't take his silence as proof of his guilt.* ♦ *They took the rainbow as a sign from their God.*

take a'side ★ [often passive]

to take someone away from someone else they are with so that you can speak to them in a place where other people cannot watch or listen

be taken aside *I was immediately taken aside by the manager.*

take sb aside *I took Mr Murray aside to remind him of his responsibilities.*

,take a'way ★★★

1	remove an object
2	move sb using force
3	travel with sb
4	make sth bad disappear
5	in maths
+	**takeaway** noun

1 to remove something from a place
= REMOVE
take sth away *Take that animal away –
it's disgusting.*
take away sth *Don't take away any of
these books from the library!*

2 if people in authority take you away,
they force you to go to a place such as
prison or hospital
take sb away *The guards came in the
night and took him away.*

3 to take someone with you when you
travel to another place, especially on
holiday
take sb away *We're taking our
grandchildren away with us when we go
abroad this year.*

4 to make something unpleasant such as
a pain or a bad taste disappear
take away sth *If you swallow this it
should take away the pain in your tooth.*
take sth away *I had to have a drink of
milk to take the taste of the chilli away.*

5 to remove one number or quantity from
another number or quantity = SUBTRACT
≠ ADD
take sth away *Think of a number and
then take fourteen away.* ♦ **+from** *Take
the smaller number away from the larger
number.*
take away sth *If you have five bags of
sugar and you take away two, how many
are you left with?*

■ **takeaway** /ˈteɪkəˌweɪ/ **noun** [C]
British **1** a meal that you buy in a
restaurant or shop and take home to
eat. The American word is **takeout**:
Let's get a takeaway. **2** a shop that sells
meals that you take home to eat: *There's
a Chinese takeaway on the corner.*

,take a'way from

1 to remove someone such as a child from
the people who are looking after them
take sb away from sb *I can't imagine
anything worse than someone taking
your children away from you.*

2 *informal* to reduce the positive effect or
success of something
take away from sth *A few rowdy fans
couldn't take away from the team's
success.*

,take 'back ★★★

1	return sth you have bought
2	accept sth that a customer returns
3	give sb the job they left before
4	admit that you said sth wrong
5	remind sb of the past

1 to take something that you have bought
back to a shop because it is broken or not
suitable = RETURN
take sth back *If you don't like the scarf,
I can take it back.*

2 if a shop takes back something that you
have bought there, they accept it and give
you the money you paid for it because it
is broken or not suitable
take sth back *If the shoes have been
worn, they won't take them back.*
take back sth *Most DIY stores will take
back unused rolls of wallpaper.*

3 to accept someone again after they have
left a relationship, job etc and want to
return to it
take sb back *She had an affair, but then
he took her back.* ♦ *If you ever want to
work for the company again, they might
not take you back.*

4 *informal* to admit that something you
said to or about someone was wrong
= WITHDRAW
take sth back *I didn't mean what I said –
I take it back.*
take back sth *I take back everything I
said about Jim being lazy.*

5 to remind someone of something in the
past
take sb back *Those 1960s clothes take me
back.* ♦ **+to** *This song always takes me
back to when I was a teenager.*

,take 'down ★★★

1	separate the parts of a big structure
2	write sth
3	lower underwear/trousers
4	hit/shoot sb
5	take a prisoner to prison

1 to separate a large structure into pieces
so that it cannot be used = DISMANTLE
≠ PUT UP
take down sth *As soon as the concert has
finished, we take down all the scenery.*
♦ *The platform was taken down for safety
reasons.*
take sth down *They took the old wall
down and built a new one.*

2 to write down information or a
statement
take down sth *The police took down our
addresses and phone numbers.*
take sth down *I'm just going to take a
few notes down.*

3 to lower your underwear or trousers without taking them off = DROP ≠ PULL UP

take sth down *Ask mummy to help you take your pants down.*

4 *informal* to hit or shoot someone so that they fall down

take sb down *He took the men down one by one.*

5 [always in imperative] *British* to remove a prisoner from a court and take them to begin their punishment in prison

take sb down *My recommendation is that you spend the rest of your days in prison. Take him down.*

'take for ★

to believe something, usually wrongly, about someone or something

take sb/sth for sb/sth *She looks so young I took her for your sister.* ♦ *Do you take me for a complete idiot?*

'take from ★★

1 to remove something from someone or something

take sth from sb/sth *He took a book from the shelf.* ♦ *Do you mind if I take some flowers from your garden?* ♦ *Can you take some of this shopping from me? It's really heavy.*

2 to remove a number or quantity from another number or quantity

take sth from sth *What do you get if you take twenty seven from thirty seven?*

3 [often passive] to get something from a book or a collection of things

be taken from sth *Today's reading is taken from St John's gospel.*

take sth from sth *Linguistics takes its subject matter from a wide variety of languages.*

PHRASE **take it from sb** to accept an explanation or something someone says without discussing it or arguing about it: *He's a fast learner. Take it from me.*

‚take 'in ★★★

1	include sth
2	allow sb to stay
3	understand and remember sth
4	make sb believe sth false
5	make clothing narrower
6	accept sth
7	look at sth
8	do work for sb else
9	go to an event
+	**intake** noun

1 to include something = INCLUDE

take in sth *The book takes in the period between 1891 and Lenin's death.* ♦ *The focus of discussion was expanded to take in more issues.*

2 to allow someone to stay in your house or your country

take in sb *We decided to take in lodgers.* ♦ *The country has taken in more refugees than any other.*

take sb in *Everyone in her family refused to take her in because of her drugs problem.*

3 [usually with a negative] to understand and remember something that you hear or read = ABSORB, GRASP, UNDERSTAND

take sth in *She nodded, not taking much of what he said in.*

take in sth *I'm not sure how much of his explanation she took in.*

4 [usually passive] to trick someone into believing something that is not true = DECEIVE, DUPE

be/get taken in *Don't be taken in by their promises.* ♦ *He has tricked hundreds of people out of their savings and police are warning the public not to be taken in.*

5 to make a piece of clothing more narrow or tight, so that it fits you ≠ LET OUT; *British* TAKE OUT

take sth in *If the skirt is too loose I can take it in for you.*

take in sth *I need to take in these trousers a bit.*

6 to accept something as real or true = ABSORB

take in sth *He still hasn't really taken in his father's death.*

take sth in *I was so shocked I couldn't take everything in.*

7 to spend time looking at something = ABSORB

take in sth *We sat there taking in the scenery.*

take sth in *She looked him up and down, taking every detail in.* ♦ *He watches them play, taking it all in, remembering what it was like.*

8 to do work in your home for someone else

take in sth *She has started taking in ironing.*

9 *mainly American* to go to an entertainment or sport

take in sth *We took in a couple of movies.* ♦ *Maybe we can take in a baseball game while we're in town.*

■ **intake** /'inteik/ *noun* **1** [singular] the amount of something that you eat or drink: *Reduce your intake of salt, sugar, and junk foods.* **2** the amount of a chemical or another substance that enters your body: *a good intake of vitamins* ♦ *Cut down your calorie intake.* **3** [C] the part of a machine or engine where air or fuel is taken in: *the engine's air intake* **4** [singular/U] *education* the number of people accepted by an institution such as a school, university, or company at one time: *this year's intake of students* PHRASE **an intake of breath** a sudden act of breathing in, especially when you are shocked by something: *A comment like that would produce a sharp intake of breath from the committee.*

,take 'into ★★★

1 to make someone become involved in something
　take sb into sth *It was that advice that had taken him into the army.*

2 to put someone or something into a particular state
　take sb into sth *The police had **taken** one of the men **into custody**.* ♦ *The animal was **taken into captivity** ten years ago.*

3 to make or allow someone or something to continue or last as long as a particular time in the future
　take sb/sth into sth *Another £1 million would take them into the next year.* ♦ *It needed a new manager to take them into the future.*

,take 'off ★★★

1	remove clothing etc
2	aircraft: start flying
3	become successful/popular
4	not go to work
5	leave suddenly
6	copy sb's behaviour for fun
+	**take-off** noun

1 to remove something, especially a piece of clothing = REMOVE ≠ PUT ON —*picture →* PUT ON
　take sth off *I'd better take my shoes off.*
　take off sth *They took off all their clothes and jumped in the river.*

2 if an aircraft takes off, it leaves the ground and starts flying ≠ TOUCH DOWN, LAND
　take off *The plane should take off on time.*

3 to become successful or popular very fast
　take off *Her business has really taken off.* ♦ *She never expected her career to take off in the way it did.*

4 to have a particular amount of time away from work
　take sth off *I'm taking Monday off to go to the game.* ♦ *We haven't taken any time off since last summer.*

5 *informal* to leave a place suddenly

take off *As soon as she saw George arrive, she just took off.* ♦ *+towards I watched as the bike took off towards the main road.*

6 *informal* to copy the way someone speaks or behaves, in order to entertain people = IMITATE
　take off sb *Beth can take off Judy Garland brilliantly.*
　take sb off *He's always taking the teachers off.* ♦ *A lot of people do Bush, but no-one takes him off like John Culshaw.*

take off (sense 2)

■ **'take-off** noun **1** [C/U] an occasion when a plane leaves the ground and starts to fly: *The pilot speaks to you again just before take-off.* **2** [C] an occasion when someone copies the voice or behaviour of someone else in a humorous way: *Sam launched into a take-off of Clinton.* **3** [C] an occasion when someone's feet leave the ground as they jump: *He appeared to twist his ankle at take-off.*

,take 'on ★★★

1 to start to employ someone = RECRUIT ≠ DISMISS
　take on sb *We're not taking on any new staff at the moment.*
　take sb on *When I took him on, he knew nothing about selling.*

2 to develop a particular character or appearance = ACQUIRE
　take on sth *Our website is taking on a new look.* ♦ *The war took on a different meaning for everyone involved.*

3 to accept some work or responsibility = UNDERTAKE
　take on sth *I can't take on any more work at the moment.* ♦ *If you don't have any spare time you shouldn't have taken on the job.*
　take sth on *Tina just keeps taking more and more responsibility on.*

4 to fight or compete against someone = CHALLENGE
　take on sb *This evening Manchester United take on Barcelona.*

take sb on *No other fighter is good enough to take him on.*

PHRASE take it on yourself *see* take upon

take 'out ★★★

1	remove sth from a pocket etc
2	take sb to a restaurant/cinema etc
3	get sth official from a bank/court etc
4	kill sb or destroy sth
5	make clothing looser
+	out-take noun; takeout noun

1 to remove something from a pocket, bag, container etc
take out sth *Henry took out his wallet.*
take sth out *The officer started to take her notebook out.* ♦ **+of** *She took some of the sauce out of the saucepan.*

2 to take someone to a place like a cinema or a restaurant and usually pay for them —*picture* → ASK OUT
take sb out *Can I take you out some time?* ♦ **+for** *She's taking her parents out for dinner.*

3 to get something officially, especially from an insurance company, bank, or law court = OBTAIN
take out sth *When you take out an insurance policy, read the small print.* ♦ **+against** *Beth took out an injunction against her ex-husband.*
take sth out *They took a loan out to pay for their wedding.*

Nouns often used as objects with
take out 3

■ **injunction, insurance, loan, mortgage, patent, summons**

4 *informal* to kill someone or destroy something = DESTROY, KILL
take out sb/sth *The night bombing raid took out the bridge.*
take sb/sth out *They hired someone to take him out.*

5 *British* to make a piece of clothing more loose, so that it fits you = LET OUT ≠ TAKE IN
take out sth *She put on a few pounds and had to take out all her clothes.*
take sth out *Could you take these trousers out a bit for me?*

■ **'out-take** **noun** [C] a part of something such as a television or radio show that is taken out before the show is broadcast: *The album includes live tracks, out-takes, and demos.*

■ **takeout** /ˈteɪkaʊt/ **noun** [C] *American* a takeaway: *The kids don't want any more takeout pizza.*

take 'out of

to change the nature of something by removing a particular quality
take sth out of sth *The move had taken some of the excitement out of her life.*
♦ *Take the worry out of studying with these new study guides.*

PHRASES take sb out of themselves to make someone forget their problems and feel happy and relaxed: *A day by the sea would take her out of herself.*
take it out of sb or **take a lot out of sb** to make someone very tired: *Looking after children can really take it out of you.*

take 'out on ★

to make someone suffer because you are angry, upset, or tired, even though it is not their fault
take sth out on sb *When he's under pressure at work, he takes it out on me.*

take 'over ★★★

1 to begin to do something that someone else was doing
take over *You've been driving for hours. Do you want to take over for a while?*
♦ **+from** *I'll take over from you for a moment.* ♦ **+as** *Jane took over as director after Richard retired.*
take over sth *Can you take over the cooking while I walk the dog?* ♦ *Ms Rice will be taking over responsibility for the company's finances.*

Nouns often used as objects with
take over 1

■ **command, control, duties, leadership, management, reins, responsibility, role, running, task**

2 to take control of something
take over sth *IBM is taking over the smaller company.* ♦ *Gibraltar was taken over by Spain in 1462.*
take sth over *The building was a private nursery until social services took it over.*

■ **overtake** /ˌəʊvəˈteɪk/ **verb 1** [T] to take control of someone or something: *He was overtaken by violent anger.* **2** [T] to become better than another person: *The women students seem to be overtaking the men.* **3** [T] to go past a particular limit: *Sales look like overtaking last year's total.* **4** [I/T] *British* to go past another vehicle that is travelling in the same direction: *That's a dangerous place to overtake.*

■ **takeover** /ˈteɪkˌəʊvə/ **noun 1** a situation in which one company takes control of another company by buying a majority of its shares: *The business is vulnerable to a hostile takeover.* **2** an act of taking control of a country or organization by an army, group etc, especially by force: *Accusations of corruption against the government resulted in a military takeover.*

take 'through *informal*
to explain to someone in detail how something should be done, what something is about etc = WALK THROUGH
take sb through sth *Here's my report. I'll take you through it if you like.*

'take to ★★
1 to begin to like someone or something = WARM TO ≠ DISLIKE
take to sb/sth *I took to John immediately.* ♦ *He never really took to long distance running.*

2 to start doing something as a habit = BEGIN
take to doing sth *Recently he's taken to wearing a hat.* ♦ *She had taken to reading in the afternoons.*

3 *old-fashioned* to go to a place, especially your bed
take to sth *The passengers took to the lifeboats.* ♦ *Joanne says she's ill, and she's **taken to her bed**.*
PHRASES **take to the air** to begin to fly: *A small flock of geese sat watching us for a while then took to the air.*
take to your heels to run away from someone, especially because you have done something wrong: *The burglars had evidently taken to their heels.*
take to sth like a duck to water to learn a new activity very easily, as if you have been doing it for a very long time: *He took to schoolteaching like a duck to water.*

take 'up ★★★

1	start doing sth new
2	use space/time
3	accept an offer etc
4	make clothing/curtains etc shorter
5	continue dealing with sth
+	PHRASES
+	**take-up** noun; **uptake** noun

1 to start doing something new as a habit, job, or interest
take up sth *Chris has taken up jogging.* ♦ *I took up smoking when I was eighteen.* ♦ *The new surgeon will take up her post in May.*
take sth up *You're a natural at selling. It's a shame you never took it up.*

Nouns often used as objects with **take up 1**

■ **appointment, directorship, duties, employment, position, post**

2 to fill a particular amount of space or time = OCCUPY
take up sth *These files take up a lot of disk space.* ♦ *I'll try not to take up too much of your time.*
take sth up *I don't have much free time and the children take it all up anyway.*

3 to accept an offer or a challenge (=an offer to fight or compete) that someone has made to you
take up sth *One of our greatest athletes has taken up a new challenge.* ♦ *Schools are taking up the offer of cut-price computers.*
take sth up *It's a great opportunity for anyone who's willing to take it up.*

Nouns often used as objects with **take up 3**

■ **challenge, invitation, offer, option**

4 to reduce the length of a piece of clothing or some curtains = SHORTEN ≠ LET DOWN
take up sth *I've still got to take up the lounge curtains.*
take sth up *If the dress is too long you can always take it up.*

5 to continue to discuss or deal with an idea, problem, or suggestion = CONTINUE, CARRY ON WITH
take up sth *She fell silent, and her brother took up the story.*
take sth up *The final chapter takes the theme of deforestation up again.*
PHRASES **take up arms** *formal* to start a battle using weapons: *He refused to take up arms for his king and country.*
take up the cudgels to take action to support or defend a person, idea, political movement etc: *She took up the cudgels on behalf of farmers.*
take up residence *formal* to start living somewhere: *A family of mice had taken up residence in our attic.*

■ **'take-up** noun [U] the number of people who accept or buy something that is offered, for example by a government or a company: *The Department admits that take-up has been disappointing.*

■ **uptake** /'ʌpteɪk/ noun [singular/U]
1 *British* the number of people who want to do something such as use a service or study a particular subject: *There was an especially high uptake in the Business Management course.* **2** *technical* a process in which living creatures use substances such as food or water to breathe, produce energy etc: *Vitamin C increases your **uptake** of minerals such as iron.* PHRASE **be quick/slow on the uptake** *informal* to take a very short or long time to understand or realize

something: *He's hardworking but a bit slow on the uptake.*

,take 'up on

to accept an offer or invitation that someone has made

take sb up on sth *I've decided to take you up on that job offer.* ♦ *He's invited us to his house in Spain. Maybe we should take him up on it.*

,take u'pon

PHRASE **take it upon/on yourself** to decide to do something without asking permission from anyone else: *My mother took it on herself to invite some friends of hers to our wedding.*

,take 'up with

1 *informal* to become friendly with someone, especially someone who could have a bad influence on you

take up with sb *I don't want you to take up with the wrong crowd.*

2 [always passive] to be busy doing, discussing, or thinking about something

be taken up with sth *A lot of my time is taken up with administrative work.* ♦ *The whole meeting was taken up with arguing about the budget.* ♦ *She was completely taken up with her own worries.*

be 'taken with

to like someone or something, especially someone who you have just met or something that you have just got or heard about

be taken with sb/sth *You could tell he was taken with your sister.* ♦ *You could see she was quite taken with the idea.*

TALK /tɔːk, *American* tɔk/
talks, talking, talked

'talk about

to discuss something in writing = DEAL WITH, DISCUSS

talk about sth *Chapter 3 talks about the causes of the war.*

PHRASE **be talking about sth** *informal* used for emphasizing something: *We're talking about people's lives here!*

,talk a'round (*also* ,talk 'round *British*)

to discuss something in a general way and without dealing with the most important issues

talk around sth *You are talking around the real issue here.*

'talk at

to talk a lot without letting someone else say anything

talk at sb *It was the kind of conversation where they just talk at you.*

,talk a'way

to continue to talk for a long time

talk away *Nobody's listening, but she just keeps talking away.*

,talk 'back

to reply quickly and rudely to something someone says. This expression is used especially about children who are being rude to their parents = ARGUE

talk back *How many times do I have to tell you not to talk back like that?* ♦ **+to** *Melanie, don't talk back to your mother!*

■ **'back talk** noun [U] *American* a rude way of answering someone who is telling you what to do: *Don't give me any of your back talk.*

,talk 'down ★

1 *informal* to speak to and calm someone who is upset or nervous, especially because they have taken an illegal drug

talk sb down *You are supposed to talk suicides (=people trying to kill themselves) down gently.*

2 [usually passive] to use a radio to explain to someone who is flying a plane how to land it

be talked down *They were talked down by air traffic controllers on the ground.*

3 *informal* to persuade someone to lower the price of something

talk sb down *He's very good at talking salesmen down.* ♦ **+to** *He wanted five thousand pounds, but I talked him down to four.*

4 to talk about someone or something in a way that makes people think they are not as good as they really are = RUN DOWN ≠ TALK UP

talk down sb/sth *Why are you always talking down your achievements?*
talk sb/sth down *She talks her husband down and makes jokes about him all the time.*

,talk 'down to

to talk to someone as if you think they are not as intelligent or important as you are

talk down to sb *Try not to talk down to your employees.*

,talk 'into ★ [often passive]

to persuade someone to do something ≠ TALK OUT OF

be talked into sth *Don't be talked into something you'll later regret.*
be talked into doing sth *The parents were talked into helping to pay for the deposit.*

talk sb into sth *It wasn't hard to talk him into another whisky.*

talk sb into doing sth *She had talked me into looking after the kids for the day.*

,talk 'out

to discuss a problem thoroughly with someone who disagrees with you about it

talk sth out *also* **talk out sth** *Let's meet up tomorrow to talk things out.* ♦ *You need to sit down with her and talk this out.* ♦ *Both partners need to sit down and talk out the decision.*

,talk 'out of [often passive]

to persuade someone not to do something
≠ TALK INTO

be talked out of (doing) sth *We were talked out of making a decision now.* ♦ *Peter would never be talked out of his plan.*

talk sb out of (doing) sth *I'm sure we can talk her out of filing a formal complaint.* ♦ *They did try to talk me out of the decision.*

,talk 'over ★★

to discuss a problem or a plan

talk over sth *You both need to talk over what happened that day.*

talk sth over *I know you're still angry; let's talk it over tonight.*

,talk 'round British

1 to succeed in persuading someone to agree to something = PERSUADE, BRING ROUND

talk sb round *She's not very happy about it, but I'm sure I can talk her round.*

2 *same as* **talk around**

,talk 'through ★★

1 to explain to someone in detail how something should be done

talk sb through sth *He talked me through the whole process of sending email.* ♦ *If you need help installing the software, call our helpline and we'll talk you through it.*

2 to discuss a plan or situation in a detailed way

talk through sth *The president talked through all the military options.*

Nouns often used as objects with
talk through 2

■ anxieties, emotions, feelings, ideas, issues, plans, problems

PHRASE **be talking through your hat** *informal* to be saying a lot about a subject you do not really understand: *That's nonsense, Will. You're talking through your hat.*

'talk to ★★★

1 to have a conversation with someone
= TALK WITH

talk to sb *I saw her talking to the teacher.* ♦ *If there's a problem, talk to me about it.*

2 to tell someone that they have done something wrong and that you are angry or dissatisfied about it

talk to sb *I'll talk to the boys later.*

PHRASE **like talking to a (brick) wall** used for saying that someone does not listen or react to you when you talk: *I tried to tell her, but it's like talking to a brick wall.*

■ **'talking-to** noun [singular] an occasion when you speak angrily to someone because they have done something you do not approve of: *He needs to give these players a good talking-to.*

,talk 'up

to talk about someone or something in a way that makes them seem more important or better than they really are
≠ RUN DOWN, TALK DOWN

talk up sb/sth *also* **talk sb/sth up** *The government are trying to talk up the economy.* ♦ *Some optimists are still talking the market up.*

'talk with ★★

to have a conversation with someone
= TALK TO

talk with sb *I talked with my aunt for a while.*

TALLY /ˈtæli/
tallies, tallying, tallied

,tally 'up

if you tally numbers or amounts up, you calculate their total

tally sth up *also* **tally up sth** *Officials are just tallying up the scores.*

TAMP /tæmp/
tamps, tamping, tamped

,tamp 'down

to press a substance down by hitting it several times with something heavy

tamp sth down *also* **tamp down sth** *Fill the tray with soil and tamp it down to produce a flat surface.*

TAMPER /ˈtæmpə, American ˈtæmpər/
tampers, tampering, tampered

'tamper with ★★

to touch something that you should not

touch, and change it in some way, often because you want to spoil it = INTERFERE WITH

tamper with sth *It was clear that someone had tampered with the computer.* ♦ *There is a possibility that evidence might have been tampered with.*

TANGLE /'tæŋg(ə)l/
tangles, tangling, tangled

be/get ,tangled 'up

1 if something is tangled up, or if it gets tangled up, its parts become twisted around each other or around something else so that they look untidy and are difficult to separate

be/get tangled up *The bedclothes were all tangled up on the floor.* ♦ **+with** *The ribbon got tangled up with her hair.*

2 to be involved, or become involved, in a difficult situation

be/get tangled up in sth *He had got tangled up in a family dispute that would probably end in bitterness.*

get tangled up

'tangle with *informal*
to become involved in a fight or argument with someone

tangle with sb *I wouldn't tangle with him if I were you.*

TANK /tæŋk/
tanks, tanking, tanked

,tank 'up *mainly American*
to fill a vehicle with petrol

tank up *I tanked up before we set off.*

■ **,tanked 'up** adj *British very informal* extremely drunk: *You don't go into a job interview tanked up.*

TAP /tæp/
taps, tapping, tapped

'tap for *informal*
to persuade someone to give you money

tap sb for sth *James was trying to tap me for money.*

,tap 'into

1 if you tap into something such as someone's ability or a supply of information, you use it or get some benefit from it

tap into sth *PC users can tap into a wealth of information via the Internet.* ♦ *There is a supply of skilled workers that they can tap into.*

2 to understand and express something such as people's beliefs or attitudes

tap into sth *The company had managed to tap into concerns over job security.* ♦ *They feared the senator's ability to tap into the American psyche.*

,tap 'out

1 to use your fingers to do something such as call a telephone number or write something using a computer keyboard

tap out sth *also* **tap sth out** *She picked up the receiver and started to tap out his number.* ♦ *I could hear him tapping out another job application.*

2 to create a particular pattern of sounds by hitting a surface gently with your fingers

tap out sth *also* **tap sth out** *He tapped out a slow rhythm with his feet.* ♦ *Max tapped the beat out while I sang.*

3 *American* to make you feel very tired

tap sb out *The pace of life in New York sometimes taps you out.*

4 *American* to use all the money that someone or something has available

tap out sth *also* **tap sth out** *How can we buy a new house without tapping out our savings account?*

TAPE /teɪp/
tapes, taping, taped

'tape to
to stick something onto a surface using tape (=a long thin band of plastic that is sticky on one side)

tape sth to sth *I taped a note to his door.*

,tape 'up

1 to fasten something using tape (=a long thin band of plastic that is sticky on one side)

tape up sth *also* **tape sth up** *Make sure you tape up the envelope securely.*

♦ *Screw on the lid tightly, then tape it up.*

2 [usually passive] to wrap a part of your body tightly with a special band of cloth because it is injured or weak
be taped up *His right leg had to be taped up after the game.*

TAPER /ˈteɪpə, *American* ˈteɪpər/
tapers, tapering, tapered

ˌtaper ˈoff

to gradually become less
taper off *Spending has tapered off from £844 million to £557 million.*

TART /tɑːt, *American* tɑrt/
tarts, tarting, tarted

ˌtart ˈup *British informal*

1 to decorate something in order to improve the way it looks, especially in a way that other people think is ugly
tart up sth *also* **tart sth up** *She's always trying to tart up her bedroom.* ♦ *They bought a house and spent a fortune tarting it up.*

2 to try to hide the fact that something is bad by showing or describing it in a positive way = DRESS UP
tart sth up *also* **tart up sth** *It's a terrible song however you try to tart it up.* ♦ *He had tarted up his past to make it sound a lot more wild than it really was.*

3 to try to make yourself look more attractive, for example by wearing nice clothes. This expression is often used for showing that you think a woman has made herself look less attractive.
tart yourself up *She tarted herself up in a short skirt and tight top.*

TASK /tɑːsk, *American* tæsk/
tasks, tasking, tasked

ˈtask with [usually passive]

to give someone a particular responsibility
be tasked with sth *The secretaries were tasked with organizing the data.*

TAX /tæks/
taxes, taxing, taxed

ˈtax with *formal*

to accuse someone of doing something wrong
tax sb with sth *She taxed him with neglect of his family.*

TEAM /tiːm, *American* tim/
teams, teaming, teamed

ˌteam ˈup

1 if two people or groups team up, they do something together = GET TOGETHER, PAIR UP ≠ SPLIT UP
team up *How did the two of you come to team up?* ♦ *If you know other people in the same situation, it may help you to team up.* ♦ **+with** *She has teamed up with her brother to record her latest album.*

2 to put two people or groups together to do something = PAIR UP
team sb up *Whose idea was it to team those two up?* ♦ **+with** *The coach teamed me up with a really fast runner.*
team up sb *We try and team up people with similar experience.*

TEAR[1] /teə, *American* ter/
tears, tearing, tore /tɔː, *American* tɔr/,
torn /tɔːn, *American* tɔrn/

ˌtear aˈpart ★★

1	make sb sad/worried
2	make people stop being friends
3	break sth into pieces
4	search a place thoroughly
5	criticize sb/sth

1 to make someone feel very sad, upset, or worried = DISTRESS
tear sb apart *All this fighting with your brother is tearing your mother apart.*
♦ *It just tears me apart to see you suffering like this.*

2 to make people argue and damage their relationship = DESTROY
tear sth apart *This issue is tearing their marriage apart.*

3 to damage or destroy something completely by breaking it into pieces = RIP APART
tear sth apart *The explosion tore the building apart.*
tear apart sth *The animal tore apart the deer with its teeth.*

4 to search a room or building very thoroughly, moving things in a careless way that causes damage
tear sth apart *The police tore the place apart looking for the money.*

5 to criticize someone or something very strongly
tear sb apart *His boss tore him apart in his last appraisal.* ♦ *If you make the slightest mistake, the press will tear you apart.*

'tear at

to pull very strongly at something
tear at sth *His eager hands tore at her clothes.* ♦ *The wind tore at her hair.*
PHRASE tear at sb's heartstrings to make someone feel a lot of love or sympathy: *They show you videos designed to tear at your heartstrings.*

,tear a'way

to force yourself or someone else to leave or stop doing something **= DRAG AWAY**
tear yourself away *She was so intrigued by what he was saying, she couldn't tear herself away.* ♦ **+from** *'Sorry,' said Douglas, tearing himself away from the conversation.*
tear sb/sth away *He's always on his computer. It's impossible to tear him away.* ♦ **+from** *She was unable to tear her eyes away from him.*

be 'torn between ★★

if you are torn between two possibilities, you cannot decide which one to choose
be torn between sth *He was torn between two careers: soccer and rugby.*
♦ *She was torn between rage and a desire to laugh.*

,tear 'down ★

to destroy or remove a structure or part of a structure **= DEMOLISH ≠ CONSTRUCT**
tear down sth *They tore down the old buildings and replaced them with concrete cubes.*
tear sth down *Demonstrators tore the barricades down.*

'tear into

1 to physically attack someone or something **= LAY INTO**
tear into sb/sth *He tore into the other kid, punching him furiously.*
2 to criticize someone or something very angrily **= CRITICIZE, LAY INTO ≠ PRAISE**
tear into sb/sth *She really tore into me for forgetting to send her letter.* ♦ *I was surprised at the way he tore into my work.*
3 to start doing something with a lot of energy or enthusiasm **= GET STUCK INTO**
tear into sth *The girls tore into their chores and were finished within an hour.*

,tear 'off ★★

1 to remove clothes quickly and carelessly
tear off sth *The boys tore off their clothes and jumped into the water.*
tear sth off *The girls tore his trousers off, leaving him completely naked.*
tear sth off sb/sth *She tore the baseball cap off her head and threw it at him.*

tear up

2 to remove something by pulling it away from something else with force
tear off sth *The hurricane tore off the roof.*
tear sth off *Farm machinery is very dangerous. It can tear your limbs off.*
tear sth off sth *The wind was threatening to tear the gate off its hinges.*
3 to move somewhere very quickly, especially in an excited or uncontrolled way
tear off *The boys went tearing off down the street.*
PHRASE tear sb off a strip/tear a strip off sb *British informal* to criticize someone angrily for doing something wrong: *She was tearing her husband off a strip for coming home drunk.*

,tear 'out

PHRASES be tearing your hair out to feel very worried or very annoyed about something because you do not know what to do about it: *Where have you been? You mother's been tearing her hair out, imagining all sorts of terrible things.*
tear sb's heart out *literary* to make someone extremely sad: *It tears my heart out when I think about that little girl losing her mother.*

,tear 'up ★★

1 to destroy something such as a piece of paper or cloth by pulling it into pieces **= RIP UP**
tear up sth *I tore up all the photos of my ex-boyfriend.*
tear sth up *I tore the letter up as soon as I'd read it.*
2 to lift or remove something in a way that damages or destroys it **= RIP UP**
tear up sth *He tore up the floorboards and tried to rewire the house.*
tear sth up *They tear the trees and*

hedges up to make way for new houses.
♦ *There were fields here once, until the developers tore them all up.*

3 to refuse to accept something such as an agreement any longer = DESTROY
tear up sth *We will tear up the whole treaty rather than accept this clause.*
tear sth up *He threatened to tear his employment contract up.*

4 to make someone feel very unhappy or upset = DISTRESS
tear sb up *I had never seen him so upset and it tore me up.* ♦ **+to do sth** *It tears me up to leave you.*

TEAR² /tɪə, *American* tɪr/
tears, tearing, teared

,tear 'up
to almost start crying
tear up *Don began to tear up when he talked about his son.*

TEASE /tiːz, *American* tiz/
teases, teasing, teased

,tease 'out
1 to succeed in discovering something difficult, complicated, or secret
tease out sth *also* **tease sth out** *I managed to tease out the relevant details.*
♦ *There's a lot of material and you have to tease this information out.*
tease sth out of sb *We'll have to tease the address out of him.*

2 to separate a group or knot of pieces of hair, string etc into individual pieces
tease sth out *We tease the wool out into longer and straighter fibres.*

TEE /tiː, *American* ti/
tees, teeing, teed

,tee 'off
1 *informal* if something tees off, it begins = KICK OFF
tee off *The event tees off with a children's competition.*

2 to hit a ball off a tee in golf, especially for the first time at the very beginning of a game
tee off *The first pair was due to tee off at eight o'clock.*

3 *American informal* to make someone angry or annoyed = ANNOY
tee sb off *also* **tee off sb** *We were late, which teed the teacher off immediately.*
♦ *Any such suggestion is likely to tee off the audience.*

■ **'teed off** **adj** *American informal* angry

or annoyed: *I was really teed off by his constant interruptions.*

,tee 'up
to put a golf ball on a tee, ready to hit it
tee up *I was just teeing up at the first hole when it started to rain.*
tee up sth *also* **tee up sth** *Jack teed the ball up and prepared to swing at it.*

TEEM /tiːm, *American* tim/
teems, teeming, teemed

'teem down [usually progressive] *British*
if it is teeming down, a lot of rain is falling = POUR DOWN
be teeming down *When I woke up, it was teeming down.*

'teem with
to contain an extremely large number of people, animals, or objects that are all moving around
teem with sb/sth *These rivers teem with fish.*

TELL /tel/
tells, telling, told /təʊld, *American* toʊld/

,tell a'gainst *British*
if a quality or feature tells against someone, it makes them less likely to succeed in achieving something = COUNT AGAINST
tell against sb *I'm sure it was my age that told against me.*

,tell a'part
to recognize the difference between two people or things that are very similar
= DISTINGUISH BETWEEN ≠ CONFUSE WITH
tell sb/sth apart *The two women are so similar that only their husbands can tell them apart.* ♦ *I could hardly tell the two pictures apart – they looked almost identical.*

'tell from
to recognize the difference between one person or thing and another = DISTINGUISH FROM ≠ CONFUSE WITH
tell sth/sb from sth/sb *Can you tell butter from margarine?* ♦ *The sisters are so alike I can hardly tell one from the other.*

'tell of ★★
1 [often passive] *formal* to inform someone about something = INFORM
be told of sth *I was told of his death by a fellow officer.*
tell sb of sth *She told us of her doubts regarding the policy.*

2 *mainly literary* to mention or talk about something
tell of sth *The legend tells of a mysterious city beneath the sea.*

,tell 'off ★★ [often passive]

to criticize someone angrily for doing something wrong = REBUKE, REPRIMAND
be/get told off *I'm going to get told off for being late.*
tell sb off *All she'll do is tell me off.*
♦ **+for doing sth** *The teacher told me off for talking in class.*

tell off

■ ,telling-'off noun [C] *informal* an occasion when you tell someone you are angry with them for something they have done: *I had to give one boy a telling-off.*

'tell on

to tell someone such as a parent or teacher about something bad that someone else has done = SPLIT ON
tell on sb *She threatened to tell on me.*

TEND /tend/
tends, tending, tended

,tend to'wards ★

1 to usually have a particular quality or attitude
tend towards sth *Her study found that sociologists tended towards liberalism.*
2 to change or develop in a particular direction
tends towards sth *Schools are tending towards stricter control in the classroom.*

TENSE /tens/
tenses, tensing, tensed

,tense 'up

if you or your muscles tense up, your muscles become tight in an uncomfortable or painful way, for example because you are feeling nervous
tense up *I could feel him tensing up.*
■ ,tensed 'up adj *informal* not relaxed: *Max is all tensed up.*

TEST /test/
tests, testing, tested

,test 'out ★

1 [often passive] to try using something in order to find out whether it works correctly or is satisfactory
be tested out *It can't go on sale until it has been fully tested out.*
test out sth *He's been diving in the area to test out equipment.*
test sth out *Test the colour out first on a small area of wall.*
2 to say things that are designed to find out what someone's opinions, reactions, or abilities are
test sb out *I could see she was testing me out.*

TESTIFY /'testɪfaɪ/
testifies, testifying, testified

'testify to

to provide evidence that something exists or is true
testify to sth *These ruins testify to the existence of Roman occupation.*

THAW /θɔː, *American* θɔ/
thaws, thawing, thawed

,thaw 'out

1 if someone's body or a part of it thaws out, it becomes warmer after being very cold
thaw out *My fingers are beginning to thaw out now.*
2 if frozen food thaws out, it becomes softer and ready to cook
thaw out *I hope the meat thaws out in time for dinner.*

THIN /θɪn/
thins, thinning, thinned

,thin 'down

to make a thick liquid become less thick by adding water or another liquid to it
thin sth down *If the soup's too thick, thin it down with a little lemon juice before serving.*

,thin 'out

1 if people or things thin out, they gradually become fewer, for example because some of them have left or have been taken away

think over

thin out *The crowd started to thin out.*
♦ *At this point, the trees thin out quite a bit.*

2 to remove plants, leaves, trees etc so that they do not fill an area or space completely

thin sth out *also* **thin out sth** *Thin the plants out to one every six inches.* ♦ *We thinned out the young bean plants.*

THINK /θɪŋk/
thinks, thinking, thought /θɔːt, *American* θɒt/

'think about *same as* think of

,think a'head ★

to make plans about things that will or may happen in the future, so that you will be prepared for them

think ahead *These reviews encourage managers to think ahead.* ♦ **+to** *We're thinking ahead to the next meeting.*

,think 'back ★★

to think about something that happened in the past

think back *Thinking back, I realize I was wrong.* ♦ **+to** *I've been trying to think back to that last evening.*

'think of ★★★ (*also* 'think about)

1 if you think of something such as a fact or a possibility, it comes into your mind
= COME UP WITH

think of sth *I used every method I could think of.*

2 [often passive] to have a particular opinion of someone or something

think of sb/sth *What did you think of her performance?* ♦ *I'd like to know what she thinks of her new job.*

think of sb/sth as sth *People think of Latin as a dead language.*

be thought of as sth *Australia is thought of as an exciting place to live.*

3 to consider doing something

think of doing sth *We're thinking of selling the house.*

4 to consider the feelings or wishes of a particular person

think of sb *We rarely think of others in these situations.*

think of yourself *It's clear he was thinking only of himself.*

> PHRASES **I wouldn't think of doing sth** or **I would never think of doing sth** used for saying that you would not consider doing something, for any reason or in any situation: *She would never think of going against her father's wishes.*
>
> **what was sb thinking of?** *informal* used for saying that you think someone has done something stupid: *Why did you say that? What on earth were you thinking of?*

,think 'out ★★ [often passive]

to consider all the important facts in a situation before deciding or doing something

be thought out *Each stage has to be carefully thought out.*

think out sth *He was thinking out his next move.*

think sth out *Think it out properly before you make a decision.*

,think 'over ★★

to consider a problem or decision carefully
= CONSIDER, REFLECT ON

think sth over *Let's think the proposal over before we see him again.*

think over sth *When you're thinking over a problem, ask yourself these questions.*

think 'through ★★

to consider the facts about something in an organized and thorough way
= CONSIDER

think sth through *Have you had time to think things through?*
think through sth *There was no time to think through all of these issues.*

think 'up ★★

to invent or imagine something, especially an excuse = INVENT

think up sth *I had to think up a plausible reason for not going.*
think sth up *It's a great scheme, and they thought it up by themselves.*

THIRST /θɜːst, American θɜrst/
thirsts, thirsting, thirsted

'thirst for *literary*

to want something very much

thirst for sth *She thirsted for words of love from him.*

THRASH /θræʃ/
thrashes, thrashing, thrashed

thrash a'bout (*also* thrash a'round)

to move your body in a violent and uncontrolled way

thrash about *Someone was thrashing about in the water.*

thrash 'out ★

to discuss something until you find a solution or reach an agreement = HAMMER OUT

thrash out sth *Both sides hope to thrash out an agreement by next week.*
thrash sth out *We're going to thrash things out over the next few days.*

THRILL /θrɪl/
thrills, thrilling, thrilled

'thrill to

to feel very excited and pleased about something

thrill to sth *Scottish audiences have thrilled to his music.*

THRIVE /θraɪv/
thrives, thriving, thrived or throve /θrəʊv, American θroʊv/, **thrived or thriven** /θrɪv(ə)n/

'thrive on ★★

to become successful or happy in a particular situation, especially one that other people would not enjoy

thrive on sth *Some couples thrive on conflict.*

THROTTLE /'θrɒt(ə)l, American 'θrɑt(ə)l/
throttles, throttling, throttled

throttle 'back

1 to reduce the speed of a vehicle by reducing the supply of fuel to the engine

throttle back *He had to settle for third after throttling back because of problems with his front tyre.*

2 to start to use less energy or effort

throttle back *He declared his feelings too early. Now he would have to throttle back a little.*

throttle 'up

to increase the speed of a vehicle by increasing the supply of fuel to the engine

throttle up *He fixed his eyes firmly on the speedometer as he began to throttle up.*

THROW /θrəʊ, American θroʊ/
throws, throwing, threw /θruː, American θru/, **thrown** /θrəʊn, American θroʊn/

Throw is often used with adverbs and prepositions when it means 'to use your hand to send an object through the air': *She **threw** the letter **into** the fire.* ♦ *I **throw** the ball **to** you and you **throw** it **back** to me.* These uses are not included here.

throw a'round ★ (*also* throw a'bout *British or* throw 'round *British*)

1	move yourself in uncontrolled way
2	say sth to people
3	throw in different directions
4	move sb with force
5	throw ball to sb
+	PHRASES

1 to move your body, or part of your body, in a violent or uncontrolled way

throw yourself around *She sings loudly and throws herself around.*
throw sth around *He throws his arms around in the air.*

2 *showing disapproval* to say something to a lot of people, usually something that you have not considered carefully

throw sth around *The teacher was throwing accusations around.*

3 to throw things in different directions because you are angry

throw sth around *The animals go mad and start throwing straw around.*

4 [usually passive] if you are thrown around, the violent movement of something, especially a vehicle you are in, causes your body to move in an uncontrolled way

be thrown around *We spent an hour being thrown around on a dusty track.*

5 if people throw a ball or similar object around, they throw it to each other

throw sth around *Some boys were throwing a ball around in the sun.*

PHRASES **throw a cordon/barrier around sth** to enclose a place so that people cannot enter or leave: *Police threw a cordon around the offices to keep away members of the public.*

throw your arms around sb to put your arms around someone in a sudden and excited way, usually because you love them: *She threw her arms around my neck.*

throw (your) money around to spend a lot of money in a way that is very careless or is intended to impress other people: *From his bank statements, we could tell he'd been throwing money around.*

throw your weight around to use your authority or influence in order to make people do what you want, in a direct or cruel way that annoys or offends them: *He was a manager who enjoyed throwing his weight around.*

,**throw a'side** [usually passive]
to refuse to accept or continue something

be thrown aside *All her plans to go to university have been thrown aside.*

'**throw at**
if you throw something such as questions, ideas, comments etc at someone, you suddenly ask them or mention them

throw sth at sb *Reporters were throwing personal questions at her.*

,**throw a'way** ★★★
1 to get rid of something that you no longer want, for example by putting it in a dustbin = BIN, DISCARD, THROW OUT

throw sth away *Have you thrown the papers away?*

throw away sth *I threw away all the broken toys.*

2 to waste something such as an opportunity or advantage, for example by doing something silly = WASTE ≠ MAKE THE MOST OF

throw away sth *They lost the game after throwing away a fourteen point lead.*

throw sth away *I don't want to see her throw an opportunity like this away.*

■ **throwaway** /ˈθrəʊə.weɪ/ adj **1** a throwaway product has been made to be used for a short time only and then thrown away. A more usual word is

disposable: *The latest idea is throwaway clothes.* **2** used about societies, activities etc in which people use a lot of throwaway objects: *the modern throwaway society we live in* **3** a throwaway remark, comment etc is something you say suddenly and without thinking carefully about it

,**throw 'back** ★★
1 to push the covers on a bed away from you, for example before you get out of bed

throw back sth *She threw back the duvet and jumped up.*

throw sth back *I watched him throw the covers back and leap out of bed.*

2 if you throw back a drink, you drink it quickly, usually swallowing it all at once = KNOCK BACK

throw back sth *She threw back the brandy I gave her.*

throw sth back *He poured himself another and threw it back before speaking.*

PHRASE **throw back your head** to move your head backwards suddenly, usually because you are laughing very loudly: *Colin threw back his head and roared with laughter.*

■ **throwback** /ˈθrəʊbæk/ noun
[singular] someone or something that seems to belong to an earlier period of time or that makes you think of an earlier period of time: *The film seems to be a throwback to the 1970s.*

,**throw 'back at**
to remind someone of a bad or stupid thing they did in the past

throw sth back at sb *His colleagues were continually throwing this back at him.*

,**throw 'back on** [usually passive]
to force someone to use their own abilities, powers etc because there is nothing else to use

be thrown back on sth *When the business failed he was thrown back on his own resources.*

,**throw 'down** ★
to drop something that you are holding in your hand quickly and with a lot of force

throw down sth *I'm ordering you to throw down your weapons.*

throw sth down *She threw the book down and stood up.*

PHRASE **throw down the gauntlet** or **throw down a challenge** to invite someone to compete or fight with you: *The government was throwing down the gauntlet to the BBC.*

throw 'in ★★

1 [often passive] to include something extra with something that you are selling, without asking for more money = INCLUDE

be thrown in *Buy a computer now and get a free printer thrown in!*

throw in sth *Sellers may throw in certain items such as carpets and curtains to settle a price.*

throw sth in *They throw that in with the price.*

2 to add a remark, question etc in a conversation

throw sth in *I just threw in a few comments occasionally.*

throw sth in *The reason I throw that in is that I know a lot of people agree.*

3 in football, if a player throws in or throws the ball in, they throw it back onto the field after it has gone out

throw in *Owen threw in quickly, taking the opposition by surprise.*

throw sth in *He threw the ball in, aiming for Beckham.*

PHRASES **throw sb in at the deep end** to force someone to deal with something difficult without being prepared for it: *How would they respond if they were thrown in at the deep end?*

throw in the towel to stop trying to do something because you think it is too difficult, or because you think you cannot win: *This is not the time to go throwing in the towel.*

- **'throw-in** noun [C] in football, an occasion when a player throws the ball back onto the field after it has gone out: *Hutchison will take the throw-in.*

throw 'into ★★★

1 to cause someone or something suddenly to be in a particular bad state

throw sb/sth into sth *One small error can throw the whole system into confusion.* ♦ *It's the kind of news that can throw you into a panic.*

> Nouns often used as objects with **throw into 1**
>
> ■ **chaos, confusion, disarray, doubt, question, panic, turmoil**

2 to start to do something with a lot of energy, often so much energy that you ignore everything else

throw yourself into sth *Her response was to throw herself into her work.* ♦ *The youngster threw himself into the task.*

3 to put someone into prison

throw sb into prison/jail etc *He was thrown into a police cell until he had calmed down.*

throw 'off ★★

1	remove clothing
2	get rid of sth that prevents freedom
3	escape from sb
4	get rid of illness
5	produce heat/smell etc
+	PHRASE

1 to quickly remove a piece of clothing = FLING OFF

throw off sth *Dieter threw off his clothes and dived into the water.*

throw sth off *She threw the jacket off.*

2 to get rid of something that has prevented you from doing what you want to do or behaving in the way you want = SHAKE OFF, SHED

throw off sth *I can't throw off this feeling of sadness.* ♦ *India had **thrown off the shackles** of colonial rule.*

throw sth off *The country had accepted foreign rule until it was strong enough to throw it off.*

3 to escape from someone who is chasing you = ELUDE, SHAKE OFF

throw off sb *He threw off his pursuers and fled across the border.*

throw sb off *I managed to throw them off in Basel.*

4 if you throw off a slight illness, you become healthy again = SHAKE OFF

throw off sth *I still haven't managed to throw off that cold I caught at the weekend.*

throw sth off *If I could just throw this wretched cold off.* ♦ *With rest, you'll soon throw it off.*

5 to produce something such as heat or a smell

throw off sth *also* **throw sth off** *Light bulbs throw off heat and can affect your air conditioning.*

PHRASE **throw sb off the scent/track** to stop someone from finding you or discovering the truth about something by using a clever plan or trick: *Detectives were thrown off the scent after the evidence was destroyed.*

throw 'on

to quickly put on a piece of clothing = FLING ON

throw on sth *also* **throw sth on** *I threw on my coat and rushed out.* ♦ *Get washed and throw some clothes on.*

throw 'out ★★★

1 to get rid of something that you no longer want, for example by putting it in a dustbin = BIN, THROW AWAY, DISCARD

Through has several different meanings when it is used as part of a phrasal verb. Some of these meanings are literal, but many are figurative. This diagram shows how all these meanings are connected, and how the figurative meanings develop from the literal ones.

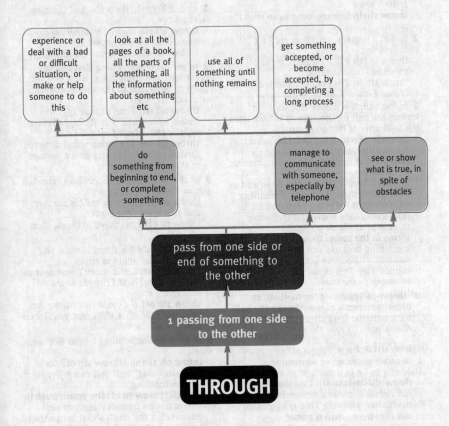

experience or deal with a bad or difficult situation, or make or help someone to do this

look at all the pages of a book, all the parts of something, all the information about something etc

use all of something until nothing remains

get something accepted, or become accepted, by completing a long process

do something from beginning to end, or complete something

manage to communicate with someone, especially by telephone

see or show what is true, in spite of obstacles

pass from one side or end of something to the other

1 passing from one side to the other

THROUGH

Main meanings	Example verbs		
1 passing from one side to the other			
pass from one side or end of something to the other	break through	plough through	score through
	cut through	rip through	strike through
	pass through	run through	swing through
Protesters tried to **break through** police lines. ♦ _If we **cut through** the park, we'll save some time._			
do something from beginning to end, or complete something	breeze through	rattle through	sleep through
	carry through	romp through	take through
	follow through	run through	talk through
	gallop through	rush through	think through
We still have a lot of work to **get through** this afternoon. ♦ _I sat **through** the whole lecture, even though I was bored to tears._	get through	sail through	wade through
	go through with	see through	walk through
		sit through	whizz through
experience or deal with a bad or difficult situation, or make or help someone do this	carry through	live through	see through
	get through	pull through	win through
	go through	put through	work through
Doctors don't expect him to **pull through**. ♦ _It's not fair to **put** children **through** so much stress._			
look at all the pages of a book, all the parts of something, all the information about something etc	comb through	page through	shuffle through
	flick through	pick through	sift through
	flip through	plough through	skim through
	go through	read through	sort through
She sat in the waiting room, **flipping through** the pages of a magazine. ♦ _Would you **read through** the essay and give me your opinion?_	leaf through	rifle through	thumb through
	look through	run through	wade through
use all of something until nothing remains	get through	go through	run through
I don't understand how two people can **go through** so much toilet paper.			
get something accepted, or become accepted, by completing a long process	force through	muddle through	rush through
	get through	push through	scrape through
	go through	put through	squeak through
Republicans promise to **push** tax reform **through** Congress. ♦ _The new law just **squeaked through**._			
manage to communicate with someone, especially by telephone	come through	get through	phone through
	fax through	patch through	put through
She said she tried to call but she couldn't **get through**. ♦ _Could you **put** me **through** to Mr Walker, please?_			
see or show what is true, in spite of obstacles	break through	see through	shine through
He didn't fool me – I could **see** right **through** him. ♦ _Her kindness and generosity **shone through**._			

throw out sth *I've thrown out my old boots.*

throw sth out *She'd thrown all my photographs out.*

2 [often passive] to force someone to leave a place or group = EXPEL

be thrown out *Anybody who misbehaves will be thrown out.*

throw sb out of sth *She threw him out of the house.*

3 [often passive] if someone in authority throws out a plan, proposal etc, they refuse to accept it = REJECT

be thrown out *The first two designs were thrown out.*

throw out sth *The judge threw out their claim.*

throw sth out *It's the second time in two years a ban has been considered: last time the council threw it out.*

4 to produce something such as heat or light = GIVE OFF, GIVE OUT

throw out sth *The lamps weren't throwing out enough light.*

throw sth out *The big fire threw heat out like a furnace.*

> **PHRASE** **throw the baby out with the bathwater** to get rid of the good and useful aspects of something without intending to, while you try to get rid of its negative aspects: *Investment companies have shown that it's possible to throw the baby out with the bathwater.*

throw out (sense 2)

,throw 'over [often passive] *old-fashioned* to end a romantic or sexual relationship with someone

be thrown over *He's already been thrown over by his girlfriend.*

throw sb over *He was thinking of throwing her over.*

,throw 'round *British same as* **throw around**

,throw to'gether ★

1 [often passive] to make something quickly because you do not have much time
= COBBLE TOGETHER, KNOCK TOGETHER

be thrown together *It feels like this course has been thrown together.*

throw together sth *I can easily throw together some lunch.*

throw sth together *We had to throw a list together at the last minute.*

2 [usually passive] if a particular situation or event throws people together, it causes them to meet and get to know one another

be thrown together *They were thrown together by chance.*

,throw 'up ★★★

1	when food comes out through your mouth
2	cause sth new to exist
3	about dust/water etc
4	build sth quickly
5	leave your job/home

1 *informal* if you throw up or throw something up, food and drink comes back up from your stomach and out of your mouth = *formal* VOMIT

throw up *I've been throwing up all night!*

throw sth up *She ate a good breakfast then threw it all back up.*

2 *British* to produce something or someone new or unexpected

throw up sth *This system has thrown up a few problems.* ♦ *The years after the war threw up some amazing new artistic talent.*

throw sth up *The report was to throw a few surprises up.*

> Nouns often used as objects with **throw up 2**
>
> ■ difficulties, evidence, issues, possibility, problems, surprises

3 to cause something such as dust or water to rise into the air

throw up sth *The car wheels threw up a shower of gravel.*

throw sth up *Horses throw clouds of dust up into the clear blue sky.*

4 [often passive] to build something such as a house quickly and not very well

be thrown up *A wall was hastily thrown up to provide some shelter.*

throw sth up *They'll have to throw a new stadium up in around six months.*

throw up sth *They claimed the land and immediately started throwing up houses.*

5 to suddenly leave something such as your job or your home = ABANDON

throw up sth *They threw up the whole city lifestyle.*
throw sth up *She felt like throwing everything up and starting a new life.*

THRUST /θrʌst/
thrusts, thrusting, thrust

ˌthrust aˈside
to pay no attention to something
thrust sth aside *also* **thrust aside sth** *You have to thrust these feelings aside.* ♦ *They learn to thrust aside their differences and co-operate.*

ˌthrust ˈinto
to put something somewhere with a quick hard push
thrust sth into sth *The man thrust his hands into his pockets.*

ˈthrust upon [usually passive]
to force someone to do or accept something
be thrust upon sb *Even more responsibility was now thrust upon her.*

THUMB /θʌm/
thumbs, thumbing, thumbed

ˈthumb through
to quickly turn the pages of something such as a book, magazine, or newspaper
thumb through sth *She was thumbing through the new exam paper.*

THUMP /θʌmp/
thumps, thumping, thumped

ˌthump ˈout *informal*
to play a tune very loudly, especially on the piano
thump out sth *also* **thump sth out** *Someone was thumping out songs from 'Oklahoma'.*

TICK /tɪk/
ticks, ticking, ticked

ˌtick aˈway
1 tick away or **tick by** if time ticks away, it passes
tick away *We need an answer now. The minutes are ticking away.*
2 if a clock ticks away, it shows that time is passing
tick away *Mortimer watched the clock ticking away.*

ˌtick ˈoff ★
1 *British* to put the symbol ✓ next to something on a list in order to show that you have dealt with it

tick off sth *Tick off people's names as they arrive.*
tick sth off *We ticked possible locations off on the map.*
2 [often passive] *British informal* to speak angrily to someone who has done something wrong = TELL OFF; *formal* REBUKE
be/get ticked off *She gets ticked off by the teacher occasionally.*
tick sb off *They tick you off for not trying.*
3 *American informal* to annoy someone
tick sb off *The noise was beginning to tick me off.*

■ ˌticked ˈoff **adj** *American informal*
annoyed: *She sounded really ticked off about it.*

■ ˌticking ˈoff **noun** [singular] an occasion when someone speaks angrily to a person who has done something wrong: *He was used to getting a ticking off from Brian.*

ˌtick ˈover ★ [usually progressive] *British*
1 if a car engine is ticking over, it is operating but the car is not moving
be ticking over *The engine was ticking over nicely.*
2 *informal* to operate steadily but not very well
be ticking over *Business was ticking over.*

TIDE /taɪd/
tides, tiding, tided

ˌtide ˈover
to help someone to get to the end of a difficult period of time, especially by giving them money until they can get some more
tide sb over *Could you lend me £50 to tide me over until pay day?*

TIDY /ˈtaɪdi/
tidies, tidying, tidied

ˌtidy aˈway
to put things back in their correct place after you have been using them = CLEAR AWAY
tidy away sth *also* **tidy sth away** *It's time to tidy away your toys.* ♦ *Have you tidied those papers away yet?*

ˌtidy ˈout
to make a room or cupboard look better by removing things that you do not want
tidy out sth *also* **tidy sth out** *We were tidying out the garage.* ♦ *I spent the day tidying the studio out.*

ˌtidy ˈup ★★

1 to make a place look better by putting things in the correct place = SORT OUT
tidy up sth *I must tidy up the house tonight.*
tidy sth up *We need to tidy this room up a bit.*
tidy up *They never tidy up afterwards.*

2 to make small changes to something in order to make it better = SPRUCE UP
tidy up sth *The government needs to tidy up the law surrounding this issue.*
tidy sth up *We'll have to tidy her spelling up a bit.*

3 to make yourself look better by washing your face, brushing your hair etc
tidy yourself up *Sara went to her room to tidy herself up.*

ˌtidy ˈup ˌafter

to make a room look tidy after someone else has made it untidy = CLEAN UP AFTER
tidy up after sb *I go round the house tidying up after my children.*

TIE /taɪ/
ties, tying, tied

ˌtie ˈback

to tie something such as hair or a curtain so that it does not hang straight down
tie sth back *also* **tie back sth** *I prefer to tie my hair back.* ♦ *Use shorter cords to tie back the curtains.*

ˌtie ˈdown ★

1 to stop someone from being free to do what they want
tie sb down *I don't want a relationship that ties me down.*

2 to force a group of soldiers to stay in one place
tie down sb *A small rebel force is tying down thousands of government troops.*
tie sb down *Their gunners tied us down for over an hour.*

ˌtie ˈin with

1 to combine with something
tie in with sth *This project ties in with the language research he is doing.*

2 to provide more evidence that something is true
tie in with sth *Your findings tie in with our own satellite observation reports.*

■ **'tie-in** noun [C] a product such as a toy or book connected with a successful film or television programme: *Over $500 million was made from tie-ins alone.*

ˌtie ˈup ★★★

1	tie ends together
2	make sb busy
3	traffic: delayed
4	make not available for use
5	complete an arrangement
6	use rope to prevent sb from moving
7	fasten an animal with rope
8	boat: go into a port and stay
+	PHRASE
+	**tie-up** noun

1 to tie the ends of something together = FASTEN ≠ UNTIE
tie up sth *Tie up your shoelaces before you trip over them.*
tie sth up *You haven't tied them up properly.*

2 [usually passive] to make someone very busy, so they are not able to do anything else or go anywhere else = OCCUPY
be tied up *I'm afraid he's tied up this morning.* ♦ **+with** *I'll be tied up with clients all day.*

3 [usually passive] *American* if traffic is tied up, the vehicles are in a long line and waiting to continue moving
be tied up *Traffic was tied up for miles.*

4 [usually passive] to be already using something, especially an amount of money, for a particular purpose, so that it cannot be used for another purpose = LOCK UP
be/get tied up *All their spare cash was already tied up.* ♦ *The photocopier's been tied up all morning.* ♦ **+in** *Don't get all your money tied up in long-term investments.*

5 to make all the arrangements that are necessary for a deal to be completed = COMPLETE
tie up sth *I've just tied up the final part of the deal.*
tie sth up *We're tying the remaining few details up today.* ♦ *She was hoping to tie it up here and now.*

6 to fasten rope around someone so that they cannot move or escape ≠ UNTIE
tie sb up *They blindfolded us and tied us up.*
tie up sb *You would expect them to tie up all hostages.*

7 [often passive] to fasten an animal with rope to something such as a post = TETHER
be tied up *A couple of horses were tied up nearby.*
tie up sth *This is where you tie up your horse.*
tie sth up *They just tie the donkey up outside.*

8 if a boat ties up or is tied up, it has

stopped sailing and is fastened to
something in a place such as a port = MOOR
be tied up *It's just one of the luxury
motor cruisers tied up in the marina.*
tie up *The bigger cruisers tie up at the
island's western end.*
PHRASE **tie up (the) loose ends** to deal
with the last few things that have to be
done before you can finish something:
*We needed a lawyer to tie up these loose
ends.*

■ **'tie-up** noun [C] **1** an agreement
between two or more companies or
organizations to become business
partners: *a tie-up with a Dutch
company* **2** *American* a situation where
something cannot move, make
progress, or work normally: *There seems
to be a communications tie-up of some
kind.*

,**tie 'up with** [usually passive]
to connect something with something else
be tied up with sth *The illness seems to
be tied up with events in her childhood.*

TIGHTEN /'taɪt(ə)n/
tightens, tightening, tightened

,**tighten 'up** ★★
1 to be stricter or more serious about
something such as a policy or rule
tighten up sth *They tightened up the law
on public protests.* ♦ **+on** *My first
priority is to tighten up on discipline.*
2 to turn something such as a screw or
lid until it is tight and you cannot turn it
any more
tighten up sth *Make sure you tighten up
the caps.*
tighten sth up *I've tightened all the nuts
up.*
3 if a muscle or a part of your body
tightens up, it becomes stiff and
uncomfortable or painful
tighten up *Your shoulders are
tightening up.*

TILT /tɪlt/
tilts, tilting, tilted

'**tilt at** *literary*
to criticize someone or something
tilt at sb/sth *We listened to him tilting
at the system.*
PHRASE **tilt at windmills** to waste time
dealing with problems that do not really
exist: *Is there a real crisis here, or are
we all tilting at windmills?*

TINKER /'tɪŋkə, *American* 'tɪŋkər/
tinkers, tinkering, tinkered

'**tinker with** (*also* ,**tinker a'round with**
or ,**tinker a'bout with** *British*)
to make small changes to something in
order to improve or repair it
tinker with sth *I tinkered with the
engine.* ♦ *Problems can arise when you
start tinkering around with the
management structure.*

TIP /tɪp/
tips, tipping, tipped

'**tip down**
PHRASE **be tipping (it) down** *British informal*
if it is tipping down, or tipping it down,
a lot of rain is falling: *Towards the end
of the game, it was really tipping down.*

,**tip 'off** ★ [often passive]
to give someone a warning or secret
information about something = WARN
be tipped off *They were arrested after
the police were tipped off.*
tip sb off *Someone must have tipped them
off.*

■ '**tip-off** noun [C] **1** *informal* a warning
or secret information that you give to
someone: *The police arrested him after
an anonymous tip-off.* **2** in basketball,
an occasion when the ball is thrown
into the air in order to start play: *James
goes up for the tip-off.*

,**tip 'onto**
to pour something from one place or
container onto another
tip sth onto sth *She opened her case and
tipped the clothes onto the bed.*

,**tip 'over**
if something that is upright tips over, or
if someone or something tips it over, it
falls onto its side, usually by accident
tip over *Be careful that the vase doesn't
tip over.*
tip over sth *also* **tip sth over** *The baby
tipped over her milk.* ♦ *I tipped the barrel
over onto its side.*

,**tip 'up**
1 to turn a container upside down so that
the things inside it come out
tip sth up *also* **tip up sth** *When I tip the
container up, nothing comes out.* ♦ *I
tipped up the dish.*
2 if something tips up, one end of it moves
upwards, especially because something
heavy has been put at the other end
tip up *The heavy handle makes the buggy
tip up.*

tip up (sense 2)

TIPTOE /ˈtɪptəʊ, American ˈtɪpˌtoʊ/
tiptoes, tiptoeing, tiptoed

ˌtiptoe aˈround
1 to avoid dealing directly with a problem
tiptoe around sth *The government should stop tiptoeing around the issue of health care.*
2 to be very careful about how you behave towards someone because you are afraid of offending or annoying them
tiptoe around sb *The rest of us tiptoe around him.*

TIRE /ˈtaɪə, American ˈtaɪr/
tires, tiring, tired

ˈtire of ★
to become bored with someone or something
tire of sb/sth *You'll soon tire of their music.* ♦ *We were rapidly tiring of his company.*
PHRASE **never tire of (doing) sth** to always enjoy something, or always enjoy doing something: *I never tire of hearing stories about his travels.* ♦ *We could never tire of New York.*

ˌtire ˈout
to make someone feel very tired = EXHAUST, WEAR OUT
tire sb out *also* **tire out sb** *All that exercise really tired me out.* ♦ *It's enough to tire out the fittest swimmer.*

TODDLE /ˈtɒd(ə)l, American ˈtɑd(ə)l/
toddles, toddling, toddled

ˌtoddle ˈoff *British informal*
to leave in order to go somewhere
toddle off *They toddled off to school.* ♦ *I toddled off home.*

TOG /tɒg, American tɑg/
togs, togging, togged

ˌtog ˈout (*also* ˌtog ˈup) [usually passive]
British informal
to dress yourself or someone else for a special occasion or activity
be togged out *They were all togged out in their best clothes.*

TOIL /tɔɪl/
toils, toiling, toiled

ˌtoil aˈway
to do something that involves a lot of effort
toil away *We toiled away but achieved very little.* ♦ **+at** *I toiled away earnestly at the tasks I was given.*

TONE /təʊn, American toʊn/
tones, toning, toned

ˌtone ˈdown ★
1 to make something less severe, shocking, or offensive = MODERATE
tone down sth *Both sides agreed to tone down their speeches.*
tone sth down *You'll have to tone your language down a little.*
2 to make the colour, flavour etc of something less strong
tone down sth *Can you tone down the decorations?*
tone sth down *We need something to tone the lemon taste down.*

ˌtone ˈin with (*also* ˈtone ˈwith) *British*
if something tones in with something else, they look good together because their colours are similar
tone in with sth *A subdued pattern will tone in with the surroundings.*

ˌtone ˈup
to make your body, skin, or muscles more firm and healthy = FIRM UP
tone sth up *also* **tone up sth** *He'd lost some weight and toned his body up.* ♦ *It would help if you toned up your stomach muscles.*
tone up *I just want to tone up a bit.*

ˈtone with *same as* tone in with

TOOL /tuːl, American tul/
tools, tooling, tooled

ˌtool ˈup
1 to prepare to do something, usually by getting the tools or equipment needed, or to prepare someone or something to do something in this way

tool up *The company was tooling up for the introduction of the euro.*

tool sb/sth up *They'd built new factories and were tooling them up.*

2 [usually passive] *British informal* to provide someone with a weapon, especially so that they can commit a crime

be/get tooled up *The men with us were tooled up.*

TOP /tɒp, *American* tɑp/
tops, topping, topped

,top 'off
1 to finish something in a satisfactory way by doing one final activity or adding one final detail

top sth off *also* **top off sth** *Another brandy would top the evening off nicely.*
♦ *We went for a walk to top off a pleasant afternoon.* ♦ **+with** *We topped off the evening with a carriage ride.*

2 *mainly American* to completely fill a container that is already partly full = TOP UP

top off sth *also* **top sth off** *I just want to top off the tank before we head into the desert.*

,top 'out
1 if a rate or an amount tops out, it reaches its highest level

top out *We're expecting the level to top out soon.* ♦ **+at** *Mortgage rates topped out at 10% before falling last spring.*

2 [usually passive] to finish building something by adding the last part to the top

be topped out *The new office building will be topped out tomorrow afternoon.*

,top 'up ★★
1 to completely fill a container that is already partly filled = *mainly American* TOP OFF

top up sth *I'll just top up the teapot.*
top sth up *Let me top your glass up.*

2 to add more liquid to someone's glass or cup in order to make it full

top sb up *Can I top you up?*
top sb up *Would you like me to top up your drink?*
top sth up *Can I top it up for you?*

3 to add more to something in order to bring it up to the level you want or need

top up sth *This is a nice way to top up your earnings.*
top sth up *Start thinking about topping your savings up.*

■ **'top-up** noun [C] *British* **1** an amount of liquid added to a glass or cup that someone is drinking from in order to

refill it: *Would you like a top-up?* **2** an amount of money added to other money in order to reach the necessary level: *a top-up loan*

be 'topped with
to be covered at or on the top with a layer of something

be topped with sth *My pizza is topped with pepperoni.* ♦ *The hills are topped with clumps of trees.*

TOPPLE /'tɒp(ə)l, *American* 'tɑp(ə)l/
topples, toppling, toppled

,topple 'over
to stop being steady and fall, or make someone or something do this

topple over *Marie shoved Simon, and he toppled over.*
topple sth over *His weight on the end of the bench toppled it over.*

TOSS /tɒs, *American* tɔs/
tosses, tossing, tossed

,toss a'round (*also* ,toss a'bout *British*)
1 [often passive] to discuss something such as an idea, often in an informal way = BAT AROUND

be tossed around *This problem has been tossed around for a century.*
toss sth around *also* **toss around sth** *We tossed some thoughts around for a while.*
♦ *Part of learning is tossing around ideas and theories.*

2 [usually passive] to make something move in a violent or uncontrolled way

be tossed around *Yachts were tossed around like toys.*

,toss a'side
1 [often passive] to stop accepting or believing in something, especially when the situation makes this inconvenient for you = REJECT

be tossed aside *His principles are tossed aside in difficult situations.*
toss sth aside *She soon tosses this idea aside.*
toss aside sth *We have tossed aside the notion of America as a land of freedom.*

2 to throw something that you have been holding or using to one side, often angrily

toss aside sth *also* **toss sth aside** *He tossed aside the book and went to the door.* ♦ *She tosses the towel aside and stands up.*

,toss a'way
to get rid of something, especially carelessly

toss sth away *also* **toss away sth** *He*

opened a window and tossed the cigarette away. ♦ She had tossed away her diet books.

,toss 'back ★

1 to move your head up and back with a sudden strong movement, for example when you start to laugh
> **toss sth back** She tossed her head back proudly.
> **toss back sth** She tosses back her long golden hair.

2 toss back or **toss down** to drink something, usually alcohol, quickly, swallowing it all at once
> **toss back sth** He's been tossing back beers all day.
> **toss sth back** Wilkes poured himself another vodka and tossed it back.

'toss for

to make a decision about which of two people will do or have something, based on which side of a coin is facing upwards when it lands after the coin has been thrown into the air
> **toss for sth** We decided to toss for it.
> **toss sb for sth** You toss your opponent for the right to serve first.

,toss 'off *informal*

1 to produce something written quickly, easily, and without much effort
> **toss off sth** also **toss sth off** I can toss off a couple of articles a month. ♦ She can toss a few thousand words off in an afternoon.

2 British offensive to touch or rub your own or someone else's sexual organs so that you or they become sexually excited = *formal* MASTURBATE

,toss 'out

1 *informal* to say or suggest something
> **toss sth out** I just tossed that phrase out to get the discussion going.

2 mainly American informal to get rid of something you do not want, for example by putting it in a dustbin = THROW OUT
> **toss sth out** also **toss sth out sth** The bread was all mouldy, so I tossed it out. ♦ She's tossed out the bathroom scales!

,toss 'up

to throw a coin into the air and make a decision based on which side the coin falls on
> **toss sth up** Neil tossed the penny up; she called 'heads' and won.
> **toss up** Let's toss up to decide who drives.

■ **'toss-up** noun [singular] *informal* the act of throwing a coin into the air and making a decision based on which side

the coin falls on: It was decided by a toss-up. **PHRASE** **be a toss-up** used for saying that you do not know which of two things to choose or which of two things will happen: It's a toss-up between going to India or China.

TOT /tɒt, American tɑt/
tots, totting, totted

,tot 'up *informal*

to add numbers together = ADD UP
> **tot up sth** also **tot sth up** Let's tot up how many hours we've spent on it. ♦ Give me the figures and I'll tot them up.

TOTAL /'təʊt(ə)l, American 'toʊt(ə)l/
totals, totalling or **totalled**, American **totaled**

,total 'up

to add several numbers or amounts together in order to find a total
> **total up sth** also **total sth up** At the end of the day, please total up your receipts.

TOUCH /tʌtʃ/
touches, touching, touched

,touch 'down

if an aircraft or space vehicle touches down, it lands = LAND ≠ TAKE OFF
> **touch down** The plane touched down in Sydney at midday.

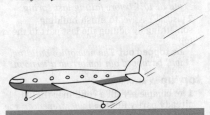

touch down

'touch for *British informal*

to get or borrow money from someone
> **touch sb for sth** He tried to touch me for a few pounds.

,touch 'off

to make something unpleasant or dangerous happen
> **touch off sth** The raid touched off angry protests.

'touch on ★★ (also 'touch upon)

to mention something when you are talking or writing = DEAL WITH, MENTION
> **touch on sth** He did not touch on the issue of immigration.

Nouns often used as objects with **touch on**

■ aspect, issue, matter, point, problem, question, subject

,touch 'up

1 to make a surface look better with small improvements = RETOUCH
touch up sth *also* **touch sth up** *Touch up the paintwork before you try and sell the house.* ♦ *This software lets you touch up your photos.* ♦ *It'll look like new once I've touched it up a bit.*
2 *informal* to touch someone in a sexual way without their permission
3 to improve the look of your make-up by adding a little more
touch up sth *Ella was touching up her lipstick in the mirror.*

'touch upon *same as* touch on

TOUGH /tʌf/
toughs, toughing, toughed

,tough 'out

PHRASE **tough it out** to stay in a difficult situation because you are very determined: *I was prepared to tough it out for a while.*

TOUGHEN /'tʌf(ə)n/
toughens, toughening, toughened

,toughen 'up

1 to make something more strict
toughen up sth *also* **toughen sth up** *Universities are toughening up their entrance requirements.*
2 to become mentally or physically stronger, or to make someone mentally or physically stronger
toughen sb up *also* **toughen up sb** *Prison life has toughened him up.* ♦ *The programme is designed to toughen up the troops.*
toughen up *She needs to toughen up a bit.*

TOUT /taʊt/
touts, touting, touted

,tout a'round

to make people interested in something by telling them that it is good
tout sth around *Hallin touted the band around in 1987.*

be 'touted as

to be described in a particular way, usually a good way
be touted as sth *She's being touted as a possible challenger for the title.*

'tout for

to try to persuade people to buy something you are selling
tout for sth *Street vendors were touting for business.*

TOW /təʊ, American toʊ/
tows, towing, towed

,tow a'way [usually passive]

to take a vehicle away from a place by pulling it behind another vehicle, especially because it is parked illegally
be towed away *If you're not careful, it'll be towed away.*

TOWER /'taʊə, American 'taʊr/
towers, towering, towered

'tower over (*also* 'tower above)

1 to be much taller than the people or things that are near you
tower over sb/sth *At 1.95 metres, Gregson towers over his team-mates.*
2 to be much better, more famous, more important etc than other people or things of a similar kind
tower over sb/sth *As an athlete Kelly towers over her contemporaries.*

TOY /tɔɪ/
toys, toying, toyed

'toy with ★★

1 to keep touching or moving something with your fingers, usually because you are nervous = PLAY WITH
toy with sth *Jerry toyed with the stem of his glass as he spoke.*
2 to consider an idea in a way that is not serious or definite = FLIRT WITH
toy with sth *I've been toying with the idea of setting up in business.*
3 to pretend that you like or love someone when really you do not = FLIRT WITH
toy with sb *We suspected she was toying with him.*
4 to keep pushing food around on your plate, instead of eating = PLAY WITH
toy with sth *He spent the whole meal toying with his potatoes.*

TRACK /træk/
tracks, tracking, tracked

,track 'down ★★

to find someone or something after a long search = FIND
track sb/sth down *I finally managed to track him down in Manchester.*
track down sb/sth *By the time we'd*

tracked down a decent hotel, it was ten o'clock.

TRADE /treɪd/
trades, trading, traded

,trade 'down
to sell something in order to buy something of the same kind that is less expensive and of a lower quality
> **trade down** *People find themselves in the position of having to trade down.*

,trade 'in
to give something old as part of the payment for something new = EXCHANGE
> **trade sth in** *How much would you get if you traded it in?* ♦ **+for** *She traded her old Ford in for a new Honda.*

■ **'trade-in** noun [C] something such as a car or piece of equipment that you give as part of the payment for something new: *You can use your old vacuum cleaner as a trade-in.*

,trade 'off
1 to accept a disadvantage so that you can have a benefit
> **trade off sth for sth** *also* **trade sth off for sth** *They traded off a positive rate of inflation for a lower unemployment rate.*
> **trade off sth against sth** *also* **trade sth off against sth** *You trade that improvement off against an overall decline in sales.*
2 *American informal* to share a responsibility or piece of work between two or more people, each doing some of the work in turn
> **trade off** *She wasn't willing to trade off.*

■ **'trade-off** noun [C] **1** the fact that you can only have one of two things, or the degree to which you can have both: *the trade-off between efficiency and quality*
2 an agreement to do something if someone else does something: *Each person helps the other. It's a trade-off.*

'trade on
to get an advantage, often an unfair one, by making use of something
> **trade on sth** *They are trading on their reputation.*

,trade 'up
to sell something in order to buy something of the same kind that is more expensive and of a higher quality
> **trade up** *We thought we could afford to trade up.*
> **trade up sth for sth** *We want to trade up our apartment for a house.*

TRAFFIC /'træfɪk/
traffics, trafficking, trafficked

'traffic in
to buy and sell things such as drugs and weapons illegally
> **traffic in sth** *He was tried and convicted for trafficking in illegal drugs.*

TRAIL /treɪl/
trails, trailing, trailed

,trail 'after *same as* trail behind

,trail a'way (*also* ,trail 'off)
if someone's voice or words trail away, they gradually become silent
> **trail away** *Her voice trailed away as she realized he wasn't listening.*

,trail be'hind (*also* ,trail 'after)
to move slowly and in a tired or unhappy way a short distance behind someone else = LAG BEHIND
> **trail behind sb** *Her husband usually trails glumly behind her.*

,trail 'off *same as* trail away

TRAIN /treɪn/
trains, training, trained

'train on [often passive]
to point something such as a gun, camera, or light at someone
> **be trained on sb/sth** *Hundreds of cameras were trained on them.*
> **train sth on sb/sth** *In 1609, Galileo constructed his first telescopes and trained them on the heavens.*

,train 'up
to make someone ready and able to do something by teaching them the necessary skills
> **train sb up** *also* **train up sb** *We're training them up for the extra work ahead.*
> ♦ *You'll have to train up a successor.*

TRAMPLE /'træmp(ə)l/
tramples, trampling, trampled

'trample on
to behave in a cruel or unfair way towards someone or something
> **trample on sth** *You have no right to trample on people's feelings!*

TRANSFER /træns'fɜ:, American træns'fɜr, 'trænsfər/
transfers, transferring, transferred

trans'fer to ★★★

1 to move someone or something from one place to another
transfer sb/sth to sth *Wait until the cakes cool before transferring them to a plate.* ♦ *Our tour group was transferred to the hotel by bus.*

2 [often passive] to move from one job, office, school etc to another
be transferred to sth *I'm being transferred to another department at the end of the month.* ♦ **+from** *Helen was transferred from marketing to sales.*
transfer to sth *I'm transferring to our Japan office next year.*

TRANSLATE /træns'leɪt/
translates, translating, translated

trans'late into ★★★

1 to cause a particular situation or result
translate into sth *Recent economic problems are beginning to translate into a demand for reforms.*

2 [often passive] to change something into a different form or to express something in a different way
be translated into sth *These earnings, translated into pounds, represent half of our total profits.*
translate sth into sth *There was an attempt to translate Marxist ideas into practice.*

TRANSPORT /træns'pɔ:t, American træns'pɔrt/
transports, transporting, transported

trans'port to

to make you imagine or feel as if you are in a different place or time
transport sb to sth *The show transported Alvin back to the nightclubs of the 1920s.*

TRAP /træp/
traps, trapping, trapped

,trap 'into

to trick someone in order to make them do or say something they did not want to
trap sb into (doing) sth *We trapped her into admitting that she had lied.* ♦ *I hoped to trap them into a confession.*

TREAT /tri:t, American trit/
treats, treating, treated

'treat with *formal*

to have a formal discussion with someone in order to try to reach an agreement about something
treat with sb *Ambassadors would be qualified to treat with foreign princes or ministers of state.*

TRESPASS /'trespəs, American 'tres,pæs, 'trespəs/
trespasses, trespassing, trespassed

'trespass on (*also* 'trespass upon) *formal*

to use more of someone's time or accept more of someone's kindness than is fair
trespass on sth *I don't want to trespass on your generosity any more.*

TRICK /trɪk/
tricks, tricking, tricked

,trick 'out (*also* ,trick 'up) [usually passive]

to decorate something in a particular way or dress someone in a particular set of clothes
be tricked out *The shop was tricked out like a Middle Eastern bazaar.*

TRICKLE /'trɪk(ə)l/
trickles, trickling, trickled

,trickle 'down

to have an effect gradually or after a long time
trickle down *The theory is that this wealth trickles down.* ♦ **+to** *This type of attitude trickles down to the children.*

■ **'trickle-down** adj relating to the belief that people at the lowest level of society or an organization always benefit from the money or advantages that people at the highest level have: *The Conservatives are great believers in the trickle-down effect.*

TRIFLE /'traɪf(ə)l/
trifles, trifling, trifled

'trifle with

1 to deal with something in a way that shows you do not have a serious attitude towards it
trifle with sth *You should never trifle with your health.*

2 [usually passive] to treat someone in a way that shows you do not respect them
be trifled with *Susan was a woman **not to be trifled with**.*

TRIGGER /'trɪgə, American 'trɪgər/
triggers, triggering, triggered

,trigger 'off ★
to make something happen suddenly,
usually something bad = SPARK OFF ≠ HALT
trigger off sth *The news of his death
triggered off further violence.*
trigger sth off *In a climate of fear, it
doesn't take much to trigger these
reactions off.* ◆ *We know what happened.
We just don't know what triggered it off.*

TRIM /trɪm/
trims, trimming, trimmed

,trim a'way *same as* trim off

,trim 'down
1 to reduce something by removing some
parts of it
trim down sth *also* **trim sth down** *You
need to trim down the first chapter.*
◆ *We've trimmed the budget down a bit.*
2 if someone trims down, they become
thinner by losing weight
trim down *Anne had already trimmed
down to a reasonable weight.*

'trim from
to reduce the amount of something you
use or spend on something
trim sth from sth *The company has
trimmed $500,000 from its advertising
budget.*

,trim 'off (*also* ,trim a'way)
to remove something that is not wanted
by cutting it
trim off sth *also* **trim sth off** *Trim off all
the fat before cooking.* ◆ *Trim any excess
mortar off with your trowel.* ◆ *If there
are any loose fibres, trim them off.*

TRIP /trɪp/
trips, tripping, tripped

,trip 'out *American very informal*
1 to start behaving in a silly or wild way,
often because you are frightened or
worried = FREAK OUT
trip out *That was the summer she
tripped out and went to New Mexico.*
2 to experience strange things because of
the effects of a powerful illegal drug
trip out *We smoked pot and everybody
was tripping out.*

,trip 'up ★
1 to make a mistake or cause someone to
make a mistake
trip up *Von Bruning continued with his
questions but Davies was careful not to*
trip up at all. ◆ **+on** *I tripped up on a
couple of questions.*
trip sb up *The tests are designed to trip
people up.* ◆ *If he asked the right question,
he might trip us up.*
trip up sb *He disapproved of his boss's
attempts to trip up interviewees with
tough questions.*
2 to hit your foot on something and fall
down = STUMBLE
trip up *I tripped up and fell when I was
running after the dog.* ◆ **+on** *Bill tripped
up on a cable and seriously injured his
knee.*
3 to make someone hit their foot on
something and fall down
trip sb up *She deliberately tripped me
up!*
trip up sb *She was caught trying to cheat
in the race by tripping up her competitors.*

TROLL /trɒl, trəʊl, American troʊl/
trolls, trolling, trolled

'troll for *informal*
to try to find or get something in a relaxed
way
troll for sth *I spent the evening trolling
for more details on the Internet.*

TROT /trɒt, American trɑt/
trots, trotting, trotted

,trot 'off *informal*
to leave a place, walking quite quickly
trot off *She trotted off down the drive.*

,trot 'out *showing disapproval*
to provide an explanation, excuse, or piece
of information that has been used a lot of
times before, and expect people to accept
it
trot sth out *also* **trot out sth** *They trot
the same old arguments out time and
time again.* ◆ *'Tomorrow's always
another day,' she said, trotting out one
of her many sayings.*

TRUMP /trʌmp/
trumps, trumping, trumped

,trump 'up [often passive]
to deliberately make up information that
suggests that someone is guilty of a crime
be trumped up *Walker insists that the
charges have been **trumped up**.*
trump up sth *Since her arrest, they've
trumped up charges against her, and
she's been deported to Beirut.*

■ 'trumped-up *adj* [only before noun]
deliberately made up in order to
suggest wrongly that someone has

committed a crime: *He was faced with a whole string of **trumped-up charges**.*

TRUNDLE /'trʌnd(ə)l/
trundles, trundling, trundled

,trundle 'out [often passive] *showing disapproval*
to give information, reasons, or a list of things that you have given a lot of times before

be trundled out *The same old arguments were trundled out to support their claim.*
trundle out sth *We expect them to trundle out some excuse to do with lack of funds.*

TRUSS /trʌs/
trusses, trussing, trussed

,truss 'up [often passive]
to tie someone's arms and legs very tightly so that they cannot move

be trussed up *He was trussed up with rope and bundled into the boot of a car.*
truss up sb *also* **truss sb up** *The robber trussed up both of the bank staff before leaving.*

TRUST /trʌst/
trusts, trusting, trusted

'trust in ★
to be sure that you can rely on someone or something totally

trust in sb/sth *They had trusted in the opinion polls, but these turned out to be completely wrong.*

'trust to *formal*
to depend on something to help you to achieve something, usually because you have no other choice

trust to sth *I'm trusting to luck that the shops will be open.* ♦ *We'll just have to trust to her usual good sense.*

TRY /traɪ/
tries, trying, tried /traɪd/

'try for
to attempt to get or achieve something difficult, or something that you want very much

try for sth *My father encouraged me to try for a Harvard scholarship.* ♦ *The couple had been trying for a baby for seven years.*

,try 'on ★★
to put on a piece of clothing in order to see how it looks and whether it fits
—*picture* → PUT ON

try sth on *What a cute dress! Why don't you try it on?*
try on sth *She must have tried on every pair of shoes on the shop.*

PHRASE try it on 1 to behave badly in order to see how annoying or unreasonable you can be before someone gets angry: *If you're a new teacher, the kids will always try it on.* ♦ *He's like a strong-willed boy **trying it on with** his parents.* **2** to attempt to start a sexual relationship with someone: *I'd slap him if he tried it on.* ♦ *He's **tried it on with** several of the new students.* **3** to attempt to get something from someone by behaving dishonestly or tricking them: *Don't let her have anything. She's just trying it on.*

,try 'out ★★★
to test someone or something to see what they are like or whether they are suitable or effective = TEST

try out sth *John hopes to try out his new running shoes this weekend.*
try sth out *You get the chance to try the software out before you buy it.* ♦ *If he sees a car he likes, he walks in and asks to try it out.* ♦ **+on** *Why don't you try your Italian out on Francesca?*

■ **'try-out noun** [C often plural] **1** a test to see what someone or something is like or whether they are suitable or effective: *Some work was arranged for me as a try-out.* **2** a test for someone who wants to become a member of a team or wants to get a part in a play or film: *Evans said they should get Jack Nicholson for the role and he was invited in for a try-out.* ♦ *I'm going to go to the try-outs for the basketball team this afternoon.*

,try 'out for
to try to become a member of a team or get a part in a play or film by showing someone how well you can play or perform = AUDITION FOR

try out for sth *Rita's trying out for the school play again.*

TUCK /tʌk/
tucks, tucking, tucked

,tuck a'way ★★
1 [often passive] to put something in a place where it is not easy to find or see

be tucked away *The candy was tucked away on the top shelf.*
tuck sth away *I tucked the photos away where the kids wouldn't find them.*

2 [usually passive] to put money in a safe place so that you can use it later be **tucked away** *I bet Grandma's got quite a bit tucked away.*

3 *British informal* to eat a lot of something quickly, because you like it or because you are hungry

tuck away sth *Before he knew it, he had tucked away the whole packet of biscuits.*
tuck sth away *She tucks more food away than anyone I've ever seen.* ♦ *It looked like enough food for a scout camp, but our three tucked it away admirably.*

4 [always passive] if a building is tucked away somewhere, it is in a quiet place away from other people or buildings

be **tucked away** *The cabin was tucked away in the woods behind the hills.*

‚tuck 'in ★

1 tuck in or **tuck into** or **tuck up** [often passive] to put a child into bed and make sure they are warm and comfortable by covering them well

be **tucked in** *The kids are all tucked in for the night.*
tuck sb in *I'll be right upstairs to tuck you in.*

2 *British informal* to eat food with enthusiasm because you like it or because you are hungry = DIG IN, DIVE IN

tuck in *Everybody tuck in before it gets cold!*
tuck into sth *I tucked into bacon and eggs.*

3 to put the end of something such as a piece of clothing under or behind another piece in order to make it tidy

tuck sth in *Tuck your shirt in!* ♦ *Put a vest on and tuck it in.*
tuck in sth *She came up to make sure I'd tucked in my vest.*
tuck sth into sth *He had tucked his trousers into his socks to keep them dry.*

tuck in (sense 2)

TUMBLE /ˈtʌmb(ə)l/
tumbles, tumbling, tumbled

‚tumble 'down ★

1 to fall downwards or to the ground
tumble down *Her hair tumbled down in dark swirls.*

2 if something tumbles down, or comes tumbling down, it ends or it is destroyed
tumble down *We shook the political structure until the leaders tumbled down.* ♦ *Soon afterwards, their marriage came tumbling down.* ♦ *The world seemed about to come tumbling down around our ears.*

■ **tumbledown** /ˈtʌmb(ə)ldaʊn/ **adj** a tumbledown building is old and in bad condition: *The materials are stored in a tumbledown shed round the back.*

'tumble into

if you tumble into a situation, you get into it without really trying to or without knowing what you are doing
tumble into sth *I never studied acting – I just kind of tumbled into it.*

'tumble to

1 *informal* to suddenly realize or understand something
tumble to sth *I didn't tumble to what she was on about until later.*

2 if you tumble to something such as a solution, you suddenly think of it
tumble to sth *Then I tumbled to a way of getting what we wanted.*

TUNE /tjuːn, *American* tun/
tunes, tuning, tuned

‚tune 'in ★★

1 to listen to a radio broadcast
tune in *Millions of people tuned in when the results were to be announced.* ♦ **+to** *Don't forget to tune in to Radio Five for live coverage of the game.* ♦ **+to do sth** *They would secretly tune in to listen to foreign news broadcasts.*

2 *informal* to understand something such as a situation or other people's feelings
tune in *When she mentions the cost of a new house, Alan tunes in right away.*
be **tuned in** *You're more tuned in to the subject than most people.*

‚tune 'out *informal*

to stop paying attention
tune out *I just tune out and let Chrissie take over.*

‚tune 'up

to make small changes to a musical instrument in order to make sure that the basic notes it plays are accurate

tune up sth *also* **tune sth up** *People think if you play percussion you don't have to tune up your instrument.* ♦ *He was in the next room, tuning his guitar up.*

tune up *The orchestra is tuning up in preparation for the performance.*

■ **'tune-up** noun [C] **1** a series of small changes made to a vehicle's engine so that it will work better: *He's taken the other car in for a tune-up.* **2** something that you do as a preparation for something else: *Williams will treat the semi-final as a tune-up.*

,tune 'up for

to prepare for an event or a situation

tune up for sth *The team is tuning up for another busy season.*

TURF /tɜːf, *American* tɜrf/
turfs, turfing, turfed

,turf 'out [often passive] *British informal*
to force someone to leave a place or an organization = KICK OUT, THROW OUT

be turfed out *If we don't keep the noise down, we'll get turfed out.*

turf sb out *also* **turf out sb** *She turfed him out when they split up.*

TURN /tɜːn, *American* tɜrn/
turns, turning, turned

Turn is often used with adverbs and prepositions when it means 'to change the position of your head or body so that you are facing in a different direction': *Lopez just glared at him and* **turned away.** ♦ *The girls in front* **turned round** *and grinned at us.* ♦ *Maria* **turned to the** *reporters and waved.* These uses are not included here.

,turn a'gainst ★

1 to stop liking or supporting someone or something and start opposing them

turn against sb/sth *The rival factions turned against each other in a bitter struggle for power.*

2 to make someone stop liking or supporting someone or something

turn sb against sb/sth *She's managed to turn your whole family against you.*

,turn a'round ★★ (*also* **,turn 'round** *British*)

1 to stop being unsuccessful and start being successful, or make something do this

turn around *That's the moment when the game turned around, Miami coach Kevin Loughery said.*

turn sth around *The £400 million loan will help turn the Russian economy around.*

2 to complete a piece of work, process, or activity within a particular time

turn sth around *Could they turn that amount of work around in one week?* ♦ *We can produce quality work and turn it around very quickly.*

3 to consider or express something in a different way

turn sth around *If you turn this argument around you'll see that it's equally valid.* ♦ *It's an awkward question to answer, so let me turn it around.*

PHRASE **turn around and do sth** to react to something, especially in a way that is surprising or not helpful: *It was your idea, so don't turn around and say you're too busy.*

■ **turnaround** /'tɜːnəˌraʊnd/ noun **1** [C] an important change in a situation that causes it to improve: *an economic turnaround* **2** [C] an important change in opinions or attitudes: *People want an explanation for this turnaround.* **3** [C/U] the time it takes a company or an institution to complete a process: *We're working to a three-day turnaround.*

,turn a'way ★★

1 [often passive] to refuse to let someone come into a place = SEND AWAY ≠ WELCOME

be turned away *Reporters who visited the team's training camp were turned away.* ♦ **+from** *A busload of Canadian tourists was turned away from the border.*

turn sb away *They're family – I could hardly turn them away!*

turn away sb *He wouldn't turn away an old friend, would he?*

2 to not help someone who has asked for help = SEND AWAY

turn away sb *Doctors are having to turn away hundreds of very sick people.*

turn sb away *We will not turn any child away.*

,turn a'way from

to refuse to accept or use something any longer = REJECT

turn away from sth *Many shoppers turned away from products that were not environmentally friendly.*

,turn 'back ★

1 [often passive] to return the same way that you came instead of continuing on your journey, or make someone do this

be turned back *Refugees who reach the border may be turned back.*

turn back *Bad weather forced the pilot to turn back.*
turn sb back *Border guards managed to turn the rebels back.*
turn back sb *Officials may turn back anyone who does not have the correct documents.*

2 to stop doing something and return to the situation you were in before you started it ≠ CONTINUE
turn back *I've gone too far to turn back now.* ♦ *The decision was made and there was no turning back.*

turn 'down ★★★

1 to not accept an offer or request
= REFUSE, REJECT
turn down sth *How could you turn down such a fantastic job?*
turn sth down *He was offered the chance to go but turned it down.* ♦ *Alex had already been asked and had turned the position down.*
turn down sb *I didn't understand how they could turn down such an experienced candidate.*
turn sb down *I don't believe it: he turned me down flat!*

Nouns often used as objects with
turn down 1

■ application, chance, invitation, offer, opportunity, proposal, request

2 [often passive] to reduce the amount of sound, heat, or light produced by a piece of equipment by pressing a button or moving a switch ≠ TURN UP
be turned down *The lights were turned down low.*
turn sth down *Can you turn the music down a bit?*
turn down sth *Bring to the boil, turn down the heat and simmer for one hour.*

3 [often passive] to fold the edge of something = FOLD BACK
be turned down *The top sheet had been neatly turned down.*
turn sth down *One of the jobs is turning the beds down.*

■ **downturn** /ˈdaʊntɜːn/ **noun**
[singular] a reduction in economic or business activity: *There has been a sharp downturn in demand in recent months.*

turn 'in ★★★

1	tell the police about sb
2	produce sth
3	point inwards
4	give sth to sb in authority
5	go to bed
6	give sth to its owner

1 to tell the police about someone who has committed a crime, or take someone or yourself to the police to be arrested
= *formal* DENOUNCE
turn sb in *His own brother turned him in.*
turn in sb *The boy turns in a member of his own family.*
turn yourself in *Police are appealing to the gunman to turn himself in.* ♦ **+to** *She turned herself in to the local police.*

2 to produce something, especially something good
turn in sth *Bicknell turned in a fine all-round performance.*

3 [often passive] to point inwards, or make something do this
be turned in *He does press-ups with his hands turned in.*
turn sth in *Turn your toes in, like this.*
turn in *Don't let your feet turn in too much.*

4 *mainly American* to give something to the person who has officially asked for it or who is in charge = HAND IN
turn in sth *You're the only person who hasn't turned in their report for the quarter.* ♦ **+to** *Mitro turned in his resignation to the President.*

5 *informal old-fashioned* to go to bed at night ≠ RISE
turn in *I might try to get a bit more work done before I turn in.*

6 *mainly American* to return something to the person it belongs to, especially something that was lost or was lent to you
turn in sth *I think Mr Watkins has already turned in his security pass.*
turn sth in *At the end of the trip, you have to turn your ticket in.* ♦ **+to** *Someone may have turned your briefcase in to the lost-and-found department.*

turn 'in on

to start to think only about yourself and your own problems and forget about other people and their problems
turn in on yourself *Isn't there a danger that the country might turn in on itself and ignore what's happening in other countries?*

‚turn 'into ★★★

1	change/develop
2	make sth change/develop
3	a period of time: get longer
4	change by magic
5	make sth change by magic

1 to change or develop into something different

turn into sth *What started out as an enjoyable holiday turned into a nightmare.*

2 [often passive] to make someone or something change or develop into something different = MAKE INTO

be turned into sth *His first novel was turned into a television film.*

turn sth into sth *The freezing temperatures had turned the water in the lake into ice.*

3 if one period of time turns into another longer period of time, the amount of time that passes increases in a way that is noticeable

turn into sth *As the days and weeks turned into months, he found great comfort in her presence.*

4 to change into something else as a result of magic

turn into sth *With one wave of her magic wand the mice turned into strong white horses.*

5 [often passive] to make someone or something change into something else using magic

be turned into sth *the tale of a prince who is turned into a frog by his wicked stepmother*

turn sb/sth into sb/sth *He threatens to turn the girl into a rabbit.*

‚turn 'off ★★★

1	make equipment stop working
2	stop water/gas/electricity from flowing
3	leave a road
4	make sb bored
5	make sb not sexually attracted
6	stop paying attention
+	**turn-off** noun

1 to stop a piece of equipment working temporarily by pressing a button or moving a switch = SWITCH OFF ≠ TURN ON

turn sth off *Will you turn the television off, please?* ♦ *I've asked you to turn the music off, so turn it off.*

turn off sth *It is now safe to turn off your computer.*

2 to stop using a supply of water, gas, or electricity by turning a tap, pressing a button, or moving a switch ≠ TURN ON

turn off sth *The emergency crew has turned off local power and gas supplies.*

turn sth off *Go and turn the tap off before the bath overflows.*

3 to leave the road you are travelling along in order to go along another one that leads away from it = BRANCH OFF

turn off *Let me know when it's time to turn off.* ♦ **+at** *Turn off at the next junction.*

turn off sth *They turned off the main road towards the beach.*

4 to make someone feel bored or no longer interested in something = PUT OFF

turn sb off *This sort of talk could turn a lot of voters off.*

turn off sb *An experience like that could turn off the most hardened holidaymaker.*

5 to stop someone feeling sexually attracted to someone ≠ TURN ON

turn sb off *His bad breath really turns me off!*

6 *informal* to stop paying attention to something or someone = SWITCH OFF

turn off *When people lose interest they just turn off.*

■ **'turn-off** noun [C] **1** a road that leads off a main road or motorway: *We'll take the next turn-off.* **2** *informal* something that stops you feeling sexually attracted or excited: *Some men think facial hair is a turn-off.*

‚turn 'on ★★★

1	make equipment start working
2	make water/gas/electricity flow
3	use a quality you have
4	direct sth at sb/sth
5	be the thing that sth depends on
6	behave angrily towards sb
7	attack sb
8	make sb sexually attracted
9	make sb interested
+	PHRASES
+	**turn-on** noun

1 [often passive] to make a piece of equipment such as a television start working by pressing a button, turning a switch etc = SWITCH ON ≠ TURN OFF

be turned on *Is your answering machine turned on?*

turn sth on *Turn the radio on.*

turn on sth *He turns on the TV as soon as he gets in.*

2 to start using a supply of water, gas, or electricity by turning a tap, pressing a button, or moving a switch ≠ TURN OFF

turn sth on *Have they turned the water back on yet?* ♦ *The gas won't come out if you don't turn it on.*

turn on sth *Turn on the outside tap, will you?*

3 to make a deliberate effort to use a special quality that you have in order to achieve something

turn on sth *He'll have to turn on all his charm to persuade her.*

turn sth on *The Yankees turned the power on in the late innings to defeat the Red Sox 12–10.*

4 [often passive] to direct something at someone or something = DIRECT AT

be turned on sb/sth *The hoses were turned on the demonstrators.*

turn sth on sb/sth *The press turned their attention on the Whitewater affair.*

5 to be the issue, fact, or point that something depends on most

turn on sth *The trial turned on the medical evidence presented by the defence.* ♦ *Prospects for a rate cut will now turn on tomorrow's fourth-quarter output figures.*

6 to suddenly start angrily criticizing someone or shouting at them = ROUND ON

turn on sb *Danny turned on her, accusing her of betraying him.*

7 to suddenly attack someone violently

turn on sb *The dog suddenly turned on its owner, causing serious injuries.*

8 to make someone feel sexually attracted or sexually excited = AROUSE ≠ TURN OFF

turn sb on *He's very nice, but he just doesn't turn me on.*

9 *informal* to make someone become interested in something ≠ TURN OFF

turn sb on *Astronomy doesn't turn most viewers on.*

PHRASES **turn on the waterworks** to start crying, especially in order to get someone's sympathy: *He'll turn on the waterworks, but don't be persuaded.*

whatever turns you on *informal* used for saying that something that interests someone else does not interest you: *Some people truly enjoy going to casinos and gambling. Great! Whatever turns you on.*

■ **'turn-on** noun [C] *informal* something that makes you feel sexually attracted or excited: *Do many people really find black leather a turn-on?*

,turn 'out ★★★

1	how sth develops/ends
2	make a light stop shining
3	be present at an event
4	produce sth
5	force sb to leave
6	remove sth from a container
7	direct sth outwards
8	how sb is dressed
9	when you discover the truth
10	remove things from pockets/bag
+	turnout noun

1 to develop in a particular way or have a particular result = *informal* PAN OUT

turn out *Obviously, I'm disappointed at the way things have turned out.* ♦ *I'm sure it will all turn out well in the end.* ♦ *As it turned out, the storm missed Puerto Rico.*

2 to stop using a light by pressing a button or moving a switch ≠ TURN ON

turn out sth *The caretaker had turned out all the lights.*

turn sth out *Someone turned the lights out.* ♦ *What about the hall light? We can turn it out if it'll bother you.*

3 to go somewhere in order to be present at an event or take part in an activity = TURN UP, ATTEND

turn out *Though the rally was widely advertised, only a few people turned out.* ♦ *+to do sth Thousands of screaming fans turned out to welcome the champions home.*

4 to produce something, especially in large numbers = PRODUCE

turn out sth *The company plans to turn out 2,000 small planes a year.*

turn sth out *Anyone who can use a computer can easily turn these leaflets out.*

5 [often passive] to force someone to leave a place, especially their home = EVICT

be turned out *If they don't pay the rent, they could be turned out next week.*

turn sb out *Our landlord turned us out on the street.*

6 to remove something from a container by turning it upside down

turn sth out *Turn the dough out onto a floured board.*

7 to point or be directed outwards, or make something do this

turn sth out *Keep your back straight and turn your toes out.*

turn out *The animal's feet turn out slightly.*

turn sth out *You're turning out your knees.*

8 [always passive] to be dressed in a particular way

be turned out *He is immaculately turned out in a dark grey suit with a white shirt.* ♦ *Their children are always very **well turned out.***

9 to be discovered to be something, have something etc = *formal* TRANSPIRE

turn out *It all turned out to be a mistake.* ♦ *The tape turned out to contain vital information.* ♦ *+that It turned out that I was right all along.*

10 *British* to remove everything from your pockets or a bag = EMPTY

turn out sth *The police made them turn out their pockets.*

turn sth out *We were instructed to produce our passports and turn our bags out.*

■ **turnout** /'tɜːnaʊt/ noun [U] **1** the number of people who come to an event: *Sunny weather helped boost the turnout at Sunday's rally.* **2** the number of voters in an election: *We're expecting quite a low turnout for the local elections.*

turn 'over ★★★

1	turn a page
2	move in a lying position
3	watch a different television station
4	let sb use sth
5	give sth to sb in authority
6	earn an amount of money
7	engine: start to operate
8	think about sth carefully
9	steal things
+	PHRASE
+	**turnover** noun

1 to turn something such as a page in a book or a sheet of paper so that the other side is towards you

turn over sth *You may turn over your exam papers and read the questions.*
turn sth over *When I turned the painting over, I saw a name printed on the back.*

2 when you are lying down or sleeping, to change the position of your body so that you face the opposite direction

turn over *She turned over and fell out of bed.* ♦ *I could hear one of the children turning over.*

3 *British* to stop watching one television station and start watching another

turn over *Let's turn over – this is really boring.*
turn sth over *Do you mind if we turn the TV over? ♦ Turn it over. There might be some football on the other side.*

4 to allow something to be used for a particular purpose or by a particular person = HAND OVER

turn over sth *They have turned over the*

Hall to be used by a local community group.

turn sth over *People were forced to turn their property over to the army.*

5 to give something to someone in authority, especially because they have ordered you to = HAND OVER ≠ HOLD ONTO

turn over sth *The journalist was ordered to turn over all the information he had.* ♦ *+to You will have to turn over all your records to the investigating authority.*
turn sth over *They expect you to turn all your paperwork over.*

6 to make a particular amount of money in a particular time

turn over sth *The 17-year-old runs his own computer firm in Bath and turns over around £60,000 a year.*

7 if an engine turns over, or if you turn it over, it starts or continues to operate

turn sth over *He turned the engine over to check that it would start without any problems.*
turn over *The car was turning over nicely.*

8 to think carefully about all the details of something = MULL OVER

turn over sth *As I ate, I turned over some of what he'd told me.*
turn sth over *He began to **turn the scheme over in his mind.***

9 [usually passive] *British informal* to enter a place illegally and steal things from it = BURGLE

be turned over *We got back to find the flat had been turned over.*

PHRASE **turn over a new leaf** to change your life by starting to be a better person or stopping a bad habit: *We're expected to believe that hardened criminals such as Thomas can turn over a new leaf.*

■ **turnover** /'tɜːnˌəʊvə/ noun **1** [C/U] the value of the goods and services that a company sells in a particular period of time: *a company with an annual turnover of over £150 million* **2** [C/U] the rate at which people leave a place and new people arrive: *a high turnover of personnel* **3** [C/U] the rate at which a shop sells products: *Advertising has a dramatic effect on your turnover.* **4** [C] a sweet food like a small pie, filled with fruit: *a cherry turnover*

turn 'over to

1 [often passive] to take someone who has committed a crime to the police or other person in authority to be arrested

be turned over to sb *She'll be turned over to the proper authorities in the morning.*

turn sb over to sb *The local police turned him over to the FBI.*

2 to stop speaking at a meeting and allow someone else to speak

turn over to sb *Are there any more questions before I turn over to Susan?*
turn sth over to sb *I'd like to say a few words and then turn it over to you, Mike.*

,turn 'round British same as **turn around**

'turn to ★★★

1	ask sb for help
2	change/develop
3	give your attention/thoughts to sth
4	do sth different
5	look for a page
6	use sth when you need help
7	start discussing sth
8	a period of time: get longer

1 to go to someone for help when you are in a difficult situation

turn to sb *I'm sorry, but I had no one else to turn to.* ♦ **+for** *There are plenty of people you can turn to for advice.*

2 to change or develop into something different

turn to sth *Shock at the killings quickly turned to anger.* ♦ *The traffic lights turned to green.*
turn sth to sth *Days of rain turned the roads to mud.*

3 to direct your attention, thoughts etc towards someone or something

turn sth to sth *It is time he turned his mind to more serious problems.* ♦ *The astronauts are now turning their attention to scientific experiments.*

4 to start doing something new or different from what you were doing before

turn to sth *Karras is the ex-football star who later turned to acting.*

5 to look for a particular page in a book

turn to sth *Turn to page 17 for our prices.*

6 to start to do or use something in an attempt to help yourself when you are having difficulty dealing with a situation = RESORT TO

turn to sth *He turned to drugs after his wife left him.* ♦ *She spent much of her life in prison after **turning to crime** to support a drug habit.*

7 to start thinking about or discussing something

turn to sth *Let's turn to more important matters now.*

8 if one period of time turns to another longer period of time, the amount of time that passes increases noticeably

turn to sth *The minutes turned to hours and still no one came.*

,turn 'up ★★★

1	increase power/sound etc
2	go to an event
3	arrive unexpectedly
4	be found after being lost
5	happen unexpectedly
6	make clothing shorter
7	pull clothing up
8	find sth
+	PHRASE
+	**turn-up** noun; **upturn** noun

1 to increase the amount of sound, heat, or light produced by a piece of equipment such as a television or oven by pressing a button or moving a switch ≠ TURN DOWN

turn up sth *Could we turn up the sound?*
turn sth up *Don't turn the fire up – it's boiling in here!* ♦ *If you can't hear the music, turn it up.*

2 to go to an organized event = formal ATTEND

turn up *How many people do you think will turn up?* ♦ **+at/to** *Over 500 people turned up to his funeral.*

3 to come somewhere unexpectedly or without making a firm arrangement = APPEAR, SHOW UP

turn up *There is no need to book – just turn up on the night.*

4 to be found, especially by accident and after being lost = COME TO LIGHT ≠ DISAPPEAR

turn up *Don't worry – your cat's bound to turn up eventually.* ♦ **+in/on/under** etc *An original Van Gogh turned up in a junk shop in a Parisian backstreet.*

5 to happen unexpectedly or by chance

turn up *You'll get another job – something's bound to turn up soon.*

6 to make a piece of clothing or cloth shorter by making a fold along the bottom edge and fastening it with stitches = HEM, SHORTEN ≠ TURN DOWN

turn up sth *I'll need to turn up these jeans.*
turn sth up *Do you think Anne would turn my skirt up for me?* ♦ *Don't worry if the sleeves are too long. We can turn them up.*

7 to open a fold along the edge of a piece of clothing ≠ TURN DOWN

turn sth up *She turned her collar up against the cold.*
turn up sth *Turn up the collar on your jacket.*

8 to find something by looking for it = DISCOVER

turn up sth *The police haven't turned up anything new, have they?*
turn sth up *As soon as we turn something up, we'll let you know.*

PHRASE **turn up like a bad penny** if someone you do not like turns up like a bad penny, they always seem to appear in situations where you do not want them: *At these times, Petula turns up like the proverbial bad penny.*

■ **'turn-up** noun [C] *British* a fold on the outside of the bottom of the leg of a pair of trousers, for fashion = *American* CUFF: *My old trousers had turn-ups.*
PHRASE **a turn-up for the books** a surprising event: *A victory for Stoke would certainly be a turn-up for the books.*

■ **upturn** /'ʌptɜːn/ noun [singular] an increase in something such as business or economic activity: *Last month saw an unexpected upturn in property prices.*

'turn upon
to be the issue, fact, or point that something depends on most
turn upon sth *The whole matter turned upon whether the boy had lied or not.*

TYPE /taɪp/
types, typing, typed

,type 'in
to type information on a keyboard so that it is recorded by a computer and appears on its screen = KEY IN
type in sth *also* **type sth in** *Type in the name of the program, then press 'Return'.* ◆ *Have you typed your password in?*
type sth into sth *She typed the instructions into the computer.*

,type 'out *old-fashioned*
to write the whole of something using a keyboard or typewriter
type sth out *also* **type out sth** *I'll have to type the whole letter out again!* ◆ *She wants me to type out each paragraph separately.*

,type 'up
to type something that someone has written using a pen or pencil
type up sth *also* **type sth up** *I need to type up my report.* ◆ *She got into the habit of typing her notes up in the evening.*

Uu

UPDATE /ʌp'deɪt/
updates, updating, updated

up'date on
to tell someone about what has been happening recently and how things have developed
update sb on sth *We'll try to update you on progress at least once a week.*

URGE /ɜːdʒ, *American* ɜrdʒ/
urges, urging, urged

,urge 'on
to encourage someone to put more effort into something or to not stop trying to do something
urge sb on *also* **urge on sb** *James' father urged him on from the side of the court.*
◆ *They shout to urge on their team.*

USE /juːz, *American* juz/
uses, using, used

,use 'up ★★★
to use all of a supply of something ≠ *formal* CONSERVE
use up sth *I've used up all my vacation days for this year.*
use sth up *They had used all their fuel supplies up by the end of the week.* ◆ *Is there any cream left, or have we used it all up?*

USHER /'ʌʃə, *American* 'ʌʃər/
ushers, ushering, ushered

,usher 'in *mainly journalism*
to start a period of time in which a particular activity or process will take place = HERALD ≠ SEE OUT
usher in sth *The talks ushered in an era of international co-operation.*

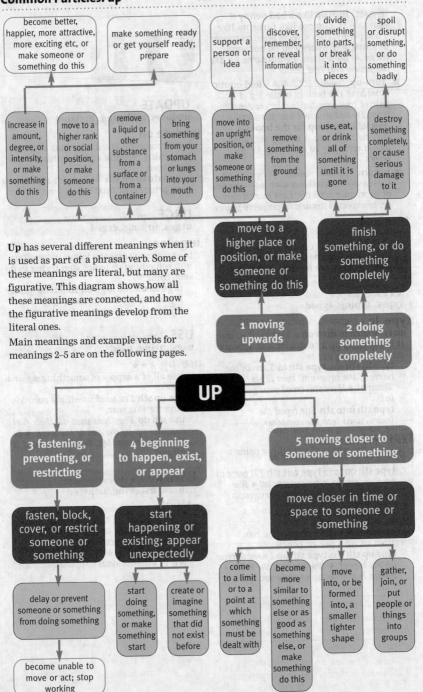

become better, happier, more attractive, more exciting etc, or make someone or something do this

make something ready or get yourself ready; prepare

support a person or idea

discover, remember, or reveal information

divide something into parts, or break it into pieces

spoil or disrupt something, or do something badly

increase in amount, degree, or intensity, or make something do this

move to a higher rank or social position, or make someone do this

remove a liquid or other substance from a surface or from a container

bring something from your stomach or lungs into your mouth

move into an upright position, or make someone or something do this

remove something from the ground

use, eat, or drink all of something until it is gone

destroy something completely, or cause serious damage to it

Up has several different meanings when it is used as part of a phrasal verb. Some of these meanings are literal, but many are figurative. This diagram shows how all these meanings are connected, and how the figurative meanings develop from the literal ones.

Main meanings and example verbs for meanings 2–5 are on the following pages.

move to a higher place or position, or make someone or something do this

finish something, or do something completely

1 moving upwards

2 doing something completely

UP

3 fastening, preventing, or restricting

4 beginning to happen, exist, or appear

5 moving closer to someone or something

move closer in time or space to someone or something

fasten, block, cover, or restrict someone or something

start happening or existing; appear unexpectedly

delay or prevent someone or something from doing something

start doing something, or make something start

create or imagine something that did not exist before

come to a limit or to a point at which something must be dealt with

become more similar to something else or as good as something else, or make something do this

move into, or be formed into, a smaller tighter shape

gather, join, or put people or things into groups

become unable to move or act; stop working

Main meanings	Example verbs		
1 moving upwards			
move to a higher place or position, or make someone or something do this **Pick up** your clothes and put them away. ♦ *Without warning, the horse **reared up** and charged.*	bob up hang up hike up hitch up jack up	lift up pick up pin up pop up rear up	ride up shin up shoot up stick up tip up
increase in amount, degree, or intensity, or make something do this *It looks like they're **putting up** the price of oil again. ♦ You need to **hurry up** or we'll be late. ♦ Could you **speak up**? We can't hear you in the back.*	beef up build up bump up fatten up flare up heap up	hurry up mount up pile up put up ramp up rachet up	speak up speed up stack up stock up swell up whip up
become better, happier, more attractive, more exciting etc, or make someone or something do this ***Cheer up** – it's not that bad. ♦ I really need to **brush up** my maths skills before the test.*	bone up brighten up brush up cheer up dress up	freshen up jazz up liven up perk up polish up	sex up smarten up spice up spruce up tidy up
make something ready or get yourself ready; prepare *The show was about to begin, and the band was **tuning up**. ♦ It took me a while to **psych** myself **up** for the interview.*	build up to butter up firm up gear up limber up	line up psych up saddle up soften up sweeten up	tee up tool up tune up warm up work up to
move to a higher rank or social position, or make someone do this *I hope to **move up** to a management position within five years.*	bump up	go up	move up
remove a liquid or other substance from a surface or from a container *Who's going to **mop up** this water? ♦ The kitten **lapped up** the milk.*	lap up mop up	soak up sop up	sweep up wipe up
bring something from your stomach or lungs into your mouth *She ran to the toilet and **threw up**. ♦ He keeps **coughing up** blood.*	bring up cough up	puke up sick up	spit up throw up
move into an upright position, or make someone or something do this *Everyone **stood up** and joined hands. ♦ They've **thrown up** the whole building in just a few months.*	get up hold up jump up	prop up put up sit up	stand up straighten up throw up
support a person or idea *It's important to **stand up for** what you believe in. ♦ If you don't believe me, Kevin will **back** me **up**.*	back up bolster up	prop up shore up	speak up for stand up for
remove something from the ground *Authorities have **dug up** two bodies in the back garden.*	dig up	grub up	pull up
discover, remember, or reveal information *Police have **turned up** some new evidence. ♦ If the divorce comes up in conversation, fine, but I'm not going to **bring it up**.*	bring up call up dig up	dredge up look up point up	rake up turn up yield up

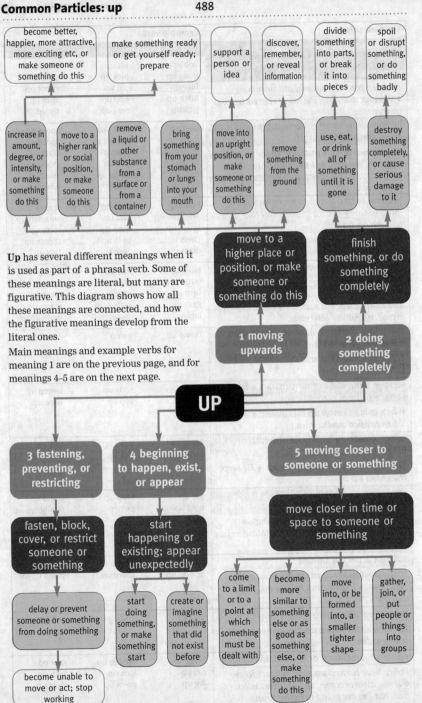

become better, happier, more attractive, more exciting etc, or make someone or something do this

make something ready or get yourself ready; prepare

support a person or idea

discover, remember, or reveal information

divide something into parts, or break it into pieces

spoil or disrupt something, or do something badly

increase in amount, degree, or intensity, or make something do this

move to a higher rank or social position, or make someone do this

remove a liquid or other substance from a surface or from a container

bring something from your stomach or lungs into your mouth

move into an upright position, or make someone or something do this

remove something from the ground

use, eat, or drink all of something until it is gone

destroy something completely, or cause serious damage to it

Up has several different meanings when it is used as part of a phrasal verb. Some of these meanings are literal, but many are figurative. This diagram shows how all these meanings are connected, and how the figurative meanings develop from the literal ones.

Main meanings and example verbs for meaning 1 are on the previous page, and for meanings 4–5 are on the next page.

move to a higher place or position, or make someone or something do this

finish something, or do something completely

1 moving upwards

2 doing something completely

UP

3 fastening, preventing, or restricting

4 beginning to happen, exist, or appear

5 moving closer to someone or something

fasten, block, cover, or restrict someone or something

start happening or existing; appear unexpectedly

move closer in time or space to someone or something

delay or prevent someone or something from doing something

start doing something, or make something start

create or imagine something that did not exist before

come to a limit or to a point at which something must be dealt with

become more similar to something else or as good as something else, or make something do this

move into, or be formed into, a smaller tighter shape

gather, join, or put people or things into groups

become unable to move or act; stop working

Main meanings	Example verbs		
2 doing something completely			
finish something, or do something completely *We **ended up** selling the house for less than we paid for it.* ♦ *A development company **bought up** all the land to the west of town.*	buy up break up clean up dry up end up	fill up finish up load up pack up shut up	sum up swallow up top up wash up wind up
use, eat, or drink all of something until it is gone *Running can **burn up** a lot of calories.* ♦ *Someone **used** all the toothpaste **up**.*	burn up drink up eat up	finish up gobble up soak up	swallow up take up use up
destroy something completely, or cause serious damage to it *The gears of the machine had **chewed up** his right arm pretty badly.* ♦ *The bridge was **blown up** by terrorists.*	bang up blow up chew up churn up	cut up mess up plough up rip up	shoot up smash up swallow up tear up
divide something into parts, or break it into pieces *One winter they had to **chop up** furniture for firewood.* ♦ *We still haven't decided how to **divide** the money **up**.*	break up carve up chop up	cut up divide up divvy up	hack up saw up split up
spoil or disrupt something, or do something badly *He **tripped up** when he tried to pronounce her name.* ♦ *She got into drugs and really **messed up** her life.*	botch up break up bust up foul up	jumble up louse up mess up mix up	muck up screw up slip up trip up
3 fastening, preventing, or restricting			
fasten, block, cover, or restrict someone or something *Two dogs were **chained up** in the yard.* ♦ *The window **fogged up** and I couldn't see anything.*	bandage up bind up block up board up brick up bundle up bung up button up chain up clog up do up fog up freeze up	gum up hitch up hook up ice up jam up lace up lock up mist up nail up pack up parcel up seal up sew up	shut up silt up snarl up steam up stitch up stop up tangle up tape up tie up truss up wall up wrap up zip up
delay or prevent someone or something from doing something *She got **held up** at work and missed the show.* ♦ *The accident **backed up** traffic for miles.*	back up bottle up	choke up hold up	slow up tie up
become unable to move or act; stop working *She **froze up** as soon as the cameras started rolling.* ♦ *The photocopier's **packed up** again.*	freeze up	pack up	seize up

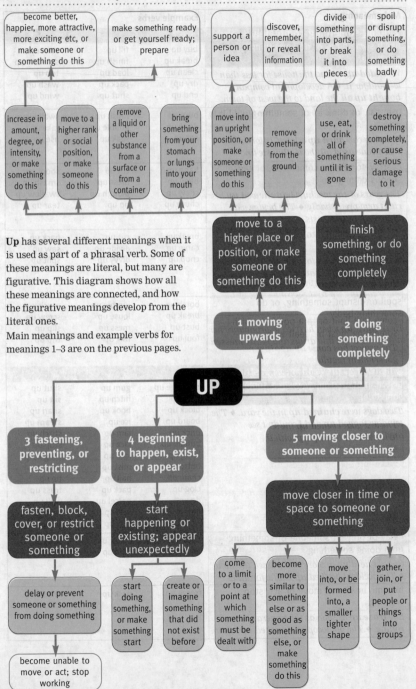

become better, happier, more attractive, more exciting etc, or make someone or something do this

make something ready or get yourself ready; prepare

support a person or idea

discover, remember, or reveal information

divide something into parts, or break it into pieces

spoil or disrupt something, or do something badly

increase in amount, degree, or intensity, or make something do this

move to a higher rank or social position, or make someone do this

remove a liquid or other substance from a surface or from a container

bring something from your stomach or lungs into your mouth

move into an upright position, or make someone or something do this

remove something from the ground

use, eat, or drink all of something until it is gone

destroy something completely, or cause serious damage to it

Up has several different meanings when it is used as part of a phrasal verb. Some of these meanings are literal, but many are figurative. This diagram shows how all these meanings are connected, and how the figurative meanings develop from the literal ones.

Main meanings and example verbs for meanings 1–3 are on the previous pages.

move to a higher place or position, or make someone or something do this

finish something, or do something completely

1 moving upwards

2 doing something completely

UP

3 fastening, preventing, or restricting

4 beginning to happen, exist, or appear

5 moving closer to someone or something

move closer in time or space to someone or something

fasten, block, cover, or restrict someone or something

start happening or existing; appear unexpectedly

delay or prevent someone or something from doing something

start doing something, or make something start

create or imagine something that did not exist before

come to a limit or to a point at which something must be dealt with

become more similar to something else or as good as something else, or make something do this

move into, or be formed into, a smaller tighter shape

gather, join, or put people or things into groups

become unable to move or act; stop working

Main meanings	Example verbs		
4 beginning to happen, exist, or appear			
start happening or existing; appear unexpectedly	blow up	shoot up	sprout up
	crop up	show up	strike up
*Several problems **cropped up** just as we were finishing. ♦ Manny wasn't invited – he just **showed up**.*	pop up	spring up	turn up
start doing something, or make something start	boot up	pipe up	speak up
	light up	power up	start up
*Mary has just **taken up** knitting. ♦ Dad got into the car and **started up** the engine.*	open up	set up	take up
create or imagine something that did not exist before	brew up	dream up	rig up
	build up	knock up	rustle up
	come up with	make up	summon up
*It turns out she **made** the whole story **up**.*	conjure up	muster up	think up
♦ *The two boys **cooked up** a plan to steal the bike.*	cook up	open up	throw up
	draw up	put up	whip up
5 moving closer to someone or something			
move closer in time or space to someone or something	budge up	creep up on	move up
	bunch up	cuddle up	sneak up
	catch up with	draw up	snuggle up
*Don't **sneak up** behind me like that! ♦ We're now **coming up to** the second stage of the process.*	close up	keep up	steal up
	come up to	lead up to	step up
come to a limit or to a point at which something must be dealt with	come up against	face up to	run up against
*The project has **come up against** new government regulations. ♦ She needs to **face up to** the fact that he's not coming back.*			
become more similar to something else or as good as something else, or make something do this	come up to	live up to	measure up
	even up	make up	square up
	keep up	match up	stack up
*The last goal **evened up** the score. ♦ Jeff has to work hard to **keep up** with the other kids in his class.*			
move into, or be formed into, a smaller tighter shape	crumple up	fold up	screw up
	curl up	roll up	scrunch up
***Roll up** the mats and put them in the corner. ♦ The bed **folds up** into a sofa.*			
gather, join, or put people or things into groups	call up	hook up	round up
	join up	link up	sign up
	gang up	meet up	take up with
*My brothers and sisters used to **gang up** on me. ♦ Nadia and Claudine are **meeting up** at the museum this afternoon.*	gather up	pair up	team up

V v

VEER /vɪə, American vɪr/
veers, veering, veered

,veer 'off
to suddenly move in a different direction
veer off *The Volkswagen veered off the road and crashed into a fence.*

VEG /vedʒ/
vegges, vegging, vegged

,veg 'out *informal*
to sit and relax and do nothing
veg out *We collapse on the sofa and veg out for the evening.*

VERGE /vɜːdʒ, American vɜrdʒ/
verges, verging, verged

'verge on ★ (*also* 'verge upon *formal*)
to be almost reaching a particular state or level, especially an extreme one = BORDER ON
verge on sth *He has a footballing talent that verges on genius.* ♦ *The test was so difficult it was verging on the ridiculous.*

VIE /vaɪ/
vies, vying, vied

'vie for
to compete with other people for something that is difficult to get
vie for sth *Five players are still vying for the last position on the team.*

'vie with
to compete with someone for something that is difficult to get
vie with sb for sth *You can see these two boys are vying with each other for her attention.*
vie with sb to do sth *Law firms vie with each other to hire the best students.*

VIEW /vjuː, American vju/
views, viewing, viewed

'view from [usually passive]
to look at or watch something from a particular place
be viewed from sth *Viewed from the road, the wall looked much too high to climb.*

VISIT /'vɪzɪt/
visits, visiting, visited

'visit on (*also* 'visit upon *formal*) [usually passive] *literary*
to make something very unpleasant happen to someone
be visited on sb *Violence was relentlessly visited upon innocent civilians.*

VOTE /vəʊt, American voʊt/
votes, voting, voted

,vote 'down [often passive]
to stop or end something as the result of a vote
be voted down *The proposal was voted down by a massive majority.*
vote sth down *also* **vote down sth** *He knew the others would vote the motion down.* ♦ *They're likely to vote down any proposal that sounds overtly political.*

,vote 'in (*also* ,vote 'into)
to give a person or political party a position of power by voting = ELECT, PUT IN
vote in sb *also* **vote sb in** *It's only for that reason that they voted in Thatcher.*
♦ *Would people be willing to vote the Tories in again?*
vote sb into sth *We're the ones who voted him into office.*

,vote 'off [usually passive]
to remove someone from a position on something such as a committee by voting
be voted off sth *Parsons was voted off the board.*

,vote 'out [usually passive]
to remove a person or political party from a position by voting
be voted out *He was voted out of the National Assembly in the 2002 election.*

,vote 'through [usually passive]
to make something accepted officially by voting
be/get sth voted through *We need to get the budget voted through.*

VOUCH /vaʊtʃ/
vouches, vouching, vouched

'vouch for ★
1 to say that something is true, correct, or good based on your own knowledge or experience
vouch for sth *We can vouch for the software – everyone here uses it.* ♦ *I can't vouch for the food – I've never eaten there.*
2 to say that you believe someone is good

and will behave well in the future
vouch for sb *Are you willing to vouch for him?*

Ww

WADE /weɪd/
wades, wading, waded

wade 'in (*also* **wade 'into**) *British informal*
to become involved in someone else's discussion, argument, or fight in a confident way that people may not like
wade in *She just waded in and gave the kid a smack.*
wade into sth *You can't just go wading into someone else's marital problems.*

'wade through
to read or deal with a lot of boring information = PLOUGH THROUGH
wade through sth *I spent the day wading through piles of data.*

wade through

WAFFLE /'wɒf(ə)l, *American* 'wɑf(ə)l/
waffles, waffling, waffled

waffle 'on *British informal*
to talk or write using a lot of words but without saying anything interesting or important = RAMBLE ON
waffle on *He waffled on for another ten minutes about the importance of standards.*

WAIT /weɪt/
waits, waiting, waited

wait a'round (*also* **wait a'bout**)
to do nothing because you are expecting something to happen and you cannot do

anything until it does = HANG AROUND
wait around *The officials kept us waiting around all day before they would see us.* ♦ **+for** *I don't feel like waiting around for him to decide.*

wait be'hind
to stay somewhere after everyone else has left = STAY BEHIND
wait behind *He decided to wait behind and help clean up.*

'wait for
PHRASE **wait for it** *British informal* used for saying that you are about to tell someone something that is silly, funny, or surprising: *Tonight's lucky winner will go away with a cheque for – wait for it – £100,000!*

wait 'in *British*
to stay at home to wait for someone to arrive
wait in *I waited in all morning, but no one showed.* ♦ **+for** *I have to wait in for a delivery this morning.*

'wait on ★ (*also* 'wait upon *formal*)
1 to do a lot of personal jobs for someone, especially things that most people would do for themselves
wait on sb *She was employed as a maid to wait on the princess.* ♦ *He seems to expect me to wait on him every minute of the day!*

2 to wait for a particular thing to happen
wait on sth *Foreign investors are waiting on election results there.*

3 [often passive] *mainly American* to serve people in a restaurant = SERVE
be/get waited on *What do we have to do to get waited on here?*
wait on sb *Who's waiting on table 4?*
PHRASES **wait on sb hand and foot** *showing disapproval* to do everything for someone so that they do not have to do anything for themselves: *He obviously loved her, and waited on her hand and foot.*
wait on tables *British* to serve people in a restaurant or café: *I spent the summer waiting on tables in a West End restaurant.*

wait 'out
to stay where you are until something ends, usually something bad
wait out sth *also* **wait sth out** *Let's go to the basement and wait out the storm there.* ♦ *You have no choice but to wait the scandal out.*

wait 'up

1 to not go to sleep until someone comes home

wait up *I'll probably be very late tonight, so don't wait up.* ♦ **+for** *I'm pretty tired, so I won't wait up for you, if you don't mind.*

2 *American informal* used for asking or telling someone to stop so that you can speak to them or walk with them

wait up *Heather, just wait up a second please.*

'wait upon *formal same as* wait on

WAKE /weɪk/
wakes, waking, woke /wəʊk, *American* woʊk/, **woken** /ˈwəʊkən, *American* ˈwoʊkən/

wake 'up ★★★

1 to stop sleeping or make someone stop sleeping = WAKE

wake up *When I woke up the sun was shining brightly.* ♦ *He sounded as if he'd only just woken up.* ♦ *Wake up! There's someone at the door for you.*

wake sb up *The sounds from the street below woke me up.* ♦ **+at** *The alarm clock woke her up at 7 o'clock as usual.*

wake up sb *Turn that music down! You'll wake up the whole neighbourhood!*

2 to start to feel more lively or make someone feel more lively = REVIVE

wake sb up *Another cup of coffee will wake me up.*

wake up sb *I woke up a rather sluggish class with a few stretching exercises.*

3 to start to pay more attention to something, or make people pay more attention to something

wake sb up *It takes a serious crisis like this to wake people up.*

wake up sb *The only way of waking up this rather dozy committee is to tell them the unpleasant truth.*

  PHRASE **wake up and smell the coffee** *mainly American informal* used for telling someone they need to pay attention to what is happening in a situation they are in, usually a situation that is not good: *Sippl went to the Unix International members' meeting to deliver a simple message. Wake up and smell the coffee, guys. There's no time left.*

wake 'up to

to start to realize something

wake up to sth *They need to wake up*

to the fact that the sport has completely changed.

WALK /wɔːk, *American* wɔk/
walks, walking, walked

Walk is often used with adverbs and prepositions when it means 'to move forwards by putting one foot in front of the other': *I like to walk around the lake at sunset.* ♦ *He walked slowly and unsteadily down the hall.* ♦ *Howard walked in with two men I'd never seen before.* These uses are not included here.

walk a'way ★

to leave a place or bad situation = WALK OUT

walk away *If you see any trouble, the wisest thing to do is walk away.* ♦ **+from** *You can't just walk away from all this mess you've created!*

walk a'way with

1 to feel a particular emotion when you leave a situation

walk away with sth *We can all walk away with a clear conscience.*

2 **walk away with** or **walk off with** to win something easily

walk away with sth *United could walk away with the championship.*

3 **walk away with** or **walk off with** to steal something

walk away with sth *Someone walked away with my purse!*

walk 'in on

to walk into a room where someone is doing something private or secret = BURST IN ON

walk in on sb *More than once, he walked in on them kissing.*

'walk into

1 to accidentally hit a part of your body against something when you are walking

walk into sth *I walked into a table and got a nasty bruise.*

2 to get a job easily

walk into sth *She walked into a top position within the company.*

walk 'off ★★

1 to leave somewhere, usually angrily or without telling people that you are going to leave = WALK OUT

walk off *Don't walk off yet, I haven't finished my story!*

2 to get rid of a bad feeling or condition by going for a walk

walk off sth *He went to the beach to try to walk off his hangover.*

walk sth off *I can usually manage to walk the pain off.*

,walk 'off with *same as* walk away with 2, 3

,walk 'on
to continue walking in your intended direction
walk on *She walked on without a backward glance.*

■ **'walk-on** noun [C] **1** a small acting part in a film or a play, especially one with no words to say: *She had a five-second walk-on in his first film.* **2** an actor who has a walk-on part: *He's been a walk-on in most of the big soaps.*

,walk 'out ★★
1 to suddenly leave a relationship, your family, your job etc = WALK AWAY
walk out *My mother walked out when I was five and I haven't seen her since.*
♦ **+on** *Her husband had walked out on her a year before.* ♦ **+of** *He famously walked out of a Broadway production he was starring in.*
2 to stop working as a way of protesting about something = GO ON STRIKE
walk out *All the workers walked out on Friday night.*
3 to leave a meeting, performance etc before the end, usually because you are angry or bored
walk out *Several members of the audience walked out.* ♦ **+of** *The delegation from the opposition party walked out of the talks yesterday.*

,walk 'over
PHRASE **walk all over sb 1** to treat someone badly and make them do what you want without caring about their feelings: *I'm not about to let them walk all over me.* **2** to defeat someone easily = TROUNCE: *We expected Williams to walk all over her.*

,walk 'through
to teach or tell someone about a process by explaining its individual stages from beginning to end = TAKE THROUGH
walk sb through sth *She walked James through the basics of money management.* ♦ *Can you walk us through your reasons for wanting the job.*

,walk 'up
to go to where someone is standing, in order to talk to them
walk up *She just walked up and asked to borrow the car.* ♦ **+to** *What do you do when a stranger walks up to you and asks for help?*

WALL /wɔːl, *American* wɔl/
walls, walling, walled

,wall 'in [usually passive]
to surround something with a wall
be walled in *You'll see the garden has been walled in on three sides only.*

,wall 'off [usually passive]
to separate a small space from a larger one by building a wall
be walled off *Several rooms were walled off to save money on heating bills.*

,wall 'up
1 [usually passive] to permanently block in the windows or doors of a room or house using bricks
be walled up *Most of the old building's windows have been walled up.*
2 to put someone in a room or space in which all the entrances have been permanently filled with bricks
wall sb up *We discover that he's walled the body up somewhere in the house.*

WALLOW /'wɒləʊ, *American* 'wɑloʊ/
wallows, wallowing, wallowed

'wallow in *showing disapproval*
to spend a lot of time thinking or talking about something bad that has happened to you, especially because you want sympathy
wallow in sth *Three years on, he still seems to be wallowing in self-pity.*

WALTZ /wɔːls, *American* wɔlts/
waltzes, waltzing, waltzed

,waltz 'off with *informal*
to take something without asking permission
waltz off with sth *Someone has just waltzed off with my drink.*

'waltz through *informal*
to deal with something very easily
waltz through sth *The rest of us waltzed through our duties.*

WANDER /'wɒndə, *American* 'wɑndər/
wanders, wandering, wandered

,wander 'off
to move away from a place where you are usually, or where people expect you to be
wander off *It's a safe place where kids can wander off on their own.*

WANT /wɒnt, American wɑːnt/
wants, wanting, wanted

'want for *formal*
PHRASE **not want for sth** to have as much of something as you need
want for sth *I'll make sure they never want for money.* ♦ *Her children **wanted for nothing** (=had everything they needed).*

,want 'in *informal*
1 to want to enter a place
want in *I think the cat wants in.*
2 to want to take part in a situation, plan, or activity
want in *This is the last time I'm asking you – do you want in or not?*

,want 'out *informal*
1 to want to leave a place
want out *Would you open the door? The dog wants out.*
2 to want to leave a situation or relationship and no longer be involved in it
want out *This is all getting a little scary. I want out.* ♦ **+of** *She wants out of the marriage.*

WARD /wɔːd, American wɔrd/
wards, warding, warded

,ward 'off
to do something to prevent someone or something from harming you = DEFEND AGAINST
ward off sth *also* **ward sth off** *The herb can be used to ward off biting insects.*
♦ *He saw the blow coming and raised his arm to ward it off.*

WARM /wɔːm, American wɔrm/
warms, warming, warmed

,warm 'through
to heat food until it is warm in all parts
warm sth through *Warm the sauce through just before serving.*

'warm to
to begin to like someone or something = TAKE TO
warm to sb/sth *She's the kind of person you warm to immediately.* ♦ *It might take them a while to warm to the idea.*

,warm 'up ★★

1	make sth warm
2	become warm
3	become more interesting
4	practise before doing sport
5	compete in smaller events first
6	make an engine ready to use
7	make an audience ready
+	**warmed-up** adj; **warm-up** noun

1 to make something warm or warmer
warm up sth *The morning sun soon warmed up the air in the camp.*
warm sth up *Shall I warm the sauce up again?* ♦ *I've put the plates in the oven to warm them up.*
2 to become warm ≠ COOL OFF
warm up *Drink this and you'll soon warm up.* ♦ *The birds begin to return as soon as the weather warms up.*
3 if an event or situation warms up, or if something warms it up, it starts to become enjoyable, interesting, or busy = LIVEN UP
warm up *By midnight the party had really warmed up.*
warm sth up *A bit of music might warm things up.*
warm up sth *Something is needed to warm up this rather lacklustre production.*
4 to prepare for a sport or activity by doing exercises or practising just before it starts = LIMBER UP
warm up *The players are already on the field warming up.*
warm up sth *First of all, let's do some stretching exercises to warm up your calf muscles.*
warm sth up *We start by warming the knees up with a few bends.*
5 to prepare for a race, game, or competition by competing in less important events first
warm up *She warms up with an unscheduled appearance in an Indonesian tournament.* ♦ **+for** *The boys warmed up for their big game with a 4–0 win at Derby last week.*
6 if you warm up a machine or an engine, or if it warms up, you turn it on and wait for a short time until it is ready to be used
warm up *You may need to let the engine warm up for a while.*
warm sth up *I'd better warm the car up first.*
warm up sth *A shift arrives in the afternoon to warm up the presses for the evening run.*
7 if someone warms up an audience, they put the audience in the right mood for the main performance, for example by making them laugh

warm up sb *DJ Chris Hopkins will be warming up the crowd from 10.30 onwards.*

warm sb up *Scott's job was to warm the crowd up while the band got themselves fired up.*

■ ˌ**warmed-up** adj **1** ready to do a sport or other activity: *He shakes hands with an eager and warmed-up Keane on the touchline.* **2** if food is warmed-up it has been heated again after going cold, to make it warm enough to eat: *A jacketed waiter served them a warmed-up airline meal with little bottles of wine.*

■ '**warm-up** noun **1** [C] a set of exercises that you do just before you start to play a sport, in order to prepare your body: *There's a ten-minute warm-up before the class gets going.* **2** [C] an occasion when you prepare yourself for an activity: *The match against Latvia will serve as a useful warm-up.* ♦ *The letter was a warm-up for the one he was going to write to Johnson.* **3 warm-ups** [plural] *American* a loose jacket and trousers that you wear for doing sports or for staying warm after sports = *British* TRACKSUIT: *Peter always looked good in warm-ups.*

WARN /wɔːn, *American* wɔrn/
warns, warning, warned

'**warn against**
to tell someone not to do something, because it may be dangerous or it may cause problems
warn against (doing) sth *Eisenhower warned against any attempt to find some quick and easy solution.* ♦ *The Belgian government warned against eating British beef.*
warn sb against (doing) sth *The teacher warned us against reading such books.*
♦ *He warned people against becoming directly involved with political movements in the region.*

ˌ**warn a**'**way**
to warn someone not to come near, because of a possible problem or danger
warn sb away *also* **warn away sb** *The male bird sings to warn other males away.* ♦ *The noise warns away intruders.*

ˌ**warn '**off ★
to tell someone not to do something because it may cause something bad to happen to them = DETER FROM
warn sb off *I suddenly realized that Steve had been trying to warn me off.*
warn sb off sth *My parents warned me off a career in acting.*

warn sb off doing sth *She warned Sam off making any trouble.*

WASH /wɒʃ, *American* wɑʃ/
washes, washing, washed

ˌ**wash a**'**way** ★★
1 to get rid of unhappy or painful feelings
wash away sth *Drugs can't help, and whisky won't wash away the pain.*
wash sth away *Time hadn't washed that desire away.*
2 [often passive] if something such as rain or a river washes something away, it moves it away with great force
be washed away *Thousands of homes were washed away in the floods.*
wash away sth *Heavy rains have washed away the bridge.*
wash sth away *The untamed river washed cars and buses away.*
3 to remove something with water, especially by washing it
wash sth away *The sun blistered the paint and the rains washed it away.*
wash away sth *Be careful to wash away any trace of blood.*

ˌ**wash '**down
1 [often passive] to drink something after putting food or medicine in your mouth, especially so you can swallow more easily
be washed down with sth *He had a large slice of pizza washed down with beer.*
wash sth down *also* **wash down sth** *Here are your pills and here's a glass of water to wash them down.*
2 to wash the whole surface of something = CLEAN
wash down sth *also* **wash sth down** *Use hot water and detergent to wash down kitchen worktops.*

ˌ**wash '**off ★
if you wash dirt off something or if dirt washes off, you remove it by washing
wash sth off sth *Wash the soil off potatoes before you cook them.*
wash off *Don't worry about the dirty marks. They'll wash off easily.*

ˌ**wash '**out ★★
1 to wash something quickly, especially the inside of a container
wash out sth *Don't you ever wash out your coffee cups?*
wash sth out *Wash the bowl out before you put food in it.* ♦ *The fridge was looking grubby, so I spent the afternoon washing it out.*
2 if dirt, a mark, or a substance washes out of cloth, it can be removed by washing

wash out *Permanent dyes won't wash out.* ♦ **+of** *All the colour has washed out of these old curtains.*

3 [usually passive] if an event is washed out, rain prevents it from taking place or from continuing
be washed out *It looked like the first game of the season would be washed out.*

■ **,washed-'out** adj **1** *informal* someone who is washed-out looks very pale and ill or tired: *For all his show of energy, he suddenly looked old and washed-out.*
2 washed-out clothes have lost a lot of their colour because they have been washed so often: *He arrives in a grey sweater and washed-out jeans.*
3 *American* a washed-out road has been damaged so much by rain or a flood that people cannot drive on it: *The shack was another half mile along a washed-out track.*

,wash 'up ★★

1 *British* to wash plates, cups, spoons etc after a meal
wash up *I can help to cook and wash up.*
wash up sth *Haven't you washed up the breakfast things yet?*
wash sth up *It won't take long to wash these few things up.*

2 [often passive] if the sea washes something up somewhere, it carries it and leaves it there
be washed up *Two whales have been washed up on the beach.*
wash up *Some of the oil has washed up on a neighbouring island.*
wash up sth *The North Sea washes up all sorts of treasures along this coastline.*
wash sth up *Something is thrown overboard off Rotterdam and the sea washes it up in Hastings.*

3 *informal* if someone washes up somewhere, they arrive there unexpectedly after a long time
wash up *He stays out for four days solid and eventually washes up at his brother's house.*

4 *American* to wash your hands, for example before a meal
wash up *I'll go wash up before we eat.*

■ **,washed-'up** adj *informal* someone who is washed-up will never be popular or successful again: *She became an actress, a real actress not a washed-up joke like her mother.*

■ **,washing-'up** noun [U] *British* **1** the activity of washing the dishes and other things used for a meal: *I don't mind doing the cooking, but I hate doing the washing-up.* **2** things such as dishes,

wash up

cups, knives, and forks that need to be washed after a meal: *Where did all this washing-up come from?*

WASTE /weɪst/
wastes, wasting, wasted

,waste a'way
to gradually become thinner and weaker over a period of time, usually because of an illness = WITHER
waste away *Sarah seemed to waste away over the next few months.*

be 'wasted on [always passive]
if something is wasted on someone, they do not understand it or realize how good or valuable it is
be wasted on sb *There's really no point in giving expensive toys to very small children. They'll just be wasted on them.*

WATCH /wɒtʃ, American wɑtʃ/
watches, watching, watched

'watch for ★★ (*also* ,watch 'out for)
to pay attention so that you will see something when it arrives or happens
watch for sth/sb *He seemed to be watching for any signs of nervousness.*
♦ *She stood by the gate, watching for her mother.*

,watch 'out ★★ [often in imperative]
to be careful = LOOK OUT
watch out *Watch out! Those mushrooms could be poisonous!* ♦ *You could have a nasty accident if you don't watch out.*

,watch 'out for ★★

1 to be careful of something or someone that could cause you problems or harm
watch out for sth/sb *Watch out for snakes!* ♦ *I was told to watch out for people who seem too ready to agree with me.*

2 to pay attention so that you will see something when it arrives or happens
watch out for sth/sb *Watch out for big discounts and clearance sales at this time of the year.*

3 *informal* to make sure that nothing bad happens to someone = LOOK OUT FOR
watch out for sb *People in my family have always watched out for one another.*

,watch 'over

to guard, protect, or be in charge of someone or something
watch over sb/sth *Soldiers arrived to watch over the city and maintain peace.*

watch over

WATER /'wɔːtə, *American* 'wɔtər/
waters, watering, watered

,water 'down ★

1 to make something such as a statement or newspaper article less offensive, powerful, or detailed = TONE DOWN ≠ BEEF UP
water down sth *The editors have watered down some of the more forthright sections of the book.*
water sth down *Members of the family were urging me to water the letter down.*

2 [often passive] to add water to a drink or liquid in order to make it less strong or thick = DILUTE ≠ THICKEN
be watered down *The beer tasted as if it had been watered down.*
water sth down *Water the fruit juice down if you're giving it to young children.*
water down sth *If you water down the emulsion, it goes on more smoothly.*

■ **,watered-'down** adj **1** made less offensive, powerful, or detailed than the original: *They gave us only a **watered-down version** of his speech.* **2** a watered-down drink, especially an alcoholic drink, has been made weaker with water: *a glass of warm, watered-down lager*

WAVE /weɪv/
waves, waving, waved

,wave a'round (*also* ,wave a'bout
British)
to shake or swing your arms or something that you are holding in different directions
wave sth around *He kept waving the gun around.* ♦ *He shouted and waved his arms around in the air.*

,wave a'side
to ignore someone's ideas, feelings, or opinions because you do not think they are important
wave aside sth *also* **wave sth aside** *Whenever I mention finances, he just waves aside my concerns.*

,wave a'way
to wave your hand in order to show that you do not want to speak to someone or do not want something that is being offered to you
wave away sb/sth *also* **wave sb/sth away** *Waving away the waiter, he stood up to leave.* ♦ *Karen waved the bottle of wine away.*

,wave 'down
to ask a vehicle to stop by making a signal with your arm or hand at the driver
= FLAG DOWN
wave sb/sth down *I waved a passing car down and asked for help.*

,wave 'off
to say goodbye to someone by moving your hand as they leave
wave sb off *I went to wave them off at the airport.*

,wave 'on
to make a signal with your hand in order to tell someone to continue moving forwards
wave sb on *The officer waved us on.*

,wave 'through

1 to make a signal with your hand that shows you are allowing someone to go through a gate or other entrance
wave sb through *The policeman on duty waved me through.*

2 [often passive] to give permission or approval immediately and often without checking or considering something properly

wear off

be waved through *His bid was waved through in a matter of days.*
wave sth through *Most countries have waved the legislation through.*

WEAN /wiːn, *American* wiːn/
weans, weaning, weaned

ˌwean ˈoff
to make someone gradually stop depending on something that they like and have become used to, especially a drug or a bad habit
wean yourself off (doing) sth *We're trying to wean ourselves off watching too much television.*

be ˈweaned on
to get used to something when you are young
be weaned on sth *The daughter of a musician, she was weaned on classical music.*

WEAR /weə, *American* wer/
wears, wearing, wore /wɔː, *American* wɔr/, **worn** /wɔːn, *American* wɔrn/

ˌwear aˈway [often passive]
to gradually disappear or get thinner, or make something gradually disappear or get thinner by using or rubbing it = ERODE
be worn away *The grass has been worn away by the constant tramp of tourists' feet.*
wear away *The inscription on the ring had almost worn away.*

ˌwear ˈdown ★ [often passive]
1 to make someone gradually lose their energy or confidence = UNDERMINE
be worn down *They were worn down by the stress of feeding five children.*
wear sb down *Slowly he wore his opponent down.*

2 to make something gradually disappear or become thinner by using or rubbing it = WEAR AWAY
be worn down *The old stone steps had been worn down by years of use.*
wear down sth *This type of road surface will wear down ordinary tyres pretty quickly.*
wear sth down *The increased volume of water is wearing the rocks down faster.*

ˌwear ˈin
1 to make a hole or mark in something by using it or rubbing it a lot
wear sth in sth *The constant flow of water had worn a channel in the middle of the path.* ♦ *She had worn another hole in her sweater.*

2 if you wear in something such as a pair of shoes, you wear them until they fit your feet better and are more comfortable
wear in sth *also* **wear sth in** *It's always so painful wearing in new shoes.*

ˌwear ˈoff ★★
if something such as a pain or feeling wears off, it gradually disappears
wear off *The numbness in his shoulder was starting to wear off.* ♦ *I got bored with the job once **the novelty wore off** (=when it stopped being new and exciting).*

> Nouns often used as subjects with **wear off**
> ■ drug, effect, excitement, feeling, novelty, shock

ˌwear ˈon
if time wears on, it passes
wear on *My headache grew worse as the evening wore on.*

ˌwear ˈout ★★
1 [often passive] to make someone feel very tired = EXHAUST, TIRE OUT ≠ INVIGORATE
be worn out *She was worn out from*

1st Floor 8th Floor 22nd Floor

be worn out (see wear out)

looking after her elderly mother.
wear yourself out *You need to slow down
a little or you'll wear yourself out.*
wear sb out *All the excitement of the day
had worn them out.*

2 to use something a lot so that it no
longer works, or can no longer be used
wear sth out *He's played the old record
so many times he's worn it out.*
wear out sth *The kids wear out their
shoes within weeks.*
wear out *The rear tyres had worn out.*

3 to make a hole in something, or make
it thinner and weaker, by using or
rubbing it a lot
wear out sth *He'd long since worn out
the knees in his old jeans.*
wear sth out *All these people going up
and down have worn the stair carpet
out.*

■ **outworn** /aʊtˈwɔːn/ **adj** no longer
useful or important: *outworn industries*

wear 'through [often passive]
if something such as a carpet wears
through or is worn through, holes appear
in it because it has been used a lot
be worn through *The carpet's worn
through: we really have to replace it.*
wear through *The linoleum had worn
through to the floorboards.*

WEARY /ˈwɪəri, *American* ˈwɪri/
wearies, wearying, wearied

'weary of *formal*
to become tired of something or bored
with it
weary of sth *I soon wearied of his endless
chatter.*

WED /wed/
weds, wedding, wed or **wedded**

be 'wedded to
to strongly support an idea or enjoy doing
something very much
be wedded to sth *The tactic worked for
a while but it was madness to remain
obstinately wedded to it.*

WEED /wiːd, *American* wid/
weeds, weeding, weeded

weed 'out ★
to remove the people or things from a
group that are not good enough or have
not reached a high enough standard
= REMOVE ≠ SELECT
weed out sb/sth *We need a process that
weeds out corrupt police officers.*
weed sb/sth out *Of course we get a few
people who can't do the job, but we try
to weed them out in the early stages.*

WEIGH /weɪ/
weighs, weighing, weighed

weigh a'gainst ★
1 [often passive] to carefully consider how
good or important one thing is in relation
to another thing before making a decision
be weighed against sth *These elements
have to be weighed against each other.*
weigh sth against sth *I had to weigh my
principles against these risks.*

2 to be a quality or feature that makes
someone or something less satisfactory or
impressive = COUNT AGAINST
weigh against sb/sth *That is one point
that weighs against them.*

weigh 'down [often passive]
1 if something weighs you down, it is very

heavy, and so it is difficult for you to
carry it easily

be weighed down *The waiters were
weighed down by huge trays of food.*
weigh sb down *Leave the bags in the
hotel – we don't want them weighing us
down all day.*

2 to cause problems or worries for
someone or something = BURDEN, WEIGH ON
≠ BUOY UP

be weighed down *Wall Street has been
weighed down by economic uncertainty.*
weigh sb/sth down *The pressures
weighing him down were becoming
unbearable.*

be weighed down

weigh 'in

1 to have your weight checked before you
take part in a sport such as boxing or
horse racing
weigh in *Have you weighed in yet?* ♦ **+at**
Bowen weighed in at 241 pounds.

2 to become involved in something such
as a discussion in an enthusiastic way
weigh in *At this point the Chancellor of
the Exchequer weighed in.* ♦ **+with** *The
cousins all weighed in with their own
suggestions.*

■ **'weigh-in** noun [singular] an occasion
when someone who is taking part in a
sport such as boxing or horse racing is
officially weighed: *I talked to him at the
weigh-in.*

weigh 'into

1 to become involved in something such
as a discussion in an enthusiastic way
weigh into sth *The Institute of Directors
has weighed into the campaign.*

2 to start to criticize or blame someone
angrily
weigh into sb *The organization weighed
into companies for not making these
conditions clear to clients.*

'weigh on

to cause problems or worries for someone
or something = WEIGH DOWN, BURDEN
≠ HEARTEN

weigh on sb/sth *The responsibility of
her new job had begun to weigh on her.*
♦ *The high price of property weighs
heavily on many businesses.* ♦ *The
decision to move has been weighing on
Eric's mind (=he has been worrying
about it).*

weigh 'out

to measure an exact amount of something
weigh out sth *also* **weigh sth out** *He
weighed out every portion of sugar, flour,
and dried fruit.*

weigh 'up ★★

to consider the good and bad aspects of
something in order to reach a decision
about it = ASSESS

weigh up sth *Before buying, weigh up
the advantages and disadvantages of
each type.*
weigh sth up *I knew the situation before
I went out there. I weighed it all up and
made my decision.*

> Nouns often used as objects with **weigh up**
>
> ■ **advantages, consequences, costs, factors,
> merits, possibilities, pros and cons**

WEIGHT /weɪt/
weights, weighting, weighted

weight 'down

to make something heavier by putting a
weight on it, especially in order to stop it
from moving
weight sth down *A blue mug weighted
the papers down.* ♦ **+with** *He had
weighted the bag down with rocks.*

WELL /wel/
wells, welling, welled

well 'up

1 if feelings well up inside you, they
become very strong
well up *He felt his face reddening and
anger welling up.* ♦ *A sense of hurt and
outrage welled up inside him.*

2 if a liquid wells up, it comes to the
surface and begins to flow
well up *Water began to well up from the
hidden spring.*

3 if tears well up, they come into your
eyes so that you want to cry
well up *I could feel tears welling up in
my eyes.*

WELSH /welʃ/
welshes, welshing, welshed

'welsh on
to not do what you promised or agreed to do. Many Welsh people consider this word offensive.
> **welsh on sth** *I'd never welsh on our agreement.*

WHACK /wæk, *American* wæk, hwæk/
whacks, whacking, whacked

ˌwhack 'off *British impolite*
if a man whacks off, he rubs his penis in order to get sexual pleasure

WHALE /weɪl, *American* weɪl, hweɪl/
whales, whaling, whaled

'whale at *American informal*
to criticize someone or something strongly
> **whale at sb/sth** *She's always whaling at me about something.*

'whale on *American informal*
to hit someone or something very hard
> **whale on sb/sth** *The other boys were whaling on him.*

WHEEL /wiːl, *American* wil, hwil/
wheels, wheeling, wheeled

ˌwheel a'round
to turn around quickly where you are standing = SWIVEL AROUND
> **wheel around** *She wheeled around and glared at me.*

ˌwheel 'out
1 [often passive] to mention or use someone or something that has been mentioned or used many times before, often so many times that people are now bored with them
> **be wheeled out** *This same argument was wheeled out again in 1909.*
> **wheel out sb/sth** *The station is wheeling out some real oldies to broadcast.*
> **wheel sb/sth out** *She's still popular, and they wheel her out at every party conference.*

2 to show people something new, or make something new available, for the first time
> **wheel out sth** *Unix is wheeling out its new system next week.*
> **wheel sth out** *The makers wheeled their latest offering out in London yesterday.*

WHILE /waɪl, *American* hwaɪl/
whiles, whiling, whiled

ˌwhile a'way
to spend time in a relaxed way when you have nothing else to do = PASS
> **while away sth** *also* **while sth away** *We whiled away the afternoon sitting by the lake.*

WHIP /wɪp, *American* wɪp, hwɪp/
whips, whipping, whipped

ˌwhip 'into
PHRASES **whip sb into a frenzy** to make a person or group of people become very excited: *The players whip each other into a frenzy of enthusiasm.*
whip sb into line to use strict methods to make someone do what you want them to do: *The government wants to whip teachers into line.*
whip sb/sth into shape to use strict methods in order to make someone or something improve: *They've got a new coach to whip the team into shape.*

ˌwhip 'off
to remove something very quickly
> **whip sth off** *also* **whip off sth** *They whipped off their shirts and plunged into the river.*

ˌwhip 'out
to remove something or take something from somewhere very quickly
> **whip out sth** *also* **whip sth out** *Smiling, she whipped out her purse.* ♦ **+of** *He whipped the gun out of its holster.*

ˌwhip 'through
to do something very quickly
> **whip through sth** *Congress whipped through the budget discussions.*

ˌwhip 'up ★
1 to deliberately make people feel a strong emotion such as anger, excitement, or fear = STIR UP
> **whip up sth** *The newspapers have been accused of whipping up hysteria against migrant workers.*
> **whip sth up** *I don't believe this feeling exists of itself. I believe it's the media that whips it up.*

2 *informal* to prepare something to eat very quickly = RUSTLE UP
> **whip up sth** *I can easily whip up something before we go out.*
> **whip sth up** *You can whip this delicious sweet up in five minutes.*
> **whip sb up sth** *If you're hungry, I can whip us up some lunch.*

WHISK /wɪsk, American wɪsk, hwɪsk/
whisks, whisking, whisked

,whisk a'way (also ,whisk 'off) [often passive]
to remove someone or something very quickly
> **be whisked away** *The President was immediately whisked away by his security guards.*
> **whisk sb/sth away** *The police whisked her away in a van.*

WHISTLE /'wɪs(ə)l, American 'hwɪs(ə)l/
whistles, whistling, whistled

'whistle at
to make a high sound by forcing air through your mouth in order to show that you think someone is sexually attractive
> **whistle at sb** *Up on the scaffolding, the two men whistled at her.*

WHITTLE /'wɪt(ə)l, American 'hwɪt(ə)l/
whittles, whittling, whittled

,whittle a'way [often passive]
to gradually reduce the amount or importance of something = EAT INTO
> **be whittled away** *The team saw their lead whittled away during the second half.*
> **whittle away sth** *also* **whittle sth away** *She accused the government of whittling away these tax breaks.* ♦ **+at** *The regime was whittling away at the rights of citizens.*

,whittle 'down [often passive]
to reduce the number of people or things, or the size of something = CUT DOWN
> **be whittled down** *Costs have been whittled down, but we need to make further savings.* ♦ **+to** *The list of 50 candidates was finally whittled down to four.*
> **whittle down sth** *also* **whittle sth down** *The director of the exhibition has whittled down the number of works on display.*

WHIZZ /wɪz, American wɪz, hwɪz/
whizzes, whizzing, whizzed

'whizz through *informal*
to do something very quickly and not very carefully
> **whizz through sth** *David whizzed through his homework before going out.*

WHOOP /wuːp, American wup, hwup, hup/
whoops, whooping, whooped

,whoop 'up
PHRASE **whoop it up** *informal* to enjoy yourself in a noisy way, especially with a lot of other people: *She needs someone more outgoing, someone who likes to whoop it up a bit.*

WIMP /wɪmp/
wimps, wimping, wimped

,wimp 'out *informal*
to decide not to do something because you are frightened or not confident enough
= CHICKEN OUT
> **wimp out** *I was going to ask her to come with me but I wimped out.*

WIN /wɪn/
wins, winning, won /wʌn/

,win a'round *same as* win over

,win 'back ★★
to get back something that you lost
> **win back sth** *We hope to win back the trophy we lost last year.*
> **win sth back** *I'd do anything to win her trust back.*

,win 'out *same as* win through

,win 'over ★★ (*also* ,win a'round *or* ,win 'round *British*)
to persuade someone to agree with you or be sympathetic towards you = BRING ROUND
> **win sb over** *His easy charm soon won her over.* ♦ **+to** *We've finally won him over to our point of view.*
> **win over sb** *The most important thing is to win over the jury.*

,win 'through (*also* ,win 'out)
to succeed in doing something in spite of difficulties or strong opposition
> **win through** *I always knew she'd win through in the end.*

WIND /waɪnd/
winds, winding, wound /waʊnd/

,wind a'round (*also* ,wind 'round *British*)
to wrap or twist something around something
> **wind sth around sth** *I wound the scarf tightly around my neck.*

,wind 'back
to make a video or a music tape move

back towards the beginning or an earlier place = REWIND
> **wind sth back** also **wind back sth** *Wind the tape back ten minutes.*

,wind 'down ★★

1 to end gradually or to make something end gradually
> **wind down** *The party started to wind down around 2.00 am.*
> **wind down sth** *The UN has decided to wind down the peacekeeping operation.*
> **wind sth down** *The factory will wind production down before closing next year.*

2 to relax after a period of excitement, worry, or hard work = RELAX, UNWIND
> **wind down** *It usually takes me an hour or so after work to wind down.*

3 *British* to turn a handle or press a button in order to make a window in a vehicle go down ≠ WIND UP
> **wind down sth** *She wound down the window and shouted to the man.*
> **wind sth down** *He drove up to us and wound the window down.*

■ **wind-down** /'waɪnd ˌdaʊn/ **noun** [singular] *British* the time or process when you gradually do less of an activity because you are preparing to stop completely: *She's looking forward to the wind-down at the end of the season.*

,wind 'forward (also ,wind 'on)

to make a video or a music tape move forward towards the end
> **wind sth forward** *He slotted the tape in and wound it forward.*

,wind 'round *British same as* **wind around**

,wind 'up ★★★

1	end sth
2	be in a place/situation at the end
3	trick sb
4	make sb angry/upset
5	make a clock/watch etc work
6	close a business
7	close a vehicle's window
8	in baseball
+	**wind-up** adj, noun

1 to end something ≠ BEGIN
> **wind up sth** *I'd like to wind up the meeting soon.*
> **wind sth up** *She was hoping to wind the entire affair up with the minimum delay.*

2 to be in a particular place or situation, not because you choose to but because of other things that have happened
> **wind up** *You'll never guess where we wound up last night.* ♦ **+in** *There were no hotels available in San Francisco, so we wound up in Oakland.* ♦ **+doing sth** *Ted*

wound up owing almost $50,000 in loans for graduate school.

3 *British informal* to trick someone by telling them something that is not true
> **wind sb up** *At first I thought they were winding me up.*
> **wind up sb** *It's so easy to wind up gullible people like her.*

4 *informal* to deliberately make someone angry or upset = ANNOY
> **wind sb up** *Please don't wind him up – he causes me enough trouble.*
> **wind up sb** *Why do you always try to wind up your father like that?*

5 to make a watch, clock etc work by turning a part of it around and around
> **wind up sth** *He used to wind up his old grandfather clock every evening.*
> **wind sth up** *You must have forgotten to wind your watch up this morning.*

6 [often passive] *British* to close a business = LIQUIDATE
> **be wound up** *The firm was later wound up with debts of £104,000.*
> **wind sth up** *In 1993 he wound the business up and joined the Navy.*
> **wind up sth** *At this meeting the creditors will be asked to endorse the resolution to wind up the company.*

7 to turn a handle or press a button in order to make a window in a vehicle go up
≠ WIND DOWN
> **wind sth up** *Make sure you wind up all your windows before you go through the car wash.*
> **wind sth up** *It was getting cold, so he wound the window up.*

8 to prepare to throw the ball in baseball
> **wind up** *Moore wound up and threw to Henderson.*

■ **wind-up** /'waɪnd ˌʌp/ **adj** a wind-up toy or machine is one that works when you turn a key several times: *a wind-up radio*

■ **wind-up** /'waɪnd ˌʌp/ **noun** [C]
1 *British* something that you say or do to deliberately annoy or trick someone: *When they said I'd won I thought it was a wind-up.* **2** the process of ending something: *In the wind-up of the debate, she said that the situation must change.*

WINK /wɪŋk/
winks, winking, winked

'wink at

to pretend that you have not noticed something or do not know about it
> **wink at sth** *Princess Diana often winked at royal tradition in her choice of clothes.*

WINKLE /ˈwɪŋk(ə)l/
winkles, winkling, winkled

,winkle 'out *British informal*

1 to get something such as information from someone when they did not intend to give it to you = EXTRACT

winkle out sth *also* **winkle sth out** *Before the interview, prepare a list of questions to winkle out facts not covered by the application form or c.v.* ♦ **+of** *We tried to winkle an apology out of them.*

2 to try to force someone or something out of a place

winkle sb/sth out *also* **winkle out sb/sth** *Don't be long down there. I don't want to have to come and winkle you out.*

WINNOW /ˈwɪnəʊ, *American* ˈwɪnoʊ/
winnows, winnowing, winnowed

,winnow 'out

to separate the useful or important people or things from the rest of a group

winnow out sb/sth *Maybe a process of natural selection had winnowed out the overworked and discontented.*

WIPE /waɪp/
wipes, wiping, wiped

,wipe a'way ★

to remove something by wiping it with a cloth or with your hand

wipe away sth *She shook her head and wiped away her tears.*

wipe sth away *He wiped the blood away with a handkerchief.*

,wipe 'down

to clean a surface with a cloth

wipe down sth *also* **wipe sth down** *He scrubbed the kitchen floor and wiped down the surfaces.*

'wipe from [often passive]

to remove information from a record, a tape, a computer's memory etc

be wiped from sth *Several entries seem to have been wiped from the accounts.*

wipe sth from sth *It's not too difficult to wipe downloads from your hard disk.*

,wipe 'off [often passive]

to reduce the value of something by a large amount

be wiped off sth *Over $3 billion was wiped off the value of the company's stock yesterday.*

wipe sth off sth *Recession and the Gulf War wiped 62% off pre-tax profits.*

,wipe 'out ★★★

1	destroy sth
2	kill many people
3	clean inside sth
4	make sb tired
5	fall when riding sth
+	wiped out adj; wipeout noun

1 to destroy or get rid of something completely = *formal* ERADICATE

wipe out sth *Our ultimate aim is to wipe out child poverty.*

wipe sth out *You can't wipe the past out as if it didn't exist.*

2 [often passive] to kill a lot of people or animals

be wiped out *Thousands of people were wiped out by the new viruses brought in by European settlers.*

wipe sb/sth out *Pollution threatens to wipe this species of fish out entirely.*

wipe out sb/sth *They seemed intent on wiping out the whole population.*

3 to clean the inside of something with a cloth

wipe out sth *Just wipe out the fridge with a damp cloth.*

wipe sth out *I'd wipe the box out before putting the linen in it.*

4 [often passive] *informal* to make someone extremely tired = EXHAUST

be wiped out *By the end of the day I was completely wiped out.*

wipe sb out *These early morning meetings really wipe me out.*

wipe out sb *The games in the garden wiped out most of the younger children.*

5 *informal* to fall and have a serious crash when you are riding something such as a snowboard or surfboard

wipe out *Two downhill racers had already wiped out on this slope.*

■ **,wiped 'out** adj *informal* extremely tired: *By the end of the day, I felt totally wiped out.*

■ **wipeout** /ˈwaɪpaʊt/ noun [C/U]
1 total destruction or failure: *the wipeout suffered by tomato growers* **2** a crash or fall when you are riding something such as a snowboard or surfboard: *He had survived his first wipeout.*

,wipe 'up

to remove a liquid from a surface using a cloth = MOP UP

wipe up sth *also* **wipe sth up** *I wiped up the spilt juice.*

WIRE /ˈwaɪə, *American* ˈwaɪr/
wires, wiring, wired

,wire 'up

1 to connect someone or something to a piece of electrical equipment or to an electricity supply
wire up sb/sth *also* **wire sb/sth up** *We wired up the students with miniature heart and blood-alcohol monitors.* ♦ *The burglar alarm system is quite sophisticated, with all the windows being wired up.* ♦ **+to** *The patients are wired up to various machines for tests.*
2 to connect the wires inside a piece of equipment
wire up sth *also* **wire sth up** *I watched the mechanic wire up the car battery.*

WISE /waɪz/
wises, wising, wised

,wise 'up *informal*

to learn or understand the unpleasant truth about something = SMARTEN UP
wise up *If he doesn't wise up soon, it'll be too late.* ♦ **+to** *When are they going to wise up to the fact that people aren't interested?*

WISH /wɪʃ/
wishes, wishing, wished

,wish a'way [usually with a negative]

to make something stop or disappear just by hoping that it would do this
wish away sth *also* **wish sth away** *You can't just wish away your debts.*

'wish for

1 *formal* to want something
wish for sth *They do not wish for pity.* ♦ *What more could anyone wish for?*
2 to hope that something you want will happen by magic or by the power of your thoughts
wish for sth *We know what she'll be wishing for on her birthday.*
PHRASE couldn't wish for sb/sth more/better etc used for saying that someone or something is the best you could possibly have: *You couldn't wish for a better friend.* ♦ *He could not have wished for a more pleasant holiday.*

,wish 'on (*also* ,wish up'on *formal*) [usually with a negative]

to wish that something, usually something bad, will happen to someone
wish sth on sb *It's such a disgusting job that I **wouldn't wish it on my worst enemy.***

WITHDRAW /wɪðˈdrɔː, *American* wɪðˈdrɔ/
withdraws, withdrawing, withdrew /wɪðˈdruː, *American* wɪðˈdru/, **withdrawn** /wɪðˈdrɔːn, *American* wɪðˈdrɔn/

with'draw from

1 to stop taking part in something, or to make someone do this
withdraw from sth *The injury forced him to withdraw from the competition.*
withdraw sb from sth *Parents are entitled to withdraw their children from religious education in schools.*
2 if armed forces withdraw from an area, or if someone withdraws them, they leave that area
withdraw from sth *Troops began to withdraw from the northern region.*
withdraw sb from sth *The UN is urging the government to withdraw its forces from the area.*

WITHER /ˈwɪðə, *American* ˈwɪðər/
withers, withering, withered

,wither a'way

to become weaker or smaller and then disappear
wither away *They worry that honoured traditions will wither away.* ♦ *Their love was withering away.*

WITNESS /ˈwɪtnəs/
witnesses, witnessing, witnessed

'witness to *legal*

to formally state that something is true, especially in a court of law
witness to sth *Are you prepared to witness to the honesty of your informant?*

WOLF /wʊlf/
wolfs, wolfing, wolfed

,wolf 'down *informal*

to eat something very quickly = *formal* DEVOUR
wolf down sth *also* **wolf sth down** *The girls wolfed down the pizza in minutes.*

WONDER /ˈwʌndə, *American* ˈwʌndər/
wonders, wondering, wondered

'wonder at

to admire someone or something and feel surprised by how beautiful or unusual they are
wonder at sb/sth *It's hard not to wonder at the miracle of a newborn baby.*

WORK /wɜːk, *American* wɜrk/
works, working, worked

,work a'gainst ★

1 if something works against you, it makes it harder for you to achieve something
work against sb *This was another fact working against him.*

2 to make something less likely to succeed or make progress
work against sth *The new laws work against Scottish interests.*

,work a'round (*also* ,work 'round *British*)

to deal successfully with a problem that might prevent you from achieving your aim
work around sth *A skilled craftsman can work around these difficulties.*

,work a'round to (*also* ,work 'round to *British*)

to gradually start to talk or write about a particular subject in a conversation or piece of writing, especially because it is embarrassing = GET AROUND TO
work around to (doing) sth *She suspected that he had something important to say and could not work around to saying it.*

'work at ★

to try hard to develop or improve something
work at sth *Successful relationships don't just happen. You have to work at them.*
work at doing sth *If she works at improving her game, she could be a champion.*

,work a'way

to keep working hard, or keep trying hard to do something, for a long time
work away *John was working away quietly in the corner.* ♦ **+on** *She's still working away on her assignment.* ♦ **+at** *He works away at Latin and Greek.*

,work 'in (*also* ,work 'into)

1 to add one thing or idea to another, or include one thing or idea in another
= INCORPORATE
work in sth *also* **work sth in** *If you can work in the word 'objective', that would be good.*
work sth into sth *They work a lot of Brazilian sounds and rhythms into their music.*

2 to mix one substance gradually into another one
work in sth *also* **work sth in** *Whisk 2 egg*

whites to stiff snowy peaks, gradually working in the sugar.
work sth into sth *Butter or cream are sometimes worked into the cheese to give a more rounded taste.*

,work 'off

1 to pay someone what you owe them by doing a job for them instead of giving them money
work off sth *also* **work sth off** *They were forced to work off their debts.*

2 if you work off something such as a feeling or some of your weight, you get rid of it by doing something that involves a lot of physical activity
work off sth *also* **work sth off** *She generally works off stress by going for a run.*

'work on

1 to spend time producing or improving something
work on (doing) sth *He'll have to work on getting fit before the game.*

2 to try to influence someone
work on sb *We'll have to work on Joey to find out what's going on.*

3 to use an idea or theory as a basis for action, even though you do not know if it is true
work on sth *Police are working on the assumption that he will try to leave the country.*
PHRASE **I'm working on it** *informal* used for saying that you are dealing with something: *Don't worry about that: I'm working on it.*

,work 'out ★★★

1	whether sth ends successfully
2	manage to do sth
3	do physical exercise
4	understand sb/sth
5	calculate
6	deal with sth
7	solve a problem
8	used for giving a cost/value
9	decide sth
+	**workout** noun

1 to be successful or to end in a particular way
work out *If it doesn't work out, you can always come back here.* ♦ *Things worked out pretty well in the end.*

2 to find a satisfactory way of doing something = *formal* DEVISE
work out sth *We need to work out a way of getting the message across without offending anyone.*
work sth out *They're still trying to work a peace plan out.*

3 to do physical exercise as a way of keeping fit

work out *He works out at the local gym every day.*

4 to understand someone or something = FIGURE OUT, MAKE OUT

work sb/sth out *I can't work him out.*

5 to solve a problem by doing a calculation = CALCULATE

work out sth *Work out how much we'll have left after we've paid for the flight.*
work sth out *Have you worked the total out yet?*

6 to deal with a problem in a satisfactory way = RESOLVE

work out sth *I think we've managed to work out our differences.*
work sth out *They're trying to work their marital problems out.*

7 to solve a problem by considering the facts

work out sth *I can't work out what to do.*
work sth out *We'll have to work a strategy out by tomorrow.*

8 used for saying what the actual cost or value of something is when you calculate it

work out *Taking the train works out more expensive than going by car.*

9 [often passive] to decide or agree on something

be worked out *The exact details of the event haven't been worked out yet.*
work out sth *We haven't worked out a date for the meeting.*

work out (sense 3)

■ **workout** /ˈwɜːkaʊt/ noun [C] an occasion when you do physical exercise: *I gave myself a tough workout.*

work ˈout at
to add up to a particular amount
work out at sth *The mortgage works out at about £360 a month.*

work ˈover *informal*
to injure someone severely by hitting them

work sb over *We'll work him over and then dump him in the river.*

work ˈround *British same as* **work around**

work ˈround to *British same as* **work around to**

work through
to deal with something such as a problem or a strong feeling by thinking and talking about it

work through sth *also* **work sth through** *He needs to work through some of the guilt he's feeling.*

work toˈwards ★★
to do things that help you to make progress towards something that you want to achieve

work towards sth *Both countries are working towards peace in the region.*
♦ *Europe was working towards economic integration.*

work ˈup ★★

1 to develop a particular feeling such as hunger or interest

work up sth *I just can't work up any enthusiasm for this trip.* ♦ *We went for a long walk to work up an appetite (=make us feel hungry and ready to eat).*

2 *mainly American* to develop something
work up sth *I'd like you to work up the next set of guidelines.*
work sth up *He's working his notes up, hoping to get a book out of them.*

3 [often passive] to make yourself feel upset, angry, excited, or nervous
be/get worked up *She's so worked up she can't bring herself to talk to them.*
♦ **+about** *He always gets worked up about the state of the neighbourhood.*
work yourself up *Stop working yourself up like that. You know it's nothing.*
♦ **+to/into** *The kids had worked themselves up to a fever pitch of excitement.* ♦ *She was working herself up into a state again.*

PHRASE **work up a head of steam** to start to become active and successful: *It has taken the project a while to work up a head of steam.*

■ **worked ˈup** adj upset, angry, or excited: *He gets all worked up about nothing at all.*

■ **workup** /ˈwɜːkʌp/ noun [C] *American* a series of tests to find out if someone has medical problems: *The doctor was completing her workup.*

,work 'up to

1 to prepare yourself to do something difficult, or to try to prepare someone for bad news

work up to (doing) sth *Are you working up to telling me that you can't pay?*

2 to develop or increase and reach a particular level

work up to sth *The plane's engines were working up to take-off power.*

WORM /wɜːm, *American* wɜrm/
worms, worming, wormed

,worm 'out of

to gradually get information from someone who does not want to give it to you

worm sth out of sb *I eventually managed to worm a few details out of him.*

,worm 'into

PHRASE **worm your way into sth** to get yourself into a particular state or situation gradually, often using clever or dishonest methods: *She had wormed her way into Charles's affections.*
♦ *They wormed their way into the confidence of the owners.*

WORRY /'wʌri/
worries, worrying, worried

'worry at

1 *British* if you worry at a problem, you keep thinking about it and trying to solve it

worry at sth *I kept worrying at the problem, juggling the pieces in my mind.*

2 if a dog worries at an object, it holds the object in its teeth and shakes it

worry at sth *The terrier was worrying at the rat it had caught.*

WRAP /ræp/
wraps, wrapping, wrapped

,wrap a'round (*also* ,wrap 'round *British*)
[often passive]

to put something around something else

be wrapped around sth *Couples were strolling down the street with their arms wrapped around each other.* ♦ *Each cake has a bright red ribbon wrapped around it.*

wrap sth around sth *He grabbed a towel to wrap around his waist.*

■ **wraparound** /'ræpə,raʊnd/ **adj**
1 wrapped around your body and tied rather than being fastened with buttons etc: *wraparound skirts* **2** wraparound

objects curve around the sides of whatever they are fitted to: *wraparound sunglasses*

■ **wraparound** /'ræpə,raʊnd/ **noun**
1 [C] a wraparound skirt: *Helen was wearing some kind of silky wraparound.*
2 [U] an instruction to a computer to start a new line of text automatically after you type the last letter on the previous line: *Of course, on a typewriter, there's no wraparound.*

,wrap 'in ★★

to cover something by putting something such as paper or cloth around it

wrap sth in sth *They usually wrap the fish in newspaper.*

,wrap 'up ★★

1	cover sth with paper/cloth
2	wear clothes for cold weather
3	put warm clothes on sb
4	end a meeting/discussion etc
5	achieve a victory/agreement etc
+	wrap-up noun

1 to cover something by putting a material such as paper or cloth around it
≠ UNWRAP

wrap up sth *We've just finished wrapping up Susie's birthday present.*
wrap sth up *It would mean taking the bandage off her ankle, but she could always wrap it up again.* ♦ **+in** *He carefully wrapped the figure up in a cloth and placed it in the box.*

2 to wear enough clothes to keep you warm

wrap up *I could hear my mother telling me to wrap up warm.*

3 [often passive] to put warm clothes on a child

be wrapped up *Keep the baby well wrapped up in the early weeks.*
wrap sb up *Wrap her up warmly. It's cold outside.*
wrap up sb *Wrap up the little ones for me, will you?*

4 [often passive] to finish something such as a meeting, ceremony, or discussion
= CONCLUDE

be wrapped up *Each meeting is wrapped up with a speech from the manager.*
wrap up sth *Can we wrap up this question so that we can get back to the main point at issue?*
wrap sth up *I thought you wanted to wrap things up quickly.*

5 *informal* to achieve something such as a victory or an agreement

wrap up sth *Negotiators are confident they can wrap up a deal soon.*

wrap sth up *They had enough chances to wrap the game up in the first half.*

wrap up

■ **'wrap-up** noun [C] *American* a short summary at the end of something, especially a news programme: *It was Alan's job to write the sports wrap-up.*

be ,wrapped 'up in
to spend so much time doing something or thinking about it that you do not notice anything else = BE IMMERSED IN, BE ABSORBED IN
be wrapped up in sth *He's completely wrapped up in his work.*

WRESTLE /'res(ə)l/
wrestles, wrestling, wrestled

'wrestle with
to try to deal with or solve a difficult problem
wrestle with sth *Philosophers have been wrestling with the question of human consciousness for centuries.*

WRIGGLE /'rɪg(ə)l/
wriggles, wriggling, wriggled

,wriggle 'out of
1 to take off a piece of clothing by twisting or turning quickly
wriggle out of sth *He desperately tried to wriggle out of his shorts.*
2 to escape from a person or place by twisting or turning quickly
wriggle out of sth *The child wriggled out of her grasp and ran off.*
3 to avoid doing something that you should do by thinking of reasons for not doing it
wriggle out of (doing) sth *Don't try and wriggle out of doing your homework.*

WRING /rɪŋ/
wrings, wringing, wrung /rʌŋ/

'wring from (also 'wring out of)
to get something from someone with great difficulty
wring sth from sb *She survives on the money she wrings out of the state.*

,wring 'out
to twist and squeeze something in order to remove liquid from it
wring out sth *also* **wring sth out** *I'll just wring out this jumper and hang it up.*

WRITE /raɪt/
writes, writing, wrote /rəʊt, *American* roʊt/, written /'rɪt(ə)n/

,write a'way
to write to an organization asking them to send you something = WRITE OFF
write away *I'm going to write away immediately and ask for more information.* ♦ **+for** *Rose helped Maggie to write away for the forms.*

,write 'back ★
to send a reply to someone who has sent you a letter
write back *We wrote back saying we would be delighted to come.* ♦ **+to** *I wrote back to her at once, accepting her invitation.*

,write 'down ★★★
to write something on a piece of paper = RECORD
write down sth *Write down seven words that describe how you feel.*
write sth down *I quickly wrote the number down as the car sped off.*

,write 'in ★
1 to write to an organization, for example because you want information about something
write in *Hundreds of people wrote in, complaining about the poor service.* ♦ **+to** *I wrote in to the programme to ask for more details.* ♦ **+to do sth** *Several people wrote in to tell us about their own experiences.*
2 to add words or numbers that are missing from something
write in sth *Write in the letter that is missing from each word.*
write sth in *Write the total in at the bottom of each page.*

,write 'into [usually passive]
to include a particular feature in an official document such as a contract

be written into sth *The right to withdraw is written into the agreement.*

ˌwrite ˈoff ★★★

1	tell sb not to pay money
2	realize that sb will never pay you money
3	stop helping sb
4	write a letter to ask for sth
5	damage a vehicle very badly
6	about tax
+	**write-off** noun

1 to say officially that someone does not have to pay an amount of money = CANCEL
write off sth *He urged the industrialized countries to write off the loans to the poorest countries.*
write sth off *The US government agreed to write the debts off.*

2 [often passive] to accept that you will not get back money or something else that you have given someone
be written off *The £500 they have spent will have to be written off.*
write off sth *Liverpool won't want to write off all these millions spent on recruiting a new manager.*
write sth off *We saved our shareholders from having to write the lot off.*

3 [often passive] to decide that someone or something will not succeed, and stop trying to help or improve them
be written off *At school he felt he had been written off.* ♦ **+as** *I'm ashamed to say I had him written off as a failure.*
write off sb/sth *Don't write off the idea until you know more about it.*
write sb/sth off *My teachers all wrote me off and look at me now!*

4 to write to an organization asking them to send you something = WRITE AWAY
write off *She spotted an advertisement for the festival in the paper and wrote off at once.* ♦ **+for** *Why don't you write off for more details?*

5 *British* to damage a vehicle so badly that it cannot be repaired = WRECK
write off sth *In the 1991 race one team wrote off their raft in an unfortunate accident.*
write sth off *He had to tell his parents he'd written their car off driving home after a party.*

6 to claim the value of something that you have paid for against the amount of tax you have to pay
write sth off *After five years you can write the equipment off for tax.*

■ **ˈwrite-off** noun [C] **1** a period of time when you fail to achieve anything: *Today was a write-off as far as work is*

write off (sense 5)

concerned. **2** *British* a vehicle that is so badly damaged that it cannot be repaired: *The other driver's car was a complete write-off.* **3** an agreement that allows someone not to pay back the money they owe: *The clients are arguing for a write-off.*

ˌwrite ˈout ★★

1 to complete an official document by writing information on it = MAKE OUT
write out sth *It only takes a minute to write out a prescription.*
write sth out *The traffic warden was still writing my ticket out when I got back to the car.*

2 to write something again, usually in a more detailed way
write out sth *Could you write out exactly what you need me to do?*
write sth out *I'm going to have to write my essay out more neatly.*

3 [often passive] to remove a character from a television or radio series by writing stories that do not include them = KILL OFF
be written out *Ratings fell when the star was written out of the show.*
write sb out *There are rumours they're writing her out at the end of this series.*
write out sb *If they carry on like this, they'll have written out half the cast by Christmas.*

ˌwrite ˈup ★★

1 to write a report, article etc using notes that you wrote earlier
write up sth *The police officers wrote up the accident at the station.*
write sth up *I'm planning to write the report up this evening.*

2 *American* to officially report that someone has done something wrong
write sb up *The police officer wrote him up for disturbing the peace.*
write up sb *The company wrote up*

workers for smoking in bathrooms.

■ **'write-up** `noun` [C] an article in a newspaper or magazine that gives the writer's opinion about something such as a new book, play, or film = REVIEW: *Write-ups in the national press have been largely positive.*

X /eks/
X'es, X'ing, X'ed

,X 'out *American informal*
to draw an X over something that you have written to show that you do not want or need it

X sth out *also* **X out sth** *Students X out the options they don't want.*

YEARN /jɜːn, *American* jɜrn/
yearns, yearning, yearned

'yearn for *mainly literary*
to want something a lot, especially something that you know you may not be able to have

yearn for sth *He yearned for her love.*

YELL /jel/
yells, yelling, yelled

,yell 'out
to shout loudly or shout something loudly = SHOUT

yell out sth *also* **yell sth out** *Suddenly, Terry yelled out, 'Mind your head!'*
♦ *Someone yelled my name out and I turned around immediately.*
yell out *She yelled out in pain.*

YIELD /jiːld, *American* jild/
yields, yielding, yielded

,yield 'up *literary*
to finally allow people to see or know about something that has been hidden

yield up sth *also* **yield sth up** *The latest dig has yielded up over a hundred pieces*

of fine Roman silverware. ♦ *The ocean does not* **yield up** *its secrets easily.*
♦ *Was the wreck finally about to* **yield** *its treasures* **up**?

Zz

ZERO /'zɪərəʊ, *American* 'zɪroʊ/
zeroes, zeroing, zeroed

,zero 'in on
1 to start to give all your attention to a particular person or thing

zero in on sb/sth *The newspapers have now zeroed in on his private life.*

2 to aim directly at someone or something with a gun or missile

zero in on sb/sth *Just zero in on the target and squeeze the trigger.*

ZIP /zɪp/
zips, zipping, zipped

,zip 'through
to deal with or complete something very quickly

zip through sth *I zipped through the first three questions in ten minutes.*

,zip 'up ★
1 to fasten or close something with a zip (=a long narrow metal or plastic object with two rows of teeth) ≠ UNZIP

zip sth up *He just zipped his trousers up and left.*
zip up sth *She zipped up her dress.*

2 to fasten or close with a zip (=a long narrow metal or plastic object with two rows of teeth) ≠ UNZIP

zip up *It zips up at the back.*

3 to close a zip (=a long narrow metal or plastic object with two rows of teeth) on a piece of clothing for someone

zip sb up *Do you want me to zip you up?*

■ **'zip-up** `adj` closed by means of a zip (=a long narrow metal or plastic object with two rows of teeth): *a zip-up sweatshirt*

ZONE /zəʊn, *American* zoʊn/
zones, zoning, zoned

,zone 'out *American informal*
to stop paying attention and just look in front of you without thinking, especially because you are tired, bored, or have taken drugs

zone out *Sorry, I was just zoning out for a minute.*

ZONK /zɒŋk, *American* zɑŋk/
zonks, zonking, zonked

,zonk 'out [often passive] *informal*

to become very tired and start to sleep, or to make someone do this

be zonked out *He fell asleep immediately. He must have been really zonked out.*

zonk out *I was so tired I just zonked out.*

INDEX OF SINGLE-WORD EQUIVALENTS

This index lists over 1,000 English verbs and – for each one – gives one or more phrasal verbs that express the same meaning. The purpose of this list is to enable you to take a single-word verb that you already know (such as **prepare** or **interrupt**) and find an equivalent phrasal verb that you may be able to use instead.

It is rare for two words to be *exact* equivalents, so there are two points to remember when you are using this list:

- the meaning of one word may be more *limited* than the meaning of the other. For example, **resemble** (meaning 'to be similar to someone or something else') has the equivalent **take after**, but **take after** is used only to talk about people in the same family who resemble each other.

- there is often a difference in *register*. For example, the phrasal verb may be more informal than the single-word verb, as in the case of **discharge** (a rather formal word meaning 'to do something that you have a responsibility to do') and its less formal equivalent **carry out**.

It is important, therefore, always to read the entry for the phrasal verb before deciding whether it is the right verb for you to use.

Single word	Phrasal verb	Single word	Phrasal verb	Single word	Phrasal verb
abandon	call off	**allow**	permit of	**apportion**	share out
	give up	**amplify**	flesh out	**approach**	border on
	throw up	**amuse**	break up		come at
abolish	do away with		crack up		come up
absorb	take in 3		crease up	**approach**	come up to
	take in 6	**anaesthetize**	put under	**argue**	talk back
	take in 7	**annoy**	get to	**arise**	come up 2
abuse	interfere with		hack off		come up 3
accelerate	speed up		tee off		come up 4
accept	bow to		wind up	**arouse**	stir up 1
accumulate	add up	**anticipate**	look forward		stir up 3
	pile up		to		turn on
acquire	take on	**appear**	break out	**arrange**	fix up
add	add up		come across		line up
address	deal with		come along	**arrest**	pull in
admire	look up to		come off as		run in
admit	let in		come out	**arrive**	come in
	let on		come over		draw in
advance	get ahead		roll up		get in 1
afflict	strike down		spring up		get in 9
agree	come around	**apply**	put on		pull in
alight	light on	**appoint**	put in	**ask**	call on

Single word	Phrasal verb	Single word	Phrasal verb	Single word	Phrasal verb
assemble	bring	**block**	cut off	**close**	shut up
	together		fill in	**clown**	fool around
	piece		pen in	**cohabit**	live together
	together	**boost**	build up	**collapse**	break down
	put		buoy up		cave in
	together 2		pump up		fall apart
	put		soup up		fall down
	together 3	**borrow**	check out		flake out
assess	size up	**bother**	play up		keel over
	weigh up	**bribe**	buy off	**collect**	get together
assign	put on		pay off		pick up
attack	beat up	**brighten**	light up		rack up
	do over	**bring**	bring along		scrape
	go for		bring round		together
	lay about	**broadcast**	put out	**communicate**	put across
	lay into	**broaden**	broaden out		put over
	set about		open out	**complete**	fill in
	set on		open up		fill out
attend	turn out	**burden**	weigh down		finish off
	turn up		weigh on		tie up
attract	bring in	**burgle**	break into	**comprehend**	catch on
	bring into		turn over		cotton on
	pull in	**calculate**	work out	**conceal**	blot out
audition	read for	**call**	call up		paper over
avoid	keep off		phone up	**conclude**	wrap up
back	back up 5		ring up	**concoct**	dream up
	back up 6	**cancel**	call off	**confess**	cough up
	side with		cry off		own up
bankrupt	clean out		write off	**confine**	shut in
bark	rap out	**capitulate**	cave in	**conform**	fit in
begin	break into	**capsize**	keel over	**confuse**	mix up 1
	kick off 1	**catch**	go down with		mix up 3
	kick off 2		pick up		muddle up
	lead off	**cause**	bring about	**connect**	hook up 1
	set about		bring on		hook up 4
	start off		set up		put through
	strike up	**challenge**	take on	**conscript**	call up
	take to	**chew**	chew up	**consider**	chew over
benefit	cash in	**choke**	choke up		look at
betray	give away 3	**choose**	go for		mull over
	give away 6		opt for		think over
	grass on		pick out		think through
	grass up		plump for	**constitute**	amount to
	rat on	**chuck**	pack in		make up
bin	chuck out	**clean**	go over	**constrain**	box in
	throw away		wash down		hem in
	throw out	**clog**	clog up	**consume**	eat up 1
block	block up	**close**	board up		eat up 2
	bung up		push to		eat up 3

Single word	Phrasal verb	Single word	Phrasal verb	Single word	Phrasal verb
consume	put away	**deliver**	drop off	**discuss**	talk about
contain	bottle up	**demand**	call for	**disguise**	dress up
continue	go on 1	**demolish**	knock down	**disgust**	gross out
	go on 11		pull down	**disinherit**	cut off
	go on 12		tear down	**disintegrate**	fall apart
	take up	**denounce**	turn in	**dismantle**	take apart
contract	come down	**deposit**	pay in		take down
	with	**depress**	bring down	**dismiss**	boot out
contribute	chip in		get down		brush aside
	kick in	**destroy**	kill off		brush away
convey	get across		take out		brush off
	pass on		tear apart		kick out
	put across		tear up		lay off
copy	back up	**detach**	break off 4		shrug off
corroborate	back up		break off 5		sweep aside
couple	hook up	**detain**	keep in	**disparage**	do down
cover	deal with	**detect**	smell out		put down
crash	fall over	**deteriorate**	go down	**dispatch**	send off 1
	go down		go off		send off 2
	keel over	**detonate**	let off	**display**	lay out
criticize	lay into		set off		set out
	take apart	**develop**	bring on		show off
	tear into		build up	**disregard**	put aside
cross	pass through	**devise**	work out	**distinguish**	make out
dampen	damp down	**devote**	dedicate to		mark off
date	go with		put in		mark out
deal	deal out	**devour**	gobble down		set apart
deceive	put on		gobble up	**distract**	put off
	string along		wolf down	**distress**	tear apart
	take in	**die**	pass away		tear up
decelerate	slow down		pass on	**distribute**	dish out
decline	fall off	**dilute**	water down		parcel out
decrease	come down	**dim**	go down		pass out
	fall away	**disappear**	fade away		share out
	fall off		go away	**disturb**	break into
	go down	**disappoint**	let down	**ditch**	pack in
dedicate	devote to	**discard**	cast off	**diversify**	branch out
defeat	dispose of		throw away	**divide**	break up
	knock out		throw out		split up
	put out	**discern**	make out	**do**	carry out 1
	see off	**discharge**	carry out		carry out 2
defect	cross over	**discount**	factor out	**dock**	put in
defend	stand up for		mark down	**down**	drink down
	stick up for	**discover**	find out		knock back
deflate	let down		sniff out	**download**	pull off
deflect	fend off		spy out	**downplay**	play down
delay	hold up		turn up	**draft**	call up
	put off	**discuss**	deal with		draw up
delete	cross out		go into		rough out

Single word	Phrasal verb	Single word	Phrasal verb	Single word	Phrasal verb
draw	pull in	**enter**	go in for	**experience**	come up
drop	fall back		go into		against
	take down		key in		go through
dry	dry off		put in for	**explain**	account for 1
	rub down	**entice**	lead on		account for 3
dupe	take in	**equalize**	even up	**explode**	go off
dwindle	tail off	**equip**	fit out		let off
earn	pick up		fit up	**exploit**	capitalize on
ease	smooth over		kit out	**expose**	catch out
eavesdrop	listen in	**eradicate**	root out	**extend**	add on
ebb	go out		stamp out		add on to
elect	put in		wipe out		drag out
	vote in	**erase**	rub out		spread out
elicit	bring forth	**erect**	put up	**extinguish**	put out
	call forth		set up		stamp out
eliminate	do away with	**erode**	eat away	**extract**	squeeze out
	weed out		eat into		winkle out
elude	shake off		wear away	**face**	face up to
	throw off	**erupt**	flare up		stand up to
embarrass	show up	**escape**	get away	**fail**	conk out
embellish	embroider on	**establish**	carve out		fall down
emerge	come out		set up 1		fall through
	leak out		set up 8		give out
emit	give off		start up		go under
	give out	**evict**	turn out		strike out
	let off	**evoke**	bring back	**faint**	black out
	let out		call up		pass out
	pump out		conjure up	**fall**	come down 2
	send out	**examine**	look at		come down 4
emphasize	point up		pore over	**fasten**	do up
empty	turn out	**exceed**	go beyond		tie up
enact	act out	**exchange**	trade in	**fell**	cut down
encounter	come across	**exclaim**	burst out	**fetch**	go for
	come on	**exclude**	count out	**finalize**	nail down
	come upon		cut out	**find**	track down
	run into		factor out	**finish**	come in
encourage	cheer on		freeze out		get through
	egg on		keep out		knock off
end	break up		rule out	**fire**	fire off
	run out	**excuse**	let off		loose off
endure	live through	**exhaust**	tire out	**fit**	put in
	ride out		wear out	**flatten**	level off
energize	liven up		wipe out	**flatter**	butter up
enjoy	lap up	**exit**	log off		play up to
enlarge	blow up	**expand**	broaden out 2	**fleece**	rip off
enlist	join up		broaden out 3	**fold**	fold up
enter	come in	**expel**	drive out	**follow**	abide by
	come on		throw out		adhere to
	go in				stick to

Single word	Phrasal verb	Single word	Phrasal verb	Single word	Phrasal verb
forge	carve out	**include**	build in	**involve**	draw in
forget	leave behind		count in	**isolate**	cut off 4
form	make up		factor in		cut off 5
frame	fit up		take in	**issue**	put out
	set up		throw in	**join**	fall in with
	stitch up	**inconvenience**	put out	**kill**	bump off
freeze	ice over	**incorporate**	build in 1		cut down
frisk	pat down		build in 2		dispose of
fulfil	carry out		work in		finish off
gain	put on	**increase**	bump up		gun down
get	come by		crank up		put away
grab	snap up		go up		rub out
graduate	pass out		jack up		take out
grasp	take in		scale up	**lambast**	land on
gut	burn out		step up	**lampoon**	send up
handle	deal with 1	**indicate**	point out	**land**	bring down
	deal with 2	**induce**	put up to		put down
	deal with 4	**indulge**	pander to		touch down
harvest	gather in	**inflate**	blow up	**last**	hold out
hatch	hatch out 1		pump up		last out
	hatch out 2	**inform**	tell of	**lead**	head up
head	head up	**inherit**	come into	**learn**	mug up
heal	close up	**initiate**	set up		pick up
hem	turn up	**inspect**	check out	**leave**	check out
herald	usher in		look over		draw out
hesitate	hang back	**install**	put in		get away
hide	hide away	**intend**	start out		get off
	hole up	**intensify**	hot up		get out
highlight	bring out		step up		go off
	pick out	**interrupt**	break into		head off
	point up		butt in		move on
hinder	hold back		cut in		move out
	keep back		cut into		pull out
hit	lay into		cut off		set forth
hoard	salt away		jump in		set off
identify	pin down		put in		set out
ignore	pass over	**intervene**	step in	**like**	care for
illuminate	light up	**introduce**	bring in		go for
imitate	take off		roll out		go in for
impress	bowl over	**intrude**	muscle in	**linger**	stick around
	knock out	**invent**	cook up	**liquidate**	wind up
improve	buck up		make up 1	**list**	heel over
	come on		make up 2	**listen**	listen up
	look up		think up	**lose**	go down
	pick up	**invest**	put into	**lower**	bring down
improvise	cobble	**investigate**	dig into		let down
	together		inquire into	**mail**	post off
	rig up		look into		send off
inaugurate	swear in	**invoke**	call down on	**maintain**	keep up

Single word	Phrasal verb	Single word	Phrasal verb	Single word	Phrasal verb
make	rack up	**overact**	ham up	**produce**	knock out
maltreat	rough up	**overcome**	break down		turn out
manage	get by		break through	**profit**	cash in
masturbate	beat off		get over	**progress**	come along
	jack off	**overflow**	boil over		come on
	jerk off		brim over 1		move along
	toss off		brim over 2		move on
match	accord with		run over	**prolong**	draw out
	come up to		spill over		string out
	live up to	**overrun**	run over	**promote**	move up
mature	grow up	**oversleep**	sleep in	**propose**	put forward
maximize	play up	**overthrow**	bring down	**prosecute**	haul up
meet	come together	**overturn**	set aside		have up for
mend	patch up	**pack**	pack up	**protrude**	jut out
mention	bring up	**part**	split up		stick out
	rake up	**participate**	join in	**provide**	lay on
	touch on	**pass**	hand over	**prune**	cut back
minimize	play down		while away	**publish**	bring out
misbehave	act up	**perform**	go through		get out
	play up	**persevere**	soldier on		put out
mislead	fob off	**persuade**	prevail on	**pursue**	come after
mist	mist over		talk round		go after
moderate	tone down	**phone**	call up		run after
moor	tie up		phone up	**quell**	put down
neaten	straighten up		ring up	**raise**	bring up 1
need	depend on	**plateau**	level off		bring up 2
nerve	psych up	**plug**	fill in		bring up 4
notice	pick up on	**ponder**	chew over		bump up
	spy out		mull over		put up
obey	abide by		puzzle over	**reach**	arrive at
	keep to	**post**	post off		get at
obstruct	block off		send off	**rebel**	rise up
	block up	**postpone**	hold over	**rebuke**	tell off
obtain	come by		put back		tick off
	take out		put off 2	**recall**	dredge up
occupy	take up		put off 3		look back
	tie up	**precede**	lead up to	**receive**	pick up
occur	go on	**prepare**	cook up	**recite**	reel off
offset	balance out		make up	**recline**	lie back
	cancel out		rustle up	**record**	write down
omit	leave out	**press**	force on	**recover**	bounce back 1
	miss out	**pressurize**	lean on		bounce back 2
open	come out	**pretend**	make out		claw back 1
	open up	**prevent**	head off		claw back 2
organize	set up	**produce**	bring forth	**recruit**	sign on
outdistance	leave behind		churn out		sign up
outdo	rise above		come across with		take on
outgrow	grow out of		come up with		

Single word	Phrasal verb	Single word	Phrasal verb	Single word	Phrasal verb
recur	come around	**repress**	fight back	**rob**	knock over
	come back	**reprimand**	speak to		stick up
redeem	cash in		tell off	**rouse**	knock up
reduce	boil down	**request**	ask for		wake up
	bring down		send for	**ruin**	mess up
	cut back 1	**require**	call for		muck up
	cut back 2	**resemble**	take after	**sacrifice**	give up
	cut down 1	**reserve**	keep back	**satisfy**	fill up
	cut down 2		put aside	**score**	chalk up
	cut into		set aside		put away
	knock down	**resign**	stand aside		rack up
	mark down		stand down	**scorn**	look down on
	scale down	**resolve**	sort out	**search**	look around
refrain	hold back		work out		scout around
refuse	turn down	**respond**	come back	**select**	pick out
register	check in 1	**restore**	bring back	**separate**	break up
	check in 4	**restrain**	hold back		split up 1
	pick up on		hold in		split up 2
rehearse	go through	**resuscitate**	bring back	**serve**	serve up
	run over	**retain**	keep back		wait on
	run through		keep on	**set**	go down
reinforce	bolster up	**retaliate**	fight back	**shed**	slough off
reinstate	bring back 2		hit back 1		throw off
	bring back 3		hit back 2	**shoot**	blow away
reject	knock back		strike back	**shorten**	cut down
	shoot down	**retouch**	touch up		take up
	throw out	**retreat**	back away		turn up
	toss aside	**retrieve**	dig out	**shout**	call out
	turn away		get back		cry out
	from	**return**	give back		yell out
	turn down		go back	**show**	put out
relax	chill out		send back	**shut**	push to
	kick back		take back	**silence**	shut up
	wind down	**reveal**	give away	**sink**	bury in
release	bring out		let on		go down
	put out	**reverse**	back up	**skim**	dip into
relinquish	hand over	**revive**	bring back	**soar**	shoot up
remain	stay on		bring round	**socialize**	go out
remember	look back		bring to	**sound**	go off
remove	cut out		wake up	**spot**	pick out 2
	take away	**revolve**	go around		pick out 3
	take off	**rewind**	wind back	**spread**	pass on
	weed out	**ring**	call up		put about
repay	pay back		phone up		put around
replace	put back		ring up	**squander**	fritter away
represent	act for	**rise**	get up		gamble away
	stand for		go up	**stabilize**	calm down
	sum up		stand up		level off
		rob	hold up	**stage**	put on

Single word	Phrasal verb	Single word	Phrasal verb	Single word	Phrasal verb
start	break out	**surrender**	give up	**unleash**	set off
	crank up		hand in	**unroll**	roll out
	cut in	**survive**	come	**unwind**	wind down
	kick off 1		through	**vent**	act out
	kick off 2		get by	**violate**	go against
	lead off		get through	**visit**	call by
	set about		last out		call in
	start out		live on		call on
steal	knock off		live through		call round
	rip off		pull through		come around
stifle	gulp back	**switch**	change over		come by
stipulate	lay down	**table**	put down		come over
	provide for	**tackle**	deal with		drop in
stop	cut out	**tackle**	go about		pop over
	dry up	**tease**	have on	**volunteer**	come
	give over	**telephone**	call up		forward
	jack in		phone up		step forward
	lay off		ring up	**vomit**	bring up
	leave off	**test**	try out		chuck up
	pull in	**tether**	tie up		heave up
	pull up	**thrash**	take apart		puke up
store	lay in	**tolerate**	live with		sick up
strengthen	beef up		put up with		throw up
	firm up		stand for	**wait**	hang on
strike	come out	**topple**	bring down 1	**wake**	wake up
stumble	trip up		bring down 4	**warn**	tip off
stun	knock out 4	**total**	add up to	**wash**	freshen up
	knock out 5		amount to	**waste**	fritter away
subside	die down		come to		throw away
subtract	take away		count up	**widen**	broaden out
succeed	come off	**transform**	shake up		open out
	get on	**transpire**	turn out		open up
suggest	put forward	**trap**	pen in	**win**	carry off
summarize	sum up	**trip**	fall over		pick up
summon	call in 3	**trust**	swear by	**withdraw**	bottle out
	call in 4	**uncover**	dig out		pull back
	call out		get at		pull out 1
	conjure up	**undergo**	pass through		pull out 2
	send for	**undermine**	wear down		take back
support	back up		latch on	**wither**	waste away
	bear out	**understand**	make out	**withhold**	hold back
	get behind		take in		keep back
	hold up	**undertake**	take on	**wreck**	smash up
	speak up for	**unearth**	dig out		write off
	stand by		dig up 1	**wring**	squeeze out
	stick up for		dig up 3	**yell**	cry out
suppress	choke back	**unfold**	open out	**yield**	back down
	cover up		open up		cave in
	put down	**unite**	pull together		give in